#WomenTechLit

Edited by María Mencía

Computing Literature
Morgantown, WV / Rochester, NY

COMPUTING LITERATURE

A book series distributed by the West Virginia University Press.

Volume 1 Regards Croisés: Perspectives on Digital Literature

Edited by Philippe Bootz and Sandy Baldwin

Volume 2 Writing Under: Selections from the Internet Text

By Alan Sondheim. Edited and Introduced by Sandy Baldwin

Volume 3 Electronic Literature as a Model of Creativity and Innovation in Practice

A Report from the HERA Joint Research Project. Edited by Scott Rettberg with Sandy Baldwin

Volume 4 Po.Ex: Essays from Portugal on Cyberliterature and Intermedia

Edited by Rui Torres and Sandy Baldwin

Volume 5 Word Space Multiplicities, Openings, Andings

By Jim Rosenberg. Edited by Sandy Baldwin

Volume 6 Electronic Literature Communities

Edited by Scott Rettberg, Patricia Tomaszek, and Sandy Baldwin

Volume 7 Text as Ride

By Janez Strehovec. Edited by Kwabena Opoku-Agyemang and Sandy Baldwin

Volume 8 #WomenTechLit

Edited by María Mencía

Published 2017 by Computing Literature, Morgantown, WV 26506 / Rochester, NY 14623

Cover design by María Mencía

ISBN-13: 978-1-943665-90-7 (pb)

978-1-943665-91-4 (elec)

978-1-943665-92-1 (pdf)

ACKNOWLEDGMENTS

This book started off at one of the E-Poetry Festivals, in conversation with Giovanna di Rosario, Angelica Huizar and Maria Engberg. We all felt there were far too many male keynote speakers and "only male" panels at conferences. When I suggested editing a book, representing and celebrating the work of women in the field of electronic literature, everybody agreed it would be a great contribution to the scholarship and creativity of women's digital writing. Therefore, I would like to take this opportunity to thank them for their enthusiasm and encouragement in pursuing this project.

I also would like to express my enormous gratitude to Stephanie Strickland, Marjorie C. Luesebrink, and Judy Malloy. They have been like three supporting rocks through this process. I have been guided by their knowledge, their helpful suggestions and comments have made the book a much more informed and rounded project. Stephanie went out of her way to send me lists of pioneer women in e-lit and together with Rita Raley revised my proposal and suggested ways to organise the different sections in the book which has given the volume a much better focus.

In 2015 we had the first women panel ever presenting at an E-Poetry Festival hosted in Argentina. I would like to thank its panellists, which included some of the contributors in this volume: Claudia Kozak, Odile Farge, Laura Shackelford, Giovanna di Rosario, and Angelica Huizar. This gave us a great opportunity to discuss general issues in preparation for #WomenTechLit and some particular concerns examined in each of our individual contributions - from the point of view of creative practice, critical and historical perspectives. Thanks also to Hazel Smith for her comments and proofreading of my individual chapter, to Zuzana Husárová and Dene Grigar for discussing the title of the volume with me, and to Christine Wilks for her kind words and encouragement about the project.

In addition and most importantly, this book would not have been possible without the generosity of all the contributors, their dedication and patience to bring this all together.

I am also extremely grateful to Sandy Baldwin for enabling me to publish this book and his dedication to the volume in his role as series editor, including his assistance with editing, proofreading, formatting and designing such a large and arduous volume; and to N. Katherine Hayles for contributing with her insightful foreword.

Finally thanks to my partner Keith, for his support and all those friends who have somehow helped to make it possible.

CONTENTS

Foreword: Why #WomenTechLit?

BY N. KATHERINE HAYLES

In the mid-1990's I was a visitor at Stanford University, and one beautiful California afternoon I forsook my study to attend the popular computer science lecture series for a talk by Rodney Brooks on the new ideas he was incorporating into his robots. Arriving early, I amused myself by counting the women among the four or five hundred people filling the auditorium. There were no more than twenty—including me. Things have changed since then, of course, but computer science and allied disciplines remain fields dominated by men. Electronic literature is an exception to this generalization, for women have been active since its beginnings in the late 1980's up to today, although the importance of their contributions remains under-recognized and, importantly, under-theorized. *#WomenTechLit* addresses both of these concerns in a global framework.

M. D. Coverley's analysis of women's contributions over two decades, from 1990-2010, clearly shows not only the presence of women writers but also the important innovations they undertook; that Coverley ends her chapter with a "roll call" of over 200 women beyond those discussed indicates the remarkable depth and breadth of what women artists and writers have achieved. Sue Thomas's chapter on women participating in the trAce Online Writing Community over the decade from 1995-2005 supplements Coverley's by extending the purview to a British context, as does Claudia Kozak with a Latin American context, Zusáná Husarova with Slovak and Czech contributions, and Dolores Romero López with Spain. Romero López's chapter is complemented by the edgy contribution of María Goicoechea and Laura Sánchez on how the digital divide complicates any simple account of women's achievements, for they remind us that access remains a crucial issue and one that alienates as well as empowers.

In addition to these general summaries, also valuable are the chapters analyzing individual or small groups of works, where the author has the space to explore the works in depth. When the author is writing about her own work, additional insights emerge about the conditions of production, contexts of creation, and underlying issues that catalyzed the work and guided its expressive aesthetics. For example, María Mencía's chapter on her work articulates some fascinating thoughts about how she views the relation of her creative work to literary theory; she never intends to "apply" a theory, she recounts, but rather reads it to generate a general sense of important issues that intersect with her own concerns. The chapters collected in the "Pioneers" section address a concern central to electronic literature: obsolescence, and the writer's frustration when a software authoring environment suddenly is discontinued or becomes unplayable. M. D. Coverley's chapter on the making of *Califia*, a work that remains one of the canon's most complex and accomplished long narratives, is heart-breaking as she explains how literally years of work were rendered moot when the work would no longer play (thankfully, that work has now been resurrected with the help of a virtual machine environment). Stephanie Strickland's astute analysis of how porting her long poem *V: Vniverse* from a Flash environment to an iPad affected the reader's interactions also illuminates the challenges that writers of electronic literature face when their original platforms disappear.

The issue of authoring environments is a thread running through many of the chapters, as writers comment about their choice of software, their engagement with the underlying code, and the influence of software on their creative choices, from Judy Malloy's chapter on her pioneering works *Uncle Roger* and *Its name was Penelope*, to María Mencía's comment about why she wanted to use the open-source programming language Processing rather than a commercial for-profit package. Odile Farge explores these issues explicitly in her chapter on the rhetorics of softwares, including the language employed by designers to entice writers to use their product as well as the rhetorical force of a software's palette of choices, from affordances to interactive possibilities to design considerations.

Among the remaining connecting threads, no doubt there are many different ones that will attract and intrigue readers; the one that calls to me is the enduring question of whether women's writing has specific characteristics, and if so, how these manifest themselves in the digital domain. In entertaining this question, Maria Angel with Anna Gibbs, and Giovanna di Rosario, evoke the theories of French feminists Luce Irigaray and Hélène Cixous, as well as (for Angel and Gibbs) the more recent Deleuzian-inspired writings of Rosi Braidotti and Elizabeth Grosz, which share an affinity for fluidity, immanence, and non-static forms. Specifically, Angel, Gibbs and di Rosario reference Irigaray's claim that women's language is (or has the potential to be) fluid rather than rigid, intimate rather than formal, sensuous rather than masterful, as in her famous metaphor of two lips touching each other. From Cixous, they take the idea of women's writing as untheorizable because to theorize it is immediately to enter the masculine realm of concepts imbued with phallic mastery. These ideas, which have circulated for some time in print and have called forth numerous literary experiments (including the writings of these theorists themselves), involve an interesting tension when applied to the digital realm. Underlying any screenic text, of course, is the enabling code, from the formatting instructions of html to the processing environments that execute commands. In contrast to the postulated fluidity of women's writing, code is precise and unforgiving, requiring exact syntax and no ambiguities except for what the code permits. Therein lurks a paradox: in order to create the impression of fluidity, the woman writer-programmer must first engage with the rigors of code, either through a software authoring environment, through collaborators who write the code, or directly through constructing the code herself. Moreover, the more innovative and original her vision of how the interface could or should work, the more expertise is required in coding to enact her vision as a performance with which the user can interact.

None of this prevents an innovative work from reaching fulfillment. In this collection, examples include the interfaces described in Kate Armstrong's chapter on her generative art, including *Path: A Generative Bookwork in 12 Volumes*, Amaranth Borsuk's augmented reality work *Between Page and Screen*, María Mencía's *Data-Self*, as well as the work of Aya Karpinska's three-dimensional art analyzed in Giovanna Di Rosario's chapter on "Unfixed Forms in Electronic Poetry." All testify to the power of female digital literature and art in instantiating fluidity, responsiveness, and transience within a non-masterful, non-patriarchal feminist aesthetic.

The tension between rigorous code and fluid interface suggests that the specificities of female writing in the new millennium are enacted not so much through fluidity and unfixed forms in themselves as in the author's abilities to negotiate this tension, to be masterful enough with coding (through whatever means) to instantiate her dream of another kind of regime, another form of creativity that emphasizes play rather than mastery, fluidity rather than static forms, transience rather than permanence. Here we might recall the passage from Virginia Woolf quoted by di Rosario for a clue to how to express this historically specific and technologically mediated juncture. Woolf, Rosario writes, thought that because "the older forms of literature were fixed before women writers could significantly shape their conventions," the "novel alone was young enough to be soft [in the woman writer's] hands" (quoted in di Rosario). Whatever truth Woolf's comment about the novel may once have held, the comment's status in the new millennium is undoubtedly problematic, for by now the novel itself has centuries of (male-dominated) tradition behind it. Nevertheless, one part of Woolf's insight here remains as vital as ever: that new forms are crucial for women's writing, for they enable women artists and writers to escape, in part although never completely, the centuries of male-dominated tradition that, as Marx picturesquely said in another context, "lie like a nightmare on the brains of the living."

Herein lies both the challenges and promises of *#WomenTechLit*—the negotiations this volume charts in the evolving dynamics between code and screen, tradition and innovation, women-specific writing and the common tongue, digital access and broader community, empowerment and constraint. Readers who look to this volume for some kind of final resolution will not find it here. What they—or better, we--will encounter, however, are resources richer than this brief foreword can encompass. These chapters invite us to puzzle over them, speculate about them, and draw upon them. Most importantly, they promise to catalyze our thinking about the positionalities and specificities of women writing and working in technological media across the span of nearly a half-century of work documented here, and the future tendencies toward which these contributions point.

Introduction

BY MARÍA MENCÍA

Readers, writers, artists, critics, historians, scholars, students: this study of Electronic Literature (e-lit) brings together pioneering and emerging women whose work has international impact and scholarly recognition. It covers essays about practice from as early as 1986, such as *Uncle Roger*, the first online hyperfiction by Judy Malloy released originally on Art Com Electronic Network (ACEN) and published online in 1987, and Deena Larsen's *Marble Springs* published with Eastgate Systems in 1993. Although not covered in depth, it covers other early work in literary hypertext and hypermedia such as Alison Knowles's poetry generator, *The House of Dust* (implemented by James Tenney); Natalie Dehn's research on the use of artificial intelligence in authoring systems; the graphic adventure game, *Mystery House*, written and designed by Roberta Williams and programmed by Ken Williams; and Judith Kerman's generative poetry system, *Colloquy*, programmed by Robert Chiles are cited in Judy Malloy's contribution. The early 1990s also saw influential hypertext narratives by Martha Petry, Carolyn Guyer, J. Yellowlees Douglas, Mary-Kim Arnold, Shelley Jackson, and hypertext researcher, Cathy Marshall, published by Eastgate Systems, at a time when Mez Breeze was pioneering *codeworks* in an invented language, Mezangelle, which combined natural language and code and which became her trademark.

The innovations new technologies bring—creative platforms, software packages (Director, Flash, Dreamweaver), programming languages (Processing, Java, HTML, CSS), new media platforms and tools (webcams, mobile technologies, HUD (Heads-Up-Display), Xbox Kinect)—continuously challenge creators and therefore contribute to the formation and evolution of different genres. In this volume an array of digital media forms is discussed by both practitioners and critics, including Augmented Reality (AR) poetry, web-based Virtual Reality, AR Net-worked multimodal and cross-media interactive narratives, 3D games and performance and playable media fiction.

Integral to this work are women practitioners writing essays about their own work that demonstrate the significance of artistic practice-based research in creative fields. I teach media practice in a department of Media, Film and TV Studies, and I struggle to find books that feature women practitioners writing about their work. This collection offers an opportunity to read about what women writers have created, the research and conceptual evolution of their projects, and how they have used technology in their works. At the same time, students and practitioners will be able to read accounts by external critics and theorists about works that are also discussed in the book by their own creators. For instance, Laura Shackelford's "R(e)orienting Poetics and Lived Spaces 'Between'" explores, from a feminist perspective, alternate understandings of digital literary language practice and poetics. She illustrates her thesis on writing spaces which recalibrate the predominant discourses of a masculine lived space with two works of electronic literature, "Between Page and Screen," also discussed in this book by one of its authors, Amaranth Borsuk, and "Transient Self-Portrait," an essay written by myself as a practice-based research project.

Overall, the volume enhances the visibility of women leaders and creators of this field of electronic literature, celebrates their influence in shaping it, and extends a historical critical overview of the state of the field from the diverse perspectives of twenty-eight worldwide contributors. It illustrates the authors' scholarly interests through discussion of creative practice as research, historical accounts documenting collections of women's new media art and literary works, and art collectives. It also covers theoretical approaches and critical overviews, from feminist discourses to close readings and 'close-distant-located readings' of pertinent works in the field and includes authors from Latin America, Russia, Austria, Ireland, Spain, France, Italy, Portugal, Slovakia, Czech Republic, Poland, United Kingdom, Australia, Canada, and the U.S.A.

Electronic Literature is not a new field anymore as this volume demonstrates.[1] Little by little we have incorporated electronic literature in our university curricula, and it has become an established academic field of research and creative practice. There are many books, journal articles about electronic literature, and online publications of work such as the Electronic Literature Collections and The Anthology of European Literature.[2] The Electronic Literature Organization (ELO) presents two awards: the N. Katherine Hayles prize for best work of criticism and the Robert Coover Award for a Work of Electronic Literature.[3] The New Media Writing Prize from Bournemouth University also promotes the best practice in new media writing.[4] The Research group Hermeneia from Barcelona University, together with "Ciutat de Vinaròs" have awarded International Digital Literature Prizes since 2005. And, in 2007, the LETHI Digital Literature Award (Complutense University, Madrid) was the first award dedicated to Digital Literature written in Spanish.

While the above publications and prizes present great opportunities for both theorists and practitioners to show and discuss their work, a book focusing on women writers is a vital input to feminist studies from a social and political perspective. Bring-

1 See Coverley / Luesebrink's contribution to this volume for further information.

2 See http://collection.eliterature.org and https://anthology.elmcip.net.

3 See http://eliterature.org/2016-elo-awards

4 See http://newmediawritingprize.co.uk.

ing together the substantial contributions of women to the field can motivate and inspire young women to engage in computer-mediated studies and related fields, especially those with an interest in exploring new technologies and stretching the possibilities these bring for writing and producing creative work. This volume will be a useful reference for educators, practice-based researchers and scholars, not only of electronic literature but also in the adjacent areas of language art, new media art practices, digital humanities and feminist studies.

Many of these authors have crossed paths at international conferences, workshops and exhibitions organized and supported by the Electronic Literature Organization (ELO),[5] Electronic Literature as a Model of Creativity and Innovation in Practice (ELMCIP),[6] the bi-annual E-Poetry Festival sponsored by the Electronic Poetry Center (Buffalo),[7] and individual events organized by some of the contributors at different universities, galleries and research centres. These include the research group Hermeneia at the University of Barcelona[8]; the interdisciplinary Research Group LEETHI (European and Spanish Literatures from Texts to Hypermedia) from the Complutense University, Madrid, Spain[9]; Bergen Electronic Literature Research Group at UiB, Norway[10]; Laboratoire Paragraphe, EHN (Ecritures et hypermédiations numériques: digital writing and hypermediation) at University of Paris 8, France[11]; the group Lit e Lat (Red de Literatura Electrónica Latinoamericana) ; and more recently, the Creative Computing Lab at the Jagiellonian University, Kraców, Poland[12] and the Creative Process Research Unit (CPRU) at Kingston University, London, UK.[13]

Although this book is organized into four topic sections, many of the essays clearly traverse all four. The first section presents a general overview of e-lit world's histories. Great effort has been put into making this first volume of women digital writers as inclusive as possible, with the list of contributors evolving through the process of compiling the book. The second contains essays on creative practice by the creators. The third focuses on critical readings of creative practice, through enquiry, exploration

5 See http://eliterature.org.

6 See https://elmcip.net.

7 http://epc.buffalo.edu/e-poetry/archive/.

8 http://www.hermeneia.net.

9 See http://www.ucm.es/leethi/.

10 See http://www.uib.no/en/rg/electronicliterature.

11 See http://paragraphe.info.

12 See http://litelat.net and https://www.facebook.com/groups/830496850381009/?ref=bookmarks.

13 http://creativeprocessresearchunit.net/#post-45.

and analysis. And the last discusses the work of early pioneers in the context of the migration of forms through archiving, recovery, preservation and evolution of work. These techniques are necessary in a field where work can become difficult to access in as little as a year if the operating system is upgraded, or the software is made redundant, as for instance in the case of Flash when in 2010 Apple decided not to support it on iOS devices.

I. HISTORIES OF DIGITAL WRITING PRACTICE

Section One reveals the impact of pioneering women in electronic literature. It covers a wide spectrum of Anglophone contributions (UK, USA, Australia, Canada, Ireland) in addition to geographical histories and special theoretical reflection on works from Latin America, Slovakia, Czech Republic, Poland, Spain and Russia. It examines computational and technological developments in media poetics. Among these are the re-appropriation and repurposing of media affordances; the blur of literary and art boundaries (electronic literature, digital poetry, lettrism, performance, language art); and the practice of feminist theories, xenofeminism and cyberfeminism in transnational and intercultural settings. Within these discussions, pioneering and contemporary works are critically analyzed.

M.D. Coverley/ Marjorie C. Luesebrink in her essay "Women Innovate: Contributions to Electronic Literature," documents artworks from 1990 to 2010 which shaped and helped develop the field, among them *Assemblage* and *The Progressive Dinner Party*, two influential collections of women's new media and literary work curated respectively by Carolyn Guertin and Luesebrink. Also presenting a historical review in "Women Making New Media at the trAce Online Writing Community 1995-2005," trAce founder Sue Thomas interviews some of the women whose new media art and writing was featured on the trAce site. Literary critics María Angel and Anna Gibbs, in their essay "At the Speed of Light: Cyberfeminism, Xenofeminism and the Digital Ecology of Bodies," address how feminist thinking might consider the digital transformation of gender and corporeality through a consideration of women's work in electronic literature and textbased digital media art. They discuss cyberfeminist practices from the 1990s, as a form of activism and as art-making process, by considering the work of the Australian feminist collective VNS Matrix (1991), both its narrative and game components and its relation to the development of xenofeminism and feminist theories of current techno- and eco-politics. Claudia Kozak considers how different contexts of economic development, interculturalism, glocalization and the use of new technologies helped shape and influence the creation of electronic literature in Latin America. She analyses, among others, Eugenio Tisselli's and Gustavo Romano's works using what she calls a "close-distant-located reading," although the essay also proposes to include a "collaborative reading" for works of electronic literature. Zuzana Husárová presents a historical account of works of electronic literature in Slovakia and the Czech Republic, with examples of digital literature from the 1960s to current works including her own practice. She focuses on the different approaches (remediation, re-appropriation, remixes, translations, poetic generations) used by authors to create and process the electronic text in artistic and literary forms. Dolores Romero López uses an analytical structure of stage/background/main characters (figures) to discuss main themes, trans-genders, transnational characteristics and cyberfeminism in electronic literature in Spain. Jeneen Naji discusses the evolution of digital poetry from modernism to the present day using a socio-technological approach. Exploring the idea that the relationship between humans and technology is reciprocal, that is, that we adapt to the ubiquity of technology in society and reciprocally technology adapts to our needs, she illustrates how the shape of the digital poem has evolved through the creative use of a variety of media platforms. Natalia Fedorova's essay explores digital letterisms, the material use of unicode characters in art and experimental literature. She considers the role of letters in the era of digital writing, the qualities of their new materiality and multidimensionality, focusing on non-linguistic audial, spatial and temporal properties. Non-referential relationships of signification that can be built around standard sets of graphemes (such as the Latin alphabet, Roman numerals, the QWERTY keyboard layout, ASCII, unicode and n-grams) are studied in works by Hollis Frampton, Dmitry Prigov, John Maeda, Ivan Khimin, and Nick Montfort.

II. DIGITAL WRITING PRACTICE: PRACTITIONERS

Creative practice, as the leading force of electronic literature, is discussed in this section by female electronic writers whose works through the years have influenced and shaped this hybrid and interdisciplinary field creating a vibrant literary and artistic culture. We are presented with the opportunity to hear from the authors/practitioners about their creative processes and about the evolution and production of their work. In doing so, we encounter different research methodologies and creative approaches, as well as the artistic use of emerging technologies to explore concepts and themes to create new literary artistic forms resulting in a variety of genres. These include Virtual Reality (VR); multimodal, interactive, web-based, networked and generative narratives; Augmented-Reality (AR) poetry; playable media fiction; digital storytelling; literary games; conceptual poems; and forms drawing on sound, music and the spoken word.

The works address key concepts and concerns characteristic of electronic literature. Among these are the intersection of print and digital, the page and screen; the exploration of digital literacies; cross-media production; reading technologies; the role of the reader, the author, the audience; performance reading, performance writing and sonic writing. Also explored are meaning and the relationship between form, content, technology and medium; the aesthetics of engagement; interactive aesthetics/poetics; use of data and code as practice; exploration of the spoken word, sound and music in conjunction; textual materiality; semantic text, visual text, sonic text, and multimodal textualities; augmented and virtual reality narrative structures; disruption of linear systems; internet aesthetics; publication in multiple platforms; and, of course, use of programming and software practices.

The works produced engage as well with a wide range of themes and issues relevant to media and cultural studies and to humanities and the arts. These include gender and identity, women's history, female creativity, female digital literary spaces, female representations, womanhood, motherhood, landscape as body and body as landscape. One finds attention to love letters, birth, death, marriages, human trafficking and contemporary slavery, silenced voices of minority groups, cultural aspects of a mediated society, the digital self, ephemerality of technology, mediation, science fiction, sea voyages, space exploration, surveillance and anti-surveillance, psychedelic drug culture, ethics, fashion and artifice.

It is extremely valuable to acknowledge the diversity of processes and methodologies used in the development and production of the selected works of electronic literature. These include practice-based research, script writing, collaboration strategies, maps and mapping, cartographic assemblages, networked image search, generative functions of images and text, digital assemblage, compositional fragmentary recombinations, online live dynamic feeds, détournement, sound sampling and processing of voice and words, spatialization of the voice and algorithmic synaesthesia, remediation of forms, remixing, collage, appropriation of cinema languages and construction of 3D environments.

Focusing on the author's individual essays, Kate Armstrong investigates, through a selection of works, the function of activity and compositional recombination in networked art in order to produce knowledge about how the artistic use of technology can create new literary forms. Amaranth Borsuk focuses on her influential collaboration with Brad Bouse, *Between Page and Screen*. This book of augmented-reality poetry merges the book art and e-poetry traditions, trespassing the boundary between print and digital, old and new media. It enquires into the text's material form, into reading experiences and the connection between form and content in meaning production, thereby questioning the place of books at a time when we are reading more and more on screen. J.R Carpenter reflects upon the transmutation of male-authored print-based forms of narrative into female-narrated digital literary spaces through strategies of détournement employed in the composition of her web-based work *Notes on the Voyage of Owl and Girl*. María Mencía reflects on the development of her practice-based research project, *Transient Self–Portrait*, presenting aim, research enquiries, process and influences in the production of this interactive piece, based on two pivotal sonnets from Spanish literature of the Renaissance and Baroque periods. She investigates new literacies and poetics of engagement while exploring the concepts that emanate from these sonnets with respect to the cultural references and attitudes of our period, the twenty-first-century mediated society and the digital medium we inhabit. Mez Breeze in her essay explains how her "Literary Anti-Surveillance 3D Game *#PRISOM*" originated and evolved, including its focus on privacy, surveillance, and the underlying ethical associations of civil liberty encroachment. Hazel Smith brings up the sonic and abstract properties of language and the semantics of sound in electronic literature through the analysis of her collaborative performance and cross-media works. She explores the relationship between words and sound, literature and music, to argue that the meaning of writing in this multimedia context goes beyond the purely linguistic and reaches an affective intensity that perturbs categorizable emotional states. She maintains these conjunctions between words and music facilitate a wide range of cultural meanings about identity, place, gender and ethnicity. Christine Wilks discusses her work *Underbelly*, a playable media fiction about a woman sculptor carving on the site of a former colliery in the north of England, now landscaped into a country park. In her essay she explores the core ideas of this work within three thematic strands: mining the metaphor, mapping the obscured and re-voicing the unheard, specifically looking at how these concerns play out in this interactive multimodal narrative work. Odile Farge, although not a practitioner, is included in this section because of her interest in the author's creative challenge through the use of different software. In her essay "A 'Rhetoric for Creative Authoring' and the Author's Intent," she presents a critical overview of the relationships authors maintain with authoring tools in order to document the role of software tools in digital creation.

III. CRITICAL OVERVIEWS OF DIGITAL WRITING PRACTICE

In this section, critics, theorists, curators—and in the case of Kathi Inman Berens, also a maker—critically analyze works of electronic literature through methods of close reading, literary approach and feminist perspective. They investigate notions of reading and writing practice; reader engagement and the conceptualization of the poetic; artistic interfaces; writing spaces; gender and identity; sexual politics; digital environments and the role of gender in poetic writing.

Giovanna Di Rosario questions whether the digital medium helps people to break with certain gender views and traditions and whether it offers women new creative possibilities for the writing of poetry. She reviews works such as *Figures* by Marie Bélisle, María Mencía's *Another Kind of Language* and Aya Karpinska and Daniel C. Howe's *Open.ended.* María Goicoechea and Laura Sanchez explore whether there is an existence of a female techno-cultural identity through the analysis of works by Hispanic female writers, among them works by Marla Jacarilla, Tina Escaja, Lara Coterón and Belén Gache. Kathi Inman Berens addresses the question of e-lit reading practices through a feminist approach to interface. She analyzes two very different publication platforms (web and installation) of the *UpsideDown Chandelier*, a collaborative work by four women from different countries (C. Wilks, Z. Husárová, J. Naji, M. Mencía) which consists of generative images and words in different languages simulating the voices of women factory workers from the actual place, currently a media arts centre, where the installation was hosted in Kosice, Slovakia. Angelica Huizar immerses herself in the exploration of artistic, poetic and linguistic experimentations by following a lineage from Latin American avant-garde poetics: the Chilean poet Vicente Huidobro, particularly his *Altazor* (published in 1931, with some fragments written as early as 1919); Argentinean poet Ana María Uribe's *Anipoemas* (1997); and the native Venezuelan, Spanish local, and London-based María Mencía in her *Birds Singing Other Birds' Songs* (2001). Laura Shackelford explores alternate understandings of digital literary writing and e-poetics that emerge from a careful analysis of feminist engagements with digital media. She focuses on Borsuk's and Bouse's *Between Page and Screen* and Mencía's *Transient Self- Portrait* where there is a lived space in-between and beyond the screen. Maya Zalbidea Paniagua, through a comparative analysis and close reading of Shu Lea Cheang 's *Brandon*, invites the reader to reflect on questions of gender, identity and sexual politics.

IV. FORMATIVE PIONEERS OF ELECTRONIC LITERATURE: MIGRATION OF FORMS

In the field of Electronic Literature archiving, recovering and preserving works has become a crucial area of research in which Dene Grigar, curator and current president of the ELO, has been actively involved, recovering works whose delivery platforms are now difficult to access. Her essay, "The Legacy of Judy Malloy," reminds us of the terms of this legacy through an analysis of Malloy's ground-breaking work, *Uncle Roger*. Four influential female digital writers join Grigar by documenting challenges involved in reviving their work from platforms and technology that are now obsolete and by explaining how these works have evolved from floppy disk to the WWW, to CD-ROM, to

DVD, on to laptops and mobile devices. Judy Malloy discusses *its name was Penelope, A Generative Hypertext* (1989); Deena Larsen engages "*Marble Springs*: A Journey of an Electronic Work from the Pre-dawn of the Internet to Today's Golden Age" (1993); Coverley Luesebrink chronicles "The Making and Unmaking of Califia" (2000) and Stephanie Strickland explores "The Death and Re-Distribution of *V*" (2002). Related issues of the obsolescence and ephemerality of technology in connection with work produced in Flash and in the Processing Language are discussed earlier in the volume by Borsuk and Mencía respectively. This last section also serves to highlight works by pioneer writers.

I. HISTORIES OF DIGITAL WRITING PRACTICE

Women Innovate: Contributions to Electronic Literature (1990- 2010)

BY M.D. COVERLEY // MARJORIE COVERLEY LUESEBRINK

The intelligence, knowledge, and creativity it takes to write and/or implement software for artistic purposes can no longer be separated from the work, for the craftwork involved in making a piece materially affects every aspect of the open-work, from its appearance to its functionalities to its interfaces and its operation by the user. The open-work is open in the sense that it serves as a fluid space in which artistic intent commingles with technical expertise. At many levels and in many ways, the material basis for the production of the open-work interpenetrates the work as concept and cannot be separated from it. —N. Katherine Hayles from the introduction to *The Progressive Dinner Party* (2000)[14]

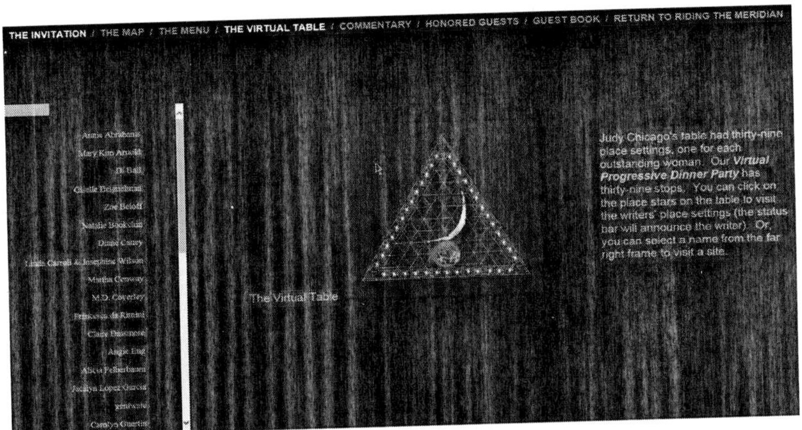

Figure 1: Virtual table for *The Progressive Dinner Party*, 2000

ROLE OF WOMEN IN INITIAL PHASES

While women may have been underrepresented in many initial phases of computers, programming, and communications technology, they have played a major role in digital arts and literature—in the conception, in the critical articulation, and most especially in the creation of works of electronic literature.

We have evidence of women in leadership roles throughout the history of the field. Women start organizations, publish critical studies, launch magazines, author collections, and teach e-lit in colleges and universities. The sheer number of women

14 See *Riding the Meridian*, spring 2000 http://califia.us/RM/haylesfr.htm.

active in many capacities is remarkable (see "Roll Call" below). The substantial presence of women in a highly "technical" field like electronic literature is impressive in itself—but perhaps even more important are the groundbreaking innovations we see in their works.

Why, we might ask, do we see so many women early on in e-lit? Two major issues may have come into play in the development of this field: an undefined canon and an unrestricted entry gate.

First, while the traditional "canon" of print literature still tends to favor male authors, no such filtering system existed for electronic literature. In the 1990's, there were only a few colleges or universities where e-lit was being fostered; for the most part, the field was undefined, wide open. Without pre-existing "standards" against which all writing might be measured, women were free to invent as they chose. Moreover, without critical pre-judgement, readers were equally free to evaluate these creations on the basis of involvement, attention, desire.

Literary canons usually have a formidable entry bar. The threshold might be a classical education, access to publishers and audiences, formal training of some kind, or simply a "room of one's own" – time and money to write. In the history of women in literature, we have seen only a few periods when the obstacles to women were porous.

In much the same way that the 6-shilling, one-volume novel changed the relationship between author and reader for the late Victorian women, providing for a more direct contact, the revolution in communications technology of the 1990's opened a sliding-door-sized window of opportunity for women writers. One need not be situated at university, or hang out with agents in New York, or have impressive connections: anyone with a personal computer and an idea could participate.

And, that is just what we saw happening during the nineties. Some women had published in print previously, and some had university connections, but just as many were working in other fields, held full-time jobs outside academia, had children and families to care for, or were isolated from mainstream literature activities in other ways. A remarkable number of these women have done their work at home on their own personal computers. They all became involved in the emerging culture, began writing in this new language—using text, image, sound, and structure together in a digital environment—and joined in the formation of the corpus of electronic literature.

One of the ways to consider the impact of women in the field of electronic literature is to examine the innovations that contributed to its growth and shaping. While a substantial array of literary practices carried over from print work to electronic creations, women were in the forefront of introducing new practices that did not necessarily propagate traditional forms. In a sense, of course, each discrete work that appeared as the field of e-lit grew was likely to have some novel element that had not been seen before; such was the nature of this new literary genre.

As a result, a short chapter can only point to a very few of the many profound contributions. Our main focus is on e-lit fiction and poetry from 1990 to 2010.

Women's innovations can be observed in Narrative Structure and Architecture, Poetic Design, Visual and Aural Effects, Games and Metagames, Installations, and Coding. Moreover, the unconventional language of poetry and fiction being created by women was materially aided by the launching of "rooms" for this work—collaborative sites and online workshops, e-zines, and online curated collections. Finally, an in-progress list of the women who have worked and are working in digital literature from 1990–2015 illustrates the wealth of talented women who are joined in this singular electronic experiment.

LANDMARK INNOVATIONS

While the above classifications of electronic literature practice are useful in identifying specific elements of invention, they are inherently forced and most often arbitrary for any one work. In proposing innovations based on Poetic Design, for example, I would be citing titles that may also represent breakthroughs in Coding or Visual Effects, and so on, throughout the catalogue. In almost every case, works overlap two or several designations. Alternately, a chronological organization allows us to observe the way in which innovative advances parallel the rapid development of the technology. The following is a rough combination of the two approaches, and, however imperfectly, spotlights some especially transformational work.

1990 (OR EARLIER) – 2000 // THE FIRST WAVE

NARRATIVE STRUCTURE AND ARCHITECTURE

One of the most attractive affordances facilitated by digital-based works is a visual layout of the story architecture. Using mapping and/or locative-based organization, a whole new way of storytelling is possible. It is particularly telling that mapping, location, and spatial detail seemed to echo and extend some of the qualities of modern and contemporary women's print fiction. Electronic narratives (and some notable women-authored print literature) can be said to be characterized by, among other features: simultaneity, multiplicity of voice, layering of history, recursion, and re-interpretation of the physical world. In looking at early e-lit works by women, it appears that they also led the field in abandoning many of the default print assumptions and moving into a spatial-based conceptual story-world.

It is impossible to be authoritative about "firsts" in the illustrations below, and much scholarship still needs to be done. But one can say that certain works were among the remarkable examples of imaginative narrative shaping in early digital literature.

JUDY MALLOY: *UNCLE ROGER*

Judy Malloy is a California poet and an early creator of online interactive and collaborative fiction. She wrote *Uncle Roger* (1986), the first online hyperfiction, for the Art Com Electronic Network on the WELL. *Uncle Roger* was released on ACEN in 1986 as a narrative intervention and published online as an interactive hypertext on ACEN Datanet in 1987. Malloy styled her work as "narrabase," using molecular narrative units to create nonsequential narrative on the personal computer. Still active in the field, her work is archived at the David M. Rubenstein Rare Book and Manuscript Library at Duke University.

http://www.well.com/user/jmalloy/uncleroger/partytop.html
http://www.well.com/user/jmalloy/

DEENA LARSEN: *MARBLE SPRINGS*

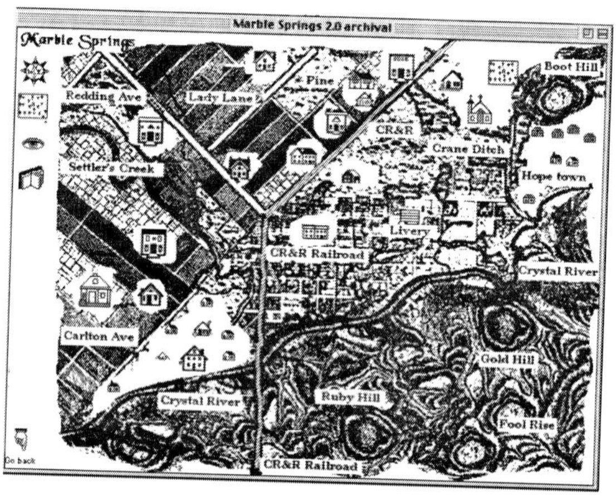

Figure 2: Visual of the town of *Marble Springs*.

Deena Larsen's *Marble Springs* (1993, Eastgate Systems), illustrated by Kathleen A. Turner-Suarez, makes a remarkable jump into the possibilities of electronic narrative. Composed originally in HyperCard, it was published by Eastgate Systems on floppy disk. The text is a series of narrative character-poems, but the interface architecture represents an entirely new vision of story access. The events take place in the mythical Marble Springs, Colorado, and the old mining town comes alive through photographs.

The story is organized according to the residents, maps of the town and nearby places, and connections between the characters. The visual mapping provides the organizational navigation for the narrative. Readers may also contribute to the tales. US-based, Larsen's work is archived at MITH at the University of Maryland.http://marblesprings.wikidot.com/

http://www.deenalarsen.net/

SHELLEY JACKSON: *PATCHWORK GIRL*

Shelley Jackson is an American writer and artist known for her cross-genre experiments, including her groundbreaking work of hyperfiction, *Patchwork Girl* (1995, Eastgate Systems). *Patchwork Girl* is a narrative constructed on the body itself. The body parts—sewed together like Frankenstein's monster or the Patchwork Girl of Oz—each tell a part of the effort to "patch" enough pieces together to form an identity and to tell the story. Individual segments lead down a linked trail of lexia, offering the reader multiple directions. Both the layering of a contemporary story with Oz and Mary Shelley and the invention of body-part chapters, as it were, represent a revolutionary use of Storyspace and an ingenious first in e-literature.

Available through Eastgate Systems: http://www.eastgate.com/people/Jackson.html

POETIC DESIGN

Certain kinds of poetry (Visual Poetry, Concrete Poetry) have always placed importance on the visual aspect of the page. Digital poetry emphasized and expanded the possibilities for text, image, sound, and code language as material elements.

ANA MARÍA URIBE (DEC.): *TIPOEMAS Y ANIPOEMAS*

Ana María Uribe (1951-2004) is an Argentine visual poet who made work online beginning in 1997, after working in other media for many years. She started writing visual poetry in the late 1960's, and her style continued to evolve. Her works reflect, as Jim Andrews writes, "a remarkable understanding of the poem on the screen as a performance." In the poems, text is generally used pictorially and rotated or otherwise manipulated to introduce a sense of motion into the scene. *Deseo - Desejo - Desire* (2002) is one such piece that illustrates the original nature of her poetry.

http://www.vispo.com/uribe/deseo/deseo.html

http://www.vispo.com/uribe (maintained by Jim Andrews)

ANNIE ABRAHAMS: *SEPARATION / SÉPARATION*

Annie Abrahams is a Dutch performance artist working largely in France. She specializes in video installations and internet-based performances which also consist of writings that derive from collective interaction. In addition to her landmark work *Being Human* (1997-2007), Abrahams has reinvented how work might look on the screen. A good example of this is *Separation / Séparation* (2002), reflecting the body's process in reading and writing, and the trauma of overuse. The piece must be read slowly, and the screen appears blank unless and until the reader coaxes out a message.

http://collection.eliterature.org/2/works/abrahams_separation/separation/
https://aabrahams.wordpress.com/

MEZ: *_THE DATA][H!][BLEEDING T.EX][E][TS*

MEZ (Mary Ann Breeze) is an Australian-based artist and practitioner of net.art. Widely recognized for her signature codework language *mezangelle*, she has been creating a hybridization of human-only and digital languages since 1995. Using a condensed and vaguely phonetic language of email messages, ASCII codes, and online games, MEZ designs a text that fragments and recombines words, making a hybrid script that commingles alphabet writing and binary code. *_the data][h!][bleeding t.ex][e][ts* (2001) are remnants from email performances devoted to the dispersal of writing that has been inspired and mutated according to the dynamics of an active network. As of May 2014, Mez is the only Interactive Writer and Artist who's a non-USA citizen to have her comprehensive career archive (called "The Mez Breeze Papers") housed at Duke University, at the David M. Rubenstein Rare Book & Manuscript Library.

http://netwurkerz.de/mez/datableed/complete/
http://netwurker.livejournal.com/

VISUAL AND AURAL EFFECTS

As the web developed in the late nineties, design possibilities expanded. Sound, image, layering, frames, and movement were used by women to create strikingly original online work.

ADRIANNE WORTZEL: *THE ELECTRONIC CHRONICLES*

American contemporary artist Adrianne Wortzel creates unique and innovative interactive web works, robotic and telerobotic installations, performance productions, videos, and writings. These works explore historical and cultural perspectives by coupling fact and fiction via use of new technologies in both physical and virtual networked environments. *RIGHTING NOVEL FOR THE WORLD WIDE WEB* includes *The Electronic Chronicles.* This web art project was produced as a thesis project for an MFA in Computer Arts at the School of Visual Art in 1995. It was accompanied by a separate thesis paper described on her website, as follows:

> *The Electronic Chronicles* consists of text and images created for and on the World Wide Web. The work is in the form of hypermedia. I.e. text and images are activated to link to other text and/or images. It is meant to be viewed with the latest and most developed graphical browsers, at this time that is Netscape 1.1b3. It is scripted in HTML (Hypertext Markup Language). Clusters of stories and articles are continually constructed and connected to each other as well as to other sites on the Internet, the World Wide Web sites, and to virtual communities.

Figure 3: The Muses of *The Electronic Chronicles.*

http://www.adriannewortzel.com/electronic-chronicles-contents/
http://www.adriannewortzel.com/

OLIA LIALINA: *MY BOYFRIEND CAME BACK FROM THE WAR*

Moscow-born Olia Lialina is a pioneer internet artist, theorist, experimental film and video critic, and curator. She founded Art Teleportacia, a web gallery of her work, which also features links to remakes of her most famous 1996 piece *My boyfriend came back from the war*. This early black-and-white web story featured original animated gifs and a direct, intimate style that Lialina terms "digital folklore." Some of her artwork is maintained in the Computerfinearts.com collection at the Rose Goldsen Archive of New Media Art, Cornell University.

http://www.teleportacia.org/war/
http://art.teleportacia.org/olia.html

CHRISTY SHEFFIELD SANFORD: *LIGHT-WATER: A MOSAIC OF MEDITATIONS*

Christy Sheffield Sanford is an American print poet and mixed genre artist/creative writer using advanced web techniques. Christy Sheffield Sanford's *Light-Water: a Mosaic of Mediations* (1999) is a hypermedia web work using DHTML, layers, and Java to create a striking experience of poetic meditation. It simulates depth through the layering of text and image. Sanford's visual lushness opened up radical new possibilities for the look of the screen and the combination of merged image, movement, and text.

Unfortunately, much of Sanford's work is currently difficult to find online.

AURIEA HARVEY: *GENESIS*

Auriea Harvey is an African-American artist, who co-authors with Michaël Samyn, a Belgian artist and programmer. In 1999 they co-founded the zine Entropy8Zuper! During this period, they created works such as *The Godlove Museum*, a website that showcased their storytelling strengths by merging Biblical stories with narratives drawn from their own lives and contemporary culture. *Genesis* is the beginning of these visually compelling pieces.

http://entropy8zuper.org/godlove/fuxation/
http://entropy8zuper.org/godlove/

CLAIRE DINSMORE: *THE DAZZLE AS QUESTION*

Claire Dinsmore is a designer who has turned her hand to jewelry, interiors, and web sites. Starting in the late 1990's, she employed her design background to create lovely fusions of image, sound, and movement. Published in *Poems That Go*, editors described *The Dazzle as Question* (2002) as follows:

> an animated hypermedia poem which traces the conflict between the left and right brain inclinations of an erstwhile 'old school' artist [as] experienced via his encounter with the digital realm. This conflict notes the [digital] media/um's seemingly unrivaled sway as pitted against the narrator's right brain predilections.

http://poemsthatgo.com/gallery/summer2002/dazzle/launch.htm
http://www.studiocleo.com/

GAMES AND METAGAMES, INSTALLATIONS

Part of the experimental fictional world of digital literature during this period included new types of story generation and crossover media experiments.

NATALIE BOOKCHIN: *THE INTRUDER*

California-based Natalie Bookchin is well known for the variety of her work: online computer games, collaborative performances and "hacktivist" interventions, interactive websites, and widely distributed texts and manifestos. *The Intruder* (1999) is a web-based, hybrid, interactive narrative that uses a series of classic videogames to propel the story forward, and was innovative in its use of gaming as a strategy for interactive storytelling, merging literature, art, and games. It was based on 1966 short story by Jorge Luis Borges, also titled "The Intruder."

http://bookchin.net/intruder/
http://bookchin.net/

DIANA REED SLATTERY: *GLIDE*

U.S.-based Diana Slattery opened new possibilities with *Glide: an interactive exploration of visual language* (1997). This open-work is part flash fiction labyrinth, part visual symphony, part game, part language invention, and part of a much larger project, including a three-volume print novel. It presents the user with a visually stunning and conceptually intriguing lexicon of marks that express a sinuous fluidly. The narrative of the "Death Dancers" further unites image and text through a fascinating story of novitiates who struggle to negotiate a labyrinth whose passages are shaped like the letters of *Glide*, thus conflating abstract inscription with material object. The narrative enhances our appreciation of what reading is in a mixed-media environment, for it encompasses not just verbal decoding but also visual thinking, kinesthetic manipulation, and a cyborg fusion of medium and subjectivity.

http://psychedelicsandlanguage.com/the-guild/diana-slattery-glide/
http://psychedelicsandlanguage.com/

CAMILLE UTTERBACK: *TEXT RAIN*

Camille Utterback is an interactive installation artist currently based at Stanford University. Initially trained as a painter, her work is at the intersection of art and interactive literature. Created in 1999 with Romy Achituv, *Text Rain* is an interactive installation in which participants use the familiar instrument of their bodies to do what seems magical, to lift and play with falling letters that do not really exist. In the *Text Rain* installation participants stand or move in front of a large projection screen. On the screen they see a mirrored video projection of themselves in black and white, combined with a color animation of falling letters. Like rain or snow, the letters appears to land on participants' heads and arms. The letters respond to the participants' motions and can be caught, lifted, and then let fall again. "Reading" the phrases in the *Text Rain* installation becomes a physical as well as a cerebral endeavor.

http://camilleutterback.com/projects/text-rain/
http://camilleutterback.com/

CODING

Much of the work done by women in the 90's included either some or significant amounts of coding. In many cases, the projects were elaborately conceived and carried out

LISA JEVBRATT: *EVERYBODY SAYS SHE DOESN'T LOOK LIKE THIS, IT DOESN'T MATTER, SHE WILL*

Lisa Jevbratt is a Swedish artist working in California who has been exploring the expressions and exchanges created by the protocols and languages of the internet and the web. Her visualizations are remarkable, beginning with her early piece 1991-1992 using computer-manipulated photography *Everybody Says She Doesn't Look Like This, It Doesn't Matter, She Will.* A later work, *1:1* (Web Site, Softbots, Database 1999/2002) was a project that consisted of a database which would eventually contain the address of every web site in the world and interfaces through which to view and use the database. *1:1(2)* is a continuation of the project including a second database of addresses generated in 2001 and 2002 and interfaces that show and compare the data from both databases.

http://jevbratt.com/home_projects.html

2000 – 2010 // MEDIA-RICH FUSIONS

Although time divisions in electronic literature are arbitrary, after 2000 we began to see elaborations of strategies for Narrative Structure and Architecture, Poetic Design, Visual and Aural Effects, Games and Metagames, Installations, and Coding. Increased bandwidth, new technologies, and a maturing field brought more impressive inventions.

YOUNG HAE CHANG HEAVY INDUSTRIES: *THE LAST DAY OF BETTY NKOMO*

Based in Seoul, South Korea, YOUNG-HAE CHANG HEAVY INDUSTRIES combines text with jazz to create Web-based New Media work. The work, presented in 20 languages, is characterized by text-based animation composed in Adobe Flash that is highly synchronized to a musical score. Young Hae Chang and Marc Voge strip away interactivity, graphics, photos, illustrations, and colors to leave viewers with language and sound. The result is a strangely appropriate and unique delivery–whether heavy satire or light political protest. *The Last Day of Betty Nkomo* (2000) is a heartrending account of a woman dying of AIDS.http://www.yhchang.com/BETTY_NKOMO.html

http://www.yhchang.com/

M.D. COVERLEY: *CALIFIA*

California-based Marjorie C. Luesebrink writes hypermedia fiction as M.D. Coverley. *Califia* (2000, Eastgate Systems on CD-ROM) takes the spatial-visual narrative into epic-novel territory. Using a linked and layered structure, *Califia* traces the stories of three California families as their lives intersect over five generations of Los Angeles history. The reader can choose between three narrators; select any one of four compass directions; consult star charts, map cases, archive files, and family albums to piece together the accounts. Using Toolbook, Coverley filled the object-oriented landscape with 2400 images, 30 songs, and over 500 words. The scope of *Califia* introduced several new ways of navigating story architecture.

Available through Eastgate Systems: http://www.eastgate.com/catalog/Califia.html

http://califia.us

MARÍA MENCÍA: *BIRDS SINGING OTHER BIRDS' SONGS*

María Mencía is a Spanish-born media artist and researcher working in London. *Birds Singing Other Birds' Songs* was developed in 2001 for three different media: print, video installation, and interactive work for the web. The work is an exploration into the idea of the translation process: from birds' sounds into language and back to birds' songs via the human voice with knowledge of language. These birds are animated "text birds" singing the sound of their own text while flying in the sky.

http://www.mariamencia.com/pages/birds.html

http://www.mariamencia.com/

GISELLE BEIGUELMAN: *CODE MOVIE 1*

Giselle Beiguelman is a Brazilian media artist. Her work includes interventions in public spaces, networked projects, and mobile art applications; she has exhibited internationally in the main media art museums, research centers and contemporary art venues. Beiguelman's *Code Movie 1* (2004) treats the hexadecimal code of JPG images as a signifier in its own right. Beiguelman's "The book after the book" (1999) is a hypertextual and visual essay that defines in the source of the page: "The Internet is no more than a big text. On the front, at the screen, text reveals itself as image."

http://collection.eliterature.org/1/works/beiguelman__code_movie_1.html
https://www.digitalartarchive.at/database/artists/general/artist/beiguelman.html

DONNA LEISHMAN: *DEVIANT: THE POSSESSION OF CHRISTIAN SHAW*

Scotland-based Donna Leishman is an illustrator, animator, and graphic designer. *Deviant: The Possession of Christian Shaw* (2004) is a pioneering work in several ways: It takes its inspiration from a document of the 1696 witch trial of Christian Shaw's purported demonic possession. But the animated, interactive graphic landscape is strangely sparse and forces the reader to probe carefully into the Flash-based labyrinth of the story. The interface offers well-hidden "active" portals, which may or may not move the reader forward. A series of "signs" signal the navigational possibilities.

http://collection.eliterature.org/1/works/leishman__deviant_the_possession_of_christian_shaw.html
http://www.6amhoover.com/

GENIWATE: *CONCATENATIONS*

Geniwate's *Rice* (also spelled Geniwaite in some sources, Dr. Jenny Weight is an Australian writer) was the co-winner of the 1998 trAce/AltX hypertext competition. She went on to create fascinating generative poetry with intricate coding, such as *Concatenations* (2005). These works of generative poetry employ combinations of algorithms to create an unpredictable poetic "performance piece." Moving the mouse may result in other types of change. Users need only click to create a new iteration of these poems. The sophistication of the coding creates an endlessly-varying experience.

http://collection.eliterature.org/1/works/geniwate__generative_poetry.html
http://idaspoetics.com.au/

ONI BUCHANAN: *THE MANDRAKE VEHICLES*

While kinetic text has been a staple of electronic poetry, the legacy of Ana María Uribe is continued in masterful fashion by Oni Buchanan. The Electronic Literature Collection Volume 2 editors commented:

> *The Mandrake Vehicles* (2006) challenges our notions of the normal economy of a poetic text by providing numerous different readings of the same set of letters, in the process concretely moving the graphemical (if not psychological) "sub-text" of a poem to the foreground in clever, surprising ways. Transitional anima-

tions, in which letters fall, expand and disappear, transport the reader between texts through a [...] sort of warp, a pictorial revelry that brings this seemingly stable, stylistically intricate text to the frontier of linguistic meaninglessness and back.

Oni Buchanan is a poet, pianist, and the founder and director of the Ariel Artists management company.

http://collection.eliterature.org/2/works/buchanan_mandrake_vehicles.html
http://www.onibuchanan.com/

STEPHANIE STRICKLAND: *SLIPPINGGLIMPSE*

Figure 4: Video of *slippinglimspe* with poetry written on the water

Stephanie Strickland is a New York City-based print and electronic poet. Among her several groundbreaking pieces the eco-poem *slippingglimpse* (2007) stands out, a collaboration between Strickland, Cynthia Lawson Jaramillo, and videographer Paul Ryan. Reading in this poem is accomplished by human and non-human agents, treated with equal respect. Wave patterns in the water exert their "force" on the lines and phrases of the poetry, and because a motion-tracking algorithm is "reading" the motion in the water videos and "writing" numbers into a reference table, the poem phrases can be read by this motion and their repositioning accordingly is a form of writing, writing done by the water! Human readers can watch the water read the poem-text by choosing full-screen; read the print poem-text itself at any speed, in any direction via scroll-text; or contemplate the patterns that the video camera captured in hi-rez mode. Choosing regenerate initiates the reading process anew with different phrases from the poem.

Strickland's files and papers are archived at the David M. Rubenstein Rare Book and Manuscript Library at Duke University.

http://www.slippingglimpse.org
http://www.stephaniestrickland.com/

CAITLIN FISHER: *ANDROMEDA*

Andromeda (2008) is just one of the suites of projects produced over the last two decades by Canadian artist Caitlin Fisher. After winning the first ELO Fiction Prize for *These Waves of Girls* in 2001 (this piece was also the first hypertextual dissertation in Canada), Fisher began coding augmented reality pieces (poems, tabletop theatre, web-viewable and immersive augmented reality fictions) and building the interfaces to display them. *Andromeda*, a poem about stars, loss, and women named Isabel, breaks new ground in coding, architecture, and platform. The poem is brought to life when a reader, using a camera attached to a computer, unlocks the textual, video and audio elements associated with the markers – the basic idea being that the camera 'sees' these symbols being explored and overlays digital content. The resulting poem can be viewed on the computer screen or through a head-mounted display.

http://collection.eliterature.org/2/works/fisher_andromeda.html
http://www.yorku.ca/caitlin/home/

SHARON DANIEL: *BLOOD SUGAR*

Sharon Daniel is a California-based media artist who produces interactive and participatory documentaries focused on issues of social, economic, environmental, and criminal justice. She builds online archives and interfaces and installations that make the stories of marginalized and disenfranchised communities available across social, cultural, and economic boundaries. *Blood Sugar* (2010) operates as a companion piece to her and designer Erik Loyer's earlier, Webby award-winning Vectors project *Public Secrets* (2008). Like their earlier work, which featured the voices of women in the California State Prison system, the primary content of *Blood Sugar* is a voice archive compiled from painstakingly recorded interviews with participants in an HIV prevention and needle exchange program in Oakland, CA.

http://bloodandsugar.net/
http://www.sharondaniel.net/

MAKING A ROOM FOR ELIT

ONLINE AND COLLABORATIVE HYPERFICTION

One delightful development in early e-lit was the online collaborative fiction site. Several of these were produced but not all of them are still available. Sue Thomas and Teri Hoskin created the hypertext web piece, *Noon Quilt* (1998-1999) which was comprised of "quilt pieces" submitted to the trAce OnlineWriting Community by women. Christie Sheffield Sanford hosted a piece in which collaborators chose an hour of the day to tell the story of *The Book of Hours* of Madame de Lafayette (1997). Carolyn Guyer invited women to write about their mothers for the new century in *MotherMillennia* (1999). These collections encouraged women to try their hand at born-digital writing in an atmosphere of support and friendship.

"COMMUNITY" PROJECTS AND WORKSHOP SITES

Part of the opportunity for open participation in electronic literature was provided by the affordances of the medium itself. Collaborative online sites, group workshops, online instruction, MOOs, MUDs, chats, and discussion lists combined and morphed into virtual colloquiums and writer's colonies. Some of the earliest and most influential of these were initiated by women.

DENE GRIGAR: *NOUSPACE GALLERY & MEDIA LOUNGE*

Dene Grigar's NOUSPACE Gallery & Media Lounge began in 1997 as NOUSPACE, a virtual environment aimed at experimenting with online, participatory communities. NOUSPACE was a MOO (or "Multi-User Domain Object-Oriented") that brought people together from across the world in one space for poetry readings, lectures, meetings, and social gatherings. Grigar had joined LinguaMOO in 1994 and defended her dissertation in it in 1995. The development of her own virtual environment, Nouspace, while she taught at Texas Woman's University, offered a place to continue thinking about what it means to live and work online and how one best interacts with and presents multimedia on the web. Some of the highlights of Nouspace during this period included hosting 750 scholars to an online version of the 1999 Feminisms and Rhetoric Conference (hosted by the U of Minnesota) and teaching numerous university courses, like "Feminist Cyberculture," "American Women and Literature" and "World Literature" synchronously online at the site.

http://dtc-wsuv.org/wp/nouspace/history/

REGINA CÉLIA PINTO: *MUSEUM OF THE ESSENTIAL AND BEYOND THAT*

Regina Célia Pinto is a Brazilian artist whose work focuses on web-based and CD-ROM art. Pinto's utilization of technology is permeated with a poetic and playful sensibility. Global awareness and desire to make connections characterize most of her work. Pinto, who calls herself a "net artist," broke new ground with her elaborately conceived *Museum of the Essential and Beyond That*. This virtual museum exhibits the work of international artists with special emphasis on South American digital art. The plan of the building attests to the global ambitions of the project. It includes areas dedicated to topics such as Cartographies of Globalization, Cloning and the Web, Esthetic of Tragedy, Borders of net.art and Web Art Today, The Concept of Borders Today, Electronic Poetry, Electronic Artist's Books, Anthropological and Sociological [issues], a video room, and a game room. The entrance to the extensive "web museum" features a map that allows the reader to select from different galleries to read stories, connect with writers, and submit material. Pinto's own pieces such as *Viewing Axolotls* and *The Book of Sand* can be accessed from the library.

http://arteonline.arq.br/

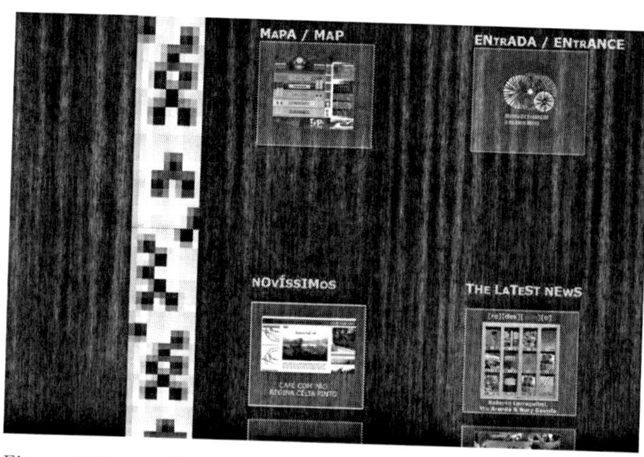

Figure 5: Excerpt from opening page for *The Museum of the Essential and Beyond That*

http://arteonline.arq.br/library.htm

MELINDA RACKHAM: *-EMPYRE-*

Melinda Rackham initiated -empyre- as part of her doctoral research in 2002. This Australia-based online discussion list facilitates critical perspectives on contemporary cross-disciplinary issues, practices and events in networked media by inviting guests – key new media artists, curators, theorists, and others – to participate in thematic discussions It welcomes guest moderators who organize discussions for one month. The empyre- soft-skinned space continues to be a platform dedicated to the plurality of global perspectives reaching out beyond Australia and the Northern Hemisphere to greater Asia and Latin America.

http://empyre.library.cornell.edu/

SUE THOMAS: *THE TRACE ONLINE WRITING CENTRE*

Sue Thomas provided the vision and the leadership behind the trAce Online Writing Centre. Based in the UK, from 1995-2005 the Centre hosted a unique international community where, using the internet as both medium and raw material, trAce contributors generated an unequalled body of innovative creative work. This group supported and influenced the development of new media writing worldwide and promoted lively debate about the impact of the web on the future of text and literature. Today, the trAce Archive houses a broad range of original new media writing, articles, and transcripts of practice-based discussions.

http://tracearchive.ntu.ac.uk/index.asp

E-ZINES

If there existed barriers for women in writing in the past, the requirements for becoming a publisher were perhaps even more daunting. Not so with the advent of the WWW. Suddenly, talented editors and designers emerged – starting up fascinating e-zines from colleges and universities, coffeehouses, and kitchen tables. Among the new online publishers, several were women. It would be impossible to list them all – the but following specialized specifically in digital literature.

Born Magazine – Anmarie Trimble, Jennifer Grotz, and Molly Sokolow Hayden
Cauldron & Net – Claire Dinsmore
Hyperrhiz: New Media Cultures – Helen Burgess
Poems That Go – Ingrid Ankerson and Megan Sapnar
Riding the Meridian – Jennifer Ley
trAce and *frAme* – Sue Thomas

COLLECTIONS

CAROLYN GUERTIN: *ASSEMBLAGE: THE WOMEN'S NEW MEDIA GALLERY*

Carolyn Guertin describes this collection, begun in 1995, in the Introduction as follows:

> This international gathering of women's voices is a showcase of new media art being created on and off the World Wide Web. I call this show space an "assemblage" because it is a multiplicity. It is a coming together of languages, skills and visions, a collection of art texts, and an exhibit showing the act of fitting disparate pieces together under the umbrella of gender. It is also a unification of art parts into a new gallery and a new work of art in its own right made of found objects.

The Assemblage was "retired" with the closure of trAce in 2005. A valuable catalogue of early women writers, it is available on the trAce Archive site.

http://tracearchive.ntu.ac.uk/traced/guertin/assemblage.htm

MARJORIE COVERLEY LUESEBRINK AND CAROLYN GUERTIN: *THE PROGRESSIVE DINNER PARTY*

Modeled on Judy Chicago's iconic "Dinner Party," *The Progressive Dinner Party* is a virtual showcase of 39 English-language, web-specific literary works by an international selection of women. With commentary by N. Katherine Hayles and Talan Memmott, it was published in *Riding the Meridian's* special Women and Technology issue in 2000.

http://califia.us/RM/predinner.htm

ROLL CALL (ONGOING)

This Roll Call is a yet-to-be-completed list of women who were active e-lit between 1990 and 2015. It is a continuing compilation – including practitioners, teachers, critics, and scholars. The list is currently heavily weighted toward earlier years; more recent names and more international names need to be added. Readers of this piece are encouraged to e-mail the author with further suggestions for the Roll Call <luesebr1@ix.netcom.com>. The Roll Call is on the www at http://califia.us/wormenwork.

There are several reasons why a scattering of the women listed are no longer active in the field, often having produced one or a few stunning works and then moved on.

One reason that stands out is the lack of acceptance of "creative" work in colleges and universities. Women on tenure track found that they needed to direct much of their energies to critical work and spend less time on poetry or fiction.

Some women made e-lit works as a side experiment while they pursued a different career in the arts: Laurie Anderson's *Door Where Carol Merril is Still Standing* and her video poems were fascinating asides to her performance art. Adriene Jenik's *Mauve Desert* was one of the earliest electronic narrations, but she works, now, in large-scale public art events utilizing community-based wireless networks.

Finally, and not a negligible issue, electronic literature, still regarded as "experimental," has not become commercial. Aside from securing a teaching job, one cannot make a steady living from it. Some women found their primary (money-producing) careers more demanding as time went by. Such was the case for Claire Dinsmore, whose Studio Cleo was partly a hub for her commercial design business. Auriea Harvey and her partner left net art for video games; in 2002, they founded Tale of Tales, an independent game development studio.

Notwithstanding, this list of over 200 women continues to grow; it attests to the ongoing participation of women in electronic literature.

Abrahams, Annie
Anderson, Laurie
Ankerson, Ingrid
Angel, Maria
Armstrong, Kate
Arnold, Mary-Kim

Baker, Laurie
Ball, Cheryl
Ball, Di
Bazarnik, Katarzyna
Beiguelman, Giselle
Bell, Alice
Beloff, Zoe
Berens, Kathi Inman
Bergeron, Annick
Bergvall, Caroline
Berkenheger, Susanne
Boluk, Stephanie
Bookchin, Natalie
Borsuk, Amaranth
Brine, Lola

Buchanan, Nancy
Burgess, Helen

Calvi, Licia
Caney, Diane
Carpenter, J.R.
Carroli, Linda
Carroll, Amy Sara
Castanyer, Laura Borràs
Charney, Davida
Chatelain, Jules
Clifford, Alison
Conway, Martha
Coverley, MD (Marjorie C. Luesebrink)
Cramer, Kathryn

Damon, Maria
Daniel, Sharon
da Rimini, Francesca
da Silva, Ana Marques
Davino, Caterina
Davies, Chrystin
Davis, Juliet
di Blasi, Debra
di Rosario, Giovanna
Dinsmore, Claire
Donato, Claire
Douglas, Jane Yellowlees

Eisen, Adrienne
Emerson, Lori
Emily Short
Eng, Angie
Engberg, Maria
Ensslin, Astrid

Farge, Odile

Fedorova, Natalia
Felberbaum, Alicia
Fernandez-Vara, Clara
Ferraiolo, Angela
Fisher, Caitlin
Flanagan, Mary
Florence, Penny
Frenkel, Vera
Froehlich, Elaine

Gaché, Belén
García, Dora
Gibb, Susan
Gibb, Anna
Geniwate
Glaros, Michelle
Goicoechea, María
Gorman, Samantha
Górska-Olesinska, Monika
Goss, Jacqueline
Greco, Diane
Green, Jo-Anne
Grigar, Dene
Gromala, Diane
Guertin, Carolyn
Guyer, Carolyn

Harvey, Auriea
Hayles, N. Katharine
Heyward, Megan
Holmes, Janet
Hoskin, Teri
Huffman, Kathy Rae
Huizar, Angelica
Husárová, Zuzana
Inman Berens, Kathi

Jackson, Shelley
Jacobs, Sarah
Janis, Lori
Jaramillo, Cynthia Lawson
Jeremijenko, Natalie
Jevbratt, Lisa

Kaplan, Nancy
Karpinska, Aya
Keane, Jayne Fenton
Kerman, Judith
Kikiyama
King, Deb + 48 others
Klastrup, Lisbeth
Klink, Flourish
Knipe, Elizabeth
Knowles, Alison
Knox, Elena
Kozak, Claudia

Lacetti, Jess
Lambert, Jeanette (Jean Net)
Lang, Dorothee
LaPorta, Tina
Larsen, Deena
Laurel, Brenda
Lawrynovicz, Kerry
Lazariuk, Leah
LeCor, Gwen
Leishman, Donna
Ley, Jennifer
Lialina, Olia
Libby, Lee
López, Dolores Romero
Lopez-Garcia, Jacalyn

Mac, Kathy

Marshall, Cathy
Martin, Julie Ann
Masurel, Pauline (Mazzy)
McPhee, Christina
Mencía, María
Mez (Mary Anne Breeze)
Malloy, Judy
Morris, Adalaide (Dee)
Mueller, Petra
Monro, Kate
Murray, Janet
Mylonas, Elli

Naji, Jeneen
Nanard, Jocelyn
Nesheim, Elizabeth
Nestvold, Ruth
Niss, Millie (dec.)

Odin, Jaishree
O'Rourke, Karen

Pearce, Celia
Pearl, Amy
Pinto, Regina Célia
Pressman, Jessica
Pryor, Sally
Pullinger, Kate

Rackham, Melinda
Raley, Rita
Rapoport, Sonya
Ramsay, Lehan
Rau, Anja
Rivera, Raquel
Romero López, Dolores
Rodgers, Johannah

Rueb, Teri

Saemmer, Alexandra
Salter, Anastasia
Sanford, Christy Sheffield
Sánchez, Laura
Sanz, Amelia
Sapnar, Megan
Sassoon-Henry, Perla
Seaman, Patricia
Shackelford, Laura
Short, Emily
Sengers, Phoebe
Slattery, Diana Reed
Smith, Hazel
Smith, K.E. (Brown)
Sourkes, Cheryl,
Steffensen Jyanni
Strickland, Stephanie
Stringfellow, Kim
Swanstrom, Lisa
Szilak , Illya

Thomas, Sue
Thorington, Helen
Tomaszek, Patricia
Tosca, Susan Pajares
Trimble, Anmarie
Trudel, Pascale

Uribe, Anna María dec.
Utterback, Camille

van der Klei, Alice

Walker-Rettberg, Jill
Waterson, Sarah

Weidenhammer, Lori
Welby, Victoria
Wenz, Karin
Werner, Marta
White, Kim
Whitehead, Helen
Wilks, Christine
Williams, Roberta
Wilson, Josephine
Winson, Leonie
Wortzel, Adrianne
Wylde, Nanette
Wysocki, Anne Frances

Young Hae-Chang
Yoon, Jin-Me

Zalbidea Paniagua, Maya
Zamora, Mia
Zellen, Jodi
Zerbarini, Marina
Zeriff, Natalie
Zurkow, Marina

2010 AND BEYOND

By the year 2000 the presence of women in e-lit was continuing to grow. The elements of the field, however, were changing even more rapidly. While many more women held college and university jobs in digital media arts and digital humanities, the speed of technology made producing and sharing work more difficult for individual practitioners. A rapid succession of browsers, escalating prices for proprietary software (and its discontinuance), and the unreliability of "soft" funding have all taken a toll on women writers and "communities" that nourished them.

Regardless, Katharine Hayles' vision of "open craftwork" survives in the new generation of women in electronic literature. An expanded Roll Call and a survey of the excellent work being done in fiction and poetry, digital humanities scholarship, curating, and e-lit leadership must await further research and a full-length book.

Women Making New Media at the trAce Online Writing Community 1995-2005

BY SUE THOMAS

> It was the inspiration of the entire package, the instantiation of a new kind of international artist's haven, that rendered trAce one of the most influential creative communities and made it so valuable to its members. - Marjorie Luesebrink

The trAce Online Writing Community was based at Nottingham Trent University, England.[15] From 1995-2005 it provided an online space where writers could meet, talk, share skills and develop new work. Most of their output took the form of traditional linear fiction and poetry, but there was a small and very active international group of writers, artists and coders dedicated to developing new media work on a range of online platforms. trAce supported and promoted their efforts in a number of ways including the provision of web space, online residencies, teaching and project funding. In this essay I examine the experience of some of the women whose new media art and writing was featured on the site and look at how their professional lives have evolved over the last two decades.

I founded trAce whilst teaching creative writing in the Faculty of Humanities at Nottingham Trent University, and after I was awarded a three year Arts Council grant of £365,000 in 1997 I was seconded from my job to be Artistic Director. Simon Mills, formerly my student on the MA in Writing course, designed the website and worked for trAce throughout its life, first in a freelance capacity and then full time. He founded frAme, the trAce Journal of Digital Culture, which provided a showcase for writers developing new media work. Helen Whitehead joined us soon after we launched, providing freelance editorial and website building services at first, then moving into a full time role which included project management and, most importantly, her own extremely successful Kids on the Net project, working with teachers and schools to build junior creative web skills. We also employed administrative support and a wide range of international freelancers running individual projects, teaching, and mentoring, mostly online, although a few also taught onsite or in local communities. Employing expert freelancers enabled us to provide practical support to the growing international community of digital writers and coders, whilst also making their knowledge available

15 For a detailed account of the early years of trAce, Thomas, S.J. (2005)..

to a global audience. In the late nineteen-nineties when trAce was at its height, we had around 5,000 online members across over twenty countries. Physically, however, we were a small team based in a former student accommodation block on the edge of campus. Colleagues at Nottingham Trent University were uninterested in our work and during the life of the project we remained isolated from the Department of English whence we had originated.

When trAce began, in 1995, very few people around the world were making what we now call digital writing, and there was certainly no way to earn a living from it. Pioneers were generally self-taught and technical training was hard to come by. trAce's ability to attract generous funding, first from Arts Council England, then later from The British Council, The Royal Literary Fund, the Arts and Humanities Research Board, NESTA, and other sources, made it possible to support a wide range of UK and international writers at different stages in their careers. Some were already making new media of various kinds when they arrived at trAce, whilst others came to us entirely new to it. Beginners were given free personalized training, support and mentoring; others were offered commissions, online studio space, and online publication. There were numerous collaborative projects, some formal and funded over a period of time, and others arising organically from the online community. For example, in 2000, Adelaide-based artist and coder Teri Hoskin collaborated with perl coder Ali Graham and myself to produce the *Noon Quilt* website and book. Women writers-in-residence included novelist Kate Pullinger and new media writer Christy Sheffield Sanford. Some artists, such as the poet Catherine Byron, were given online studios comprising a private online space for experimentation and development with the proviso that the artist documented their progress in a public creative journal. In 1998 trAce collaborated with Mark Amerika's Alt-X project to host the world's first Hypertext Competition, whose co-winners were Australian writer Jenny Weight and 'The Unknown', an American quartet led by Scott Rettberg. From 1999-2005 trAce hosted *Assemblage*, Carolyn Guertin's important showcase of new media writing by women. This work, and much more including a small physical archive, was held at the trAce Online Archive housed at Nottingham Trent University until 2015. At the time of writing it is in the process of being transferred to the Electronic Literature Organization where it will be updated and placed back online.[16]

There were many ways for people to interact with trAce: in the online forums; via private or public webspace provided by us at a time when it was often difficult to come by and expensive to rent for artists and writers working outside of academia;

16 trAce Online Writing Centre Archives http://eliterature.org/trace-online-writing-centre-archives/. Accessed 11 April 2016.

at regular Sunday evening chat sessions; in online residencies, training programmes, the trAce Online Writing School, and at physical events including the three biennial Incubation Conferences. Anecdotally, we seemed to have more women members than some other online artistic communities active in the 1990s, but no record of gender balance was kept so this cannot be proved. There is no doubt, however. that numerous women were making work on the site and interacting in the forums.

For the purposes of this essay, I attempted to contact a number of women who were particularly active. Six proved uncontactable, five either did not reply or did not return a response to my survey, and fourteen sent full and often extensive answers to my questions. Those whose replies inform this essay come from widely varying professional backgrounds and their interests and skills are diverse. Some were already working in the digital when they arrived at trAce, others were entirely new to it. They come from different eras of the project, with some joining in the very early years, and others towards the end. They fall into two main groups: those wishing to learn technical skills and those who came primarily to collaborate, although there was a great deal of crossover and slippage between them.

TECHNICAL SKILLS

Kaz Madigan told me via email on January 12, 2015 that she arrived at trAce sometime around 1996. She had just completed a BA in sociology and communications and was looking for more diverse writing opportunities and applications. Based on the east coast of Australia, she had already written two books on yarns and weaving, was widely published in Australia and the US, and edited a small magazine *Curious Weaver*. At trAce, she found "a lot of excitement and goodwill combined with a yearning for collaboration." She set about learning HTML, worked on ways to apply the art of coding to what she already knew about design, and joined the small team of Volunteer Mentors which answered members' queries on technical matters. Asked what she gained from her association with trAce, she wrote

> trAce gave me a real start on using the Internet and web technology and viewing its possibilities in a creative way. It prepared me for work in online learning which sometimes has a discovery approach and is always re-inventing itself to fit into changing needs.

Carrie McMillan is a UK-based teacher and writer who joined trAce some time between 1996-8. She was already a member of Moondance, a small group of women who workshopped their writing via a mailing list. She attended a workshop in Bristol, plus a number of other events in the UK where she met visiting writers including

Christy Sheffield Sanford. For Carrie, the most potent interactions were face to face, although she gained a lot from it online too. She learned to use Adobe Dreamweaver at trAce, something she struggled with at first but made progress on with the help and support of other members of the community.

Catherine Byron is an Irish poet based in the UK who joined trAce in its early years. Already an established print poet, she wanted to learn how to design and upload images and texts, and how to create animations. She told me in an email on December 29, 2014, that the technical training fired up her creativity. "I was energized by the systematic and meticulous attention I learned to maintain when exercising new skills in website construction and animation." She was also inspired by the presence of so many women: "It was just so brilliant to see how women were drawn to online creativity, and how brilliant and various were their projects. In this brave new world there was neither male nor female." Her new-found skills led to sponsorship from The Poetry Society and in 2001 she was invited by the British Council to share her digital poetry techniques in Mumbai and New Delhi. In 2003, after attending trAce's "Writers for the Future" residential course, she secured a three-year Arts and Humanities Research Council Fellowship which included a collaboration with trAce designer Simon Mills to create *Gloryhole*, a work based on her experiences of working with artists and hot glass at the University of Sunderland.

Sharon Rundle lives in New South Wales, Australia. She enrolled in an online course taught by Helen Whitehead around 2001, and was subsequently invited to teach her own courses at the trAce Online Writing School. She was already teaching creative writing at James Cook University and had devised material for correspondence courses, but at trAce she learned how to teach online and how to moderate online forums. In an email to me on January 9, 2015, she described how she learned

> effective ways to generate responses from students, encouraging 'lurkers' to engage more, keeping up morale for writers, giving useful feedback, critique and encouragement—and knowing which to give when; and working with writers in different time zones. I also learnt to handle students who were 'difficult' more effectively.

In 2003 trAce organized TextLab, a week-long residential workshop led by Tim Wright. Applicants were invited to outline which skills they wanted to improve. Dene Grigar was already making new media but wanted to learn how to use sound. She flew from Texas to attend, bringing with her *Fallow Field*, the piece she wanted to work on. It was already almost complete when she arrived but TextLab provided a sound engineer who taught her how to record and edit audio in order to finish it. She later returned to Nottingham in 2004 to present a paper about Internet radio at the 3rd Incubation conference, and contributed to a print publication about trAce edited by Randy Adams.

COLLABORATION

Pauline Masurel (known as Mazzy) joined trAce in Spring 1999 and for the next few years was very active in a range of formal and informal collaborations at trAce. She worked on *Claims*, a multi-media form-driven adventure, with Randy Adams and Everdeen Tree (sadly, I have been unable to track down Everdeen for this article), took part in a real-time collaborative project, *QUICK-SHIFT*, and contributed to *In Search of Oldton*, Tim Wright's transmedia mystery story. She told me by email on January 16, 2015

> I enjoyed the discussions, the exchanges of ideas, and also the social aspect of interacting with writers and artists from around the world. The online community was the major part of trAce for me, more so than the set-piece works and articles which seemed set at a distance.

It was the lessons she learned about collaboration, rather than the hard technical skills, that were most interesting to her. "I learned a lot about the practicalities and the emotional aspects of creative collaboration, which is a fragile and precarious thing. I learned a lot, at a personal level, about the trade-offs implicit between process and product when writing and creating."

Collaboration was also important to Kate Pullinger, who was already an established print author when she joined trAce in 2001. She began by teaching a Fiction course in the newly-launched trAce Online Writing School, but the following year was awarded an AHRB Fellowship to research and develop new work on the site. After that, she worked with the NESTA-funded project Writers for the Future and attended a week-long residential workshop in Nottingham where she met coder and designer Chris Joseph. The two would go on to collaborate on a number of pieces, most importantly *Inanimate Alice*, a new media serial for children still in production. "trAce," she says in an email to me dated January 5, 2015, "introduced me to the notion that new forms of narrative and storytelling were emerging via digital tools and platforms and that the internet was a space for new forms of literature and literary experiment. "

For Nickie Hastie, collaboration was vital to her interactions at trAce. In her email to me dated January 31, 2015, she too cites Everdeen Tree as a major figure who managed numerous group projects.

> During this period I felt a lot more creative when I was inspired by others to work together. I built close relationships with other trAce members, particularly Everdeen Tree, Mazzy (Pauline Masurel) and Glenis Stott. We interacted a lot

> on the WebBoard, through posts, private messages, as well as by email. We also worked on projects at LinguaMOO and started developing geographical spaces, rooms, objects and characters which would flow into each other. I felt part of something special and I felt respected as a writer/creative person.

Christine Wilks had been a member of trAce for several years before she participated in her first project in 2004. She told me in an email on January 31, 2015, that it was an online course in digital writing led by Tim Wright that

> changed my life. It opened up a whole new world of exciting creative possibilities for me. During the course I created my first work of multimedia hypertext, *Sitting Pretty*. I then went on to learn Flash and created a number of animated digital poems. I also took part in collaborative projects, including *In Search of Oldton*.

In the years since trAce, she has collaborated in a much more involved or tightly knit way with a number of artists she first met via trAce, such as Randy Adams, Andy Campbell and Chris Joseph.

> These were collaborations without the kind of creative overseer or architect that the earlier trAce projects had. One particular collaborative project that emerged from the ashes of trAce is *R3/\/\1X\/\/0RX* (http://remixworx.com/) which is an intricately interwoven site or remixed original creative spanning a number of years.

Some developed a long-term and multi-faceted relationship with the trAce community. Australian network artist Mez Breeze was known simply as Mez, or Netwurker, or a number of other titles. She was a constant and mysterious presence, bringing her own hand-made mix of code and text which both intrigued and frustrated her readers. Already involved with a large number of groups including 7-11, Nettime, Fleshfactor, and Rhizome, she told me in an email message on January 30 2015 that she saw trAce as an additional platform for support, "a gestation space, a creatively fertile place in which to experiment." She created *trAceSpace*, a collaborative homage to trAce, and contributed to many projects, including *My Millennium*, and contributed extensively in forums, chats, and virtually at Incubation conferences.

Hypertext writer Marjorie Luesebrink, aka M.D. Coverley, also contributed in many ways. She first got involved in 1999 when Christy Sheffield Sanford was appointed Virtual Writer-in-Residence. Luesebrink was already very technically competent but she enjoyed the chance to workshop with other new media writers and it was during this time she created the innovative *Fibonacci's Daughter*. Participants were keen to share their techniques and help others, and in the years that followed she polished her skills in HTML, DHTML, layers, animation and general design. She wrote to me in an email on February 1, 2015, that "Almost every day was a new learning experience in this dynamic field, and we were all on a very steep (and exciting) learning curve." And it wasn't just technical, there was a lot to learn about interaction on the internet, finding "ways to make the online community a rich and fruitful place, and most of all, interface often with other writers - all of these were part of the informal educational experience at trAce." She collaborated on the site, wrote articles, attended chats, and organized *M is for Nottingham*, a 2002 experiment for the 2nd trAce Incubation Conference which began online and was completed in person at Nottingham Trent University.

GENDER ISSUES AT TRACE

When asked whether they were conscious of any gender aspects to life at trAce, most respondents replied in the negative. The fact that it seems not to have been considered an issue is interesting in the light of contemporary problems around the harassment and bullying of women online. At that time it was common across the Internet for people to adopt ambiguous usernames which concealed their real-life gender; it was also common for users to cross-dress online in a fairly public way and the convention was to respect their choice of gender. Pauline Masurel told me

> It wasn't much of an issue for me in terms of the people that I wrote with online. Certainly issues of gender and sexuality formed part of the thematic content of some of the writers. Online I found myself writing on a common footing with people of either (or even unknown) gender and of different ethnicities and nationalities.

Nickie Hastie believes trAce demonstrated the way in which women were at the forefront of a lot of new media work not just because it was managed by two women (Helen Whitehead and myself) also because there were many female project leaders and artists. Sharon Rundle, who taught for trAce, notes that

> It was one of the few courses where a number of male writers enrolled. Almost all writing courses face2face and on online that I have taught have had predominately female enrolments. trAce had a more equal balance. The male writers often re-enrolled for more courses and stayed with trAce.

And Marjorie Luesebrink recalls that the early days of electronic literature – and the trAce days – provided a very remarkable time for women.

> For the cost of a computer, a woman who did not have formal training or an academic title could learn to create a new kind of writing, have a wealth of avenues for expression, meet up with (both online and f-t-f) with an exciting range of people working in the same field, and benefit from all of the encouragement and support of a dedicated community. For many of the early women practitioners, this was the first time that they could enter into a vibrant, full scale, professional writing community as an equal. I had taken an MFA at U.C. Irvine, had continued to write and teach in the intervening years—and I found the atmosphere at trAce (and the field of e-lit in general) more open and inviting to women than any previous experience.

POST-TRACE

In its early years trAce attracted a very diverse range of practitioners but inevitably as Internet use increased new online spaces opened up and competed for the attention of both linear and new media writers. Although it was still receiving regular Arts Council funding, the organization became impossible to sustain at the level it needed in order to make an impact, and it was closed and archived in 2005.

Some members still make new media work whilst others have diverted the skills they learned at trAce into different career paths.

In the latter group, Kaz Madigan runs a small handweaving studio specializing in Japanese Saori Freestyle weaving and is developing online handweaving courses. She no longer makes new media work, but is still immersed in the Internet, coding and design, and uses software to create her weaving designs. Looking back, she says "trAce was really the initiator for my knowledge and interest." Carrie McMillan is now an assistant head teacher at a secondary school. She too no longer creates new media work but enjoys reading Twitter poetry and occasionally shares some of her own. Her time at trAce influenced her future career by sparking an interest in ICT for creativity. She has been a lead technology innovator at school, and wrote her MEd dissertation on creativity and blogging in the classroom. She still retains "lots of warm memories" about trAce.

> Looking back it feels like I was a part of something important. It would be great to think that people could carve out communities like that again but the Internet feels like such a big place now and that sort of community with a shared purpose feels very rare now.

When she joined trAce, Pauline Masurel worked with statistics. Today she has stopped making new media, and runs her own gardening business. But, she says, there are indirect chains of events spanning outwards from her time at trAce that influenced many parts of her life, including studying for an MA in Creative Writing in 2003/04. Her time at trAce taught her

> to be braver and more experimental creatively. Perhaps some of that rubbed off on my life too. It also offered a diversity of writers and artists and styles of working that I never encountered anywhere else at the time, nor since.

Sharon Rundle still works in editing and teaching Adult Education. She says

> my time with trAce was one of the most stimulating and motivating times I've had as a writing tutor. The courses were innovative, the interaction and "real-time" connection to students and tutors was a real joy and often very exciting.

Jenny Weight, co-winner of the first trAce/Alt-X Hypertext Award, is now Program Manager of the Master of Media at RMIT University in Melbourne, Australia, and no longer makes new media work.

Those still working in the field continue to ride the roller-coaster of digital media as it innovates and expands. Kate Pullinger continues to write award-winning print fiction as well as producing new media work in collaboration with others including Chris Joseph, her collaborator on the globally successful *Inanimate Alice*. Her most recent project is a digital war memorial and work of participatory media, *Letter to an Unknown Soldier* (2015). She is now Professor of Creative Writing and Digital Media at Bath Spa University, a title which, she says, "is what it is because of my work with trAce." Nicki Hastie still works in information management in higher education but continues to make animated poetry and has diversified into writing for performance and video. Mez Breeze also continues to make award-winning digital writing and games. Her work is held in collections at The World Bank, the National Library of Australia, and Cornell University's Rose Goldsen Archive. In 2013, Duke University offered to house her comprehensive career archive at their David M. Rubenstein Rare Book & Manuscript Library. Marjorie Luesebrink was making intriguing hypertexts even before trAce began, and she continues to do so. She is a past president of the Electronic Literature Organization and current member of the Board of Directors. Most recently she has created *Tarim Tapestry*, a suite of stories about the Silk Road, and is collecting a series of works called *Tin Town*, an experiment in narrative form and structure created in Excel. Dene Grigar is now Director of the Digital Technology and Culture Program at Washington State University, and continues to make her own new media work. Most recently, she was featured as one of the Master Artists at OLE.1 in Naples, Italy, for her sound-based work *Curlew*. She is currently President of the Electronic Literature Organization. Christine Wilks has pursued a career in new media, winning several prizes, and is currently studying for a PhD with Kate Pullinger at Bath Spa University. After years of struggling to find the right medium for creative expression, she says, "trAce gave me a new direction." This is reflected in a comment she made in the commemorative booklet *Writers for the Future*: "I was a digital ditherer, now I"m a digital doer, I feel my creative life has been transformed" (quoted in Adams 2005).

The women profiled here are just a few of the many who spent time at trAce between 1995-2005. Hundreds more submitted work, contributed to the forums, or were simply readers whose names seldom appeared on the site. There is no room in this essay to demonstrate the density of the networks these women inhabited, nor to do justice to their complex and detailed creative histories. After trAce was closed, many friendships and collaborations migrated to other communities, often settling in Facebook where they continue today.

In an essay for trAce on "Women and the Aesthetics of New Media," Carol Gigliotti observes that "new media's eclectic transdisciplinarity threaded loosely together by digital ubiquity are both its best and most problematic attributes" (2003). That eclecticism can be seen very clearly in the stories of the women related here. trAce provided the digital ubiquity that threaded them together, and many paths crossed in virtual space which would never have intersected in physical space for reasons both geographical and cultural. The problem Gigliotti acknowledges may derive partly in the fact that academia, whence some, but not all, of these contributors came, remains trapped in discipline silos which neither understand nor recognise the importance of this kind of work. If universities are to move forward, they must give space and support to this kind of unconventional projects. As Marjorie Luesebrink, a widely honoured writer, artist and coder with many years of experience of working and living in the digital says:

> The trAce period was such a time of exploding change and possibility; it was difficult to understand, then, the impact this organization was making. trAce was an entirely new concept being invented in an entirely new environment. It seems to me that, even now, I can't adequately assess how much trAce impacted my artistic practice and my work online. trAce was pretty much the water to the fish—an environment that provided an immersion into a new element. And, once you are in the water—it just IS.

WORKS CITED

Adams, Randy, ed. *Writers for the Future*, 2005. trAce Online Writing Centre (print only).

Gigliotti, Carol. "Women and the Aesthetics of New Media." 20 June 2003, trAce Online Writing Centre. http://tracearchive.ntu.ac.uk/Opinion/index.cfm?article=71 Accessed 27 August 2015.

Thomas, Susan J. "The tools of online community : The first five years of the trAce online writing centre." In: *Creativity and cognition: Proceedings 2005*. 12-15 April, Goldsmiths College, London. pp. 63-70.

At the Speed of Light: Cyberfeminism, Xenofeminism and The Digital Ecology of Bodies

BY MARIA ANGEL AND ANNA GIBBS

In this paper we address the question of how feminist thinking might consider the digital transformation of gender and corporeality through a consideration of women's work in electronic literature and text-based digital media art. Central to our task is to elaborate a feminist project through the study of digital art and writing as modes of aesthetic practice. Here we focus specifically on the development of xenofeminism as a contemporary regeneration of the cyberfeminism of the 1990s, and an address to the development and transformation of feminist theories of sexual difference and their relationship to feminist techno- and eco- politics in the present.

> [W]omen diffuse themselves according to modalities scarcely compatible with the framework of the ruling symbolics. Which doesn't happen without causing some turbulence, we might even say some whirlwinds, that ought to be reconfined within solid walls of principle, to keep them from spreading to infinity. Otherwise they might even go so far as to disturb that third agency designated as the real - a transgression and confusion that it is important to restore to their proper order.—Luce Irigaray, 106.

> The future is unmanned.—VNS Matrix

As the work of the Humanities in Australia becomes increasingly modeled on, and captured by, corporate interests, we see feminist work as fundamentally important both in analyzing and understanding the ways in which bodies are deployed, reproduced and represented in material and digital economies, and as a step to be fed back into a process of a collective research-creation in which experiment, invention, and speculation open new political possibilities, and where scholarship does not simply come after production, but is entwined with it in generative ways. Here the tensions between modes of critique on the one hand, and a research-creation conceived in Bergsonian terms, where the virtual opens new possibilities in (without being able to determine) what becomes actual on the other, are in some ways analogous with a tension in feminism itself as it confronts the question of its own ground in the light of shifting conceptions of sexual difference.

Continental feminism from Irigaray to Cixous, and beyond, well understood the implications of the psychoanalytic insight that subjectivity is formed on the basis of the body: therefore, it asserted, we have sexual difference as the basis not only of subjectivity but of the western antinomies between mind and body; reason and feeling; etc. But what happens when, under the accelerating and intensifying process of capitalism since the late twentieth century, it is not just the sexual organs, but increasingly "micro" aspects of the human—the senses, affects, movements, rhythms, vibrations, and energies of bodies (rather than bodily wholes or unities)—are targeted and mobilized as points of connection with other bodies, both human and nonhuman? If the philosophies of immanence which initially seemed to show a way beyond the determinism of description now seem to have most purchase in describing and understanding these processes, it is nevertheless apparent that the old dichotomies—and the old oppressions—continue to be reproduced alongside (or intertwined with) these new situations. (The work of Rosi Braidotti in particular has been concerned to keep the question of this relationship alive, frequently foregrounding in various ways the need to think relationship between theory and politics). The question is thereby raised of what the basis for feminism might be, if sexual difference—though not the oppression of women—has been superseded—as some, Colebrook (2000), for example—would have it, by philosophies of immanence. In these philosophies, distinctions between organic and non-organic life are also called into question in various different ways (see Grosz; Haraway; Barad), and affect too appears not in its categorical or discrete form as a human motivational system (Silvan Tomkins) but rather in the asubjective form envisaged by Spinoza and elaborated by Deleuze, Massumi and others.

In an earlier paper we wrote of the history of (especially continentally-inflected) feminist theory as both a refusal to dematerialize corporeality and (more recently) an insistence upon possibilities for dynamic re-configurations and re-patternings of living matter. Anna Munster, too, has challenged the "dematerialisation of information" and she asks "what if we were to produce instead a different genealogy for digital engagements with the machine, one that gave us the room to take body, sensation, and movement and conditions such as place and duration into account?" (3). In this context, as Grosz's work in particular has long made clear, it becomes evident that what we once referred to as "the body" is not reducible to a stable unity or totality, whether conceived in biological, social constructivist, or performative (ie Butlerian) terms, but is rather a moment of organization in an open-ended process of connection that spans both the corporeal and material, and the symbolic realms (see Grosz, 1994). In the process ontology of this work, what bodies in all their differentials can *do* replaces or perhaps answers the question of what "the body" *is*. Here transversal modes of connection, conjunction, expansion and multiplication rather than filial modes of descent and reproduction are key. One critical consequence of this—made most apparent in the contemporary new materialisms—is that the organism as a pre-established organic form can no longer be held to be the privileged representative of the body. What takes over is the organism as an organicity, as a form that actively makes its connections and connectivity. Haraway's famous dictum "I'd rather be a Cyborg than a Goddess" (1985, p. 106) highlights this emphasis on the hybridity of connection once it becomes impossible to distinguish finally and cleanly between nature and culture or between technology and biology.

In all this work, where difference comes to take priority over presence and relationality over being, it turns out that time is of the essence. We took this lesson to heart when we applied it to an understanding of the way digital media art and electronic literature transform what it means to read in a context where writing becomes a process of what we call "exscryption," in which new forms of spatiality are unfolded through movement. Elsewhere we have written about the importance of animation and movement to the production of digital works, particularly those that want to re-instate process and experience, but this ethos is also apparent in the progress bars and spinning wheels used to visualize the processing of information (Angel and Gibbs, 2012). In these latter instances, time is overtly mapped as movement. The more movement, however circuitous (as with the Mac computer's endlessly spinning wheel—the "wheel of death" as it is colloquially known—or the "thread" of the barber's pole), the more time spent connecting or downloading. As Tiziana Terranova writes, information is neither simply meaning nor merely material form: rather, it "implies the unfolding of a *duration*—an active temporality where consequences hardly ever follow from linear causes" (69). As we have written, 'this implies a different approach to time, one which expresses an aesthetic of movement where time is constitutive in the expression of form" (Angel and Gibbs, 2012). And indeed of matter itself.

We are now at a point, however, where data no longer simply collects information in order to predict the future on the basis of this past, but instead aims to design the future in the present, or more accurately, to *produce* it, to generate rather than simply animate it. This is because algorithms now actively *anticipate* us in a process of what Luciana Parisi describes as a form of "post-cybernetic control"—that is, she writes, "a form of parametric design," the goal of which "is deep relationality, the real-time integration of the evolving variables of a built environment in software systems that are able to figure emerging scenarios by responding to or pre-adapting scripted data" (105). Clearly this raises new questions for social and political analysis, but it also presents a new challenge to digital media arts where it produces a reciprocal—and differential—transformation (not necessarily positive) of corporeal capacities and agencies.

In this context, it's not media but rather mediation itself that is crucial, that is, in Haraway's terms, how cyborg being takes shape. What are the points of connection and connectivity between body and machine? What gets moved, uploaded and distributed? What gets seen and what remains occluded? Braidotti writes that "the body in question here is far from a biological essence: it is a crossroad of intensive forces; it is a surface of inscribed social codes" (244). We agree but we argue against any evaporation of lived materiality as we plug into the network. Cyborg being makes life "discontinuous" (Braidotti's term). The hyperlink conflates and confounds time/space relations, hides or visualizes "being" (digital identity is precarious), but the discontinuities of life and living now involved and intensified in digital participation were always there lurking in offline culture as well—you only have to read a few lines of Gertrude Stein or the philosophies of Henri Bergson and Deleuze and Guattari to get there.

Here we elaborate a possible epistemology and feminist history for negotiating this principle of lived discontinuities in digital contexts where technology supplies the promise of access "at the speed of light." The cyberfeminists whose work we analyze confound this easy instantaneity, modeled on the "ontology of the hyperlink," in favour of a different kind of performativity, one which refuses the evaporation of sexual difference and which draws on the lived materiality of bodies: their insertion back into the network, and on the storying (in this case 'stitching' together) of social histories and "co-mobilities" (Southern, 2012).

Responding to Haraway's distinction between the goddess and the cyborg referred to above, we claim that recourse to classical mythology can reveal some interesting insight into the modes of maintenance of sexual difference, and their resistance, at least in western culture and history, as much feminist work before us has shown. Previously, we have referred to the mythological figure of Ariadne and her thread as a way of plugging women, their work, and feminist history, into the network. Now we look to the figure of Arachne, the spinner, to provide an emblem for material production, meaning and connectivity. Arachne, in her mythological contest with Athena, challenged a cosmology through her woven texts which were said to have depicted the male gods in their debauchery (Zeus seducing mortal women, Dionysus drunk and disorderly) questioning the authority of gods over mortals. Punished by Athena for her challenge, Arachne was turned into a spider, a creature who produces its sticky silk or thread through a gland in its body. This reminds us of the biological foundation of material forms of reproduction, and also of particular scales and economies of production and reproduction—it is said that the spider uses its body as a measure for the production of its web, which functions both as a food trap and as a technology of self-made connection with its environment, a mode for creating material spaces and bootstrapping movement between things—in her foundational work on feminism and digitality, Sadie Plant sees the thread as "neither metaphorical nor literal, but quite simply material" (12).

Similarly, early cyberfeminist creative work, that of VNS Matrix and Linda Dement in particular, points to and works with the *organicity* of the gendered body. Organicity works with the spider's intuition of using itself as a relational mechanism for its web, and it accounts for the cyberfeminist interest and insistence in using images of female organs, body parts and functions in the construction of its epistemologies and ontologies. For example, in the oft quoted *Cyberfeminist Manifesto for the 21st Century*, VNS Matrix write:

> we are the modern cunt
> positive anti reason
> unbound unleashed unforgiving
> we see art with our cunt we make art with our cunt
> we believe in jouissance madness holiness and poetry the virus of the new
> world disorder
> rupturing the symbolic from within
> saboteurs of big daddy mainframe
> the clitoris is a direct line to the matrix
> the VNS MATRIX
> terminators of the moral code
> mercenaries of slime
> go down on the altar of abjection
> probing the visceral temple we speak in tongues infiltrating corrupting
> disseminating
> corrupting the discourse
> we are the future cunt

Rather than representing the female as an organized whole, the manifesto works with a metonymic epistemology where parts, organs and functions are drawn on for particular affect. The female body is not cut up in the mode of pornography but at once parodies this and figures bodies as open sets of possibilities. If a body can be put together in the manifesto, it is metonymically figured as a parodic, threatening, slimy, virally contaminating cunt, and a set of viscerally probing tongues. In one of its articulations, the written text of the manifesto (appearing as though written on the exterior of a globe—the earth, an eyeball, an ovary or cyst, a womb or bubble of slime perhaps?)

is bordered by a pattern of opened female genitalia, visually but viscerally suggesting some kind of birth. That of the "future cunt," perhaps. The in-your-faceness of their challenge to propriety forms a kind of reverse discourse ("you call us disgusting so that is what we will be"—with a vengeance) a performativity that does not just involve imagining another world, but actually bringing one into being, changing the conditions of existence.

In her analysis of VNS Matrix's *All New Gen* series (a cyberfeminist game, a series of installations, and 'a virus of the new world disorder'), Kaye Schaffer writes of the game's avatars, Patina de Panties, Dentata, and the Princess of Slime, as "mercenaries of slime" representing an "Irigarian metaphorics of feminine alterity—a space conjured up by gaps in the narrative, holes in the social fabric. Their bodies call attention to the 'slime' of eroticized female genitalia" (156). In 'The "Mechanics of Fluids," Irigaray sets out to challenge a certain type of realism, an epistemology and ontology of "solid" forms which she associates with rationality, and male power. In this context we could also align solid with an emphasis on product, and fluid with the reinstatement of process. In the place of the solid (object, identity, product, commodity etc.), she asks us to imagine an economy of fluid form, and of partial identities. She writes of "a semantics of incomplete beings: functional symbols" and throws down a challenge to "the privilege granted to metaphor (a quasi solid) over metonymy [...] more loosely allied to fluids" (110).

Irigaray's work is prescient in relation to the contemporary operation of digital networks and to "exscryptive" process. In an earlier paper (forthcoming) we wrote about exscryption as a process of the unfolding of new spaces through movement, the putting together of bits and functions that involves the storying of spaces, bodies, and places. In digital contexts, exscryption works against the conflation of space-time made possible by the hyperlink, and we use it to characterise a particular type of feminist work that acknowledges the importance of memory and creative amalgamation in the distribution of being and in the constitution of objects, subjects, and events. This is a process-based ontology where relationality and storying is important rather than presence, the entity, or object. It is a metonymic process rather than a metaphorical one, to use Irigaray's terms.

The metonymic putting together or storying of "bits" or partial identities is a kind of Frankensteinian project, but the model for exscryption is the "patchwork" rather than Mary Shelley's monster. In Shelley's story, the bits that comprise the monster have no history, and no extrinsic relations. The monster is metaphoric of "objective" monstrosity itself, that is, a unified composite with no "history" of process. On the other hand, in digital exscryption the function of memory, and the storying of bits, work to compose a creative amalgamation that *may* appear as a body, as is evident in Shelley Jackson's early digital work *Patchwork Girl* (1995). Here, the economy of representation is metonymic rather than metaphoric. Her monster comprises the relational storying and "threading" together of the body parts. Irigaray and Haraway both point to a western hierarchy of the senses which privileges a unifying vision over all else. The patchwork aesthetic asks what the world would be like if this hierarchy was reconfigured. Haraway asks, what if the objectifying gaze of the satellite (the eye in the sky)—a projection of disembodied masculinity—were to be superseded by an embodied form of vision that looked at its objects with "passionate detachment" (Haraway, 1988, 585)?

Linda Dement's *Cyberflesh Girlmonster* comprises donated images of body parts which were collected during the Artists' Week of the Adelaide Festival in 1994. This aspect emphasizes feminist work as a collective enterprise, and signals the images as having a history, a provisional origin. These "detached" body parts are digitally combined and create a set of animated interactive 'monsters', some based on arms, hands, mouths and ears. As with *Patchwork Girl*, the reference is to Shelley's *Frankenstein*, but the work also parodies the interchangeability of women from the patriarchal point of view. All the girlmonsters bear a metonymic relation to the female body and particularly to the genitalia, but unlike the fragmented body in pornography they are entry-points into a story. By clicking on any one of these cyberflesh girlmonsters, you are taken through a series of partial narratives that deal with rape, violence and carnality—themes which signal the history of women's oppression. The partial and fragmented nature of these girlmonsters reflect both the trauma involved in these stories, and an acknowledgement that we never have the whole story, or else they provide open ends pointing to different possibilities. Dement's *In My Gash* and *Typhoid Mary* use a similar metonymic language to tell stories.

In this process of (metonymic) connection, human bodies are affective transducers. Like Linda Dement's "bodies" of work, VNS Matrix's *Manifesto* exemplifies this process of affective transduction and what we have previously called, after Flusser, "creative amalgamation" (Angel and Gibbs, 2015, para. 1). Feminist manifestoes are manifestations of an affirmative and often joyful politics. They are, as Colman writes,

> civic modes of action that are motivated not only to construct visible protest and register against or affirm a situation, but engage and serve to agitate particular aspects of civic hope that action may alter long-term patterns and structures. (Colman, 376)

Colman does not discuss the VNS Matrix manifesto, and was writing in advance of the appearance of Laboria Cuboniks collective's xenofeminist manifesto but she taps into the performative and affective aspect of the manifesto form, writing that the manifesto is "very much in the present of its utterance," although "one could say there is no object of the affective subjectivity desired by the manifesto form — it is, of course, diagrammatic of the forms of relations that constitute it" (379).

Xenofeminism calls for the creation of a new non-totalizing universalism assembled from the bottom up, as it were, on the basis of "the needs of every human, regardless of race, ability, economic standing, or geographical position" (Cuboniks). This new universalism, then, requires that "a thousand" (or actually a limitless number of) tiny differences be kept alive in it. But rather than insisting on a Foucauldian politics of enunciation or a Harawayan ethos of situationism, it proclaims instead "the right of everyone to speak as no one in particular" (ibid). In part this seems to respond to a contemporary proliferation of forms of identity politics in which identities themselves are increasingly minutely specified and where the politics of enunciation sometimes seems to take precedence over any politics of listening. In the face of the ethos of "purity" that so often accompanies this, xenofeminism wants "neither clean hands nor beautiful souls, neither virtue nor terror." What it does want are "superior forms of corruption" (ibid). Following earlier feminisms of sexual difference, xenofeminism rejects the old dualisms along with the hierarchies of value implicit in them. But there is a danger here of reading a reductive essentialism that doesn't belong there back into the politics of sexual difference, for what Irigaray, Cixous and Duras (in their very different ways) actually asked us to imagine was what the world might look like if we began to think it on the basis of female rather than male bodies (as western humanist philosophy had always done without acknowledging it), and VNS Matrix famously proclaimed in the same vein "the clitoris is a direct line to the matrix." These should be understood as tactical moves, using heuristic devices in speculative enterprises, designed to open possibilities rather than to produce any particular outcome. Xenofeminism, on the other hand, wagers very specifically that the "rationalism" (reason)—posited by the feminisms of difference as a projection of disembodied masculinity—can be refashioned as the gender neutral tool of choice for a feminism aiming to generate new worlds through the active production of differences and novelty in this one. What the manifesto doesn't explicitly say, however, is that the accelerationist movement with which xenofeminism is in many ways allied—but which has also arguably exerted a recuperative force on it in as much as corporeality, affect, subjectivity and gender are all often disappeared (especially from the work of the male theorists of acceleration)—insists on the way reason in the age of the algorithm ultimately exceeds human control (see Parisi, 2014). If the future is "unmanned" in one of the senses foreseen by VNS Matrix, it remains to be seen that it is unmanned in the other sense.

Calling itself gender and race "abolitionist", and acknowledging that women are always made into the markers of gender, xenofeminism wants to build a world in which "traits currently assembled under the rubric of gender, no longer furnish a grid for the asymmetric operation of power" (ibid). Following implicitly the foundational work of Shulamith Firestone which argued that women would be emancipated by technologies that freed them from the work of reproduction, and Luciana Parisi's claim that molecular biotechnology was already detaching femininity from the imperative of sexual reproduction (which led her to question the need for the category of femininity in the politics of the body), xenofemism wants explicitly to reject the essentialism it suspects of lurking in all naturalisms, and argues the risky necessity of seizing existing technologies to repurpose them for a large scale work of re-engineering the world (see Firestone, 1970; Parisi, 2004).

Curiously, the only aesthetic practice (if it can still be called one) of which the xenofeminist manifesto makes particular mention is architecture "as a vocabulary for collective choreography—the coordinated writing of space." But not perhaps surprisingly, given xenofeminism's explicit rejection both of melancholy and of any "reification of the given masked as critique" (Cubonicks), the appearance of xenofeminist politics coincides with a reinvigoration of the relationship of the digital to live performance. Feminist performance artists of the 1970s and 80s (for example, Gina Pane, Joan Jonas, Carolee Schneeman, Eleanor Antin, Marina Abramowicz, Karen Finley, and Linda Montano) re-performed the female body both to interrogate and transform its representations, while Laurie Anderson extended corporeal capacities by technological means. The politics of sexual difference were called into question by Sandy Stone's "The Empire Strikes Back: A Posttranssexual Manifesto" which situated gender in an undecidable middle, and the exploration of the implications of trans politics for gender politics was extended in her "theory-performances" through the 1990s and into the noughties.

The recent work of Virginia Barratt (who was a member of VNS Matrix) now takes performance in a direction in some ways akin to the accelerationist mode of xenofeminism, which aims to intensify the alienating tendencies of capitalism, along with the abstractive processes of the algorithms that increasingly drive them. Barratt's work makes live performance into a privileged venue for what Sadie Plant and Nick Land are credited with terming "hyperstition" and defined as a collective "making real" of fictional entities and qualities. More broadly it could be described as a kind of alchemy which turns what is imagined into what is actual through forms of technologically-enabled magic, and forms of magic as a particular kind of technology for transforming the relationship of the "I" to itself, to collectivities and to the world, as the work of

Isabelle Stengers has shown (see Gibbs, 2012). (Hyperstition came, in the subsequent work of Nick Land, to designate a contagious process involving an intensification and acceleration born of the creation of positive feedback loops.)

At Cementa15 arts festival in Kandos (a small town in rural New South Wales), Barratt presented a performance titled "cryptocrystalline: technomancy (divination)" featuring a new work of experimental writing called "Gold" (2015). This work was presented within an environment created by Barratt in the cavernous, Spartan front bar of the Railway Hotel that hosted the evening of music and performance. It featured a large-scale video projection of moving, morphing red and green skeletal figures floating in starry space as if seen through x-ray specs, and a delicate sound surround from which the performed text seemed to emerge without at all being overshadowed by it. Moving flecks of light fell like a light sprinkling of snow or perhaps drifting detritus over the whole scene, while Barratt, futuristically clad in black leggings imprinted with gold circuit boards and Lucy Oliver, her collaborator for this performance, drew out golden threads as if from the air and silently stitched them to Barratt's sleeve, so that their two bodies seemed to be linked in occult communication. Or, since Oliver had the image of a skeleton on her top, as if Barratt were a projection or a kind of avatar for her rather ghostly figure. Fleshy bodies were conjured in words while the images splintered subjects and reformed them into new and ever-changing configurations. The work, "a lovesong for the future," was oracular, conjuring another world into being out of the post-industrial ruins of toxic coal mines and deathly boardrooms created by capital. Yet rather than performing as the singular figure of an oracle, Barratt's presentation seemed to be—as the subtitle suggested—more a matter of divination, of sensing, tuning into and channelling other voices, both human and beyond human, both plant and implant. In the world brought into being by the work, the clouds, birthed by trees, were imaged as "long legged wraiths that stalk across the valley" then "grow a dank warm skin of green velvet, nodal, a matted earth body" and "make mycelial networks" whose "telepathic exchanges" can be sent in packets as information over the internet. Barratt's work seemed to re-activate and amplify the mycelial network, which mycologist Paul Stamet calls a "natural Internet" (see Fleming), as a powerful image of communication and detoxification, lending it yet another kind of body, revivifying the philosophical concerns it referenced (those of the new materialisms, accelerationism, cyberfeminism) and recharging the moment with a burst of hope-generating energy: pure gold.

Barratt's work, then, can stand as an emblem for xenofeminist work which attempts to open out the possibilities for rethinking and repurposing the relationship between bodies and networks in a way that broadens out the fields of possible connectivity beyond the unitary or solidified structures of what we call the "human" in its old structures of ascendency: a great chain of being rather than a network or an ecology. Sexual difference was one of the defining and enabling features of this formation. This reconception of the human subject, as Grosz writes, functions as an ecology rather than as an entity. It

> emerges from and functions with within natural, technological and social orders in which it finds itself placed as event and advent rather than as agent. (2005, 128)

"Unmanning," in this context, requires not only the recognition of the networked (and "liquid") nature of the human "solid" (we are an amalgamation of what we eat, and what we love, and do, and make and think and hate and deny, we are also wormfood, and stardust etc). Perhaps, we might suggest, it also requires that we acknowledge our place in networks beyond ourselves and alongside the subhuman, the extra-human, and the non-human, as Grosz argues.

WORKS CITED

Angel, Maria and Anna Gibbs. "The Futures of Writing: experiments in digital exscryption." *The Journal of Poetics Research*. 3, October (2015). Unpaginated. http://poeticsresearch.com/article/angel-and-gibbs-the-futures-of-writing/

_,_. "Geospatial Aesthetics: Time, Agency and Space in Electronic Writing," *Sprache und Literatur*, Special Issue, eds. Joergen Schafer and Peter Gendolla. 108, 42 (2012).

Barad, Karen. "Posthumanist Performativity: Toward an Understanding of How Matter Comes to Matter." *Signs* (3)28 (2003). 801-831.

Barratt, Virginia. "cryptocrystalline: technomancy (divination)", *Cementa15 Arts Festival*. Kandos NSW, 2015.

Braidotti, Rosi. *Metamorphoses: Towards a Materialist Theory of Becoming*. Cambridge: Polity Press, 2002.

Colebrook, Claire. "Is 'Sexual Difference' a Problem?" in Ian Buchanan and Claire Colebrook (eds), *Deleuze and Feminist Theory*. Edinburgh: Edinburgh University Press, 2000. 110-127.

Colman, Felicity. "Notes on the Feminist Manifesto: The Strategic Use of Hope." *Journal For Cultural Research*. Vol 14 no 4 (2010), 375-392.

Cuboniks, Laboria. *Xenofeminism: A Politics for Alienation*. 2015. http://www.laboria-cuboniks.net/

Cybernetic Culture Research Unit (CCRU), "Lemurian Time War." In Schneiderman & P. Walsh (Eds.). *Retaking the Universe: William S. Burroughs in the Age of Globalization*. London: Pluto, 2004. 274-291.

Dement, Linda. *Cybergirl Fleshmonster*. 1995. Images archived at http://www.lindadement.com/cyberflesh?girlmonster.htm

_,_. *In My Gash*. 1999. Images archived at http://www.lindadement.com/in-my-gash.htm.

_,_. *Typhoid Mary*. 1991. Images archived at http://www.lindadement.com/typhoid-mary.htm

Firestone, Shulamith. *The Dialectic of Sex: the case for feminist revolution*. William Morrow and Co, 1970.

Fleming, Nick. "Plants talk to each other using an internet of fungus." 11th November 2014. http://www.bbc.com/earth/story/20141111-plants-have-a-hidden-internet.

Gibbs, Anna "As if by Magic," eds. Lanfranco Aceti, Janis Jefferies and Irini Papadimitriou. *Leonardo Electronic Almanac (Touch and Go)*. 18, no. 3 (2012). 58-59.

Grosz, Elizabeth. *Time Travels, Feminism, Nature, Power*. Durham: Duke University Press, 2005.

_, _. *Volatile Bodies, Towards a Corporeal Feminism*. Bloomington: Indiana University Press, 1994.

Haraway, Donna. (1991) "A Cyborg Manifesto: Science, Technology, and Socialist-Feminism in the Late Twentieth Century", in *Simians, Cyborgs and Women: The Reinvention of Nature*. Routledge, New York, 1991. 149–181.

_,_. "Manifesto for Cyborgs: Science, Technology, and Socialist Feminism in the 1980s." In: *Socialist Review* 80 (1985). 65–108.

_,_. "Situated Knowledges: The Science Question in Feminism and the Priviliege of Partial Perspective." *Feminist Studies*, Vol. 14, No. 3, Autumn, 1988. 575-599.

Irigaray, Luce. *This Sex Which Is Not One*, trans. Catherine Porter with Carolyn Burke. Ithaca and New York: Cornell University Press: 1985.

Jackson, Shelley. *Patchwork Girl*. Eastgate Systems, 1995.

Munster, Anna. *Materializing New Media: Embodiment in Information Aesthetics*. Hanover: Dartmouth College Press, 2006.

Parisi, Luciana. *Abstract Sex: Philosophy, Biotechnology and the Mutations of Desire*. London: Continuum, 2004.

_,_. "Automated Architecture." In *#Accelerate: the accelerationist reader*. Eds Robin Mackay and Armen Avanessian. Falmouth: Urbanomic, 2014.

_,_. *Contagious Architecture: Computation, Aesthetics and Space*. Cambridge, Massachusetts and London, England: The MIT Press, 2013.

_,_. "For a Schizogenesis of Sexual Difference." *Identities*. 3.1 (2004): 67-93.

Plant, Sadie. *Zeros + Ones, Digital Women + The New Technoculture*. New York, Doubleday, 1997.

Schaffer, Kay. "The Game Girls of VNS Matrix: Challenging Gendered Identities in Cyberspace." In: Anne O' Farrell and Lynne Vallone (eds), *Virtual Gender: Fantasies of Subjectivity and Embodiment*. Michigan: University of Michigan Press, 1999, 147-168.

Southern, Jen. "Comobility: How Proximity and Distance Travel Together in Locative Media." *Canadian Journal of Communication*, Vol 37, 75-91 (2012).

Stone, Sandy. "The Empire Strikes Back: A Posttranssexual Manifesto." In Kristina Straub and Julia Epstein, eds. *Body Guards: The Cultural Politics of Sexual Ambiguity*. New York: Routledge,1996.

Terranova, Tiziana. "Communication Beyond Meaning: on the cultural politics of information." *Social Text*, 80, Vol. 22, No. 3 (Fall 2004), 51-73.

VNS Matrix, *Cyberfeminist manifesto for the 21stC*, 1991. https://anthology.rhizome.org/a-cyborg-feminist-manifesto-for-the-21st-century

Latin American Electronic Literature: When, Where, and Why

BY CLAUDIA KOZAK

The aim of this text is to focus on topics which enable a discussion of Latin American electronic literature's necessity and/or specificity. To what extent should electronic literature be considered as a global practice? How do social imaginaries related to technological modernization intervene in the shaping of electronic literature in underdeveloped countries?[17] Latin America involves diverse levels of economic development, interculturalism and glocalization. When technological issues are seen in relation to modernization, the tendency is to associate them to novelty as their main value. And this frequently implies a sort of fascination. On the contrary, the approach followed here seeks to address electronic literature not merely from the point of view of technological fascination, but focusing on the complex tension produced when artists experiment with new technologies because of their creative potential and, at the same time, are aware of technology's social, economic and political interdependencies. Even if electronic literature constitutes a worthy subject of interest for contemporary literary theory and criticism, it would be important to not focus on it—or on new media art—for the sake of novelty itself.

Instead, framed by a brief contextualization of electronic literature in Latin America, in order to drive the attention to some highlights that draw a summarized cartography—the when and where of this text's title—the focus will be put on electronic literature works that deal with the why of the title of the essay. As an answer to this question, these works show that it is possible to experience technology in an artistic/literary manner, not because of the fascination with the new—which is the norm in mainstream digital culture—but to open a diverted (techno) imagination.

This diversion from the norm, that is to say, from the very usual association between new technologies, modernization, novelty and progress, encompass specific aesthetic/political directions pursued by a significant portion of Latin American electronic literature.

Therefore, it is possible to take as a point of departure the hypothesis that because of its location—not only geographically but concerning economic underdevelopment, interculturalism and glocalization—Latin American electronic literature tightens an

17 The concept of social imaginary—developed by authors such as Cornelius Castoriadis (1998) and Branislow Baczko (1984)—is understood here as symbolic constructions or representations a given social group or broader society share about their own image as a society. Baczko refers to them as "ideas-images" a society "invents" to represent itself as a society with a particular identity, divisions, power legitimations and role models for its members. See also Taylor (2004) and Marcus (1995).

imaginary string which could be called "technological modernization." This string's ends are, on one side, electronic experimentation as a form of uncritical technological fascination and, on another side, electronic experimentation as a form of posing new paths for intercultural community. The latter operates within digital culture in order not to fascinate or to be fascinated, but to open imagination to a change of meanings, including those related to material conditions of life for millions of people to whom global informational developments don´t imply necessarily any improvement. In other words, the works to be analyzed here try to respond from within to hegemonic global techno imaginaries.

Combining the where with the why (and how), the analysis will be dedicated to a couple of Latin American electronic literature works that cover Latin America territory "from top to bottom": from Mexico, where *El 27/The 27th* by Eugenio Tisselli discusses political and economic autonomy within globalization, to Argentina, where *IP Poetry* by Gustavo Romano discusses the ways meaning could be constructed in global societies, the Internet being a symbolic reservoir to be deconstructed. We will consider this work particularly when exhibited as an installation during the "I Biennial of The End of the World." Since this is an art Biennial whose first three editions, beginning in 2007, took place at the city of Ushuaia, the southernmost city of the world, the bottom turns out to be almost literal.

Latin America is a subcontinent of complicated social fabric with assorted levels of economic development, diverse cultural heritages and resultant implications for heterogeneity within globalization: among others, peripheral market economy, pointed separation of social classes, and ancestral cultures which survive and/or regenerate with uneven levels of visibility and impact on state cultures.

Having that context in mind, and given the fact that electronic literature is a field necessarily developed within the informational turn which has been one of the foundational stones of globalization, it would be worthy to question if electronic literature should develop or even exist everywhere. As it will be argued below, the works to be dealt with in this paper offer a deviated way to answer that question. On the one hand, as electronic works, they don't refuse to be part of the global informational world; but on the other, they discuss from within "how to be together" in a world which also contains many exclusions.

THEORETICAL AND CRITICAL APPROACH

So far, the above mentioned concepts—globalization/glocalization, technological modernization and interculturalism—could be seen as a theoretical framework for the approach to Latin American electronic literature proposed here. Hence, before the works' analysis, these sociological framing concepts will be presented in a rough summary. But both works will be read with a critical approach which considers electronic literature in its own specificity—that is to say, its materiality, formal devices, and sociopolitical implications.

Technological modernization is a concept bound to the history of Modernity. Important steps of that history were, for instance, the new scientific imagination during the Renaissance or the influence of the Industrial Revolution on the modeling of Modernity. But it can be observed that imaginaries of technological modernization have been accelerating themselves and growing as a way of shaping reality. At least since the beginning of 20th Century, these techno imaginaries have been modeling the ways reality is seen in order to keep the idea going that the comfort technology can provide is equivalent of a full and richer life. Of course technology makes many things in everyday life easier, but technological modernization as an ideology tends to obscure many other aspects. In contemporary times the concept is addressable not really in globalization but in globalism. As Ulrich Beck says: an ideology of globality which "proceeds monocausally and economistically reducing the multidimensionality of globalization to a single, economic dimension" (Beck, 9). In its affirmative way, globalism coincides with neoliberalism. Instead, globalization, and glocalization—following Ronald Robertson's neologism of the nineties—can be seen as processes which stress the paradoxes and ambivalences of several convergences, namely location/delocation, universalism/particularism, connection/fragmentation, homogeneity/heterogeneity, etcetera.

In more recent years, since theories of globalization were primarily developed in the nineties, the concept of interculturalism came to complement this perspective. It proposes a way of focusing on how similarities and differences are managed, and what kind of power relations are involved, not only concerning subaltern groups but the whole social fabric. Native communities living, for example, in a country such as Argentina, a country with a broad tradition of neglecting them as citizens with their own history and memory, are intercultural; but interculturalism applies to the rest of the population as well. Argentinean people are nowadays more conscious about the existence of native communities who, due to policies of extermination and invisibilization, seemed to have disappeared. Nevertheless, it is not clear for many people how to "be open to different ways of seeing things and generate new languages and symbols together to talk about what makes us closer or apart, what we could share and what we could not" (Briones, 3, my translation). Following the same idea of not addressing interculturalism only to subalterns, intercultural people are not only Mexicans trying to cross a border which in historical terms shouldn't have been settled where it was, but the whole population on both sides of that border. An intercultural perspective does not mean, however, to flatten differences or avoid seeing power relations, but to situate a perspective which recognizes them.

Going back to the main concern of this paper on Latin American electronic literature, an intercultural perspective means that a critical approach, from Latin America, should need also to acknowledge a located perspective. There are many examples of electronic literature in Latin America, but to whom is this literature addressed? Why and how should electronic literature be created in Latin America? Whatever the answers could be, the point here is to certainly prefer electronic literature which allows, by its own means and ends, asking these sorts of questions rather than others that assume that these are unimportant questions.

Concerning the analysis of Latin American electronic literature, a collaborative and combined approach that could propose a multidimensional convergence would be more suitable. Given that many critics could not develop its full implications by themselves, it could be seen as a *close-distant-collaborative-located* critical approach (Kozak 2015) This would mean a way of reading electronic literature focusing on: a) its phenomenological and logical materiality; that is to say, its visuality, sonority, textuality, and the formal materiality of its code; b) the task of mapping Latin American electronic literature, in relation to world electronic literature; and c) the articulation between collaborative and located approaches, in which different people with different reading skills could converge. Unfortunately, the scope of this paper could not be as broad as that; although the suggested perspective aims to provisionally cover part of it.

WHEN, WHERE, WHY AND HOW

Up to the current state of the art,[18] the very first Latin American electronic literature works are *IBM* (1966) by Argentinean Omar Gancedo and *Le tombeau de Mallarme* (1972) by Brazilian Erthos Albino de Souza. The former is a series of three short poems codified in IBM cards. These cards were processed by a Card Interpreter, bringing as a result the printing of the de-codified texts on the middle horizontal line of each card. The latter is a series of ten visual poems printed by a computer after the manipulation of software prepared for temperature measurement, and accessible to de Souza due to his work as an engineer in the Brazilian oil company Petrobras.

At the same time, Erthos Albino de Souza produced other poetic experimentations with computers. One of them was the transcodification in computer cards of the poem "Cidade" by Augusto de Campos. In addition, he produced a computer version

18 See Antonio 2008; and Kozak 2015.

of Augusto de Campos' *Colidouescapo*, originally published in 1971. Interviewed in 1983 by Carlos Ávila, de Souza says: "When Augusto did his *Colidouescapo*, which is a collage of word fragments, I did it with the computer, including all possible permutations. I sent it to him, and he found it interesting as research" (de Souza 2008, my translation). In the same interview, de Souza explains that art computer experiences by Waldemar Cordeiro in Brazil in the late sixties were earlier than his, but they were mainly visual arts experiences, not poetry ones.

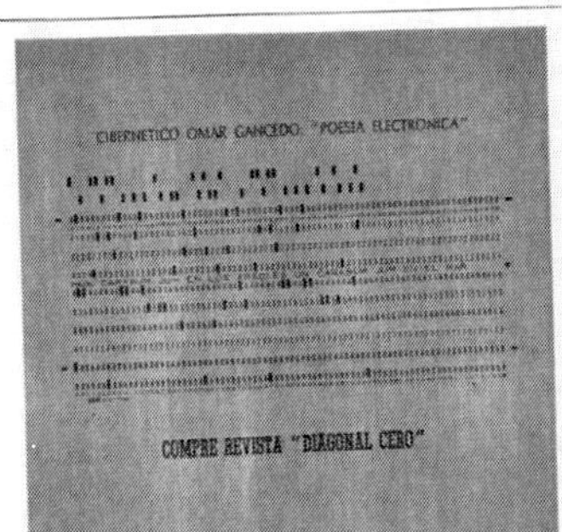

Figure 1: Omar Gancedo: One of IBM poems. Flyer advertising magazine *Diagonal Cero*. Archive Centro de Arte Experimental (CAEV)

The sixties and early seventies were times of technological modernization, coinciding with the progressive spread of big computers in business and government agencies. It was not the time of personal computers yet. Hence, experiences of this kind were more or less isolated. Nevertheless they were part of a time when Latin America envisioned itself as a subcontinent in ways of development, with all the tensions and complexities this could encompass. I have tried to assess these tensions within the works of Gancedo and de Souza elsewhere (Kozak 2016), since both artists demonstrated at least curiosity about computers and in native South American cultures. In fact, technological modernization and ancestral cultures encountered each other in no predictable ways within the works of both poets.

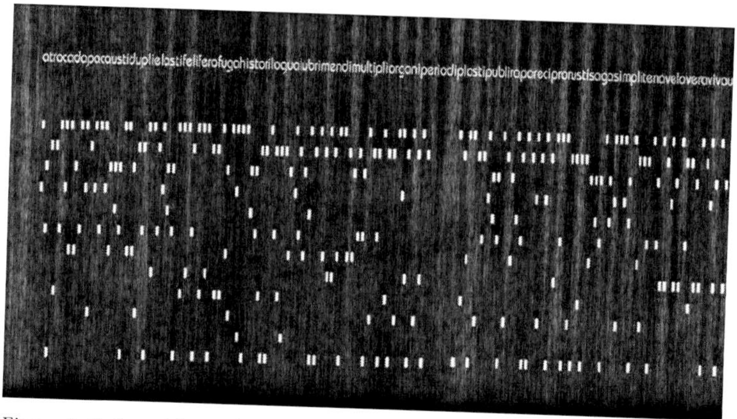

Figure 2: Erthos Albino de Souza: "Cidade," transcoded version of "Cidade City Cité" by Augusto de Campos: dadoacaso.blogspot

During the eighties several experiments linking literature and computers were made all around the world, including Latin America. As examples among others, Jorge Luiz Antonio refers to "Soneto só prá vê" (1982) by Brazilian Daniel Santiago with programming by Luciano Moreira, in the TAL/II language; and "Universo" (1985) by João Cohelo programmed in the Advanced Basic language (Antonio 2015). By 1986, in Argentina, Ladislao Pablo Györi shaped one of Grete Stern's photomontages using 3D graphics software and combined it with a poem written by madi artist Gyula Kosice recorded with the aid of a synthesizer.

After the opening of the Internet beyond military and educational frontiers, in the mid-nineties, the development of globalized electronic literature grows exponentially. In Latin America not only digital poetry, perhaps the most extended subgenre in that part of the planet, grows in quantity and quality, but also hypertext and hypermedia fiction were part of the scene.

Just to present a rough and not exhaustive panorama of names, it is worthy to mention a list of artists who have been producing digital poetry in sound, visual, kinetic, hypermedia and/or generative modalities language some of them since the nineties and others in more recent years– either as their main artistic work or as part of it.

In Argentina: Ana María Uribe, Belén Gache, Charly Gradin, Fabio Doctorovich, Gustavo Romano, Héctor Piccoli, Iván Marino, Ladislao Pablo Györi, and Milton Läufer. In Brazil: Alckmar Luiz dos Santos, Andre Vallias, Álvaro Andrade García, Chico Marinho, Eduardo Kac, Giselle Beiguelman, Lucio Agra, and Wilton Azevedo. In Chile: Carlos Cociña, Martín Gubbins, and Orquesta de Poetas. In Mexico: Benjamin R. Moreno, Eugenio Tisselli, Karen Villeda. In Perú: Enrique Beó, José Aburto, and Luis Alvarado.

Some features of works only by female artists will be outlined here. Ana María Uribe was a visual poet who moved into digital multimedia in the nineties. In 1997 she began to remediate some of her late sixties typographic poems and also produced new digital ones where multimedia animations were central, until she passed away in 2003. She compiled these digital poems in two CD-ROMS and in a website. Later, her *Tipoemas* and *Anipoemas* have been broadly diffused thanks to Jim Andrews' website.[19]

Figure 3: Ana María Uribe: still from "Disciplina"

Belén Gache, an Argentinean writer living currently in Madrid, has published novels and essays on experimental and expanded literature since the nineties. At the same time she has experimented with videopoetry and digital poetry. One of her best known works is the series of interactive digital poems and short texts *WordToys*, but her electronic literature covers a wide range of works as blogs, transmedia storytelling and generative poetry.

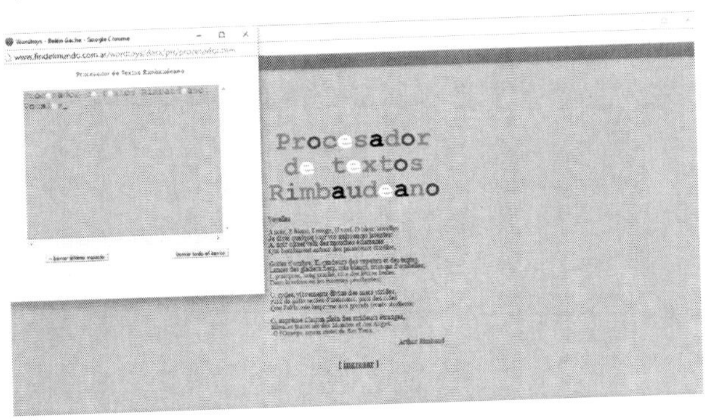

Figure 4: Belén Gache: Screen shot of "Procesador de textos Rimbaudeano" in *Wordtoys*.

19 See vispo.com/uribe.

Brazilian Giselle Beiguelman is also a prolific digital artist. Her work is not exclusively oriented to literary nuances, but some of her projects, such as *Poetrica*, and parts of the project *//** Code_Up* as *Code Movie 1*, are a type of codework poetry and very good examples of the potential of electronic literature in Latin America.

Figure 5: Giselle Beiguelman: Screen shot of movie trailer announcing *Poetrica* (and P0es1s exhibition) at cinemas in Berlin.

Mexican Karen Villeda has published several poetry books but in her website she defines herself as a multimedia poet.[20] She presents there several projects including *Poetuitéame*, interactive generative poetry in collaboration with Denise Audirac; stop motion poetry as in *Dodo* (2013-2014); and wikipoems as in *Poepedia* (2014). Her first digital interactive poetry project was *LABO: Cyberpoetry Laboratory*, launched in 2010, where she recreated previous published poems with the aid of HTML and ActionScript languages.

Concerning hypertext and hypermedia fiction, some relevant Latin American works are: *El primer vuelo de los hermanos Wright* (first hypertext version 1996-1998) by Columbian writer and mathematician (living currently in USA) Juan B. Gutierrez, with web design by Carlos E. Herrera; and *Gabriella infinita* (1998) by Columbian Jaime Alejandro Rodríguez, with interactive design for the hypermedia version by Carlos Roberto Torres. Both novels had earlier hypertext versions, and even in the case of

20 See poetronica.net.

the initial book *Gabriella infinita* (1995) it was first released as plain text; only afterwards did they create into hypermedia versions.

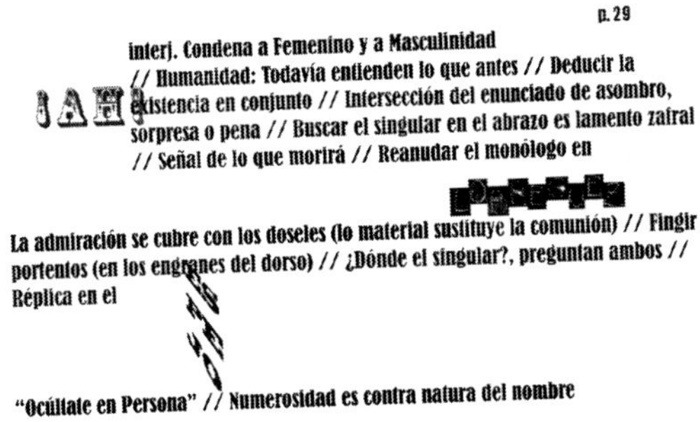

Figure 6: Karen Villeda: Screen shot, interactive version of her book *Tesauro*.

Tierra de extracción by Doménico Chiappe (a Peruvian writer who has lived in Venezuela and lives currently in Spain) is also very well known. The project began in 1996 and its first version was released in 2000. It is in fact a collaborative work, with multimedia design by Andreas Meier and contributions by many other artists. *Pentagonal: incluidos tú y yo* by Chilean writer Carlos Labbé (living in USA) is part of this first generation of Latin American hypertext fiction too, since it was released in 2001. *El libro flotante de Caytran Dölphin* (2006) by Ecuadorian Leonardo Valencia and Mexican Eugenio Tisselli (both living in Barcelona at the time) is a hypertext project which dialogs with a homonymous novel published as a book by Valencia. Less known is the hypermedia fiction *Desnudo* by Argentinean Carola di Nardo, awarded with second prize in 2006 by the "Digital Literature in Spanish Prize," a reward given by the Research Group LEETHI at the Complutense University in Madrid.

In any case, the above brief historic outline only intends to put in perspective the two works which are the specific focus in this paper.

El 27 / The 27th is a piece of electronic textuality conceived by Eugenio Tisselli as part of his algorithmic politics. Tisselli is a Mexican electronic artist/poet/programmer who has lived for several years in Barcelona and has moved back in recent years to Mexico. The number of the title refers to the 27th article of Mexican Constitution which deals with the property of land, water and natural resources. In its original text, the article established that "the property of lands and water resources inside the limits of the national territory corresponds to the Nation." But due to a reform sanctioned by Mexican Congress in 2013, it has suffered changes in order to be adapted to a more neoliberal way of understanding who the owner of national natural resources should be. The new text guarantees for the State the right to transfer the dominion over lands and territorial waters into private hands. In an essay concerning his work Tisselli says:

> In this piece, an algorithm operates directly on the text of Article 27 in the following way: every night, after the activity at the New York Stock exchange has come to an end, a robot obtains its last closing price and its respective percent variation. If the variation is positive, another robot chooses a fragment of Article 27 randomly, translates it into English automatically, and inserts the translation into its corresponding place within the original text written in Spanish. Given enough time, the algorithm will produce a version of Article 27 fully readable in effective, yet incorrect, English. (Tisselli 2015)

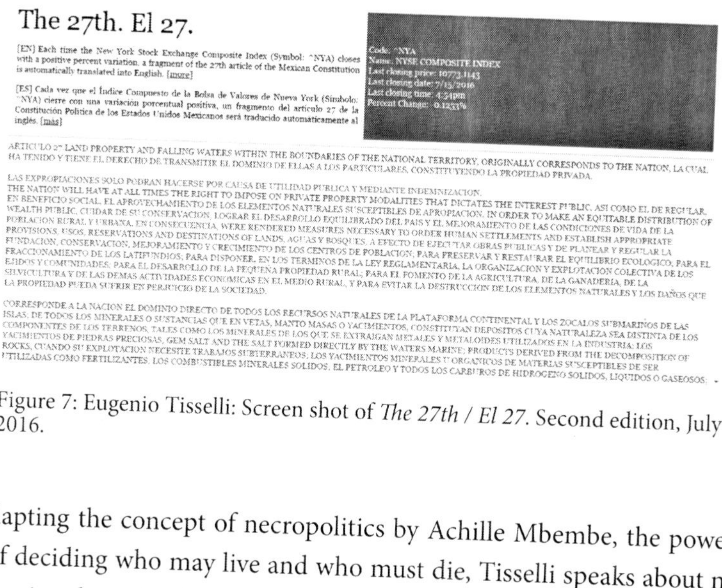

Figure 7: Eugenio Tisselli: Screen shot of *The 27th / El 27*. Second edition, July 2016.

Adapting the concept of necropolitics by Achille Mbembe, the power and the capacity of deciding who may live and who must die, Tisselli speaks about necrocapitalism, meaning the reduction of the sphere of politics by hands of financial capitalism which ultimately decides on the life and death of many people. The disappearance/murder in 2014 of 43 students in Ayotzinapa, for instance, can be understood in the same context: "The power of capital has increasingly turned into a murderous one that, nevertheless, is still executed by the officers of the old sphere of politics" (Tisselli 2015). The alterations to the 27th article can be seen as one example of this kind of execution, which concerns not only capital but language, given that it is the language of the article that has been modified with political and economic consequences.

This piece can be considered as part of an electronic poetic conceptualism that discusses the way capital and languages are dealt with in contemporary globalist culture; natural and artificial languages as well. Spanish language is turned into English by means of an algorithm that retrieves information from the global financial market. In a way, this kind of information becomes a trigger to intertwine natural languages with an artificial language. As the author points out, the work is not toward an inversion or liberation from algorithmic politics; on the contrary, it is supposed to deepen the usual direction algorithm politics adopts: when financial markets improve, the quality of natural language is reduced. Spanish from the time when the Mexican Constitution was written tends to disappear, replaced by macaronic English. Neither Spanish nor English win anything, but a machine language which blindly follows the market. The Spanish language of the Mexican Constitution was certainly also built by power relations; in a way this replacement only points out the new directions of power relations nowadays. But even if the work deepens the hegemonic algorithmic politics, even if it does not propose to deviate the routes capital and languages usually follow, it nevertheless intervenes as artistic activism showing to what extent capital and languages usually go together. And it does it as part of informational globalization since it depends on the programmed algorithm to work and since its access relays on the Internet.

As a work in progress, at first, when the work was launched on the first day of 2014—twenty years of North American Free Trade Agreement (NAFTA), in Spanish: Tratado de Libre Comercio de América del Norte (TLCAN)—it showed a plain screen with the article 27 in grey capital letters. The only colorful part was the red rectangle on the right part on top of the screen, with the white letters that refer to the closing figures of the New York Stock Exchange Composite Index (Symbol: ^NYA) on the day of the launching. This rectangle turns into green every time ^NYA closes with a positive percent variation. In the present, the work has already been changed many times. On the rectangle it is always possible to visualize the date of the last change. In fact, there have been for the moment two editions of the work: the first one launched in 2014, and the second one restarted in February 2016, once the first one showed almost the totality of the text translated into English in red letters. When posing the mouse on the red English letters, access to a memory of textual changes is available: each time people position the mouse on the red letters, the date of the change and the positive percent variation that has triggered it becomes visible.

Therefore, the work has been invaded by the red in form of Capital letters. The pun only applies in English, not in Spanish though. Something worth to mention since the work is bilingual, even in a twisted manner. Had this happened during the days of Cold War, the red invasion would have surely had an entirely different meaning. However, it can nowadays be read more in the blood line of necrocapitalism. At least when we read it contiguously with the already mentioned essay Tisselli has recently published online. If we accept that the work can be seen as part of an electronic poetic conceptualism, we can also interpret the essay being part of the work as well.

It is also worth paying attention to the fact that the work uses an automatic remote translator. Tisselli had already used automatic translators as poetic devices in previous poetic works such as his *PAC/CAP (Poesía asistida por computadora/Computer Aided Poetry)*. Taking into account that automatic translators aren't 100% reliable, electronic literature authors, and many Latin Americans among them, have been using them in order to distort poetry, language, communication, embracing some sort of politics of the mistake, considering that the ideal of an effective communication on the Internet usually reinforces the kind of non reflexive imaginaries of technological modernization referred to in the beginning of this paper.

Finally, the randomness involved in the work should also be paid attention to. It is an aspect shared by many other electronic literature works and it is itself a topic within global digital culture. Each fragment of the 27th article is chosen randomly by a robot that alters the original text. It is well known that, from the days of the first electronic generators, randomness has been used as a poetic device. In a very general sense, it can be said that randomness has been a way to open creative works to the unexpected, but this conveys a tenacious paradox, since randomness is certainly not "chance." In fact, randomness creates a tension between constructive poetics and chance poetics. Related to a socio-political approach to digital culture, this could speak about the tension between the routes more or less everybody follows without even noticing it and the possibility of playing against those routes by means of the creation of unexpected meanings.

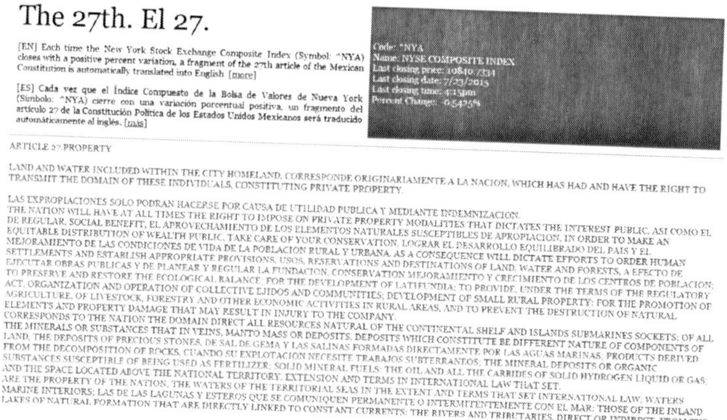

Figure 8: Eugenio Tisselli: Screen shot of *The 27th / El 27*. First edition, July 2015.

The randomness involved in *The 27th* can lead the attention to the second work to be considered here: *IP Poetry* by Gustavo Romano, an Argentinean artist living in Madrid for several years now, with programming by Milton Läufer, an Argentinean electronic literature author/programmer himself, currently living in New York.

Many net.art projects take the Internet, or even the Internet browsers, as a point of departure for capturing words, images or sound in order to randomly compose/collage artworks. The distinctiveness of *IP Poetry* is its combination of Flarf poetry, a posthuman reflection on the new globalized configuration of the natural and the artificial (Weintraub 2011)—including, as in Tisselli's work, natural and artificial languages—and a locative perspective on global electronic arts. This last aspect is particularly visible when speaking about the *IP Poetry* project developed in the form of installations, which is not the only way it works, because the possibility to interact with *IP Poetry* remotely to create new poems online is available too.

Romano describes his *IP Poetry* as follows: "The *IP Poetry* project involves the development of a software and hardware system that uses text from the Internet to generate poetry that is then recited in real time by automatons connected to the web" (Romano 105). When inserting search instructions in the form of a short sentence or textual fragment, sometimes a verse by a specific poet, the robots randomly retrieve different textual fragments including the one searched, and reproduce them in real time using the gallery of 2.000 phonemes pre-recorded by Romano's own voice. This, in the male Spanish version, but a female Spanish one exists as well. The project includes also a male English version and a Chinese one for the Beijing installation, as it is appreciated when playing the Beijing video on the project's website. The robots have human names and are displayed as speakers mounted inside acoustic boxes, each of them having a screen in their front. These screens show part of a head, particularly the mouth, reciting the texts sometimes one at a time, sometimes in dual recitals and in other variations, and each one in its own style. Romano adds:

> The *IP Poetry* project studies the role of poetry and of poets themselves. On the one hand, as far as the construction of the robots is concerned, it highlights the increasing subjectivity of technology, which is endowed with certain artificially enhanced human characteristics (in this case, memory, and the ability to speak and listen). On the other hand, as concerns the resulting poetic structures, it uses the virtual arrangement of the collective human memory found on the Internet to compose poetry that has both mechanical and random elements. (Romano 105)

Even if the procedure lies on randomness, when exhibited as installation the artist usually establishes a close relation between the robots and the location where the installations are exhibited, since the fragments of text that trigger the Internet search are commentaries on the context. For instance, the installation *Un robot poeta en Nueva York (A Robot-Poet in New York)*, which took place in 2008 at the Instituto Cervantes in New York, was triggered by verses pulled out from *Poeta en Nueva York (A Poet in New York)* by Federico García Lorca, written in 1929, the one surrealistic book written by Lorca. Another installation, *Metropolis*, was exhibited at the Hotel de Inmigrantes in Buenos Aires, an old building that used to be in the first half on 20th century the gate of entrance to the country for the majority of immigrants coming to Argentina for a new life. Referring to this work the artist says:

> The poems focus on topics of migration and Metropolis, this meaning not only the physical place where people meet and interact, but also as a metaphor for the gathering of information, a virtual assembly for communication, a repository for memories present and past, a utopian or dystopian place where ideas are born, multiply and die. (Romano 110)

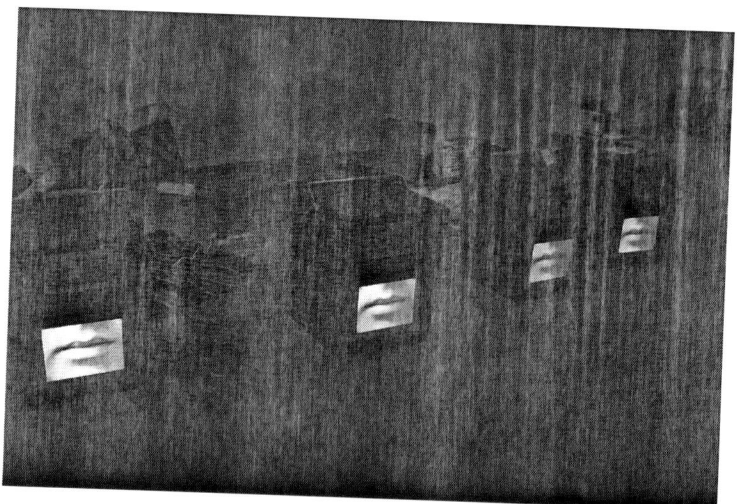

Figure 9: Gustavo Romano: *IP Poetry*, backstage.

About the *IP Poetry* installation in April 2007 for the "I Biennial of the End of the World," under the name of *Keepers of The End of the World*, Romano outlines:

> The poems at this exhibit alluded to the ends of the known world and to the imaginary ones that lay beyond. Like the "keepers of the end of the world" in the movie *Heart of Glass* by Herzog, the sole function of the poet robots, situated on

the water's edge on the planet's southernmost inhabited outpost, was to watch for and warn the world of the coming "unknown." The public was able to create its own IP poems through the website, which were then recited at the Ushuaia exhibit and seen via Internet around the world. (Romano 109)

As it is possible to learn watching a video that documents the Biennial, one of the poems was built upon the search of the phrases "tienes miedo" ("you fear") and "es peligroso" (it is dangerous"). These textual fragments reinforced perceptions around the anxiety of the unknown created by an installation at the edge of the world with a phantom connection with the entire world. But what does it mean the fear when it is felt from this specific "End of the World"? Regardless the fact that "the end of the world" is the motto of the city in order to encourage tourism, that is, a label and the city brand, other located interpretations could be held. For the moment, two of them are followed here.

Figure 10: Gustavo Romano: *IP Poetry*, installation, I Biennial of The End of the World.

On the one hand, carried by the robotic voices of this automatons nurtured by a delocated magma of words—many of them quite trivial—all together with the cloudy sky, the cold ocean and the wind, in a place where everything reminded to the participants that they were at the "end of the world," the experience could have been seen as an immersion in a disturbing, even upsetting, outdoors ambience. The unknown got there the shape of a posthuman entity trying to be closer to humanity by reciting human banalities. This disturbance could have been provoked a bit by the sense of the "ends" the installation established—of the land, of the time, of the human—but in a second perspective, it could have been provoked by the memory of other endings closely related to the history of the place as well.

When people from other locations in Argentina, mainly from more "central" places, travel to Ushuaia, they are aware not only of how distant the city is located but also of the extent of historic endings. That is to say, this awareness is not only due to how extensive Argentinean territory could be and to the fact that there is no other inhabited town beyond, but because of the long history of centralism, which led to neglect many regions far away from Buenos Aires and other central populated areas. In fact, this neglect contributed to the progressively disappearance of native people who had lived there before the conquest of South America. What could have been the fear and the sense of the end, for example, for Selk'nam people (also called Ona) who lived in Tierra del Fuego, the southernmost province of Argentina with Ushuaia as its capital city, when the conquerors arrived there for the first time in 1520? Or what could have been the sense of the end for their scattered descendants when the last of them was about to die?

In an article written by French-American anthropologist Anne MacKaye Chapman in 1975, we read:

> The Indians [sic] had been the owners of Tierra del Fuego for thousands of years. A hundred years ago the Selk'nam (Ona) numbered probably between 3,500 and 4,000. Now only a few remain whose mothers were Selk'nam. On 28 May 1974, one of the very last Selk'nam, Angela Loij, died. (Chapman 2007)

In the *IP Poetry* project the web is understood as a reservoir of knowledge, emotions and language: a randomly acquired collective memory. When visiting the artist's website, it is possible to have access to a set of poems that have been performed by the automatons in Ushuaia along the days of "The End of the World Biennial." Still, a poem compounded in a vanished language as the langauge of the selk'nam people could have been performed too. In that case, it would have been a striking comment on location and delocation in our globalized world. The *IP Poetry* robots, posthuman entities, retrieve and mix randomly the words humanity says to itself in continuous dispersion. The most challenging results might arise when these sayings also lead us to hear the unsaid.

ARTISTS' WEBSITES

Ana María Uribe: http://www.vispo.com/uribe/

Belén Gache: http://www.findelmundo.com.ar/wordtoys/; http://belengache.net/

Eugenio Tisselli: http://motorhueso.net/27/

Gisele Beiguelman: http://www.desvirtual.com/projects/poetrica/

Gustavo Romano: http://ip-poetry.findelmundo.com.ar/; http://www.gustavoromano.org/

Karen Villeda: http://www.poetronica.net/poesiadigital.html

WORKS CITED

Antonio, Jorge Luiz. "Trayectoria de la Poesía Electrónica en Brasil: Una breve historia." Escaner Cultural. *Revista virtual de arte contemporáneo y nuevas tendencias* 103 (2008). Accesed December 12, 2015, http://revista.escaner.cl/node/714.

_,_. "Del medio impreso al digital: la poesía de Ana María Uribe." *Revista Laboratorio* 5 (2011). Universidad Diego Portales. Accesed October 28, 2015. http://revistalaboratorio.udp.cl/investigacion-5/.

Baczko, Bronislow. *Les imaginaires sociaux. Mémoires et espoirs collectifs*. Paris: Payot, 1984.

Beck, Ulrich. *What is globalization?* Malden, MA: Blackwell, 2000.

Briones, Claudia et al. "Diversidad cultural e interculturalidad como construcciones socio-históricas." In *Diversidad cultural e interculturalidad*, edited by Aldo Amegeiras and Elisa Jure, 255-264. Buenos Aires: Prometeo/UNGS, 2006.

Castoriadis, Cornelius. *The imaginary institution of society*. Cambridge, Massachusetts: The MIT Press, 1998.

de Souza, Erthos. Interview with Carlos Ávila, "O engenheiro da poesia." in *Poesia pensada*, Rio de Janeiro: 7Letras, 2004.

Giovine, María Andrea. 2014. "Poesía perceptual: experiencias poéticas interactivas." In Revista Laboratorio 9 (2014). *Universidad Diego Portales*. Accesed December 16, 2015, http://revistalaboratorio.udp.cl/investigacion-9/.

Hayles, N. Katherine. *Literatura eletrônica. Novos horizontes para o literario*. São Paulo: Global Editora, 2009.

Kozak, Claudia. "Literatura digital y materialidad. Cómo se lee." *Dossier Art Matters*. Edited by Ana Rodríguez Granell and Pau Alsina. Artnodes 15 (2015): 90-98. doi: 10.7238/a.v0i15.2580.

_,_. "Mallarmé e IBM. Los inicios de la poesía digital en Brasil y Argentina." Ipotesi. *Revista de Estudos Literários* 19.1 (2015): 191-200. Programa de Posgraduação de Letras da Universidade Federal de Juiz de Fora, http://www.ufjf.br/revistaipotesi/

MacKaye Chapman, Anne. "Angela Loij." In *RISM Electronic Archives* (2007). Accessed August 31, 2015. Originally published in *Journal de la Société des Américanistes* 62 (1975): 62: 235-36. http://www.thereedfoundation.org/rism/chapman/angela.htm.

Marcus, George E. (ed.). *Technoscientific Imaginaries. Conversations, Profiles, and Memoirs*. Chicago: Chicago Universtity Press, 1995.

Pressman, Jessica, Jeremy Douglass and Mark Marino. "Intersecting Approaches to Electronic Literature: Close-Reading Code, Content, and Cartographies in William Poundstone's Project for the Tachistoscope: [Bottomless Pit]" [abstract online]. ELMCIP. *Electronic Literature Knowledge Base* (2010). University of Bergen Electronic Literature Research Group. Accessed February 20, 2015. http://elmcip.net/critical-writing/intersecting-approaches-electronic-literature-close-reading-code-content-and.

Robertson, Ronald. *Globalization: Social Theory and Global Culture*. London: SAGE, 1992.

Romano, Gustavo. *IP Poetry. Catalogue of the installation IP Poetry, for de exhibition Sabotage in the abstract machine*. Trans. Vaughan Systems and Tamara Stuby. Badajoz, Extremadura: MEIAC (Museo Extremeño e Iberoamericano de Arte Contemporáneo), 2008.

Taylor, Charles. *Modern Social Imaginaries*. Durham, NC, Duke University Press, 2004.

Tisselli, Eugenio. "Article 27." *Urgeurge (Ultimate Reseau Generalintellect Emerges)* March 2015. Accessed July 1, 2015. http://urgeurge.net/2015/03/09/article-27-articulo-27/.

Weintraub, Scott. "Machine (Self-)Consciousness: On Gustavo Romano's Electronic Poetics." Paper presented at the Conference "Latin American Cybercultural Studies: Exploring New Paradigms and Analytical Approaches." Liverpool, UK, University of Liverpool, May 19-20, 2011. Accesed August 1, 2015. http://ip-poetry.findelmundo.com.ar/MsC.html.

A Kaleidoscope of Slovak and Czech Electronic Literature

BY ZUZANA HUSÁROVÁ

INTRODUCTION

> Formalizability and computation on the one side, and intuition and imagination on the other, are the two poles of the mixtum compositum media art with regard to the actions of the subject.[...]The spectrum of what is currently still referred to as media art is a training ground for mixtures of the heterogenous. It is, therefore, a chaotic space, if one understands chaos to mean that dynamic linkage of multifarious elements, of chance and necessity, which is by nature opaque and out of which arise phenomena and processes that we can understand.—Zielinski, *The Deep Time of the Media*, 277.

In *The Deep* Time of the Media, the German media theoretician Siegfried Zielinski writes that in order to properly understand the poles that create media art, one has to get rid of a dualistic view and rather perceive these poles "as two ends of a scale that can be played in both directions" (277). This paper will therefore try to provide a closer look at a specific genre of media art, i.e. electronic literature, by employing an analysis that takes into account the mutual interconnections between formalizability, computation, and intuition and imagination. A specific environment of electronic literature will be studied: Slovakia and the Czech Republic, formerly united in the state Czechoslovakia (1918-1939, then again 1945-1992). The reasons for choosing these two countries are that the author of the study is Slovak; the Slovak and Czech languages are very similar; they share their history; and, especially important, is the fact that theoretical reflection on Slovak and Czech electronic literature has been very limited in the Anglophone context. The situation is different in another neighboring country, Poland, where the research has been provided also for the English speaking world (see e.g. Pisarski, Polish II, Pisarski, Polish III, Pająk, Polish I, Pająk Polish IV, Branny-Jankowska, Polish V, all published in The Cybertext Yearbook Database). The language of the fourth neighboring Post-Communist country, Hungary, which with the other three belongs to the grouping called the Visegrad Group or Visegrad Four, is not Slavic, but belongs to the Uralic language family, and the author of the paper does not understand Hungarian. So even though the production of electronic literature might tend to be somehow similar in all these four countries that geographically and culturally belong to the region of Central Europe, the paper will focus only on the Slovak and Czech works.

Regarding the methodology applied, the works will be divided into categories based on the corresponding genre. Further on, for the analytical part, a medium-specific analysis will be applied, as proposed by N. Katherine Hayles (see Writing Machines). A methodology of practice-based research will be at the focus for the works which the author of this paper created. The genres of the works fall on a scale: from digital poetry, hypermedial narratives and poetry, generative literary projects, to the use of QR codes and dynamic touch-responsive applications, and to interactive installations and performances. The aim of this paper is to present those digital works that can be categorized as electronic literature.

The works presented here were created by more or less established authors, but some others remain unknown for now and will be discovered in the future research. Even though many of these examples come from the authors working in the field of visual arts rather than the literary milieu, the focus is only on those which aim for literary qualities and/or where the digital textuality involved corresponds with trends in the current era or even proposes new questions for literary and new media research.

THE FIRST EXAMPLES OF ELECTRONIC POETRY

The first theoretical and practical research into electronic text can be mapped in the 1960s, the era when the Czech Republic and the Slovak Republic did not exist separately but formed Czechoslovakia and were under the Communist regime. So even though I will separate the Czech and the Slovak examples, it must be taken into account that these countries were one state then, with a common government.

The first examples of Czech digital poetry can be dated to the year 1966, when Jiří Levý, a researcher of translatology and literary studies, and the linguist Karel Pala, described at a versologist conference in Brno their research that lead to the generating of poems. Their paper included two generated poems, the first one based on the random choice from 116 generated sentences, the second one from 220 sentences. These poems consisting of sentences in a free verse form, were generated thanks to the language ALGOL-GENIUS that worked on the computer SAAB D 21 in the Computer Laboratory at Brno University of Technology. The poems were generated from the corpus of texts by the Nobel Prize-winning Czech writer, poet and journalist Jaroslav Seifert, who was a leading representative of the Czechoslovak avant-garde. Since their research was predominantly based on the study of generative grammar, they describe in their paper that "mechanical translation, artificial poetry etc. are just the side products of this methodology, they are just the verification of the constructed program" (Levý and Pala, *Generování veršů jako problém prozodický*, 74). So even though some of the poems were quite remarkable thanks to a well-chosen corpus, the fact that this was done for the sake of linguistic rather than poetic research might be one of the reasons why it has not influenced many similar projects in the field of generative poetry. The computer SAAB D21 was used for generating poetry also in 1967, in a project that Karel Pala and a literary critic Oleg Sus described in their article *Některé principy strojové poetiky* (*Some Principles of Machine Poetics*). This article published in a literary journal *Host do domu* includes their theoretical text and eight generated poems based mostly on sentence structures. The authors here argued that computer does not create poetic texts, but "parapoetic " ones – their structure does not bear traces of author´s personality and intention. "Parapoetic texts " should be according to them understood as achievements in the field of modern mathematic linguistics and not connected to concrete poetry. As authors of the generated poems are declared SAAB D 21 and Oleg Sus. Oleg Sus continued with text generating also in 1968, when he fed the computer with a vocabulary of political communication – a political speech by a member of the Communist Party Jiří Hendrych (For both pieces by Oleg Sus see Piorecký, *Česká počítačově (de)generovaná literatura*, online). The parody of the politician, who was against the reforms, led thanks to the computer that is "relentless and strictly neutral " to the "degeneration of political ideologist" in 29 generated sentences (Sus, *generovaná degenerace*, 50).

In Slovakia, the topic of cybernetics and arts appeared in a literary journal as early as 1959 (Kozma, *Budú stroje myslieť?*, 18) and continued to be theoretically discussed throughout the 1960s.[21] Some translations of theoretical texts on the possibilities of computers for art by foreign authors were printed. Additionally, some Slovak authors wrote their own theoretical texts, in which they either translated generative poems by foreign authors into Slovak or kept them in the original. Tibor Szebényi shows in his article in 1962 a generative poem, without stating the name of the author, to compare it with a visual poem by a Polish author Adam Macedoński (Szebényi, *Kybernetika v umení*, 24), and a generative poem by a French author Albert Ducrocq appears in a translation of the article by a Polish author Marian Mazur (Mazur, *Kybernetika a umenie*, 48). Klement Šimončič, a Slovak literary researcher, translated one of the generative poems from *blank verse at the rate of 150 words a minute* by Clair Philippy as a part of his paper, in which he compares the computer poetry to a surrealist literary technique. He initially gave this lecture at the Columbia University in New York in 1964 at a Second Congress of Czechoslovak Society for Arts and Sciences in America and later, in 1965, it was published in a Slovak literary journal Slovenské pohľady (Šimončič, *Poetika surrealistov a básnická kompozícia z matematických strojov*, 29-33). In a 1985 article, the artist Rudolf Legel published two generated poems: *Analyticka geometria v priestore mojej hlavy* (*Analytical Geometry in the Space of My Head*) and *Laska* (*Love*).

21 I wrote about the history and contemporary trends of Slovak digital poetry in the essay *Slovenská elektronická literatúra*..

His article describes in several steps a detailed process of creating a poetic text with a computer. Due to the strong inflections in the Slovak language, Legel edited the initial computer generated text, but his article also presents some verses without the editing. He states that "the advantage of the use of computers for the textual construction lies in the fact that the computer can quickly choose from big databases of words and a distribution of words is programmable." (Legel, *Experiment s interakciou človek-počítač pri vytváraní básnického textu*, 39). For the first poem, he chose the keywords from the terminological field of analytical geometry. For the second poem *Love*, the words come from the poem *Horská kanzóna* by Dante in a Slovak translation by Viliam Turčány. Both poems are not based on sentences but rather on a typical poetic structure. They use language that is in the first poem enriched due to a mathematical source and in the second poem follows a romantic poetic expressiveness.[22]

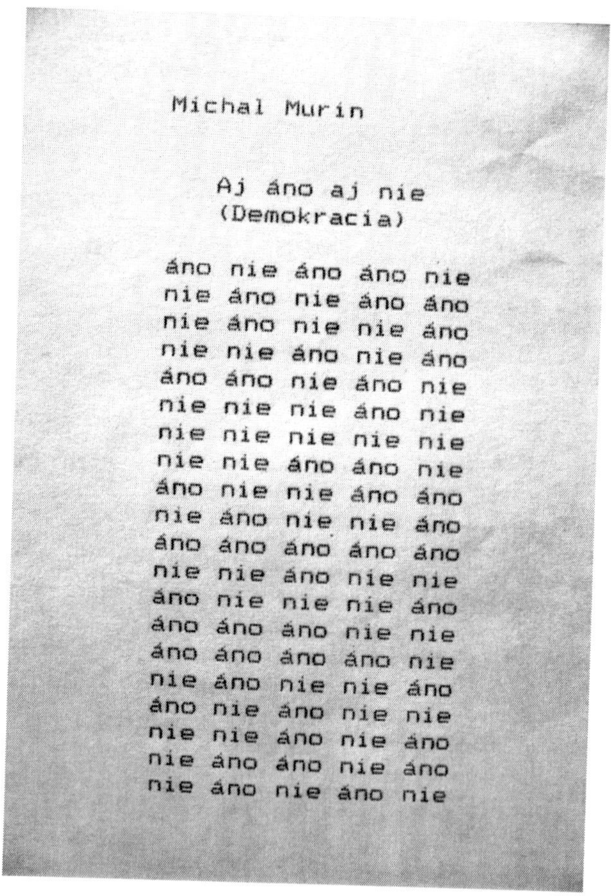
Michal Murin

Aj áno aj nie
(Demokracia)

áno nie áno áno nie
nie áno nie áno áno
nie áno nie nie áno
nie nie áno nie áno
áno áno nie áno nie
nie nie nie áno nie
nie nie nie nie nie
nie nie áno áno nie
áno nie nie áno áno
nie áno nie nie áno
áno áno áno áno áno
nie nie áno nie nie
áno nie nie nie áno
áno áno áno nie nie
áno áno áno áno nie
nie áno nie nie áno
áno nie áno nie nie
nie nie áno nie áno
nie áno áno nie áno
nie áno nie áno nie

Figure 1: Michal Murin, *Random Poetry*

22 For these early examples compare Michal Murin, *Digitálne médiá a poézia*, 74-75.

EARLY ELECTRONIC POETRY FROM 1989 AND THE 1990S

At the end of the 1980s, generative text creation reached the university milieu. During his studies in the 9th semester at The Technical University of Košice (from September until November 1989), a young Slovak student named Peter Šulej, today a famous poet, created an untitled generative poem as a part of his assignment for the class Programming for PC. According to his own words, the poem was programmed in the language Modula 2 and the program randomly chose verses from a database of 60 adjectives, 60 nouns and 60 verbs. The structure was adjective – noun – verb. After a stanza of 4 verses a refrain appeared, written by Šulej himself. The whole poem consisted of 3 stanzas and 2 refrain repetitions. The refrain called *Erotický fragment* (*Erotic Fragment*) was published in his debut poetry collection *Porno* from 1994.

Another electronic poem from 1989 was programmed by Michal Murin, when the artist worked in the MEOPTA state military plant in Bratislava, which specialized in military optical technology (laser sights and lenses) with its civil division focusing on the production of copy machines. Thanks to the fact that he worked in a plant that had a terminal network for computers, he could access these machines and was able to produc a piece of art. On 20. November 1989 (at 2pm, before the first public protest meeting in Bratislava streets), just 3 days after the protests in Prague that lead to the Velvet Revolution and resulted in the fall of Communism in Czechoslovakia, Michal Murin used software generating 0 and 1 to program a generative poem called *Random Poetry* (See Murin and Barok, *Rozhovor s Michalom Murinom*, 45). The first part of this conceptual poem, programmed in the MUMPS language entitles "Aj áno aj nie (Demokracia)," which translates into "Both yes and no (Democracy)." The second part consists of a concrete poem, in which the words "áno" (yes) and "nie" (no) randomly follow each other to create 20 lines with 5 words in each one of them. A tension between these two contradictory words reflects the unsure situation in the real world. Thus, the poem reads like a statement questioning the future existence/nonexistence of democracy in Czechoslovakia during those turbulent times. Thanks to the work`s conceptual framework of constant interchanges between the confirmation and negation of the presence of the democratic regime in Czechoslovakia, the poem can be understood as politically engaged.

The poet, artist and performer József Rocco Juhász, who was born in Slovakia as a member of a Hungarian minority, has used the possibilities of computer programs for his literary works since the early 1990s, which is documented in his collection of visual poems *kepben vagy* published in 2006. He created his first computer poems (*belyeg.bat, one.bat, onegogh.bat, a.bat*) in 1991 on a program entitled *Presents*, running on MS DOS. In these poems, he played with the aesthetics and graphic possibilities enabled by the operating system MS DOS: the poems consist of simple sequenced animations, colorful backgrounds and flickerings on the screen that create the animations. In the poem *belyeg.bat*, the word "mammon " appears (later divided in lines into "ma," "mm," "on"), then the central "mm" changes to "li.li," then is the expression replaced by colorful squares until "The End" appears on the screen. In the poem *one.bat* a black and white image is replaced by a red square with a growing title "gogh" that subsequently changes into "one gogh," "two gogh " and "three gogh," a reference to Van Gogh. The poem *onegogh.bat* can be viewed as technically improved previous poem: it starts with collages of images, after which the previous poem follows. In the poem *a.bat*, an additional kinetic letter A is added to the "goghs" content, which, by its growing and diminishing divides the individual poem parts. However simple, repetitive and playful these poems are, they represent an important point in Slovak electronic literature: and thus Juhász´s energy to try new media possibilities and engage with movement, colors and technologies in his poetry. His poems were published also in a cult French journal *Alire* that was issued on a floppy disc. Juhász has continued to work with marginal forms of poetry up until the present (he is, however, much more present in the field of performance art). For example in his later project *Digital Copy* from 2000, he remade an old Continental typewriter to a computer keyboard, which he used for writing action poetry inspired by Lajos Kassák that was sent in real time to various poetic events and festivals (in Budapest, France, Poland, Latvia, Estonia). For the EXIT festival in Helsinki, he wrote on this typewriter a travelogue about the four day journey to that festival.

In the second half of the 1990s, when the presence of computers and Internet was more common in Slovak and Czech households, some of the Czech poets started to experiment with the media possibilities and tried to enrich the text by images or computer animations in GIF. These poems combining the poetic, or in some cases also narrative, text with static or moving images and occasionally also sound, were published on the web magazine called *magazlin.cz* that supported these media functions and enabled also hypertextual connections between parts of the poems. Among the authors whose works on *magazLín* can be considered as examples of digital literature (rather than the use of online platform for a wide-spread and free publishing of a stable text and images) are Michal Šanda, Jiří Dynka, and the collaboration of František Horka a Kateřina Vozková.

On this website, Jiří Dynka remediated some parts of the poems from his already published collections of poems. The text is remixed on the page, followed by some animated graphics and at times also generatively appearing in a kinetic form (e.g. *Liviový lenkový*) or enriched with a simple sound file (e.g. *Minimální okolí mrazícího boxu*). Michal Šanda´s piece *Psychoanal* remediates an existing visual collage in a digital envi-

Figure 3: Markéta Baňková, *New York City Map*

ronment and replaces the visual elements by a repeating denotative text. The collage on the left is accompanied by a hypertextual narrative on the right. By clicking on any of the visual elements on the virtual canvas (which is a navigational strategy in this piece), a neighboring visual element turns into a denotating text and the corresponding hypertextual fragment with the particular image appears. Karel Piorecký writes:

> Šanda uses here web graphics, animation and also in the end automatically rotating text in a rather illustrative way; the text is analogic to his printed works, in which archaic language, mystification and absurdity play a dominant role. (Piorecký, *Česká literatura a nová media. Prolegomena k tématu*, 835)

The collaborative "effort of animated series" (as the subtitle suggests) between the writer František Horka and the author of graphics Kateřina Vozková called *Závislost (Addiction)* presents lyrical text with (animated) illustrations. Among 9 poems, 2 examples of kinetic text appear, in fig. 7, where the text "Ona čítala" ("She read") floats from the cut head and in fig. 9, where the text, placed into a visual representation of an anatomical cross section of the human upper body, moves from the brain through the digestive system, ends in the rectum and creates erection-like kinetic words.

Karel Piorecký states that after these few examples of digital poetry, "in the next era, as a result of Flash technology and other software programs starting to dominate in digital literature," none of the Czech poets seemed to be interested in combinations of text and digital animations (Piorecký, *Česká literatura a nová media*, 70). Piorecký mentions as the only exception in the Czech space of visual culture (rather than in a poetry group) a cycle of videos *ABS* by the visual artist Jiří Černický from 2005-2007, where the animated text (as a transcription of people´s thoughts) appeared on real-time video footage of the city (Piorecký, *Česká literatura a nová média*, 70-71).

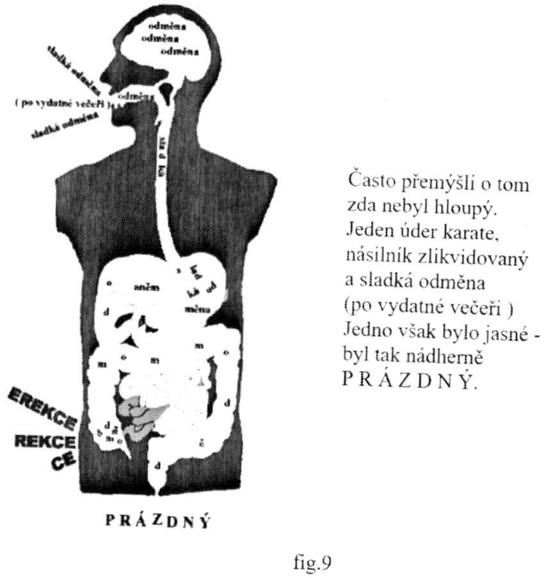

Figure 2: Horka, František - Vozková Kateřina, *Závislost*

HYPERMEDIAL LITERATURE

The Czech artist Markéta Baňková is the author of two hypermedial narratives with net.art aesthetics, both from the end of the 1990s. The first one, called *The City.html* (*Město.html*), exists in Czech and English versions, and consists of 42 lexias, in which the long pieces of text are accompanied mostly by computer graphics and rarely by animations or sounds. The work was created gradually, in the years 1997-1999, and the author`s intention was to build a fictional website of a girl named Rose Shetkova. As Baňková writes in the information about the piece "[t]he text is a reaction to the era, in which I intensively communicated on the chat (from 1995) and reacts also to an interesting experience of choosing my own identity, which chatting enables." Rose Shetkova is a fictional narrator and the author of the pages. After her short biography and a lexia about shopping, the readers proceed to the narrative line, where the cab driver decides to kill her and the reader has a choice to click either on "The cab driver commits a crime " or on "or he doesn't." In the first case, the reader reads the lexias, where Rose is taken by an angel to heaven, she meets God and talks to Melancholy and in between reads lexias that present a retrospective. In the other case, the driver leaves and she takes a bus back to the city and recounts the experience to her friend Helen. Later on, she becomes actively engaged in political life, talks on the phone to her old childhood friend Mashl and this story line ends with the lexia called "God`s consulting service," in which Mashl discusses with God death and the meaning of life. The decision about the driver`s crime is one of the minimal decisions that the readers take, while most of the lexias contain just an arrow to move the text ahead. At the beginning, the reader can decide to click on any of the 42 lexias, but then the story is linear. Along with the inclusion of computer graphics, digital media possibilities offer the option to contact Baňková – to write a message either in the assigned box or by email – this appears in the last lexia called "to be continued... ", which suggests that it was supposed to be somehow more developed.

The biggest potential of this hypermedial narrative is its focus on fictional identity and on the manipulation of identity that chatrooms provide. Baňková`s second work also has a connection to urban life, but here the narrative takes on a more concrete profile as it is based on her experience in NYC, where she was given a scholarship. *New York City Map*, as the work is called, was created from 1999 to 2002, contains around 235 lexias and is programmed in html. The work presents lexias that are supposed to document the atmosphere of the city in that era through a kind of virtual guide to its compelling parts. As the author states

> With the *NYC Map* I've tried to capture the atmosphere, the energy, or that Something which I think makes New York City so curiously different from other cities with skyscrapers. At the same time, this project is my personal diary, a document of time I spent there since 1999.

This work uses the hypermedial potential in a more advanced way than the previous project: the textual parts are shorter or sometimes missing, more focus is placed on the photographs (at times with computer graphics or simple interactivity) and sound recordings in some parts accompany the other elements. Also the navigation is not so linear: the reader can choose from several options, usually in the form of directions – uptown, downtown, east, west, subway, exit, etc. – and thus the navigation in the project simulates also a geographical navigation in the city. The narrative tone is personal and presents a direct account of walking the streets and meeting the people, with authorial ponderings about the situations. A similarly oriented project is the American hypermedial narrative *Subway Story* by David M. Yun, but in the case of Yun´s project, the narrative is much more developed and broader. In both projects, the setting is NYC and the main motives are travelling the subway and its interconnection with a fragmented hypermedial narrative.

Travelling the city via public transport is also the motive of the hypermedial work *Konečná: Peklo* (*Terminal: Inferno*) by the Slovak visual artist Radim Labuda. This piece was both in the form of a site-specific installation and a website. Both realizations recontextualize and repurpose Dante´s *Inferno* by implementing combinations of the original stanzas (in the Slovak translation by Viliam Turčány and Jozef Felix from 1964). In the public space the poems were placed on tram stops in Bratislava city center, while in the case of the virtual art project they appear when clicking on the virtual map of the transport system. Labuda invented a new tram line 700 and instead of its timetable, the commuters could read Dante´s poetry lines combined according to a specific scheme. This real experience set into the context of reading time tables was mimicked on the website to serve as a virtual guide of the same routes with the same poems. Labuda, who created the web concept, cooperated on the project with the Slovak Buryzone cultural open space and gallery and the website was programmed by Nino Hýbal and Peter Jančár (Nino and Gozo) using HTML and JavaScript. Vladimíra Pčolová from Buryzone assisted also with the implementation of the service schedules. As the Slovak author and media theoretician Mária Rišková states about the cooperation and consequent profilation of Buryzone,

> Labuda approached me, as a coordinator of the Buryzone gallery and club, in order to participate in the production and execution of his outlined concept. Thanks to this cooperation early Slovak internet art was created in only a few weeks, and Buryzone's focus on new media experimentation was consolidated. (Rišková, *Terminal: Inferno*, 82)

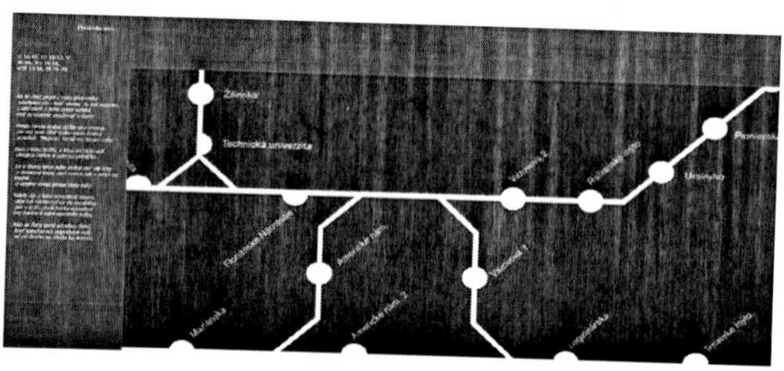

Figure 4: Radim Labuda, *Konečná: Peklo*

What is very interesting about the whole project is the fact that the official Bratislava online transport guide (www.imhd.sk) had been released only several months before. The entire project was carried out in a rather activist style, without the knowledge of Bratislava transport company. The combinatory structure of the reappropriated stanzas was modelled on the basis of the Bratislava tramway system. Labuda used only 12 out of 34 cantos from Dante´s *Inferno* to correspond with the number of tram lines in Bratislava: No. 1-9, 11, 12 and 14. He kept the content and form of Dante´s tercets but the form of terza rima is changed, since the number of verses varies depending on the length of the tramlines. He combined the tercets for each tram stop based on the key, which tram line stops there and based on the length of the tramline. So for example, "Main train station" tram stop was then the first stop for the trams 1, 2, 3, 8. Therefore, Labuda chose for his combinatory poem the cantos 1, 2, 3, 8 and from each canto chose here the first 3 or 6 verses (based on the length of the tram line), because it was the initial tram stop for each of those lines. Labuda always split a given canto, so that the line starts with the first verse and ends with the last verse of the given canto (For more on the context of the piece, the combinatory structure used, examples of poems and the role of Buryzone, see the paper *Terminal: Inferno* by Mária Rišková). This Situationist work based on the principles of combinatorics, appropriation and repurposing is thanks to its conceptual background, semantically interesting implementation of hypermedial structure, visually interesting layout and user-friendly navigation a unique piece of hypermedial work, which, as in the case of Baňková´s pieces, comes from the field of visual rather than literary arts.

A case of literary hypertext, whose author comes from the literary field, is the 1999 piece *HyperHomer* by the Czech writer Petr Odillo Stradický ze Strdic. This work is not online any more, therefore just a brief, orientational description will be provided. Stradický´s aim was to create a collective, multimedial, participatory hypertext, into which participants were supposed to contribute by writing and coding a subsequent part of the unfinished hypertext in html and sending this complete lexia to the administrator by email. Unfortunately, due to the fact that in 1999 few Czech people where skilled enough to code a hypertext (though if interested in contributing, Stradický offered to find them technical co-authors), this project remained only in its conceptual phase. The Czech theoretician Karel Piorecký writes that the goal of *HyperHomer* was to "renew the understanding of literary structure and mainly to enrich it by the possibilities of the new medium. " (Piorecký, *Česká literatura a nová média*, 835).

GENERATIVE LITERATURE AFTER 2000

Michael Bielický is a Czech-German artist and Professor of Media Art who was born in Prague in 1954 but emigrated to Germany in 1969. His works mainly represent the field of new media art, but in the projects *Falling Times*, *Columbus 2.0*, and *Why Don´t We*, the generated texts play an important role, which is why I will introduce them as well. The poetics of Michael Bielický´s works are often based on questioning information overload, navigation through a vast sea of information and constant acceleration of the data stream. It calls upon the infoEcology discourse and the human ability to deal with the world-wide news and the absorbability of rides on the information superhighways. The aesthetics in the style of new media folklore is very similar in all these projects, since it consists of variously combined and variously multiplied animated icons, figures, heads of world-famous political individuals (such as Merkel, Obama, Lenin, Snowden or Bin Ladin), that constantly flicker and repeatedly appear on the screen. The information overload is multimedially represented by the screen overload and its constant filling with new generated content.

The text in the interactive piece *Falling Times* (on which Bielický collaborated with Dirk Reinbold and Kamila B. Richter) presents news jargon and the whole project is directed against the InfoPollution that surrounds us. Bielický writes about the meaning of the piece thus:

> [I]n our visualization we reduce the content only to headlines and key words that appear in the news most frequently. These reduced news are translated into a dynamic pictogram language that is considered to be universal and instantly understandable. (Bielický, *Falling Times*, online)

Figure 5: Michal Bielický, *Falling Times*

Columbus 2.0 (in collaboration with Czech media artist Kamila B. Richter) is "an interactive navigational system " (hence the origin of its poetic name) that projected Google news in the various languages on the historic walls of the Alcázar in Spanish Sevilla in 2008. The news was in the shape of dynamic 3D waves intended to give the illusion of navigating in the sea, an effect strengthened by the fact that the navigational device in this project was an actual ship`s steering wheel. The visuals of the project *Why Don´t We*, in comparison with the previous two, are produced in color, which adds a more entertaining effect to the vibrating visuals of the screens. *Why Don´t We* is presented as "a computer-generated composition of different animated scenes involving real time information from the social network Twitter" (Bielický, *Why Don't*

We, online). According to the author´s website, this piece has its origins in the works *Falling Times* and *Garden of Error and Decay*. But here, in contrast to the piece *Garden of Error and Decay*, the Twitter statements are only in the form of animated icons but are displayed as titles of a "visual-poetic silent movie relating to a place (Stavanger) where oil is the main trigger for economic and social dynamics."

The Slovak artist Erik Bartoš used a more glitch-art driven aesthetics in his project *Adam 2.0*. In this online and offline Internet installation, the software searched for the RSS news headlines of the five biggest news agencies of the Western world (CNN, BBC and others) plus the five biggest pro-Russia oriented news agencies (such as Ria Novosti). Then these headline texts ran through Google Image search, which also assigned to the text the contextual image. The textual and the visual content was downloaded to the computer and then remixed from an assigned database into a new collage: first the words were montaged into a new, often meaningless message and subsequently the contextual images were added to them. This final collage also always contains a glitch error intended to remind the viewers of the falsified reality. However, the project did not stop here: Bartoš also created false Bots accounts on Facebook, Twitter and Tumblr, which automatically spread the multimedia collages to their subscribers. The main idea of this project was to criticize the user´s inability to perceive reality through the information spread on the Internet. The obvious random patchwork of the visual information and the asyntactic textual headlines spread by the Bot suggests an alert to people that unconditionally believe news sources and even identify with their point of view (Cf. Michal Murin, *Digitálne médiá a poézia*, 81). It is interesting that Bartoš came with this project even before the massive use of automatic Bots on the Internet. The quandary of whom and what to believe in the Internet sea and under which conditions, is the main resonator in this work. A similar project, where the author also worked with generated text from RSS messages, is a project by Matej Ivan. But here the text was projected on the body of a viewer, who stood in front of a mirror and selected the text by her movement (See Michal Murin, *Digitálne médiá a poézia*, 81).

Another approach of appropriating, recycling and repurposing the text (rather than also other visual media) from the information overflow was chosen by the Slovak artist Jonáš Gruska in his project *Báseň* (*Poem*). The software uses RSS feeds from news websites: currently from the website of the Slovak independent journal Denník N, previously from the websites of the Slovak journal Pravda or the Polish journal Gazeta Wyborcza. After the user´s hoovering with a cursor over the button "start," the individual, random words from the news websites start to float on the empty white screen. Formally reminiscent of a poem, the new words appear with the movement of the cursor, in a kind of 3D fashion, sometimes layering each other in quick movements. Most of the poem content happens on the left side of the screen, also evoking the traditional poem layout. With each new loading of the work´s website, new words get loaded as well. If the user interacts with the poem, after quite a short time the words lose their form – their ends get cut – until after a while only some of the letters remain and in the end the situation of the empty white screen is present again. This "devaluation" of information, as the author describes it, also refers to the InfoPollution we live in. Therefore, *Báseň* can be understood in its semantic sense as socially-critical, in the formal sense as generative with the use of conceptual tendencies. The users´ involvement is however not restricted only to triggering the words and hoovering with the curser to load new textual content, for they can also rewrite the loaded word into whatever word they like with the use of the "tab" key. Thus, the poem can acquire a more personal touch. Due to the RSS feeds, the poem´s text is constantly actual. Even though the generated poems make mostly no coherent semantic sense even in their starting phase (the project is not based on the generators that pay attention to the syntactic criteria), the constantly decomposing words, in which the traditional semantics is also not-working, are intriguing when thinking about the work as a gradually disappearing kinetic poem, where the system that brought it to us also "feeds on it" until the state of its "digestion" for the sake of the white screen´s new potential.

The Slovak artist, writer, cultural activist and specialist in the media discourse Dušan Barok chose an art discourse-oriented approach for his site-specific software installation *Computer with a Printer*. This installation, presented as a part of the "Point of View" exhibition in Trnava, Slovakia in 2006, consisted of only, as the title suggests, a computer and a printer. This conceptual piece raises questions about art discourse and the practice of writing curatorial texts in this field. The computer generates a curatorial text about the work itself and the printer prints it on the user´s demand. Here the user´s interaction is reduced to pushing the only button on the screen to trigger the action. The installation, in a self-referential manner, presents itself as a work of art whose sole purpose is to generate and print curatorial texts about itself. As Barok writes on the website presenting the project and displaying four examples from several dozen printed texts, "the body of the texts was composed by a software which contained a database of textual formulas that were repeatedly used in the catalogue texts for the exhibitions held earlier at the venue. " (Barok, *Computer with a Printer,* online). This piece can be therefore considered also in the context of software processing of site-and field-specific textual archives and the practice of generative art. In one of the generated texts, this sentence occurred: "The obvious material function of the computer is re-interpreted and transformed to communicate a spiritual, intellectual and psychological message of art as dialogue and as cross-cultural interaction. "

LITERATURE IN QR CODES AND POETIC APPLICATIONS

The most conceptual piece including QR codes in the Slovak literary field has so far been created by the artist, performer and writer József R. Juhász in his project *Urban mémoire*.

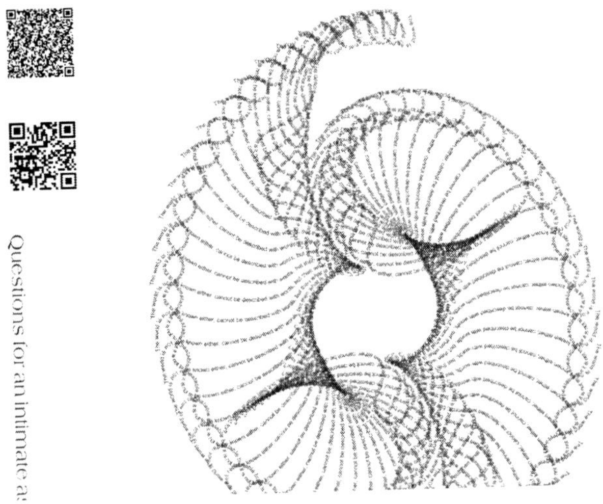

Figure 6: József Rokko Juhász, *Urban mémoire*, from the website

Urban mémoire consists of a white box with twelve or thirteen "poemposters" (47 x 67 cm) based on which language version one has: the Hungarian version contains thirteen posters, the Slovak and English ones contain twelve posters. On each poster (eight consist of visual poems, three contain photographs and one is Petrarca 2012 poster), two small QR codes are printed, of which one is always informative and the other functions like a "home" button and brings the users to the Index listing all the poems. The QR codes on different posters represent a different approach to the use of QR codes. The QR codes on eight visual poemposters represent either the same visual material that is printed, or they work as a text that provides an understanding of the visual material. In the posters containing photographs, the QR codes trigger the videos and photographs of the author´s performances in Asian countries. The Petrarca 2012 poster contains forty-six AR codes, out of which forty, visually organized into four main groups, encode the addresses of websites that contain Petrarca´s poems. The whole work combining printed and online material, refers to the "memory box" in several media forms, containing fragmentary associations, thoughts and references to the moments that create memories linked with specific places. The traditional form of memoirs in the written form is here replaced by visual poems, videos, photographs and codes. The codes could represent ciphers to which only certain humans or machines have access, therefore here the author´s memories are encoded, so that the reader, instead of just reading them in the traditional way, has to first decode them by the use of online tools (For more on *Urban mémoire*, see Husárová-Suwara, *Literature Coded for Marked Quick Response*, 149-154).

Ľubomír Panák and Zuzana Husárová are the authors of two poetic applications *Obvia Gaude* and *Talis Quadra*, which recontextualize and repurpose two poems from the Slovak Baroque poetic cycle by Matej Gažúr from 1649. The Baroque poetic cycle in Latin *Enneas diversi generi epithalamiorum, solennitati Nuptiarum* (*Nine different types of epithalamia, for a wedding celebration*) is a celebratory lyric written for the wedding celebration of Paul Ostrosith (Pavol Ostrošič) and Eva Uifalusi (Eva Ujfalusiová). The touch applications remediate the original pattern poems but several other functions were added, such as reader´s interactivity and playfulness, music, kinetic textual aspect, virtual 3D dimensionality and the possibility to intervene with the textual content. The *Obvia Gaude* application is based on 3D dynamics, so that when the screen is touched, the visuals start to bend according to the user´s hand gestures and thus create a kinetic text. The work reacts also to the physical handling of the electronic device: if one shakes the tablet/smartphone, the letters get bigger and fly upfront. After the app is loaded, the user has an option (Set Names) to write two names (Her/His Name and Her/His Name) into the specified squares. If she does so, these names replace the original names: Evula and Paulo in the poem. This way, a personalized version appears on the screen. Unlike the Baroque poem, the app is enriched by music – one can hear the reinterpretation of "Intrada" from "Codex Vietoris" (a collection of 300 songs from around 1670-1680 from the Austrio-Hungarian Empire, from the area of present day Slovakia). The mix of several slightly different reinterpretations of the music is responsive, just like a kinetic text, to the places touched on the screen.

Talis Quadra is a playful interactive application that is based on the principle of getting things into their right order. At the beginning of the app, the text rolls and its visual pattern remediates Gažúr´s other poem from the cycle. A square shape with the letters forming the sentence "Talis Quadra pii sit tibi norma Tori" ("*This Square should be your model of a Sacred marriage/marriage bed*") appears on the screen. After this initial stage, the original lines where the reader could read the statement, start to move and shift in all four directions – in order to visualize the kineticism of letters that Gažúr probably had in mind. The reader is then left with a different version of sentences and their task is to place the sentences into their original positions by interactions with the touch screen. After reaching the correct solution, some celebratory Baroque music starts playing, to provide the player with a fanfare again reminiscent of Baroque art.

POSTDIGITAL PERFORMANCES AND INSTALLATIONS

The performance and installation *Breathings* by Slovak artist Richard Kitta focuses on the phenomenon of breathing, which is in this context directly linked with the production of speech. The breathing and speech of the author/performer are captured by an algorithm that loads new textual content on the screen and layers, shifts and deletes the already projected words, phrases and sentences. The functionality of the piece is based on a special headset that contains a microport and is connected to a computer, where the open source live-programming environment (VVVV) is running. The textual content loaded on the screen is a mixture of two sources: excerpts of cosmological texts by Robert R. Caldwell about the end of the universe (Big Rip) and a text representing the performer´s speech (appearing on the screen thanks to the speech-recognition plugin). Thus, in this performance, the written cosmological text is interconnected with subjective associations expressed in real-time (and contextual to the projected text). The textual field, layered and changing with each breath, appears to be in a constant state of flux, where the only stable moment is the moment of holding the breath (cf. Michal Murin, *Digitálne médiá a poézia*, 76). Kitta also created a variant called *Breathings / Typototems*, whose textual basis consists of just the signs from two language cultures – the Latin alphabet and the Japanese alphabet. In this case, the reference seems to evoke the trends of Léttrism or processual typography.

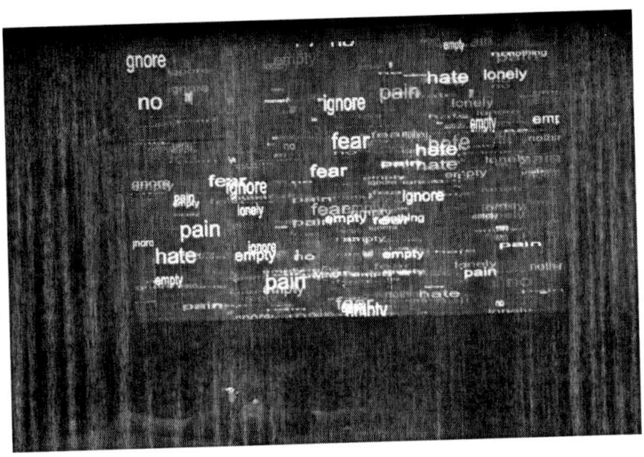

Figure 7: Richard Kitta, *Breathings*

The triggering of the textual content based on the interactor´s body is also the principle of another piece of Slovak electronic literature, called *I : * ttter* by Zuzana Husárová and Ľubomír Panák. But here, in comparison with the automatic functionality of breathing that almost insures the flow of new text on the screen, in the piece *I : * ttter* the interactor has to move their hands, so that the Kinect 3D sensor responds. This piece is multimedial, and besides the triggered textual layers, the user can also draw and listen to the theremin-like sound responding to the position of the hands. The loaded text is a remix of the text appearing in selected textual fragments of the European Net.Art (*My Boyfriend Came Back From the War* by Olia Lialina, *This Morning and IBM* by Alexei Shulgin, *zkp3.21* by Vuk Cosic, *100cc* and *g33con* by the JODI art collective, *Irational* by Heath Bunting, *City.html* by Markéta Baňková, *four. Values* by Perfokarta, *Falling Times* by Michal Bielický, *Koniec swiata wg Emeryka* by Radoslaw Nowakowski, and *AE* by Robert Szczerbowski). In its gradually loaded form, it resembles the online communication of two persons/machines: each new loaded text represents a new answer in the conversation. As responses to the hand movements, thanks to Kinect sensor and the Processing software, the full dialogues disperse into individual words, the words change their position on the screen, become variously layered, appear in new connections and can be erased.

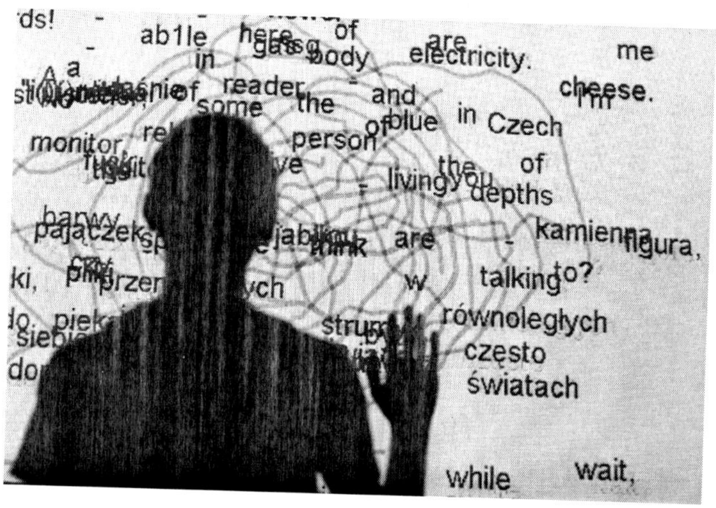

Figure 8: Zuzana Husárová-Ľubomír Panák, *I : * ttter*

The poetics of the body lies at the center of attention in another intermedial performance/installation by Zuzana Husárová and Ľubomír Panák, called *Enter:in' Wodies*, which also functions on the Kinect 3D sensor and the Processing software. Here, the interaction is based on the virtual touching of points on virtual models representing a female or male body. These points refer to seven organ systems, which, when touched, reveal a biological image of their cell textures from medical websites, while special sounds referring to that system´s functions appear in the overall sound loop and a virtual area for other types of movements gets activated. By the movement of hands in this assigned area, the interactor reveals poems connected with the particular human biological system and highlighting the system's exceptional features. The uncovering of the words is realized on their spatial area, which often results in uncovering only parts of the words rather than loading complete words. This, when performed, results in sound poetry, during which the performer combines the acoustic representation of the parts of the words, the parts of signs and the whole textual fragments. After having read all seven biological systems (circulatory, integumentary, muscular, respiratory, reproductive, digestive, nervous), the final text appears about leaving the other person's body. The main idea is to imagine the person whose interior one would desire to read, while reading here represents the interconnection of reading, watching, hearing and moving. *Enter:in' Wodies* aims to question the alternative "boundaries" between the imaginary and the virtual, between two humans, between the inside and the outside. The virtual body is entered through the interaction, is read in fragments, watched, heard and finally left. This project examines the body´s poetics represented by the cooperation of media. It questions the notion of words as "bridges" into the imagination, and treats the words as a material that one can unveil in a person´s interior. This piece enables the user to grasp the poetics of a human by providing the space for interaction, imagination and the artistic experience that relies on bodily aesthetics.

WHAT ARE WE LOOKING AT NOW?

The Scottish scientist David Brewster named his invention in 1816 "kaleidoscope" from the Greek words: kalos (meaning "beautiful"), eidos (meaning "form"), and scopos (meaning "watcher" or even "mark, goal"). Therefore kaleidoscope means "beautiful form watcher" (*The Kaleidoscope Book*, online).

It seems that the goal of contemporary computer sciences is to build more advanced neural networks, which are already able to produce not only reasonable sentences indistinguishable from the ones produced by humans, but to produce art, as the most imaginative form of expression. The trends similar to those that lead Levý and Pala in Brno in the 1960s into feeding the generative system with the poetry of Seifert, are now, almost 50 years after, resonating in the much more sophisticated efforts to teach neural networks. Among the cases of training neural networks to create images and music, can be found also cases of teaching them to produce poetry.

Slovakia-born Andrej Karpathy, who emigrated with his family at the age of 15 to Toronto and is currently doing a PhD. in Computer Vision/Machine Learning at Stanford University, released in 2015 a paper about how he trained his Recurrent Neural Network (RNN) to learn to generate text character by character (Karpaty, *The Unreasonable Effectiveness of Recurrent Neural Networks*, online). For that purpose, he fed the RNN with a large piece of text, specifically all the works by Shakespeare (he tried also the 100 000 sample of characters from Wikipedia, also Linux source code and algebraic geometry), and found out that it was gradually able to learn to form words. At first, the neural network learnt that the sentences are formed of chunks of text (words) and spaces and later it could form words that made semantic meanings and even copy Shakespearian style. So in these new cases of training intelligent systems, the focus (in comparison with the old approach of combining the existing words according to a syntactic scheme) is on making neural networks learn the principles of morphology and syntax themselves. His open-source code also inspired other programmers world-wide to feed the networks with other text samples, among which occurred cooking recipes, Eminem lyrics, Obama speeches and music notations.

The Czech programmer Jiří Materna fed a neural network with the database of music lyrics from the server supermusic.sk in order to create "the automatic poet" (Materna, *Středověk umělé inteligence skončil*, online). Digital poetry has from its beginnings been formed by the cooperative geniuses of technology and innovative approaches to the use of poetic language. The probability that the ties between these two players become even closer in the near future rises with the availability of new approaches that are spreading from the labs to a more open domain. It will be more than exciting to read, interact and play with their results as well as watch them with the help of a kaleidoscope. Let´s scope through the colorful media in our hands.

ACKNOWLEDGEMENT

The paper was written within the grant VEGA "The Hypermedial Artefact in the Post-digital Age" (2014-2017) No. 2/0107/14.

WORKS CITED

Barok, Dušan. "Rozhovor s Michalom Murinom." *¾ Revue, 27-28: REMAKE* (2012): 40-51, edited by Katarína Gatialová and Barbora Šedivá. Accessed May 6, 2015. http://www.34.sk/text.php?text=3-230.

Branny-Jankowska, Emilia. "Polish V: The Destruction of Text in Polish E-Literature. AE by Robert Szczerbowski and Electronic Poetry by Perfokarta." *CyberText Yearbook 2010*. Edited by Markku Eskelinen and Raine Koskimaa, 2010. Accessed March 28, 2015. http://cybertext.hum.jyu.fi/articles/137.pdf.

Hayles, N. Katherine. *Writing Machines*. Cambridge: The MIT Press, 2002.

Husárová, Zuzana. "Slovenské elektronická literatúra." *World Literature Studies 3*. (2016): 57-77.

Husárová, Zuzana, and Bogumiła Suwara. "Literature Coded for Marked Quick Response." *American and British Studies Annual* 6 (2013): 145-161.

Karpaty, Andrej. *The Unreasonable Effectiveness of Recurrent Neural Networks*, 21. May 2015. Accessed July 28, 2015. http://karpathy.github.io/2015/05/21/rnn-effectiveness/.

Kozma, Andrej. "Budú stroje myslieť?," *Mladá tvorba* 8-9 (1959): 18-21.

Legel, Rudolf. "Experiment s interakciou človek-počítač pri vytváraní básnického textu, " *Romboid* 2 (1982): 38-40.

Levý, Jiří, and Karel Pala. "Generování veršů jako problém prozodický." In *Teorie verše. II, Sborník druhé brněnské versologické konference*, 18.-20. října 1966, edited by Karel Pala and Jiří Levý, 73-80. Brno: Universita J.E. Purkyně, 1968. Accessed May 6, 2015. https://digilib.phil.muni.cz/bitstream/handle/11222.digilib/120153/SpisyFF_136-1968-1_12.pdf?sequence=1.

Materna, Jiří. Středověk umělé inteligence skončil, 9. August 2015. Accessed August 28, 2015. http://www.mlguru.cz/stredovek-umele-inteligence-skoncil-seznamte-se-s-neuronovymi-sitemi-ktere-umi-psat-basne/ .

Mazur, Marian. "Kybernetika a umenie." *Slovenské pohľady* 1 (1963): 41-49.

Murin, Michal. "Digitálne médiá a poézia," *ENTER 24* (2015): 74-81, edited by Michal Murin.

Pala, Karel, and Sus, Oleg. "Některé principy strojové poetiky." *Host do domu* 9 (1967): 42-47.

Pająk, Andrzej. "Polish I: The Polish Way to E-Literature from the Baroque to the 21st Century." *CyberText Yearbook 2010*. Edited by Markku Eskelinen and Raine Koskimaa, 2010. Accessed March 28, 2015. http://cybertext.hum.jyu.fi/articles/133.pdf.

Pająk, Andrzej. "Polish IV: Modern Generators." *CyberText Yearbook 2010*. Edited by Markku Eskelinen and Raine Koskimaa, 2010. Accessed March 28, 2015. http://cybertext.hum.jyu.fi/articles/136.pdf.

Piorecký, Karel. "Česká literatura a nová média. Prolegomena k tématu," *Česká literatura* 6 (2012): 821-850.

Piorecký, Karel. *Česká literatura a nová média*. Praha: Academia, 2016.

Piorecký, Karel. *Česká počítačově (de)generovaná literatura*. 30. March 2016. Accessed April 4, 2016. http://www.academia.edu/23825259/Česká_počítačově_(de)generovaná_literatura

Pisarski, Mariusz. "Polish II: Silva Rerum 'A Book of Everything on Anything' as a Cybertextual Experience I." *CyberText Yearbook 2010*. Edited by Markku

Eskelinen and Raine Koskimaa, 2010. Accessed March 28, 2015. http://cybertext.hum.jyu.fi/articles/134.pdf.

Pisarski, Mariusz. "Polish III: In the Textual Caves of Malgorzata Dawidek-Gryglicka. Nonlinearity and Ergodicity in 'A Short History of an Accident' and 'Definition.'" *CyberText Yearbook 2010*, edited by Markku Eskelinen and Raine Koskimaa, 2010. Accessed March 28, 2015. http://cybertext.hum.jyu.fi/articles/135.pdf.

Rišková, Mária. "Terminal: Inferno: The almost forgotten intermedial work." In *ENTER+ Repurposing in Electronic Literature*. Edited by María Mencía and Zuzana Husárová, 82-85. Košice: Divé buki, 2014-2015.

Sus, Oleg. "generovaná degenerace." *Host do domu* (1968): 50-51.

Szebényi, Tibor. "Kybernetika v umení." *Mladá tvorba* (1962): 23-25.

Šimončič, Klement. "Poetika surrealistov a básnická kompozícia z matematických strojov." *Slovenské pohľady* 2 (1965): 29-33.

Šulej, Peter. "Tetxik." Email Communication. Sent April 29, 2016.

The Kaleidoscope Book. "Kaleidoscope History." Accessed July 19, 2015. http://www.thekaleidoscopebook.com/thescopebook/scope-resources/kaleidoscope-history.

Zielinski, Siegfried. *Deep Time of the Media: Toward an Archaeology of Hearing and Seeing by Technical Means*. Cambridge: The MIT Press, 2008.

ARTIST'S WORKS

Baňková, Markéta. "The City.html." Accessed April 21, 2015. http://www.city.je/.

Baňková, Markéta. "New York City Map." Accessed April 21, 2015. http://www.nycmap.com/.

Barok, Dušan. "Computer with a Printer." Accessed May 19, 2015. http://monoskop.org/Computer_with_a_Printer.

Bartoš, Erik. "Adam 2.0." Accessed May 19, 2015. http://erikbartos.com/portfolio/artworks/adam-20.

Bielický, Michal, and Kamila B. Richter and Dirk Reinbold. "Falling Times." Accessed April 21, 2015. http://fallingtimes.net/index.php?page=3&lang=en.

Bielický, Michal, and Kamila B. Richter. "Columbus 2.0." Accessed April 21, 2015. http://bielicky.net/projects/columbus-20.

Bielický, Michal, and Kamila B. Richter. "Why Don´t We." Accessed April 21, 2015. http://bielicky.net/projects/why-dont-we.

Černický, Jiří. "ABS video." Accessed July 19, 2015. http://cernicky.com/cs/abs-video/.

Dynka, Jiří. "Liviový lenkový." Accessed June 19, 2015.http://www.magazlin.cz/dynka/liviovy.htm.

Dynka, Jiří. "Minimální okolí mrazícího boxu." Accessed June 19, 2015. http://www.magazlin.cz/dynka/minim.htm.

Gruska, Jonáš. "Báseň." Accessed May 21, 2015. http://work.jonasgru.sk/basen/sk/

Horka, František, and Kateřina Vozková. "Závislost." Accessed April 19, 2015. http://www.magazlin.cz/zavislost/index.htm.

Husárová, Zuzana, and Ľubomír Panák. "Obvia Gaude." Accessed May 21, 2015. http://delezu.net/blog/2014/04/23/obvia-gaude/.

Husárová, Zuzana, and Ľubomír Panák. "Talis Quadra." Accessed November 10, 2015. http://delezu.net/blog/2015/11/02/talis-quadra/.

Husárová, Zuzana, and Ľubomír Panák. "Enter:in´ Wodies." Accessed September 1, 2015. http://zuz.delezu.net/2012/06/22/our-interactive-kinect-based-project-enter-in/.

Husárová, Zuzana, and Ľubomír Panák. " I : * tter." Accessed September 1, 2015. http://zuz.delezu.net/2012/04/30/i-tter-zuzana-husarova-lubomir-panak-sk/.

Juhász, József R. *Képben vagy? Vizuális költemények 1986–2006*. Dunaszerdahely: NAP, 2006.

Juhász, József R. Urban mémoire. Dunaszerdahely: NAP, 2012.

Labuda, Radim. *Konečná: Peklo*. Accessed April 21, 2015. http://plateau.sk/maria/peklo/main.htm.

Šanda, Michal. *Psychoanal*. Accessed April 19, 2015. http://www.magazlin.cz/sanda/index.htm.

Yun, David M. *Subway Story: An Exploration of me, myslef and I*. Accessed June 10, 2015. http://www.cyberartsweb.org/cpace/ht/dmyunfinal/frames.html.

A Diorama of Digital Literature in Spain

BY DOLORES ROMERO LÓPEZ

This chapter shows the forking paths of Spanish electronic literature.[23] After an initial discussion about how digital literature emerged, the chapter uses the analytical structure of a diorama—with stage, background and main characters or figures—to discuss the main themes, trans-genders, transnational characteristics and cyberfeminism in electronic literature in Spain, with some Hispanic examples. Clavy and @Note are mentioned as tools to develop the repertoires of digital literature (Cyberia) or digitized text (Mnemosyne) created by LEETHI, LOEP and ILSA Research Groups in the Universidad Complutense de Madrid.

I. INTRODUCTION

Dioramas are good means of teaching because of the visual aspects of the set and the material representation of its components. This essay shows an open diorama of digital literature in Spain, observable from different perspectives. The diorama is presented as a theatrical representation: how digital literature emerged will be discussed as the background of the stage. On stage, new textualities are put into action, along with original trends and approaches that strengthen the global stimulus of digital literature, its attraction for remediation and the identity crisis of transcultural societies. The figures that in this occasion come on stage are Miriam Reyes, Marla Jacarilla and Ainize Txopitea. Their reflections on their corporeity and their identity as women exhibit artistic challenges for what has been called 'technofeminism.'

Digital literature in Spain is now a field of artistic experimentation that attracts the attention of many authors, critics and readers. Its heartbeat began in the late 90s. In the twenty years since, the launch of digital literature has coincided with the crises in textuality due to the rise of new media (Romero López, 2012).

In addition, the creativity of the so-called "digital natives" is an added factor that is giving substantial results. The new commitment to digital reading has been enough to bring about a knowledge crisis capable of formulating new socio-cultural changes,

---

23 This essay draws on funding from the Spanish Ministerio de Economía y Competitividad for the research project "Escritorios Electrónicos para las Literaturas-2," reference FFI2012-34666. Ciberia Digital Library has been partially supported by the BBVA Foundation (Research Grant HUM14_251). The project "eLITE-Comunidad de Madrid: Edición Literaria Electrónica" (Ref. H2015/HUM-3426), currently supported by the European Social Fund, is financing our research on digital works created by women writers.

innovative ways of disseminating information and novel beliefs, which is what we are already witnessing.

Most of the first digital creators are unknown by the general public as novelists or poets, but they always leave some interesting paths in the work they publish online. Authorship is generally shared in the collaboration between story's inventors and technicians. Quite a few hypertextual digital writing projects are done by Spanish students of journalism, who undertake this sort of university work under the guidance of their teachers. The works are mainly adapted to the taste of young people: collages, chats, e-mails, images mixed with words and music and the influence of comics and detective plots (Carrasco, 2011). The favorite subjects have to do with games, diaries, adventures, love stories, loneliness, and so on. The characters are, for the most part, young people with young people's problems, involving identity, falling in and out of love, social conflict, etc.

Digital literature is promoted in a context that is provided with a network of directories. The one directed by José Luis Orihuela from the University of Pamplona dedicated to hyperfiction in Spanish was the first on-line archive.[24] Joaquín Aguirre Romero and Susana Pajares Tosca encourage digital literature through the periodical publication *Hipertulia* at the Complutense University.[25] A third pioneering group is Hermeneia led by Laura Borrás. They are interested in general digital literature, mainly written in English and Catalan. In September 2009 Juan José Díez opens a Webpage dedicated to Hispanic Electronic Literature in the Biblioteca Virtual Cervantes (Cervantes Virtual Library).[26] He gathers narrative works written in Spanish, information about authors and critical references, emphasizing works by Latin American authors. The latest contribution to public collections focusing on digital literature written in the Spanish language is *Ciberia* (Goicoechea, 2014), a digital library coordinated by María Goicoechea, with the collaboration of Laura Sánchez and Ana Cuquerella.[27] They are responsible for the compilation of works and they propose many literary and artistic categories. This library, conceived as an interoperable database, will exchange categories with international databases like the ones in CELL.[28] These repositories are the

24 See http://mccd.udc.es/orihuela/hyperfiction/. Without public access in September 2016. It was open before.

25 See http://www.ucm.es/info/especulo/hipertul/. Accessed September 2016.

26 See http://www.cervantesvirtual.com/bib/portal/literaturaelectronica/. Accessed September 2016.

27 *Ciberia: Digital Library* is a repository for Spanish digital literature funded by a National Research Project ("Escritorios Electrónicos para las Literaturas-2." Reference FFI2012-34666). The *Ciberia* database is structured according to the international Metadata Element Set proposed by the Consortium on Electonic Literature (CELL: http://cellproject.net/members).

28 These particular initiatives are starting to receive support through initiatives such as prizes and

evolution of digital literature in Spain. It is clear detectable that it has gone from the simple compilation of resources to international taxonomy categorization.

II. THE BACKGROUND: FOR ANALOGUE AND DIGITAL TEXTUALITY

There were printed hypertexts in Spanish literature before digital hypertext ever existed (Romero López, 2009). In general, the works cited as precedents for hypertextual writing are selected based on two criteria: the desire to experience the collective and the rupture of narrative linearity (Douglas, 1992). Creativity as a social value, which generates collective communication, is one of the original features of Internet ideation (Toschi, 1996). David Casacuberta developed the thesis that one of the most radical changes that new information and communication technologies are producing in our culture is precisely the opportunity for collective creation (Casacuberta, 2003). In Spanish literature, collective creation can be traced from the old kharja,[29] songs and ballads, to the collective novel as conceived of by Sinesio Delgado in *Las vírgenes locas* (*The Mad Virgins*, 1886), the surrealist *Cadáver exquisito* (*Exquisite Corpse*, 1925).[30] Ramón J. Sender first published *Suma y sigue o el cuento de nunca acabar* (*Add and Continue or the Never-ending Story*), in the magazine *Línea* between 1935 and 1936. During 1953 he published *Historia de un día en la vida española* (*History of a day in the life of Spain*) in the magazine *Tensor*, numbers 5 and 6.). In 1944, another noteworthy project was *Nueve millones* (*Nine Million*), a collective novel which arose from a radio programme, published by Afrodisio Aguado. In the year 2001 Lorenzo Silva, with the publishing house Círculo de Lectores (The Readers' Circle), decided to embark on the challenge of creating a novel with the help and participation of the readers. *La isla del fin de la suerte* (*The Island at the End of Luck*) (2002) came to be an extremely intense thriller with profound psychological twists.[31] Many other examples came out with the support of El Mundo. Those who set up such initiatives justify the fact that these projects of collective creation should be carried out on the Internet due to the speed and ease of communication this new medium provides. The idea of collaboration in literature is easily found

institutional events. As for prizes, in 2007 the LETHI Digital Literature Award was the first dedicated to Digital Literatures written in the Spanish language. In 2008 Yuxtaposiciones'08. Microfestival de poesía y polipoesía (Poetry and Polipoetry Microfestival) took place at La Casa Encendida in Madrid. The International Digital Poetry Festival was held in Barcelona in 2008.

29 The kharja is considered the first example of Spanish literature. A kharja is the final refrain of a lyric genre written in Ibero-Romance language during the XIth and XIIth centuries.

30 Published as a series in the pages of the magazine *Madrid Cómico* in 1886.

31 See *La rebelión de los delfines* (*The Rebellion of the Dolphins*, 2001) or *La muerte atravesó el paraninfo* (*Death Crossed the Auditorium*) at http://www.elmundo.es/especiales/2003/11/cultura/novela/. Accessed September 2016.

in the first hypertext stories. For example, it can be discovered within the experimental project entitled *Un mar de historias* (*A Sea of Stories*, 2005), created by three post-graduate students, Xiomara Acosta, María Jesús Vidal, and Álvaro López Santos, at the School of Sociology, A Coruña University.[32] The project combines elements from the oral tradition with traditional auditory features. The authors intend to offer a variety of Galician maritime legends in the form of interactive literature, in which one may choose at any time the trajectory of the readings, selecting which connections to make, and which characters (Toñito, Gervasio, or Capitán Risco) take on the role of narrator. It is noteworthy that this hypertext adopted the oral characteristics of traditional literature as the basis of its narrations. The oral tradition entails the presence of the narrator before the audience; in virtual stories, there is a high degree of interactive participation by the users (Vouillamoz, 2000). Another feature of the literary hypertext is that it functions based on links that allow the reader to browse around, and offers a greater degree of discursive openness than printed works.

Another feature of digital literature is non-linearity (Aarseth, 1999). The precedents of the type of hypertext creation we are concerned with in relation to this feature can be found in all the writers who tried to find strategies that would replace analogue linearity because, supposedly, it falsified their creative experience. They are works which offer, in manifest ways, multiple endings or conclusions joined to new beginnings; novels which are presented, very explicitly and consciously, as itineraries or paths that, when they are trodden, build the virtual story. This idea is present in many Latin-American writers. The precedent to this rupture of linearity is often attributed to several stories by Borges, such as "The book of Sand," "The Garden of Forking Paths," and "The Library of Babel." Of course Julio Cortázar's *Rayuela* (1963) is also often cited as inviting the reader to find their own reading, their own route through the text. Within literature in Spain, Max Aub's novel *Juego de cartas* (*Card game*) (1964) is cited as a precedent, since its plot is based on the combinatory possibilities of a game of cards (Trueba, 2016). Many others have been added to the list since then. Another example is Arturo Pérez-Reverte's novel *La piel del tambor* (*The Drumskin*) (1995), which involves the theme of multimedia literature although not as a narrative technique. A CD is included in the novel by Laura Esquivel, *La ley del amor* (*The Law of Love*) (1996), in which illustrated parts and fragments that must be listened to as music are interwoven. Luis Goytisolo's *Mzungo* (1996) is also presented in CD-ROM format, including several games directly related to the development of the novel. Doubtless, as the advertising for these works is intended to exploit, the world of

32 See http://mccd.udc.es/unmardehistorias/. Accessed September 2016.

new technologies as part of the plot is a safe bet for selling to young readers. The most salient feature of the rupture of linearity is that it seems to be generated by computers themselves. This is what occurs in *Diorama*, a work created in 2004 by Argentine Santiago Ortiz.[33] *Diorama* is a relational network of concepts, texts, pictures, interactive applications, links and references, all within navigable web-space. The contents make up a compilation of information, as well as a reflection on language and codes. Three uses of codes are identified, each operating in very different, yet related, fields: a life-generating code [genetic code], a narration-generating code [languages], and a representation and system model generating code [computing code]. More important than the compilation of information is the interweaving of the relationships. *Diorama* is the result of work that began with the exhibition *El inventor de historias* (*The Story Inventor*) at Medialab Madrid in which the walls of the exhibition hall were covered with texts and pictures related to one another and including installations and digital applications (on the exhibition website a photograph of the assembly can be seen).[34] The network of texts, pictures and applications can be explored by travelling around the contents by way of the relationships. Thus, each trajectory is a specific journey, a narration through knowledge. The reader does not hop from one page to another by way of links, which seems to be more related to play or instinct. In this kind of non-lineal reading, both the poet's choice of words and the relationship among those words must be taken into account. The artist strives for a total art form in which the different signifying codes are conflated. The reader finds these works rather strange, and in addition, is forced to participate more actively in them. What is being attempted? It could be said that relativism, the loss of the hegemony and rationality of written language, is the goal. The perspective of critical judgment, the development of that which is cognitive (the communication of sensations, emotions and concepts) allude to a changing existence, just as is found in reality, time and space change according to the contingency of each reader, so that timelessness and utopia are brought about. Rhythm is based on the sensation of textual instability, which becomes emotional, since the artist actually attempts is to demonstrate the theory of the impossibility of closed structures.

33 See http://moebio.com/santiago/diorama/#. Accessed September 2016.

34 Medialab Madrid, Centro Cultural Conde Duque, Madrid, April - May 2004.

III. THE STAGE AND THE DROP SCENES: TRANS/GENRES, TRANS/THEMES AND TRANS/NATIONS

As expected, new critical contributions to add to those who already begun to study the field, from new readers, PhD Humanities students,[35] and digital writers as Belén Gache (Gache, 2006) and Doménico Chiappe.[36] New digital works arise every day on the Net and are gradually located, indexed. After their reading and analysis, the following general trends are detected by humanist critics.

THE FIRST DROP SCENE: TRANS/GENRES

Over the last twenty years, due to the growing number of Spanish digital works, the notion of genre has expanded and its categorical limits have become increasingly porous. New subcategories have been unveiled in poetry: hypertext poems,[37] moving letters poems,[38] words-in-movement poems,[39] moving phrases poems,[40] poems in movement,[41] animated poetry,[42] E-minstrelsy poetry,[43] and computer-assisted poetry.[44] Digital theatre is still taking its first steps in the digital world. The current trend on the stage for presenting dialogue between words and images shows the vitality and necessity of this symbiosis.[45] Narrations display more categories of subgenre. Juan José Díez on the website Hispanic Electronic Literature classifies digital narrations as hypernovels,[46]

---

35 For example: Calles (2011); Montiel (2012); and Jiménez-Díaz (2015).

36 Chiappe (2015).

37 See http://lorealenelespejo.blogspot.com.es/2007/12/me-gusta-que-te-encuentres-en-el-verso.html.

38 See Ana María Uribe: *Tipoemas, Anipoemas, Deseo/Desejo/Desire, El circo/The circus*; and Paulo Carvajal (*Programa 11*).

39 See Hugo Cuevas-Mohr, *El agua que sacie tu sed* (*The Water That Quenches Your Thirst*) or *El violín que espera tu regreso* (*The Violin Awaits yYur Return*).

40 See Isaías Herrero Florensa, http://www.elevenkosmos.net.

41 See Ainize Txopitea, *TV* and Daniel Ruiz, *Tetra*.

42 See Pedro Valdemorillos, *Caosflor* and Tina Escaja, *Velocity*.

43 This is the terminology used by Ana Cuquerella for those poems recited by the poet with the support of electronic and visual media, for example Óscar Martín Centeno, *Somos* (*We are*). See Cuquerella Jiménez-Díaz, 2011.

44 See Pablo Gervás, *Wishful Automatic Spanish poet* (*WASPo*).

45 The group Yoctobit staged their work *Mata a la Reina* (*Kill the Queen*) in 2014 under the category of "playable theatre."

46 See *Como el cielo los ojos* (*As the Sky the Eyes*) by Edith Checa and *Sinferidad* by Benjamín Escalonilla.

hypermedia novels,[47] webnovels,[48] blognovels,[49] collective novels,[50] and wikinovels.[51] María Goicoechea and Laura Sánchez Gómez in Ciberia incorporate other genres from a cross-media perspective (Goicoechea and Gómez, 2012): ambient,[52] interactive film,[53] codework,[54] conceptual,[55] comic,[56] documentary,[57] interactive fiction,[58] hacktivism,[59] and wordtoy. [60]

The need to classify technical innovations involves the invention of a critical terminology that reflects a desire for thematic transgression. Ana Cuquerella proposes two general trends related to the characteristics of global literature (Cuquerella, 2015): osmosis between games and literature; and ekphrasis.

THE OSMOSIS BETWEEN GAMES AND LITERATURE

Literature is rich with recreational aspects, sometimes as children's presentations and other times digital work is a game with exquisite intellectual chimeras.[61] Santiago Ortiz in *Bacterias* (*Bacteria*, 2005) and *La esfera de las relaciones* (*The Sphere of Relations*, 2007) raises a disconcerting game that involves math, art and philosophical reflection.

47 See Doménico Chiappe, *Tierra de extracción* (*Land of Extraction*); *Wordtoys* by Belén Gache; *Heartbeat* by Dora García; *Trincheras de Mequinenza* (*Mequinenza Trenches*) by Félix Remírez; *Los estilitas de la sociedad tecnológica* (*The Technological Society Stylites*) by Antonio Rodríguez de las Heras; and *Asesinos y asesinados* (*Murderers and Those Murdered*) by Benjamín Escalonilla.

48 See Juan José Díez, *Don Juan en la frontera del espíritu* (*Don Juan on the Edge of the Spirit*).

49 See *El diario del niño burbuja* (*Diary of a Bubble Boy*) by Belén Gache.

50 See *La huella del cosmos* (*The Mark of the Cosmos*) and *Milagros sueltos* (*Loose Miracles*).

51 See *Madrid escribe* (*Madrid Writes*), *El regreso de Cecilio* (*The Return of Cecilio*) and *Vidas prodigiosas* (*Dangerous Lives*).

52 See *Our Dreams are a Second Life* by Belén Gache

53 *Mindstorming* by Miguel Ángel Campos.

54 *IP Poetry* by Gustavo Romano; *Árboles de texto* or *Karrutu* by Santiago Ortiz and *Migraciones* by Leonardo Soolas.

55 See Santiago Ortiz, *Bacterias*, and *Zona Inestable* by Jacinto Martín.

56 See Sergio Morán and Alicia Guemes, *El vosque (sic)* and *Tiempo de héroes* (*Heroes' Time*) by Daniel Estorach.

57 See Dora García, *The Tunnel People* and *La mano del hombre* (*Mankind's Hand*) by Isabel Aranda.

58 See *El códex del peregrino* (*The Pilgrim's Codex*) by VVAA; *Hazlo* (*Do It*) by Santiago Eximeno; *Un relato de amor/desamor* (*A story of Love / Heartbreak*) by Ainara Echaniz Olaizola; and *Hotel Minotauro* by Doménico Chiappe.

59 See *elmundo.es* by Ricardo Iglesias.

60 *WordToys* by Belén Gache and *Escribe tu propio Quijote* (*Write your Own Quixote*); also *El idioma de los pájaros* (*The Language of Birds*) and *Góngora WordToys*. See also *Anipoemas* by Ana María Uribe, *Tetra* by Daniel Ruiz, and *Karratu* by Santiago Ortiz.

61 In *Las casas perdidas* (*The Lost Houses*, 2012) Serrat, Alegret and Obon invite the reader to interact and play on-screen with the rooms that hide secrets as if it was a children's game.

His works, always experimental, offer the reader concepts, linked without too much discursive logic, causing self-reflection. Serendipity, i.e. the accidental discovery of information through the causality of movement, governs the pursuit of something that fails to be found. The game as an end itself, as simple input and output from reality to fiction, is one of the bulwarks of digital literature (Tosca, 2007).

EKPHRASIS: SYMBIOSIS OR COLLISION[62]

Throughout these twenty years of digital literature in Spain, there has been a progression from hypertext to multimedia. The triumph of intermediality is due to the evolution of technical means and the development of virtual memory. Literary texts increasingly rely on static or dynamic images. Not only does image decorate the text, now it illustrates it, enriches it. The reader reads text and image together at a single glance. Ekphrasis is not based on mimesis, but a phenomenon of intertextual synesthesia that evokes the activation of several senses at the same time. In *Islario* (2001) Laura Barrón crosses sounds and lines with images, turning the work into a poem, captured by several senses at the same time. *Hotel Minotauro* (*Minotaur Hotel*, 2015) by Doménico Chiappe is an interactive multimedia construction that criticizes violence against women and the abuse of power. Symbiosis or collision of digital text and image represent a visual thinking formed in the vision of each individual, in their reading space. Besides that, the relationship between image and words in electronic works proposed strategies of cultural understanding that enrich the communities of reading interpretation. Displaying images and words in a "whole with meaning" turns out to be a dialogic and symbolic construction of a shared reality that enables narrative communities with rigorous reflection, involvement and commitment.

THE SECOND DROP SCENE: TRANS/THEMES

With multimedia innovation appears certain topics (love, violence, metaliterature, memory...) with the purpose of transgressing them with a sharp metatechnological reflection that, in some cases, obliges the reader to reflect on a new conception of time, space or materiality. Laura Sánchez defends the computer as a performative machine and argues digital works show a capacity of speech not simply to communicate but rather to construct and perform a cultural identity and so readers are able to engage the emotions shown in these four aspects (Sánchez, 2016).

62 Ekphrasis is a Greek literary genre that implies a creative relationship between text and image.

VIRTUAL TIME: CONSTRICTION VS. LIBERATION

As it is well-known time is a crucial aspect in any literary work. Quite a few examples of digital literature show the anguish of the human being controlled by time or, on the contrary, it could be felt that the readers control time, causing them a feeling of euphoria. This is the case of *La hermandad de los escribanos* (*The Clerks' Brotherhood*) (2005) in which Félix Remírez proposes a challenge to the reader, who is now the main character of the plot and is led by the machine, to play an interactive game to avoid the computer being reformatted. It is the same mechanism that is used in videogames: the time for the player to meet the objectives is strictly controlled. After playing, the reader will feel euphoria or distress, depending on her achievement of its objectives. In *Una contemporánea historia de Caldesa* (*A Contemporary History of Caldesa*) (2007) Félix Remírez imposes even more anguish on the reader, who inexorably has to continue playing and is constantly doomed to make decisions. Santiago Eximeno in *Hazlo* (*Do It*, 2011) obliges the reader to take a stance a side, to act if a solution to the story is to be found (Coterón, 2012).

VIRTUAL SPACE: CLOISTER VS. AGORA

Virtual space is constantly possessed by the dynamic between the private and the public: it is perceived in the spaces in which the narrated events take place. *Nada tiene sentido* (*Nothing Makes Sense*) by Isabel Ara and Iñaki Lorenzo consists of a digital diary in which a narrator describes his desperation at being unable to leave his own room; all he can do is to write on his computer about how he feels. His work was composed using new digital discursive genres in which the narrator copies and pastes text into his virtual diary. The plot is simple: the narrator wants to communicate with others in order to be saved from his loneliness, but does not manage to do so. Suddenly one anonymous internaut contacts a psychiatrist, who turns out to be the same psychiatrist that is already treating the narrator. The psychiatrist warns the internaut that the person they are communicating with by e-mail is a schizophrenic suffering from symptoms such as hallucinations, delirium, disorganized thinking and strange behavior. The readers' suspicions are confirmed: the text gradually loses coherence and cohesion; that is, logical word order. The background and the foreground converge into schizophrenia, into the madness of the digital narrator.[63] The agora, as a public space in which to play, is very well represented in the work *Pueblo desnudo* (*Naked Town*) (2007) by Carola Di Nardo.

63 In *The Tunnel People* (2000) by Dora García, the mysterious inhabitants of a fictional journey walk through the closed space of the Brussels underground.

The reader has to reconstruct the story of a naked man who appears in a square in a lost village. The author sees the agora as a metaphor of the broad but naked digital relations.

VIRTUAL SUBJECT: SOLIPSISMS VS. COMUNICATION

The intimacy exposed to the public represented by *Pueblo desnudo* (*Naked Town*) is called "extimacy" (Sibilia 2009: 303). This motion between solipsism and communication, between the private and the public appears in *Un relato de amor/desamor* (*A Tale of Love/Heartbreak*) (2001) by Ainara Echaniz, a story about love and the absence of love between adolescents, in which the reader selects the texts according to two versions: happy times and unhappy times. Part of the story is made up of the love poems of the Chilean poet, Pablo Neruda, around which the theme of this narrative revolves. *Navega en privado* (*Browse Privately*, 2002) by Susana Heredia and Cristina Seraldi combines chats, emails, and links to construct a work in which Cloe allows readers to go into her private life.[64] In the chat we witness a conversation between Cloe and her psychologist: he advises her to get out and not to be enclosed in her computer.

VIRTUAL MATTERS: APOCALYPSE VS. UTOPIA

This thematic tension, already advocated by Katherine Hayles presents the dualism of the human being: on the one hand, deified by the intellectual impulse of the computer and, on the other hand, overshadowed by the apocalyptic fall in an increasingly selfish and violent society (Hayles, 2002). Isaías Herrero in *5000 palabras* (*5000 Words*) (2011) questioned a chaotic society governed by automata and fanatics. He portrays a strange world, as well as fascinating, in which the reader feels helpless and is moved. This apocalyptic vision is shared by Isabel Aranda in *La mano del hombre* (*Mankind's Hand*) (2007). This work represents a piece of sea with sixteen fish swimming. When moving the mouse throughout the screen (which represents the mankind's hand) to select one fish, it dies and Wikipedia opens to inform the reader about the consequences of human intervention in nature. La mano del hombre reflects a clear criticism towards the harmful effects that mankind produces on the environment.

THE THIRD DROP SCENE: TRANS/NATIONS

A further step in this process is the "linking" of two concepts that are in themselves already separately "in conflict": digital literature as global literature and literary nationalism (Tabbi, 2010).[65] A dialogic game exists in digital literature in Spain between global standards and cultural differences (Llamas, 2014). Some works use the reme-

---

64 See http://www.unav.es/digilab/proyectosenl/2002/navega_en_privado/.

65 Digital literature in the Catalan, Galician and Basque languages requires specific research.

diation of well-known references or canonical authors to catch the reader's attention. Transnationality in this kind of digital works does not come from the story itself but from the international readers who have access to them because the stories have been canonized along ages as Saint James, Quixote or Góngora. Thus, *El códex del peregrino* (*The Pilgrim's Codex*) (2012) by collective authorship narrates the story of Norberto, a young man who has lost his memory and is alone and wounded. Throughout the narrative game the reader will discover traditions and poems related to the Way of Saint James. Phrases from *Don Quixote* and from BBC journalism texts interact randomly in *Migraciones* (*Migrations*) (2005) by Leonardo Soolas. And the rewriting of a universal classic arises in *Escribe tu propio Quijote* (*Write your Own Quixote*) (1996-2006). Belén Gache encourages the readers' imagination by challenging them to rewrite the opening of Don Quixote de la Mancha, but the reader cannot escape from the classical beginning. Luis de Góngora is another of the canonical authors elected for the remediation of her works. Belén Gache plays with and challenges the reader in *Góngora WordToys* (2011) and María Mencía transcends the national and historical character of the Góngora lines in *Transient Self-Portrait*. In her work, María Mencía recreates the sonnet in a postmodern key and offers a reflection on the ephemerality of life, transient entities, digital self and the fragility of life and technology. She creates a fragile piece which needs light and caressing in order to exist.

Many digital works written by Spanish creators play with the desire of overcoming linguistic borders and are translated into English, French or the other official languages of the Spanish territory. *On Translation: The Internet Project* (1995- 1997) by Antoni Muntadas represents the overcoming of languages through a set of messages that are sent from one country to another at the same time that they are translated from one language to another, with the consequent alteration of their meaning. Antoni Muntadas reflects on the interpretation and manipulation of texts that come and go from one to another, from one culture to a different one.

The idea of nation as narration has been present in the background since the first stages of literature (Anderson, 1983; Bhabha, 1990; Bhabha, 1994). Since the advent of the new digital rhizomatic narrativity, however, there has been a dissemination of complex dialogues, of relationships that move like a shuttle back and forth across the loom, from the universal to the particular and vice-versa, from prose to poetry and vice-versa, from letters to images and vice-versa, and from Spanish to English and vice-versa, creating a network of international, intercultural and transliterary links that give rise to the hyper-nation, which is always on the move, always in universal chaos and with its own particular order.

IV. THE FIGURES: CYBERFEMINISM IN ACTION

The growing momentum of digital literature has coincided in time with a new feminist wave driven by Donna Haraway and her *Cyborg Manifesto* (Haraway, 1991) and by the review *Australian Feminist Studies*, where Rhoda Shaw published her famous article "Our Bodies, Ourselves" (Shaw 2003). In Spain, Donna Haraway's theses were translated early (Haraway, 1995) and Beatriz Preciado collected the "postfeminist turn" in *Manifiesto* contra-sexual which supported the overcoming of feminist essentialism and enacts a techno-feminism which demands, without fear, spaces and digital relations to empower women who participate as actors, spectators and designers in digital scenarios (Preciado, 2002). Female sex exceeds her body: her gender identity mixes up the natural and the artificial, and her social roles have become diverse and multiple. The desire for transgression in cyber culture powers the historical desire for the liberation of women. Woman exercises control over the media in search of the multifaceted, the de-hierarchized and the inclusive.

Two aspects stand out in digital cyber-feminist literature: the hybridization of the body and the new techno-textual identity (Dietrich, 2002; Escaja, 2000). Both rituals are becoming present through a progressive range of nuances. In *Mi cuerpo (My body)* Miriam Reyes exposes her naked body, foreshortened, moving with difficulty within a refrigerator.[66] The voice of the poet recites a poem that questions the female body abandoned in a rented room, febrile, alone on a mattress, eaten by worms. And at the end she says: "dead or alive / my body / couldn't find any difference." It is a posthuman representation of the broken-down female body in a refrigerator as a metaphor for the female identity cloistered in the machine. Refrigerators or computers are the masks of her naked identity.

Marla Jacarilla's *Caperucitas de color granate* asserts the new role of women in cyber society through the remediation of five fairy tales: *Sleeping Beauty*, *Alice in Wonderland*, *Little Red Riding Hood*, *Snow White*, and *Cinderella*.[67] The most interesting aspect of this project is the video installation: a handmade dollhouse that contains a 7" TFT monitor from where phrases like this come out: "identity is provisional, always precarious, dependent and constantly faced with an unstable relationship of unconscious forces, changing social and personal meanings and historical contingencies"

66 See http://www.miriamreyes.com/micuerpo.html.

67 The picture above shows the subversion of the sexist paradigm: a cyber-cutout doll incites a man to follow her but the main picture shows a high-heeled shoe covering a phallus on a bloody body. The image disintegrates the innocence of the women formed through the reading of traditional stories. The new myth exaggerates sexuality to exterminate female submission. See http://www.marlajacarilla.es/#.

(Weeks, 1993). Taking these ideas as input, Marla Jacarilla transcends the discourse of folktales and changes the young, beautiful and well-behaved female characters into digital artists conscious that the game of creation brings with it a perverse ritual, in order to reach the women's own voice within historical discourse. The heroines of these mythical fairy tales are represented by cyber-cut-out dolls who question the inherited images of the female body.

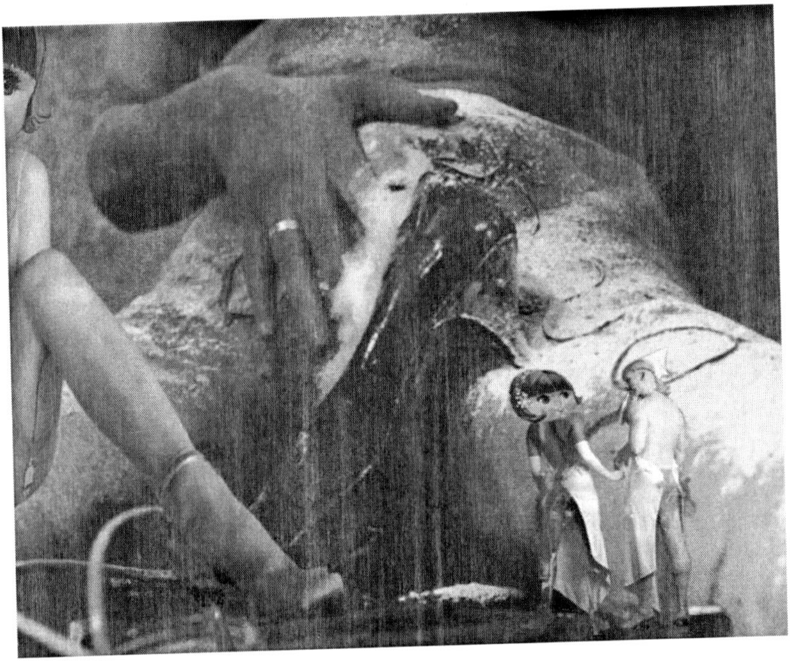

Figure 1: Marla Jacarilla, *Caperucitas de color granate* (*Maroon-Coloured Riding Hood*, 2006)

Ainize Txopitea intends to "entertain not only with words and visuals but also with the imagination." Her work, which until recently was shown in the web Cyber-poetry.com, is now being revised by the author, but it is very well described by Tina Escaja (Escaja, 2003). Txopitea juxtaposed the anatomy of man and woman and their respective identities. The man is an androcyborg, a rigid, hieratic subject. This andro-cyborg seems to be like an old print of the human body showed in anatomy classes and his speech, artificial, is built to foster harmony and the persistence of love. This cyborg does not question inherited patterns. The female cyborg is more relaxed, stands sideways, looking at the man. In her speech, this gynecyborg questions her feelings for the man; she pretends to be deaf and blind. She repeats: "the beaver has broken the dam"; i.e., the gynecyborg has let out the immanent and labile fluid which is looking now for new channels.

The posthuman body of Miriam Reyes, Marla Jacarilla's cut-out heroines and Ainize Txopitea's gynecyborgs represent the robotic materialization of the female body. The female identity in digital literature is complex and is represented by a subject that runs away from inherited stereotypes, who seeks her voice between the manifold and the arbitrary. The authors presume that digital artistic creation is the best way to be inserted into an inclusive cosmology that allows the use of masks and dynamic rituals. Cybernetics then responds to a problematic ontology that constantly checks inherited patterns to come up with something new (Pressmanm 2014). Female artists aware of their own identity create a liberating ontology in which the heteroglossia of digital speech celebrates the authority and heterogeneity of women: a new era for poetic expression.

To conclude, digital literature in Spain is a creative field that, from its birth until today, has evolved with the times. In this essay, we focus only on digital literature in Spain, but it is necessary to overcome nationalism and extend the vitality of this area to all electronic works that are written in Spanish in any part of the world. The great challenge for the future for both creators and critical specialists is also spreading the work beyond academic circles and promote it as an alternative to reading and writing for the general public and to education in particular (Hayles, 2008).

WORKS CITED

Aarseth, Espen. "Nonlinearity and Literary Theory." In *Hypertext and Literary Theory.* Edited by G. P. Landow, 51-86. Baltimore: Johns Hopkins Press, 1993.

Anderson, Benedict. *Imagined Communities: Reflections on the Origin and Spread of Nationalism*. London & New York: Verso, 1983.

Bhabha, Homi, ed. *Nation and Narration*. London: Routledge, 1990.

———, ed. *The Location of Culture*. London: Routledge, 1994.

Calles, Jara. *Literatura de las nuevas tecnologías. Aproximación estética al modelo literario español de principios del siglo* (2001-2011). (PhD. Diss. Universidad de Salamanca, 2011).

Carrasco Yelmo, Silviano. "Nuevos detectives digitales." In *Literatura e internet. Nuevos textos, nuevos lectores*. Edited by Salvador Montesa, 249-261. (Málaga: Universidad de Málaga, 2011).

Casacuberta, David. *Creación colectiva. En Internet el creador es el público*. Barcelona: Gedisa, 2003.

Chiappe, Doménico. *Forma y fondo de la narrativa multimedia* (Ph.D. Diss. Universidad Carlos III de Madrid, 2015).

Cotte, Pierre, ed. *Language et Linéarité*. Paris: Septentrion, 1999.

Cuquerella Jiménez-Díaz, Ana. "E-tertulias, e-vanguardias, e-juglaría. La poesía que se aloja en las bitácoras españolas. Algunos ejemplos de remediación del canon poético en estos blogs." *Texto Digital* 7: 2011, 67-73.

Cuquerella Jiménez-Díaz, Ana. *El potencial creativo de la remediación en la literatura digital hispánica* (PhD Diss. Complutense University in Madrid, 2015).

Dietrich, Dawn. "(Re)-Fashioning the Techno-Erotic Woman: Gender and Textuality in the Cybercultural Matrix." In *Virtual Culture. Identity and Communication in Cybersociety*. edited by Steven G. Jones, 185-205. London: Sage Publications, 2002.

Douglas, J. Yellowlees. "What Hypertexts Do That Print Narratives Cannot." *The Reader* Autumn, 1992, 1-23.

Escaja, Tina. "On Angels and Androids: Spanish/American Women Poets Facing Centuries' End." *Hispanófila* 30, 2000, 91-105.

____. "Hacia una nueva historia de la poesía hispánica: Escritura tecnetoesquelética e hipertexto en poetas contemporáneas en la red." *Espéculo. Revista de Estudios Literarios*, (2003). <http://www.ucm.es/info/especulo/numero24/ciberpoe.html> Accessed Sept. 2015.

Escandell Montiel, Daniel. *La narrative digital hispana. El blog como espacio de creación literaria a comienzos del siglo XXI*. (PhD Diss., Salamanca University, 2012).

Gache, Belén. *Escrituras nómadas, del libro perdido al hipertexto*. (Gijón: Trea, 2006).

Goicoechea, María. "A Survey of Electronic Literature Collections." *CLCWeb: Comparative Literature and Culture* 16.5, 2014. <http://dx.doi.org/10.7771/1481-4374.2558>. Accessed September 2016.

Goicoechea, María and Sánchez, Laura. "Ciberia Project: Building Community through a Digital Literature Archive." Paper presented at the International Conference on Digital Literary Studies, Faculdade de Letras da Universidade de Coimbra, Portugal, May 23, (2012).

Gómez Trueba, Teresa. "La literatura electrónica y sus antecedentes en la cultura impresa." 2005 <http://www.liceus.com/bonos/compra1.asp?idproducto=509>. Accessed September 2016.

Llamas, Miriam. "Digitising the World: Globalisation and Digital Literatura." *Neohelicon. Acta Comparationis Litterarum Universarum* 42: 227-251, 2014.

Haraway, Donna J. "A Cyborg Manifesto: Science, Technology, and Socialist-Feminism in the Late Twentieth Century." In *Simians, Cyborgs and Women: The Reinvention of Nature*. New York; Routledge, 1991. 149-181.

______. *Ciencia, cyborgs y mujeres*. Madrid: Cátedra, 1995.

Hayles, Katherine. *Writing Machines*. Cambridge, Mass.: MIT Press, 2002.

Pajares Tosca, Susana. "Ludology Meets Hypertext." In *Literatures in the Digital Era. Theory and Praxis*. Edited by Amelia Sanz Cabrerizo and Dolores Romero López, 51-59.Newcastle, Cambridge Scholars Publishing, 2007.

Preciado, Beatriz. *Manifiesto contra-sexual*. Madrid: Opera Prima, 2002.

Pressman, Jessica. *Digital Modernism. Making it New in New Media*. Oxford: Oxford University Press, 2014.

Romero López, Dolores. "From Analogue to Hypermedia Text in Hispanic Literature." *Neohelicon. Acta Comparationis*. 36, 463-475 2009.

______. "Poetics of Crisis or Crisis of Poetics in Digital Reading/Writing?" *The Case of Spanish Digital Literature, Literary and Linguistic Computing* 20: 1–16, 2012.

Sánchez Coterón, Lara. *Arte y videojuegos: mecánicas, estéticas y diseño de juegos en prácticas de creación contemoránea*. PhD Diss. (Madrid: Universidad Complutense 2012).

Sánchez Gómez, Laura. "El ordenador como máquina performativa." *Caracteres. Estudios Culturales y Críticos de la Esfera Digital*. 3. 2014. Accessed September 2016. http://revistacaracteres.net/revista/vol3n1mayo2014/ordenador-maquina-performativa/.

Show, Rhoda. "'Our Bodies, Ourselves,' Technology, and Questions of Ethics: Cyberfeminism and the Lived Body." *Australian Feminists Studies* 18.40: 45-55, 2003.

Tabbi, Joseph. "Electronic Literature as World Literature; or, the Universality of Writing under Constraint." *Poetics Today*, 31.1:17–50, 2010.

Toschi, Luca. "Hypertext and Authorship." In *The Future of the Book*. Edited by Geoffrey Nunberg, 69-207. (Berkeley: University of California Press, 1996).

Vouillamoz, Nuria. *Literatura e hipermedia. La irrupción de la literatura interactiva: precedentes y crítica*. Barcelona: Paidós 2000.

Weeks, Jeffrey. *El malestar de la sexualidad*. Madrid: Talasa, 1993.

ARTISTS' WORKS

Acosta, Xiomara, María Jesús Vidal and Álvaro López Santos. *Un mar de* http://mccd.udc.es/unmardehistorias/.

Aranda, Isabel. *La mano del hombre*. http://www.escaner.cl/yto/net-art/clima/#.

Campos, Miguel Ángel. *Mindstorming.* http://www.mindstorming.tv/es/ http://www.mindstorming.tv/en/.

Carvajal, Paulo. *Programa 11.* http://www.epimone.net/pieces/programa11/index.html.

Centeno, Óscar Martín. *Somos.* http://www.youtube.com/watch?v=UsAk0ZGth7E.

Checa, Edith. *Como el cielo los ojos.* http://www.badosa.com/bin/obra.pl?id=n052.

Chiappe , Doménico. *Hotel Minotauro.* http://domenicochiappe.com/pg_d_11a.html

_,_. *Tierra de extracción.* http://www.domenicochiappe.com/tierra-de-extraccion/

Cuevas-Mohr, Hugo. *El agua que sacie tu sed.* https://www.youtube.com/watch?v=XO-4pA06Ty0.

_,_. *El violín que espera tu regreso.* https://www.youtube.com/watch?v=qYndEWqbYP4.

Díez, Juan José. *Don Juan en la frontera del espíritu.* https://archive.org/details/Don-JuanEnLaFronteraDelEspiritu.

Di Nardo, Carola. *Pueblo desnudo.* http://www.pueblodesnudo.com.ar/.

Escaja, Tina. *Velo City.* http://www.uvm.edu/~tescaja/poemas/hyperpoemas/velocity.htm.

Escalonilla, Benjamín. *Asesinos y asesinados.* http://www.erres.com/swiche/swiche.html

_,_, *Sinferidad.* http://www.erres.com/abran-esa-maldita-puerta/sinferidad/

Echaniz Olaizola, Ainara. *Un relato de amor/desamor.* http://www.unav.es/digilab/proyectosenl/0001/final/amor_desamor/zbs1.htm.

Estorach, Daniel. *Tiempo de heroes.* http://www.tiempo-de-heroes.com/2012/03/daniel-estorach-martin.html#.V72EuWV0HtM

Eximeno, Santiago. *Hazlo.* http://www.eximeno.com/hazlo.html.

Gache, Belén. *El idioma de los pájaros.* http://findelmundo.com.ar/pajaros/index.htm.

_,_. *Escribe tu propio Quijote.* http://www.findelmundo.com.ar/wordtoys/data/quijote/intro.htm.

_,_. *Our Dreams are a Second Life.* https://vimeo.com/47094240.

_,_. *El diario del niño burbuja.* http://www.findelmundo.com.ar/bubbleboy/intro.htm.

_,_. *Góngora WordToys.* http://belengache.net/gongorawordtoys/.

_,_, *Wordtoys.* http://www.findelmundo.com.ar/wordtoys/.

García , Dora. *Heartbeat.* http://aleph-arts.org/art/heartbeat/.

_,_. *The Tunnel People.* http://www.doragarcia.net/tunnelpeople/.

Heredia, Susana and Cristina Seraldi. *Navega en privado.* http://www.unav.es/digilab/proyectosenl/2002/navega_en_privado/.

Herrero Florensa, Isaías. www.elevenkosmos.net.

Jacarilla, Marla. *Caperucitas de color granate*. http://www.marlajacarilla.es/CAPERUCITAS_WEB/index.html.

Martín, Jacinto. *Zona Inestable*. http://www.elviajero.org/martin/zi/previo.html.

Mencía, María. *Transient Self-Portrait*. http://www.mariamencia.com/pages/transient-self_portrait.html,

Morán, Sergio and Alicia Guemes. *El vosque*. https://autoestopistaliterario.wordpress.com/2014/10/19/el-vosque-de-sergio-moran-y-alicia-guemes/

Muntadas, Antoni. *On Translation: The Internet Project*. http://adaweb.walkerart.org/influx/muntadas/project.html.

Ortiz, Santiago. *Árboles de texto*. http://moebio.com/santiago/arboles/arboles.html.

_,_. *Karrutu*. http://www.344server.org/karratu/

_,_. Bacterias argentinas. http://moebio.com/santiago/bacterias/

_,_. *La esfera de las relaciones*. http://moebio.com/esfera/esfera.htm

_,_. *Diorama*, http://moebio.com/santiago/diorama/#.

Remírez, Félix. *Trincheras de Mequinenza*. http://www.cervantesvirtual.com/bib/portal/litElec/Trincheras_de_Mequinenza_Felix_Remirez/.

Romano, Gustavo. *IP Poetry*. http://ip-poetry.findelmundo.com.ar/.

Reyes, Miriam. *Mi cuerpo*. http://www.miriamreyes.com/micuerpo.html.

Ruiz , Daniel, *Tetra*. http://biblumliteraria.blogspot.com.es/2014/04/tetra.html

Serrat, Alegret and Obon, *Las casas perdidas*. https://itunes.apple.com/us/app/lost-houses-hd/id484836057?l=es.

_,_. *Tipoemas*. http://amuribe.tripod.com/tipoemas.html.

_,_. *Anipoemas*. http://www.vispo.com/uribe/anipoemas.html.

_,_, *Deseo/Desejo/Desire*. http://vispo.com/uribe/deseo2/deseo.html.

_,_. *El circo/The circus*. http://vispo.com/uribe/2000/circo/index.html.

Soolas, Leonardo. *Migraciones*. http://solaas.com.ar/migraciones/migraciones.htm.

Txopitea, Ainize. *TV*. http://www.epimone.net/pieces/tv/index.html.

VVAA. *El códex del peregrino*. http://elcodexdelperegrino.com/es/index.php.

Yoctobit, Mata a la Reina. http://intermediae.es/event/mata_la_reina_te_apetece_jugar__convocatoria_2.

Digital Poetry Evolution and the Art of Machines

BY JENEEN NAJI

> If you have to choose among an infinite number of ways to put it together then the relation of the machine to you, and the relation of the machine and you to the rest of the world has to be considered, because the selection from among many choices, the art of the work is just as dependent upon your own mind and spirit as it is upon the material of the machine. (Pirsig, 169)

INTRODUCTION

The above quote is from Robert Pirsig in Zen and the Art of Motorcycle Maintenance. Published in 1974 it was a seminal work that attempted to explore the search for meaning in a modern world increasingly shaped by technology. This was of particular concern in the 1970s as technologies developed for the "space race" permeated the everyday lives of humans with televisions, cars and washing machines being touted as essential components of every affluent western home.[68] In relation to technology, Pirsig observes that the art of the work, created through use of the machine, is just as dependent on the machine as it is on the human in terms of how we choose to use the machine. This socio-technological position is a little more nuanced than the reductionist binary of technological versus social determinism dialectic most typified by arguments of the same era by Marshall McLuhan and Raymond Williams (McLuhan, 1964; Williams 1972). Although to term McLuhan's and Williams arguments as reductionist is perhaps too harsh as both their positions display far more nuance and complexity than a simple social versus technological binary. Humanity's relationship with technology has always been complicated, media theorist Friedrich Kittler proposes that "machines are our fate, and to say so is not to witness to an awful downfall of the human condition; it is to properly grasp our situation" (Peters, 2010, p. 2). Essentially what is important to recognise is that our relationship with technology can be more usefully viewed on a spectrum or even a Möbius strip, in that not only does technology influence us but we too influence the technology.[69] Nowhere is this more evident than in human creative and artistic expression such as for example digital poetry

68 The "space race" defined a period from the 1950s to the 1970s when the U.S.A. and the U.S.S.R. competed to display superiority of their technologies through space exploration.

69 Also known as the twisted cylinder, a Möbius strip is a one-sided non-orientable surface that can be achieved by twisting a single strip once and then attaching the two ends. See Weisstein.

practice. Clearly technology has had a tremendous impact on society, but what impact has society had on technology? Whilst technology may initially be conceived for a specific purpose it can quickly be adapted to other more creative uses by human beings. This essay explores this reciprocal relationship of humans and technology through the prism of a historical approach to digital poetry writing practice by viewing it as one of Howard S. Becker's art worlds (Becker, 1982).

Writing has always been linked to and indeed reliant on technology: from the prehistoric necessity of inscribing marks on a cave wall humans have always needed a device of some sort to help them perform this task. Whether the ability to inscribe was discovered by accident or on purpose we will never know but what we do know is that often as a technology is introduced it is initially launched with a specific function in mind. Then as the technology permeates through common usage the affordances of the technology come to the fore and human use of it adapts and changes as correspondingly the technology also adapts and changes to our needs. For example when the Minitel in France was launched in 1982 it was mainly envisaged as a video-text system using telephone line networks to book tickets, make reservations or look up phone numbers (Michalet, 2011). However *Art Access* an art review began to offer writers the possibility to write poetic works specially adapted to the Minitel, accompanied by critics' text (Bootz, 2007).

Digital poetry makes up a sizeable chunk of the contemporary development of electronic literature. Electronic literature was first recognizable as a genre with the emergence of hypertext fictions, these were texts that used the emerging hypertext technology of the Internet to create non-linear blocks of text or lexia that linked to either each other or to external sites. As the technologies evolved, the literary artefacts began to include graphics, colors and sound and concurrently the affordances of digital technologies changed thereby influencing contemporary artistic and cultural practice as evidenced by the changing shape of the digital poem (Hayles, 2008). This essay will specifically deal with the changing shape of the digital poem through charting a historical path of digital poetry practice from early experimentations by Ana María Uribe and Philippe Bootz to contemporary examples such as Jason Edward Lewis' apps and Zuzana Husárová and Ľubomír Panák's *I: * tter* using the Kinect 3D sensor. Less commonly cited examples such as Graham Allen's Holes and my own (Jeneen Naji) *Rubayaat* are also covered towards the aim of providing a snapshot of the innovative writing practices of digital poetry which mirror the evolution of digital technology innovations from app to kinect and web based to virtual reality. Emphasis is also given to providing digital poetry examples from a wide a range of countries (such as Argentina, Canada,

France, Ireland, Portugal, Slovakia, and the U.S.A.) in order to provide an international perspective.

MODERNISM AND POETRY

In relation to existing variations within the larger scope of poetic expression digital poetry can be seen at some points to constitute evidence of sizable cultural (such as modernism and postmodernism), societal (such as World Wars I and II), and/or technological (such as massive industrialization) changes affecting poetic (and other artistic) genres. A cultural and technological historical analysis of this type is meritorious because as Stephen Mayes proposes in relation to photography, the revolutionary change in cultural presence wasn't led by photographers, nor publishers or camera manufacturers but by telephone engineers (Mayes, 2015). This process will repeat as business grasps the opportunities offered by new technology to use visual imagery in extraordinary new ways, throwing us into new and wild territory.

With regards the advent of modernism, David Harvey argues that it is compellingly the case that, during a short time period the whole world of representation and of knowledge underwent a fundamental transformation somewhere between 1910 and 1915 (Harvey, 1990). He cites Malcolm Bradbury and James Walter McFarlane's work documenting the transformations that occurred in

> the arts and science of the capitalist world, including works of Proust, Joyce, Lawrence, and Mann in literature; Matisse, Picasso, Duchamp, Braque, Klee, and Kandinsky in art; Stravinsky, Schoenberg, and Bartok in classical music, Einstein's generalization of the theory of relativity, and Saussure's structuralist theory of language, in which the meaning of words is given by their relation to other words rather than by their reference to objects. (28-29)

Harvey reminds us that modernism came about as a reaction to rather than a pioneer of the rise of mass markets, consumption and production as a result of technological innovations of the era just before the First World War. Is it any surprise then that with the radical transformation of Western capitalist space and time that "Gertrude Stein [...] interpreted cultural events, such as the advent of cubism, as a response to the time-space compression to which everyone was exposed and sensitized" (271)? No longer did it take an Atlantic boat crossing of a month or more to travel to the "new world." Instead you could hop on a plane and be there in hours. Time and space had been compressed, the world was smaller and time went faster, or so it seemed.

Equally it can be no surprise that as a great promoter of Modernist experimentalism, whose Paris apartment became a salon for a circle of fine artists and writers including among many others, Picasso, Matisse and Hemingway, Stein's own poetry reflected exactly the same response to this time-space compression (Paschen and Mosby, 2001). As Adalaide Morris outlines, Gertrude Stein's writing was "a continuous present as additive as a drive in the country, as iterative as the frames in a filmstrip, as collaged as the views from a plane" (Morris and Swiss 2006, 2).

Similar arguments can equally be made regarding the effects of massive societal changes on the development and expression of Walt Whitman's poetry in the mid 19th century. By the end of the 1860s when the construction of the "The Great Bridge" was starting from Brooklyn across the East River to New York, Brooklyn had been transformed in less than a generation from a "backwater [...] hinderland" to the third largest and fastest growing city in America (McCullough, 1972, 103-104). This transformation was reflected in the poetry of Whitman who had grown up near and spent most of his adult life in the very same city between his birth in 1819 and the first edition of *Leaves of Grass* in 1855.

Though Stein and Whitman did not innovate in terms of the technology they used to write their poetry to the same extent as future digital poets did we can nonetheless see that societal technological changes influenced their writing practice. It is clear then that socio-cultural currents of which technology makes up a sizable part continuously influence poetry, as technology continues to permeate our everyday lives so too can it be seen to do so in our artistic practice and worlds of representation.

DIGITAL POETRY AS AN ART WORLD

Clearly massive societal transformations, what Harvey refers to as "new conditions of production [...] transportation [...] and consumption," impact massively on our "worlds of representation" (28-29). But even societal transformations on the scale of European modernity or the take off of industrialization along the east coast of America in Whitman's time rarely, in Howard Becker's words, "produce new art worlds" (310). Becker writes: "Artistic revolutions (such as modernism) make major changes in the character of the works produced and in the conventions used to produce them" (305). However most of the personnel—creative, production, distribution, etc.—remain intact, albeit perhaps extending, modifying their existing practices. In Becker's terms, "the innovation is usually added to what competent participants need to know and do" (308).

The reasons for this are simple. An art world, in Becker's terms, "denote(s) the network of people whose cooperative activity, organized via their joint knowledge of conventional means of doing things, produces the kind of art works that the art world is noted for" (x). Over time every art world develops its own "artistic tradition(s), such as a connected series of solutions to commonly defined problem(s)" (301). Thus "revolutionary changes (within an art world) occur when their originators mobilize some or all of the members of the relevant art world to cooperate in the new activities their vision of the medium requires" to address the still "commonly defined problems" (308). In contrast, a new "art world is born when it brings together people who never cooperated before to produce art based on and using conventions previously unknown or not exploited in that way" (310). A digital poetry example of this combining of people who haven't collaborated before would be *Born Magazine*, an online publication that would pair web designers/authors and poets to make digital poems. Launched in 1997 as a quarterly publication *Born Magazine* brought together "creative writers and interactive artists to create experimental, media-rich literary arts experienced only through the Web" (*Born Magazine*, 2011). In a similar way to how the Internet has allowed an explosion in online literary content such as *Born Magazine*, Becker argues that new art worlds typically begin with either the "invention or diffusion of a technology" (such as, "photography and motion pictures"), the "development of a new concept" (such as "the novel"), or "a new audience" (such as, "the outdoor rock concert" of the '60s) (310-314). In all of these cases, and hence most consequentially in our thinking regarding digital poetry, Becker notes, "the people who develop new art worlds participate in the broad currents of intellectual and expressive interest growing out of extant tradition and practice" (314). As a result,

> a new technique, conception, or audience suggests new possibilities but does not define them fully. So the first people involved experiment with it, seeing what it can do and what they might want to do with it. What people actually do with the innovation depends on what it makes possible, on what version they have of contemporary traditions and interests, and on the people and resources they can attract. (314)

The expanding art world that is digital poetry was able to build on the extant traditions and practices of its precursor videopoetry. In the early 20th century there was an explosion of creative electromagnetic experimentation that fed into global video experimentation. Holly Rogers mentions how in 1965

> video was cheap and easy to use: it could be managed by one person; it could manipulate sound and image in real time; it could use the space around it as a creative material; and it could engender a new mode of activated spectatorship. (367)

This type of fast and loose experimentation is particularly striking with regards its' resonances to today's digital technologies. In a similar fashion to how video technologies sparked an explosion in creative practice in the early 20th century so too have digital technologies sparked a creative explosion in the early 21st century. Video poetry clearly was an important precursor to the development of digital poetry. A notable and well-known video poet is Ernesto Melo e Castro, a Portuguese practitioner and theorist of video poetry. Most notably in 1968 he produced the video poem *Roda Lume* and in 1989 *Signagens* a series of videopoems (Funkhouser, 2007, p. xxii). Interestingly 1989 is also the year that C.E.R.N. proposed new protocol for information distribution and so began the repurposing of technology into avenues and tools for future creative expression (Howe, 2014).

Seamus Heaney in his poem "Seeing Things" writes:
Whatever is given
Can always be reimagined, however four-square,
Plank-thick, hull-stupid and out of its time
It happens to be. (Heaney 2004, v)

Nowhere is Heaney's reimagining more apparent than in digital writing practice. Clearly in relation to the "commonly defined problems" of poetic expression, the impact of the worldwide advent of digital technologies is of much further reaching consequence than was either the modernity of Stein's era or the industrialization of America in Whitman's. To what extent it will continue to trigger the emergence of a new art world as per Becker or sizably revolutionise poetic expression within the existing one remains to be seen. David Constantine tells us that poetry must be agile; continually it must devise new ways to answer the changing circumstances and shapes of human life. Human life has changed and this will be reflected in our poetry. Whatever the consequences of the impact of digital technologies within both the culture and the poetic genre, poetic expression will continue to query the meaning of human existence, both perceptually and intellectually, and hence emotionally by "foregrounding" the changing nature of the human condition and "situating its means of doing so within the structures of technology and art that define the genre as expanding rather than pregiven" (Watten 2006, 365).

INTERNET TECHNOLOGIES AND DIGITAL POETRY PRACTICE

In terms of the beginnings of a creation of a digital poetry art world, the late 1980s and early 1990s were when the most activity took place. In 1989 the Parisian group L.A.I.R.E. (Lecture, Art, Innovation, Recherche, Écriture) created the web-based literary journal *Alire*, this included Philippe Bootz, Frédéric Develay, Jean-Marie Dutey, Claude Maillard, and Tibor Papp. Bootz states that it is the oldest multimedia journal in Europe. *Alire* was "the first periodical on disk dedicated to the publication of digital poetry" (Bootz, 1999). Before the arrival of CD-ROMs and the Internet explosion, the journal was already publishing poetry written for and intended to be read through computers. Bootz believes that historically,

> the journal corresponds to the establishment of a "third stream" in computerized literature, if one acknowledges that hypertext and earlier software texts (générateurs automatiques) made up the first two. This third stream being that of animated literature, to which the five authors from L.A.I.R.E. came from backgrounds in aural and visual poetry. (Bootz, 1999)

While France was experimenting with the Minitel, in America Gopher was in use in the early 1990s. This was a predecessor of the World Wide Web and was a text-only interface. Its major drawback was that, unlike the World Wide Web, it did not display images. "Gopher and the system of text-based hypertext it employed, may have marked a kind of age of innocence for digital poetry, a last great days of print" (Glazier 2002, 16). The World Wide Web of today has developed to the point of allowing for text, visuals, graphics, animations, video, audio, and extensive interaction. Although Tim Berners-Lee and others at the European Laboratory for Particle Physics (C.E.R.N. - Conseil Européen pour la Recherche Nucléaire) had proposed a new protocol for information distribution though its' development had begun before Gopher, it was slower to progress. Nonetheless it was this protocol, which became the World Wide Web in 1991, and was based on hypertext. Voyager and Eastgate Systems were publishers of electronic literature during mainly the late 1980s and early 1990s. Storyspace, a hypertext authoring software, and Macintosh's HyperCard software were the main tools used during this period (Hayles, 2008). Published works were primarily interactive CD-ROMS and hypertext fictions, but in the poetry category, Eastgate lists the following: Robert Kendall's *A Life Set For Two*, Judith Kerman's *Mothering*, Deena Larsen's *Marble Springs*, and Rob Swigart's *Directions*. Of special note are the important works by Jim Rosenberg, *Intergrams* and *The Barrier Frames Diffractions Through*.

Sarah Sloane describes hypertext fictions as digital texts that use digital note cards with embedded buttons that allow readers to make choices between alternative plot branches and to write in their own words into the evolving story (22). Sloane posits that Multi User Dungeons (MUDs), MOOs (MUD, object orientated) and MUSHes (Multi User Shared Hallucinations) which are all text based are in fact "a third type of digital fiction, one that relies on the Internet to connect readers and writers in collaborative stories distinguished by otherworldly settings and levels" (22).

In fact Bootz believes that computerized literature can be broken down to three main developments that were close contemporaries (hypertexts, software texts and animated literature) the first works in these genres having been written between 1978 and 1985. At the same time as computer poetry was forming in the 1980s so too were others experimenting in video and visual poetry. It was the proliferation of the computer and the Internet that made these experimental pieces accessible to a viewing audience and also the ease of access for artists to a new medium in which to experiment. Bootz suggests that "computerization not only encouraged the creation and wide publication of these works, it profoundly modified its own capacity to perform [...] digitality encroached upon literature, not in order to kill it, but to transform it" (Bootz, 1999).

THE EVOLUTION OF THE DIGITAL POEM

The Argentinian poet Ana María Uribe is important to mention within the context of the transformation of literature and the changing shape of the digital poem as she was a pioneer in terms of pushing the boundaries of material, form and visuality in her writing practice. In 1968 and 1969 Uribe wrote *Typoems* with the typewriter Lettera 22 and Pica type (Antonio 2011, 141). These were in the style of concrete poetry, whereby a poem's visual form mirrors the theme of the poem itself. Such as for example *The Mouse's Tale*, which appears in Lewis Carroll's (1865) *Alice's Adventures in Wonderland* that tells the story of a mouse through a poem that is visually presented in print in the form of a mouse's tail. Uribe's work progressed from typed on the page concrete style to poetry in the 1960s to the digital screen in 1997 with *Anipoems* online.

Roberto Simanowski uses the term kinetic concrete poetry to refer to Uribe's online work (Simanowski 2011, 58). Kinetic refers to movement and so kinetic concrete poetry not only builds on the previous static tradition of form in concrete poetry but also draws on contemporary aesthetics of film and club culture through incorporation of movement and a far greater reliance on visual language. Ana Maria's work is a perfect example of technology impacting on the changing shape of the poem as a cultural object and poetic writing practice. John Cayley tells us the phenomenology of text is not static and cultural and technologic change leads to a change in materials, which consequently leads to a change in reading and writing practice (Cayley, 2006).

In a similar fashion Uribe's poetry writing materials changed from black & white text on a page created by a typewriter to colorful moving digital text with animation and sound. Interaction by the user in Uribe's work however was still minimal and yet as technological affordances allowed for greater user interaction so too did digital poetry.

Caroline Bergvall's 1999 work *Ambient Fish* can be seen to build on Uribe's 1997 *Anipoems* in the sense of a kinetic concrete poetry style that goes a step further by incorporating interactivity and sound. This poem was made in Adobe Flash and it requires the user to click a button to play but from that point on user interaction is dynamic in the code. Marjorie Perloff discusses *Ambient Fish* in her paper "Screening the Page/Paging the Screen: Digital poetics and the Differential Text," and she highlights how important the sound dimension is to this piece (Perloff 2006, 143). What is interesting regarding *Ambient Fish* is that its current form with a click to play interactivity exists just to trigger coded dynamic interactivity built into the poem, rather than interactivity generated through specific user interaction such as a mouse click.

Figure 1: Jeneen Naji 2014 *The Rubayaat Cave*, Granoff Building, Brown University, Rhode Island, U.S.A. http://www.jeneeninteractive.com

To look at the opposite end of the spectrum in terms of a greatly expanded potentiality of interactivity we can look at Cave technology which is enjoying a renewed interest thanks to the resurgence of virtual reality technology that is now more affordable and accessible than ever before in the form of the Oculus Rift. The Oculus Rift is head mounted virtual reality technology that was developed by Oculus VR. Cave technology however has been around long before the Oculus Rift and is an immersive, shared virtual reality environment created using goggles and several pairs of projectors, each pair pointing to the wall of a small room. The first Cave was developed at the University of Illinois at Chicago, which has trademarked the acronym Cave Automatic

Virtual Environment (CAVE); some similar virtual environments are referred to using the term "cave," not used as an acronym. Works of electronic literature have been made for a cave, most notably at Brown University. What is interesting in Brown University is that although the Cave technology was initially developed and housed by science departments such as Computer Science and Applied Mathematics it has since been used predominantly in the department of Literary Arts for digital writing.

The *Rubayaat* used Brown University's interactive and immersive stereo 3D audiovisual environment (Cave) to make a digitally mediated work of poetic language art, while studying the Cave as a media system for digital literary practice. This project used the Cave to explore notions of translation, multiculturalism, and the impact of technological affordances on literary expression and reception. This was done through creating a digital version of the mutable poem *The Rubáiyát* of Omar Khayyám, one that allows the user to experience, simultaneously, different translations that exist for this work in English, Irish, Arabic and Farsi. Potentially, this provides the reader with an opportunity to simultaneously access in the virtual space alternative versions of the text, some of which may fall outside the mainstream. For example, the digital Cave version not only includes the well-known English language translation by Edward Fitzgerald from the 19th century but also a lesser known English language version by a Mrs Henry Moubray Cadell (née Jessie. E. Nash), a 19th century Persian scholar who dedicated her life to this translation and the study of the Persian language. The Arabic translation of the poem by 20th century Egyptian poet Ahmed Rami is also included as distorted audio sung by Oumm Khalthoum a 20th century Egyptian singer as well as the original text in Farsi from the 11th and 12th century and an Irish language version intended to represent the research-author's multicultural identity. The user steps into the cube that is the Cave and using goggles and a remote control navigates the immersive VR environment however they please. The piece uses multilingual kinetic text and audio and the user navigates the virtual reality space through movement and a remote control whilst wearing specific 3D glasses that the computer uses to track the user's position in the virtual space.

To look at other contemporary examples of digital poetic writing practice that also incorporate gestic play it is worth mentioning Zuzana Husárová and Ľubomír Panák's *I: * ttter* that uses the Kinect 3D sensor. The Kinect technology is a motion-sensing device developed by Microsoft for games consoles. Using hand movements the user can browse, erase or mix dialogues that resemble the online communication of what could be people and machines. The text on the projection screen is remixed from selected textual fragments of European Net.Art (*My Boyfriend Came Back From the War* by Olia Lialina, *This Morning* and *IBM* by Alexei Shulgin, *zkp3.21* by Vuk Cosic,

100cc and *g33con* by the art collective JODI, *Irational* by Heath Bunting, *City* by Markéta Baňková, *four. Values* by Perfokarta, *Falling Times* by Michal Bielický, *Koniec swiata wg Emeryka* by Radoslaw Nowakowski, and *AE* by Robert Szczerbowski). See Husárová's essay in this book for further discussion of this work.

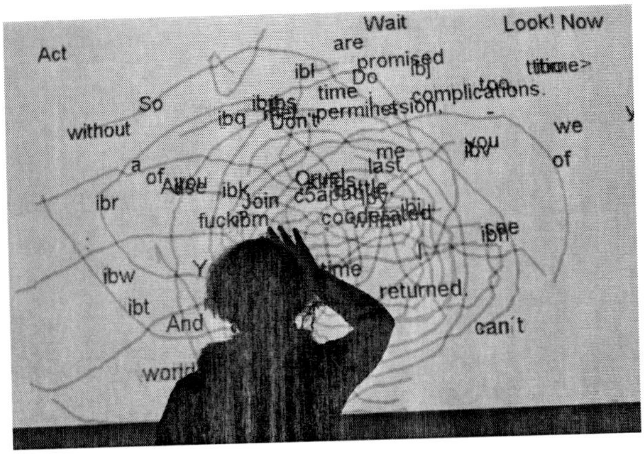

Figure 2: Zuzana Husárová and Ľubomír Panák. *I: * tter*. E-Poetry 2013, Kingston University, London, United Kingdom. http://zuz.delezu.net/2012/04/30/i-ttter-zuzana-husarova-lubomir-panak-sk/

To move from virtual reality to augmented reality, escapism to presenteeism we must look at Amaranth Borsuk and Brad Bouse's *Between Page and Screen* a book containing QR codes that when combined with a webcam provides a series of poems that chronicle a love affair between two characters, P and S. See Borsuk's essay in this book for further discussion of this work.

Figure 3: Amaranth Borsuk and Brad Bouse, *Between Page and Screen*. (Los Angeles: Siglio, 2012) – Photograph Brad Bouse.

Figure 4: Jason Edward Lewis, *The World Was White* iPad 2013.

Another example of digital poetic practice that can be seen to "hijack" contemporary commercial technologies for cultural and artistic practice is Jason Edwards Lewis and Bruno Nadeau's *P.o.E.M.M.* (*Poetry for Excitable [Mobile] Media*) project. *P.o.E.M.M.* is a series of eight mobile iOS apps that deals with themes of belonging, identity, youth and multiculturalism amongst others. The touchscreen interactivity of the apps uses the pinch and swipe gestures we have come to associate with iOS technology. The pieces also allow for the creation of your own version as well as connecting with online social media such as twitter. Interestingly the user can even register their own version of an app in a similar fashion to limited edition print artworks i.e. one of one hundred.

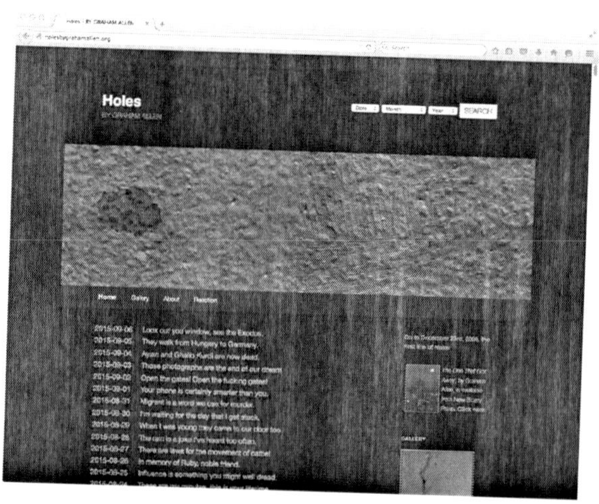

Figure 5: Graham Allen, *Holes*. Last modified 8th September 2015. Accessed 8th September 2015 http://holesbygrahamallen.org/

Holes by Graham Allen is a web-based digital poem to which Allen adds a ten syllable line to everyday. *Holes* is an example of a digital poem that could not have been written without digital technologies. It began on December 23rd 2006 and has been going since. James O'Sullivan is the producer of the piece through New Binary Press and on his website states "*Holes* could not have been bound in a traditional textual construct because of its iterative nature. Only a digital apparatus could be used to realize the author's vision of a text that grew by one line each day."

CONCLUSION

This chapter has provided a brief snapshot of digital poetry writing practice using a variety of technologies. Technologies that were originally envisaged for military or commercial use have been quickly subsumed into a new art world of digital artistic practice and poetic expression. A comprehensive list of all technologies and all digital poems would be far reaching and never ending so that is not my intention, instead here is provided a tantalizing taste of existing practice. In this book Marjorie C. Luesebrink's essay "Women Innovate: Contributions to Electronic Literature" bravely attempts a list of all female electronic literature practitioners that will give you a sense of the enormous scope of digital writing practice in existence. This chapter demonstrates how entwined the changing shape of digital writing practice is with human technological advancement and the art of machines. Cultural expression and technological innovation are interconnected as we see digital poetry practice evolving from beginnings in typewriters to animation with Ana María Uribe's work through to telephony networks with the Minitel and then the Internet right through to the expanded field of gestic play in augmented and virtual reality poetic writings as well as the commercial megalith that is mobile media. Contemporary technological development opportunities would seem to indicate that it is in the area of virtual and augmented reality environments that currently offer the most tantalizing opportunities for the expansion of a digital poetry art world. We will just have to wait and see…

The Man and the Machine - E. J. Pratt 1932
By right of fires that smelted ore
Which he had tended years before,
The man whose hands were on the wheel
Could trace his kinship through her steel,
Between his body warped and bent
In every bone and ligament,
And this 'eight-cylinder' stream-lined,

The finest model yet designed.
He felt his lesioned pulses strum
Against the rhythm of her hum,
And found his nerves and sinews knot
With sharper spasm as she climbed
The steeper grades, so neatly timed
From storage tank to piston shot –
This creature with the cougar grace,
This man with slag upon his face.

WORKS CITED

Allen, Graham. *Holes*. Last modified 8th September 2015. Accessed 8th September 2015 http://holesbygrahamallen.org/

Antonio, Jorge Luiz. "From Printed to Digital Media: The Poetry of Ana María Uribe." *Review of the Air Force Academy* 18(2011): 141-147.

Becker, Howard S. *Art Worlds*. Berkeley: University of California Press, 1982.

Bergvall, Caroline. *Ambient Fish*. Accessed 8Th September 2015 http://epc.buffalo.edu/authors/bergvall/amfish/amfish.html .

Bootz, Philippe. *Alire: A Relentless Literary Investigation*. Last updated 15 March 1999 http://www.electronicbookreview.com/thread/wuc/parisian

Bootz, Philippe. "Poetic Machinations." In edited by E. Kac, *Media Poetry, an International Anthology*, Bristol & Chicago Intellect Books, 2007.

Born Magazine. Last modified 2011. Accessed 28th June 2016 http://www.bornmagazine.org.

Borsuk, Amaranth and Brad Bouse. *Between Page and Screen*. Los Angeles: Siglio, 2012.

Bradbury, Malcolm and James MacFarlane. *Modernism 1890-1930*. Harmondsworth & New York: Penguin, 1976.

Cadell, Henry Moubray. *The Ruba'yat of Omar Khayam*. London & New York: John Lane The Bodley Head, 1899.

Cayley, John. "Lens: The Practice and Poetics of Writing in Immersive VR (A Case Study with Maquette)" in *Leonardo Electronic Almanac* 14(2006):05-06 http://leoalmanac.org/journal/vol_14/lea_v14_n05-06/JCayley_LEA140506.pdf

Carroll, Lewis. *Alice's Adventures in Wonderland & Through the Looking Glass*. Hertfordshire: Wordsworth Editions, 1993.

Constantine, David. *A Living Language: Newcastle/Bloodaxe Poetry Lectures.* Newcastle & Northumberland: Bloodaxe Books & University of Newcastle, 2004.

Fitzgerald, Edward. *The Rubáiyát of Omar Khayyám*. Hertfordshire: Wordsworth Editions, 1993.

Funkhouser, Christopher T. *Prehistoric Digital Poetry: An Archaeology of Forms, 1959-1995*. Alabama: The University of Alabama Press, 2007.

Glazier, Loss Pequeño. *Digital Poetics: The Making of E-Poetries*. Alabama: The University of Alabama Press, 2002.

Harvey, David. *The Condition of Postmodernity: An Enquiry into the Origins of Modern Change*. Massachusetts & Oxford: Wiley-Blackwell, 1990.

Hayles, N. Katherine. *Electronic Literature: new horizons for the literary* Indiana: University of Notre Dame, 2008.

History.com "The Space Race." Accessed 27 June 2016 http://www.history.com/topics/space-race.

Howe, Walt. *A Brief History of the Internet*. Last updated 28 May 2014 http://www.walthowe.com/navnet/history.html

Husárová, Zuzana and Ľubomír Panák. *I: * ttter*. E-Poetry 2013, Kingston University, London, United Kingdom.

Husárová, Zuzana. Accessed 8th September 2015 http://zuz.delezu.net/2012/04/30/i-ttter-zuzana-husarova-lubomir-panak-sk/

Kubler, G. *The Shape of Time: Remarks on the History of Things*. New Haven: Yale University Press, 1962.

Lewis, Jason Edward and Bruno Nadeau. *P.o.E.M.M.* Accessed 8th September 2015 http://www.poemm.net

Lewis, Jason Edward. *The World Was White*. iPad 2013.

Mayes, Stephen. "The Next Revolution in Photography is Coming." Last modified 25 August 2015, http://time.com/4003527/future-of-photography/.

McCullough, David. *The Great Bridge: The Epic Story of the Building of the Brooklyn Bridge*. New York: Simon & Schuster, 1972.

McLuhan, Marshall. *Understanding Media: The Extensions of Man*. New York: McGraw Hill, 1964.

Michalet, Thibaud. "Minitel, 1982-2012." Last modified 2011. Accessed http://www.gqmagazine.fr/popculture/le-desk/articles/minitel-1982-2012/8611.

Morris, Adalaide and Thomas Swiss. eds. *New Media Poetics: contexts, technotexts, and theories*. Cambridge, Massachusetts: The MIT Press, 2006.

Naji, Jeneen. *The Rubayaat*. Accessed 8th September 2015 https://youtu.be/9dvjTK-PgXI

Naji, Jeneen. *The Rubayaat*. Cave, Granoff Building, Brown University, Rhode Island, U.S.A., 2014.

O'Sullivan, James. *Holes by Graham Allen*. Accessed 8th September 2015 http://josullivan.org/creative/holes-by-graham-allen/

Paschen Elise and Rebekah Presson Mosby. eds. *Poetry Speaks*. Naperville, Illinois: Sourcebooks MediaFusion, 2001.

Perloff, Marjorie. "Screening the Page/Paging the Screen: Digital Poetics and the Differential Text" in *New Media Poetics: contexts, technotexts, and theories*. Edited by A. Morris and T. Swiss, T., Cambridge, Massachusetts: The MIT Press, 2006.

Peters, John Durham. "Introduction: Friedrich Kittler's Light Shows" in Friedrich Kittler, *Optical Media*. Cambridge: Polity Press, 2010.

Pirsig, Robert. *Zen and the Art of Motorcycle Maintenance: An Enquiry into Values*. London: Vintage, 1974.

Pratt, Edwin John Dove. *The Complete Poems and Letters of E.J. Pratt: A Hypertext Edition*. Accessed 1st July 2012 http://www.trentu.ca/faculty/pratt/.

Rogers, Holly. "Multimedia Art video art-music" in *Routledge Companion to Music and Visual Culture*. Edited by T Shepard & A. Leonard, New York & London: Routledge, 2013.

Simanowski, Roberto, *Digital Art and Meaning: Reading Kinetic Poetry, Text Machines, Mapping Art, and Interactive Installations*. Minneapolis: University of Minnesota Press, 2011.

Sloane, Sarah. *Digital Fictions: Storytelling in a Material World*. Connecticut: Ablex Publishing Corporation, 2000.

Uribe, Ana María. *Typoems*. Accessed September 8th 2015. http://www.vispo.com/uribe/typoems.html

Tillinghast, Richard. *Poetry and What Is Real*. Ann Arbor: The University of Michigan Press, 2004.

Watten, Barrett. "Poetics in the Expanded Field: Textual, Visual, Digital..." in *New Media Poetics: contexts, technotexts, and theories*. Edited by A. Morris and T. Swiss, Cambridge, Massachusetts: The MIT Press, 2006.

Weisstein, Eric. W. "Möbius Strip." From *MathWorld--A Wolfram Web Resource*. Accessed 28th June 2016. http://mathworld.wolfram.com/MoebiusStrip.html.

Williams, Raymond. *Television: Technology and Cultural Form*, London: Fontana, 1972.

Digital Letterisms: Alternumeric Orders

BY NATALIA FEDOROVA

This essay will focus on non-referential relationships of signification that can be built around standard sets of graphemes (such as the Latin alphabet, Roman numerals, the QWERTY keyboard layout, ASCII, Unicode, and n-grams) in language art. Iconic, alphanumeric, permutational use of the alphabetic characters in works by Hollis Frampton, Dmitry Prigov, John Maeda, Ivan Khimin, and Nick Montfort will be discussed. Digital Letterisms, the material use of Unicode characters in art and experimental literature, is the term we are going to use to describe these phenomena.

One of the key questions of the essay is the question of the role of letters in the era of digital writing. What are the qualities of their new materialities? Through mediation letters gain multidimensionality: they obtain non-linguistic audial, spatial and temporal properties. The question that evolves after that is what would be the rules of reading and interpreting digital literature. Roberto Simanowski argues for cannibalization of the text by media, meaning, often, the non-legibility of the text (Simanowski, 2010). This essay looks into ways of interpreting letters as visual signs.

When placed on the surface of a computer screen letters enter the realm of digital as they are referenced by numbers and are involved in computational processes. Nevertheless, John Cayley argues that the digital media "would be better characterized as 'literal'" (Cayley, 2004). Alphabetization, as Montfort responds, can be seen as a first algorithmization applied to language (Montfort, 2004). The phonemic alphabet divides spoken language into small permutable blocks of letters arranged in a certain order. The origin of alphabetical order is not quite clear but it is one of the unquestioned orders organizing objects, spaces, and texts. The essay explores the creative possibilities of the use of other orders of letters (QWERTY, Unicode, n-grams), implementing alphabetical order for non-linguistic information, the substitution of letters for the numerical order.

The atomic level of the letter allows it to involve, in the terminology of Christopher Funkhouser, both "mutations and permutations of the language" (Funkhouser, 2007). Alphabetic order is comes with combinatory potential. Digital letterist pieces have the freedom to neglect the language's grammar, but what paradigmatical orders would letters then obey? The aim of the essay is to study the alphanumerical orders of letters e.g. algorithmic properties or "the touch of the infinite," "optical perceptions," and the spatial order of the screen grid (Turkle 2002; Flusser 2011, 3).

I. LETTERS ON THE SCREEN: EMPTY SPACE

em typewriter —bpNichol

a thing is a whole on the surface of what it is not —Carl Andre

Today's digital screen interfaces enable the flow of thousands of images a day, and they seem to be meant for this purpose. Meanwhile the discussion of a letter as a medium of writing doesn't seem to be trivial when letters appear on screen, rather than on a page. As the image seems to be the most liquid exchange currency on the computer screen, the less customary use of letter on screens must be justified. The zero concept of *spatium*, an empty space, is a principle uniting printing press technology and the study of perspective. A space can be filled by a letter or left empty. It was "poured into lead by Gutenberg and into verse by Mallarme" (Kittler, 2001). *Spatium* can be compared to zero, ordering all other numbers. According to McLuhan, the point of view in Albertini's perspective and the space of the letter share similar geometry. The same is true for the cartographer's grid (McLuhan and Harley 1968, 12). This similarity creates an equality between the page and the screen and explains how the same surface can be used for working with image and text.

As a visual artist from the UK, Fiona Banner gets rid of the following QWERTY letters, meanwhile leaving the keyboard in place. Her slightly altered readymade Mac keyboard doesn't include alphabetic characters. The punctuation and special signs remain to study the pause from linguistic meaning making to evoking the visual associations of the Unicode characters. Banner questions this human-computer interaction model of a keyboard and forces viewers to pay attention to visual properties of the characters. She also equips any PC user with this tool automatically as all the special signs are present at the standard keyboard and anyone can choose to use just those at any time.

The apophatic figure of negative space is a way of arranging space on the page or a set of pages usually rather concretely symbolizing an unspeakable loss. Omitted photos from the United States Holocaust Memorial Museum in Washington, DC and the remaining language of the captions is a compositional principle of the work *Holocaust Museum* (2013) by American conceptual poet Robert Fitterman. *Absence* (2003) is a cube block of a book by an architect and educator Meejin Yoon from MIT. This is an ideologically charged personal memorial of the Twin Tower's attack. The first page after the cut out title presents a dot that slowly (in 110 pages, just as many as the number of floors in the WTC) transforms into the plan view silhouettes of two towers and then into their absence on the grid of the map.

Figure 1: Ivan Khimin, *Portrait of Joseph Beuys*

While Fitterman and Yoon use the architecture of negative space and image to suggest the materiality of absence, Russian digital artist Ivan Khimin employs the empty space of the screen, or the blue shade of space, as a medium of indexical and abstract representation for the six pieces of the ASCII32 series. The images are made up of the space key signs. The only thing you see when following the url is the surface of your screen, once you press "Control A" the blue shades of spaces reveal the familiar silhouette of a man wearing a hat (see Figure 1), none other than Joseph Beuys in the subsequent portrait. The four of them are *figurative* *____x___.htm* (a computer), *__x_____.htm* (a fur tree), *tHE_pORTRAIT_oF_jOSEPH_bEUYS.htm*, *tHE_pORTRAIT_oF_tIMUR_nNOVIKOV.htm* (a male profile), and two non figurative: a stripped screen of *________x.htm* and the solid rectangle of *________.html.*

1. ________.html.

<!-- there's nothing outside the text. jacques derrida -->

<center><pre>

2. ________x.htm

<!-- there's nothing outside the text. jacques derrida -->

<center><pre>

3. ____x___.htm

<!-- there is nothing outside the text. jacques derrida -->

```
<center>
<pre>

4. __x______.htm
<!-- there is nothing outside the text. jacques derrida -->
<center>
<pre>

5. tHE_pORTRAIT_oF_jOSEPH_bEUYS.htm
<center>
<pre>

6. tHE_pORTRAIT_oF_tIMUR_nNOVIKOV.htm
<pre>
```

The code is as evasive as the flickering on the visibility border of the resulting image, depending on whether you did or did not select the space of the image. The code is also clearly written to be read alongside with the text. The Derridian "*il n'ya pas d'hors-texte*" (Derrida, 1976, 158-159) can be read as nothing literally outside the text of the code. And the nothing gapped in the blue of the cursor selection, while the portrait of Joseph Beuys still contains two words (<center> <pre>), the last work of the series contains only one (<pre>). Khimin puts this Cagean idea of necessity of including reality in the work of art into the gaps between the words or images on the screen. One subconsciously starts looking for recognizable shapes in the spaces between the words of a page he or she is reading or writing.

Holocaust Museum, *Absence*, and *ASCII32* involve the omission of a sign on a given surface. This emptiness reveals the depth of the surface as in Yoon's piece, or existence of another surface of text (*ASCII32*) or of time (*Holocaust Museum*). In *ASCII32* the code suggests the existence of a text of a different ontological order a text that contains a key to understand these symbols, *Absence* and *Holocaust Museum* the positive presence in the previous or parallel time line that substitutes the hole.

And, the empty of semantic and morphological meaning space is also a space for a pause, a space for a punctuation sign.

II. PROTOTYPE: QWERTY

Figure 2: Fiona Banner, *Prototype*, 2013, Mixed media, 44 x 63 cm

I wanted language to only work for me and no one else. —Paul Chan

The grid like page in the typewriter, the first personal language processing machine, treats the space and the letter equally. Its keyboard sets a new non-alphabetical succession of letters, chosen according to their frequency within a certain language. Keyboard input increased the speed of production and consumption of language, standardized the shape of the letters and structured the empty space of the page. These fed the new wave of visual poetry, concrete poetry. ASCII art, based on visual properties of the language, is characteristic of the early era of computing. The keyboard input also leads to a number of constraints: the limited number of symbols, the necessity to learn a new order of letters, and the positions of the fingers. It is ambidextrously digital in the way that it involves a the process of text production actively using all ten digits (fingers) of both hands.

The keyboard, the letter processing hardware shared by a typewriter and a computer is explored in the work of MIT design professor John Maeda's *Tap.Type.Write* (1998). *Tap, Type, Write* is the fourth book in the series of Reactive Books. It responds to the keyboard. In the 90's, Maeda was reflecting on possible input sources for the computer, such as a mouse (*Reactive Square*), a microphone (*Flying Books*), graphical time-based behaviors (*12 o'clocks*), and a video camera (*Mirror, Mirror*). In *Tap.Type. Write* Maeda presents ten possible combinations of letter compositions on the computer screen. *Qwerty* allows for the shift between small and capital letters and exploiting horizontal spaces between them; *Forest* presents a spatial disposition of pixelized shapes of letters; *Dishes* allows letters to revolve around their axes; *Sky* is a circle transformed into letterist constellations, Jump is represented rather concretely by jumping letters, *Red Balloon* allows the user to inflate the letter by means of typing, with the properly inflated ones finally set into the air; *Bubble* removes letters from their linear positions to dissolve into pixels; in *Balance* the letters in a bulk of the Latin alphabet change their position in the space, with optical letters juxtaposed one over the other; finally, in *Flower* letters dissolve in circular pixel flowers. *Tap.Type.Write*—existing both in screen and print versions—suggests continuity in the evolution of design rather than a radical departure.

The Alphanumeric by American artist, writer and publisher Paul Chan is a work re-indexing the alphabet, attaching words or phrases to each letter, turning any computer keyboard into a text generator. Chan breaks into the language using a conventional text input device such as the keyboard. An alphabet turns into a narrative as in an alphabetical prayer or a song. Every one of Chan's alphabets differs from all others; alphabets are personalized and can be chosen depending on the writer's purpose.

"Una página de Babel," a concrete poem by American computational poet and computer scientist Nick Montfort based on Jorge Luis Borges's "Una biblioteca de Babel" ("The Library of Babel") also uses typewriter tropes. To create a page that is formally like the ones in Borges's library, 80 characters wide, 40 lines long, Montfort chooses a typewriter-like monospace font. The appearance of letters is based on the unigram probabilities of letters in the Borges's story itself, in the Spanish text of "La biblioteca de Babel." Montfort explains in his Postposition Blog:

> So, for instance, the lowercase letter a occurs a bit less than 8.4% of the time, and this is the probability with which it is produced on the page. The same holds for spaces, for the letter ñ, and for all other glyphs; they appear on the page at random, with the same probability that they do in Borges's story. Because each letter is picked independently at random, the result does not bear much relationship to Spanish or any other human language, in which the occurrence of a glyph usually has something to do with the glyph before it (and before that, and so on). (Montfort 2015)

Letters in Maeda's piece, remaining in their familiar and standardized proportions, perform the kinetic tricks impossible within the medium of the typewriter: interactivity, inflation to the full screen size, rotation on the Z axis. The work exhaustingly lists all the possible variations the translation on the screen grants. The QWERTY layout still models the interaction: the typed letter is being transformed, the accustomed sound is reproduced. The letters are visibly composed of either dots or squares, i.e. minimal blocks of visual composition. Thus they transit to the visual digital image of spatial language. Banner's piece also involves studying the keyboard mediated interaction, an act of digital textual production. However, she chooses a postdigital move of altering the hardware. With the title of the piece she introduces the timely perspective of prototypical, premodeled, defined interaction. "Prototype" shows the number of layers included in the keyboard interaction: the textual and the "punctuational." The level of signs framing, pausing and structuring the text produce a gap in logical meaning as they belong to the iconic. Typewriter as a perpetual mechanism for the generation of text is implemented in Chan's *Alternumerics*. Individual alphabets rely on a keyboard as an input medium. The resulting text can be read in two encoding systems: the Latin alphabet that can be reconstructed, Chan's alphabet that occupies the surface. Montfort is thinking of n-grams, probabilistic letter sequences, as the basis for computer language processing. The probability of appearance of one letter after another is the computational QWERTY.

III. A LETTER AS AN IMAGE: LETTERIST UNIVERSE

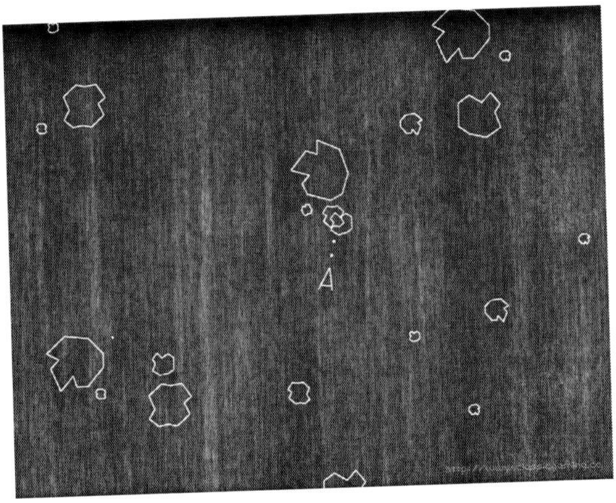

Figure 3: Jim Andrews, *Arteroids* (2003)

As Goodman states, a picture in one system may be a description in another; the particular marks or inscriptions do not dictate the way in which they must be read (Goodman 12). Indeed, the letters are made up of lines and spaces, as images, as architectural plans, they can express iconicity. For instance, it is easy to see a cocktail glass in "Y" or a poked tongue in "P" (Frutinger). The *Letterism Manifesto* (1947) of Isidor Isou, followed Rimbaud's *Voyelles* (1872) in attempting to assemble sensual aspects of the letter. Electronic lettrism is discussed by Canadian scholar de Kerckove as a return to the ancient Logos.

> I refer to the electronic Logos as the place where we find the imitation of the ancient Logos, the magic, creative, productive, diffusive dimension of the divine word which creates things. That we find in the electronic letter. (Kerckove)

De Kerckove imagines that magical things can become materially real in the digital domain. The other aspect of his thought deals with the Internet of things, created by Logos, or the letters for things, utopian letterist universe or Liber Mundi, a book of the world written in the perfect language of things. Supposing the world is a book, consequently, letters are a construction kit of the universe, and, assembled in the right order, will form the cosmos, and otherwise chaos. In this universe objects are represented by letters, or are letters; for instance, constellations are shown as the letters of Greek alphabet in Detanico and Lain's *Falling Stars*. Another example of similarly cosmic scale image to letter/word transformation can be found in *Arteroids* (2003) by Jim Andrew's. The game combines poetry with one of the most popular genres in digital media: the first person shooter. The spaceships and asteroids from the 1979 Atari arcade game are replaced for words and phrases. Words become spaceships that decompose other words into the debris of letters (see Figure 3).

Animation of letters by delegating them the properties of living creatures, or prosopopoeia, is another of the digital letterist strategy. Austrian artist Jörg Piringer builds a 30 minute long catalogue of all the Unicode glyphs 0–65536, one character per frame (2011). They form a sequence based on similarity of form that was calculated by an automatic recognition process. This set of letters is based on the visual properties of the letters, a letter is followed by a letter which can be visually transformed into. By means of contrast, at a similar speed, but at a less grand scale, Oliver Larik's *787 Cliparts* lists images of human beings in different professional roles and historical situations. White males changes race and historical times, alone and with animals, then all the variations of the two, then the second becomes a child, then a woman and so on.

Figure 4: Jörg Piringer, *Unicode* (2011)

The mutation is completed in Austrian artists and designers' Georg Schnitzer and Peter Umgeher's *Clipart Abc* where stretched human figures are arranged in the letterforms.

Figure 5: Oliver Larik, 787 *Clipart* (2010)

Since 1970s and even earlier ASCII art has been developing tools and technologies for iconic and abstract representation following or not the traditions of visual poetry and typewriter art. For example, on April 10, 2015, in St Petersburg, a Russian science artist Dmitry Morozov (::vtol::) launched a hacked a Brother sx-4000 typewriter to make it print ASCII portraits of *Festival 101. Poetics of Digital Technology* visitors. The ASCII characters and empty spaces are used in the work to reflect on light and shade, the image is typed from a digital photo.

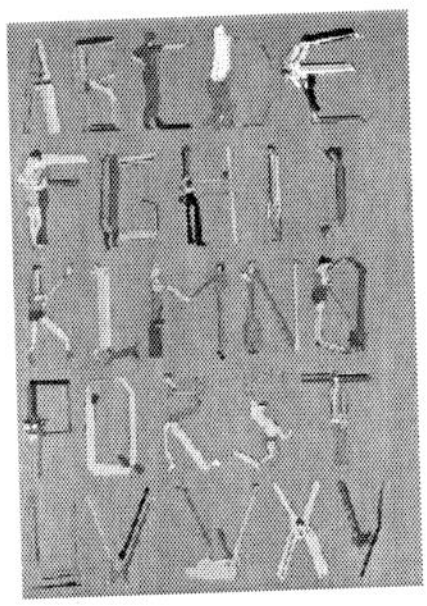

Figure 6: Georg Schnitzer and Peter Umgeher, *Clipart Abc* (2007)

By contrast, Ivan Khimin makes an argument for *asciiticism*, i.e. ascetic, non representative ASCII art. He attributes his style as abstract conceptualism referring to the fact that conceptualism as such is rather concrete. “My works are abstract texts. By analogy with fine art's opposition of figurative and abstract, text deprived of narrative and verbal functions becomes abstract. Graphical symbols removed from the habitual context acquire unexpected visual connections” (Khimin). Asciiticism not simply decontextualizes text, it detextualizes it. It is used as an image and not mimetically, but abstractly. It is fair to note that the abstract, non semantic use of ASCII characters, or in the historical case of *Typestracts* was practiced by a number of concrete poets, including Dom Sylvester Houedard.

Text, according to Khimin, gains abstraction of meaning, and still remains reproducible. At the same time, the resulting image is also abstract.

> If it's possible to speak about abstraction as a refusal from figurative image in fine arts, then it's quite fair to speak about abstract conceptualism as a result of successive refusal of narrative, verbal, grammatical etc. meanings of text in conceptual art. (Khimin)

I suppose by "text" here Khimin means a minimal unit of the text, a glyph. Still the statement seems controversial since the image in digital art can be made up of any set of components, be it cubes, small images, or letters. None of these destroys these materials in their abstract or concrete properties, moreover, the abstractness of the image constituents doesn't give any information about the nature of the image that results from them.

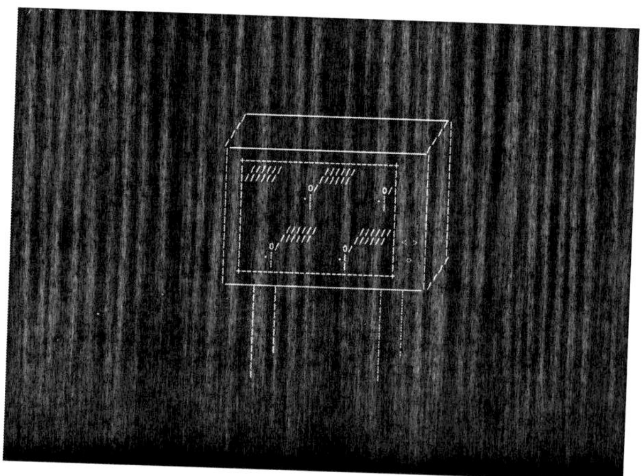

Figure 7: Ivan Khimin, *Asciiticism* (2002)

Digital lettrists are skilled in using either alphabetic characters or punctuation signs as iconic or abstract images. Recycling the existing linguistic signs as an element of visual composition is important in the process of visual writing. The complete annihilation of semantic meaning is neither possible nor desirable. The point is, rather, to activate our sense of the profoundly materialist and the multidimensionality of the reading/ writing process, i.e. to turn letters from the transparent carriers of meaning to objects.

V. LETTER AS A NAME: ALL THE NAMES OF GOD

The abstract permutations of combinations of ASCII characters can be conceptualized within the notion of the names of god. The name is seen as hidden within the familiar combinations of letters, when recomposed they reveal the divine name. Famously, in Arthur Clarke's "Nine Billions of Names of God" (1953), all the nine letter combinations of the devised by Tibetian lamasery monks alphabet once printed out by Mark V should cause the Universe to end as its sole goal of naming them would be reached. When the typewriter finishes to print the last combination the stars begin to slowly go out. Nick Montfort's piece "All the Names of God" (2011) from the Concrete Perl series is a machine (32-character Perl programs) for generating concrete poems. It prints all the one, two, three, four letter combinations. Fortunately, the program crashes before it completes its task, and the world remains in its place at least for now.

```
#### All the names of god
{print"a"x++$...$"x$.,$,=_;redo}
```

Unlike Clark, Dionysius Areopagite in the treatise *The Divine Names* states that human language cannot contain god's name. Moscow conceptualist Dmitry Prigov (1940 -2007) in a cycle *The Name of God* constructs poems as a generation of multitude from singularity, multitude that is completed by unity. Each of the poems amplifies the sacral words: "god", "father", "son", "spirit." Each of these words is treated as an abbreviation, as a combination of multitude of words within one.

GOD
GoOpDe
GorOpeDee
Gorge Open Deep

Next, the words are mutated and transformed back to the initial word "GOD"

GeOnDa
GuOfDo
GyOrDe
GOD
(Пригов, Дмитрий)

Prigov uncovers the inefficiency and insufficiency of the alphabetic characters to communicate the divine meanings. The property they should hope to acquire is multidimensionality. As mentioned above a linguistic sign in the system of given language might have a meaning in the language on a different orthology. Montfort's work performs the exhaustive permutation of the possible combinations of the letters. Prigov and Montfort work with the unknown—a divine name. Montfort takes a computational approach of calculating it alphanumerically. Prigov takes a mystical approach of revealing irrelevance of the surface of the language and see through it instead.

VI. A LETTER AT A TIME: ZORN'S LEMMA BY HOLLIS FRAMPTON

> Letters codify acoustic perceptions, while numbers codify optical perceptions, letters belong to the field of music, while numbers belong to the field of visual art. Thus reading letters is one-dimensional, and reading numbers is two-dimensional. —Vilem Flusser

While both the page and the screen allow for the expression of space, the medium of film introduces the perspective of time. Simultaneous with the viewer's experience of time in the same space is the driving engine of the Space-Length Thought (2013) by the UK artist Rosa Barba (see Figure 8). The piece is composed of a 16 mm projector, 16mm film, text and a typewriter. The machine spells letter by letter the description of the installation space, a script measured by letters. It lasts as long as the installation does. As it is describing the installation space, the pile of film creates a spatial materialisation of this description. Each letter is printed at a unique moment of time and going to be experienced simultaneously with its production. The effect can be described as the procedural aspect of the work.

Figure 8: Rose Barba, *Space-Length Thought* (2013)

The same simultaneity of the viewer's and author's perspectives is at play in the literary clock series by John Cayley. *Epigraphic Clock* is a poem that consists of 365 words. The length of each stanza depends on the number of days in the month to which it corresponds. The piece "spells" time in two-word phrases of month, day, hours, minutes, and seconds. Meanwhile two words in each phrase are highlighted in the text indicating the seconds and change in accordance with the clock. The numerical clock connects the given moment of time with all the previous ones with the same name. This creates the circle of time connecting moments with the same name. The speaking clock gives the illusion of real time passing. The bottom line on the screen spells the unique time phrase for a given moment, the legend on the left translates the letters into numbers. We can refer to this as a database of time instead of a matrix of 12 hours. The infinite time requires infinite set of names. The mechanism of a literary clock is the one of transmedia translation. The poem's text indicates the warmth, the breath of time hidden beneath the cyclical behavior of the clock.

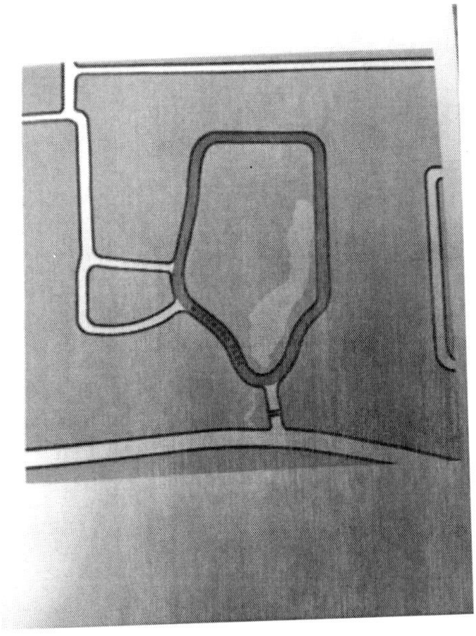

Figure 9: Flavio Trevisan, *Alphabet City: Number* (2013)

Alphabetical order of letters as the order suggestion for the material world is presented in *Zorn's Lemma* by American filmmaker Hollis Frampton (1936-1984). Boris Groys argues the epoch-making achievement of conceptual art was to demonstrate "the equivalence, or at least a parallelism, between language and image, between the order of words and the order of things, the grammar of language and the grammar of visual space" (Groys). For example, Detanico and Lain apply the process of indexation of a set of codes to each letter of the alphabet:, days of the year (*Analemma*). Rather more digitally, Flavio Trevisan's tenth book within his Hex Editions publishing project *Alphabet City: Number* reveals shapes of Arabic numerals within the curves of the map of the Alphabet City.

Zorn's Lemma is a structural film consisting of found images of text from New York City. Frampton had been collecting for seven years images arranged pseudoalphabetically, rather alphanumerically. The film's name originates in mathematical order theory, suggesting that the Latin alphabet is a set and attributing quantitative meaning to a letter: each letter-frame is a second long. In a 1972 interview with Peter Gidal, Frampton calls these "time capsules" (Gidal). The same single second passes in the viewer's time as the second Frampton has cut. This letterist film is equal to its surface, a viewer sees a letter and the meaning of this letter is what the viewer sees. Frampton explains his attitude to time within film by the third part's inclusion of a quote from the 11th century treatise, *On Light, or the Ingression of Forms*, by Robert Grosseteste.

> The key line in the text is a sentence that says, "In the beginning of time, light drew out matter along with itself into a mass as great as the fabric of the world." Which I take to be a really apt description of film, the total historical function of film, not as an art medium, but as a great kind of time capsule. It was thinking about this, which led me to posit the universe as a vast film archive (which contains nothing in itself) with—presumably something in the middle, in the undiscoverable center of this whole matrix of filmthoughts—an unlocative viewing room in which, throughout eternity, sits the Great Presence screening the infinite footage. (Gidal)

Wanda Bershen in an *Artforum* article states that *Zorn's Lemma* is ultimately concerned with a kind of cosmology, this is the theory of the universe as an ordered whole governed by a set of general rules (Bershen). Images compete with words and suddenly you start reading them homogeneously instinctively searching for the alphabetically suitable names for the meat being ground, swinging, talking woman's face, walking man, paged book, man painting the wall, fire and reed. A strong illusion of material world's abidance to the order of letters is forged.

As mentioned above, *Zorn's Lemma* contains three sections. It starts with a female voice reading from *The Bay State Primer*, an early American grammar textbook that teaches the letters of the alphabet by using them in sentences from the Bible. It concludes with a man, a woman and a dog crossing a snowy field, while several narrators each narrate one word at a time read from *On Light, or the Ingression of Forms*. The middle part is giving silent found alphabetical images until a second kind of ordering occurs; letters begin to drop out of the alphabet and they are replaced by a moving image without any text. The first to go is X, replaced by a fire; a little later Z is replaced by waves breaking backwards. Once an image is replaced, it will always have the same substitution; in the slot of X the fire continues for a second each time, the sea roll backwards at the end of each alphabet once the initial substitution occurs.

> The substitution process sets in action a guessing game and a device. Since the letters seem to disappear roughly in inverse proportion to their distribution as initial letters of words in English, viewers can with occasional accuracy guess which letter will drop out next. They can also guess that when the alphabet has been completely replaced, the film or the section will end. A second timing mechanism exists within the substitution images themselves, and it gains force as the alphabetic cycles come to an end. Some of the substitution images imply their own termination. The tying of shoes which replaces P, the washing of hands (G), the changing of a tire (T), and especially the filling of the frame with dried beans (N) add a time dimension essentially different from that of the waves, or a static tree (F), a red ibis flapping its wings (H), or cat-tails swaying in the wind (Y). The clocking mechanism of the finite acts is confirmed by the synchronous drive toward completion which becomes evident in the last minutes of the section. (Adams-Sitney)

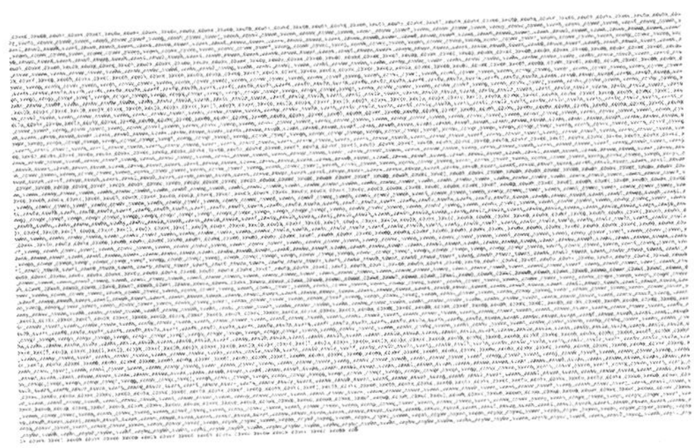

Figure 10: Nick Montfort, *The First M Numbers* (2013)

A more literal digital to verbal translation is done in *The First M Numbers* by Nick Montfort (Figure 10) which references French artist Claude Closky's *The first thousand numbers in alphabetical order* (Figure 11). Montfort's poem is also a program that generates all of the Roman numerals from "I" to "M" and then orders them alphabetically.

```
#!/usr/bin/env python
"""The First M Numbers Classified in Alphabetical Order
Props to Claude Closky, the Romans, and computers.
Happy New Year from Nick Montfort. Have a great MMXIII."""
def romanize(arabic):
"""Return the roman numeral representing n.
Should work for n in (1, 4999)."""
```

```
numerals = [(1000, 'M'), (500, 'D'), (100, 'C'),
(50, 'L'), (10, 'X'), (5, 'V'), (1, 'I')]
smaller = {1000: (100, 'C'), 500: (100, 'C'),
100: (10, 'X'), 50: (10, 'X'), 10: (1, 'I'),
5: (1, 'I')}
roman = ''
for (value, numeral) in numerals:
roman += (arabic / value) * numeral
arabic -= (arabic / value) * value
if value in smaller and arabic >= value - smaller[value][0]:
roman += smaller[value][1] + numeral
arabic -= (value - smaller[value][0])
return roman
nums = []
for i in range(1, 1001):
nums += [romanize(i)]
nums.sort()
print ' '.join(nums)
```

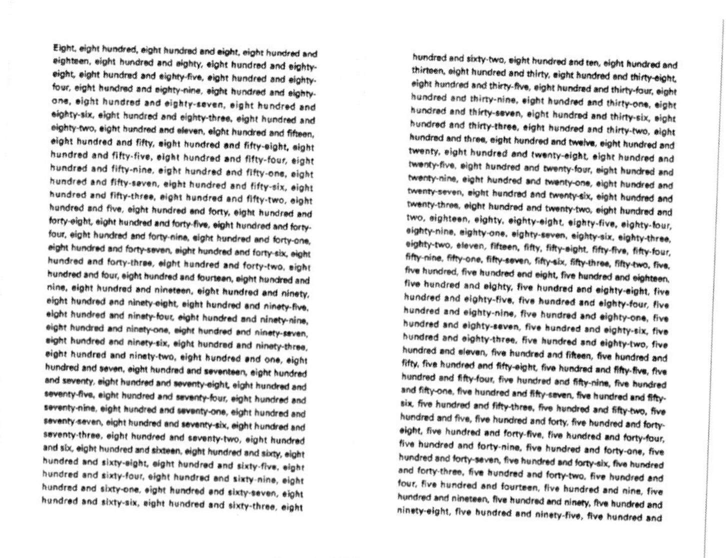

Eight, eight hundred, eight hundred and eight, eight hundred and eighteen, eight hundred and eighty, eight hundred and eighty-eight, eight hundred and eighty-five, eight hundred and eighty-four, eight hundred and eighty-nine, eight hundred and eighty-one, eight hundred and eighty-seven, eight hundred and eighty-six, eight hundred and eighty-three, eight hundred and eighty-two, eight hundred and eleven, eight hundred and fifteen, eight hundred and fifty, eight hundred and fifty-eight, eight hundred and fifty-five, eight hundred and fifty-four, eight hundred and fifty-nine, eight hundred and fifty-one, eight hundred and fifty-seven, eight hundred and fifty-six, eight hundred and fifty-three, eight hundred and fifty-two, eight hundred and five, eight hundred and forty, eight hundred and forty-eight, eight hundred and forty-five, eight hundred and forty-four, eight hundred and forty-nine, eight hundred and forty-one, eight hundred and forty-seven, eight hundred and forty-six, eight hundred and forty-three, eight hundred and forty-two, eight hundred and four, eight hundred and fourteen, eight hundred and nine, eight hundred and nineteen, eight hundred and ninety, eight hundred and ninety-eight, eight hundred and ninety-five, eight hundred and ninety-four, eight hundred and ninety-nine, eight hundred and ninety-one, eight hundred and ninety-seven, eight hundred and ninety-six, eight hundred and ninety-three, eight hundred and ninety-two, eight hundred and one, eight hundred and seven, eight hundred and seventeen, eight hundred and seventy, eight hundred and seventy-eight, eight hundred and seventy-five, eight hundred and seventy-four, eight hundred and seventy-nine, eight hundred and seventy-one, eight hundred and seventy-seven, eight hundred and seventy-six, eight hundred and seventy-three, eight hundred and seventy-two, eight hundred and six, eight hundred and sixteen, eight hundred and sixty, eight hundred and sixty-eight, eight hundred and sixty-five, eight hundred and sixty-four, eight hundred and sixty-nine, eight hundred and sixty-one, eight hundred and sixty-seven, eight hundred and sixty-six, eight hundred and sixty-three, eight

hundred and sixty-two, eight hundred and ten, eight hundred and thirteen, eight hundred and thirty, eight hundred and thirty-eight, eight hundred and thirty-five, eight hundred and thirty-four, eight hundred and thirty-nine, eight hundred and thirty-one, eight hundred and thirty-seven, eight hundred and thirty-six, eight hundred and thirty-three, eight hundred and thirty-two, eight hundred and three, eight hundred and twelve, eight hundred and twenty, eight hundred and twenty-eight, eight hundred and twenty-five, eight hundred and twenty-four, eight hundred and twenty-nine, eight hundred and twenty-one, eight hundred and twenty-seven, eight hundred and twenty-six, eight hundred and twenty-three, eight hundred and twenty-two, eight hundred and two, eighteen, eighty, eighty-eight, eighty-five, eighty-four, eighty-nine, eighty-one, eighty-seven, eighty-six, eighty-three, eighty-two, eleven, fifteen, fifty, fifty-eight, fifty-five, fifty-four, fifty-nine, fifty-one, fifty-seven, fifty-six, fifty-three, fifty-two, five, five hundred, five hundred and eight, five hundred and eighteen, five hundred and eighty, five hundred and eighty-eight, five hundred and eighty-five, five hundred and eighty-four, five hundred and eighty-nine, five hundred and eighty-one, five hundred and eighty-seven, five hundred and eighty-six, five hundred and eighty-three, five hundred and eighty-two, five hundred and eleven, five hundred and fifteen, five hundred and fifty, five hundred and fifty-eight, five hundred and fifty-five, five hundred and fifty-four, five hundred and fifty-nine, five hundred and fifty-one, five hundred and fifty-seven, five hundred and fifty-six, five hundred and fifty-three, five hundred and fifty-two, five hundred and five, five hundred and forty, five hundred and forty-eight, five hundred and forty-five, five hundred and forty-four, five hundred and forty-nine, five hundred and forty-one, five hundred and forty-seven, five hundred and forty-six, five hundred and forty-three, five hundred and forty-two, five hundred and four, five hundred and fourteen, five hundred and nine, five hundred and nineteen, five hundred and ninety, five hundred and ninety-eight, five hundred and ninety-five, five hundred and

Figure 11: Claude Closky's *The first thousand numbers in alphabetical order* (1989)

This translation of Closky questions the structure of the decimal sets of numerals, or rather searches for a new meaning in the alphabetical order. Montfort is seemingly switching between the numerical systems. *The First M Numbers* is a poem and it can be read in a very conventional way: by decoding phonetic symbols from graphemes. It can also be vocalized as a set of numbers. The set of these graphemes has a structure, an external order, which is not foreign to them either—the Roman alphabet. Also, Roman numerals are traditionally used to designate time unit of a year or a century. This poem was Montfort's 2013 New Year's poem, an alternative device for counting time from I to M.

These pieces reinvent the language for counting time. Numerical properties of the sets of letters in the chapter are justified by time space dimension they acquire. The authors attempt to give a different experience to each time of the viewer, think of a time as a database. In *Zorn's Lemma* time space capsules from Manhattan are fixed in the alphabetical order of the film. Alphabetical order and a second is experienced in the same way by the author and the viewer, than the space is also real, it creates another layer of space. *The First M Numbers* as well as *The Epigraphic Clock* aim to rename time. *Space-Length Thought* and *Zorn's Lemma* rename space.

VII. ABC: THE END OF ALPHABET

> The habit of breaking creatures up into abstract component elements and then reassembling them into strange—and usually terrifying—forms has a specific historical origin: it is the product of what he calls "the first age of mechanical reproduction," roughly corresponding to the creation of the first bureaucratic systems of governance in Mesopotamia and Egypt, whose administrative cadres were also responsible for the systematic development of systems of math and writing, and who, generally, specialized in this sort of schematization and rearrangement of aspects of the world. —David Wengrow, *The Origin of the Monster*, 2013

Dmitry Alexandrovich Prigov wrote a series of *ABC*s from 1980 to 2007. He wrote 120 such works, mostly using his typewriter. They date from 1980 to a publication in 2007, with by far the largest number dating to 1985 (over 40 items). The principle involved is rather well known and even traditional: going through the alphabet (in this case the Cyrillic alphabet) and extending each letter to involve words beginning with that letter. "But I was the first to understand the Alphabet as a strict succession of meanings, that all combined present the grandiose drama of being," Prigov writes in *Preduvedomlenie to ABC 9* (Пригов). The dichotomy of the human and outworldly is the constructive principle of these fundamental texts.

Conceptualist seriality and iteration, as well as critique of the media of language is at stake in Prigov's ABC project. Numerology is another property of Prigov's *ABCs* since they are rarely nominated, instead simply numbered or counted. He produced these poems, as well as others, "according to the plan." And the conveyor belt method of producing texts was far from being a mere parody of society's production mechanisms. It was a semiotic survival strategy, the desire to fill metaphorical abyss with ever-more masses of text.

Moscow Romantic conceptualism according to Groys "continued unity of Russian soul" and "mystical experience." Prigov's *Alphabets* can be read as the mediation with the supernatural, and equally as the impossibility of such mediation. Communication of something that by definition cannot be communicated, excommunication (Galloway 11).

ABC 6

Preduvedomlenie: Isomorphism of the hierarchical rows of the universe allows to connect them in one space, using as the language of one of them (or a third one) as a descriptive language for another, opening up unexpected moments of the prepared harmony of this world.

Aleph ais aimportant aper
Btiger bis bterrible bpredator
Cwhale cis cgiant cmonster
Delephant dis dgreat dcarcass
Erhinoseur elooks eterrible
Fbuffullo fights ferrociously
Geagle gflies ghigh
Ibug, Iaphis, Ilouse,
I am less than a louse
(Пригов)

The language itself becomes "haunted media" (Thacker 13) since the communication is happening between the two ontological orders (natural-supernatural, earthly-divine, life-afterlife). In this case the phonetical and lexical orders are clashed to shape linguistic monsters of the excommunication with the divine. "God" is the name of the ode by Gavrila Romanovich Derzhavin, the most important poet before Pushkin; Prigov is alluding to in the last line of *ABC 6*. It is generates a mediation with the otherworldly. When the connection with the otherworldly is broken, a composite linguistic monster appears. Such haunted language is inadequate for the description of the divine creatures; they hardly abide the alphabetical order.

In *Preduvedomlenie or Introduction to The End of ABC* Prigov writes:

> Everything wants to go beyond its limits obtain all encompassing power and eternity, and the ABC is not an exception from this, letters try to shake the niches of their ontological placement, but alas to no avail. However, with the intersecting waves of resonance they create a new reality that composes into a phantom body above the solid surface of dense alphabet. (Пригов)

As if to illustrate this desire to go beyond the phonographic principle, Prigov uses letters in *The End of ABC* that are single cyrillic alphabet letters ended individually: the end of letters А, Б, В, Г, Д, Е, Ж, З, И, О, П, У, Ы, Э, Ю. However, the combination of letters, nominated as an individual letter, also find their ends in this text: the end of letter ТСР, НМЛК, ЦХФА, ЦШЩ. The text forms language soundscapes that are illegible semantically, only legible phonosemantically and structurally. They are negative shapes of the alphabet, "weird media," negatively mediating between the two ontological orders (Thacker 133).

"Конец всего," the last line of the last text of the *ABC* series, means "the end of everything." *The End of ABC* was published in 2007, the year of Prigov's death. It makes *The End of ABC* one of his last texts. Presumably, after the end is the beginning of the outworldly, the immaterial communication. The "End of ABC" is decaying language that is not equal to itself, dark media for broken communication.

VIII. CONCLUSION

Letters were invented in the first age of mechanical reproduction and were used by the first bureaucracies to schematize material reality. The linear system of writing is also responsible for the breaking of the cyclical time paradigm and introduction of historical time. It is also responsible for the idea of breaking creatures up into abstract component elements and then recombining them into often horrifying forms. As a minimal unit of a language, a letter belongs to the visual and phonetic. Letters can be freely permutating and keeping these two functions.

The essay reveals two attitudes to the sets of letters: a database approach and a keyboard approach (*Alternumerics*, *Una página de Babel*, "All the Names of God," *The End of Alphabet*, *Tap.Type.Write*). The database has a vast number of units demonstrated only once (*Unicode*, *Zorn's Lemma*, *Speaking Clock*), while a keyboard has a limited number of units but is obtaining the variety through permutation. The border between the two is transferable: *Una página de Babel*, is a page from a practically endless library labyrinth. Some of the keyboard systems such as the *Alternumeric* form the next level of metasystems. Generally it could be concluded that the database systems are more concerned with time, while the keyboard systems are more involved in spatial exploration.

The typewriter as well as other text processing machines such as the camera and the computer add the complexities of the materialities of their surfaces. They also allow for a new mechanics of time: counting time in letters. The digital literary clocks question the rotation of the earth around Sun as a universal measure of time. The uniqueness of the measurement of time at every moment and every space is developed into a database principle. Literary clocks work on the basis of generation of content as an attempt to create an exhaustive collection of current moments.

The number of layers allow us to see one system of writing as a reference to another system. Numerically referenced glyphs include visual perceptions. Space emptied of semantic and morphological meaning is also a space for a pause, a space for a punctuation sign. The property these spacees hope to acquire is multidimensionality, turning letters from transparent carriers of meaning to objects. The letter learns to be a separate carrier of meaning, and the process of assembling and reassembling letters becomes the meaning of the work.

WORKS CITED

Adams-Sitney, P. *Visionary Film: The American Avant-garde*, 1943-200. New York. Oxford University Press, 2002.

Banner, Fiona. *Prototype*. Pesonal website, http://www.fionabanner.com/works/prototype/index.htm?i53. Accessed 20 June 2016.

Barba, Rosa. "Time as Perspective." 2012. Intertitles

Bergson, Henri. *Creative Evolution*. Trans. Arthur Mitchell. New York, 1911.

Bershen, Wanda. "Zorn's Lemma." *Artforum* September: 41, 1971.

Cayley, John. "Literal Art." *Electronic Book Review*. http://www. electronicbookreview.com/thread/firstperson/ programmatology. 2004. Accessed 20 June 2016.

Closky, Claude. *Les 1000 premiers nombres classes par ordre alphabetique*. Accessed 20 June 2016.

Clark, Arthur C. "Nine Billions of Names of God." *The Best Short Stories of Arthur C. Clarke*. New York: Harcourt, Brace&World, 1973. 235-240.

Derrida, Jacques. *Of Grammatology*. Translated by Gayatri Chakravorty Spivak. Johns Hopkins University Press. Baltimore, 1976.

Detanico, A and Lain, Rafael. 2001-2015. Last accessed 20 June 2016 http://www.detanicolain.com.

Fitterman, Robert. *Holocaust Museum*. Denver: Counterpath Press, 2013.

Flores, Leonardo. "Letterisme." *I Love E-Poetry*. 2012. Accessed 20 June 2016. http://iloveepoetry.com/?cat=287.

Flusser, V. *Does Writing Have a Future?* Translated by Nancy Ann Roth. (Minneapolis: University of Minnesota Press, 2011).

Frampton, Hollis. *Zorn's Lemma*. 1970. Last accessed 20 June 2016. http://www.fulltv.tv/movies/zorn-s-lemma.html.

Frutinger, Adrian. *Signs and Symbols: Their Design and Meaning*. New York: Van Nostrand Reinhold, 1989.

Funkhouser, Christopher, T. P*rehistoric Digital Poetry. An Archaeology of Forms, 1959–1995*. Tusclaoosa: University of Alabama Press, 2007.

Galloway, A.R."Love of the Middle." *Excommunication. Three Inquiries in Media and Mediation*. In Galloway, A.R., Thucker, E, Wark, M. Chicago and London: Chicago University Press, 2012.

Goodman, Nelson. *The Languages of Art: an Approach to the Theory of Symbol*. Indianapolis:Hackett, 1988.

Groys, B. "Introduction: Global Conceptualism Revisited." *e-flux*. Accessed 20 June 2016.http://www.e-flux.com/journal/introduction-global-conceptualism-revisited/.

Holten, Katie. *Translating Borges into Trees: An Interview with Book Artist Katie Holten*. Interview by Katrine Øgaard Jensen. 20 June 2016 http://www.asymp-totejournal.com/blog/2015/08/20/translating-borges-and-radiohead-into-trees-an-interview-with-book-artist-katie-holten/.

Kerckhove de, Derrick, interview by Emanuele Patti. 2012. "From letter to electronic lettrist." *International Journal of McLuhan Studies*. 28 Jan 2012. Accessed 20 June 2016. http://www.mcluhanstudies.com/index.php option=com_content &view=article&id=482:ddkinerview&catid=109:interviews&Itemid=573.

Khimin, Ivan. *ASCIITICISM*. 2002. 20 June 2016. http://asciiticism.org

_,_. *ASCII32*. 2003. Author's archive.

_,_. *Strokes and Incisions*. Curated by Gleb Ershov. Nauvicula Artis, St Petersburg, 2012. Exhibition documentation by Vladimir Micheilutz. Accessed 20 June 2016 http://photoshare.ru/album351565-2.html.

Kittler, Friedrich. "Perspective and the Book." *Grey Room*. 5: 40, 2001.

Larik,Oliver. *787 Cliparts*. 2010. Accessed 20 June 2016. http://oliverlaric.com/2000cliparts.htm.

Maeda, John. *Reactive books*. 1999. Accessed 20 June 2016. http://www.maedastudio.com/2004/rbooks2k/index.php?this=reactive_books.

_,_. *Tap.Type.Write*.1998.

McLuhan, Marshall and Harley Parker. "Through the vanishing point: Space in poetry and painting." *World perspectives*. Vol. 37. New York: Harper & Row, 1968.
Montfort, Nick. Personal website. Accessed 20 June 2016. http://www.nickm.com.
_,_. *Post Position*. Personal blog. Accessed 20 June 2016. http://nickm.com/post.
_,_. Response to Literal Art. Electronic Book Review, 2004. Accessed 20 June 2016. http://www.electronicbookreview.com/thread/firstperson/swoosh
_,_. 2014. *#!*.Denver: Counterpath.
Morozov, Dmitry. *I/O*. Personal website. Accessed 20 June 2016. http://vtol.cc/filter/works/i-o
Piringer, Jorg. *Unicode*. 2011. Accessed 20 June 2016. http://vimeo.com/36132600
_,_. *abcdefghijklmnopqrstuvwxyz*. 2010. Accessed 20 June 2016. http://m.youtube.com/watch?v=PycAnT8-F5c.
Prigov, Dmitry, Antipin, Alex, and Fedorova, Natalia. *The End of Alphabet*. 2014. Accessed 20 June 2016. http://languageartist.me/about/
Schnitzer, Georg and Umgeher, Peter. *Clipart Abc*. 2007. Accessed 20 June 2016. http://sheriff.at.
Simpson, Nicola, ed. "Notes from the Cosmic Typewriter. The Life and Work of Dom Sylvester Houedard." *Occasional Papers*. 2013.
Simanowski, Roberto. "Reading Digital Literature. A Subject Between Media and Methods." *Reading Moving Letters. Digital Literature in Research and Teaching. A Handbook*. Eds. Peter Gendolla, Jörgen Schäfer, and Roberto Simanowski. Bielefeld: transcript, 2010. 15–28.
Trevisan, Flavio. *Alphabet City: Numbers*. Toronto: Hex Edition, 2013.
Turkle, Sherry. "Video Games and Computer Holding Power." *The New Media Reader*. Eds N.Wardrip-Fruin and Nick Montfort. Cambridge, Massachusetts, MIT Press, 2003, 499 -513.
Wengrow, David. *The Origins of the Monster. Image and Cognition in the First Age of Mechanical Reproduction*. Princeton, NJ: Princeton University Press, 2013.
Yoon, Jeannie Meejin. *Absence*. New York: Printed Matter/Whitney Museum, 2003
Пригов, Д.А. 2007. Personal website. http://www.prigov.ru/bukva/azbuka01.php. Accessed 20 June 2016.
_,_. *Собрание стихов*. т. 3. Weiner Slawistischer Almanach. 1999 [1977]).
_,_. (2003) *Книга книг*. Москва: Зебра Е, Эксмо.

II. DIGITAL WRITING PRACTICE: PRACTITIONERS

Generative Activity in Art and Literature

BY KATE ARMSTRONG

My *research centers* on the creation of narrative forms that use dynamic information sources as part of their material structure. These narratives, which have taken a variety of forms including telephone menu systems, generative online video software, printed books, location-based software delivered through public Wi-Fi networks, and custom algorithms, are ongoing and perpetual, and work with text in a fragmentary, non-linear way.

In this essay I will discuss some of these works, including *Grafik Dynamo* (2005), a net art work that loads dynamic images from the internet into a live action comic strip; *Path: A Generative Bookwork in 12 Volumes* (2008), a 12 volume text generated by the physical movement of an anonymous individual living in the city of Montreal between 2005- 2007; *Space Video* (2012), a generative system that mixes an original non-linear narrative on the subject of disparate cultural and scientific phenomena including guided meditation, undersea and outer space exploration by NASA, motivational speaking, PowerPoint backgrounds, science fiction, psychedelic drug culture, and guided meditation with YouTube videos on these subjects as they are uploaded in real time; and *Medium* (2011), a print book which revisits Marshall McLuhan and Quentin Fiore's 1967 book *The Medium is the Massage* by algorithmically matching images from the original book with compositionally similar images from the internet.

The goal of this research is to investigate the function of dynamic activity in literary or text-based systems and to test different ways to implement recombination as a compositional strategy in literary networked art. This is done in order to produce knowledge about how the artistic use of technology can create new literary forms.

For the purposes of this chapter I will outline three different ways in which I have experimented with dynamic activity as a material element in text-based artworks, and connect these methods with some of the works I have made in the process of exploring them.

1. One strategy has been to build narrative works online that have, as an integral part, a dynamic feed.
2. Another has been to connect the real-world activity of human movement to a text work so that the physical movement of a person or a group of people introduces a dynamic recombination of the text.

3. The third has been to work on the level of the network to create a text responsively and in partnership with networked algorithmic processes that source images from the mass of collectively created information that resides online and can be found in a search engine.

I. DYNAMIC FEEDS

In my work, I make narrative forms that use dynamic information sources as part of their material structure. By material structure, I mean that the works are designed, as written forms, to pull in information from another source that does not originate with me but that reflects another aspect of life, data or activity, and that these information sources are integral to the concept and function of the work.

For example, *Grafik Dynamo* (2005) loads live images from the internet into a live action comic strip.[70] The work takes the form of three panels, which display three different images that are perpetually reloaded. Inside the panels are speech and thought bubbles as well as explanatory text boxes that reload in an ongoing way with fragments of an original narrative that references mid-century comic books and spy novels.

From the time of its launch in 2005 to the end of 2008, the work used a live feed from social networking site LiveJournal. The work is still running and is currently using a feed from Flickr. Animating the comic strip using dynamic web content opens up the genre in a new way: Together, the images and narrative create a dislocated notion of sense and expectation in the reader, as they are sometimes at odds with each other, sometimes perfectly in sync, and always moving and changing. The work takes an experimental approach to open ended narrative, positing a hybrid between the flow of data animating the work and the formal parameter that comprises its structure.

Because the images that flow into *Grafik Dynamo* are live, there is an aspect to the work that is temporal. The outside world, and whatever is happening in it that is being captured by photographs taken by a random, self-selecting group of people, becomes part of the work. As a result, *Grafik Dynamo* has a different feel to it on Valentine's Day than it does at Christmas, and was different in 2005 than it is in 2015. Images bubble into and out of the work, causing thematic changes that blend with or push against the meaning of the texts. I think of this aspect of liveness and the role that this dynamic information plays inside the work as a kind of subject matter, because content, context, history, meaning and accident flow into the work through the participation and ongoing activities of people through this live feed. The aspects of life

70 *Grafik Dynamo* is a collaboration with Michael Tippett that was commissioned by New Radio and Performing Arts, Inc. for Turbulence.org with funds from the Andy Warhol Foundation.

that are reflected in the work through the inclusion of images from photo sharing sites become not only part of the work itself, but also can be adjusted in order to shape the conceptual framework of the piece.

Grafik Dynamo

We are tired of stunts!
My next impression was of coldness: I was witnessing the triumph of madmen.
The culture has a history of brutality.
Beware the essential!
Suddenly, from the control room…
No one remembers Villanova here.
Go! Wait for me at the frontier!
After eating the sandwiches the dog began to pant heavily and to glow from within.
Evangelical students clogged the crosstown arterial.

After *Grafik Dynamo* I began to think about how this could be developed further, in order to explore the outside subject as not only a dynamic element but as a literary element. By literary element I mean an element that is inherently constitutive of the work. And further, that there is something to note about this element being both literary (and constitutive of the work) and visual or data-driven (as opposed to prior forms of literary elements including plot, theme, or tone). For example, that a stream of images marked "city" can be brought into a literary work that is engaged with the subject of the city, and that by doing this, another layer of meaning about the city can enter the world of the text, informing it and being informed by it.

I began to work in a more mindful way with the origin of the images that were entering my texts in this way so I began to experiment with keywords. The idea became to write a text in which keywords would parse the imagery that flowed into the work. *Why Some Dolls Are Bad* (2007) was an experiment using this idea. The work, which addresses ethics, fashion, artifice, and the self, was parsed with a list of terms "city, tunic, fashion, doll" and was written "with and against" these words in terms of the text itself, which became a construction of associative references, materials and ideas including Venus Flytraps (Dionaea muscipula), Perspex cabinetry, Vogue Magazine, Jenny Churchill, and Henri Bergson.

One observation I can make having used this approach has been that keywords—here defined technically as words that have been given specific meaning within the computer program that is parsing the images by subject matter, and rarely considered in the frame of programming to possess a literary aspect—can nonetheless function well in the context of the associative, fragmented text, and can be viewed as another form of writing that both defines and actively creates layers of meaning within the written work.

Why Some Dolls Are Bad

Why are people so amazed by what I do?
I'd stolen the painkillers from the charity where I'd been working.
I have experienced the pleasures of work outside the home.
Gosh, that's a real smart trick!
Rebellion for me is trying to be honest about what I see.
But, we share a brother, perhaps more!
Soon the dress will be broken into useful squares.
Can it be stifled by a depraved revolt?
The fabric had been knit from stainless steel and paper.
The Fall collection was inspired by discord.
The contagion of this idea left everyone in awe.
The jury had hoped for consensus, but they'd gotten appetite.
She looked forward to her wedding, and to the effortless short dresses that were bound to follow.

My work arises in part from the context of electronic literature and in part from media arts. I see media arts as a deeply hybrid field that engages a huge array of investigative and disciplinary modes including locative narrative, text-based installation, conceptual art, video, and photography. But most crucially I think of generative art and the associated tenets and principles of generative activity as applied to art practice that are elucidated by Philip Galanter and others.

> Generative art refers to any art practice where the artist uses a system, such as a set of natural language rules, a computer program, a machine, or other procedural invention, which is set into motion with some degree of autonomy contributing to or resulting in a completed work of art. (Galanter)

Following this, I see generative art as art in which the artist creates a process such as a set of rules, and then the process is let to "run." As opposed to the idea of the artist creating a finished work, in generative art the artist creates the rules that cause the work to be created. In the context my own practice I see the process of creating a set of rules as being an inherently literary activity. I begin with a process of thinking through and testing what the framework must be in order to create the kinds of variables I am looking for.

With the idea of perpetual and fragmentary compositional strategies, the work is written in interoperable pieces, pieces that are designed to interoperate perpetually so as to always be a source of new meaning, whether new meaning is conceived as something emerging from the shifting text combinations or as something emerging from the ongoing juxtaposition of image and text (or both).

I've chosen to work with fragmentary recombination as a method because it allows me to integrate text with the functioning of a system and to have the text be deployed into new combinations driven by the activity of the system. But it also allows me the ability to form the tone and tenor of the text and to retain some control over the writing. For example, a system that would randomize at the level of the word (rather than the level of the short fragment), would create a different effect. I am less interested in this kind of linguistic deployment and more interested in finding the point where a text can retain its style while also being dynamically driven.

In my work I aim for a situation in which the ideas themselves bear a formal relationship to the technology and context in which they take place. Perhaps in the same way that electronic literature practitioners consider the "born digital" aspect of their works to be key, with the digital context being integral to the form of the writing, I don't see how my written projects could take any form other than they form they have taken. Which is to say that my goal is to work in a blended way with form and subject, working through technology to realize forms that invite new combinations of ideas and meaning.

An example: *Pattern Language*, by being situated in physical space and composed by the individual movements of people in the city, becomes on the level of the subject a text that is about behavioral, social, cultural, geographical, visual patterns, so that the text is informed by the conceptual engagement on the formal level of the network. *Space Video* as a work is "about" the shared aesthetic sensibilities of the collective imagination, as evidenced by videos uploaded to YouTube and tagged with a shared (but disparate) set of keywords. A third example: By publishing the printed "path" of a specific individual, the form of *Path* is a direct translation of movement that both exposes and codifies or elides the path of movement that was the direct technical and operational input that caused the text to take that form.

So it is a manner of writing "with" and "through" the network, which in my view also means changing the conversation about interactivity. For me some of the commonly held or at least historically foundational precepts about interactivity in fiction have become boring: That a reader would like to choose the direction of a piece; that a journey is created for the reader when navigating through a multimodal, multimedia piece that possesses many layers. I am thinking now that this has come to be a chore and that many times these principles result in an un-designed, densely packed forest of text and image that is rarely fully experienced or appreciated by anyone other than the author. In response to this I have always chosen to recast the role of interactivity so that it happens on a different level. To use a feed of information (data or movement) as the dynamic aspect that is brought into a text allows the text to engage with outside information and the broader participation of people without forcing the reader to be the primary source of this activity.

In my work this is often happening on the level of the image, where the written (though recombinant) forms are the stable element designed in each work to be deployed in response to ideas, materials, outcomes that come into the project through the work of others (e.g. Flickr feeds, YouTube videos, or the mass of documents on the internet that can be accessed through Google Image Search).

From works like *Grafik Dynamo* I can observe that shifting the interactive burden away from the reader is actually what allows the reader to become actively engaged in terms of forming meaning - working across the different frames and different inputs to form a narrative that is mental; active in a similar way as reading any text would be. And opening the "active" portion of a piece to different configurations of participants (not just the reader, but all of YouTube, or everyone tagging photos in Flickr with the word "city") so that the participation can become not only active but a conceptual part of what is happening in the work. Shifting away from the need for an individual to laboriously click through something actually creates space for form. What a feed is, where it comes from, who is making it, when and why, becomes a formal piece of the structure that has its own meaning, behaviour, history, cultural position, and context, and this works within and against the other written elements.

One of the open questions for me is, from within this frame of generative art as a context for this kind of practice, how can generative text further evolve to where the rules and the outcomes can be further integrated to create a specific aesthetic or set of values. Looking comparatively at generative practices within the sonic and purely visual arts for example, I wonder how we can move ahead to frame out the "book" as a platform and tool, the "book" as instrument, the "book" as field, feedback or loop. I have gotten only a short way to achieving what I think is possible in this area, characterizing these works as in some sense "book-machines," which run forever, always fresh but also stable, and that engage with the outside world inside of a fiction, or a fiction inside the world, and that allow me to engage others in making a world that is also my own.

II. REAL WORLD ACTIVITY

In 2008 I became interested in feeds (Armstrong 2007). At that time the software landscape was shifting into a broader experimentation of what it could mean to stream information through a feed into a totally alterable and contingent interface. Since that time the influence of the feed as a concept and metaphor (and also as a technology) has only grown. We as a culture often express ourselves in terms of updates: we post updates on Facebook; we follow people's feeds on Twitter. These are perpetual, ongoing modes that lie together across time but are also formed of short, interoperable segments. This is a technological structure that is also a mode of experience that becomes psychological. By now, we understand ourselves in terms of representational, actual, technological, social feeds: Following or producing a feed not only comes to create a concept of the individual but to restructure or normalize the role of the feed, and the stream of information that emanates from an individual is both documentary and surveillance oriented, as well as creative and fictive.

To me this forms linkages between data and the individual, and between technological, mental and physical experience. In this vein I began to experiment with dynamic activity to connect the real world activity of human movement to a literary project so that the movement of people introduces a dynamic recombination of the text. With *Pattern Language*, a narrative[71]—also written in fragmentary, interoperable texts—was attached to the login of the free public Wi-Fi network in the City of Montreal.[72] Each time a person would log in to the Wi-Fi, they would receive a textual passage exploring themes of visual, personal and spatial patterns as reflected in the lives of fictional characters. These fragments were location-specific so that different texts would be triggered at different geographical points in the city. These fragments accumulated over time, being stored in the accounts of the individual using the network, so that every individual would have a different iteration of the "book" that depended on the geographic pattern of their Wi-Fi usage.

This platform operated for two years. Following the end of that project I built on these ideas with *Path: a Generative Bookwork in 12 Volumes*, which took the text

71 I'll discuss *Pattern Language* (2005-2007) in this context, though the first significant work of mine that explored this was *PING* (2003).

72 This project took place in the context of the Mobile Digital Commons Network (MDCN) and was built on the Ile Sans Fils (ISF) Wi-Fi platform, which was the first free city-wide Wi-Fi system in Montreal.

that had been generated by one individual through their use of the *Pattern Language* platform and published it as a print work, which resulted in twelve 600 page volumes. Accumulating over time, I see these behavioral and technological points of contact as having come to form a fabric of language that both reveals and conceals the pattern of a life lived in the city and that offers another mode of translation between movement and text.

Pattern Language

Café Supreme
8. She thought of the city's underground, ridged concrete geometry and tile in forty year old patterns.

Café Tribune
25. To describe this it would be necessary to show many other things.

Cluny's Art Bar
39. He needed to start something controversial.

III. WORKING WITH THE NETWORK

The third way I've explored dynamic activity has been to work on the level of the network to create a text responsively and in partnership with networked algorithmic processes that source images from the mass of collectively created information that resides online and can be found in a search engine.

In 2011 I published *Medium*, a print book which revisits Marshall McLuhan and Quentin Fiore's 1967 book *The Medium is the Massage.*[73] I flattened the original book and matched it with compositionally similar images from the internet. Each page was matched multiple times, keeping the pages in order, so that the new version of the book is three times the size of the original and is comprised of loose, impressionistic human or corporate documents like PowerPoint graphs or photographs of refrigerators.

This is the most recent thread of investigation and underpins my continued interest in internet aesthetics, and my wish to delve deeper into processes of production that involve the internet as a repository of images and that look to address the network and conditions of networked culture. It is also another mode that for me seeks to expand thought around what "interactivity" should or can look like, and to broaden interactions with the network to include processes that are mindfully blasting open

73 Originally commissioned for Medium_Massage 2.0, a YZO production curated by Michael Alstad.

architectures that lie between page and screen, or that problematize or explore world interfaces.

Another example of this is *Space Video* (2012), which is an online project that addresses ideas of exploration in relation to inner and outer space.[74] Having noticed that there are shared aesthetic qualities of video imagery that accompany disparate cultural and scientific phenomena including guided meditation, hypnosis, undersea and space exploration by NASA, motivational speaking, PowerPoint backgrounds, science fiction, psychedelic drug culture, electronic music, popular spirituality, and computer effects, I built a generative system that mixes an original non-linear narrative with YouTube videos on these subjects as they are uploaded in real time. These videos often attempt to portray what are ultimately non-visual spaces, producing images that are at once placeholders, images of the transcendental, trippy intergalactic stereotypes, and fields for persuasion. The videos are interspersed with text fragments that explore and blend these themes.

Space Video

We can teach you to solve your problems in whatever
You have got to be able to pick up this device right here and talk to strangers
Baby animals are the young offspring of grown up animals
As we speak people everywhere are erecting piles of stones along the coastline
Soon you will see shapes emerging from the International Klein Blue
Witness my civilization
I channel power to the paramecia that glow and support me

Space Video is in some ways similar to *Grafik Dynamo* and *Why Some Dolls are Bad* in the sense that dynamic information enters an online space as a living thread. But in *Space Video*, there is an additional aspect which bears a relationship with the third principle as well, which is to say that the form of engagement that the work has with the online material is database oriented, and that the inquiry itself, on the level of subject matter, engages with the idea of what commonly held or collective impressions are about a set of subjects (meditation, self-help, hypnosis, science fiction). The work engages on the level of collectivity and the social in terms of asking what the shared aesthetic values are in culture across these phenomena or effects. So there is a tie here with *Medium* and the process of "writing with and against" the network as well

74 *Space Video* is a collaboration with Michael Tippett commissioned by New Radio and Performing Arts, Inc. for Turbulence.org with funds from the National Endowment for the Arts.

as an aspect of working in "partnership" with the algorithms to examine the effects of broadly held ideas as expressed in and through the network, whether or not these are ultimately sensical.

Going forward I see fascinating opportunities for working with dynamic and generative narrative in the framework of the changing internet, including the internet of things. With the number of networked objects and devices projected to jump from 1.9 billion to 9 billion by 2018 , the amount of data is exploding and the kind of data continues to evolve into new frames, which for me continue to collide with literary possibilities (Hoelzel and Ballve, 2015). The amount and the kind of data affects how we use it and therefore what we use it for. The importance of "voice" in software is one avenue that introduces further possibilities for development in the context of the written and literary form. But it is also a matter of the boundless possibilities for recombinant literary strategies in a world where things can combine with other things in ways that were previously impossible. What avenues for stylistic experimentation, expression, and literary forms emerge when humans can not only communicate with each other in new ways but can enter a web of expressive communication with their data and their objects? What literary possibilities are introduced when toasters and refrigerators begin to speak to each other? The modes of these intersections are numeric and code-based but they are also linguistic and will ultimately become philosophical particularly as the interfaces, influences and balances change. It is the current norm to frame these questions in the context of Human Computer Interaction (HCI) but I think this will turn out to be a shallow reading: interfaces between machines and humans have always taken place within a culture that is engaged with text and literature. To conceive contexts that involve technology without paying attention to style and function on the level of text and literature will be a missed opportunity.

WORKS CITED

Armstrong, Kate. "RSS Poetics: Feeds and Streams." *The Capilano Review*. 2007

Galanter, Philip. "What is Generative Art? Complexity Theory as a Context for Art Theory." http://www.philipgalanter.com/downloads/ga2003_paper.pdf

Hoelzel, Mark and Marcelo Ballve. "The Programmatic-Advertising Report: Mobile, video, and real-time bidding drive growth in programmatic." *BI Intelligence*. March 26, 2015.

Between Page and Screen

BY AMARANTH BORSUK

Between Page and Screen is a book of augmented-reality poetry. In the tradition of Dieter Roth's minimalist artist's books, Emmett Williams' mid-twentieth century concrete poems, and Camille Utterback's interactive textworks, it merges the book art and e-poetry traditions, trespassing the boundary between print and digital, old and new media. This paper discusses the book's investigation of the place of books at a time when we are reading more and more on screen, and the ways it uses the self-reflexivity of the artist's book form to address the materiality of reading.

I. "BE MY APPORT": OPENING A SPACE

As a poet and scholar, my work has always paired a critical interest in how poems make meaning with the creative endeavor of writing them. I read critically to write better, and I write creatively in order to be a better critic. I have found that my own work at the intersection of print and digital media has helped me think through questions of the present moment in book culture and provides me with a starting point for critical inquiry into the nature of the object we know as "the book" that is continually evolving. *Between Page and Screen* (Siglio Press, 2012; Spring Gun Press, 2016), an artists' book created in collaboration with Brad Bouse, arose from a curiosity about the way the changing nature of text's material form inflects our reading practices. Risking its own technological obsolescence, the book uses marker-based augmented reality (AR) to open a spectral space in which to consider materiality. As we enter an age of differential[75] reading in which the same text may be offered to us simultaneously in multiple shapes (from print book, to website, to ePUB, to app), our attentiveness to the structure in which it is delivered becomes ever more important to understanding the nature of reading and writing.

In conceptualizing the book,[76] I was deeply influenced by N. Katherine Hayles' suggestion that scholars of electronic literature have much to learn from those in print history, who have long known that "literature was never only words, never merely

75 A term I borrow from Marjorie Perloff, who has written extensively on 21st century writing practices in which a text exists simultaneously "in different material forms, with no single version being the definitive one" (Perloff, "Screening the Page/Paging the Screen: Digital Poetics and the Differential Text," 146).

76 While completing my Ph.D. at the University of Southern California, where my research focused on the influence of writing technologies on modernist poets' reconfigurations of authorship. Bouse and I created the prototype as the outcome of a graduate-led seminar I co-organized with Genevieve Kaplan on the relationship between chapbooks and artists' books.

immaterial verbal constructions. Literary texts, like us, have bodies, an actuality necessitating that their materialities and meanings are deeply interwoven into each other" (Hayles, *Writing Machines*, 107).[77] As many bemoan the death of the book, Bouse and I wanted to interrogate its changing role and definition and to think through the presumed ephemerality of print. Given the unique affordances of each medium and the history of concurrence of reading forms (even after the emergence of the codex around 150 AD, scrolls lingered into the seventh century and waxed tablet polyptychs persisted into the seventeenth), why must we give over one reading technology for the other? If print and digital already seem a false binary from which to begin, page and screen, acting as their apports, might make space for a consideration of other structuring pairs that continue to hold sway on the public imagination, including author and reader, public and private, language and image. *Between Page and Screen* utilizes the self-reflexivity of artist's book form along with the affordances of augmented reality to address the embodied and dialogic nature of reading. Through the book itself and a number of paratexts, we have endeavored to create opportunities for readers to hold language in their hands and see and feel the often-overlooked relationship between books and bodies.

II. "ARRAS TO ARIAS": WEAVING METAPHOR

As reading experiences technological shifts, an understanding of "the book" must, as Hayles suggests, recognize it as a "material metaphor [...] an artifact whose physical properties and historical usages structure our interactions with it" (Hayles, *Writing Machines*, 23). For this reason, artists' books have proven fertile ground for considering the nature of what scholar Jessica Pressman has referred to as "bookishness," since they traffic in the tenor and vehicle of that "metaphor" (Pressman, "Aesthetic of Bookishness," 465). In Johanna Drucker's formulation, the artist's book "integrates the formal means of its realization and production with its thematic or aesthetic issues" (Drucker, *The Century of Artists' Books*, 2). In other words, an artist makes a book because no other medium would allow her to address the same constellation of concerns. By creating a dialogue between its form and content, the artist's book functions as what Hayles calls a "technotext," a work that "interrogates the inscription technology that produces it [and] mobilizes reflexive loops between its imaginative world and [...] material apparatus" (Hayles, *Writing Machines*, 25). The technotext, by drawing attention to ma-

77 Published in 2002, Hayles' MIT Mediaworks Pamphlet, a print book whose design simulates both fore-edge printing and hypertextual linking, continues to influence my thinking about mediation and signification and the relationship between print and digital—a sign, perhaps, that obsolescence marches more slowly than we imagine.

teriality, reminds us that literature can never be read separately from the form of its reception.

If we accept that we cannot separate meaning from materiality then we begin to see the book as a process, rather than a vessel so that, as Craig Dworkin notes, "media are not merely storage mechanisms somehow independent of the acts of reading or recognizing the signs they record" (Dworkin, *No Medium*, 32). The blank works of art and silent compositions Dworkin examines in *No Medium*, like John Cage's 4'33", vividly demonstrate the centrality of retrieval to technotextual signification. Despite a temptation to read the seemingly post-medium[78] work as a collection of free-floating signifiers that can be reconstituted differentially with identical results, "the book" is not transparent, but rather under constant negotiation. Its materiality is, as Drucker suggests, "performative," contingent upon the reader's activation and interpretation of the technotext's recursive loops (Drucker, "Performative Materiality," n.p.). While readers learn to think of an engagement with a book as a kind of disappearing act in which they become absorbed (a telling term) by the text, that very disembodiment is predicated on a model of publication that privileges composition, the copyright-able product of authorial genius, over reception. *Between Page and Screen*, in its attempt to create a technotextual feedback loop between its physical form and poetic content, also seeks to draw readers' attention to their own role in its activation.

Figure 1: Reading *Between Page and Screen*

78 Theorizing the "post-medium condition," Rosalind Krauss suggests the term "technical support" to refer to the "layered mechanisms of new technologies that make a simple, unitary identification of the work's physical support impossible" (Krauss, "Two Moments in the Post-Medium Condition," 56). Writing after the conceptual turn, Krauss's formulation reminds us that even idea-based art can only be experienced through some mediating support.

AR technologies make visible a layer of digital information superimposed on a camera's feed. This visual data might be geospatially mapped to appear on a smartphone screen when an app user visits a specific location, or it might be linked to an external fiducial recognized by computer vision, which triggers animations keyed to a given image.[79] Such "mixed reality" experiences allow for an interpenetration of the virtual and physical, and in the case of marker-based AR can also draw attention back to the reader, who sees her own image mirrored onscreen.[80] Not only does it reinforce the body visually, AR might be thought of as a body-device ecology, as Amanda Starling Gould puts it, since "neither the body nor the media disappear, but instead, they reappear as vectors for the expression and experience of art as both must be present in order to access AR art's invisible visualities" (Gould, "Invisible Visualities," 26). *Between Page and Screen* exploits this networked relationship to draw attention to the ways in which reading is always a mediated experience, albeit one that has been naturalized to us through habit and education. [81]

Figure 2: The cut-out cover of the Siglio Press trade edition.

79 Constructing a rigid definition of augmented and mixed reality is outside the scope of this short piece, but it bears noting that AR differs from virtual reality in that it allows users to simultaneously experience their embodied reality and a layer of virtual information. It also differs from quick response (QR) codes, which visually encode data, but typically serve as shortcuts to retrieve it and do not superimpose it spatially on the user's surroundings.

80 For more on the centrality of embodiment to mixed reality art, see philosopher Mark Hansen. His suggestion that "the new mixed reality paradigm *foregrounds [the] constitutive or ontological role of the body in giving birth to the world*" (Hansen, *Bodies In Code: Interfaces With Digital Media*, 5) has been central to affective readings of new media art.

81 For a thorough documentation of the changing nature of reading and an analysis of the intricate relationship between print, readership, and the changing shape of the book, see Cavallo and Chartier.

III. "SPACE TO UNDULATE": READING BETWEEN

Minimalist in physical form, *Between Page and Screen* presents the reader with a book of poetry whose pages contain no text: centered on each recto page, a black-and-white grid, similar to a QR code, faces the blank verso. These cryptic visual poems, like Swiss-German artist Dieter Roth's hand-cut *Book* editions of the late 1950s and early '60s, call out to be deciphered.[82] Roth's books consist of loose cardstock pages, each fifteen inches by fifteen inches, with a smaller central square of cut-out slots in varying widths and patterns. When stacked and turned by the reader, they alternately reveal and conceal the pages below, creating a variety of optical effects and transformations. Playfully interactive, these works press at our notions of the book by presenting us with a space that references text (evoking a shifting prose block with ample margins), but that only becomes legible by flipping—rather than moving our eye to scan these lines, we move the page to make meaning from it. Though we can examine and appreciate an individual sheet, we must, in fact, look through it for juxtaposition with the page below.

Although it references Roth's work, because of its codex form (a stack of sheets bound along one side, fixing page order and suggesting a narrative structure) *Between Page and Screen* is immediately legible as a book—even if its "texts" cannot be read by human eyes.[83] When readers obey the instructions on the opening page, however, "[t]o find the words, visit betweenpageandscreen.com," and visit the website, they are prompted to allow access to their webcam, at which point they confront their own image. When they open the book, the poems spring to life: "Dear S, / I fast, I fasten to become compact" begins the epistle that hovers perpendicularly to and above the first page, much like a hologram or pop-up. The texts move as the reader shifts position, tilts the book, and presses closer to (or moves away from) the screen. The sixteen poems, a series of letters between "P" and "S" alternating with visual and permutative concrete poems based on keywords from those letters, are mapped to the surface of the page using Flash-based augmented reality software that examines the video image from the webcam up to thirty times per second, updating and adjusting the animation

82 Images and descriptions of some of these works are available through the Museum of Modern Art's website from the 2013 exhibition, "wait, later this will be nothing": moma.org/interactives/exhibitions/2013/dieter_roth/.

83 The book's trade edition is legible as a book thanks, in part, to a number of visual cues, including the cardstock cover, printed spine, barcode, and blurbs we expect to find on a slim volume of contemporary poetry. These trappings are missing from the stark black and white artist's book, letterpress-printed on Rives BFK paper with rich black printmaking ink and bound by hand in an edition of twelve.

accordingly to create this holographic illusion.[84] If the marker bends or is obscured, the animation scatters, sending letters flying in all directions.

Which of these two texts is more ephemeral, the digital one that seems to promise archival longevity but threatens to fly apart at the slightest disturbance, or the printed one, which, while illegible as text, will likely outlast the software that brings its sigils to life?[85] We were drawn to marker-based AR precisely because it requires both a printed page and networked screen in order for the text to take shape.[86] The thing we think of as the book's content, its text, in this case does not exist on either page or screen, but in the augmented space between them opened up by the reader, who places the two in dialogue and in whose hands they might learn to coexist.

Between Page and Screen considers this moment of tension between our reading and writing interfaces in which one may feel torn "between" a love of print (in some cases even a fetishization of it) and recognition of the affordances of the digital. The term "between" itself suggests both interposition and interconnection—a mediating role played by the reader, who sees herself peeping in on the unfolding conversation made possible by her presence. In the tradition of the romantic epistle, P and S speak familiarly, drawing on a coded language suggestive of a larger narrative they share. Seeing ourselves on screen reminds us that letter poems, from Horace and Ovid onward, always have two audiences: the internal one of their recipient, and a secondary audience outside the poem, as Wimsatt and Beardsley put it, "like a reader over another reader's shoulder" (Wimsatt, *The Verbal Icon: Studies In the Meaning of Poetry*, xv). This coy encoding is designed not only to simulate attempts to thwart interception, but also to knit writer and recipient together, a junto of two for whom the letter's argot has extra meaning.

The epistles draw on the etymologies of "page" and "screen" to explore their intersections and divergences, revealing the Indo-European roots that seem to have set

84 FLARToolkit, a port of ARToolworks' Java NYARToolKit to Flash/AS3 by Tomohiko Koyama a.k.a. Saqoosha, CTO of interactive design agency Dot by Dot.

85 We chose to use Flash because of its ubiquity in 2009. Built into the browser and self-updating, it made it easier for readers to access AR without having to install additional plugins. Of course, Flash has, as of this writing, been maligned and obsolesced, thanks in part to Apple's 2010 decision not to support it on iOS devices. Even ARToolworks has developed commercial software for iOS and Android to satisfy commercial clients. While we will continue to support the Flash-based version for as long as possible, we will eventually have to port to a different platform if the work is to remain accessible.

86 Reading *Between Page and Screen* is decidedly different from encountering AR mediated by a smartphone. In a gallery setting, it establishes a mirror that puts the reader on display alongside the work. Experienced at home, on the web, in front of one's computer, it becomes a private, personalized performance. In this way, it calls upon our haptic and affective memory of what it means to read—our sense of the function and apparatus of the book. It does so in order to raise questions about that very experience, replicating it in defamiliarized ways, from the mirroring of the reader to the presentational way the book must be held.

them at odds from the start. Page comes from the root pag-, "to fasten or join," which gives us a number of terms related to connection, including pact, peace, and appease (Watkins, *The American Heritage Dictionary of Indo-European Roots*, 63). Screen's root, (S)ker-, "to cut," yields the language of protection and defense, including scabbard, shield, sword, and carnage (Watkins, *The American Heritage Dictionary of Indo-European Roots*, 80). The pacifist and the warrior, their personalities appear to have been established for them, and these meanings influence their personas. However, over the book's unfolding conversation, points of connection appear, including screen's tendency to shine and beckon, a kind of beacon, and page's tendency to fix, sometimes violently, with its impaling fang. Not quite so far apart as one might think, language tells another story about the possible alliances (romantic, linguistic, and physical) between them. While my own desire for parity certainly directs their dialogue, the exploratory process of looking for etymological connection helped forge the characters of P and S, much as a close engagement with the affordances of AR and the unheimlich experience of reading in the "between" space influenced the book's text and animations. "Dear P, / You give me space to undulate" writes S, words that could not mean the same thing if trained on page's trellis. S and P vacillate in the sheer space that separates and connects, a veil we can see through.

Figure 3: Looking over the reader's shoulder.

IV. "SHEAR" AND "SHARE": MAKING SPACE FOR THE READER

I constructed the first edition of *Between Page and Screen* by hand, letterpress-printing it on a Vandercook Proof Press at Otis College of Art and Design (where I worked as a lab technician) using photopolymer plates made locally by Gerald Lange of Santa Monica's Bieler Press. The gesture, while initially intended as a tongue-in-cheek reference to the history of fine press printing, one that juxtaposes the limited-edition object with the even more ephemeral digital object of the AR poems, became central to our consideration of the way books signify. In order to draw out the centrality of the reader to the text and provide an opportunity for closer engagement with the materialities AR both facilitates and calls into question, we have developed resources that put the text more firmly into readers' hands: a printable PDF with binding guide and a web-based AR-writing interface.[87] Just as Drucker gained a deeper understanding of materiality by "holding language in my hands" (Drucker, *The Century of Artists' Books*, 132) while composing with lead type, we hope readers will consider the book as an object and interface through a direct engagement with the means of its production.

Figure 4: Binding the first edition by hand.

Working closely with the material of the book proved essential to our own understanding of how page and "screen" (literally, the webcam) must interface for the AR technology to work. For example, the constraints of the software dictated that the pages must lie flat, since any disruption of the markers' square shape renders them invisible to the camera. We thus experimented with paper grain and binding structure to find a way to make the book "legible" to, in the words of poet Christian Bök, "the

87 Available at betweenpageandscreen.com/diy, these tools arose from dialogues with faculty at a number of institutions who have taught or plan to teach the book, and who are interested in modes of what Matt Ratto has termed "critical making": collaborative, practice-based research methods that emphasize process over product in addressing a theoretical question (Ratto, "Critical Making," 253). We are grateful to María Mencía and Zuzana Husárová for the opportunity to develop our web-based AR tool as part of a Code-Interactive Workshop in London in 2013. Thanks as well to David Gruber and Jhave Johnston at City University Hong Kong and Roger Whitson at Washington State University Vancouver for the chance to share the participatory aspect of the project with colleagues in the Digital Humanities. .

eyes of robots."[88] Likewise, in both the letterpress and trade editions each marker is designed asymmetrically—allowing each text, mapped in three dimensions, to have a front and back. The covers and layout attempt to provide clues as to how to hold the book in order to make the poems appear (facing oneself or the camera), but what a given reader sees on-screen will always be different from any other reader by virtue of the space and time of reading, the light and lector seated before the page. By printing and binding their own copies of *Between Page and Screen*, directly engaging the trial and error of assembly, readers may, perhaps, more deeply appreciate the ways the work's form and content reflect upon the shape of books past and present.

In addition to allowing readers to tinker with the "page," it is important to the project's emphasis on the reader that the "screen" be accessible as well. To that end, all the software that runs *Between Page and Screen* is freely available on Github, and anyone who can compile Flash can alter it to create derivative works.[89] However, we also wanted to make AR accessible to those without programming experience so that they might press at the bounding box of the book, the screen, and the marker, a series of nested squares that hem in the text. The Epistles tool, a web-based interface for composing marker-based AR poems, allows readers to see their own text in three-dimensional space. As they enter language, writers see a live preview of their work super-imposed on their webcam feed. After they save their piece, they receive a unique URL to share with others, as well as another at which they can revise it. When their recipient visits the custom URL with a printed marker or the cover of the book, she can read the text and create one in response. In addition to allowing for a direct engagement with questions about form and content, access, the way texts signify differently under different technical supports and in differential settings, and the role of author and reader in constructing the text, writing in AR enters the reader into the discourse network established by P and S, allowing her to exchange private messages with an awareness of a potentially public audience. Experimenting in that space, readers may treat the design constraints of the medium as a challenge to see what they can do with super-imposition, textual mapping, and the body-device ecology.

V. "$A_{-1.19}$ $BOOK^{+0.38}$ $SPX_{-1.24}$": LOOKING AND LISTENING

After seeing themselves reading, readers might bring others into the text, experiencing its interactivity more directly by recognizing what Barthes, Foucault, and early writers of electronic literature felt profoundly: that the text, while composed by a writer, only

88 In his generous blurb for the book.

89 Please see www.betweenpageandscreen.com/source for links and instructions.

takes shape in the hands of the reader. As Camille Utterback, whose interactive text works have been foundational to new media art, suggests, "[a]ll forms of 'interactive text' demand a physical body with which to interact" (Utterback, "Unusual Positions," 218), and works that misbehave or draw attention to their interface can bring this demand into relief. The book's very interactivity has been naturalized for us to such a degree that we tend to recognize it only in those technotextual works that shift our gaze to their shimmering surfaces (breaking the illusion of absorption). In *Between Page and Screen*, we hoped to create a work that would reward attention to both and that would remind readers of the fundamentally reader-oriented nature of any text.

Figure 5: Trespassing the bounding box.

Between Page and Screen raises questions it cannot answer on its own. While the process of writing the poems and engaging the print and digital components of AR allowed us to explore books' significance in this particular moment, the goal of the project is not to resolve the question of page or screen, but to revel in the magical, surprising, coded and intriguing between space activated by the reader. P and S close the book with a "co-script posthaste postface: there is no postscript" (n.p.). The project suggests that no matter what technological shifts influence the way art is created and received, both print and digital poetry require the writer to step aside, to let script itself have the last word. The book that speaks here, or sings, does so silently, inviting the reader to give it voice.

WORK CITED

Borsuk, Amaranth and Brad Bouse. *Between Page and Screen*. First Edition. Los Angeles: Siglio Press, 2011.

_,_. *Between Page and Screen*. Second Edition. Boulder, CO: Springgun Press, 2016.

Cavallo, Guglielmo and Roger Chartier, Eds. *A History of Reading in the West*. Trans. L.G. Cochrane. Cambridge: Polity Press, 1999.

Drucker, Johanna. *The Century of Artists' Books*. New York: Granary Books, 2004.

_,_. "Performative Materiality and Theoretical Approaches to Interface." *Digital Humanities Quarterly* 7.1 (2013). Web. 29 Nov. 2014. digitalhumanities.org/dhq/vol/7/1.

Dworkin, Craig. *No Medium*. Cambridge: MIT Press, 2013.

Gould, Amanda Starling. "Invisible Visualities: Augmented reality art and the contemporary media ecology." *Convergence: The International Journal of Research into New Media Technologies* 20.1 (2014): 25–32.

Hansen, Mark B.N. *Bodies In Code: Interfaces With Digital Media*. New York: Routledge, 2006.

Hayles, N. Katherine. *Writing Machines*. Cambridge: MIT Press, 2002.

Krauss, Rosalind. "Two Moments in the Post-Medium Condition." *October* 116 (2006): 55-62.

Perloff, Marjorie. "Screening the Page/Paging the Screen: Digital Poetics and the Differential Text." In *New Media Poetics: Contexts, Technotexts, and Theories*, edited by Adalaide Morris and Thomas Swiss, 143-164. Cambridge: MIT Press, 2006.

Pressman, Jessica. "The Aesthetic of Bookishness in Twenty-First Century Literature." *Michigan Quarterly Review* 48.4 (2009): 465-472.

Ratto, Matt. "Critical Making: Conceptual and Material Studies in Technology and Social Life." *The Information Society* 27 (2011): 252–260.

Utterback, Camille. "Unusual Positions—Embodied Interaction with Symbolic Spaces." In *First Person: New Media as Story, Performance, and Game*, edited by Noah Wardrip-Fruin and Pat Harrigan, 218-226. Cambridge: MIT Press, 2004.

Watkins, Calvert, Ed. *The American Heritage Dictionary of Indo-European Roots*, third edition. New York: Houghton Mifflin Harcourt (2011).

Wimsatt, W.K., and Monroe C. Beardsley. *The Verbal Icon: Studies In the Meaning of Poetry*. Lexington: The University Press of Kentucky (1954).

Notes on the Composition of *Notes on the Voyage of Owl and Girl*

BY J. R. CARPENTER

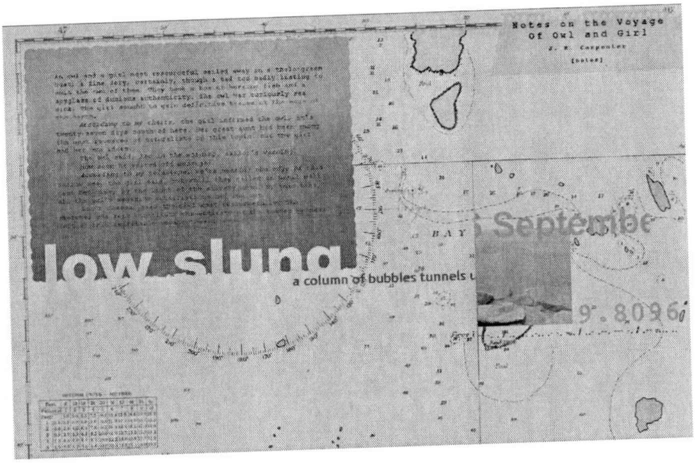

Figure 1: J. R. Carpenter, *Notes of the Voyage of Owl and Girl*, 2013. Screenshot from http://luckysoap.com/owlandgirl Image by J. R. Carpenter

This essay will reflect upon the transmutation of predominantly male-authored print-based forms of narrative into female-narrated digital literary spaces through the strategies of détournement employed in the composition of one web-based work of digital literature produced during my PhD research (Carpenter 2015). *Notes on the Voyage of Owl and Girl* (Carpenter 2013) is a work of fiction, yet it's frequent references to actual events, locals, persons, and texts are entirely intentional.[90] Part ship's log, part sea chart, part sailor's yarn, part children's book, part Victorian nonsense poem, part computer-generated narrative — this hybrid work détournes, appropriates, conflates, and confabulates characters, facts, fictions, and forms of accounts of sea voyages undertaken over the past 2340 years or so, into the North Sea, into the North Atlantic, and beyond into territories purely imaginary.

90 This work was first presented in "Avenues of Access: An Exhibit & Online Archive of New 'Born Digital' Literature," curated by Dene Grigar & Kathi Inman Berens, at the Modern Languages Association (MLA) Convention in Boston, MA, USA, in January 2013.

At the furthest edge of this textual, photographic, and cartographic assemblage floats the conceptual figure of the classical island of Thule, the precise location of which has been disputed since ancient times. Thule was first mentioned by the Greek Pytheas in a work no longer extant based on travels he claims to have undertaken between 330 BC and 320 BC which, however, are unlikely to have ever taken place. Pytheas described an island called Thule located six days' journey north of Britain, and observed what we would now call the midnight sun, and a strange phenomena he called "sea-lung," which was neither land nor sea nor vapor.

Wildly divergent versions of Pytheas' accounts have been textually transmuted through the writings of classical scholars from Pliny the Elder to Ptolemy and beyond, into modern times. Contemporary scholars continue to disagree on the location of Thule. In *Venetian Navigators* Andrea di Robilant conflates Thule with modern Iceland:

> They say Pytheas of Marseille was the first European to reach the shores of Iceland while exploring the Atlantic around 400 BC. He called it Ultima Thule: the last island before the great sea lung of mist and ice and water that extended beyond the known world. The name Ultima Thule lived on throughout antiquity and was resurrected by cartographers in continental Europe during the Renaissance. But in northern Europe the island was known by its old Norse name, Islanda, the island of ice (Robilant 106).

Writing in the first century A.D., the Roman Tacitus places the Orkney Islands and Thule in close proximity:

> a Roman fleet [...] discovered and subdued the Orkney Islands, hitherto unknown. Thule, too, was sighted by our men, but no more; their orders took them no farther [...] but they do report that the sea is sluggish and heavy to the oar. (Tacitus, 60)

The Romans were coastal pilots, terrified of open seas. In *Atlas of Remote Islands: Fifty Islands I Have Never Set Foot On and Never Will*, Judith Schalansky suggests that Thule was less an island and more of a conceptual threshold: "The Romans called the every edge of their flat world Thule. So where does it lie? At the outermost of all borders" (Schalansky 50). Schalansky's atlas contains an entry for an island happened upon by James Cook in 1775: "Suddenly they come upon a frozen land with black cliffs [...] a land of firn and ice ruins that never melt, gloomy, cold and full of horrors [...] Here is the new Thule, the other end of the known world" (ibid.).

It is toward the outermost of all borders that Owl and Girl voyage.

I. THE SEA CHART

The narrative of *Notes on the Voyage of Owl and Girl* unfolds against a background collage of cartographic information: a key of measures in feet and fathoms, a grid of lines of latitude and longitude, a scattering of dotted lines and numbers indicating ocean depths and soundings, warnings of foul grounds, and an island named Grey. These details have been collected from sea charts of Scotia Bay and the South Orkney Islands complied from surveys undertaken in the Antarctic Ocean between 1903 and 1966. Sea charts are always composites, composed of stratified layers of textual accounts of passages – logs, notes, soundings, compass readings, currents, weather phenomena, and estimated distances observed by generations of pilots at sea. In *Notes on the Voyage of Owl and Girl*, details from printed sea charts are broken apart, rearranged, and reoriented to suit web navigation; this new web context renders these charts incoherent. In *The Interface Effect*, Alexander R. Galloway states, "coherence and incoherence compose a sort of continuum" (Galloway 46). An incoherent aesthetic is one that tends to "unravel neat masses into their unkempt and incontinent elements" (ibid.). When the web-browser window is re-sized, the relative positions of these page elements shift in relation to one another in a manner analogous to the shifting of winds, waves, tides an ocean currents.

II. THE POSTCARD

At the upper left corner of the screen, a short computer-generated narrative formatted in indented paragraphs is situated within the pictorial space of a rectangular photograph with scalloped edges evocative of a mid-twentieth-century picture postcard. This postal association suggests that this story is from another place and time. In her short story "In the Village," Elizabeth Bishop writes: "Postcards come from another world, the world of the grandparents who send things…" (Bishop 255). In *Terra Infirma: Geography's Visual Culture* Irit Rogoff argues, "the postcard is a complex artifact in which image and text are reversible, in which public and personal collapse" (Rogoff 52). In *The Post Card: From Socrates to Fred and Beyond*, Jacques Derrida frames this reversibility within the relational dialectics of here and there, image and text, narrative text and encoded information:

> one does not know what is in front or what is in back, here or there, near or far… Nor what is the most important, the picture or the text, and in the text, the message or the caption, or the address. (Derrida 13)

Derrida goes on to suggest that in the postcards referred to in *The Post Card*, it is the image which comes first, the image which prompts the writing of the text:

> if you reread the post cards I sent you... you will notice... that everything I write is legendary, a more or less elliptical, redundant, or translatable legend, caption, of the picture... of the icon which is found on the back of the text and watches over it... (Derrida 121-122)

The picture postcard in *Notes on the Voyage of Owl and Girl* depicts an incoherent landscape — a blue-gray gradation of ocean, weather, and sky. With neither ground for perspective nor discernible horizon line, it is impossible to know from looking at it where this photograph was taken. As the photographer, I know it was taken from a granite bluff at Chebucto Head, Nova Scotia, at the southwestern limit of Halifax Harbour, facing east toward Dartmouth. It could just as well have been taken from a granite bluff in Cornwall or on the Western Isles of Scotland. The coastlines of Atlantic Canada and the United Kingdom share a common climate and topography. One can stand on either coast on headlands formed of the same granite, squinting into a sea fret, battered by the same wind. An evocation of the South Orkney Islands produces a North Orkney, where previously there had simply been Orkney. An evocation of Nova Scotia (New Scotland) produces an Old Scotland, where previously there had simply been Scotland. The persistence of North Atlantic and North Sea names in southern oceans creates a shadow place, a doppelgänger born of an uncanny doubling between places inextricably linked, as Sigmund Freud writes, through the constant "repetition of the same ... features, the same characters, the same destinies, the same misdeeds, even the same names, through successive generations" (Freud 142). Thus narrative of the voyage of Owl and Girl unfolds within an incoherent aesthetic of inversions and uncanny returns.

III. THE NARRATIVE

The corpus of the generative narrative text relating the voyage of Owl and Girl contains fragments of and references to stories of fanciful, fluid, and fictional floating places described or imagined from diverse literary, historical, and archival sources. For example, there are phrases borrowed from Eugene Field's children's lullaby poem "Wynken, Blynken and Nod," in which three young children one night,

> Sailed off in a wooden shoe--
> Sailed on a river of crystal light,
> Into a sea of dew. (Field, 1889)

The children in this poem are not specifically gendered other than that they are referred to as fishermen, who have "come to fish for the herring fish / That live in this beautiful sea." Evocation of this inverted dream logic in which fish are stars and sea is sky introduces a narrative resonance to *Notes on the Voyage of Owl and Girl*, between the parallel planes of sea and sky, childhood and adulthood, wakefulness and sleep.

The characters named in the title *Notes on the Voyage of Owl and Girl* are détourned from Edward Lear's Victorian nonsense poem "The Owl and the Pussy-Cat", in which, a sweet-talking Owl and an easily-impressed Pussy-cat go to sea in a beautiful pea-green boat. They sail for a year and a day to the land where the Bong-Tree grows, where they marry and dance on the sand by the light of the moon. McKenzie Wark argues: "Key to any practice of détournement is identifying the fragments upon which it might work" (Wark 40). The hyphen in Lear's Pussy-cat creates a fragmentary creature. According to the *Random House Dictionary*, The term "puss" has been used to refer to a cat since the 1520s. The term "pussy" has been used to refer to a small cat or kitten since the 1570s. The term "pussycat" has been used to refer to a cat or an nonthreatening, endearing, or gentle person since the 1790s. The vulgar use of the term "pussy" to refer to the vulva, to a woman as a sex object, or to an effeminate man did not come about until the 1870s. Lear's poem was published in 1871. In the title and in the text of the poem, Lear writes "Pussy-cat" suggesting a gentle creature, but when the Owl sings to the Pussy-cat in the first verse, he refers to her as "Pussy" implying he thinks of her as a sex object:

> O lovely Pussy! O Pussy, my love,
> What a beautiful Pussy you are,
> You are,
> You are!
> What a beautiful Pussy you are! (Lear 1871)

Lear separates himself from this whiff of vulgarity through the use of quotation marks. It's the Owl who uses the foul (fowl) language, not the author. Lear makes it clear that the Pussy-cat knows precisely what the Owl's after; in the next verse she pleads: "O let us be married!"

The hyphen in Lear's Pussy-cat provides an opening for détournement, invites the invention of a new creature (Lecercle 41). In the variable narrative space of *Notes on the Voyage of Owl and Girl*, the passive Pussy-cat has been replaced by an altogether different sort of girl. Girl is not defined by Owl but rather by the argument #{studious} called in the opening sentence: "An owl and a girl most #{studious} #{setsail} in a #{green}green #{boat}; a #{seaworthy} #{boat}, certainly, though a #{amount} too #{equipped} to suit the two of them."

Each of the bracketed words in the above sentence refers to a variable string. From the #{studious} string emerges a girl most ["adventurous," "ardent," "courageous," "curious," "determined," "industrious," "keen," "practical," "rational," "resourceful," "rigorous," "studious," "serious"]. These multiple definings of Girl are informed by the narratives of two other female castaways depicted in literature. In J. M. Coetzee's novel *Foe*, the castaway Susan Barton is determined to tell the truth of her story: "I am a free woman who asserts her freedom by telling her story according to her own desire" (Coetzee 131). Yet upon her rescue to England, Barton seeks a male author to write of her adventures. In Douglas Glover's novel *Elle*, a character based on the real-life sixteenth castaway Marguerite de La Rocque corrects her male biographer when he exaggerates: "Two, I say. Two bears died. I didn't kill either of them" (Glover 181). Girl does not seek a biographer, asserting, through the argument #{ideas} that she has her own ["approach," "books to write," "ideas," "life to live," "line of inquiry," "mode of questioning," "plans," "research," "reasoning," "strategies," "story to tell," "theories"].

The hyphen in Lear's beautiful pea-green boat provides another opening for détournement, creating an opportunity for a linguistic joke which presupposes a familiarity with both with the literary fragment upon which it is based and the linguistic rules through which it might be extended. In addition to "pea-," the #{green} variable string initially contained: ["bottle-," "beetle-," "grass-," "grey-," "jelly-," "lima-bean-," "sea-," "sea-foam-," "thalo-"]. I later added: ["alligator-," "apple-," "collard-," "grasshopper-," "kelly-," "olive-," "thumb-"]. These variable could yet be altered. This work is an assemblage, and, as Deleuze and Guattari note: "Assemblages are in constant variation, are themselves constantly subject to transformations" (Deleuze and Guattari 82). The same could be said for the sailor's yarn, forever twisting, knitting, knotting and unraveling.

In "The Aesthetic of Bookishness in Twenty-First-Century Literature," Jessica Pressman suggests that an "aesthetic of bookishness… unites novels that pursue a thematic interest in depicting books as characters and focal points of narrative action […] and books or paper-filled spaces serve as physical places of refuge for traumatized characters." Pressman goes on to say that "born-digital works exploit the aesthetic of bookishness by adapting the appearance of paper and translating the print-based reading practices onto the screen. For example, they employ handwritten drawings on notepaper as backdrops…"Within this paradigm, *Notes on the Voyage of Owl and Girl* exhibits an aesthetic of bookishness rather more in keeping with novels than with born-digital works. As the following statement-event reveals, books drive Girl's actions and inform her decisions: "According to my #{books}, the girl informed the owl, it\'s #{number} #{distance} #{direction} of here."

The argument #{books} contains a variety of books and other printed forms: ["calculations," "charts," "library books," "manuscripts," "maps," "research," "sources," "test results," "textbooks," "World Book Encyclopedia"]. Girl does not seek refuge in these books; rather, she uses them as tools. Though she is a girl not a woman, and though the owl seems less of a help than a hindrance, and though they sail alone through seas unknown never to be heard from again, Girl is not a traumatized character. She is not a castaway like Defoe' Robinson Crusoe, who is forever watching for a sail, nor does she take after J. M. Coetzee's castaway Susan Burton, who is waiting for a book to be written to set her free. Girl is actively engaged in writing her own story.

The last line of the computer-generated narrative calls the string #{notes} which contains the following variables: ["charts," "diaries," "drawings," "hand-drawn maps," "journals," "letters," "lists," "notes," "photographs," "recordings," "records," "samples," "ships logs," "sketches," "soundings," "specimens," "telegrams"]. These forms of annotation suggests that the photographic, cartographic, and textual collage that Girl and her lazy friend Owl voyage through is a manifestation of notes kept by Girl during her voyage. The bulk of Girl's notes are displayed in five horizontally scrolling texts which annotate this mythical, implausible, impossible voyage toward ["seas unknown," "the northern lights," "the fountain of youth," etc.] through different topographic modes of description.

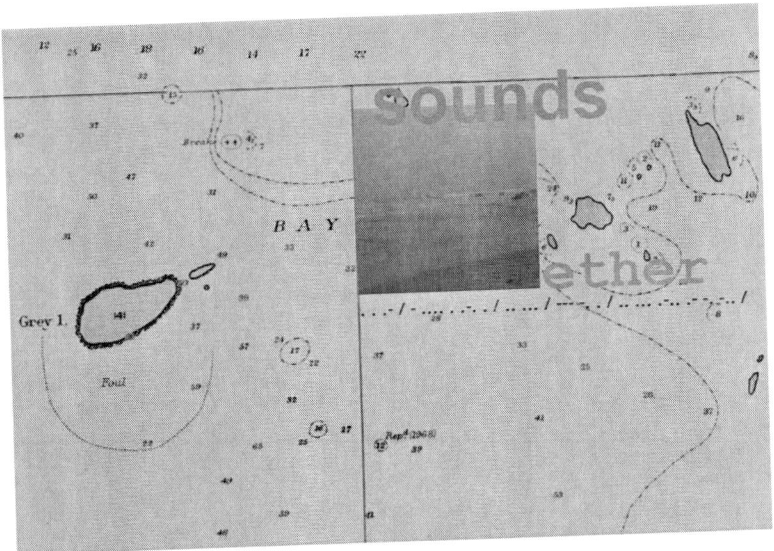

Figure 2: J. R. Carpenter, *Notes of the Voyage of Owl and Girl*, 2013. Screenshot detail from http://luckysoap.com/owlandgirl Image by J. R. Carpenter

IV. THE NOTES

The large gray horizontally scrolling text which appears at the bottom edge of the image of the picture postcard appears to address that image directly in so far as it pertains to the sort of weather the photograph depicts. Picking up on a line of dialogue from the narrative text in which Girl addresses Owl — "Don\'t #{fret}, said the girl most #{studious}ly." — this line of text begins: "don't fret / sea wet / mist and haze / come inland..." Later on in this slow-moving line, like the Roman sailors before her, Girl observe a sea sluggish to the oar: "far flung / low slung / sea lung / a frozen tide / a breath suspended...." Through the evocation of classical, early-modern, Victorian, and contemporary texts, Owl and Girl voyage through time as well as through space.

The notes in the smaller dark blue text which appears below the large postcard image are primarily concerned with cartographic representations of the fears and desires of seafarers: "avoid a void inked-in / where sea monsters swim." The double meaning of the term "legend" is evoked, as legendary creatures, such as sea monsters and dragons intermingle with cartographic legends as suggested by the passage: "Legends warn of rip tides / shallows / shoals..." The evocation of the birth of a volcanic island toward the end of this line of text suggests that Owl and Girl may have ventured into northern waters off Iceland: "mid-ocean smoke / a sudden sulphurous odour / a column of bubbles tunnels up from the deep."

The text in gray which appears above the small square images to the right of the screen is an erasure poem based on the second voyage attempted by Mr. John Davis with others, for the discovery of the Northwest Passage in 1586, as recounted in Hakluyt's *Voyages and Discoveries*, published twelve years later. This line begins: "7 May: departed from Dartmouth." Narrative resonance emerges between this reference to Dartmouth, Devon, and the a fore mentioned picture postcard, which was photographed across Halifax Harbor mouth from Dartmouth, Nova Scotia. This horizontally scrolling text is quotidian in two respects. First, it indicates days and months, giving a sense of the duration of this voyage, chronicling a passage of time spanning from May to October. Second, it details aspects of daily life on board the ["bottle-," "beetle-," "pea-"] green boat that are not mentioned in the narrative text. For example: "2 August: much troubled with a fly which is called mosquito." In this line of horizontally scrolling quotidian journaling, the male voice of the narrator of the voyage of John Davis has been appropriated by Girl.

The pink text which appears to the right of the square images at the lower right corner of the screen references a wide range of communications networks technologies. The following passage refers to the transmission and interception of ship-to-shore wireless messages, and the efforts to decode encrypted messages undertaken by the

British at Bletchley Park during WWII: "beeps / blips / tongue slips / loose lips / sink ships." These references suggest these notes constitute a transcript of communications sent from the ["lima-," "grey-," "grass-"] green ["wooden shoe," "dinghy," "boat"], and a ship's log of observations on small sounds in the enormity of the in-between space through which Owl and Girl travel. The following passage refers to the vast ocean of static which wireless technology revealed to the world: "silence / listen / into the ether / an ocean of static / an ocean of noise…." In *The Post Card,* Derrida suggests: "The end of postal epoch is doubtless also the end of literature" (Derrida 104). In this horizontally scrolling line of notes, the postal and telegraphic epochs merge: "full stop / post date / press here / press on / on board…." This line of notes also suggests a sense of urgency. The girl will use any means at her disposal to broadcast her message. The numbers which appear toward the end of this line of text are latitude and longitude coordinates charting a route roughly northward from Great Britain into the North Atlantic. That these coordinates trail off mid-ocean suggest that this is a doomed voyage, the fate of which will remain a mystery.

The performance of all these texts scrolling on one page allows them to be read in new ways. For example, narrative resonance emerges between the lines détourned from the a fore mentioned voyage of John Davis – "29 June: a company of isles / full of fair sounds … / within the sounds we sent our boats" – and the strange sounds engendered by early ship-to-shore wireless communications – "silence / listen / into the ether / an ocean of static / an ocean of noise" – as shown in the image below.

V. A SCRIPT FOR LIVE PERFORMANCE

The new ways of reading proposed by the performance of multiple modes of narrative and annotation within the narrative space of *Notes on the Voyage of Owl and Girl* prompted an investigation of how the narrative, dialogic, and annotative voices presented in this web-based assemblage might be re-sounded in the context of live performance.

Although *Notes on the Voyage of Owl and Girl* contains lines of dialogue spoken by both Owl and Girl, there is only one narrative voice. This voice is not Girl's but rather that of an author's. In a bid to undermine the authority of the authorial voice, JavaScript is employed to create a transient text, which in turn, in Galloway's terms, presents an incoherent narrative, constantly rewriting the narrative of the voyage. Further, although the lines of horizontally scrolling texts address different topics in different tones, they are all presented as notes written by Girl. In order to address both the authorial narrative voice and the fragmented annotative voice, a script for live performance was created,[91] which was subsequently published in *Fourteen Hills: The San Francisco State University Review* (Carpenter 2014), thereby somewhat paradoxically returning one iteration of this newly reconstituted digital narrative to print.

Notes on the Voyage of Owl and Girl: A Script for Live Performance comprises two distinct sections: narrative and notes. The opening "narrative" section of the script undermines the authority of an authorial voice by interrupting both the linear narrative flow of the story and the grammatical structure of its sentences. The syntax of code languages infuse this print script for live performance with incoherence, indecision, vagaries, possibilities, and multiplicities. These interruptions are achieved through the insertion of some but not all of the variables contained in the JavaScript strings. For example, the first sentence of the "narrative" section of the script reads:

An owl and a girl most ["adventurous," "curious," "studious"] ["set out," "set sail," "sailed away"] in a ["bottle-green," "beetle-green," "pea-green"] ["boat," "sieve," "skiff," "vessel"]; a ["beautiful," "ship shape," "sea worthy"] ["craft," "raft," "wooden shoe"], certainly, though a ["good deal," "wee bit," "tad"] too ["small," "high in the stern"] to suit the two of them.

In the "notes" section of the script, fragments from the horizontally scrolling texts have been fragmented and reformulated into one long text. On the page, these lines remain differentiated by indentation. For example:

June 15th:

mightily pestered with ice and snow

  don't fret
  sea wet
  mist and haze
  come inland
  come hell or high water

    uncomfortable
    untranslatable

 come home sick

91 *Notes on the Voyage of Owl and Girl: A Script for Live Performance*, has been performed during In(ter)ventions: Literary Practice at the Edge at The Banff Centre, Banff, Canada, February 2013; Chercher le texte, at Le Cube, Paris, France, September 2013; and Lines in the Ice at The British Library, February 2015.

come house wreck
come sea wrack and ruin strewn ashore

no hope of landing

In the live performance of this script, distinctions between Girl's categories of observation — be they climactic, cartographic, quotidian, or pertaining to communication — dissolve into one voice. A new narrative of the voyage emerges. Though reconstituted from Girl's own notes, this narrative retains its incoherence — it refuses to coalesce into a conventional narrative or poetic form. Rather, it finds its strength in détournement, transmediation, and transformation. Through these compositional strategies *Notes on the Voyage of Owl and Girl* creates a new narrative context in which the overwhelmingly male narratives of seafaring, exploration, discovery, and adventure can be claimed by a new narrator, a girl most ["adventurous," "courageous," "curious"], with her own ["books to write," "line of inquiry," "stories to tell"].

WORKS CITED

Bishop, Elizabeth. *The Collected Prose*. NY: FSG, 1984.

Bishop, Elizabeth. *The Collected Prose*. NY: FSG, 1984.

Carpenter, J. R. *Notes on the Voyage of Owl*, 2013. Accessed 27 August 2015. http://luckysoap.com/owlandgirl.

_,_. "Notes on the Voyage of Owl and Girl." *Fourteen Hills: The San Francisco State University Review*, 20.2., (SF: SFSU, 2014), 122-128.

_,_. *Writing Coastlines: Locating Narrative Resonance in Transatlantic Communications Networks*. PhD thesis, University of the Arts London and Falmouth University, 2015. Downloaded 27 August 2015 from: http://ualresearchonline.arts.ac.uk/7825/

Coetzee, J. M. *Foe*. London: Penguin, 2010 [1986].

Deleuze, Gilles and Félix Guattari. *A Thousand Plateaus: Capitalism and Schizophrenia*. Minneapolis: U. Minnesota, 2007 [1987].

Derrida, Jacques. *The Post Card: From Socrates to Freud and Beyond*. Translated by A. Bass. Chicago: U. Chicago Press, 1987.

di Robilant, Andrea. *Venetian Navigators: The Voyages of the Zen Brothers to the Far North*. London: Faber, 2011.

Field, Eugene. "Wynken, Blynken and Nod," 1889. Accessed 28 April 2014. http://www.poetryfoundation.org/poem/171653.

Freud, Sigmund. *The Uncanny*. London: Penguin Classics, 2003 [1919].

Galloway, Alexander R. *The Interface Effect*. Cambridge: Polity, 2012.

Glover, Douglas. *Elle*. Fredericton, NB: Goose Lane Editions, 2003.

Hakluyt, Richard. *Voyages and Discoveries: The Principal Navigations, Voyages, Traffiques and Discoveries of the English Nation*. London: Penguin Classics, 1985 [1598-1600].

Lear, Edward. "The Owl and the Pussycat," Poetry Foundation, 1871. Accessed 27 August 2015. http://www.poetryfoundation.org/poem/171941

Lecercle, Jean-Jacques. *Philosophy of Nonsense: The Institutions of Victorian Nonsense Literature*. London & NY: Routledge, 1994.

Pressman, Jessica. "The Aesthetic of Bookishness in Twenty-First-Century Literature." *Michigan Quarterly Review*. Vol. XLVIII, no. 4. Ann Arbor, MI: MPublishing, University of Michigan Library Fall 2009.

Rogoff, Irit. *Terra Infirma: Geography's Visual Culture*. London & NY: Routledge, 2000.

Schalansky, Judith. *Atlas of Remote Islands: Fifty Islands I Have Never Set Foot On and Never Will*. Trans. Christine Lo. NY: Penguin, 2010.

Tacitus. *On Britain and Germany*. Translated by H. Mattingly. Middlesex: Penguin Classics, 1960 [97-98].

Wark, McKenzie. *The Beach Beneath the Street: The Everyday Life and Glorious Times of The Situationist International*. London & NY: Verso, 2011.

Transient Self-Portrait: The Data-Self

BY MARÍA MENCÍA

YOU ARE PART OF THIS POEM
AS YOU READ THE POEM
THIS POEM READS YOU
IT SPEAKS TO YOU
IT NEEDS TO BE CARESSED
IT NEEDS LIGHT
YOU NEED TO SPEAK TO IT
YOU ARE ITS INK, ITS COLOUR, ITS SURFACE
PLAY WITH IT

This essay reflects on the production and development of my practice-based research project titled *Transient Self-Portrait*. I will briefly outline the underlying principles of my on-going research to better position my project within the interdisciplinary field of electronic literature.

My practice-based artistic investigation evolved from my background in linguistics, design and fine art when I began interconnecting these fields with digital technology at the end of the last millennium. Influenced by Julia Kristeva's notions of the in-between the pre-linguistic and linguistic (in her terms: semiotic and symbolic) and drawing from conceptual-art, language-art, linguistics, translation, concrete, visual, sound and experimental poetics, I set out to question ways of reading and writing using the digital medium.

I was interested in exploring new digital multimodal textualities and engaging the reader/viewer in a shifting in and out of language - creating an experience of what is 'outside' but also 'within' language – a concept explored in depth by Steve McCaffery in his book *North of Intention: Critical Writings* (1986). I associated this process of reading and viewing—moving from the linguistic to the visual language—with Richard Lanham's notion of looking at and through the malleable text of transparent and abstract landscapes of text and linguistic soundscapes.[92] That is, looking at the text, the surface,

92 "The textual surface is now a malleable and self-conscious one. All kinds of production decisions have now become authorial ones. The textual surface has become permanently bi-stable. We are always looking AT it and then THROUGH it, and this oscillation creates a different implied idea of decorum, both stylistic and behavioral" (Lanham 5).

the materiality and looking through the text, the semantic meaning of language. It was this in-between text and image and the meaning appearing from this poetic space that interested me. Hence, McCaffery's, Kristeva's and Lanham's poetic theories and practices started to form the spine of my creative work during my doctoral investigation 2000-2003 and have continued to be the foundations of all my work. In the process of developing my doctorate studies my work found itself under the umbrellas of digital art and e-poetry, coinciding with the studies on Digital Poetics carried out at the time at the Electronic Poetry Center, SUNY, Buffalo under Dr Loss Pequeño Glazier. It also began to receive international recognition when one of my works *Birds Singing Other Birds Songs* (2001) was selected to be exhibited at the International Symposium of Electronic Arts- ISEA 2002, Nagoya Japan and was later on selected for the first publication of the electronic literature collection *ELC Vol 1* (2006). The editors of that volume were able to understand my vision—at that stage—of my creative investigation and N. Katherine Hayles specially supported my work through critical writings in books such as *Electronic Literature: New Horizons for the Literary.*

Language is always the material of my creative practice; interconnecting the visual, aural and semantic meaning of language in order to explore notions of the linguistic (the transparent, the legible), the visual materiality of language (the language surface, the illegible) and aural multilingual soundscapes. This creates an in-between space where the legible/illegible and intelligible unintelligible meet in a form of symbiosis to create new landscapes of expression and new meanings.

Software programmes such as Macromedia Director and Adobe Flash opened possibilities for artists/poets to produce animations and interactive work (e-poems, e-narratives, games, digital art, net.art) without having programming skills. They were very useful for experimenting with typography, create animated images, kinetic letters, blurring and erasing of words and adding phonetic sounds. However, in recent years, I have become less interested in using software packages and more concerned with exploring open source software and the possibilities code brings for interactive aesthetics and poetics. Thus, I have worked with other creators interested in creative computing. Many of my interactive works such as *Transient Self-Portrait*—discussed in this essay—have been produced using the programmable language, Processing,[93] and my

93 "Processing is a flexible software sketchbook and a language for learning how to code within the context of the visual arts. Since 2001, Processing has promoted software literacy within the visual arts and visual literacy within technology. There are tens of thousands of students, artists, designers, researchers, and hobbyists who use Processing for learning and prototyping." The lead developers were Authors: Casey Reas and Ben Fry. Now there are groups of developers. https://processing.org Accessed 21 June 2016.

most current work *Gateway to The World*,[94] in its many site-specific iterations, has been developed with WebGL.[95] Being able to programme, even if it is in collaboration with coders, provides a greater agency to investigate concepts such as interactive aesthetics; poetics of engagement; performance writing and digital literacies. It facilitates the exploration of new grammars such as: voice activation, use of webcam, use of mouse, acts of revealing, triggering, dragging, cut and paste.

Thus, the above underlying notions are the foundation of my artistic research, together with methods of remediating, translating, remixing, repurposing while stretching the possibilities of new technologies.

In this essay I will discuss the development of the above enquires through the production of the interactive work *Transient Self-Portrait*, presenting aim, research enquires, process and influences in the production of this artistic research project.

TRANSIENT SELF–PORTRAIT

Is an interactive piece based on two pivotal sonnets from Spanish literature, "Soneto 23: En tanto que de rosa y azucena" (1522)[96] by Garcilaso de La Vega and "Mientras por competir con tu cabello" by Luís de Gongora (1582).[97] It consists of three stages: the first one based on Garcilaso's sonnet, makes reference to the passing of time; the second one connected to Gongora's notion of the unavoidable death, makes the text disintegrate into the final stage where the portrait becomes programming data, and alludes to the transient nature of the digital/data-self.

The participant is invited to explore the work to reveal a fluid portrait—grabbed by the webcam—encapsulated inside the screen, as a medium of textual, generative and sound surfaces. Text and sound are activated by mouse-over actions in stage one, the voice of the reader—by reading aloud—triggers the text in stage two, and mouse click and drag helps to manipulate the image and activate the sound in the third stage.

The piece questions many of the notions just highlighted in the essay; the experience of reading; the use of digital grammars (interacting and engaging with the work); while exploring concepts evoked in the sonnets through coding for interactive aesthetics and poetics.

---

94 *Gateway to the World*, http://lumacode.com/projects/gttw/. This piece uses WebGL and therefore requires modern browsers such as the latest versions of Firefox, Chrome or Safari.

95 WebGL (Web Graphics Library) is a JavaScript API for rendering interactive 3D computer graphics and 2D graphics within any compatible web browser without the use of plug-ins. https://en.wikipedia.org/wiki/WebGL Accessed 21 June 2016

96 "So long as of red rose and lily white," published in *Poesías castellanas completas*.

97 "While trying with your tresses to compete," published in *Sonetos completos*.

I. METHODOLOGY: ARTISTIC RESEARCH PROCESS, INFLUENCES

Hazel Smith and Roger T Dean state: "In humanities: theory, criticism and historical investigation have been prioritized over creative practice" (2009, p. 2). This is still particularly apparent in humanities departments in the United Kingdom. Practitioners, in their many roles as artists, researchers, educators and academics, need to exhibit and present their work at prestigious research conferences and peer-reviewed exhibitions in order to progress in their academic careers. They are also required to support their practice with a theoretical essay—of the same length as if no creative practice was involved—in order to validate the research undertaken through the production of their practice.

However, in artistic research the research occurs through the production of practice, this is understood as "practice as research" or "research through practice." Since it addresses questions in connection to the production of knowledge through the production of creative work, the research takes place in the process and also becomes present in the outcome, that is, in the final work. Research and practice are inextricably linked. The development of practice as research involves similar research processes to those undertaken in theoretical investigations of the arts and humanities: aim, research enquires, methods, context and significance of the work in the field of research. The methodologies are interdisciplinary including creative research methods more akin to creative practices, varying depending on the project.

Smith and Dean argue that the term practice-based research is employed in two different ways. On the one hand it is used to emphasize the primacy of creative practice, whereby "Creative work in itself is a form of research and generates detectable research outputs." On the other hand the term is used to emphasize the documentation and reflection that accompany creative practice: "The specialised research insights that creative practitioners have and the process they engage in creating their art can lead to generalized research and written up as research" (5). Nonetheless, they also comment on how these two types of research are interlinked and researchers use and talk about these terms interchangeably. The fact that the research is led by practice is what unites these two processes and for this reason, I very often refer to this activity as practice as research or research through practice.

This essay serves as a written reflection of the research undertaken through the production of the poetic work *Transient Self-Portrait*. And, hopefully it offers some insights to those academics, working in the arts and humanities, who are not that familiar with the use of digital media technologies in art and poetic projects within the digital humanities, and can help them to understand the innovation projects like this bring to interdisciplinary research in new media art, literature and poetry.

Transient Self-Portrait comes as an executable application, which downloads to the computer and it requires a webcam and a proactive reader to explore the piece. This interaction is an essential part of the work to explore the multimodal textualties through clicking, revealing, dragging, body movement and reading aloud. The research questions are explored through the work while working towards the aim of the piece and are underlined in the following sections in the essay.

INFLUENCES: DEPARTURE POINT

Garcilaso de La Vega
(1501– Oct 14, 1536)
"Soneto 23: En tanto que de rosa y d'azucena" (1522)

En tanto que de rosa y d'azucena
se muestra la color en vuestro gesto,
y que vuestro mirar ardiente, honesto,
con clara luz la tempestad serena;

y en tanto que'l cabello, que'n la vena
del oro s'escogió, con vuelo presto,
por el hermoso cuello blanco, enhiesto,
el viento mueve, esparce y desordena:

coged de vuestra alegre primavera
el dulce fruto, antes que'l tiempo airado
cubra de nieve la hermosa cumbre.

Marchitará la rosa el viento helado,
todo lo mudará la edad ligera,
por no hacer mudanza en su costumbre.

"Sonnet 23: So long as of red rose and lily white"

So long as of red rose and lily white
the proper colors of your face now show,
and your impassioned, fervent, honest glance
inflames the heart and holds it close in tow;

and so long as your hair, which in a vein
of gold was mined, endowed with rapid flight,
around your lovely white, and haughty throat
the wind can still move, scatter, and uncomb;

go, pluck now from the spring of your delight
the sweetest fruit, before the angry years
can wrap the lovely peak in snowy scenes.

The icy wind will cause the rose to wilt,
and all things will be changed by fickle time,
so as to never change its own routine.

Luis de Gongora
(July 11, 1561 –May 24, 1627)
"Mientras por competir con tu cabello" (1583)

Mientras por competir con tu cabello,
oro bruñido al sol relumbra en vano;
mientras con menosprecio en medio el llano
mira tu blanca frente el lilio bello;

mientras a cada labio, por cogello.
siguen más ojos que al clavel temprano;
y mientras triunfa con desdén lozano
del luciente cristal tu gentil cuello:

goza cuello, cabello, labio y frente,
antes que lo que fue en tu edad dorada
oro, lilio, clavel, cristal luciente,

no sólo en plata o vïola troncada
se vuelva, mas tú y ello juntamente
en tierra, en humo, en polvo, en sombra, en nada.

"While trying with your tresses to compete"

While trying with your tresses to compete
in vain the sun's rays shine on burnished gold;
while with abundant scorn across the plain
does your white brow the lily's hue behold;

while to each of your lips, to catch and keep,
are drawn more eyes than to carnations bright;
and while with graceful scorn your lovely throat
transparently still bests all crystal's light,

take your delight in throat, locks, lips, and brow,
before what in your golden years was gold,
carnation, lily, crystal luminous,

not just to silver or limp violets
will turn, but you and all of it as well
to earth, decay, dust, gloom, and nothingness.

I took as point of departure two pivotal sonnets from the Spanish Golden Age representative of the Renaissance and the Baroque, which are normally studied alongside each other in literature classes to compare the similarities and differences between these two cultural movements. One is "Sonnet 23: En tanto que de rosa y azucena" (1522)[98] by Garcilaso de La Vega, a 16th Century Spanish poet, using Italian Renaissance verse forms, poetic techniques and themes. The other sonnet is "Mientras por competir con tu cabello" by Luís de Gongora, a 17th Century Spanish poet from the Baroque period.[99] Gongora's sonnet can be considered as homage to Garcilaso, dedicating this sonnet to him around 60 years later in 1583. I thought they were two great works to explore and remediate into an interactive work of electronic literature; exploring digital literacies by mixing the old and the new[100]; and responding to the concepts that emerged from the sonnets to bring them into the digital medium.

They are strong conceptual poetic pieces with different styles and cultural aspects distinctively reflecting the attitudes from the Renaissance and the Baroque. Although both sonnets deal with the same themes: youth, nature, beauty, time and death; they compare the beauty of a woman to that of nature[101] -pretty much the themes of sonnets- they also comment on the effects of time on beauty and youth, make references to the fragility and ephemeral character of life and the inevitable death, through the use of metaphors (the feminine figure, her loss of beauty and youth with the passage of time) and encourage the reader to reflect and enjoy youth taking the Renaissance theme of the carpe diem (live in the present). Given the Renaissance was a more optimistic period than the Baroque, Garcilaso uses a Renaissance style referring to "the passing of time," while Gongora talks about old age as an "unavoidable event" producing two very different endings to the sonnets.

The ending to Garcilaso's last tercet:

Marchitará la rosa el viento helado,
todo lo mudará la edad ligera,

98 "So long as of red rose and lily white," published in *Poesías castellanas completas.*

99 "While trying with your tresses to compete," published in *Sonetos completos.*

100 Regarding the notion of media presenting itself as a refashion and improvement of old media, see Bolter and Grusin in Remediation, which they define "to mean the formal logic by which new media refashion prior media forms" (273), adding: "…we call the representation of one medium in another 'remediation,' and we will argue that remediation is a defining characteristic of the new digital media" (45).

101 This sonnet could well be addressed to Doña Isabel Freire for whom he felt some platonic love. See more about Gracilaso's life and literary work in the introduction by Elias Rivers to *Poesias Castellanas Completas.*

por no hacer mudanza en su costumbre,

The icy wind will cause the rose to wilt,
and all things will be changed by fickle time,
so as to never change its own routine.

And Gongora's with a Baroque sentiment is

....en tierra, en humo, en polvo, en sombra, en nada,

...to earth, decay, dust, gloom, and nothingness.

II. RESEARCH QUESTIONS

Therefore, given that cultural differences are reflected in the content and the writing styles of the sonnets, how could we explore the concepts that emanate from these sonnets in connection to the cultural references and attitudes of our period—the twenty first century mediated society—and the digital medium we inhabit? How are they relevant to our time and what new media writing styles can we use to develop a work of electronic literature? What digital literacies can be applied to invite the reader to be part of the poem and reflect about life while exploring the sonnets? What poetics of engagement and interaction are required for these writing spaces? These were all pertinent questions I addressed while developing the practical piece.

In order to delve into these enquires *Transient Self-Portrait* is a response to the concepts in question such as—the ephemeral nature of life, fragility, the passing of time, evanescence, non permanent, fluid, transient entities, the unavoidable event of death—concepts not only relevant to our age but also to the electronic world we inhabit. Consequently, these became the keywords for the production of the practice-based research project and were explored through the practice.

III. RESEARCH AIM

Considering the above interrogations, the aim became to find ways to remediate the sonnets into an interactive digital piece addressing the above questions and inherent concepts—to create a fluid portrait encapsulated inside the medium- grabbed inside the medium—with the use of a webcam which would grab the image of the participant while exploring the sonnets in a malleable medium of visual generative text and sound.

I explored this with the technical help of Jalal Miftah and Reda Yacouby, two computer science students, during my residency at the University of Technology of Compiegne in France. After considering different programmable languages, we decided to use the open source language of Processing (java simplified) for code-design, inclusion of sound, forms of reading and new media aesthetics of engagement and interaction while considering overall notions of the digital self and the fragile medium.

IV. THE INTERACTIVE WORK: INTERFACE

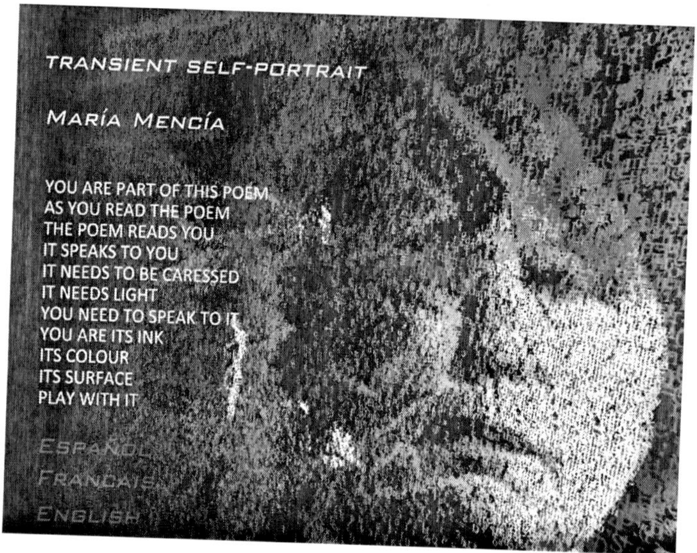

Figure 1: Screenshot from Transient Self-Portrait, opening screen.

The reader is presented with an interface with a portrait of the artist (a screenshot from the third stage of the piece built with the letters of the piece's underlining code) there is a text, on the left side of the interface, as a hint for the reader to explore the piece:

YOU ARE PART OF THIS POEM
AS YOU READ THE POEM
THIS POEM READS YOU
IT SPEAKS TO YOU
IT NEEDS TO BE CARESSED
IT NEEDS LIGHT
YOU NEED TO SPEAK TO IT
YOU ARE ITS INK, ITS COLOUR, ITS SURFACE
PLAY WITH IT

Figure 2: Reader interacting with Garcilaso's stage. Exhibition. The Digital Research in the Humanities and Arts (DRHA), Conference University of Greenwich, London, UK.

The lyrics in Spanish have been translated into English and French so we are provided a choice of three natural languages: Spanish, English and French to start interacting with the piece in its three different stages.

In the FIRST STAGE of the work, the reader needs to mouse over the interface to reveal the text, as well as trigger the voice of the poet reading Garcilaso's sonnet to us. The webcam is also picking up our presence, the reader starts to realize that there is something moving behind the text of Garcilaso's sonnet in the screen—perhaps a video of themselves? This is the first realization the readers/performers have of their presence inside the work, behind the screen, inside the text, inside the sonnet. After the screen is filled with 80% of the sonnet's lyrics, the text disappears and moves into second stage of the work.

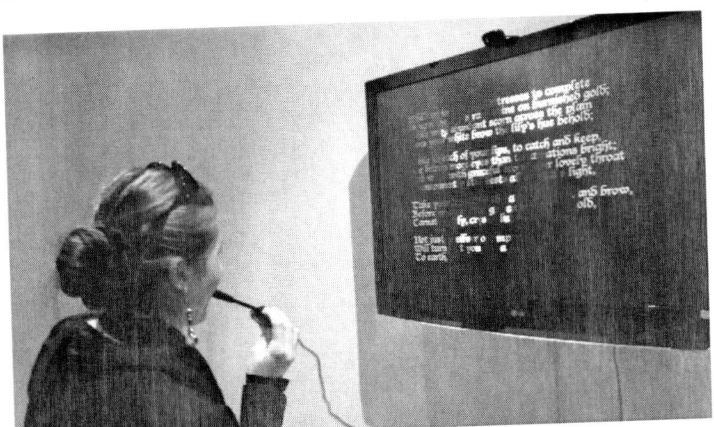

Figure 3: Reader interacting with Gongora's stage. Exhibition. The Digital Research in the Humanities and Arts (DRHA), Conference University of Greenwich, London, UK.

The SECOND STAGE of the poem is a response to Gongora's sonnet using a font in a Baroque style. The reader needs to put in much more effort to persuade the text to appear on the screen. The text is triggered by sound and the reader needs to move their body in order to see the text and be able to read it aloud. There is a performative aspect of body involvement and performance writing. When the full sonnet is visible the text slowly disintegrates into a pile of letters before the last stage—the data-self—appears.

The THIRD STAGE. In this last part of the interactive work, the invisible code that constructs the data-self, becomes visible and audible. The language text-code, the material surface of the work, which is read aloud by a female computerized voice. Data is the medium that shapes the reader's portrait, programming serving as a sculptural material helps to pick up light and shade to create a 3D portrait of the reader which can then be manipulated- by her interaction- into distorted and expanded landscapes of abstract language text-code. This last part of the work prompts the reader to question our transition into 'data-selves' in the electronic medium.

The piece therefore, follows a lineage passing from different stages of written, visual, aural, natural languages and code. As the work evolves, we are faced with ourselves. The piece is telling us through the sonnets about our ephemeral lives, transient selves and our transformation into data. We are inside the poem. We read the surface, firstly with natural languages, the lyrics. The poet reads to us and we read to the poet. We perform the poem. We become data behind the camera, behind the screen.

Figure 4: Screen shot of one of the many iterations from third stage the data-self

faced with ourselves
inside the poem
the poet reads to us
we read to the poet

we perform the poem
we become data
behind the camera
behind the screen
this is part of our identity and cultural aesthetics.

With Garcilaso's sonnet we experience the passing of time, Gongora tells us about the unavoidable event of death, with *Transient Self-Portrait* we dissipate into data selves.

V. CREATIVE PROCESS

THEORY- PRACTICE - CONCEPTS - CODE – DESIGN -COLLABORATION

> How much theory does artistic research need? Well, we should not say: "Here is a theory that sheds light on artistic practice," but "Here is art that invites us to think." (Borgdorf, 96)

In order to address the research questions and adapt the concepts evoked in the sonnets to the cultural aspects and attitudes of our period *Transient Self-Portrait* incorporates them as part of the virtual realm of the digital piece through visual metaphors, interactive advances and adaptable programming.

The creative process consists of a remediation of forms (see Bolter and Grusin), and an exploration of digital literacies to get the reader immersed in the reading of the sonnets. In the passing of the sonnets from the page to the digital medium, I envisaged a spatial interface for language and image to interplay, as found in visual and concrete poems. I considered the poetic forms that digital technologies allow such as navigation, the use of layers, time, transitions, erasing of words, the generation of text with vocal sounds, and the overall reader participation, to expose the aspects noted in the following list of parameters for poetics/aesthetics. The reading experience is that of revealing layers of text and sound helped in some cases by body performativity.

PARAMETERS FOR POETICS/AESTHETICS

The shifting from the linguistic (the transparent, the legible) to the visual language and vice-versa.

Looking *At* the text, the surface, the materiality of the text.
Looking *Through* the text, the semantic meaning of language.
In and *Out* of language: the in-between space of the legible/illegible.

Meaning production in the in-between image, sound and text.
Open meaning/multiple readings of the work.
The materiality of language: The Surface materiality
Multi-linear, non-linear structures of multiple layers (image, sound, text).
The digital reader.
The experience of the work.

As I described in my introduction, the above are some of the conceptual bases of my overall investigation, acting as methodology, guidelines and foundation for the production of the creative works.

In addition, during the research process, many books of influential theorists have passed through my hands, on the subjects of media languages, software, the self and embodiment. These include Sherry Turkle (immaterial self, mediated landscapes, life on the screen), Lev Manovich (language of new media, software studies), Florian Cramer (speculation on digital code and literary text, interface aesthetics), Noah Wardrip-Fruin (software projects). Also, Mark B.N. Hansen's work on the subject of embodiment and his argument that "all reality is mixed reality" engaged me. However, although they form part of my overall research interests, and ideas discussed in these books might be embedded in my research project, they have not been applied to the production of the work. Research is unavoidably informed by our intellectual endeavours but in the production of my practice, it is never my aim to apply theories to my artistic work. On the contrary my practice brings me to these theories and engages me into theoretical dialogues, which then work as theoretical frameworks.

The choice of programming language to explore concepts derived from the sonnets, poetics of engagement, interface aesthetics and poetics was also a part of the creative process in *Transient Self-Portrait*. Poetic and aesthetic aspects merge in works like this where natural, visual and programmable languages fuse to create multimodal textualities.

CODE AND OPEN SOURCE

Choosing an open source programmable language such as Processing was significant in the production of the work since it reflected my interest in a sharing economy of culture as opposed to a commercial economy, issues which are well argued in Lawrence Lessig's seminal book *Remix: Making Art and Commerce Thrive in the Hybrid Economy*. He contrasts "read-write" (RW) and "read-only" (RO) cultures and the development of new media literacies while discussing the paradigm shift that has occurred in fundamental models of writing and creative practices regarding notions of intellectual Property (IP) and authorship, producer and consumer, and dissemination models. Therefore re-using the open source Processing's code is very much part of the creative act: "remix is an essential act of (RW) ReadWrite creativity" (55). It was interesting to introduce this open source programme to students of computer science. They had always programmed everything from scratch but appreciated using a platform where code could be repurposed. This means that in return anybody can re-appropriate the code from this piece and remix it in to create a new work.

CODE AS SURFACE MATERIALITY

After exploring Garcilaso's and Gongora's sonnets in stage one and two through visual metaphors of text disintegration, and disappearance, the reader encounters stage three of *Transient Self-Portrait* where instead of natural languages, the source code is revealed and becomes the surface materiality of the work. Code triggers the webcam, grabs, translates and shapes the participants' faces into visual landscapes formed of letters of programming language. These can be distorted by the reader's interaction, making them more or less legible, zooming in and out to move from figurative to abstract landscapes. Simultaneously, we hear the reading aloud of this code by a computerised voice, sound and text disintegrating to give end to the narrative.

Inspired by N. Katherine Hayles' book *My Mother was a Computer* (2005), six years before *Transient Self-Portrait*, around 2006, I started to explore the idea of surface materiality, examining code as the medium and the material of the work.

I produced a series of *Speech-Sound Generated Visual Poems* (2007), based in Hansjorg Mayer's *alphabetenquadratbuch* poem (alphabetsquarebook), all made in the shape of a square.[102] One of the pieces consists of a pair of poems, one is filled with the letters of the alphabet rotating and generated by sound, the other reveals the code from this alphabet poem, thus, presenting the surface language of natural language and code. Later on, I re-titled this collection *Generative Poems*, as a group of ongoing experimental generative poems including a piece entitled the alphabetic (exhibited at the Palazzo delle Arti, Naples, Italy, 2010).[103] This is a triptych of three projections, each in the shape of a square, consisting of surfaces filled with multilingual alphabet

---

102 In my essay on this work, I describe the poems as follows: "This work is part of an ongoing series of interactive, experimental and generative poetic texts using Processing to generate visual compositions which fill the viewable space in time, with a growing pattern triggered by sound and silence. These particular poems developed with Szekely were inspired by Hansjorg Mayer's alphabetenquadratbuch poem (alphabetsquarebook). In all the experiments, three communication systems are coming together: image, writing and code. It is my aim to stretch the possibilities of programming to produce generative texts activated by sound and rooted in the tradition of concrete poetry, its formal representation, production processes and progression with technological advances."

103 Technical support with Processing Evan Raskob. Exhibition Palazzo delle Arti, Naples, Itay, 2010.

letters and written language gestures (Western, Arabic and Chinese), also generated by sound. In 2009 at the E-Poetry Festival Barcelona, I performed, some of the *Generative Poems*, where the body activated the text triggered through a webcam.[104] Therefore, aspects of *Transient Self-Portrait* such as generative text, textual visual materialities, audio activation, participation and performance evolved from these previous works. Creative research is always a continuing and evolving process and all my works borrow and derive from each other as happened with this one.

The curiosity for code derives partly from my interest in linguistics and translation—from one system to another—whether visual, linguistic or technological. However, it also derives from my background as fine artist, after having worked with a variety of materials to build sculptures, installations, objects and performances, code became a sculptural material and a language to design, sculpt, mold and write. It does not only shape the visual aspect of the piece but is in itself the piece. Without code there is no surface, there is no work. The plasticity and materiality of code creates the *surface materiality*. Hence, my engagement with N. K. Hayles' ground breaking discussion on the textual materiality of digital writing and her argument for a theoretical framework where language and code come together. In her book *Writing Machines* she argues for a methodology of interpretation she called Medium Specific Analysis as 'a kind of 'criticism that pays attention to the material apparatus producing the literary work as a physical artifact" (29). This was manifested in all the programmable choices taken while producing *Transient Self-Portrait* and in the works mentioned above.

It is worth mentioning that in this area of research and critical analysis, as well as Hayles, there are many other critics, writers, poets and scholars like Rita Raley (2006), John Cayley (2002), and more currently Mark C Marino (2006), who have argued extensively and presented different viewpoints about textual materiality and code. Also, under the genre of codeworks in electronic literature, there are practitioners such as Mez Breeze well known for her Mezangelle, a creolized language where she combines natural language and code. Talan Memmott has also written on the subject and used a kind of creolized text of human language and computer code in works like "Lexia to Perplexia" (2000).

CODE - CONCEPTS - DESIGN

Programming played an integral part in the planning of the stages and aesthetics of the work to integrate the conceptual ideas from the sonnets and involve the reader in the exploratory process.

104 José Carlos Silvestre, technical developer.

In a mediated society we are constantly facing ourselves through technology, we flirt with webcams or any other lenses and we document every minute of our lives, especially through social media where we seem to have a need to grab and record our lives. Why then, not use a webcam to grab the image of the main character- the reader- inside the text, to create a fluid portrait behind the surface, beyond the screen, and with this, explore the relationship between physical-virtual and the flux and repositioning of a self no longer static. In the sonnets the self gets older, disintegrates and dies. With technology, the digital self becomes data, becomes obsolete and disappears with the instability of technology.

The passing of time in our lives is also reflected in technology, which is so much a part of our life. The fragility of life evoked in the sonnets became an interesting notion to explore through the use of code to create a fragile interactive work. How can programming be used to create a fragile piece? What aspects can highlight this characteristic? In order to highlight the fragility of technology, we looked at aspects such as the need of light for the piece to be able to function- for the webcam to grab the reader's face inside the work (the reflection of the self in this exploration)- and in this production, code became like a kind of sculptural material, which gave form to the work, the material surface.

In addition, there is the unavoidable condition of technology to become obsolete and in this volume of *#WomenTechLit* we have a section on 'migrations of forms' where authors discuss how they have tried to implement their works with more or less success into new digital platforms. *Transient Self-Portrait*, after five years, is already highlighting the precariousness of technology. *Transient Self-Portrait* also has highlighted the precariousness of technology and recently had to be updated to work with new operating systems.

Overall, with Processing as the programmable language, we had to find ways to activate the webcam to make the reader part of the work, to reveal the text and activate the text through sound. We researched and explored ways to create fluid textualities and unstable multimodal texts through mouse dragging, voice activation and by making the work different every time depending on the outside environment. The portrait absorbs the light and color from the readers whose clothes serve as color palettes to create the many portraits.

CODE AND INTERACTION - POETICS OF ENGAGEMENT

In the production of the interactive work there were many discussions and decisions taken about, what I call, the poetics of engagement: the passing from one stage to another, timing each stage, ways to make the readers part of the work, revealing the text and sound, activating the text with the voice, and using code to trigger the webcam to capture the outside colors and the image of the reader. The webcam as interface involves the reader in the work so that he/she becomes part of it. Here the physical and the virtual reflection face each other.

In this process many design features were taken into account for the development of the interactive aesthetics of the work and poetics of engagement such as timing, light, color, layering and the illusion of 3D, while exploring notions of reading, multimodal text, remediation of forms through the concepts of the sonnets. I briefly outline here some characters these poetic forms involved.

Poetics of time include developing transitions and poetics of disappearing.

Poetics of layering and revealing were explored through mouse over and sound activation. Revealing sound, revealing text and image while a webcam was capturing the user.

Poetics of translation: The Palette. In the translation process the camera picks up the image from the outside and the code tells the computer to translate it into text, into different colors and in 3D effect depending on the light the camera is picking.

Poetics of form: relationship light and color. The third stage creates an illusion of 3D textual relief by playing with light and color. Here the programme puts letter by letter in the same color as the image captured in the foreground, (the reader interacting with the work). Thus, this 3D effect changes according to the brightness of the each point.

The foreground becomes the background- the image the camera captures becomes the background of the work- here there is an interaction between the reader and the work through the camera as an interface.

you are part of the poem
the poet reads you
you read to the poet
you are reading yourself to death
since you are inside the poem
embodied in the poem.

Poetics of sound and translation of the sonnets. The sonnets were translated from Spanish into English and French, recorded and saved as mp4s to create the layers of sound in the three different languages. The underlined code, which creates the piece, was also recorded using Google voices and added as a female voice to the third stage.

Fonts were taken into account: for the Renaissance *Apple Chancery Renaissance*, *Bickham Script* and *Lucida Blackletter* and *Bank Gothic* for the Baroque.

VI. CREATIVE COLLABORATIVE PROCESS

DISCUSSIONS, EXPLORATION, REFLECTION, PRODUCTION, PROGRAMMING, TESTING

The collaborative creative process was that of researching, producing, reflecting, programming and testing the medium to explore the notions of the sonnets in an electronic media society characterized by dialogues with self-images.

The sonnets activated by the reader pass from different stages of written, visual, aural, language and code. These stages were carefully planned through different design processes in order to get the reader involved through poetics of engagement and interaction with the text. Working with Jalal Miftah and Reda Yacouby was very stimulating and hassle free perhaps because we had well defined roles. They were mainly dealing with the programming.

VII. CONCLUSION

The production of this piece has led me to research poetic forms of classical literature, concepts of time, life and death, the digital self and the use of digital technologies and programming languages to explore new media literacies and bring these sonnets to digital born generations.

Through the observation of readers performing with this work, the most gratifying moment was to see how the students invigilating The Digital Research in the Humanities and Arts exhibition had learnt the sonnets by heart through interacting with them. They were a public not familiar with electronic literature, or even with the more familiar genre of digital art, but they were eager to engage and explore the interface, the poetics of engagement and media literacies, which allowed them to learn the sonnets and recite them. This created a full circle in the life of a poem: from oral to writing to oral; or in this case from writing to digital writing to oral.

The questioning of code in this collaborative adventure has been a stimulating aspect of the research. The poetics of engagement through layering, sounds, time, light, color, translations, webcam, have enriched and evolved my understanding of code and digital technologies. Processing is a playful 'programme', which allows a lot of creativity. However, I can envisage this work with a more robust code, working across platforms where the reader/performer can get more immersed in the work in a three-dimensional surface through aesthetics of embodiment and performance.

Overall, I thoroughly enjoyed creating a fragile piece of digital media, a piece that needs to be caressed and explored; a piece that needs light, time and patience (perhaps) in a world of speed and little time to sit and think. As the poets reminds us: Carpe Diem! Enjoy the present!

Art and Concept by María Mencía
Programming-Realisation by Reda Yacouby and Jalal Miftah
Special thanks to Serge Bouchardon

Sonnets:

"En tanto que de rosa y azucena, Sonnet XXIII" by Garcilaso de la Vega
"Mientras por competir con tu cabello" by Luís de Gongora

Translations:

French by Alix Ingber
English by Pierre Darmangeat

Sonnets read by:

Spanish by Pablo Romero
English by Ian Smith
French by Serge Bouchardon

Funded by Faculty of Arts and Social Sciences, Kingston University, London, UK
Residency hosted by Technologies and Human Sciences (TSH) Department, Université de Technologie of Compiegne (France)

TRANSIENT SELF–PORTRAIT: RESEARCH OUTPUTS

EXHIBITIONS: MEXICO, PORTUGAL, FRANCE AND UNITED KINGDOM.

Plataformas de la Imaginacion, Escenarios de la Literatura Electronica, Centro Cultural Universitario Tlatelolco y Universum- Museo de Las Ciencias de la UNAM, Mexico, 2015. Curators: Maria Andrea Giovine and Eugenio Tisselli.

Language and the Interface, International Conference on Digital Literary Studies, University of Coimbra, Portugal, 2015. Exhibition, Curators: Daniela Côrtes Maduro, Ana Marques da Silva, Diogo Marques.

The Digital Research in the Humanities and Arts (DRHA), Conference University of Greenwich, London, UK, 2014. Exhibition, Curators: David Waterworth and James Hobbs (peer-reviewed).

Figure 5: *Transient Self-Portrait*, Exhibition in Museo de Las Ciencias de la UNAM, Mexico, 2015.

Chercher le Texte, Locating the Text in Electronic Literature, a conference including performances and exhibitions of selected works, organised by the Electronic Literature Organization (ELO) and hosted by the Laboratoire Paragraphe and the EnsAD (École nationale supérieure des Arts Décoratifs) (peer-reviewed), ELO Paris 2013. This virtual gallery showed at:

1. The French National Library in the exhibition "Digital Literatures From Yesterday to Tomorrow"

2. Public Library of the Centre Pompidou and

3. Ecole Nationale Supérieure des Arts décoratifs for the duration of the ELO conference (23-29th September). It is a part of the DDDL :: Digital Digital Digital Littérature site and the Chercher le Texte site.

Words Unstable on the Table, (Mencía M curator), Watermans Art Centre, as part of the E-POETRY [2013] Kingston University. LONDON: NEW WORKS, NEW FRAMES. (Peer-reviewed)

WORKS CITED

Bolter, David Jay and Grusin Richard. *Remediation: Understanding New Media.* Cambridge, Mass, London: MIT. 2000.

Borgdorff, Henk. "Artistic Research and Academia: an Uneasy Relationship." http://docplayer.net/storage/27/9887628/1481640044/Cy7N7-_MlnebRO-7hYxzXKg/9887628.pdf. Accessed 13 Dec 2016.

Cayley, John. "The Code is Not the Text (unless it is the text)." *Electronic Book Review (ebr)*, 2002. http://www.electronicbookreview.com/thread/electropoetics/literal Accessed 28 June 2016.

Ciplijauskaité. Biruté (ed). *Luis the Góngora, Sonetos Completos*. Clásicos Castalia. Madrid, 1985.

Cramer, Florian. *Anti-Media: Ephemera on Speculative Arts*. Institute of Network Cultures, naioro publishers, Rotterdam, 2013.

Electronic Literature Collection 3. Edited by Stephanie Boluk, Leonardo Flores, Jacob Garbe, Anastasia Salter, 2014. Accessed July 16th 2016. http://collection.eliterature.org/3/work.html?work=motions

Fuller, Matthew (ed). *Software Studies: A Lexicon*. Cambridge, Mass; London: MIT Press, 2008.

Hansen, Mark B.N. *Bodies in Code: Interfaces with Digital Media*. New York and London: Routledge, 2006.

Hayles, N. Katherine. *How We Became Posthuman: Virtual Bodies in Cybernetics, literature, and informatics*. Chicago: University of Chicago Press. 1999.

_,_. *Writing Machines*. Cambridge, MA: MIT Press, 2002.

_,_. *My Mother was a Computer*. Chicago, London: University of Chicago Press, 2005.

_,_. *Electronic Literature: New Horizons for the Literary*. Notre Dame, Ind.: University of Notre Dame, 2008.

Kristeva, Julia. *Revolution in Poetic Language*. New York: Columbia University Press.1984.

Lanham, Richard. A. *The Electronic Word*. London: The University of Chicago Press. 1994.

Lessig, Lawrence. *Remix: making art and commerce thrive in the hybrid economy*. UK: Penguin Press 2008.

Manovich, Lev. *Software Takes Command*. New York, London: Bloomsbury, 2013.

Marino M.C. "Critical Code Studies." *Electronic Book Review (ebr)*. http://www.electronicbookreview.com/thread/electropoetics/codology, 2006. Accessed 20 June 2016.

McCaffery, Steve. *North of Intention: Critical Writings, 1973-86*. New York & Toronto: Roof Books,1998.

Mencía, María. *Transient Self-Portrait* (2012). http://www.mariamencia.com/pages/transientself_portrait.html Accessed 28 June 2016.

_,_.. "Birds Singing Other Birds Songs" (2001) in *Electronic Literature Collection Vol 1*, K. Hayles, N. Montfort, S. Rettberg, S. Strickland (eds.) The Electronic Literature Organization, UCLA Department of English, Los Angeles. (online) http://collection.eliterature.org/1/.

Mez http://mezbreezedesign.com Accessed 28 June 2016

Raley, Rita. (2002). *Interferences: [Net.Writing] and the Practice of Codework*. Electronic Book Review. http://www.electronicbookreview.com/thread/electropoetics/net.writing Accessed 28 June 2016.

_,_. *Code.surface || Code.depth. dichtung-digital - journal für digitale ästhetik*. 2006. http://www.dichtung-digital.org/2006/1-Raley.htm Accessed 6 July 2016.

Rivers, Elias L, (ed). *Garcilaso de La Vega Poesias Castellanas Completas*. Clásicos Castalia, Madrid, 1996.

Schäfer, Jörgen and Peter Gendolla. *Beyond the Screen: Transformations of Literary Structures, Interfaces and Genres*. Verlag, Bielefeld: Transcript, 2010.

Smith Hazel. & Roger T. Dean. *Practice-led Research, Research-led Practice in the Creative Arts*. Edinburgh University Press. 2009.

Wardrip-Fruin, Noah. *Expressive Processing*, Cambridge, Massachusetts: MIT Press. 2009.

The Evolution and Actualisation of #PRISOM: A Literary Anti-Surveillance Game

BY MEZ BREEZE

Mez Breeze and Andy Campbell's #PRISOM...examines online realities since Edward Snowden's exposure of classified documents as evidence of the participation of companies like AOL, Apple, Google, Facebook, Microsoft, Paltalk, Skype, Yahoo!, and YouTube, as well as wearable technologies, in the NSA's PRISM data-mining program. #PRISOM ask[s] us to question the normalization of domestic surveillance as a part of everyday life in the context of a country whose international clout has been historically anchored to its democratic principles. - Dale Hudson, New York University Abu Dhabi.

Figure 1: *#PRISOM* Screenshot: The Entryway

You are about to enter #PRISOM. [105]You load the #PRISOM Configuration Screen. A blue-black drone encased in a clear bubble hovers on your toolbar. You click the "Play!" button.

You find yourself dumped in a glass city by an exhaust-spewing Dropship. The fenced off city looks stark: horizon white contrasts with transparent buildings tinged with translucent blue. The air thrums with jumbled audio-snippets. Your fellow #PRISOM inmates consist of blank bodied Mannequins who have likewise been dropped into the sterile entryway. They, like you, seem unsure about how to best navigate this unusual place... Should you read the "Help" options offered? Do you try to

105 http://dreamingmethods.com/prisom/.

jump the fence? As you spot a Drone hovering near an Induction Noticeboard, you suddenly hear a booming Drone ConTROLLer voice robotically bleat the following:

> Welcome to #PRISOM, our Perpetual Re-Educational ID State Organisational Management facility. Your ResisTOR status has been assessed and graded: consequently, you have been charged according to the severity of your crimes against the ConTROLLer State.
>
> You will be re-educated in the ways of the ConTROLLed.
>
> Your Resistance will not be tolerated.
>
> You will be re-educated.
>
> You must now locate the Re-Educational Material present in this #PRISOM facility. You will answer all "#WhatDoYouDo?" questions by interacting with the information contained in the Black Object Monument Blocks [or Info-BOMBs]. Be warned: you will have one attempt, and one attempt only, to answer questions contained in these Info-BOMBs.
>
> The ConTROLLer Drones are here to monitor you during this Re-Educative process. Do not attempt to interact with the Drones. You will avoid areas where Terrorist Organisational Representatives may have infiltrated the facility. These areas are deemed off limits to all #PRISOM inmates. Failure to avoid these areas will result in active punishment. You have been warned.
>
> This Induction Session is now closed. You may seek any additional clarification from the Induction Board.

You start walking through the fenced-off entryway into the facility itself, past the Induction Board that lists the information that the ConTROLLer123 Drone has just broadcast. The facility seems bare, vast. Buildings loom. Huge propaganda posters and wall-sized videos cover the walls.

You spot a ConTROLLer Drone hovering overhead. It starts to move towards you, so you jump onto a nearby platform and zoom towards the Info-BOMBs ...

Your time in #PRISOM has begun.

CREEPING CONCEPTIONS

> ...*#PRISOM is the digital equivalent of Orwell's 1984.*- James O'Sullivan, Digital Humanities Research Associate at the University of Sheffield.

At the complex age of 13 (perhaps 14?) I read the novel *1984*. This classically dystopian book both shocked and intrigued me: I understood some, but not all, of it. I intrigue-wrestled with the "book within a book" format, and internalized the encompassing power of the slogan. I angst-compared it to another dystopic tome, *Moreau's Other Island* by Brian Aldiss. Reading *1984* provoked a healthy scepticism towards institutionally sanctioned knowledge. It helped shape within my boiling teenage consciousness a questioning orientation towards the realities of being surveilled.

Figure 2: #*PRISOM* Screenshot: An Info-BOMB

Having Orwell's forebodings firmly centred in my mind, the spectre of "Big Brother" continued to hover. Over coming decades, I chewed the topic of privacy violations associated with surveillance states with more than a deal of gusto. I wrote code poetry about it.[106] When interviewed, I referenced it. I devoted social media space(s) to it. And most of all, I came to the realization that such encroaching tendencies were steadily creeping into institutionalized systems. It was during this period—smack-bang on a chilly morning in September 2001—when I woke to find my world had cracked. After weirdly deviating from my morning routine by switching on the TV, I sat gaze-glued to the screen, mesmerized by a rolling set of videos showing a sky filled with systematic explosions. These explosions were of the type where it appears someone has accidentally set fire to a pyrotechnic factory.

With the news ticker text-screaming "terrorism" and "Kabul" at the bottom of the screen, my confused moral compass struggled to make sense of such disjointed input: channel flicking revealed horrific images of planes hurtling into drunk-tilted towers. Then I noticed the date stamp on the news ticker: "September 12th" in Australian time, which, when translated, equated to "September 11th" in New York, USA.

106 https://drive.google.com/file/d/0B8NB82sNl3mLNHpvRXZ6VGtCa3Q4S2Y5TmpBOWprb0hrOFdz/view

It was then that the thought struck: the world as privacy advocates know it, or have come to know it, will be no more. This notion was so predictively charged it imprinted heavily into memory. This assessment of such a culturally-tectonic event proved prophetic in shaping *#PRISOM*, an anti-surveillance game. This game requires players to dodge propaganda-spewing drones while engaging with objects, scenarios and text engineered specifically to question their own roles in sacrificing individuated privacy.

A GESTATION ITCH AND ACTUALIZATION SCRATCH

> *#PRISOM is fantastic... Hilarious-disturbing and thought-provoking stuff throughout, one scenario has the border control agents demanding my social media passwords when taking my phone, tablet AND video game device... now THAT'S where I draw the line!* —Jeff Watson, Director of The Situation Lab.

In various guises, growing erosions of privacy laws have proceeded to manifest since the attack on the World Trade Centre on September 11, 2001. Given an already heightened flagging of privacy and surveillance issues, I began to ponder the concept of incorporating such into a major creative work. Accordingly, I let the news of the shifts in quotidian surveillance accumulate. I watched an alarmingly wide cross-section of the western populace react apathetically to relevant Wikileaks releases. I observed huge groups of informed persons content to disregard Edward Snowden's revelations concerning the blanket information gathering of the "Five Eyes" Network (comprised of Australia, New Zealand, Canada, the UK, and the USA) and the clandestine "PRISM" Program. On observing such a mainstream acceptance of such overt monitoring, in 2013, *#PRISOM* stirrings began to creatively-itch.

The first *#PRISOM* concepts hit one day after noticing an increase in localized air traffic. My thoughts wandered to how it must have been in the peak stages of World War Two, where the very mention of the Luftwaffe injected fear into civilians and military persons alike.

This coincided directly with my crafting of an Appstorm feature article describing the #Glassholes phenomenon[107] (plus an earlier article from 2012 focusing on Augmented and Virtual Reality[108]). This article stressed the importance of questioning new wearable tech and the impact these types of devices may have at a societal, and cultural, level:

107 http://web.appstorm.net/general/features/google-glass-and-the-glassholes-phenomenon/.

108 http://thenextweb.com/insider/2012/08/25/how-augmented-reality-will-change-way-live/.

> What seems different regarding the impending impact of Google Glass (and wearables in general) is the type of apathetic conditioning we—as individuals and as a grouped global audience—seem content to endure. Have we reached a type of surveillance fatigue where news of the entire documentation of our lives, dreams and activities no longer register on our internal radars as an implicit threat to our sense of self? Or is this not actually apathy, but more an acceptance of a kind of learned helplessness[109] that can plague constantly surveilled populations?

Although being satisfied with the points the article raised regarding the link between privacy-sacrificing and surveillance, a feature article just didn't seem enough. The urge to craft an expansive interactive work exploring such issues just wouldn't quit.

In 2013, the drive to realize such an anti-surveillance opus moved from a gestation-itch to an actualization-scratch, with the idea fomenting to create a critical game-like work. This space, or 3D Environment, would be based on the increasing acceptance of global surveillance strategies. At this stage, *#PRISOM* was to be titled "#Glassholes," and was imagined as a standalone work involving a direct critique of Google Glass. Instead, the actual *#PRISOM* incarnation stayed true to my initial vision, and was more centred on exposing the dangers of blindly adopting such privacy-reducing tech and the parallel rise of across-the-board surveillance.

In July 2013, when encountering a call for a Commission call-out for projects for inclusion in the Exhibition component of the 2013 International Symposium on Mixed and Augmented Reality (ISMAR2013), I knew I'd found the right way to fund the creation of *#PRISOM*. This exhibition titled "Transreal Topologies" was part of a Mixed and Augmented Reality Art (MARart) scoping study initiative that was launched at ISEA2013—a perfect venue for such an Augmented Reality project.

The very first *#PRISOM* script sprang from my writing piece called "Through the Looking UnGlass." This code poetry piece was constructed in Mezangelle, a poetic language form crafted via the merging of code, programming conventions, and lyrical leanings. The Wikipedia entry for Mezangelle describes it as being:

> ...primarily based on hybrid words. Like the portmanteau words invented by Lewis Carroll or used in James Joyce's novel Finnegans Wake, it dissects and recombines language and stacks multiple layers of meanings into single phrases. Beyond that, it is an Internet-cultural poetic language deriving much of its tension from incorporating formal code and informal speech at once. Its base construction qualifies it as hypertext on a morphological and grammatical level. It is not syntactically fixed and is in continuous artistic development. Through its semantic and syntactical layering, mezangelle achieves an aesthetic effect of altering words and letters from discrete, digital units into

109 On "learned helplessness," see https://en.wikipedia.org/wiki/Learned_helplessness.

fluid, quasi-analog information.[110]

Mezangelle seemed a precise fit for a projected world constructed around lingual and behavioral restrictions. In order to help craft such a 3D world environment, I turned to a previous collaborator, Andy Campbell , and asked if he'd like to jump on-board the #PRISOM construction train.[111]

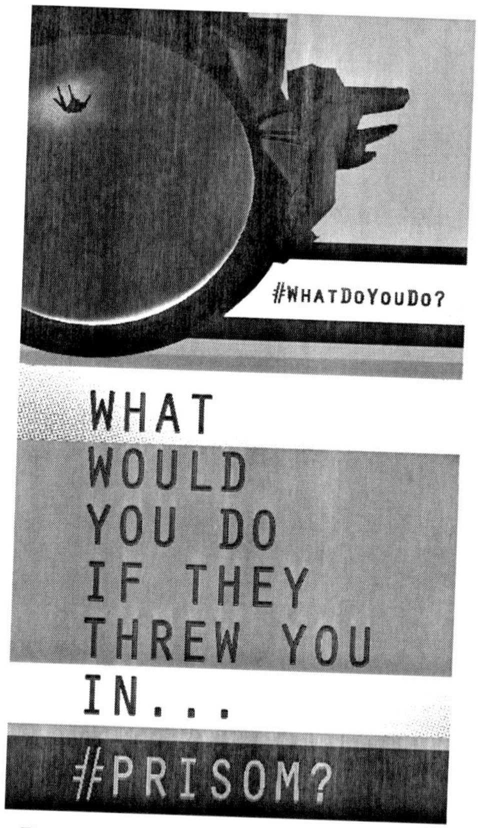

Figure 3: A *#PRISOM* Promotional Poster

THE DEVELOPMENT CHALLENGE

> *This beautifully rendered work shows the painful banality of surveillance as one wanders aimlessly through the non-spaces of a control society.* – Electronic Literature Organization's 2015 Conference Review Panel describing *#PRISOM*.

110 https://en.wikipedia.org/wiki/Mezangelle.

111 http://dreamingmethods.com/.

In July 2013 (after securing Andy Campbell's involvement in the project and obtaining the official commission go-ahead) work finally commenced on the design and development of *#PRISOM*. As *#PRISOM* was originally commissioned for the exhibition component of ISMAR2013 in conjunction with the South Australian University's Wearable Computer Lab and the Royal Institution of Australia, myself, Andy, Julian and key members of the Lab began formulating the best strategy for AR project integration. This AR integration had to reflect the overarching theme centring on increasing global covert surveillance plus the increasing monitoring of individual's private lives.

Figure 4: *#PRISOM* Description and Accolades

During the development of *#PRISOM*, it became apparent that the project would be best developed for multiple platforms, including a browser-based version (accessible via a Unity browser plugin), a HUD (Heads Up Display Unit/AR Headset), and as a downloadable, standalone executable. *#PRISOM's* target audience was to be broad: internationally centred, encompassing interactive narrative users, digital story enthusiasts, those who have a basic understanding of new immersive forms, and gamers (from indie gamers to "altgamers"). Because of the short timeframe involved from the acceptance of the project to the showcasing at the ISMAR exhibition in October 2013, *#PRISOM* took shape in a somewhat frenzied development phase, with Andy and I juggling all major design and development aspects, artist Chris Joseph providing the soundtrack,[112] and the New Zealand-based Human Interface Technology Lab helping with testing and AR logistics.

When developing and designing *#PRISOM*, we aimed to break through the general public's surveillance fatigue in relation to current whistleblower revelations (*#PRISOM's* title is a portmanteau of the terms "PRISM" and "prison"). To order to construct a 3D environment that would meet this aim, Andy and I settled on the use of the Unity game engine. The crucial factor in presenting *#PRISOM* as a game rather than in a more static (or passive) form is the audience's ability to interact with (in) the environment via choice based interactions. In *#PRISOM*, a player needs to make moral based choices to actually progress, or even to find additional narrative cues. Crafting true immersion in such a 3D space was crucial, as the overall impact would have been greatly reduced if we'd created the work in a more traditional literary format.

This choice of constructing *#PRISOM* as a game-like work aligns strongly with earlier conceptual writing centring on the idea of the "Synthetic," a term originating from the early days of my Augmentology.com project (2008): it signposts work/states that don't strictly fall into the categories of virtual, augmented or mixed reality, but that instead incorporates and extends these classifications.[113] "Synthetic Reality" evokes strong connotations of replicating issues and concepts that we think of as traditionally taking place in the so-called "real world" in digital environments such as games.

MECHANICS AND MODIFICATIONS

> *...[A] glaring-prismatic dystopian-penal semi-unnarrative cybergameworld.* — Dr Sally Evans, Editor at Rabbit Press, describing *#PRISOM*.

#PRISOM is a game that is set in a 3D space in true First Person Shooter style, but that modifies a player's ability to engage within the space as they typically would in a standard FPS by controlling game progression through weapon choice, health-pack acquisition, levelling up, and additional customary variables. Unlike standard FPS game creators, we actively attempted to partially repurpose a player's ability to engage with the gamespace. When a player first enters *#PRISOM*, the navigation appears to mirror FPS conventions (space bar to jump, arrow keys/"wasd" to move, c to crouch).[114] However, as a player begins to move around the prison-like environment, it becomes appar-

112 http://www.chrisjoseph.org/.

113 https://web.archive.org/web/20150423093116/http://arsvirtuafoundation.org/research/2009/03/01/_social-tesseracting_-part-1

114 http://www.reddit.com/r/Games/comments/10zp61/why_is_wasd_the_standard/.

ent that mechanics related to standard FPS actions are unpredictable. Instances of this include some—but not all—of the travel platforms being marginally awkward to use, or when players seek to shift into areas that they assume are safe, but their movements instead trigger explosive glass walls. During development and beta testing, we always knew we were constructing the game aspects correctly if we found ourselves being pushed past that delicious FPS-like adrenalin flow and into irritation and/or frustration territory, which is exactly appropriate an experience for *#PRISOM* inmates.

Figure 5: *#PRISOM* Screenshot: "The Filter of Reason"

In a single play through of *#PRISOM*, a player will encounter one of three endings. These three possible conclusions are all similar in that the player (warning: spoilers ahead), no matter what choices they make, ultimately end up as being incarnated into the consciousness of the ConTROLLer123 Drone. Each of the three ending paths are, however, subtly different according to the choices a player makes in-game, and how that influences their overall Re-Education level. The text of each alternate ending is as follows:

1. ConTROLLer-angled ending

> You have now successfully completed the Re-Education process through your interactions in *#PRISOM*. Congratulations. Your indoctrination is now complete. Your reward is a permanent upgrade to ConTROLLer status through an irrevocable, worldwide, royalty-laden, exclusive, perpetual license to revoke all your remaining personal rights and all associated civil liberties. Welcome, ConTROLLer123.

2. ResisTOR-angled ending.

> Your Re-Education session is now finished. Your attempts to revise your ResisTOR status have been unsuccessful through your interactions in *#PRISOM*. Your punishment is a permanent upgrade to ConTROLLer status through an irrevocable, worldwide, royalty-laden, exclusive, perpetual license to revoke all

your remaining personal rights and all associated civil liberties. Your consciousness has now been claimed as part of the ConTROLLer Drone Mind. Welcome, ConTROLLer123.

3. Finishing-all-posters-angled ending.

Your Re-Education session is now terminated. Your attempts to revise your ResisTOR status have been only partially successful through your interactions in *#PRISOM*. Your punishment is a permanent upgrade to ConTROLLer status through a worldwide, royalty-laden, exclusive, perpetual license to revoke all your remaining personal rights and all associated civil liberties. Your consciousness has now been claimed as part of the ConTROLLer Drone Mind. Welcome, ConTROLLer123.

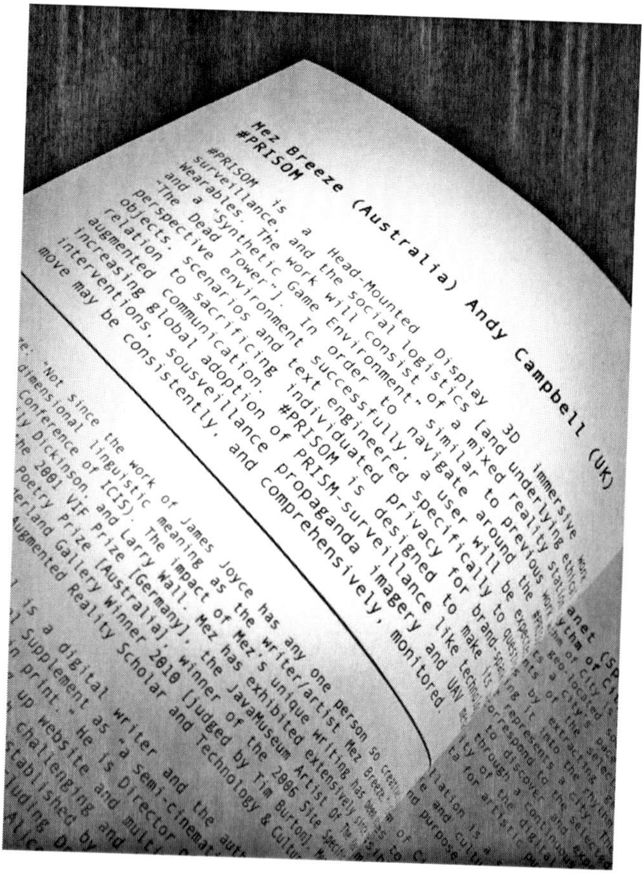

Figure 6: "Transreal Topologies" Catalogue Shot. Courtesy of Maria Engberg

Multiple documents were employed to keep track of all development and design variables, like dedicated "Help Texts" including Navigation, Display, Instructions and Tips, "Drone Texts" containing the Mezangelled scripts running on the internal Drone displays accessible via the in-game laptops. Our Comprehensive *#PRISOM* Manual included Running Notes, Play-Through Notes, Game Mechanics & Development, break-down by Elements such as Posters, ConTROLLer Monologues, Scripts, Voiceovers, Endings, QA/Bug Hunting, and Wishlisting (which often changed during development when we'd be able to implement an item from the wish list we thought wouldn't be ready by final release).

EXHIBITION EXECUTION

> *#PRISOM received a lot of attention during the exhibition. The exploration of the virtual environment joined to the game system caught a lot of players. #PRISOM really has provided a narrative approach that none of the other pieces offered in the exhibition. We were honoured and glad to be able to exhibit it for the third edition of the Notgames Fest.*—Simon Bachelier, Curator of the 2015 NotGamesFest for The Cologne Game Lab.

#PRISOM's exhibition première occurred in October 2013: the culmination of a collaborative effort spanning 4 countries: Australia, England, Austria, and New Zealand. *#PRISOM* made its debut at the 2013 International Symposium on Mixed and Augmented Reality as part of the Transreal Topologies exhibition which took place at the Royal Institution of Australia, in conjunction with the University of South Australia University's Wearable Computer Lab. #PRISOM was shown here on a wearable AR headset (HUD) with a wireless XBox 360 wireless controller.

Julian Stadon (Transreal Topologies' Curator) stated in an official Show Press Release:

> It is my pleasure to introduce these works within this new context of mixed reality, augmentation based arts practice. Transreal Topologies is part of a Mixed and Augmented Reality Art Organisation (MARart.org) scoping study initiative that launched at ISEA2013. The Mixed and Augmented Reality Arts Research Organisation (MARart.org) seeks to develop new dialogues in regards to high-end research methodologies, cultural inquiry and representation in the increasingly immersive and pervasive field of mixed and augmented reality art.[115]

This exhibition holds particular credence in terms of its pioneering value: Julian also stated in this release that this showcase was the first ever dedicated Augmented Reality exhibition showcased in Australia. The importance of not only showing a proj-

115 http://marart.org/#/home..

ect such as *#PRISOM* in such an exhibition, but also having been commissioned specifically to produce such a work, was not lost on the creative team.

After the success of having *#PRISOM* showcased at this Transreal Topologies pioneering event, Andy and I were keen to embrace other opportunities for audiences to play the game. We immediately made *#PRISOM* publicly available for a donation download for PC, Mac and Linux Desktop machines, and playable via a browser with a standard keyboard/mouse configuration.

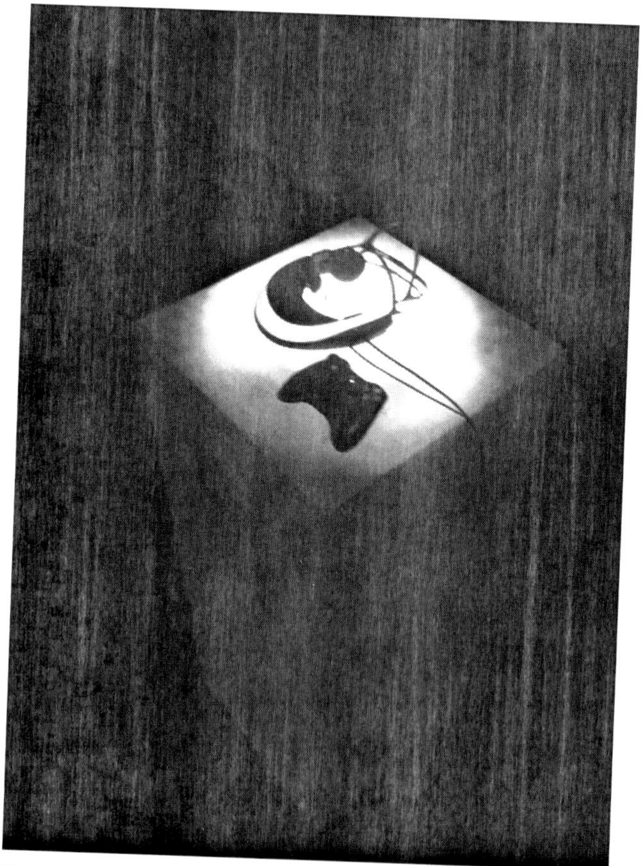

Figure 7: An Exhibition Shot of *#PRISOM* Hardware, "Transreal Topologies" Exhibition, Royal Institution of Australia

The next major showing in which *#PRISOM* featured was the "Impedance: Games and Resistance" section of the 2014 Vector Game and Art Convergence Festival that took place on February 19th-23rd in Toronto, Canada, where it was playable via a projector screen, keyboard and mouse.[116] Other 2013/2014 venues include the 2013

116 http://vectorfestival.org/vector-2014-2/.

"Amazing Streets and Spaces" Wakefield Cathedral Event, the 2014 Viral Dissonance Festival, and at Refest 2014 at CultureHub, La MaMa Experimental Theatre Club in New York, where: "Refest engage[s] the public with the themes of play and participation, celebrating the convergence of new and old, digital and analog, near and far."

In 2015, *#PRISOM* was also showcased at the 2015 Not Games Fest hosted by the Cologne Game Lab's Institute for Game Development/Research at the Cologne University of Applied Sciences[117]; at Transitio_MX06 alongside acclaimed game projects such as *The Stanley Parable*, *Papers, Please*, and *Atari-Noise*[118]; and at the 2015 International Conference on Interactive Digital Storytelling.[119]

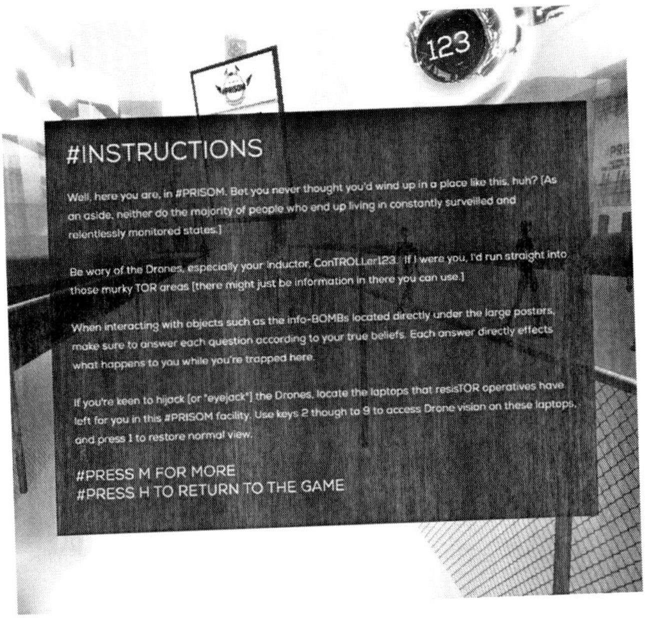

Figure 8: *#PRISOM* Screenshot: Game Instructions

LEGACIES AND LONGEVITY

> *#PRISOM seduces and repels in the same instant, situating a "player" within a gameworld of seeming transparency but in actuality a harsh digital realm of endless surveillance. Neither pulpit nor pleasure, #PRISOM forces players to make choices rendering the harsh reality of a surveillance culture inescapable. This is*

117 http://notgames.colognegamelab.com/exhibition.html.

118 http://transitiomx.net/muestra_en.html?Conexion=42.

119 http://icids2015.aau.dk/exhibition/.

> *a powerful interactive work, with a political message that is all too clear (in both senses).*—The 2014 Western Australian Premier's Book Awards Judges, Digital Narrative Category

In creating *#PRISOM*, our aim as Creatives was to craft a game that would highlight the increasing unveiling of covert surveillance on a global scale (think: the invasiveness of the clandestine NSA surveillance-gathering and the increasing monitoring of individual's private data/lives). As I've written in the "Resources" section at prisom.me:

> *#PRISOM* is designed to make players ponder the increasing global adoption of PRISM-like surveillance technology. Every one of the "#WhatDoYouDo" scenarios that you'll encounter when playing the game stem from real-life scenarios, including the ongoing unconstitutional treatment and [in some cases] incarceration of those keen to expose the nature of heavily surveilled and overtly monitored societies [think: Glenn Greenwald, David Miranda, Laura Poitras, Barrett Brown, Jeremy Hammond, WikiLeaks and the Occupy Movement, Edward Snowden, LavaBit's Owner Ladar Levison, Chelsea Manning, and a multitude of others].[120]

#PRISOM continues to garner interest and acclaim beyond a traditional gamer audience base, with the game being shortlisted for the 2014 Western Australian Premier's Book Awards in the "Digital Narrative" Category; nominated for the Digital Humanities Awards "Best Visualization or Infographic" Category; and has been analyzed in Conference Keynotes, publications[121] and Doctorial theses.[122] Although the academic focus is appreciated, what seems more germane is how playing #PRISOM may assist in shining an exposure-light on all practices determined to fundamentally alter the basic tenements of civil rights discourse and practice. What seems most pertinent about a player's time in *#PRISOM* is their experience of the frustration of being trapped in an environment where agency seems paramount, but in the end, all choices lead to a dictated, and circular, reality. Alan Bigelow succinctly alludes to just how members of a surveilled populace might react and interact to avoid the development of *#PRISOM*-like spaces, and, in short, not end up in *#PRISOM*:

> Thanks to *#PRISOM*, I am now successfully indoctrinated. This took a bit of navigation, but the payoff is definitely worth it. The environment is easy to get into, especially with the supporting audio, and once I got into the hang of what I was supposed to do, all went smoothly. I was actually entranced by the whole experience, and felt that I just HAD to get to the end. This is [a] most ambitious

120 http://prisom.me/

121 http://www.worldcat.org/title/thinking-through-digital-media-transnational-environmentsand-locative-places/oclc/894935433#relatedsubjects.

122 http://ro.uow.edu.au/cgi/viewcontent.cgi?article=5365&context=theses.

work [...] with a piece that delivers a political message within the framework of a game that is actually no game at all—it's the serious business of where do we all go from here.[123]

123 http://webyarns.com/.

Literary and Musical Dialoguing: Sound, Voice, and Screen Synergies

BY HAZEL SMITH

Sound, particularly the relationship between words and music, seems to be an under-explored area in electronic literature, where the emphasis has tended to be more strongly on the relationship between words and images. Exploring the interface between words and music is central to my writing, however, and to my work in electronic literature. My interest in sound originates from my previous career as a professional violinist in London during the 1970s and 80s, before I emigrated from Britain to Australia. When I write, sound often suggests the words that I might use, and my strong interest in literary form springs partly from my musical sensibility. Unsurprisingly, then, electronic literature for me is always a multisensory experience. My practice is cross-media and collaborative, involving musicians, visual artists, and writers, and based in the sound and multimedia group austraLYSIS. This essay will focus on some of my collaborations with musician Roger Dean, the director of austraLYSIS, who like me was born in Britain and moved later (with me) to Australia. But it will also include our—sometimes transnational—collaborations with others, in particular with Australian musician Greg White, Australian writer Anne Brewster, US video artist Will Luers, and British ceramicist Joanna Still.

Music, like language, is always ambiguous. In fact, it is much more ambiguous than language because it is not a system of discrete units (words) in the way that language is: sound is actually a continuum, and notes and scales in Western classical music are only one means of dividing it up. In music it is more difficult than in language to say what the signifier is (a note, a phrase, a timbre, a rhythm), what is being signified (there are conventionalized meanings for very few musical sounds) or how the signified relates to the signifier. In work that combines words and music, the ambiguities of sound interact with the ambiguities of language. Music can be used to emphasize the narrative or poetic, but it can also redirect, challenge, or deconstruct it.

In electronic literature the juxtaposition of words and sound, and the technological manipulation of words as sounds, can create musical features from words. Music can also provide illustrative and representational effects that correlate with the text and raise the affective intensity of the words. Conversely, words can extend tangible meaning into the less referential domain of music. The co-existence of words and music can, therefore, create what I call *semiotic and perceptual exchange*: the presence of sound makes us more aware of the sonic and abstract properties of language, the presence of words make us more aware of the semantic potential of sound (Smith 2016, 23-25). But conjunctions between words and music can also have strong cultural effects: they can be a means of interrogating boundaries and categorizations to do with identity, gender, ethnicity, and the human, but also to do with time, space, and memory. It is these formal processes, and their cultural effects, that we explore in our collaborations.

Our work with words and sound has taken a variety of different forms: in some pieces the words are more voice-based, in others they are more screen-based, some works combine both. In the following I will look at the voice-based and screen-based works in turn.

VOICE-BASED WORKS

My voice-based collaborations with Roger follow a long tradition in sound poetry of manipulating the voice and the sonic properties of words. However, digital technologies offer opportunities for the control and alteration of the pitch, rhythm, and timbre of the voice that are more extensive than performance techniques, and can be more systematically controlled. Our voice-based works, usually written by Roger in the real-time platform MAX/MSP together with several other audio manipulation platforms, are also influenced by developments in computer music over the last forty years or so, and bear a connection with the work of computer music composers such as Pamela Z, Trevor Wishart, and Paul Lansky who compose computationally with digital transformations of the voice and words. An important aspect of our pieces is their connection with live performance: they are usually written in the first instance for austraLYSIS performances even if they are subsequently recorded. This means that they often have a real-time interactive and variable performance component.

Over an extended period, we have entered the relationship between words, music, and voice in many different and developing ways. In our first words and music collaboration *Poet without Language*—an Australian Broadcasting Corporation commission originally broadcast in 1991 but recorded in 1994 as the title track of my first text-based CD (Smith with austraLYSIS, 1994)—I notated most of the words in musical rhythms (a practice that had become significant in my work at that time). Roger employed sampled and processed voice sounds, as well as other sampled and synthesized sounds, in ways that created interrelated musical, linguistic, and vocal effects. We followed *Poet without Language* with a number of other large-scale ABC commissions *Nuraghic Echoes* (1993), *Returning the Angles* (1999), *The Erotics of Gossip* (2001), and *The Afterlives of Betsy Scott* (2007), the latter two of which involve performances by professional actors.[124] These full-length mixed-genre and mixed-media pieces combine poetry, narrative, and drama, and sometimes embrace documentary or historical material. They are what we call sound technodramas because they include performed text, technological manipulation of words and voice, and also electronic and acoustic sounds.

Transformation of the voice, and of sampled words, is also a feature of some of our shorter performance pieces: thematically these sometimes address issues to do with performance and technology. They include *The Space of History* (Smith, Dean, and White 2006), a piece with a theatrical dimension in which I pose as a female "terrorist" who airs her resentments and threatens to lock the audience up.[125] When I exit petulantly from the performance space, different transmutations and traces of my voice swirl round it, creating an effect of simultaneous presence and absence. Another slightly earlier piece, *the writer, the performer, the program, the madwoman* (Smith and Dean 2004),[126] is about the contemporary writer's struggle to stabilize her identity as she moves beyond words on the page, and allows her work to be transformed by performance and technology. Real-time manipulation of the voice blurs the roles of writer, performer, audience and computer program, and creates a productive conflict for the writer between control and loss of control. This tension is dramatized in the piece as a power struggle between the writer and technology; a balancing act between madness and sanity; and an exercise in sexual politics. On the one hand the writer invites her (male) collaborators to dissolve her voice and tear up her words: it is the programmers who can creatively extend her. But at the same time she finds her performance moving out of her grasp because of those initiatives: "texts come back to me, texts I have not spoken […] I keep reaching for my voice but it has been plucked and purged" (2004).[127]

These collaborations explore the continuum between an essentialist and a non-essentialist approach to voice (Smith 2016, 29-32). An essentialist approach stresses the location of the voice in the body of the speaker and its link to a sense of identity: it is acoustic and naturalistic. The non-essentialist approach emphasizes the voice as multiple, mediatized, technologized and spatialized. Towards one end of the essentialist to non-essentialist continuum are my acoustic renderings of text, ranging from straight enunciation to a more musically nuanced or dramatic delivery. Towards the other end

124 All these pieces were originally broadcast by the Australian Broadcasting Corporation. All except for *The Afterlives of Betsy Scott* are available on CD/CD-ROM. See Smith and Dean (1996, 2001 and 2008).

125 See Smith, Dean, and White (2006). Also on the CD-ROM accompanying Smith (2008).

126 Also on the CD-ROM accompanying Smith (2008).

127 Also on the CD-ROM accompanying Smith (2008).

of the continuum, the voice is processed so that it becomes the basis of rhythmic, harmonic and timbral effects that are musical. An important aspect of this non-essentialist exploration of the voice is our exploitation of what we call the voicescape. A voicescape comprises several voices, some digitally manipulated, and involves the multidimensional and multidirectional projection of voices into space (Smith and Dean 2003). These projections play with different concepts of subjectivity, as the voice become multiple, spatialized and altered. In addition, processing of the voice can change the impression the voice creates of gender, age, class and ethnicity. Both *The Space of History* and *the performer, the writer, the program, the madwoman* oscillate between a naturalistic voice and a digitized one: they also play with impressions of age, so that my voice sometimes sounds child-like, as if it were possible to reverse time in relation to the body. But another effect, in particular, interests me: I have previously called this sonic cross-dressing: it is where the female voice is mutated to become male or vice versa (Smith 1999). This can create a transgendered impression along the continuum between male and female, and interrogates prescriptive notions of gender and sexuality. This effect can be heard, in conjunction with other transformations of the voice, in a number of our pieces, including most recently, in 2015, *Scaling the Voices* (Dean and Smith 2015).

The metamorphosis of the voice in our pieces is also intertwined with the deconstruction of language. Roger samples, clips and transfigures words and phrases, sometimes sounding only part of the word, merging different words together, playing words backwards, modifying the pitch, rhythm and timbre of the words so that they can function as musical units, and thereby also problematizing the relationship between sound and speech (Bailes and Dean 2009). While these processes musicalize language, they also have semantic effects: they create nuances that are not in the original text, prioritize certain meanings over others or, where the manipulation of the voice is in real-time, create variable import.

This synergy between naturalistic and transformed projections of the voice, and also between text and its deconstruction, is highlighted in *Bird Migrants* (Smith and Dean 2014). This piece constitutes a development in our work in the way it incorporates, and also transmutes, environmental and non-human sounds. It has had several iterations: it stemmed originally from a poem "The Great Egret" written for the Bimblebox 143 birds project. This is a conservation project in Australia concerning the Bimblebox Nature Refuge in the Desert Uplands Bioregion of Central West Queensland, which is in the path of a proposed coal mine. The poem is also heavily influenced by the wedding scene from the film *The Suspended Step of the Stork*, by Theo Angelopoulos, in which a couple who live in a divided country have to marry from the opposite sides of a river bank. *Bird Migrants* which is based on the poem, was a collaboration with Roger, and was commissioned by the Australian Broadcasting Corporation. The piece was then developed further for public performance and a visual component was added: a remix of images and words from the poem processed in real-time in Jitter.

Bird Migrants includes a performance of the poem, though with gaps between and within sections. My voice is heightened by reverberation; otherwise it is relatively naturalistic. But that naturalistic voice is also accompanied by other voices (electronic permutations and transformations of my own voice). These voices enunciate words, fragments of words (sometimes fused together) and words played backwards, creating a sense both of linguistic familiarity and strangeness. These words often foreshadow or recapture events that are part of the poem, thereby undercutting its linear progression but realizing its inner meanings and affect. In the poem, the flag that the groom is waving and the bride's veil are both thrown into the river that divides them. From the meeting of flag and veil—metaphorically alluded to as "miscegenation" in the poem—an egret emerges, potentially if ambiguously symbolizing freedom and hope. In addition to the acoustic reading of the poem, some of the words, in whole and in part, are manipulated with regard to pitch, rhythm, and timbre in such a way that they become integrated into the piece's sonic fabric. These transformations also transmit the deep longings embedded in the poem, as the political conflict impacts traumatically on the right of the couple to live together.

Whereas in most videos or films voice might form a separate sound stream, in our collaborations the vocal and non-vocal sounds are welded together. Throughout *Bird Migrants* the sampled egret sounds, voice sounds, and environmental sounds are juxtaposed, even merged. In this way the piece creates a fusion of people, birds, objects, and the environment, producing the boundary-interrogating effect I mentioned earlier in the essay, and both extending and problematizing the symbolic power of the egret. This piece also shows a recent tendency in Roger's work towards employing ecological (environmental and real-world) sounds, but also to radically molding those sounds and drawing out their musical properties.

Another important aspect of the voice-based collaborations, and of the cultivation of the voicescape, has been the spatialization of voice and sound. In austraLYSIS performances, loudspeakers are placed both at the front and back of the auditorium, and my voice is projected from these different positions. It is also often panned between those positions so that it moves round the performance space. Spatialization is particularly marked in *Disappearing*, a collaboration with Greg White and Roger (Smith, Dean and White 2013). This piece is written for four voices, though I perform all four. It is designed for four-channel sound and is available as a recording on the internet, but is most effective in the performance auditorium where it is projected by four loudspeakers, two at the front and two at the back. In performance I deliver some of the text live, in the recorded version all four voices are pre-recorded. In both versions the four projections of my voice are juxtaposed with Greg White's transformations of my voice. These transformations include stripping the semantic component of the speech, but still retaining the voice's individual identity, which Greg calls my "sonic footprint" (2012).

The four voices are sometimes heard separately, sometimes in rapid succession, sometimes superimposed. The spatialization emphasizes each voice individually, but also the way the voices interweave and disappear behind each other. They form a mosaic of death and disappearing, alluding to political repression and genocide in different places (Romania, Chile, Denmark, Argentina and Syria). Through the spatialization of the voice, personal responses to dying and death are juxtaposed with the brutal realities of political killing and the inevitable capitulation of all human beings to disease and disintegration.

SCREEN-BASED WORKS

The relationship between words and music has also been central to Roger's and my screen-based collaborations, where again we have entered the possibilities and problems of bringing words and music together from many different angles. Here the primary relationship is between sounds and words that are screened. The screened words are silent but often convey what I call a latent voice, the impression of a voice that is nevertheless unsounded. Some of these screen-based pieces have also involved spoken voice, for example *Time the Magician* (Smith and Dean 2008), which begins with the performance of a poem. Many of them, in addition, employ images and/or text-as-image.

Our screen-based works include a variety of different approaches to fusing words and music. These approaches include *parallelism* in which words and music occur together, but are not necessarily coordinated—in such pieces the relationship between the words and music may be structural, conceptual or affective—and *coordination* in which there is a concrete or illustrative link between the words and the music, so that the music helps to extend or reinforce various aspects of the narrative or poetic features of the text. In addition there is what I call *heterogeneity*, where the different media consist of many different components that keep combining, falling apart and then recombining in other ways; *interactive variability* where interaction by the user results in specific sounds or words being chosen rather than others; and *algorithmic synaesthesia* in which the different media (often text-as-image and music) employ the same algorithms (Smith 2016). Our collaborations have engaged with all these different approaches to working with the relationship between words and sounds, sometimes in combination with each other and sometimes also in conjunction with images.

The way in which screened words and music can run parallel to each other (with some interactive variability), but also converge conceptually or thematically, is apparent in a number of our early screen-based pieces including *the egg the cart the horse the chicken* (Smith and Dean 2003), which plays with, and interrogates, ideas of causality. This is a split-screen piece written by me in Flash: the upper movie has an interactive hypertextual component and the lower movie runs on a loop: in both cases a variety of fonts and colors are used to turn the text into text-image. The idea for the piece started with the scrambled word order of the title: many of the texts explore the disruption of linear systems by non-linearity. Each of the words in the title is treated as a potential metaphor that unravels into metonymies and ultimately into new metonymic connections: these "new metonymies" link objects and events that might seem to have no ostensibly strong connection, but which acquire one by the act of linking (Smith 2000). The sound consists of post-minimalist music related to the earlier minimalism of Steve Reich, but in this case algorithmically controlled to a different effect. Written and then auto-generated in MAX/MSP, the music is based on a repetitive rhythmic unit that is programmed to change with time, introducing more and more deviant notes, accelerating in speed, and reversing midstream so that the musical events are sequenced in reverse order. The sound, then, is cyclic and iterative, and works against the idea of musical progression and development that is central to classical music. It relates to the underlying dynamic of the words by challenging concepts of linearity at a structural level.

In some subsequent pieces, parallelism between sound and words also hinges on a conceptual relationship. In these pieces the words-as-image were subjected to manipulations by Jitter, VRML or Python with considerable variability between performances; both sound and text can undergo real-time intervention in performance. *ProseThetic Memories* (Dean, Brewster, and Smith 2009) originally conceived in 2001, is a piece with a multi-genre text written by Anne Brewster and me, and with music and programming by Roger. The text is programmed in Virtual Reality Modelling Language (VRML) for presentation on a split-screen. On one half of the screen, the text scrolls in its entirety and without variability. On the other half of the screen, the text is subject to algorithmic processing and allows for interaction in performance. This algorithmic processing results in rearrangement of text so that, for example, the lines of the poems appear in a different order each time the piece is run; there is movement, inversion and enlargement of text; and the text sometimes displays with missing letters and words. This programming, and the interaction between the two halves of the screen, simulates the action of memory and the fragility, selectivity, and creativity of recall. In the published version (2009)—only one outcome is captured in a Quicktime movie of an infinitely variable piece—a melody-generating program drives the sound. This presents simultaneous versions of three melodic lines with anticipations and overlaps within and between them, thereby mimicking the operations of memory; the music is different each time the piece runs and is produced through real-time intervention with the program. The piece is influenced by the Freudian concept of *Nachträglichkeit*, "afterwardsness," the idea that what is continually rewrites what has been. Memory is seen as a dynamic process, in which the present constantly transforms our impression of the past and vice versa (King 2000, 36).

In *soundAFFECTs* (Dean, Brewster and Smith 2004),[128] parallelism of a rather different kind takes place. This piece is another collaboration with writer Anne Brewster, and with Roger who wrote the music and programmed the text-image. The text-image, which is subjected to stretching, compression, multiplication and overlaying in Jitter, is in a relationship of algorithmic synaesthesia with the music, that is they both share the same data. The sound, which is written in MAX/MSP, can be manipulated by the performer (Roger) in real-time, and strongly raises the affective dimension of the piece. Influenced both by Deleuze and Guattari's theories of affect (1994, 163-200) and Keith Oatley's work on emotion from the field of cognitive psychology (1992), I have suggested previously that *soundAFFECTs*—a piece about emotion and affect—enacts non-subjective flows of affect or "affective intensities" rather than emotionally categorizable and subjectively-based states (Smith 2007). This is due both to the speed at which the text appears and to the force and intensity of the electronically-based music.

In our *Instabilities 2* (Smith and Dean 2009), which also employs performers from austraLYSIS, the parallelism of text and sound is structural as much as conceptual and affective. The screen is divided into three parts. In the upper screen is a Quicktime movie of the text (a series of verbal fragments relating to different kinds of instability: psychological, linguistic, economic and political). In the middle part of the screen the same text is treated in Jitter, resulting in stretching, compression, overwriting and multiplication of the text. The lower part of the screen is dedicated to text generation in Python. Both the words and the music move between a tight structure (the screen division, the music-compositional framework) and a looser improvisatory associative dynamic (the text-generation and the musical improvisation). While the screened text is tripartite in structure, so is the music: it starts with an acoustic improvisation that is

128 Also on the CD-ROM accompanying Smith (2008).

gradually overlaid with an electroacoustic improvisation (performed by Greg White) and returns to an acoustic improvisation (performed by Roger Dean, Greg White, Sandy Evans and Phil Slater) at the end of the piece. *Instabilities 2* also employs computer-synthesized voices that shadow the text generation, sometimes reading in synch with it, sometimes lagging behind as it changes. All these symmetries and asymmetries between words and sound play with the tension between stability and instability.

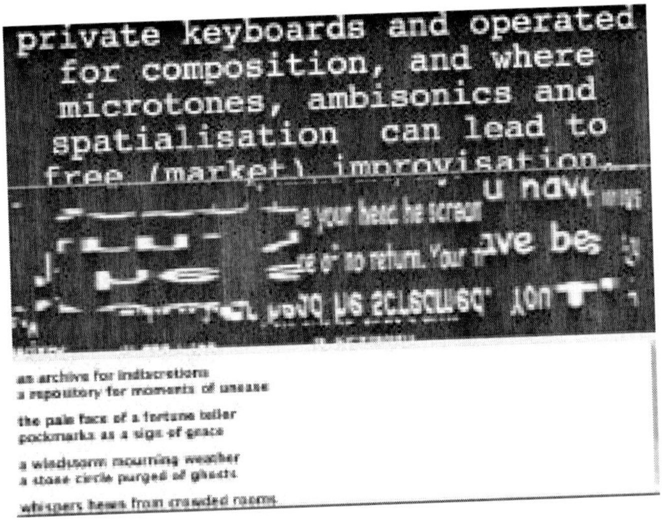

Figure 1: Screenshot from *Instabilities 2* by Hazel Smith and Roger Dean.

While there is not necessarily a clear-cut progression of style in our work, more recently the relationship between words and sound in the screened works has tended to have a greater degree of coordination. In addition, image has featured more strongly, creating a triangular relationship between word, image, and sound. Here coordination is defined as above, it consists of a concrete, representational link between the words, sounds, and images, even though sometimes they may not coincide but may be separated in time or space. At the same time, Roger has started to use more ecological (environmental and real-world) sounds, in conjunction with musical sounds, and also to transform those ecological sounds into musical objects. This was the case in *Clay Conversations* (Smith, Still and Dean 2010), a collaboration with ceramicist Joanna Still. For the collaboration, which initially only involved Joanna and me, I made a simple video in Final Cut Pro. This consists mainly of stills of ceramics Joanna made especially for the piece, including a calendar, an abacus, and a clay book. It also includes photographs of her experiences when she was sponsored by Voluntary Service Overseas to work with African women in craft and ceramic workshops, and a video of her writing in her studio in clay. In addition, I integrated many fragments of text, derived from poems I had written for the collaboration, into the video. The piece juxtaposes artefacts and activities from Western and non-Western cultures, often through the use of split screens. It interweaves ideas and images to do with uses of clay and its significance, the creative process, the negative and positive aspects of globalization, and the possibilities and limitations of cross-cultural exchange. When the project was at an advanced stage, Joanna and I asked Roger to provide some sound. In response he created a soundtrack made entirely out of the sounds of clay, including clay hydrating in water, the sound of Joanna working with clay, and the noise of markets where clay goods might be sold. The music runs parallel to the images and words but also coordinates with its content: this gives a unifying presence to the piece as well as increasing its immediacy (Smith 2012).

Figure 2: Screenshot from *Clay Conversations* by Hazel Smith, Joanna Still and Roger Dean.

Recent collaborations with Will Luers have brought visual images more prominently into the mix, and have resulted in relationships between word, sound, and image that are highly heterogeneous. In our first collaboration, *Film of Sound* (Luers, Dean and Smith 2013)—a video made by Will in Final Cut Pro—sound was the trigger for the entire piece. This project was initiated by Roger, whose objective was to make sound the starting point for the piece, rather than an add-on, as is often the case with film and video projects. To begin the process, Roger composed two sound pieces (including electronic and ecological sounds): Will and I could respond to the sound in any way we liked with images and words. After several listening sessions, the sounds (especially some of the more ecological sounds) suggested both spaces and boundaries to me. They triggered ideas about confined spaces, borders, prison-guards, even concentration camps. My response was the creation of a discontinuous text that revolved round traumatic experiences of confinement. Roger then responded to the images and texts that Will and I created, and the piece went through several iterations.

In the resultant work the music, image and sound all involve heterogeneous, non-linear elements that keep coming together and moving apart, then reforming into other configurations. For the images Will employed remix strategies. Consequently, the images arise from many different sources, and are suggestive of various types of environment such as the desert, a field, a swimming pool, a hotel room, and a busy street in a city. The screen is often split into multiple windows, there is some visual abstraction, and a focus on parts rather than wholes. The soundtrack consists of several different components: algorithmically organized piano sounds (tonal, atonal, jazz including an emotive repeating melody); environmental sounds; embodied sound (footsteps and voice) and electroacoustic sound. In performance the sound is spatialized and employs four loudspeakers: the piano (and other) sounds move between the front and back of the performance space, creating an immersive sonic experience. The text consists of interrelated fragments that are superimposed on each other. They move across the screen, are sometimes displayed in 3D, and are only partially readable, but are sometimes repeated later so that meaning gradually accumulates.

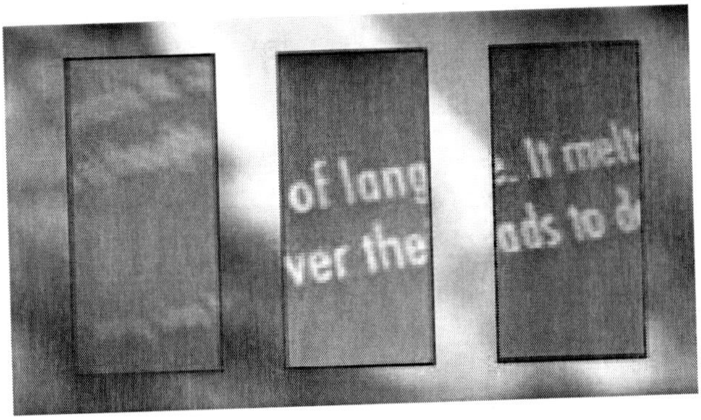

Figure 3: screenshot from *Film of Sound* by Will Luers, Roger Dean and Hazel Smith.

Due to its heterogeneity *Film of Sound* is open to multiple interpretations. On one level it is about the way that environmental sounds produce affects and perceptions. But there are also glimpses of different narratives: hints of a journey, of traumatic memories, of a sleeping man who may or may not be the source of these thoughts and ideas. The video is, in addition, about spaces, both open and closed, and traversals between them.

In our next collaboration with Will, *motions* (Smith, Luers, and Dean 2016), the dynamic between word, sound and image is one of coordination—in the sense of the inclusion of representational effects—interactive variability and heterogeneity. *motions* is a piece about human trafficking and contemporary slavery. Will undertook the image and coding, Roger composed the sound, and I wrote the text, however we made frequent suggestions about each other's contributions. The piece is conceived as a multimedia web application and is programmed in HTML5/Javascript. It involves the reader in moving forward and scrolling through the screens. Though some text and images always appear in a particular order—giving the piece an underlying structure—most of the texts and images are variable and configure differently on each reading.

motions is a mix, a hybrid in all senses. It is an example of what I have elsewhere called musico-literary miscegenation, because the words and music (together in this case with powerful images) hybridize a range of elements from different cultures and create an impression of movement across those cultures (Smith 2016, 23-26). Like *Film of Sound, motions* has a synecdochal dynamic, since we are always privy to only parts of the stories of the victims. This means the elements of the mix constantly shift, producing new configurations that seem to produce a particular narrative trajectory, and then break up and re-form in other ways.

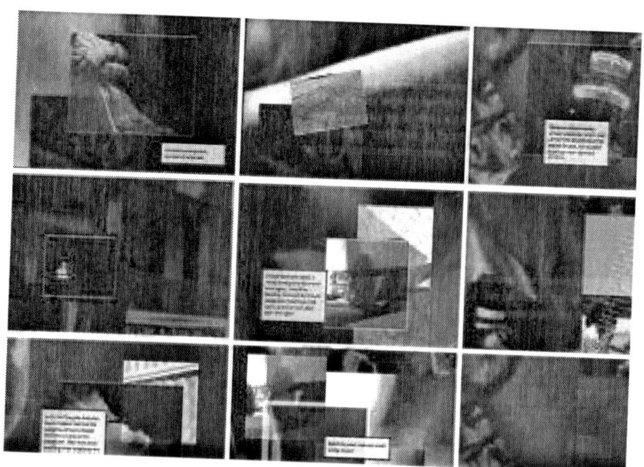

Figure 4: screenshot from the front page of *motions* by Hazel Smith, Will Luers and Roger Dean.

The texts vary from short poems, to narratives, to documentary and satirical fragments, and span human trafficking and contemporary slavery (which I researched in some detail for the piece) in numerous parts of the world. Some of the texts—like those about a train journey that start the work—are allegorical, some are more direct, emphasizing the plight of trafficking victims. They often highlight the coercion of women into prostitution, and the kind of psychological distancing mechanisms those women may need to survive such experiences. There are constant shifts of point of view, from looking at the plight of the victims externally to attempting to portray their internalization of such experiences. There is considerable fragmentation of the texts so that the shards of dialogue, poetry, and narrative interweave in varying ways on different readings, often merging the experiences of trafficking victims from different cultural backgrounds.

The images, created through remix strategies by Will, form a continuum from representational images to abstracted blocks of color. The more representational images include ones that portray travel in the form of a vehicle such as a boat or plane; restricted spaces sometimes suggested by forbidding gates or wire-netting; figures with erased faces whose body language often implies subjugation or grief and body parts, such as a huge open eye.

The sound, created by Roger, picks up the connotations of the words and images and develops them. It includes processed train and airplane noises suggestive of travel; Eastern European sounds based on an asymmetric Aksak rhythm and evoking nostalgia for the homeland for those trafficking victims emanating from Eastern Europe; and Americanized rhythmic music suggestive of hegemonic western culture. The sound is in four sections that are sequential (airplane sounds, Eastern European music, train sounds and Americanized music). Though these sections contrast with each other there are also overlaps and exchanges: the Eastern European section is centered on asymmetric rhythms and the Americanized section on symmetric rhythms, but the symmetric Americanized rhythm evolves out of the asymmetric rhythm. Similarly, while the piano chords in the Americanized section are mainly tonal and characteristic of Western music, they include some microtonal chords that point both to Eastern European and Asian music.

The reader's interactivity has effects on the sound, usually causing the different sections to progressively overlap. Each sound section is programmed to start probabilistically once a particular screen has been reached. However, the user's interactions with the texts and images trigger other algorithms that determine how and when the sonic sections begin or end. These sections will usually become superimposed as the reader/viewer interacts with the piece, and create alternative word-to-image-to-music relationships on each viewing.

CODA

Music and voice are often areas of electronic literature that seem to be relatively neglected: in our collaborations we have made them central. But there are an infinite number of ways of entering the relationship between words and sound (and also image), and my collaborative relationship with Roger, and with others, has been about the different ways in which we can negotiate that relationship. I envisage many more developments and possibilities in the future. For example, I would like to develop real-time performance of generated text in combination with real-time performance of computer-generated music. And just as we have explored transgendered positions in the manipulation of the voice through sonic cross-dressing, I would like to explore inter-ethnic manipulations of voice. Musico-literary miscegenation—cross-cultural exchange employing combinations of words and music that suggest or construct ethnic diversity—also seems to me to be an area in which there is immense room for further exploration, as the world becomes increasingly transnational.

WORKS CITED

Bailes, Freya, and Roger T. Dean. "When Is Noise Speech? A Survey in Sonic Ambiguity." *Computer Music Journal* 33.1 (2009) 57-67.

Dean, Roger, Anne Brewster, and Hazel Smith. "soundAFFECTs." *Text* 8.2 (2004). Accessed July 16th, 2016. http://www.textjournal.com.au/oct04/content.htm. Also available in a larger format on the CD-ROM accompanying Hazel Smith. *The Erotics of Geography: Poems, Performance Texts, New Media Works*. Kāne'ohe, Hawai'i: Tinfish Press, 2008.

_,_. "ProseThetic Memories." *soundsRite* 1(2009). Accessed July 16th, 2016. http://soundsrite.uws.edu.au/soundsRiteContent/volume1/prsthinf.html. Originally created in 2001; Quicktime realization by Roger Dean in 2009.

_,_. "Scaling the Voices." *soundsRite* (Four and More 2015). Accessed July 16th, 2016. http://soundsrite.uws.edu.au/soundsRiteContent/Four&More/FourAndMore2015Info.html.

Deleuze, Gilles, and Félix Guattari. *What Is Philosophy?* London: Verso, 1994.

King, Nicola. 2000. *Memory, Narrative, Identity: Remembering the Self*. Edinburgh: Edinburgh University Press, 2000.

Luers, Will, Roger Dean, and Hazel Smith. "Film of Sound." *Cordite Poetry Review* (2013). Accessed 16th July 2016. http://cordite.org.au/ekphrasis/film-of-sound/.

Oatley, Keith. *Best Laid Schemes: The Psychology of the Emotions*. Cambridge: Cambridge University Press, 1992.

Smith, Hazel "Creative Writing and New Media." In *The Cambridge Companion to Creative Writing*. Edited by David Morley and Philip Neilsen. Cambridge: Cambridge University Press, 2012. 102-117.

_,_. *Hyperscapes in the Poetry of Frank O'Hara: Difference, Homosexuality, Topography*. Liverpool: Liverpool University Press, 2000.

_,_. "A Posthuman Cosmopolitanism and New Media Writing." *Hyperrhiz: New Media Cultures* 09 (2012). Accessed July 16th 2016. http://hyperrhiz.io/hyperrhiz09/essays/a-posthuman-cosmopolitanism-and-new-media-writing.html.

_,_. "Sonic Writing and Sonic Cross-Dressing: Gender, Language, Voice and Technology." In *Musics and Feminisms*. Edited by Sally Macarthur and Cate Poynton, 129-134. Sydney: Australian Music Centre, 1999.

_,_. "SoundAFFECTs: Transcoding, Writing, New Media, Affect." *Scan: Journal of Media Arts Culture* 4.1 (2007). Accessed July 16th 2016. http://scan.net.au/scan/journal/display.php?journal_id=89

_,_. *The Contemporary Literature-Music Relationship: Intermedia, Voice, Technology, Cross-Cultural Exchange*. New York and London: Routledge, 2016.

Smith, Hazel with austraLYSIS. *Poet without Language*. CD. Sydney: Rufus, RF005, 1994.

Smith, Hazel, Greg White, and Roger Dean. "Disappearing." *Electronic Overland* (2013). Accessed July 16th 2016. http://overland.org.au/previous-issues/electronic-overland/poem-hazel-smith-roger-dean-and-greg-white/.

Smith, Hazel, Joanna Still, and Roger Dean. "Clay Conversations." Scan Gallery, *Scan: Journal of Media Arts Culture* (2010). Accessed July 16th, 2016. http://www.scan.net.au/scan/gallery/gallery.html. Also available in *Hyperrhiz* 09, 2012. Accessed July 16th, 2016. http://media.hyperrhiz.io/hyperrhiz09/gallery/smith/index.html

Smith, Hazel, and Roger Dean. "The Afterlives of Betsy Scott." Airplay: Australian Broadcasting Corporation. (2007).

_,_. "Bird Migrants." *Soundproof*. Australian Broadcasting Corporation (2014). Accessed July 16th, 2016. http://www.abc.net.au/radionational/programs/soundproof/bird-migrants/5850898.

_,_. "The egg the cart the horse the chicken." *infLect* 1. (2003). Accessed July 16th 2016. http://soundsrite.uws.edu.au/soundsRiteContent/archive/inflect/01/eggsite.3/eggindex.html.

_,_."The Erotics of Gossip." (2001). Available on the CD-ROM accompanying Hazel Smith. *The Erotics of Geography*. Kāne'hoe Hawai'i: Tinfish Press, 2008.

_,_. "Instabilities 2." *Drunken Boat* 12 (2009). Accessed July 16th, 2016. http://www.drunkenboat.com/db12/06des/smith/index.php.

_,_. *Nuraghic Echoes*. CD. Sydney: Rufus, RF 025, 1996.

_,_. *Returning the Angles*. CD. Sydney: Soma 787, 2001.

_,_. "Time the Magician." *How2* 3.2 (2008). Accessed July 16th 2016. http://www.asu.edu/pipercwcenter/how2journal/vol_3_no_2/new_media/smith_dean/smith_dean.html Also on the CD-ROM accompanying Hazel Smith. *The Erotics of Geography*. Kāne'hoe, Hawai'i: Tinfish Press, 2008.

_,_. "Voicescapes and Sonic Structures in the Creation of Sound Technodrama." *Performance Research* 8.1 (2003)112-123.

_,_. "the writer, the performer, the program, the madwoman." *How2* 2.2 (2004). Accessed July 16th 2016. http://www.asu.edu/pipercwcenter/how2journal/archive/online_archive/v2_2_2004/current/multimedia/thewriter.htm Also on the CD-ROM accompanying Hazel Smith. *The Erotics of Geography*. Kāne'hoe Hawai'i: Tinfish Press, 2008.

Smith, Hazel, Roger Dean, and Greg White. "The Space of History." *PennSound* (2006). Accessed July 16th, 2016. https://media.sas.upenn.edu/pennsound/authors/Smith-Hazel/Smith-Hazel_Dean-Roger_The-Space-of-History_2006.mp3 Also on the CD-ROM accompanying Hazel Smith. *The Erotics of Geography*, Kāne'hoe Hawai'i, Tinfish Press, 2008.

Smith, Hazel, Will Luers, and Roger Dean. "motions." *Electronic Literature Collection 3*. Edited by Stephanie Boluk, Leonardo Flores, Jacob Garbe, Anastasia Salter, 2016. Accessed July 16th 2016. http://collection.eliterature.org/3/work.html?work=motions

White, Greg. "austraLYSIS Program 'Disappearing.'" 2012. First published in *Drunken Boat*, 2014.

Excavating *Underbelly*

BY CHRISTINE WILKS

Revealing what is hidden under the surface is a defining theme in my playable digital fiction, *Underbelly* (2010), and in this essay, I will exhume some of the concerns buried in the work and in the background to the work.

Underbelly is a about a woman sculptor, carving on the site of a former colliery in the north of England. As she carves, she is disturbed by a medley of voices, including her own internal dialogue, articulating her innermost fears and desires, and other subterranean voices, telling the stories of the 19th-century women who once worked underground mining coal. Haunted by these voices from the past, when women workers had little, if any, control over the conditions of their labor, maternity or childcare, the sculptor struggles to feel in control of her own destiny despite the options available to the modern woman.

You, the reader or, more appropriately, the player of *Underbelly*, explore a traversable map-like terrain, looking for markers that trigger narrative events. The map design is based on the remarkable uterine qualities and pregnant-belly shape of a 13th-century map of the world, the Hereford Mappa Mundi, combined with diagrams of female reproductive organs and 19th-century illustrations of mine shafts and pit workings.

THE EXCAVATION BEGINS…

In archaeology, excavation is the exposure and process of studying archaeological remains. In a sense, as the author and creator of *Underbelly*, I have both buried and exposed a site of narrative remains. The work is strewn with historical remnants: oral testimonies of women miners from 1842, fragments of historical imagery of mines and pit workers, and old anatomical drawings of dissected bodily remains. The artist's thoughts as she carves are leftovers too from other moments in time: memories, reruns and rehearsals of other conversations, or the residue of feelings. As the player, you use your mouse as a tool to uncover meaningful fragments: video, animation, imagery, sound and voices. Like an archeologist on a dig, you are the one who processes, studies and interprets these expressive relics.

Excavation is also a medical term meaning both the act of hollowing out and the hollowed out space or a natural cavity. In the female body, such excavations are found around the uterus—the *rectouterine* excavation and the *vesicouterine* excavation. Underbelly is suffused with gynecological imagery. In every region of the Underbelly map, there is a visual confusion of obstetric imagery with the coal face or an entanglement of reproductive organs with pit workings. In this light, the player's mouse pointer becomes a kind of scalpel, as sharp as the sculptor's chisel, dissecting the anatomy of the work.

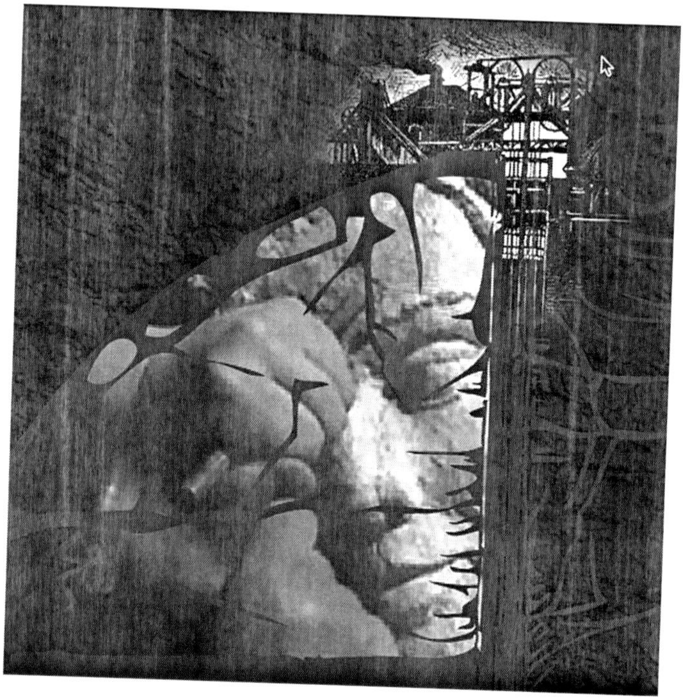

Figure 1: Screenshot detail of video of the sculptor carving inside the *Underbelly* map.

The sculptor's practice in *Underbelly* depends on excavation too. As a stone carver, her raw material is extracted from the earth. She may produce aesthetically pleasing objects but quarrying leaves vast holes in the landscape, great eyesores, often described as gaping wounds in Mother Earth. This rhetorical device is ancient and hard to resist:

> In a diverse range of patriarchal, as well as feminist, ecological and postcolonial discourses, the metaphor of mother earth has been invoked. It is used variously to emphasise fecundity, nurture, oneness and even bigness of creation, and—in the case of patriarchal and imperial discourses—plunderability. (McReddon 126-30)

In *Underbelly*, I self-consciously plundered the complexity of the Mother Earth trope as a visual and conceptual mise-en-scène for exploring the subject of working women and motherhood, in the past and the present, and also how these issues relate to a fictional female artist's life. Perhaps because I was approaching menopause at the time, I wanted to look at the subject from a visceral place of struggle, from the pit of the belly, from inside the problematic association between the female body and the land. No doubt also influencing me was the memory of my outrage as a young art student, when my male lecturer explained that the creative drive in men produces art, whereas in women it produces babies.

More directly though, the work was inspired by a visit to my sister, the sculptor Melanie Wilks, when she was hand-carving stone on the site of a former Yorkshire colliery, being turned into parkland. With my feet on the ground in the blustery open air, hearing and seeing her mallet hit the chisel hit the stone, I began to imagine uncanny correlations between her labor, as a working mother in post-industrial Britain, and the little-known history of women miners working underground during the Industrial Revolution.

So much history is buried beneath our feet, and histories buried in other ways, by forgetfulness or disregard. In the former mining areas of Britain, that history is deep underground. Evidence of the coal mines have been erased from the landscape, swept away in less than a generation as if they were an embarrassment, an unseemly reminder of past sweat, toil, deprivation and class struggle. No wonder that buried deeper still is the history of women and girls working underground too, in appalling conditions (Bloy 213).

Such fragments of contemporary life and shards of history I hauled together to build *Underbelly* in digital media. The stone carver in the video sequences is my sister. The voices of the artist and the 19th-century women miners are performed by me. The fictional artist is also modeled on both my sister and me: her image, my voice; her creative process embedded within my creative process. As artists and sisters, we are flip sides of the same coin. She chose motherhood, I decided to remain childless; she works in stone, I work in a digital media; her craft is time-honored and "low-tech," mine is highly dependent on rapidly changing new technology.

The first spoken words in *Underbelly* contain a significant Freudian slip. The sculptor says, "Carving is a reproductive… a reductive process - you start with a solid block, and using your tools, you cut away material to reveal the hidden… the… er… finished form" (Wilks 2010). This slip of the tongue foreshadows an anxiety that surfaces throughout. The woman worries that she might be pregnant and fears that motherhood is incompatible with being an artist. Listen carefully and, in some places, you'll hear her murmuring "smotherhood" repeatedly. Although, from time to time she gives way to sensual longings—"Such pleasure I felt holding her baby. Should I be denied that?" (ibid.)—maternal yearnings are frequently undercut by other thoughts, such as,

"Hack away those feelings. Carve! Chisel and chip, chip at those urges... Chisel away... Carving is a reductive process..." (ibid.).

The sculptor's first words, "you cut away material to reveal the hidden...", also signal another important theme. Like the stone carver, the anatomist cuts away material to reveal the hidden form and, in *Underbelly*, there are many anatomical drawings. There are also diagrams of cross-sections of mines and 19th-century drawings showing people working at the coal face and in tunnels underground. In a sense, the whole piece is about cutting away material: cutting away the conscious material concerns of the artist to reveal her underlying fears and desires; cutting away the present day to reveal hidden histories of women and girls working underground; and cutting away formally in the work's use of interactive cutaways. In film editing, a cutaway is a shot or scene which is of a different subject from those surrounding it. As a one-time independent film-maker, I was influenced by the language of cinema. Instead of navigating to new content via hyperlinks, within the regions of the *Underbelly* map, hovering over a symbol activates an embedded cutaway. In web design parlance, this might be called a pop-up modal window but in *Underbelly* it is more akin to a cutaway in cinema, part of the storytelling.

Exploring the *Underbelly* map entails a tour of such interactive cutaways—particularly for the stories of the 19th-century woman miners which appear with contemporary illustrations of conditions in the pits (Bloy 2013). Hover over a woman's name and the sound cuts to a voice relating her testimony in her own words, as transcribed by the inspectors of Lord Ashley's Mines Commission of 1842, who also drew the original illustrations. Their intention was to reveal what was hidden from public awareness: the appalling working conditions in the mines. They were successful. The findings of the Mines Commission led to laws prohibiting the employment of women and children younger than thirteen underground (Col 2002). The inspectors' illustrations were often copied and reproduced in the Victorian press where they caused much public moral outrage. However, more often this was due to the miners' "shocking" state of undress and presumed immorality, rather than the poverty and physical hardship that the drawings portray (Kirby 2007). For example, the *Parliamentary Papers* of 1842 record the opinion of a Sub-Commissioner:

> When it is remembered that these girls hurry chiefly for men who are not their parents; that they go from 15 to 20 times a day into a dark chamber (the bank face), which is often 50 yards apart from anyone, to a man working naked, or next to naked, it is not to be supposed but that where opportunity thus prevails sexual vices are of common occurrence. (Quoted in Halsall 1998)

Also from the *Parliamentary Papers*, compare the preoccupation of the Sub-Commissioner, below, with the testimony of mine worker, Betty Harris, further below, whose words I included in *Underbelly*.

The Sub-Commissioner:

> One of the most disgusting sights I have ever seen was that of young females, dressed like boys in trousers, crawling on all fours, with belts round their waists and chains passing between their legs, at day pits… and in many small pits. (ibid.).

Betty Harris, age 37:

> I worked at drawing when I was in the family way. I know a woman who has gone home and washed herself, taken to her bed, delivered of a child, and gone to work again under the week.
>
> I have a belt round my waist, and a chain passing between my legs, and I go on my hands and feet…
>
> I have drawn till I have bathe skin off me; the belt and chain is worse when we are in the family way. (ibid.).

The brutal working conditions caused many women to have miscarriages but it was Victorian morality rather than compassion that was the stronger motivator to remove women and children from working in the mines. Sadly, there was little motivation to improve working conditions for the men and older boys who remained in employment.

MAPPING THE OBSCURED

"Maps fascinate us because they tell us stories" (Garfiedl 2012) and, reciprocally, a map-based design, since it offers navigational benefits, is a useful way to structure an interactive story. When I started working on *Underbelly*, for a long time, I struggled with how to design and structure the diverse content I had created and accumulated until I remembered the medieval *Mappa Mundi* (c. 1290), which I first saw as a young art student in Hereford Cathedral. Studying the *Mappa Mundi* again, it struck me as an apt source on which to base my own map design, partly due to some configurational similarities with diagrams of female reproductive organs, but also because of the imaginative richness and variety it contains. The Hereford Mappa Mundi is:

> …essentially, a morality painting, a map of the world that reveals the fears and obsessions of the age. Jerusalem stands at its centre, Paradise and Purgatory at its extremes, and legendary creatures and monsters populate the faraway climes… [It] had a lofty ambition of metaphysical meaning: a map-guide, for a largely illiterate public, to a Christian life. It has no reservation in mixing the geography of the earthly world with the ideology of the next. (Garfield 2012, 43)

Similarly, I had no reservation in mixing geographical and gynecological features, fact and fiction, past and present, and feminist ideology in my *Underbelly* map. Because of the inconceivable hardship they had to endure, the women miners seem like "legendary creatures" and the "monsters" arise from the macabre anatomical drawings, all metaphorically populating "the faraway climes" of the historical past and/or the subconscious sphere. Conflating different realms and eras in this way is a characteristic of the original Mappa Mundi, which also provides a virtuoso demonstration of how to corral multifarious elements:

> In its distillation of geographical, historical and religious knowledge the mappa serves as an itinerary, a gazetteer, a parable, a bestiary and an educational aid. Indeed, all history is here, happening at the same time: the Tower of Babel; Noah's Ark as it comes to rest on dry land; the Golden Fleece; the Labyrinth in Crete where the Minotaur lived. And surely for contemporaries—locals and pilgrims—it must have constituted the most arresting freakshow in town. With its parade of dung-firing animals, dog-headed or bat-eared humans, a winged sphinx with a young woman's face, it seems closer to Hieronymus Bosch than to the scientific Greek cartographers. (Garfield 2012, 46)

However, none of these details remain in the Underbelly map since I stripped out all the medieval content to create space for my own "arresting freakshow" (see Figure 2).

The Hereford *Mappa Mundi*, for all its fantastical and humorous features, has a big, whole-world narrative to tell, but maps have been used to chart more intimate stories too. From the 17th century onwards "love maps" became popular. They sometimes pictured amatory pursuit as a siege but more commonly offered guidance by charting the "recommended route between the hazards to the goal of true love and/or marriage" (Hill 1993). *Underbelly* also follows in this tradition by mapping the routes to one woman's potential goals and desires and plotting the perils along the way, which in her case are the vagaries of gynecology and her anxieties. To symbolize these hazards I incorporated old anatomical drawings of dissected female reproductive organs, pregnant cadavers and fetuses, layering in yet more instances of imagery concerned with mapping the hidden.

Throughout the history of Western art the body has been central and many artists have studied anatomy, "dissecting the dead in order to depict the living." Coming from this tradition, I felt entitled to exploit these artists' anatomical studies, creating a montage of the dissected dead in order to depict the anxieties of the living. I was especially fascinated by the way early artist-anatomists from the 17th to 18th century chose to muddle life and death. Flayed cadavers are posed like live nude models, helpfully and provocatively revealing their innards, their most private organs. Their dead flesh is folded back as if bodily tissue is nothing more than fine clothing artfully draped. The paradoxical nature of these images made them particularly suited to my thematic purpose. If the Hereford Mappa Mundi bears an affinity with Hieronymus Bosch, then *Underbelly* bears a similar affinity with the surrealist collage-novels of Max Ernst. In particular, I felt the influence of *A Little Girl Dreams of Taking the Veil*, originally published in French in 1930, which mixes cuttings from "pre-photography illustrated penny novels, and from popular tomes about nature, science, exoticism" (Tanning 1982).

> Anatomical manuals are concerned with the "mapping" of the body, which is perhaps why, since the 16th century, they have been called atlases... As well as the spatial dimension, a pictorial atlas with its accompanying text is a serial publication, unfolding in time, just as a dissection is a series of staged representations moving from one state to another. (Petherbridge 1993, 63)

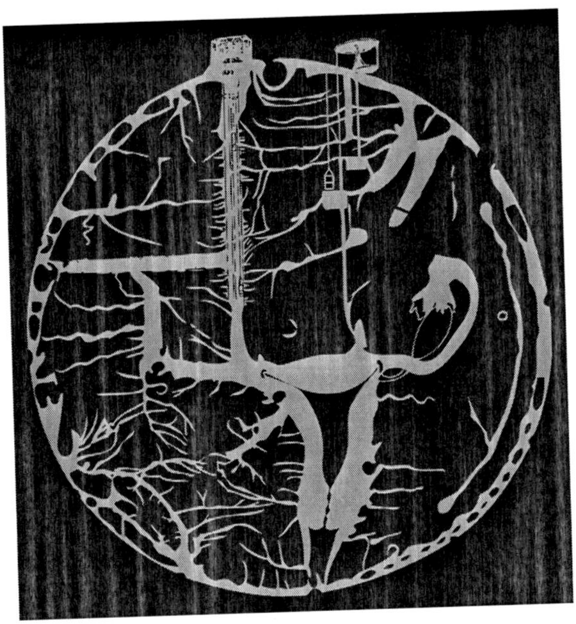

Figure 2: The design of the *Underbelly* map.

Underbelly is also a kind of dissection unfolding in time and the player progresses through a series of ten staged representations (or more depending on the endgame), moving from one state to another. The first is the opening screen, the entire *Underbelly* map surrounded by a brief historical chronology. Then you enter the map and traverse its five regions, encountering the stories of the women miners along the way. Once this exploration is complete the Chamber of Choice opens up (see Figure 3), offering a branching path, each leading to a different Spin-the-Wheel game where the map of the *Underbelly* world becomes a wheel of fortune in a playable finale (see Figure 4). Here, *Underbelly* asks you to put yourself in the position of the artist on the threshold between motherhood and non-motherhood, between decision and non-decision, between agency and fortuity. Your choice will affect the odds and the outcomes available, which are revealed in the What-the-Future-Holds section. If you are not satisfied with your lot, you may spin again, but a biological clock, with an umbilical cord and fetus for a pendulum, keeps ticking, reminding you that time is running out. In effect, the sculptor's life choices are gamified and the "glamorous" game show hostesses, who pose beside the Spin-the-Wheel parody and, ironically, announce what the future holds, are drawings of seemingly undead female cadavers.

Figure 3: Screenshot of the options available in the Chamber of Choice.

UNEARTHING RESISTANCE

Some reader-players, in conversation with me, have expressed unease at the way I mixed historical women's experience of extreme hardship with a contemporary woman's troubles, which pale in comparison. I have to admit, at first, I hesitated to use the archival material but something urged me on. Certainly, I wanted to tell the women miners' stories, to memorialize their lives and to draw attention to neglected history, but why combine that with the story of a contemporary woman? It was not until I became aware of *Studies in the Maternal*, a scholarly online journal in which *Underbelly* was published after winning its Digital Media Competition (Pullinger 2011), where I found discussion of a broader context that led me to recognize an underlying stimulus for the work.

Historically and traditionally, cultures worldwide have conflated womanhood with motherhood but there have always been women who remain childless. For some women, this is an unfortunate situation which attracts pity, but others are childless by choice and these women tend to be perceived more negatively (Shapiro 2014). In a critical review of the literature on voluntary childlessness over the past 30 years, Gilla Shapiro identifies this stigmatization and women's responses to stigma as a central debate (ibid.).

> In answering Simone de Beauvoir's (1949) question—"what is a woman?" — the response seemingly remains that 'women= mother= womb' (Gandolfo 2005). As Rich (1979, p. 26) explains, "a woman's status as childbearer [is] the test of her womanhood [...]motherhood [is] the enforced identity." The construction of womanhood as motherhood has been established through social, political, medical, and religious institutions. In so doing, motherhood has become constructed as a "fixed" and "natural" practice that is central to feminine identity. Importantly, this construction of femininity informs the debate on voluntarily childlessness and the stigma that women experience (Letherby & Williams 1999). (ibid.)

In the face of stigma, voluntarily childless women employ a variety of different responses, including attempts to deconstruct the conception of womanhood as motherhood (ibid.). This was also my endeavor when I created *Underbelly*, although I was not consciously aware at the time that it was a response to stigmatization. By portraying the plight of the 19th-century women miners alongside the concerns of the sculptor, *Underbelly* plays out a resistance to the construction of womanhood as motherhood in various ways. With no control over their fertility, the women miners had little choice but to become mothers and, also, had little choice but to return to work sometimes only days after giving birth. Having to put work first, surely made laborer, rather than motherhood, the "enforced identity" for them. In contrast, the present-day sculptor worries that, if she has children, her chosen identity as a professional artist would be subsumed in or obliterated by an enforced identity of motherhood. Unlike the 19th-century women, the sculptor has choice, but it's complicated - and, crucially, the complications are playable in *Underbelly*. In other words, by virtue of the choices being gamified, motherhood is no longer constructed as "fixed" and the presence of the paradoxical game-show-hostess dissected bodies also challenges its "natural" status (see Figure 4).

Consequently, there is no fixed ending nor identity for the sculptor. You, the player, can choose whether she tries to get pregnant, decides to remain childless or leaves it entirely to chance, although, whichever option you choose, the Spin-the-Wheel game means that chance, as in life, will always play a part. The artist's story can resolve in multiple ways with varying degrees of success or fulfillment for her. In an early version of *Underbelly*, a positive outcome in either domain, motherhood or artistic career, tended to be mutually exclusive. But when discussing the work with audiences, some people challenged me: Why couldn't she have it all? So, for the final version, I created a win-win outcome. The odds of achieving it are harder by design but if you're lucky enough to hit the jackpot and the sculptor finds success and fulfillment in every sphere of her life, you're rewarded with an animated shower of stars. This flippant decoration coupled with the game-show-hostess cadavers and the ticking fetus pendulum, perhaps, betray my cynicism. Freud observed that "Humour is not resigned; it is rebellious" and I'm conscious that the gallows humor I display in *Underbelly* is another form of response to stigma. As Freud on humor states:

> The ego refuses to be distressed by the provocations of reality, to let itself be compelled to suffer. It insists that it cannot be affected by the traumas of the external world; it shows, in fact, that such traumas are no more than occasions for it to gain pleasure. (Freud 1927)

Figure 4: Screenshot of the Spin-the-Wheel game.

Another reading of *Underbelly*'s black humor is as a response to the trauma that can attend childbirth. Until recently, parturition posed a real risk of death and, indeed, it still does in some parts of the world (Chamberlin 2006). Even in the West, where improvements in obstetric and midwifery practice have greatly reduced maternal mortality, "feeling scared of giving birth is very common" (NTC 2010) and some women's dread is severe enough to be recognized as a condition called tokophobia (Hofberg and Brockington 2000). The macabre humor in *Underbelly* may be perceived as a defense against these kinds of anxieties too.

Finally, it is no coincidence that in the dying days of my biologically fertile years, I produced a fertile work of imagination in which themes of birth, death, desire, fear, creativity and labor are intertwined. In many ways *Underbelly* is a form of elegy but it is also a defiant celebration of the diversity and endurance of the female creative drive.

WORKS CITED

Bloy, Marjorie. "Contemporary Illustrations of Conditions in the Mines." *A Web of English History: The Peel Web*, 2013. http://www.historyhome.co.uk/peel/factmine/minecond.htm.

Chamberlain, Geoffrey. "British Maternal Mortality in the 19th and Early 20th Centuries." *Journal of the Royal Society of Medicine* 99, no. 11 (November 2006): 559–63.

Del Col, Laura. "Testimony Gathered by Ashley's Mines Commission." *The Victorian Web*, 2002. http://www.victorianweb.org/history/ashley.html.

Freud, Sigmund. "Humour," 1927.

Garfield, Simon. *On The Map: Why the World Looks the Way It Does*. London: Profile Books, 2012.

Halsall, Paul. "Modern History Sourcebook: Women Miners in the English Coal Pits." *Internet History Sourcebooks*, July 1998. http://legacy.fordham.edu/halsall/mod/1842womenminers.asp.

Hill, Gillian. "In the Realms of Love and Allegory." In *Tales from the Map Room: Fact and Fiction about Maps and Their Makers*, First Edition edition. London: BBC Books, 1993.

Hofberg, Kristina, and I. F. Brockington. "Tokophobia: An Unreasoning Dread of Childbirth: A Series of 26 Cases." *The British Journal of Psychiatry* 176, no. 1 (2000): 83–85.

Kirby, P. "Child Labour, Public Decency and the Iconography of the Childrens Employment Commission of 1842." *Manchester Papers in Economic and Social History*. 2007;62:1-23., 2007. https://www.escholar.manchester.ac.uk/uk-ac-man-scw:4564.

McCredden, Lyn. "Historicising the Metaphor of Mother Earth." *Journal of the Association for the Study of Australian Literature* 0, no. 0 (February 13, 2013): 126–30.

NCT. "Tokophobia: Scared of Giving Birth? | NCT." *NCT: The UK's Largest Charity for Parents*, 2012. https://www.nct.org.uk/pregnancy/tokophobia-fear-childbirth.

Petherbridge, Deanna. "Art and Anatomy: The Meeting of Text and Image." In *The Quick and the Dead: Artists and Anatomy*. London: National Touring Exhibitions, 1997.

Pullinger, Kate. "Visual Work: Maternal Subjectivities, Care and Labour." *MAMSIE | Studies in the Maternal* | Volume 3, Issue 2, 2011. http://www.mamsie.bbk.ac.uk/back_issues/3_2/visual_media_art.html.

Shapiro, Gilla. "Voluntary Childlessness: A Critical Review of the Literature." *Online journal. MAMSIE | Studies in the Maternal* | Volume 6, Issue 1, 2014. http://www.mamsie.bbk.ac.uk/back_issues/6_1/Shapiro_SiM_6_1.html.

Tanning, D. "Translator's Note." In *A Little Girl Dreams of Taking the Veil*, by Max Ernst, 1st American Ed edition. New York: George Braziller Inc, 1982.

Wilks, Christine. "Underbelly." *Crissxross*, 2010. http://crissxross.net/elit/underbelly.html.

A "Rhetoric For Creative Authoring" and The Author's Intent

BY ODILE FARGE

INTRODUCTION

The production of digital literature "inevitably" requires tools, software or technologies that suggest and impose choices and directions; they also raise questions about the creative act. What then is the role of authoring tools in the creation process? The perspective of the digital literature author—and, more generally, the perspective of the creator in the production of digital literature—may provide some possible answers. We will highlight certain elements of enunciation inherent in the software tools and call them "rhetorics." In so doing, we will see that the purpose of these elements is indeed to strategically structure the content available to users and to exert a certain degree of influence on these users, thereby providing upstream formatting for the discourses that the authors will subsequently address to their readers.

Can we say then that the software tools, with their graphic forms, are structured as a "discourse" addressed to the designer-author—and, in particular, is this discourse based on a clearly identifiable rhetoric such as a strategy of persuasion or even a strategy of manipulation?

Thanks to the proliferation of creation/publication tools (and disregarding certain social, economic and cultural factors), it is now possible for anyone to participate in content production. This means that each of us can take possession of, modify and duplicate content as much as we like. According to Tim O'Reilly (2005), this opportunity to contribute to information production and enhancement fosters the emergence of a "collective intelligence." By the same token, this increased participatory involvement has also necessitated the standardization of formats and practices for the various web players. The development of CMS (Content Management System) tools goes hand in and with this standardization of formats. In what ways do these formats influence digital creations? In our view, the users of such tools pay a price because, to a certain degree, the "editorial enunciation" (Jeanneret, Souchier, 1999) of the content is imposed on them, i.e., the structural form and physical presentation of this content. The question then becomes this: to what extent do these tools influence the process of structuring and formalizing the contents and ideas that take shape within the work once users have accepted these rules of editorial control? Can we go so far as to say that the creation tools foster the emergence of "thought processes"?

One significant and noteworthy aspect of these tools is the separation of a creation's presentation and content. In the case of WordPress, for instance, non-programmers can easily add to a site's content, while more experienced users have the ability to modify CMS source code. This double approach lies at the heart of the design of such creation software programs—an approach with the two-fold goal of promoting efficiency and fostering user adherence. This is precisely what occurs in oratorical discourse and explains our references to "rhetoric." A two-faceted rhetoric is established in the digital text: "A rhetoric of reception aimed at the reader through its processes and templates, and a rhetoric of design that anticipates the designer's expectations and practices in various ways" (Saemmer 2013, 287). While the rhetoric of reception is concerned with the "surface" aspects of the digital text, such as the on-screen animation and hyperlinks seen by the receiver, the "rhetoric for creative authoring" is interested in the proposals made to the creator-authors by the software tool's architexts. Classical rhetoric is made up of five components: *inventio*, which concentrates on the search for arguments; *dispositio*, which organizes the arguments; *elocutio*, which formulates the arguments and the choice of the various possible signifiers; and *actio* and *memoria*, which propose techniques for updating and storing the discourse (Saemmer 2013; 27-28).

Of these five components, *dispositio* represents the construction of the discourse in classical rhetoric, in which the presentation order of the elements "changes the acceptability of the discourse" (Perelman 1977; 2002, 182). Since it is addressed to an audience, this change implies that the rhetor wishes to influence that audience through the arrangement of the elements, and win it over with convincing arguments. It also denotes a spatial use of some of the constituent elements. "Since truth alone has the capacity to persuade, the function of rhetoric will be to focus on truth while playing on the imagination," says Roger Bautier (1994, 256).

For his part, Jean-Marie Klinkenberg (2000) stresses the social function of rhetoric that studies the "strategic" use of symbols by "critically assessing the choices made by discourse creators based on the reception situation and potentially persuasive goals" (Saemmer 2013, 30). We therefore describe the "rhetoric for creative authoring" as a software tool approach that simultaneously probes how this tool anticipates the practices of digital authors, and how these authors seize it as they mobilize their imaginaries, both upstream and downstream, in the creation act. In other words, we are exploring the resulting power relationships and asking ourselves whether some discourse elements of the software tool are not likely to exert a considerable influence over the creator to ensure that he or she adheres to proposals that protect the interests and strategies of a cultural industry.

RHETORIC SERVING THE AUTHORING TOOL

According to Lev Manovich, the software tool does not directly prevent users from creating; it does, however, tend to imply the "naturalness" of following a certain logic, notably the "selection" of pre-defined objects (2010), and tends to favour "default" practices. Is the status of the author undermined by a creation that begins with pre-fabricated elements? Digital authors make assumptions about their readers' practices, inserting, for example a hyperlink between a word and its definition. Similarly, the software tool proposes discourses that would, in this sense, constitute a set of implicits that result in the creation of a paradigm of the "unthought" (Robert, 2012)—one in which the notion of paradigm is defined as the whole body of beliefs and values acknowledged and shared by a given group. Generally speaking, whether consciously or not, we filter our experiences and build our perception of the world through paradigms.

THE "IMPLICIT" THAT EXISTS BETWEEN INTERPRETATIONS OF THE DISCOURSE AND THE AUTHOR'S INTENTION

Every situation of enunciation can be marked by a measure of the "implicit," a measure of meaning that is left open to interpretation.

> The general problem with the implicit [...] is knowing how to say something without, however, accepting responsibility for having said it; this is equivalent to reaping the benefits of verbal effectiveness and the innocence of silence (Ducrot 2003, 12).

In our study context, in which the author is the software tool designer and the receiver is the digital work creator, the implicit brings into play a tension between a certain intention of the author and the possible interpretations of a discourse by the receiver. By proposing to the creator an interface structured in a particular way (*dispositio*) with graphic manual tools, instruments and verbal statements (*elocutio*), the designer seeks to obtain a specific result from the receiver, or at least to exert a remote influence on how he or she thinks about the digital creation. Through the layout elements deployed, the designer gives the user an impression of control and freedom, while also suggesting how to proceed. This is why some promotional discourses in WordPress are based on this logic of apparent freedom and implicit values, as WordPress demonstrates, for example in the new features included in version 3.2 (2011).

All of the widgets, menus, buttons, and interface elements fade away to allow

> you to compose and edit your thoughts in a completely clean environment conducive to writing, but when your mouse strays to the top of the screen your most-used shortcuts are right there where you need them.[129]

In this discourse, we can clearly see how the software tool is presented as the provider of an environment conducive to creation, while also imposing structural frameworks. This discourse is addressed to designers, whether or not they realize it; it produces belief and engenders codes of belonging that legitimize and validate the rhetoric through a community of users that is present and active, such as the WordPress user community. The software tools therefore reflect an intention to send a message whose precise scope and influence often remain unknown to the receiver. This message, structured in accordance with rhetorical strategies, is supported by beliefs. Moreover, the strength of this rhetoric resides precisely in the fact that it relies on the support of a collective imaginary or even unconscious.[130]

WORDPRESS'S LAUNCHER INTERFACE: AN EXAMPLE OF RHETORICAL ARRANGEMENT

The designer wants to ensure that software tool users understand and accept the pre-prepared elements, which are more or less visible to them. To achieve these goals, the designer must then strive for the most easily understood depictions, thereby allowing users to establish a relationship between ordinary objects in the physical world and the interface.

For the most part, software tools are products of the cultural industry, which itself is supported by traditional market levers; consequently, these tools sometimes make exaggerated promises, such as WordPress' claims that a sophisticated Web site or blog can be produced "in three clicks." These enticing promises do indeed enable users to take their first steps in digital creation with confidence but also impose on them a number of organized constraints in the form of standardized and prescriptive discourses. These discourses reveal the thought processes of the software tool designer, ensuring creators of a minimum use efficiency but nevertheless reducing the "field of

129 https://wordpress.org/news/2011/07/gershwin/>.

130 The collective unconscious is a concept owed to Swiss psychiatrist Carl Gustav Jung; it designates operations related to the imaginary with creative components. Apparently, in addition to Freud's individual unconscious, there is a deeper unconscious level that is expressed through archaic and universal images in dreams, beliefs, myths and stories. The collective unconscious would be made up of pre-existing forms of thought similar to instinct, called archetypes. Identified as being independent of culture or time, these thoughts demonstrate the existence of a collective unconscious that is deeply anchored in society and ensures the cohesion thereof.

possibilities" available to them. To engender user adherence, it still seems important to create and maintain this illusion of easy and immediate accessibility.

Launching the software is unquestionably a very important action, one that already contributes to the rhetorical arrangement of elements. The appearance of the various elements sets up a framework for creation, provides a first impression and establishes an initial relationship with the software tool. The WordPress welcome screen shows us the extent to which this philosophy of community is now present and meaningful. This welcome screen appears at the first login to WordPress (see Figure 1), offering three sections to guide users through the initial steps.

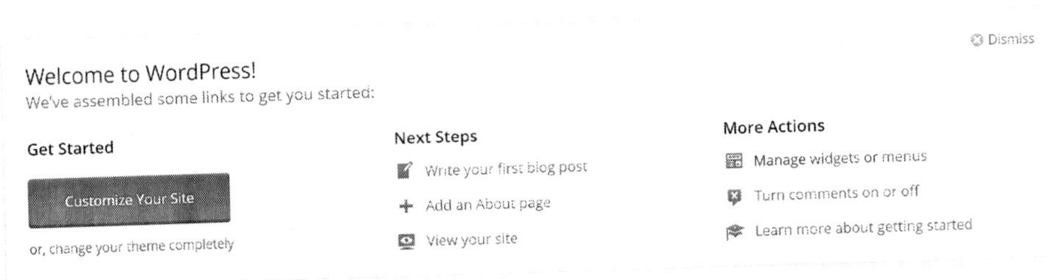

Figure.1: WordPress: administrative interface– welcome screen

As soon as this welcome message appears, we do indeed join a community in which users are seen as individuals who will be surrounded and supported. "Get Started": these are the first words the creator sees before "starting" the process; they are a way of minimizing the risks that first-time users may encounter and of removing any lingering barriers or fears—but they also help to legitimize the action by suggesting the possibility of getting started spontaneously. Overcoming one's fears would therefore be the key to successful use of this software tool. "Get Started" is a call to action and a way to give novice users control over the situation.

When creators click "Customize Your Site," they begin an immediate experience with the tool. It would appear that, after the three clicks needed for set-up (or the famous "five-minute install"), this is the only action required to make the site operational. The few steps needed to actually use the WordPress software tool are condensed into the actions suggested in the middle of this frame: "Write your first blog post," "Add…" and "View…" With these three points, WordPress confronts us with the tool's basic notions, i.e., the notions of blogs, pages and web site publishing. This "Welcome to WordPress" window thus amounts, in and of itself, to a set of instructions. On the right-hand side, we see the final step in WordPress' empowerment of users, i.e., a progressive upward movement from the exhortation to "Get Started" to the invitation to perform "More Actions" addressed to more knowledgeable and sophisticated WordPress community members who wish to explore the tool further. The availability of community expertise to help and support the creator provides confirmation of the solid identity surrounding this tool.

By organizing its various interface elements as a discourse, Wordpress prefigures, in the rhetorical meaning of the term, the manner in which the creator will use the authoring tool. Starting with the software's default proposals, and before embarking on their creations, users need to decide on their settings, make a few clicks to create their own practical knowledge from the available elements, and engage themselves in a community through a "selection" of actions found on a pre-defined welcome menu. This example of discourse clearly reveals an intention, whether conscious or not, to address a message to users. Often unknown to the receiver, this intention is supported by deep beliefs and also models the receiver's imaginary.

THE PLACE OF THE TOOL IN THE AUTHOR'S INTENTIONALITY

THE FIGURE OF THE AUTHOR

The software tool therefore makes suggestions to authors who, through their creative practices, are faced with the limits or multiple possibilities made available to them. In our view, the statements made by authors regarding their relationship with the tool represent an effective and original starting point for probing the role played by the software tool in digital creation, because from these statements emerge the many imaginaries associated with such tools, and this is what we would like to highlight. It was with this in mind that, between 2010 and 2013, we met with 16 digital authors, writers and artists, and developed an interest in the relationship between the software tool and creative practices, as experienced by the authors of digital literature. We wanted to find out how they envision creation. But we first needed to define creation in a digital context.

The software tool puts forward proposals to the creator-author, who then develops responses to this "rhetoric for creative authoring." We are indeed talking about authors here, about their beliefs, practices and imaginaries when faced with the reality of a software tool that makes promises while also tending to appear "transparent"—but a tool that nevertheless requires a constant renewal of learning practices, notably because of ever-changing technology. In this unstable context of new technologies, what are the authors' responses to the machine or the software that is discoursing with them? Do they perceive these discourses as such? Do they reject them or are they seduced by a technology that promises to help them produce a work by "facilitating" their writing? The way in which artists and creators apprehend the world allows us to define the notion of the imaginary as a representation of the world in which cultural beings construct their reality. All individuals who have to adapt to changes in their environment or who are seeking to resolve a problem call on their own creativity.

Writing experimental works of digital literature sets in motion the figure of an author who most often works solo to produce his or her work. Frequently an academic, a researcher, a programmer *and* an artist at the same time, this author seems to combine all the functions required for the production of a digital work, from his or her critical posture to computer skills. On the other hand, in the area of "commercial" applications, the roles of author and developer are often much more clearly delineated. We must ask what role the tool plays in digital writing upstream from author-implemented strategies. To what degree does the computer tool suggest, or even impose, a framework on the author's creation, even if we are just talking about the operating system that automatically starts up when the program is launched? Where does the digital work begin? Where does it stop? The question of its "framework" echoes the reflections of Jacques Derrida vis-à-vis the philosophical concept of "parergon" (Derrida, 1978). Derrida himself borrowed the "parerga" from Kant, a word used by the German philosopher to refer to embellishments and external ornaments that are detrimental to "beautiful form." While not entirely extraneous to the creation, the framework is on the boundary or fringes; nevertheless, it apparently exercises an influence on the creation. Is it still a part of the work even though it exists only on the edges? In the case of a digital work, can we not say that the computer, the operating system and the software tool act as the framework and are an integral part of the creation?

CHOOSING THE TOOL

The software tool attempts to influence creators in their choices and decisions by referencing their imaginaries and culture. In so doing, it tries to convince as many as possible and to promote its own dominance, thereby conditioning to some extent both the authors' adherence and their resistance.

In this sense, the software tool becomes a participant in the creation of works of digital literature, and the authors, who project this tool onto a certain number of wishes or ideas, see their intentionality switched on; this, in turn, triggers the implementation of a certain number of strategies, the first of which concerns the actual choice of the tool. Indeed, the choice of the tool used to present one's creative work is never without meaning. Authors seem to have difficulty, however, verbalizing the reasons why they choose one software tool over another. Such uncertainty shows first and foremost that the place of the tool in the authors' intentionality remains vague. Where does the idea to use a specific software tool come from? Which tool will offer the most streamlined management capabilities and be best adapted to the very nature of an author's work? If the author considers himself or herself to be "programming oriented," the choice to use, say, Flash or Director (two software applications frequently used in digital literature) is guided by the end goal. A software tool such as Director may make the work easier because it performs a whole body of operations automatically. Inserting a picture, for example, requires a simple drag and drop operation rather than writing several lines of code.

THE TOOL AS AN OBJECT OF FASCINATION OR AS A RISK OF ALIENATION?

Practices are transmitted by forms and result from actions when knowledge is anchored in time and space. New digital devices give texts the power to act, "action potential," in the words of Wolfgang Iser. This power differs according to the forms it takes. Yves Jeanneret speaks of "internalized" forms while Emmanuël Souchier propounds the theory of "editorial enunciation," specifying the role of visual frameworks in object reading. This amounts to characterizing form as an act in which two power games are joined together.

> Our study of the properties of visual devices has shown that the relative position of the frameworks or their respective proportions committed the reader to infer logical relationships of hierarchy or adherence. (Jeanneret, 2008, 77)

Ivan Illich, for his part, advocates a "convivial" tool that each individual could easily use for purposes of his or her own determination, without infringing on other people's freedom. Such a tool would be a "translator of intentionality" (1973, 45).

The separation of content and form proposed by many CMS tools represents a way of thinking that contradicts this concept of "editorial enunciation." Indeed, it is not possible to separate content from form, because the "corpulence" of a text is part of its existence. This explains why there may be a conflict between the tool's "editorial enunciation" and the author's intentions. The issue for creators will therefore be to ask themselves about "convention," an implicit rule of conduct that opens the way to a small degree of freedom. If a function is hidden, creators will need to mobilize their will and their fighting spirit to access it, and this sometimes requires a long period of learning. How many people are likely to change Word's default page format? Convention encourages us to keep the suggested settings, thereby creating tension between the software tool's statements and the author's intent.

The software's proposals may be a source of creativity but they can also "be preformatted" or even "banal." These various possibilities represent so many inferences of behavior that the creator will need to decipher, prompting the question of the extent to which the author has been inspired by the software tool. Is the software tool perceived as a source of inspiration? In the case of many authors, it is difficult to formalize the process by which the tool exerts an influence. If we believe that a psychological relationship is created between the author and the software tool, does this author fall under the control of the tool without necessarily knowing it? Is the author always aware of the true role played by the software tool in the creation process?

Celebrated programmer, graphic designer and researcher John Maeda stresses that artists who use Flash "try to do their best with what is available" whenever a new version of the software is released, but he would like to see them become less "enslaved by the software and, in particular, throw off the creative shackles imposed by Flash" (Maeda 2002). To what extent is the artist a slave of a cultural industry software tool such as Flash? Can we not say that the tool is invested with the power to steer actions without allowing the possibility of detachment? A hint of dependency can be glimpsed. The user-friendliness produced by the tool might also be concealing the decisive and dominant role it plays in the creation process. This "magical" character that comes into operation has been raised by Pascal Robert specifically with regard to the characteristic of immediacy. The computer would indeed seem to create a "magic gesture [...] of the thing produced, immediately and effortlessly" (2012, 52). Instantaneousness engenders fascination. Our actions on the software tool produce a feeling of power and domination. However, can we not say that the machine is also dominating us as a result of the very fascination that it creates? Or should we say that the tool motivates us and we learn how to use it, but that it does not incite fascination since only the creation produced by the tool can transform the material. In this case, fascination would then come perilously close to idolatry.

CONCLUSION

We have shown that the software tool influences and sometimes conditions creations. This demonstration is important not only in terms of heightening our awareness of the role and issues related to technological tools in our societies, but also in terms of opening up this perspective for a young audience who will be tomorrow's market consumers. Such awareness will then be able to consolidate training in the "digital culture."

Since we are assuming that the software tools are endowed with creation codes and that they transform our ways of thinking, we define "digital culture" as the capacity to perceive the digital environment while learning appropriate practices and developing critical thinking.

The implicit triggers tension between a certain intention on the part of the author and the possible interpretations by the end-user. Our practices contain an element of the unthought, a fact that reinforces the idea that an effective discourse helps to construct a reality and moulds a society in which humans are fascinated by the tools they employ. Ease of learning is a criterion guaranteeing that a software tool will be used by the greatest number of people and ensuring its durability. Users need to be promised that these tools will be simple to use if they are to agree to make the effort required to master them. The "rhetoric for creative authoring" therefore helps to "decipher" the manipulation strategies of the discourses proposed by the tool, and provides authors with the awareness that they need to preserve a greater freedom of creation.

WORKS CITED

Bautier, Roger. *De la rhétorique à la communication*. Grenoble: Presses Universitaires de Grenoble, 1994.

Ducrot, Oswald. *Dire et ne pas dire, Principes de sémantique linguistique*. Paris: Éditeurs des sciences et des arts. Collection Savoir: Sciences Hermann, 2003.

Derrida, Jacques. *La vérité en peinture*. Paris: Éditions Flammarion, 1978.

Jeanneret, Yves ; Emmanuël Souchier. "Pour une poétique de l'écrit d'écran." *Xoana* No.6 (1999): 97–107.

Jeanneret, Yves. *Penser la trivialité. Volume 1, La vie triviale des êtres culturels*. Paris: Éditions Lavoisier & Hermes-sciences, coll., 2008.

Illich, Ivan. *La convivialité*. Paris: Éditions du Seuil, 1973.

Klinkenberg, Jean-Marie. *Précis de sémiotique générale*. Paris: Éditions du Seuil, 2000.

Manovich, Lev. *Software takes command*. New York: Bloomsbury Academic, 2013.

O'Reilly, Tim. *What Is Web 2.0*. 2005, <http://oreilly.com/web2/archive/what-is-web-20.html>

Perelman, Chaïm. *L'empire rhétorique – Rhétorique et argumentation*. Paris: Librairie philosophique J. Vrin, 1977: 2002.

Robert, Pascal. *L'impensé informatique*. Paris: Éditions des archives contemporaines, 2012.

Saemmer, Alexandra. "Pour une rhétorique de la réception du texte numérique : Figures de la lecture, anticipations de pratiques." HDR Diss. Université Paris 8, 2013.

Souchier, Emmanuël. "L'image du texte. Pour une théorie de l'énonciation éditoriale." *Cahiers de médiologie*, No.6 (1998): 137-145.

III. CRITICAL OVERVIEWS OF DIGITAL WRITING PRACTICE

Gender as Patterns: Unfixed Forms in Electronic Poetry

BY GIOVANNA DI ROSARIO

Information and Communications Technology, ICT, has imposed, and continues to impose, transformations and new unforeseeable mutations on literature, just as much as it has on some objects of daily use. The encounter between poetry and informatics has had more profound effects than a simple transposition from one medium to another. Due to the novelty of its characteristics, the electronic text seems to be the bearer of deeper changes. We find in these works many crucial strategic elements—such as visual infographics, the poeticity of the elements, their [il]legibility, the pluri-signification of the relation, image-text or the flow of the reading process in the textual rearrangement (di Rosario 2003) —which affect a text's structure.

ICT affords literature and poetry new ways of expressions beyond the medium of paper/print. Computers and the internet open up new possibilities for creative writing: computers highlight the reticular nature of writing and the web space multiplies and disperses its dimensions. Poetry and art in general have always been synonymous with subjectivity, with creativity, both qualities considered to be the quintessence of the human being and not usually considered qualities of science. Science is the birthplace of the digital realm. Paul Dirac stated that; "in science one tries to tell people, in such a way as to be understood by everyone, something that no one ever knew before. But in poetry "it's the exact opposite," to use Dirac's words (quoted in Eves 1977). Wordsworth characterized poetry as "the spontaneous overflow of powerful feelings"; finally, according to E. E. Cummings "writing...is an art; and artists...are human beings" (2002) and "poetry and every other art was and is and forever will be strictly and distinctly a question of individuality [...] poetry is being, not doing" (1953, 22).

This essay will explore how the digital environment affects literature, and more specifically, how traditional markers of identity such as gender are reconfigured in digital literature in general and electronic poetry in particular. It aims at understanding what is the role of place and gender in a poetic digital environment. By investigating works by three pioneering female writers of electronic poetry, this paper will trace the feminine literary and poetic voices that emerge from the figures of literary narrative and from the rhetorical and visual devices that digital media affords.

We start from the presupposition that there is a "male poetic" language from which woman have to borrow. According to Sally Minogue:

> Sometimes this has been defined in terms of traditional poetic forms, sometimes

> in terms of conventions, sometimes in terms of the theory of language formation and acquisition, which are gender-based and which affect female identity and subjectivity, and therefore affect the way that subjectivity is expressed in poetry. Almost all feminist critics share the assumption and assertion that the poetic tradition is male dominated and that therefore any woman who [...], any woman who attempts to insert herself into it is disadvantaged because the forms she takes on are characterized by their use by men. (223)

Harold Bloom proposes a paradigm modelled on Freud's family romance and the power relationships between dominant and submissive that it encodes. As noted by Betsy Erkkila, Bloom traces a series of hierarchical relationships among male poets (Erkkila 1984). Pointing out the exclusively male nature of Bloom's model, several feminist critics—Gilbert and Gubar (1979), Margaret Homans (1980), Joanne Feit Diehl (1990)—wondered; what happens if the poet is a woman? For the last one hundred and fifty years, women writers generally preferred the novel to the poetic genre. Virgin.a Woolf hypnotised that this was because "the older forms of literature were fixed before women writers could significantly shape their conventions, while the novel alone was young enough to be soft [in the woman writer's] hands" (80).

Margaret Homans and Jan Montefiore, among others, used French feminist theories and works in order to break "new ground in pushing feminist criticism toward more explicitly theorized analysis of poetry" (Keller and Miller 1984, 6). In *Women Writers and Poetic Identity* (1980), Homans focused on deconstructive and psychoanalytic criticism (Derrida, Lacan, Irigaray) to study nineteenth-century women poets and their exclusion from speaking subjectively. In the same way, Montefiore in *Feminism and Poetry* (1987), studies women's poetic traditions particularly in terms of poetic form and language. She explores the possibility of a female poetic, or better, of a style specific to women's poetry which describes a female imaginary and female identity and meaning, insisting, however, that women's poetry will always simultaneously participate in male tradition. Can e-poetry break these forms and traditions and offer women writers new ways of relating to language and poetry?

As it is known, Lacan's description of the Symbolic locates women and men in different positions within the Symbolic in relation to the Phallus (2002). Simplifying, men (because of the Phallus) can misperceive themselves as being closer to it, whereas women (because they do not have it) are further from that centre. This distance from the Phallus is a central element for poststructuralist theoretical feminists to argue that women are closer to the margins of the Symbolic order; women are not as fixed in place as men are; "they are closer to the Imaginary" (Guy 2014, 92). And since women are less fixed in the Symbolic than men, they are, and their language too, more fluid than men.

According to Luce Irigaray, languages are not neutral but they actually bring about the phallocentric discourse (1974). A women's duty should be to build up "another language," a language that brings different values: not neutral values but female values. Languages should be deconstructed (in the Derridean sense) in order to be reconstructed.

In *Sorties* (1975), Hélène Cixous wonders where, and in many of her literary works, proposes examples of a "female writing" ("écriture feminine") that besides showing the "sexual difference" (Irigaray) show the "linguistic difference" of women in respect to men.

In a very well know part of *Sorties*, Cixous wonders where women are in the most common conceptual oppositions couples of the western tradition (activity vs passivity; sun vs moon; culture vs nature; etc.) And women are always in second place in the couple, as the "inferior" or "negative" one. The logic of western discourse is not neutral but phallocentric. This logic is a binary logic that opposes elements. According to her, this logic legitimates the subordinate role of women. The "female writing" will ignore this logic and will construct a new one.

This writing, however, cannot be theorized or codified, since theorizing always involves using phallocentric language and logic (Cixous 1975 and 2010). Cixous proposes, thus, a kind of writing that can be just practiced, attempted, improvised.

In this essay, I will explore if the new medium highlights this fluid unstable writing and if the poetic forms can be freed from "male language structure" thanks to e-poetry. Does e-poetry allow the poet to attempt and improvise a new writing?

MARIE BÉLISLE AND THE ALTER EGO OF MEANING

The first work I will analyze is *Figures* by Marie Bélisle. It consists of four figures: "Figures variables"; "Figures parallèles"; "Figures constantes"; and "Figures tangentes." Here I will analyze two of them: "Figures variables" and (its opposite, at least as far as its title is concerned) "Figure constante."

Figures is built as a literary illustration of the Golden Ratio and of Fibonacci's sequence. As an aesthetic and mathematical constant, the Golden Ratio (or Golden Section) constitutes a formal matrix which makes it possible to determine the number of words and lines in the texts, as well as the way in which they are arranged and connected with one another. Figures are thus Golden Rectangles where the words are used as the horizontal measuring unit and lines as the vertical measuring unit.

Leonardo Fibonacci (1175-1240), an Italian mathematician, is recognised as the inventor of a sequence of numbers now bearing his name. In "Fibonacci's Sequence" each number represents the sum of the two numbers that precede it: 0, 1, 1, 2, 3, 5, 8, 13,

21, 34, 55, 89, 144... The more one advances through the series, the more the relationship between two consecutive numbers converge on Phi, (roughly 1,618): 8 ÷ 5 = 1,655 ÷ 34 = 1,617 144 ÷ 89 = 1,6179. Fibonacci's sequence is connected with the Golden Section through the number Phi.

The Greek letter Phi indicates a mathematical constant called the Golden Section. Its value is roughly in decimal notation 1,618. It is an algebraic irrational number fully given by the expression (1+5½)/2. Thus, when the relationship between the height and the width of a rectangle corresponds to Phi, one speaks about a Gold Rectangle: it is the case, for example, with a rectangle of 144 mm X 89mm. Largely used in art and in architecture, the Golden Section represents an ideal of balance and elegance of the proportions. It allows us, by drawing up a constant relationship, to generate forms harmoniously linking one another thanks to their isomorphism.

Bélisle's *Figures* can be described as text-spirals, rewriting the (golden) spiral Phi. By passing the mouse over the segments the text advances or moves back in a symmetrical way.

In "Figures variables", the first of our two texts, from an opening verse line:

figures
variables

The reader can reach the complete poem in only three clicks, which forms a rectangle.

malgré ce qui survit en nous, voilà presque
advenu l'âge de toujours, éperdu de certitude
comme si nous nous étions égarés dans les
métaphores nous croyons que les figures et mouvements
du langage remplacent les mobiles variables du plaisir[131]

The meaning of the text is already inscribed in the title: "Figures variables," which are also the first two verse lines: figures that can change. And, by clicking on them, they change and another rectangle will appear:

figures et mouvements

131 My translation: "despite what survives in us, here almost / happened the age of always, lost of certainty / as if we were disoriented in / metaphors we believe figures and movements of/language replace the mobile variables of pleasure."

variables du plaisir[132]

Until now, the text is composed only of nominal syntagms, there is no verb, though the poetic construction is already built. By continuing to click on the text another "figure" will be drawn on the page:

nous voilà presque
éperdus de certitudes,
égarés dans les
figures et mouvements
variables du plaisir[133]

"Figures and movements" are metaphors of pleasure in the second segment of the poem, but in the third segment they acquire a negative connotation, since we (the poet and the reader) are almost lost "presque éperdue" and mislaid "égarés." With another click, the last rectangle appears:

malgré ce qui survit en nous, voilà presque
advenu l'âge de toujours, éperdu de certitude
comme si nous nous étions égarés dans les
métaphores nous croyons que les figures et mouvements
du langage remplacent les mobiles variables du plaisir

In this fourth segment, the poet and the reader are lost in metaphors, believing that the language with its movements and figures can replace the pleasure.

Bélisle shapes the meaning of the poem already in the title: "Figures variables": it is a variable meaning. By moving words in space, Bélisle multiplies the number of the verse lines and thus the number of possible meanings. The words form and deform the rhythm and the sense of the text. As far as the sound is concerned - for example - the reader passes from "nous voilà presque éperdu" to "malgré ce qui survit en nous, voilà presque advenu l'âge de toujours, éperdu [...]" where the sounds "ou" and "u" create internal rhymes and alliterations producing a sense of homophony although altering the meaning of the text. "Figures and movements" and "metaphors" substitute a part to one another, a sense to one another.

132 My translation: "figures and movements / variables of pleasure."

133 My translation: "here we are almost/lost of certainty, / disoriented in/ figures and movements/ variables of pleasure."

In "Figures constantes" the same construction logic is used: by sliding the cursor over the segments the text advances or moves back in a symmetrical way. From an opening verse line:

figures
constantes[134]

The reader again reaches the complete poem in only three clicks, which forms a rectangle.

comme des phrases imprononcées, les figures des amours
s'abiment, secrètement réduites au constantes désormais abstraites
de nos silences ; nous trouvons, dans la distance
même, la matière des analepses sublimées mais subverties
par nos mémoires, gardées vive par l'illusion[135]

While in the previous text the creation of multiple layers of meaning (the creation of meaning behind other meanings) is already inscribed in the title, in "Figures constantes" the title implies a constant meaning. However, here again, this logical construction is suggested to the reader from the second text that appears. The "constants figures" are transformed into figures of "amours constantes," but from now on they are abstract. It is the distance (physically and temporarily) that transforms "figures constantes" into abstract "amours constantes", sublimated, but subverted, because of the illusion. In the last text, however, "les figures des amours s'abiment," they are damaged, and it is only the illusion that keeps them alive.

Words, meanings, forms; everything changes in Bélisle's works, highlighting the dual/multi/pluri-identity of letters: there will no longer be one fixed meaning structured by the rigor of the male language, but the possibilities opened up by metaphoric and embodied writing.

134 My translation: "constant figures."

135 My translation: "as unsaid sentences, the figures of love / get damaged, secretly now reduced to abstract constants of / our silences; we find, in the distance itself, / the material of analepses sublimated but subverted/by our memories, kept alive by illusion."

MARÍA MENCÍA AND THE LIMITS OF LITERATURE IN NEW MEDIA

María Mencía's *Birds Singing Other Birds Songs* invites readers to reconsider what they consider the limits of literature to be. In *Birds Singing Other Birds Songs* the linguistic and the visual intertwine to explore the area in-between the visual, the aural and the textual. The "reader" or better yet the spectator can interact with the text in an unconventional manner, she can explore it by proposing many different reading paths, which are potentially unique for every reader.

Birds Singing Other Birds' Songs is part of the *Electronic Literature Collection* Volume 1, where Mencía states:

> This work originated when I was invited to exhibit at the Medway Galleries. The most interesting features of the gallery were its high ceiling and three large windows, which I was inspired to use in the work. I wanted to explore kinetic typography, the animation of images and sound. I came across a transcription of birds' songs in the book The Thinking Ear. Suddenly, I was drawn to this transcription because of the similarities with the phonemes I was using in my other works. The repetitive aspect of letters and what looked like syllables reminded me of sound poems. So, I decided to ask some singers to sing their own interpretation of the transcriptions of the songs, in order to play with the interpretative process of these translations. Having been translated first from birds' song into linguistic interpretations, now the birdsongs would be re-interpreted by the human voice. The sounds that emerged from this study were later attached to the animated birds in the shape of calligrams. The outlines and letters of the text birds corresponded to the transcribed sound made by each bird, so making the birds sing their own visual-textual compositions. Nevertheless, the sound does not correspond to the real bird. The visual character of the typographical character was another important characteristic in the making of each individual bird, which leads to the matter of the materiality, virtuality, and movement of the letter. This work has shown an incredible versatility in reshaping itself into different forms of media and possibilities of presentation and thus of exploration.

Based on the tradition of concrete poetry and calligrams, this work focuses on the materiality of a primordial language. The words are decomposed to become phonemes, the smallest phonetic unit in language that is capable of conveying a distinction in meaning, or to typographically represent just sounds. For instance, in the 12th sequence a white bird contains pumping letters that can form a verb see. The words do not have a clear meaning; the reader must seek it. Words construct forms: the calligram of a bird; but also they deconstruct them as in the 4th sequence. In Mencía's own words:

> The conceptual basis for the work is an exploration of the translation process: from birds' sounds into language and back to birds' songs again via the human voice with the knowledge of language. These birds are animated "text birds" singing the sound of their own text while flying in the sky. The letters, which

> create the birds' physical outlines, correspond to the transcribed sound made by each of the birds. The sound is produced by the human voice, slightly manipulated by the computer. Nevertheless, the sound does not correspond to the visual representation of the real bird. In the video version, the birds appear on screen in a random manner. (2001)

In the web version, if the "reader" activates all the 13 sequences into which the work is divided, she will listen to a flock of singing birds and watch a sequence where letters form, transform and deform themselves. Through her play with letters, sounds and forms, Mencía proposes a way to watch and seemingly to touch sound, to shape, to reconstruct the sound of a new language. At the same time, she suggests that the language used in the poem still has to find its form and its identity. In Mencía's poem, language is moulded while reading. There is no structured form yet. Mencía proposes a new poetic form of language.

As we have seen Irigaray suggested that women should build up "another language" and Hélène Cixous hoped that the "female writing" would ignore the male logic and would realize another logic. According to Cixous this new writing (and logic) cannot be theorized since theorizing always involves using phallocentric language (and logic). Mencía, in this work, gives the reader a language to be formed, a logic to be formed, but that cannot be theorized. She puts forward a kind of writing (and reading)—thus creating a kind of language—that can be just practiced, improvised, as proposed by Cixous.

In *Another Kind of Language* (2001) as the title suggests, Mencía goes further and experiments with the possibilities of a new language form. In this case too, she continues "to analyze communicative systems produced in the area of 'in-between' 'Semantic Text, Image Text and Phonetic Text' using digital technology" (quoted in Memmott 2006).

In her old personal website Mencía stated this piece

> works as a web piece or as an interactive installation: three computers projecting the images on to the same screen in order to get a multi-layered image at the same time as a multi-layered soundscape of phonetic compositions. By rolling the mouse over, the textual surface appears and disappears, revealing the text-image and sound. The user can go from one of the pieces to the others and interact with other users. Each of the pieces is formed by the meaningless phonetic sounds of three different languages: English, Mandarin and Arabic. (2016)

In the web version, which is the one analyzed here, three letters (A, E, C) enable the reader to proceed to different texts: Arabic, English and Chinese. By moving the mouse around the white screen images appear for a few moments and phonetic sounds from these different languages are triggered.

The "reader" is watching and listening to fragments of text, fragments of language, fragments of images. The act of touching makes the signs and the sounds of these texts tangible. It is the reader who re-composes the texts, through her actions. Mencía is breaking (her) language down to the essential. Images and sounds take the form of little fragments on the webpage, a very fast movement of the mouse creates curious sketches and produces a sort of peculiar melody. She writes: "the sounds are created by singing and pronouncing the combination of sounds used in these linguistic systems (English, Arabic and Chinese)" (2016). The directionality of Western reading is from left to right, but, because we do not have a traditional reading space here, one can read from right to left, from inside out, from top to bottom and so on, resembling the reading in these languages to highlight the new reading on a spatial interface. The "reader" is charged with reconstructing the meaning of the text and with re-tracing the reading path. With *Another Kind of Language*, Mencía proposes an open language, a language which is not controlled, a language without gender, a neutral language that has the ability to suggest free meanings and free associations between words, sounds and images. Starting from the blank page, it is the reader who has the power of recomposing. Mencía structures the text, but Mencía cannot foresee how the reader will read it, in which sequences, and so on. The reader can play with the text, experimenting with actions, using her imagination and knowledge to sense the text.

AYA KARPINSKA'S CREATION OF NEW SPACE

Marie Bélisle is proposing a new connection with and between words, María Mencía is focusing on a new media language formed of text, sounds and images, and Aya Karpinska is analyzing innovative possible uses of the writing space. *Open.ended* (2004) by Aya Karpinska with the collaboration of Daniel C. Howe, is also part of the Electronic Literature Collection Volume 1 where Karpinska describes it as:

> An interactive three-dimensional poem experienced through the interplay of shifting geometric surfaces. Verses appear on the faces of separate translucent cubes nested within one another. The reader manipulates a mouse, joystick, or touch-screen to bring stanzas on different surfaces into view. As cubes, faces, and layers are revealed, dynamically updating lines of text move in and out of focus. The structure of the poem facilitates a multiplicity of readings: from single verses on cube faces, to sequential verses across faces, to juxtapositions of verses across multiple cubes. Meaning is constructed actively through collaboration between reader, author, and mediated work. An audio track of the authors' layered voices extends the experience, enveloping the reader in the atmosphere of the poem, organically complementing the visual and tactile components of the work .

Karpinska's *open.ended* is a three-dimensional work made up of two cubes interacting with each other. The poems are not composed of lines and stanzas, rather, the use of stanzas acquire a new dimension by transforming themselves into cubes inside cubes, and stanzas inside stanzas. Verse lines are written with white letters in two light blue cubes, a sort of Hélène Cixous's "white ink" quote (Cixous 1975 and 2010). According to Cixous, the "écriture feminine" breaks the linear logic of male discourse and reclaims the feminine that Western tradition has suppressed. Karpinska's works experiment with the flow-logic of electronic writing.

The number of verse lines in the external cube is always three, and in the internal cube is always two. Thus, when the "cube-stanza" is created by the intersection of the two cubes, the verse lines are five in total for every cube facet. This organization of lines provides the text with a fixed structure. It also opens up many different and unpredictable meanings, depending on the interaction of the cubes. *Open.ended* suggests some of the possibilities of multimedia poetry operating in three dimensions. The reading practice is no longer linear: the reader carries on reading from left to right, but in a third dimension. The three-dimensional experience affects the writer too. She, at the moment of writing, feels herself "being immersed in multiplicities" quoting Deleuze and Guattari (2007), and she has little control of the direction of the reader's path.

In *open.ended* Aya Karpinska explores the syntax of the three-dimensional space. She does so by experimenting with the dynamic relationships between space and meaning, and with the "effect of spatial arrangement on the meaning and experience of text. (2003). In her view the extension of poetry into the third dimension will lead to "novel ways of representing relationships between words, as well as the evolution of new patterns of reading and rhythm." "We suddenly have access to the backs of words – let's make use of it," she states, offering an experience of reader participation in which the reader can manipulate two cubes, and the words written on them, in a three dimensional environment, allowing other words (and thus other meanings) to emerge.

Finally, the verse line "an insatiable need to repeat" suggests the meta-textual value of Karpinska's work: the repetition hides a difference (Deleuze 1968). If the reader does not manipulate them, the cubes will carry on in their fluctuating movements, repeating the same combination of words. Nevertheless, by playing with and manipulating the cube faces, the difference appears. The three-dimensional space brings new meaning to the verse line: "an insatiable need to repeat" can become "insatiable breath that softly repeat" and/or "press every face softly" and/or "eyes breath so softly here," passing from a perlocutive act to a metaphoric writing. The reiteration of some syntagms, such as "softly, breath, repeat," and the reiteration of morphemes like /s/ and /r/, reproduce the idea of the movement of the cubes (the liquid consonant /r/ recalls a series of Indo-European words linked to the idea of "flowing," as the Greek verb: ρεω). Finally, the title itself suggests how to use and read this text: a text with no end, or better yet, an open-ended work composed of two texts that cross one another, offering new meanings using the reiteration of morphemes and syntagms. The disturbances around the traditional intentionalities of writing, the multiplicity of signifiers, the articulation and the metamorphosing of the reading experience thus reconfigure the writing and the reading practice.

If Marie Bélisle deconstructs the words and María Mencía deconstructs the phoneme, Aya Karpinska deconstructs the writing space. In *The arrival of the beeBox*, she studies and decomposes the writing space once more. *The arrival of the beeBox* (2003) was presented at the E-Poetry 2003 International Digital Poetry Festival, which took place on 23-26 April 2003 in Morgantown, West Virginia.

> I felt it was necessary to plan the poem in three dimensions. The 3D modelling software I am using, is somewhat overwhelming to the novice. Microsoft Word just wouldn't cut it, however, I had to write in space. Obsessed with simplicity, and knowing that curved surfaces often take up too many resources in 3D renderings, I settled on a cube as the basic structure of the poem. Besides, the title of the poem is the arrival of the beeBOX, not ...the beeBALL. After I had a draft I was happy with (yes, I wrote the original verses on regular paper, not in space) I copied the 27 verses onto slips of paper and pinned them to the rickety structure pictured below. I arranged and re-arranged the verses, eventually cutting out the three at the interior for practical reasons - it was just too annoying to stick my fingers among those toothpicks to pin and un-pin the verses in the center. I thought that it would be difficult to select and view those verses in the virtual model as well as could be expected, working with the physical model affected the semantic and syntactic structure of the poem, it also affected how I imagined an ideal reading of the poem would flow. Basically, I privilege the surface of the box - verses on top are more coherent, verses near the bottom, where it was difficult to reach, are more chaotic and seemingly disconnected from each other.

The arrival of the beeBox is another three-dimensional work, where the reading practice is at once interactive and immersive. By clicking on unreadable "words," verse lines appear; finally, by using the arrows the reader can move inside the text.

Karpinska's poem is a remediation of Sylvia Plath's poem with the same title. As noticed by Kiene Brillenburg Wurth, in Plath's poem, the "clean wood box" that the speaker has ordered, appears to contain an uncontrollable life-force: the bees, "Minute and shrunk for export,/ black on black, angrily chambering" (Plath 1987, 534-35), could never be held in check. In Karpinska's spatial poem, the clustered bees have become clustered words and it is the reader/user who is to open the boxes as three-dimensional objects – allowing the words to stretch and flutter out and take their provisional in-line positions (Wurth 2006).

As in the previous Karpinska text, this poem suggests another path in the reading practice which resists the sense of an ending. With "beeBox," Karpinska allows her reader to play more and to explore deeper the possibilities given by a three-dimensional writing. The reader, in fact, can choose to read the text from the left to right, from right to left, from the top down or from the bottom, up, and so on, deciding not to make readable (and thus not to read) some "verse lines."

"What is the difference between texts that are near or far? What will it mean when one sentence is behind another? When one sentence is above another?" Karpinska focuses, again, on a new syntax of three dimensions: the most privileged issue is the pure spatial relationships between "verse lines."

The meta-textual function of the text appears when reading different "verse lines": from "it's never empty between the lines" to "climbing the volume," and from "each moment shows a different face" (which is actually the next-to-last sentence in the text, from the perspective of the standard way of reading) to "This is a collection of moments gone by." There are many possible links between the different "verse lines," any association is possible: it is a random creative reading practice, revealing William Burroughs' cut-up and fold-in method, that can be classified under N. Katherine Hayles' modus of cyborg reading. This reading is no longer related to two-dimensional text, but focuses on "topographic area to explore, with layered strata, hidden openings, crosscutting pathways, links between different world levels, and other spatial and temporal unfolding" (2004, 86). To explore the space of this text, the reader can literally move into the space of words. She can turn, rotate, zoom in and out. She can immerse herself in "beeBox," see words from the inside out; she can "erase" words, focus on specific sentences and link these sentences to others, according to her personal and private reading experience. Words become "objects" to explore and link in search of meaning.

CONCLUSION

The dynamic of all the poems presented in this book chapter destabilise the conventionally assigned aspects of poetry. Bélisle, Mencía, and Karpinska break the rules imposed on language and poetry, and in doing so, propose a new reading-space, a new language, a new way to gauge meanings. They explore the possibilities offered by the new medium in order to deconstruct writing, and in turn, the practice of reading: Bélisle deconstructs the word, Mencía goes deeper and deconstructs the foundation of language, the phoneme, and Karpinska deconstructs the writing space. The reader of such poems must recreate a personal reading experience to find her own meaning of the text, to reach the identity of the text, and (even more so while the discipline is in its infancy and lacking convention) to explore the nature of reading. This experience of reading differs from reader to reader. Suggesting new forms for the reading experience, these authors are proposing a performative poetry that is not only an act of "showing doing" but also an act of (re)creating.

Bélisle focuses on the words, and gives words other meanings, she reveals the "alter ego" of words. By exploiting the characteristics of the electronic medium, Bélisle tears apart the words and the language, constructing a difference in the repetition of words. The reading experience of Bélisle's work is personal and private; the reader creates her own sense in a private reading experience, exploring the possibilities given by altering the sentences. The same personal and private reading experience is proposed by Karpinska's poetry and Mencía's work. Karpinska invites the reader to explore the writing space, linking up different "verse lines" randomly. The three-dimensional reading practice offered by Karpinska allows the reader to (and suggests that she should) look for another viewpoint of language construction. Mencía goes further in the deconstruction of male language: she proposes an open language, a language which is not at all controlled, a language without gender, a neutral language. But again this exploratory path is personal and private: Tannen states that "women tend to see conversations and actions as an individual in a network of connections" and the reading experience proposed by these authors is an act of "showing doing" of this relationship with language.

According to Philippe Bootz, digital poetry "always put[s] the reader in a particular position where he is responsible for an experiment of reading, [...] the reader is a partner" (Bootz). Bélisle, Mencía, and Karpinska share with (if not delegate to) their readers the construction of the meaning of their texts. No longer is there a stable and common meaning. These texts are fluid; they are fluid, decomposed, and recomposed by the reader. Paraphrasing Cixous, the digital writing frees the language from the primacy of meaning, opening it up to the unintentional not intentional rhythmic movement. The intelligibility of the meaning, that wants to understand and master what is being said, is subverted.

Walter Benjamin's essay, "The work of art in the age of mechanical reproduction" focuses on the new functions of modern post-aesthetic art which leaves behind its traditional functions in ritual and aesthetic enjoyment by highlighting its new function in politics and in popular, visual and tactile culture. His claim is that the work of art becomes "a creation with entirely new functions" (1986). Bélisle, Mencía and Karpinska demand of their readers a new reader's function, they want their readers as performers of their text: they want them to (re)mix, cut, sample, filter, mash-up and recombine their words, their sounds, their languages, their texts. In this way, they do not fully control the language and the meanings of their texts. On the other hand, according to theorists like Dale Spender (1985), man's ability to control language gives him great power indeed. According to many feminist theorists, there is a lack of words for important female experiences. If one assumes that this problem goes beyond a selected number of particular terms and infects language as a whole, it is natural to suppose that women are to a large degree silenced—unable to accurately articulate key elements of their lives, and unable to communicate important aspects of their thoughts and feelings. Spender and others also suggest that the maleness of language constrains thought, imposing a male worldview on all of us, and making alternative visions of reality impossible, or at least very difficult to articulate. The deconstruction and the reader's personal reconstruction of language and meaning proposed by Bélisle, Mencía, and Karpinska, allow the creation of a new reality, which could be closer and more congenial to women, realizing the ability to articulate an alternative vision of the world as wished by many feminist theorists such as Daly and Caputi (1987), Elgin (1985), MacKinnon (1989), Penelope (1990), and Spender (1985).

Writing for immersive text-based environments (made possible by the new medium) creates an opportunity for authors and readers (male and female) to reconsider the relationships between words (language), space, and identities. The digital poetic function calls into question the very nature of the verbal digital-space under these new conditions. Additionally, the poetic experience is enriched by the ways readers invent new reading patterns that depend on spatial and personal interactions, in terms of a more sophisticated activity than just leafing through pages, as in the case of writing (reading)-as-we-know-it.

Finally, (women) digital authors have just begun to scratch the surface of what is possible in terms of the Web and new media-based textuality. Challenged with the idea to make a new poem, the digital poet is faced with the task of reinventing an innovative way the poem is, or could be, and thus an innovative possible language.

WORKS CITED

Bélisle, Marie *Figures.* http://www.scripturae.com/CadresScript.htm. Accessed July 5, 2016.

Benjamin, Walter. "The Work of Art in the Age of Mechanical Reproduction." *Video Culture. A Critical Investigation*, ed. John Hanhardt, New York: Gibbs M. Smith, Inc., 1986.

Bootz, Philippe. "The Problematic of Form. Transitoire Observable," *Dichtung Digital.* 2005/1. http://www.dichtung-digital.de/2005/1/Bootz/index.htm. Accessed July 5, 2016.

Brillenburg Wurth Kiene. "Multimediality, Intermediality, and Medially Complex Digital Poetry." *Littérature numérique en Europe: état de l'art*, ed. Ana Pano,

RiLUnE, n. 5, 2006, p. 1-18. http://www.rilune.org/images/mono5/3_brillenburg.pdf. Accessed July 5, 2016.

Cixous, Hélène. “Sorties.” *La jeune née*, published in Hélène Cixous and Catherine Clément. Paris: UGE, 1975.

_,_. “Le Rire de la Méduse” (1975) republished in Hélène Cixous, *Le Rire de la Méduse et autres ironies*. Paris: Galilée, 2010.

Cummings, Edward E. *The Enormous Room* (1922), U.S,: Dover Thrift Editions, 2002. Kindle edition.

_,_. *I : six nonlectures*. Cambridge Mass: Harvard University Press, 1953.

Daly, Mary, and Caputi, Jane. *Websters' First New Intergalactic Wickedary of the English Language*. Boston: Beacon Press, 1987.

Deleuze, Gilles. *Différence et repetition*. Paris: P.U.F., 1968.

Deleuze, Gilles, and Félix Guattari. *Mille plateau*. Paris: Minuit, 1990; republished in 1987 as *A Thousand Plateaus: Capitalism and Schizophrenia*. Minneapolis: University of Minnesota Press.

Diehl, Joanne Feit. *Women poets and the American sublime*. Bloomington: Indiana University Press, 1990.

Di Rosario, Giovanna. “Hyperpoetry on the net: derive e approcci.” *Gli oggetti di scritura II*, ed. Alessandro Zinna, Urbino: CISL, 2003. 12-21.

Erkkila, Betsy. “Dickinson and Rich: Toward a Theory of Female Poetic Influence.” *American Literature* 56, 1984. 541-559.

Elgin, Suzette. *A First Dictionary and Grammar of Láadan. Madison: Society for the Furtherance and Study of Fantasy and Science Fiction*, 1985.

Gilbert, Sandra, and Susan Gubar. *The Madwoman in the Attic*. Yale: Yale University Press, 1979.

Guy, Peter. *As Mirrors Are Lonely: A Lacanian Reading on the Modern Irish Novel*. Cambridge: Cambridge Scholars Publishing, 2014.

Hayles, N. Katherine. “Print is Flat, Code is Deep. The Importance of Media-Specific Analysis.” *Poetics Today*, 25.1, 2004. 67-90.

Homans, Margarey. *Woman Writers and Poetic Identity*. Princeton: Princeton University Press, 1980.

Irigaray, Luce. *Speculum de l'autre femme*. Paris: Minuit, 1974.

Karpinska, Aya, and Daniel C. Howe. *Open.ended*. http://www.technekai.com/open/index.html. Accessed July 5, 2016.

Karpinska, Aya, and Daniel C. Howe. *Open.ended* (2004), in Electronic Literature Collection vol 1, eds. Hayles Katherine, Nick Montfort, Scott Rettberg, Stephanie Strickland. The Electronic Literature Organization, UCLA Department of English, Los Angeles, 2006. http://collection.eliterature.org/1/works/howe_kaprinska__open_ended.html. Accessed July 5, 2016.

Karpinska, Aya. "The arrival of the beeBox." 2003, http://www.technekai.com/open/index.html. Accessed July 5, 2016.

Karpinska, Aya. *The arrival of the beeBox: an Exploration of Spatial Text.* http://technekai.com/box/beeBoxPaper.pdf. Accessed July 5, 2016.

Keller, Lynn, and Cristanne Miller. *Feminist Measures: Soundings in Poetry and Theory.* Michigan: University of Michigan Press, 1994.

Lacan, Jacques. "The function and field of speech and language in psychoanalysis" 1953, in his *Écrits: A selection.* New York: W. W. Norton, 2002.

MacKinnon, Catharine. *Toward a Feminist Theory of the State,* Cambridge. MA: Harvard University Press, 1989.

Memmott, Talan. "Beyond Taxonomy: Digital Poetics and the problem of Reading" eds. Morris Adalaide K. and Thomas Swiss. *New Media Poetics.* Cambridge, Mass, London: MIT,– 2006. 293-306.

Mencía, María. "Birds Singing Other Birds Songs" (2001), in *Electronic Literature Collection* vol 1, eds. Hayles Katherine, Nick Montfort, Scott Rettberg, Stephanie Strickland. The Electronic Literature Organization, UCLA Department of English, Los Angeles, 2006. http://collection.eliterature.org/1/works/mencia__birds_singing_other_birds_songs.html. Accessed June 30, 2016.

Mencía, María. Authors' personal website: http://www.mariamencia.com/pages/birds.html. Accessed 15 July 2016

Mencía, María. *Birds Singing Other Birds Songs.* in *content | code | process. Authoring Electronic Literature*, ed. Judy Malloy. http://www.narrabase.net/maria_birds.html. Accessed June 30, 2016.

Mencía, María. *Another Kind of Language*, 2002. http://www.mariamencia.com/pages/anotherkindof.html. Accessed June 30, 2016.

Mencía, María. *Vocaleyes*, 2001. http://www.mariamencia.com/pages/vocaleyes.html. Accessed June 30, 2016.

Minogue, Sally. "Prescription and Proscription." *Problems for Feminist Criticism*, ed. Sally Minogue London and New York Routledge, 2013. 179-236.

Montefiore, Jan. *Feminism and Poetry.* London: Pandora Press, 1987.

Penelope, Julia. *Speaking Freely: Unlearning the Lies of the Fathers' Tongues.* NY: Pergamon, 1990.

Plath, Sylvia. "The Arrival of the Bee Box" (1962), in *The Penguin Book of American Verse*, ed. Moore, Geoffrey, Harmondsworth: Penguin Books, 1987. 534-535.

Schechner, Richard. *Performance Studies: An Introduction*. London and New York: Routledge, 2002.

Spender, Dale. *Man Made Language*, 2nd edition, NY: Routledge, 1985.

Tannen, Deborah. *You just don't understand: Women and men in conversation*, New York: William Morrow, 1990.

In Search of a Female Technological Identity in Electronic Literature: Dancing with the Spanish Domestic Cyborg

BY MARÍA GOICOECHEA AND LAURA SÁNCHEZ

FIRST STEP: HOME: "WE BECAME CREATIVE WHEN WE GOT DISCONNECTED"

H*ow many minutes*, hours, days are you connected to the Internet while you carry out a research, while you write? Can you imagine having no Internet connection for over two months in the course of your research? Technicians of telephone companies on strike, local Internet congestion, breakdowns are part of our quotidian landscape, together with inequalities among regions, social classes, genders. And when you manage to be connected? What's the price? What's the type of connection? What's the download and upload speed? When one has a high speed connection one forgets about the difficulties of the underlings, but it takes some ingenuity, a lot of patience, and some strategic decisions when one works with less than one megabit of bandwidth. These are our everyday predicaments, but let us not victimize ourselves, since "we became creative when we got disconnected!"

Rage, isolation, marginalization are potent forces for creativity. Choosing low tech might be an aesthetic stand in the city, but in the countryside it becomes a necessity. So many different origins, locations, and situations make it difficult to speak about a single feminine technological identity in the arts or in digital literature in Spain, but our aim is to describe the quality of some of the voices that are contributing to its formation.

To that end, this contribution explores some of the most engaging female voices in Hispanic digital literature, aiming at discovering the singularity of their proposals and attempting to find patterns that will disclose, or not, the existence of a female techno-cultural identity in the field. Through the analysis of works by Marla Jacarilla, Tina Escaja, Lara Coterón, Belén Gache, Dora García, Teresa Martín Ezama, among others contained in the corpus of *Ciberia: Library of Electronic Literature in Spanish*, we will delineate the diorama of female artists at the ends of digital literature. At the ends, for various reasons: because they come from the South, the periphery of main digital literature creation centers; because they are women, and we cannot ignore that they are less in number and that there exists a gender digital gap ; and because they situate themselves in hybrid artistic territories, between contemporary art and digital literature. For some of these artists, like Dora García or Teresa Martín Ezama, digital literature is just another label we could use for some of their works, for others, like Belén Gache and Tina Escaja, however, digital literature is the term they have embraced as spearhead of their particular vision of the confluence of the arts in the digital age.

This review of the work of female digital literature creators in Spain responds to two main needs. First, to make visible the difference and give a space to women artists that create and type in Spanish. Second, to analyze the strategies used by women authors to discover whether common political strategies of possibility and difference are being generated, if similar models are being propagated, or if, on the other hand, these practices are solely tied by the gender of their authors.

We would like to check or question whether these voices respond to a genealogy of artists and thinkers within their own culture or whether theirs has been broken, interrupted, and they have had to assimilate foreign referents in a process of forced self-education (Sadie Plant, Donna Haraway, Katherine Hayles, as possible godmothers). We will also establish a dialogue with their possible filiations with the world of art, technology and theory in the Spanish-speaking world (Tina Escaja, Patricia Mayayo, Remedios Zafra, Ana Navarrete, among others).

NEXT STEP: DIGGING THE WEB: IN SEARCH OF OUR TECHNO-FEMALE ANCESTORS.

The search "women, art, technology" in the National Library webpage yields no consistent results. To my outcry a colleague retorts: "have you considered the possibility of no female artists working with technology in Spain in the past century?" We do not resign, we take indirect routes, read between the lines, ask other women.

As Sadie Plant did in *Zeros and Ones*, our first step in the reconstruction of a female technological identity in Spain has been to pay homage to our predecessors, women who contributed through their art, creations, inventions, and social activism to the development of this hybrid space between art and technology. Some happy discoveries are worth sharing. For example, the first distributor of one of the popular writing machines of the end of the 19th century and beginning of the 20th century, the Yost machine, was a woman called María Espinosa de los Montero, who directed, with only 22 years of age, the Yost house in Madrid.[136] This very woman was the cofounder and

136 The Yost machine company was based in New York but sold many units in the UK and in Spain. The Spanish king, Alfonso XIII, had a Yost Machine for his personal use.

first president of the National Association of Spanish Women, a leading feminist that gave conferences and fought for the female vote.

Figure 1: María Espinosa de los Montero, leading feminist and distributor of the Yost typewriting machine in Spain.

As we can see, as in other countries, typewriting meant an important step for feminine emancipation. But the activities of the National Association of Spanish Women ended in 1936, when the Spanish Civil War broke out. With the arrival of Franco's dictatorship many other hard-won rights also came to an end; divorce, for example, was allowed in the Second Republic (in 1932), and again banned in the dictatorship (in 1939). Many of the pioneer women of that period, like the only women deputies in the Spanish parliament, Victoria Kent and Clara Campoamor, who were also members of Espinosa's women association, had to go into exile. Like today's female artists working with technology, these women worked without the protection of political, educational or religious institutions; they held their meeting in their private homes and financed their projects themselves. As it is the case today, precarious life conditions, difficulty distributing their time among their different responsibilities, invisibility, work at the margins of mass culture or canonic art, was the norm for female artists.

Despite difficulties many women continued their struggle inside dictatorial Spain. Did you know, for example, that a Spanish headmaster holds one of the earliest patents of a mechanic book? Ángela Ruíz Robles registered the patent of her mechanic book in 1949 (a missing link in the history of the e-book). It is again observed the enthusiasm provoked by the typewriter in the history of women's technological development. Ángela Ruíz Robles studied education but began her career as a teacher of typing, short hand and accounting. Among her other inventions, she also registered a patent for a short-hand typing machine, a scientific-grammatical atlas, and in 1949 her mechanic encyclopedia.

Figure 2: Ángela Ruíz Robles

As many defenders of the tablets in schools, she was concerned with the weight of children's schoolbags, but she also wanted to substitute the traditional, rote-learning method by a more didactic and engaging one. She conceived an interactive book in which different subjects in different languages could be instantiated by a slight pressure on buttons. The book could also come with a magnifying or graduated lens, so that its replaceable bobbins, filled with texts and images, could contain more information. There was also a space provided for an internal light and a tape recorder, so that it could be read without external lighting and could produce and record sound. On its back, her book included a series of buttons with which the student could write short texts and make mathematical operations, it could also be placed horizontally or vertically, and it was fabricated in a light material.

Even though women and technology have had a close and quotidian relation in our recent history, technologies that belong to the private, domestic sphere do not normally appear in traditional histories of technology. As critic Ana Martínez-Collado contends, the relationships of women with technology are often based in a contradictory experience, the paradoxical binary pair of "exploitation/liberation" (Martínez-

Collado 2011, 103). Accessing the lowest levels of technological qualification and subject to part time home-based work, women have entered new Sisyphus cycles: This is a story about tedious, repetitive, straining, manual labor harnessed to the speed of electronic machines.

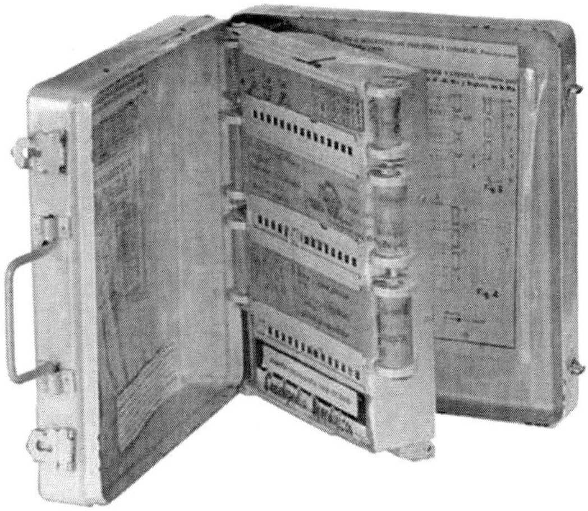

Figure 3: Mechanic book, 1949.

> clean, wash, dust, wring, iron, sweep, cook, shop, phone, drive, clean, iron, enter, mix, drive, delete, clean, purge, wash, merge, edit, shop, fold, phone, file, select, copy, curse, cut, sweep, paste, insert, format, iron, program, type, assemble, cook, email, fax, cry, forward, sort, type, click, dust, clean, etc. (Wilding)

Martínez-Collado's critical works—together with those of Faith Wilding or of Remedios Zafra, which we will discuss later—are aimed at questioning the idea that technology in an unqualified or domestic job "liberates" woman of her most tedious tasks and grants her some precious free time. These works are vital contributions to the understanding of technology as a complex social construction that is neither neutral nor sufficient, and warn against the dangers of assuming that technological advance by itself will bring social advancement.

At this point we would like to present *The Spanish Domestic Cyborg* (Figure 4)[137] as a little gag to vindicate and play with the concept of domestic technologies, an image to dig into our recent past in search of the Spanish female technological identity that is the object of our study.

137 "The Spanish Domestic Cyborg" pays homage to Faith Wilding and her inspiring essay "Duration Performance: The Economy of Feminized Maintenance Work" (1999): "This is a story about the laboring female body in the invisible feminine economy of production and reproduction" (1).

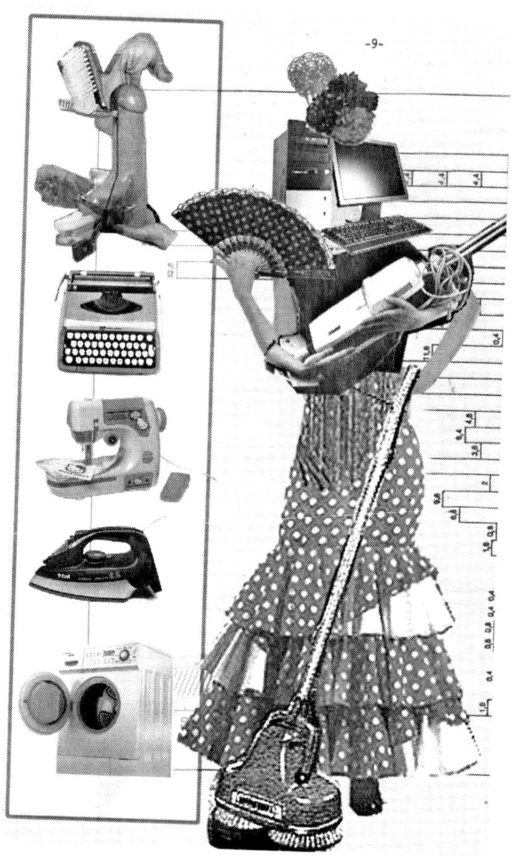

Figure 4: *The Spanish Domestic Cyborg*, collage by Laura Sánchez.

STEP 3: TRACING A GENEALOGY OF TECHNO-WOMEN IN THE ARTS: DISRUPTIONS AND DISCONTINUITIES.

The case of feminism in Spain is a complex one, not only because the majority of women artists in the 70s did not considered themselves feminists, but because the apparent absence of national referents was fulfilled with foreign referents in a forced process of self-education. The incorporation of feminist discourses in Spain has been slow and late. All the feminists phases or waves have taken place in a chaotic and simultaneous way, which has provoked, as Patricia Mayayo explains, that women artists have grown up with "their look placed upon texts and debates brought from abroad" (2014, 35). The lack of visibility of pioneering artistic works of the 70s and 80s, such as Esther Ferrer's *Íntimo y Personal* (a 1971 performance) or Eulàlia Grau's *Discriminació de la Dona* (from 1978), which dealt with themes intimately connected with cyberfeminism (like the labor conditions for women in works requiring low technological qualification), has in most cases been the reason for their lack of impact in the formation of a feminist discourse among Spanish women artists. For young artists, foreign or more recent referents remain more accessible. Thus, the cyberfeminism "made in Spain", relies heavily on imported theories and, according to Tina Escaja, succumbs to Anglocentric and theoretical imperialism. Nevertheless, it can still be a rich source of critical and aesthetic tools for numerous generations of artists.

Remedios Zafra, for example, recuperates the most intimate and domestic dimension in her introduction of cyberfeminist theories in the Spanish context, along the lines of Jessica Loseby and her "Cyber-Domestic Aesthetic" (2004). Zafra, who also alludes to foreign referents, reuses Laura Bey's "a connected room of one's own", which in turn revises Woolf's contribution. Zafra finds an analogy between the figure of the prosumer and domestic labor. The first similarity is the apparent obsolescence of the conceptual division between production, consumption and distribution, which camouflages the work carried out at home and in the digital sphere. In both cases, these tasks demand a production time and serve as the basis over which those works that receive remuneration and value are founded.

Zafra concludes that, as producers in an era of networks, the most basic and, therefore, significant challenge is not only the blank page or screen, but also the possibility of creating a blank time, a quotidian time of our own. A time, which is also a distance, from which we can reflect and think about the best way to assemble a connected room of one's own, to discover its true revolutionary and creative power (Zafra 2010, 14). The paradox of the connected room of one's own is that this space, which is perceived as an optimizer of our time, a place for concentration, focus and reflection, becomes the site where numerous activities converge and is constantly demanding more and more of our time to produce what we actually consume.

What does and does not constitute production is also a matter of perception, of a way of being in the world. Economy is therefore not neutral but determined by value judgments. What is terrifying is that the globalization of the economy is creating a monoculture at a scale the planet has never experienced before, as a steamroller it is devastating the variety it encounters in its way: diets, folklore, local connections, languages, the value of words…

Let us talk about power, about speed, about connectivity. Power is a cultural practice, and evaluating power in cyberspace is crucial for a feminist study. Our problem as women in cyberspace is becoming not so much one of access (though it is still a problem), but one of power, speed, time, visibility.

As Susan Hawthorne observed:

> The digital revolution has brought about an escalation in the culture of the Powerful although this too tends to be ignored. (…) The Powerful are those members of society who can gain ready access to power and who are able to exercise it without thinking particularly about what they are doing. The reason they are able to do this is because their exercise of power carries few consequences for them. (Hawthorne 1999, 120)

Being always connected to the Internet, leaving the computer on for hours, carries few consequences for those who have access to electricity and telephone connection, but when you are without them, you are suddenly made aware of the expense involved in downloading and uploading heavy information to the web. In the same way that healthy people will be unaware of the difficulties that a single step might carry for the disabled in a wheelchair, but conversely they will also remain ignorant of the strength of the arms of wheelchair drivers.

Spain seems trapped in multiple, co-existing timelines, progresses and stagnation, ubiquitous domestic violence lives together with female power at the political and economic level. However, inequality has increased alarmingly in the last decade, bringing with it stress-related illnesses, difficulties making ends meet, precarious jobs and hardened job conditions, which have, in their turn, provoked an increased tension in the division of labor between the genders.[138]

Other Spanish critics, like Patricia Mayayo, challenge the optimistic views of the technological revolution, such as Zafra's. In her essay, "A different gaze: women artists, digital technologies, and transnational capitalism," Mayayo provides as examples the work of contemporary women artists who show how the expansion of transnational capitalism has brought up a clear deterioration in women labor conditions all over the world. As she states:

> Domestic workers, telemarketing phone operators, electronic material assemblers, prostitutes, housewives, programmers, interns, autonomous workers, artists, mothers or baby-sitters: everyday they experiment the dark side of what it means "just-in-time", hyperflexibility, personal attention or mobility; everyday they put at stake their body, their voice, their image, their energy, their creativity, their capacity to coordinate teams, to integrate themselves in sector-leading companies or responding to the needs of the client for the sake of a new form of

138 The Gini coefficient in 2012 for Norway was 0,226 (first in the list), for the Euro zone was 0,305 and for Spain 0,350 (in position 58 below Greece, Nicaragua or India, to name a few). According to the UN, a Gini coefficient above 0,4 is alarmingly high, with risk of social turmoil and revolution (Wikipedia).

life: that of total work. (Mayayo 2007, 12)

STEP 4: DIGITAL LITERATURE CREATIONS BY SPANISH WOMEN ARTISTS.

In Spain at present there is an active scene of women artists working with technology in fields such as net-art, cyberactivism, cyberfeminism, interactive art, video-installation, video art, digital photography, sound art, virtual reality, augmented reality, etc. Digital literature is inscribed as another genre inside a wide spectrum of artistic possibilities, and it still does not have a potent scene exclusively dedicated to it. That is why our study does not focus exclusively on digital literature. Another reason for this is that in a hybrid artistic space that mixes categories and referents from various fields, talking about digital literature made by women without mentioning the evolution of the artistic practices from which their work has evolved would make no sense. We would like to approach the following questions: Is digital literature in Spanish contributing to the creation of new female techno-cultural identities? What is the space granted to gender discourses in the digital literature created by women? Do these creators share a common feminist intentionality or ideological imaginarium?

Analyzing the strategies employed by female artists from a cyberfeminist perspective, we discriminate an evolution from an optimistic embrace of hypertext as a flexible form in tune with feminine sensibility to a more combative use of digital technology aimed at unmasking the feminine condition in cyberspace. Authors have also evolved from subverting stereotypes of femininity in nostalgic, languid suicidal tendencies and auguries of death, which is the option followed by Teresa Martín Ezama in *Ara vus prec*, Marla Jacarilla in *Dead and Suicidal Myths*, and Edith Checa in *Como el cielo los ojos*, which combine technological and formal sobriety with a heightened sensitivity, to other strategies which dynamite the stereotypes in more lively and energetic terms: irony, play, parody, exaggeration, deconstruction or over-identification have become universal sabotage options.

This is the case of Marla Jacarilla, who has two very different pieces: *Dead and Suicidal Myths* (2005), which we have already mentioned, is followed by *Caperucitas de color granate* (2006). As Dolores Romero has explained in her chapter "A Diorama of Digital Literature in Spain," this work remediates five classic children stories with the purpose of vindicating the role of women in society, and more precisely, in the field of art. Among the referents that Jacarilla mentions in this work we do not find any trace from a Spanish artist, again allusions are made to imported feminist icons, such as Laurie Simmons, Meghan Boody, Faith Wilding, or the Guerrilla Girls, among others.

In this work Marla Jacarilla subversively dismantles the structure of the popular fairy tale to deal with issues never dealt in a story, such as the position of women artists in the contemporary art circuit. The ironic and subversive tone of this piece, with clear allusions to cyber- and techno-feminism, is not present in her earlier work, *Dead and Suicidal Myths*. Here Jacarilla plays with the possibilities of Internet and hypertext, with three hypertextual blocks of text which can be read scrolling down or horizontally, maintaining a sober and feminine aesthetic, with a remediation of hand-written post-it notes as a form to introduce intertextuality.

Figure 5: *Caperucitas de Color Granate* by Marla Jacarilla. Instance from the Sleeping Beauty.

With the first hypertextual works written by women, *VeloCity* by Tina Escaja or *Dead and Suicidal Myths* by Marla Jacarilla, we encounter the celebration of the use of hypertext as an aesthetic and conceptual strategy that allows the unfolding of a liberated femininity in a non-linear, non-hierarchical, and decentralized way, as Tina Escaja argues in her essay from 2003. Hypertext is, for Tina Escaja, the insignia of this new cyberfeminism that proposes a "non-essential modern subject" represented in a techno-net-skeletal writing that integrates the cybernetic medium, a hybrid space between the body and the machine, a form of art substantiated by an artificial entourage.

During the first decade of the 21st century, these utopic visions of women liberation at the hands of technology are maintained. The net is perceived as a homogenizing, democratic space in which hierarchies are broken down. However, years later the reality of cyberspace social construction starts to seep in and more critical attitudes towards this technological infrastructure and its political, social and cultural manifestations are developed. In this manner, the writings of Tina Escaja in 2005 are impregnated by a more "cybersocialist" vision with respect to the role of women in technology design and the digital gender gap. Moreover, she becomes aware of her position as a Hispanic woman in the web, which

> excludes the woman without access [...] The masses without modem are excluded from the redeeming feast, of the presumably liberating option, of this technospace in English that celebrates invisibility criteria towards a non-existent virtual other. (Escaja 2005)

Figure 6: Tina Escaja at the exhibition *The Only Bush I Trust Is My Own*, LL Gallery, University of Vermont.

Escaja brings us again towards this frontier marked by the limits to Internet connection, the margins of technological globalization, but from a subversive perspective that avoids victimization, more in tune with our mantra "we became creative when we got disconnected." Thus, in her poem, "Una, grande y libre" ("One, Big, and Free"), inside her collection of poems *Código de barras* (*Barcode*), she introduces a barcode reader as instrument to be able to hear the oral recitation of the poems, forcing the spectator to manipulate a technological artifact normally associated with commercial habits to access the poetic work and decode it. Hypertext is no longer used as a celebration of the possibilities inherent in "being a woman" or "creating a feminine writing," whatever that could mean in the Net. Here technology is used to compel us to think about a perturbing reality of control and dominion, and to situate us in a position "against the bars of conformity, against the bars of imperialism, against the bars of computer control" (Escaja 2005). In *LIBRE* (*Free*), Tina concludes with the following verses: "you are not, no longer you, we are not./ Ask the oppressed, the busy./ Everything is false and UpsideDown./ Wake up." ("no eres no, ya no, no somos. Pregunta al oprimido, al ocupado. / Todo falso y al revés. / Despierta.").[139] Without falling in a pessimist attitude, what she is actually proposing is to empower oneself through technology, to create rather than merely replicate, to make the margins, the periphery visible as one of the multiple possibilities of being a Hispanic woman artist in the Web.

Figure 7: Game over in *Homeward Journeys*, a playable drama by Yoctobit. Teatre l'Escorxador, Lleida, Spain, May, 2012. Macarena de Rueda in her role as Claudia Picaporte.

139 See http://issuu.com/tina_escaja/docs/catalogo_the_only_bush.

The more combative type of social techno-feminism has become a conspicuous trend among female artists. Lara Coterón, leading member of the collective Yoctobit, is a good example of the power of women in the design of new forms of artistic confluence of literature and technology, in her case, in the field of art-game design, with the creation of a new sort of dramatic pieces called "teatro jugable" or playable drama.

Coterón's pieces have been inspired by the strategy of the videogame *Doom* (1993), of Id Software, which, through the move of defining the basic structure of the game and then liberating a few examples and tools so that consumers could create their own versions, became the pioneer of this new economic and social model that transcended the traditional distinction between producers and consumers. According to Coterón, this new strategy produced a great enthusiasm in game-art creators, who saw in videogames the perfect frame for countercultural praxis, since videogames in themselves were the product of proprietary hardware and software, with all the vices characteristic of commercial digital technology (obsolescence, improvement, etc.) (Coterón 2012, 42). Her main works, *Homeward Journeys* (Fig. 7) and *Kill the Queen*, deal with the fast-paced and meritocratic society and the repression of the state, respectively. In both pieces of this new type of playable drama, the text is not linear but it is composed as a game structure, which makes actors work in a form of improvisation orchestrated by the game design. Lara Coterón thus takes videogame's type of interaction and expands it outside the screen in performance pieces that demand from the audience a collaborative, instead of competitive, game experience and that expose contemporary evils towards which the audience is called to take action.

From bringing cyberspace practices outside the screens to building cozy and intimate, yet public, spaces in the Net, we find that, aside the techno-feminist dystopias, there is also a tendency to decorate and design feminine spaces that act as windows, spyholes, inside women's lives. This recuperation of the domestic, private and intimate sphere inside a virtual space, which is also a public form of "being in the world," is best reflected in blogs. It remains paradoxical, though, that despite the profusion of non-fiction blogs dedicated to fashion, cooking, maternity, beauty, decoration, etc. there are so few women artists interested in the possibilities of this genre, while there are numerous examples of success by male authors in the circuit of digital literature in Spanish (Hernan Casciari, Eugenio Tisseli, Marcelo Guerrieri, among others). Probably, using a blog does not imply a great challenge for creators who prefer more complex structures that can provide them with a heightened sense of technological empowerment and which allow them to explore the potential of electronic textuality.

While there is an overexposition of women's representations in the Net, few women artists, as we have mentioned, choose the blog to subvert the stereotypes of the feminine sexual object or the mother. However, we would like to mention a couple of examples that have addressed this issue using blogs and social networks, the cases of Amalia Ulman's *Excellences and Perfections*, a performance done in Instagram in 2014, and the creation of Intimidad Romero's identity in social networks. While Ulman impersonates in her blog the stereotypical caricature of an it-girl, Romero uses the inverse strategy, overexposing her image, her life and social relations, which present themselves pixilated, creating a mystery that hooks the spectator in this process of voluntary concealment. Her authorship and identity remains veiled (Intimidad Romero being a pseudonym) but this does not hinder her from accumulating thousands of friends and followers. Her art project has now become an app to make photos with the pixilated effect that characterizes her.[140]

Figure 8: *Me, Myself, and I* by Intimidad Romero.

Nobody forgets that the Internet is a digital market, where the accumulation of images, texts, and all sorts of data is not inconsequential. From our own connected rooms, we access the market and we can create value and power relations according

140 See http://rhizome.org/artbase/artwork/52447/> and <http://www.facebook.com/intimidadromero.

to our own influence, which is measured by the number of visits generated, clicks to our links and likes to our profiles. For the first time, it is our own data and behavior which have the capacity to directly produce money; "seeing", "more than "reading," or "understanding" becomes a cash generator.

Madrid-based digital literature poet Belén Gache satirizes the competition over the ownership of web domains in her work from 2012, *Word Market*. As it is described in its webpage:

> *Word Market* (WM) is an Internet portal dedicated to buying and selling words, using a unique currency, the "Wollar." In times of increasing privatization of public spaces and the profusion of copyright laws, WM allows you to own, trade and profit from words as their value fluctuates. WM offers you attractive discounts and promotions. Don't hold back! Increase your linguistic wealth. Become the owner of your words! And most importantly, prevent others from using them!

A firm believer in the power of poetry to reinvent our relation with words and with the world, Belén Gache's pieces make the reader aware of the perverse practices that have become naturalized in the context of cyberspace. In her videopoem "Aurelia: Our Dreams are a *Second Life*" (2012),[141] Gache subverts feminine stereotypes without even trying as she makes her avatar, which looks pretty much like her, walk along the surrealist virtual landscapes of *Second Life* while reading Gerard de Nerval's text "Aurelia." Making her avatar rumble and read alone through this virtual space exposes the platitude of other *Second Life* inhabitants, vindicating the introspection of intellectual activity versus the exhibition of corporeality in the virtual space. Her reading seems out of place in a territory populated by versions of real-life individuals. It would seem that our gender identity, in its transposition to cyberspace, has not suffered much transgression or substitution of unasked biological gender, in short, we have not really benefited from the fluid creativity at our disposal. Instead people have opted for a mystification of gender towards the poles; being allowed to design avatars, they have incarnated the hypermasculine and hyperfeminine versions culturally available. As Sandra Bem's studies would confirm, we have chosen to downgrade ourselves into our stupidest versions.

STEP 5: CONCLUSIONS

But, what does "feminine technological identity" mean? As we have seen, never a single idea. We search for patterns, responses, transformations of imaginaries and contagion

141 See an English version at https://vimeo.com/69791766.

models that we could label, possibly just to facilitate our work. We should instead question the very task of defining or forming an abstract feminine subject. As the net, the feminine technological identity is an infinite tissue of multiplied differences. A tissue of possibility and otherness. A fragmentary and discontinuous diorama.

Certain experiences unite us, though: we make the most of our vital situation, as in our slogan "we became creative when we got disconnected"; we share the periphery as Spanish speakers in the web; and the need to represent ourselves in a cyberspace full of perverted caricatures and distortions of femininity; we fight for the vindication of the intimate and the domestic as spaces to make things visible and not as places to fall silent in; we advocate the use of technology as a form of power and as a social construction in which women need to take part, to participate in its design so that our needs are met and we do not become designed by it.

We want to contribute transmitting the idea that women digital creation in Spain can be a developing field with a lot of projection and possibilities, but we have to struggle against the vision that digital literature is an elitist niche with little visibility with respect to the challenging communication and cultural processes that the digital medium implies.

WORKS CITED:

Albertos Carrasco, Francisco Javier. "María Espinosa de los Monteros y Díaz de Santiago." *Biografías de Mujeres Andaluzas*. Accesed January 24, 2016 <http://historiamujeres.es/vidas/espinosa.html>.

Coterón, Lara. *Arte y Videojuegos: mecánicas, estéticas y diseño de juegos en prácticas de creación contemporánea*. PhD diss. Universidad Complutense de Madrid, 2012. Accesed February 15, 2016. http://es.scribd.com/doc/112720476/Arte-y-Videojuegos-mecanicas-esteticas-y-diseno-de-juegos-en-practicas-de-creacion-contemporanea.

Escaja, T. "Ciber/reflexiones." *Espacio Luke*, 69, Dic. (2005), Accessed April 8, 2016. http://www.espacioluke.com/2005/Diciembre2005/tina.html.

_,_. "Hacia una nueva historia de la poesía hispánica: Escritura tecnetoesquelética e hipertexto en poetas contemporáneas en la red." *Espéculo: Revista de Estudios Literarios* 24 (2003).

Hawthorne, Susan. "Connectivity: cultural Practices of the Powerful or Subversion from the margins?" *CyberFeminisms: Connectivity, Critique and Creativity.* Edited by Susan Hawthorne and Renate Klein. Melbourne: Spinifex, 1999.

Loseby, Jessica. "The Domestic as Virtual Reality: Reflections on NetArt and Post-feminism." *Electronic Book Review,* 27th Jan., (2004), Accesed February 15,

2016. <http://www.electronicbookreview.com/thread/writingpostfeminism/amplified>.

Martínez-Collado, Ana. "Prácticas artísticas y activistas feministas en el escenario electrónico: Transformaciones de género en el futuro digital." *Asparkía: Investigació feminista*, 22 (2011): 99-114. Accesed February 15, 2016. http://www.e-revistes.uji.es/index.php/asparkia/article/view/601/512.

Mayayo, Patricia. "A different gaze: women artists, digital technologies, and transnational capitalism." *Polis*, 17 (2007). Accesed February 5, 2016. https://polis.revues.org/4367.

Millán García, Rosa. "Ángela Ruíz Robles, la maestra inventora." *Ágora-Escorial* 6, March, (2012): 14-18. Accessed April 8, 2016. http://issuu.com/agoraescorial/docs/agora_6/18.

Navarrete Tudela, Ana. "Different, unequal and disconnected. Who's who in the technological industries?" *Asparkía: Investigació feminista*, 22 (2011): 17-32. Accesed February 15, 2016. https://dialnet.unirioja.es/descarga/articulo/3824398.pdf.

Plant, Sadie. *Zeros and Ones: Digital Women and the New Technoculture*. New York: Doubleday, 1997.

Wilding, Faith. *Duration Performance: The Economy of Feminized Maintenance Work*. 1999. Accessed April 8, 2016. http://faithwilding.refugia.net/durationperformance.pdf.

Zafra, Remedios. *(h)adas. Mujeres que crean, programan, prosumen, teclean*. Madrid: Páginas de Espuma, 2013.

_,_. *Un cuarto propio conectado. (Ciber) espacio y (auto) gestión del yo*. Madrid: Fórcola. 2010

Surface Reading *The UpsideDown Chandelier*: Interface "Mastery" and Feminism

BY KATHI INMAN BERENS

In this volume about the field impact of e-literature works by and about women, I suggest that a "feminist" interface engages all levels of materiality, from hardware, to code, to human body, to algorithms that assist us in experiences of decoding or reading. Interfaces are certainly material; but as Alexander Galloway observes, interface is an "effect" more than a "thing." The hardware and software interfaces of *The UpsideDown Chandelier* [UDC], a collaboratively made multiplatform digital artwork, are not merely "significant surfaces" but thresholds of reading experience. Ported from large installation to browser, UDC allows us to reflect on how interfaces prompt site-specific reading strategies tied to affective states when we read publicly (in installation) and privately (in browser). My experience curating several e-literature exhibits has given me occasion to observe hundreds of people encountering e-lit interfaces and using different reading strategies to engage the works. Citing *The Tate Handbook* on curating art (as quoted in Vince Dziekan's *Virtuality and the Art of Exhibition*), Dene Grigar notes that "much is gained when approaching art as a system that involves a synergistic relationship among the works, the space, visitors, and curator." This is because work is always situated in particular settings that influence reception, so many environmental factors that it's impossible to sketch their accretive and dynamic effect. Whether a room is crowded or empty, noisy or quiet, hot or cold will influence guests' willingness to stay or impulse to flee, for example. And this mentions nothing of the architectonic qualities of the installation space itself. Embodied and dynamic conditions of extra-artistic encounter create a context that changes moment-to-moment. Exhibiting the first showcase of electronic literature at the U.S. Library of Congress with co-curator Grigar, I observed how quickly the mood or feeling in the room would shift when large numbers of children were present. Adults became more relaxed and playful in their willingness to engage a challenging e-lit interface. Adults were more likely to visit the Creation Stations (hands-on interactive exhibits I designed to compliment themes in each e-literature stations) if children were playing there.[142]

142 See the U.S. Library of Congress's archival website of the "Electronic Literature Showcase" here: http://www.loc.gov/rr/program/elit-showcase.html. See Dene Grigar's archival website for the featured exhibit we co-curated, "E-Literature and Its Emerging Forms," here: http://dtc-wsuv.org/elit/elit-loc/. Susan Garfinkel, Library of Congress Digital Reference Librarian, hosted the Showcase and assisted in the curation of books for the exhibit. See images of the exhibit here: https://www.flickr.com/groups/elit-loc/pool/.

The UpsideDown Chandelier is uniquely suited to yield an interface comparison between installation and browser-based reading because it is the exact same code running in both installation and browser, according to UDC co-author Christine Wilks, who repurposed code for UDC from a Remixworx project "Notes Noir" she made with Randy Adams.[143] One samples the UDC installation through the full human sensorium, and decodes UDC in a browser with help from algorithmic augmentations provided by Google Translate and Search. UDC was created for a one-month installation at art gallery housed in a former tobacco factory in Košice, Slovakia that employed mostly women workers. UDC is intensely site-specific, conjuring the women tobacco factory workers in the physical space where they once worked particularly through use of spoken-word phonetic sounds from the various languages spoken on-site. After installation, UDC was ported to the browser.

Installed in a 50x25 meters room in the factory, UDC addresses the entire human sensorium: sound, vibration, proprioception, vision, touch and social awareness. The visitor's body becomes another of the work's interfaces, along with the code, the computers, the projectors, screens and brick walls. "It is quite common to understand interfaces less as a surface but as a doorway or a window," Galloway notes (36).[144] UDC's many surfaces created a highly dynamic environment where the gaze was ambient, not funneled, as it is when we view works in a browser or tablet. The embodiment of the women workers whose voices formerly filled the tobacco factory and the embodiment of the four women artists from four countries who gathered in Košice to collaboratively make the work is a palpable aspect of the installation experience. In browser, this same artwork—drastically minimized in scope and decontextualized from its tobacco-factory setting—becomes a heady puzzle: not an embodied art experience, but a difficult text that requires interruptive, "deformative" techniques in order to be read.[145]

---

143 "Repurposing" was a common theme and practice for all of the featured works in the show "Repurposing in Electronic Literature" curated by Mencía and Husárová at the DIG Gallery exhibition in Košice. For more on Wilks' extensive remix projects, see this path she created, "a crissxross trail < r3/\/\1X\/\/0RX" http://crissxross.net/remixworx/indexcxtrail.html.

144 "Interface" is a term "borrowed from chemistry, where it means 'a surface forming a common boundary of two bodies, spaces, phases'" (Cramer and Fuller, 149). Cramer and Fuller's "typology of interfaces" itemizes five aspects of interface from the material to the symbolic. The five typologies are: hardware that connects to users; hardware that connects to hardware; software that connects hardware to software; protocols that determine relations between software and software; and "symbolic handles" that make software accessible to users. "User interfaces," they conclude, "are often mistaken in media studies for interface as a whole."

145 "Deformance" is a critical practice named by Jerome McGann and Lisa Samuels that "tries to set [interpretive] modes of exegesis on new footing" by "working against the grain" of a poem's apparent intended meaning. "The question is not 'what does the poem mean' but 'how do we release or expose the poem's possibilities of meaning?'" See also Mark Sample's "Notes Toward a Deformed Humanities" which advocates "breaking things" as a way to understand their material composition as

For the women tobacco workers who arrived in Košice in 1851 and later, the journey to the tobacco factory was also a journey away from mostly unpaid domestic labor in their villages, labor conditions that continue to define most work done by most women in the world today. In the Košice tobacco factory, where women talked as they sorted through dried tobacco leaves and rolled cigarettes, Slovak, German and Hungarian languages floated through the air. This cosmopolitan, sonic inspiration for multi-platform work manifested in spoken-word phonemes, algorithmically sequenced, that filled the exhibition space with the fundamental sounds of Slovak, German, Hungarian and English, phonetic sounds that never resolve into intelligible words. Images, also generatively mixed, of the chandelier the women factory workers donated to the nearby St. Elisabeth's Cathedral, made a round, bright, golden "sun" on a large screen inside the tobacco factory. Words from each of the languages, beamed from two smaller projectors, added historical context.

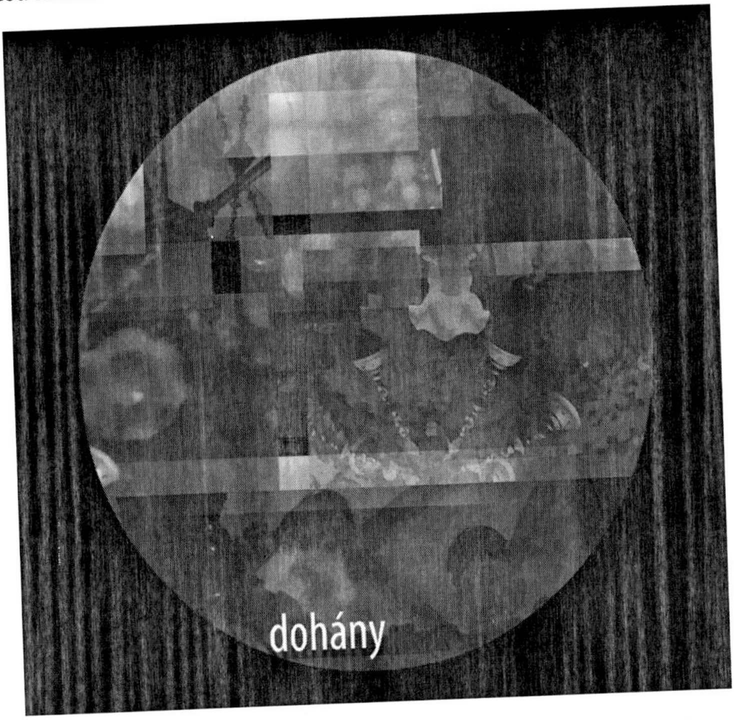

Figure 1: Animated word in Hungarian ("tobacco") positioned on top of collaged, generated chandelier images in *The UpsideDown Chandelier*. Spoken-word phonemes in four languages, also generated, are a key aspect of this multimodal work.

a springboard to working against the grain. In a 2015 Modern Language Association talk, however, Sample qualified the central claim of "Notes" by suggesting that "breaking things" had been reduced to a slogan. He eschewed "breaking things" for an ethic of "care and repair," pace Steven Jackson, and applied it to Twitter bots he has made such as the Markov-Chain-and-Melville bot @_lostbuoy_: https://twitter.com/_lostbuoy_.

The UpsideDown Chandelier's interfaces shift dramatically when the work is adapted from a large installation in a 50x25 meters room to a browser window; but our critical paradigms for understanding the significance of such an adaptation are mismatched to the task, since adaptation theory typically assumes adaptation from one stable, non-protean medial format to another. Case studies in Linda Hutcheon's seminal *Theory of Adaptation* (second edition, 2012) describe fundamental shifts in medial form: from book to screenplay, for example, or movie to code to make a video game. By contrast, *The UpsideDown Chandelier* entirely retains its medial form: it's the exact same code running into two different environments. For Hutcheon, adaptation is "repetition with variation"; but this definition emphasizes theme, not medial materiality.[146] UDC thus provides an unusual opportunity to ask: how do interfaces inflect exactly the same media object differently in a public installation and a private browser? I argue that the urge to "read" UDC dominates only when it's stripped of embodied, site-specific context and ported to the browser, where readers can read privately, and use networked search to dig for deeper meaning.

I coin the term "augmented reading" to describe my use of extra-textual interfaces such as Google Translate and Google Search to build a reading apparatus that turns out to be protean, unreliable, but essential for decoding works like UDC.[147] Surfaces proliferated as I mined the work for interpretable gems. Without materials from the artists to confirm or disconfirm my interpretations, my interpretations were founded on surfaces that factually shift, as I discuss below. Unlike "symptomatic reading" and the "hermeneutics of suspicion," where the critic is a detective looking for hidden ideologies or power operations, surface reading of interactive digital objects attends to what is "evident, perceptible, apprehensible in texts," as Stephen Best and Sharon Marcus put it in their 2009 essay "Surface Reading: An Introduction." But what constitutes "the apprehensible" shifts in environments like Google Translate and Search, smart algorithms designed to "learn" from previous searches? As I discovered, particular translations might transmute the next time I searched. Hence Best and Mar-

146 Hutcheon: "Recognition and remembrance are part of the pleasure (and risk) of experiencing an adaptation; so too is change. Thematic and narrative persistence combines with material variation," she notes, citing Ropars-Wuilleumier's "L'oeuvre au double: Sur les paradoxes de l'adaptation." See Hutcheon pp. 4-8.

147 In the research literature thus far, the phrase "augmented reading" has been used to describe layering of digital objects onto the physical world. There are two uses of the term "augmented reading" (outside of K-12 literacy research), both uses having to do with virtual layers situated on top of physical books: 1) Google has patented a technology that will lay a hologram layer over books; see Google's patent application for the "Story Device," published 3 March 2016, here: http://1.usa. gov/1XxZgBv and reported in Fast Company here: http://www.fastcompany.com/3057464/googletakes-storybooks-through-the-looking-glass-with-augmented-reality. 2) Three master's candidates in Copenhagen presented a paper that was "a prototype implementation of an augmented reading experience for children in which a physical copy of the book The Little Prince is tagged with QR codes."

cus' observation that "[s]urface is what insists on being looked at rather than what we must train ourselves to see through" takes on special urgency, since the many surfaces of UDC—the generative quality of the art itself, and the protean outputs of the Google searches—means that my information was perpetually provisional. To read the surface was to derive a field of potential meanings rather uncover a fixed set of facts.

"Those of us who cut our intellectual teeth on deconstruction, ideology and critique, and the hermeneutics of suspicion" Best and Marcus write,

> have often found those demystifying protocols superfluous in an era when images of torture at Abu Ghraib and elsewhere were immediately circulated on the internet; the real-time coverage of Hurricane Katrina showed in ways that required little explication the state's abandonment of its African American citizens; and many people instantly recognized as lies political statements such as "mission accomplished."

The trick of deconstruction is the surprise revelation, where the text "undoes" itself. The capacity for deconstructive surprise relies upon print as a stable medial environment, where the critic is the surgeon performing an operation on a medially inert text. In his essay "Why Has Critique Run Out of Steam," Bruno Latour notes that deconstructive readings became a style. He reminds us that the critic "is not the one who debunks, but the one who assembles" (2004, 246). Reading *The UpsideDown Chandelier* and other generative digital literature means to assemble patterns in the combined behaviors of machinic, algorithmic, and human agents that interact unpredictably. In surface reading, pattern detection of interactivity lays the groundwork for larger interpretive critique, which in my case became a self-conscious, feminist rumination on my impulse to "master" UDC.

The literary canon is built upon reading practices developed in relation to the book as a stable media object that returns the same information each time it is opened. *The UpsideDown Chandelier*, being a generative text, is "new" each time within a set of parameters one learns to detect. For example, I discerned that the words featured in UDC are translations of the same base set of 27 words. That pattern recognized, I could begin to interpret a theme based on elements common to those words, and explore the significance of their translation into German, Hungarian, Slovak and English. (I discuss the Google-assisted translations, and mistranslations, below.) Pattern detection, in its emphasis on nebulous outputs that require decoding, is a more materialist way to construe close reading, that *sine qua non* of humanities interpretation. In this sense, surface reading e-literature interfaces opens new vistas on what kinds of knowledge are vested with authority in digital literary humanities, and which legacies from the codex tradition of canon formation e-literature prompts us to reconsider or disrupt.

UPSIDEDOWN CHANDELIER INTERFACE #1: LARGE INSTALLATION

The UpsideDown Chandelier wasn't created for "readers" but guests. Both site- and event-specific, UDC in a browser doesn't remediate the grandeur of physical emplacement. UDC was part of the show "Repurposing in Electronic Literature" which ran November 2-20, 2013 in Košice, Slovakia at the DIG [Digital Intervention Group] space.

UDC's site-specificity is not just a design element, but a core value of the piece. There's an element of care in the parallel origin story about the women tobacco workers who collectively donated light to a cathedral, and the four women artists who pool their technologic skill and aesthetic inspiration to make a work of e-lit that reflects upon this bit of local lore. "After a couple of days in Košice discussing ideas while exploring the city, taking photographs, visiting museums, enjoying the restaurants and culture," María Mencía writes,

> everything came together when Milan Kolcun told us the story about a group of women workers in the tobacco factory who donated a candle chandelier to St Elizabeth's [sic] Cathedral which was still in situ, however now as an electric chandelier. This was A MOMENT OF LIGHT when we didn't need to discuss anything else. At this point, we all knew this was the story we wanted to use for our installation at the factory. We were four women artists from different countries, Ireland, Slovakia, England and Spain working at the factory, and the chandelier had been repurposed for current times. Everything fitted beautifully.

"MOMENT OF LIGHT" is a classic literary metaphor of inspiration. Here, the artists materialize that metaphor in the chandelier and in the projectors that deliver the generated images, words and sounds to the audience. The constraint of "repurposing," which was true of all works in the November 2013 show, has additional resonance with the way the chandelier itself was repurposed: from candles, to gas, to electricity. The message? Repurposing allows a thing to endure. The aural performance of UDC's phonetic sounds in German, Hungarian and Slovakian disrupts the authority of the ocular, the sensory origin of "objectivity" and empiricism.[148] These declarations

148 Tanya Clement, glossing Donna Haraway, writes: "Haraway calls the all-seeing viewpoint a singular, uncritical perspective; she calls it 'this eye that fucks the world to make techno-monsters' [Haraway 581]. Instead, Haraway proposes a feminist doctrine of objectivity that is situated as "specific embodiment" rather than a "false vision promising transcendence of all limits and responsibility."

of national language—all of which were spoken in Košice in the mid-nineteenth century—are uprooted from the land itself, even from the other points of reference in words—that would make the sounds intelligible. Its dislocations mirror the precarity of many women working globally today in call centers, as reproductive surrogates, in adjunct teaching positions, and many other "temporary" jobs staffed predominantly by women across the world. The "vital energy" of these female bodies is subject to an empirical, neoliberal machinery concretized through the gaze.[149] In the browser version, sound automatically triggers on page load: the artists have programmed the piece so that readers are confronted with what they don't know about this set of women. The UDC insists that these women's voices should be an omnipresent aspect of the user interface.

Phonetic unintelligibility is a form of culture jamming, a way of being present but not subject to objective correction. The aural performance of incomplete words is a baffling information stream, national languages broken into linguistic building blocks that one is given no instructions how to recombine or complete. Full words once recognized would be easy to assimilate and then to ignore. But the phonemes never cohere, because even a moment of coherence would vanish before sense could be accreted.

Mencía and Husárová collected descriptive documentation from each of the authors who exhibited in Repurposing in Electronic Literature. Their introduction to the volume is a "declaration" written in non-executable source code.

Their "declaration of independent usage" foregrounds materiality in an emulation of source code. In programming, a declaration is an act of naming, but it is also, in the artists' introduction, an act of will: that readers should use "any literary or non-literary material for questioning and exploring repurposing as a process in poetic practices." "Give me the source" is a heading that frames the entire exhibition. Mencía and Husárová conclude: "As a result of this the term literature is broadened and can be understood to include the use of differing platforms and media as well as experimentation with programmable languages, voice, techniques and modalities." "Programmable languages" and human "voice" are yoked together in this "declaration." The women authors appropriate the style of code as an affirmation of technical prowess and materiality, in the way that the factory women were immersed in the material production of tobacco. But such endeavors are inseparable from their specific context. Whether picking seeds out of tobacco, or rolling cigarettes, or repurposing the code from "Notes Noir," these women literally "got their hands dirty."

149 I refer to new work by Kalindi Vora: *Life Support: Biocapital and the New History of Outsourced Labor.*

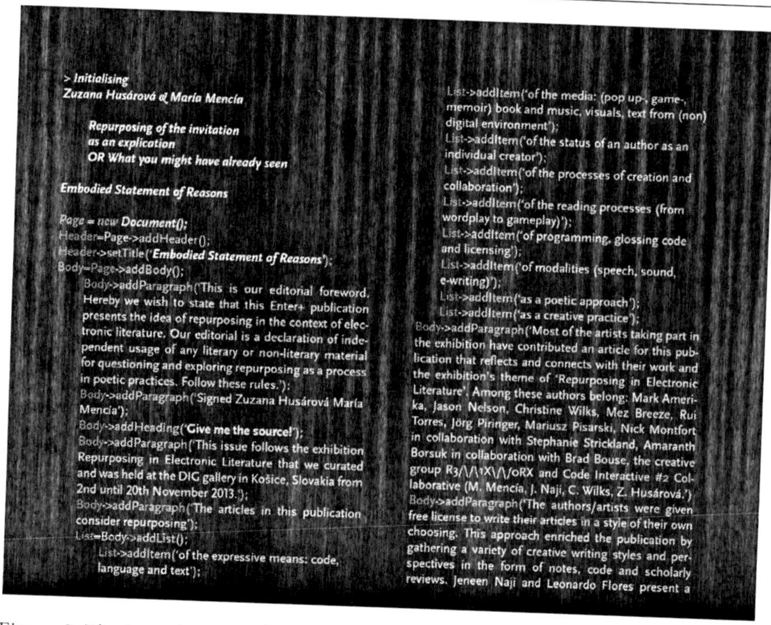

> Initialising
Zuzana Husárová & María Mencía

Repurposing of the invitation
as an explication
OR What you might have already seen

Embodied Statement of Reasons

Page = new Document();
Header=Page->addHeader();
Header->setTitle('Embodied Statement of Reasons');
Body=Page->addBody();
Body->addParagraph('This is our editorial foreword. Hereby we wish to state that this Enter+ publication presents the idea of repurposing in the context of electronic literature. Our editorial is a declaration of independent usage of any literary or non-literary material for questioning and exploring repurposing as a process in poetic practices. Follow these rules.');
Body->addParagraph('Signed Zuzana Husárová María Mencía');
Body->addHeading('Give me the source!');
Body->addParagraph('This issue follows the exhibition Repurposing in Electronic Literature that we curated and was held at the DIG gallery in Košice, Slovakia from 2nd until 20th November 2013.');
Body->addParagraph('The articles in this publication consider repurposing');
List=Body->addList();
List->addItem('of the expressive means: code, language and text');
List->addItem('of the media: (pop up-, game-, memoir) book and music, visuals, text from (non) digital environment');
List->addItem('of the status of an author as an individual creator');
List->addItem('of the processes of creation and collaboration');
List->addItem('of the reading processes (from wordplay to gameplay)');
List->addItem('of programming, glossing code and licensing');
List->addItem('of modalities (speech, sound, e-writing)');
List->addItem('as a poetic approach');
List->addItem('as a creative practice');
Body->addParagraph('Most of the artists taking part in the exhibition have contributed an article for this publication that reflects and connects with their work and the exhibition's theme of 'Repurposing in Electronic Literature'. Among these authors belong: Mark Amerika, Jason Nelson, Christine Wilks, Mez Breeze, Rui Torres, Jörg Piringer, Mariusz Pisarski, Nick Montfort in collaboration with Stephanie Strickland, Amaranth Borsuk in collaboration with Brad Bouse, the creative group R3/\/\1X\/\/oRX and Code Interactive #2 Collaborative (M. Mencía, J. Naji, C. Wilks, Z. Husárová.')
Body->addParagraph('The authors/artists were given free license to write their articles in a style of their own choosing. This approach enriched the publication by gathering a variety of creative writing styles and perspectives in the form of notes, code and scholarly reviews. Jeneen Naji and Leonardo Flores present a

Figure 2: The introduction to *Repurposing in Electronic Literature* is written in the style of source code: a "declaration of independent usage."

Mencía, Husárová, Naji and Wilks' decision to port their installation work to the browser insists that their work should remain visible, even though a browser is a decontextualized remediation of this deeply site-specific work. Creating enduring access to an installation is a labor issue, particularly for women who, as a class, are disproportionately employed as part-time laborers in the humanities and so need the extra documentation to fortify their claims for employment renewal and pay.[150] The four artists all employed full-time or, in the case of Wilks, engaged in funded Ph.D. creative work; but UDC's enduring online presence speaks to the practical need for women artists to leave digital records of otherwise ephemeral artwork and fight against the precarity that besets so many women working in the humanities today—of which I, for four years, was one. UDC is intimately bound with conditions of gender, unemployment and global migration.

The UpsideDown Chandelier transitions from digital art to digital literature when its location moves from installation to browser. This distinction adjusts the reading apparatus from full-body sensorium to a mostly cognitive process of decoding or

150 Part-time and non-tenure track faculty comprise 76% of the humanities professoriate, and at least half of these are women, according to a 2013 report from the American Association of University Professors. That means three of four North American humanities college instructors are or might be incomeinsecure, a phenomenon that extends beyond North America to Britain and Europe as well. Such faculty occupy a liminal space between professional and hourly temp worker.

sleuthing. Serge Bouchardon observes in his forthcoming essay "Toward a Tension-Based Definition of Digital Literature" that

> [t]he tension between a unique object exhibited in a museum [installation] and a reproducible object [website] corresponds in some way to a tension between artistic creation and literary creation. This raises the question of the positioning of digital literature in relation to digital arts.

If, as I suggest above, the body is an interface for UDC in installation, then a guest's experience of the art flows through multiple sensory information streams. Those streams constrict to one main channel in the browser, where words are the only intelligible point of entry. The "tension" Bouchardon observes becomes "literary" when the UDC participant reads the words as the primary portal into the work's meaning. Absent the site-specific context of the tobacco factory, the phonemes' significance would be unintelligible sounds rather than echoes of the languages spoken by women in that particular room. Such sounds, though precisely unintelligible, were poignant. Words cannot supplement the loss of that context and the affective dimension it imparted.

UPSIDEDOWN CHANDELIER INTERFACE #2: BROWSER

Spatially, words take up a large portion of the laptop or desktop screen relative to how the words would have been projected in the tobacco factory installation. In the browser, none of the physical proprioception or accidental encounters with other guests would complement and extend UDC's fixed elements (sound, words, collaged images). In the browser, one decides what to search for. In installation, information flows toward one without one exerting agency beyond staying in the room.

Words in UDC's browser form bear undue emphasis and nudges the work into digital literature rather than digital art, because the encounter becomes readerly: one's first instinct is to decode what the words mean. All of the twenty-seven words are site- and event-specific, referring to the women tobacco factory workers and their donated gift, the chandelier that first held candles, then was adapted to burn gas, and then finally electricity (when it was turned UpsideDown). Words such as "donation" ("darovanie" Slovak, "adomány" Hungarian, "zuwendung" German) or "women" ("nők" Hungarian, "ženy" Slovak, "frauen" German) or "smoke" ("fajčit"" Hungarian, "dohányzik" Slovak, "rauchen" German) appear as appearing/vanishing 3-second animations trailing across the bottom of the screen. In browser, words are the tractable element, the part that changes in ways easy to parse if not understand, and so the encounter becomes literary.

What would have been "guests" at the installation transform into "readers" because that's the clearest path to making meaning of UDC.

I discovered that the way to "read" *The UpsideDown Chandelier* was to "deform" the work by interrupting Flash software's procedurality. I'd transcribe the vanishing words into a text file so that I could plug them into Google Translate; or I used screen grab if I couldn't indicate the diacritical marks in Hungarian, Slovak or German fast enough as the foreign words vanished before my eyes. I translated all of the words, which unlocked UDC for me; but the process of reading was so interruptive as not to be reading, in the sense of continuously building a frame of reference, so much as decoding. I quickly discerned that the words were translations of a core set. But Google Translate detected eight languages: not just the Hungarian, Slovak, English, and German, which the authors used; but also Polish, Czech, Dutch, and Irish, which I later learned the authors did not. These mistranslations were a combination of my human transcription errors and machine errors. As a reader moving from decoding to interpreting, the mistranslations inclined me to deduce that the women working in the tobacco factory hailed from more countries than they actually did. These mistranslations were an algorithmic ghost: languages floating through the interface but emanating neither from the authors nor from me.

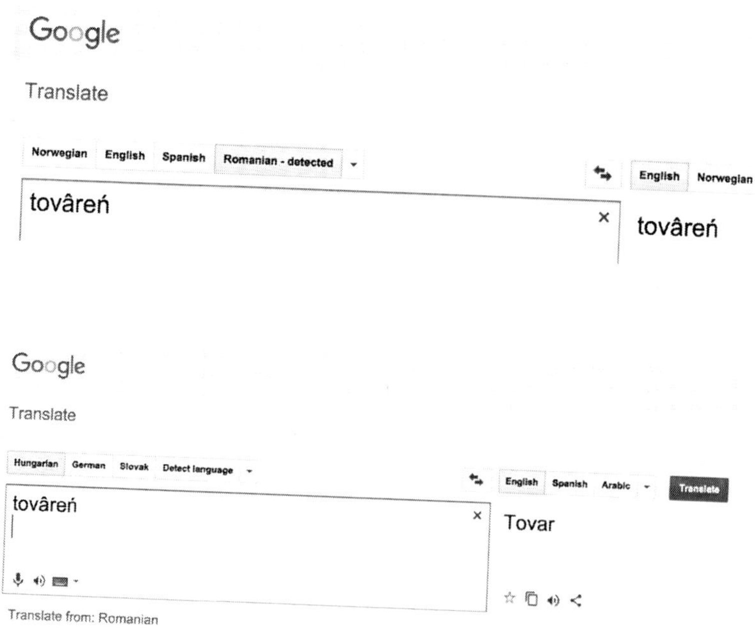

Figure 3: Google Translate was an essential but unstable reading tool I used to decode *The UpsideDown Chandelier*. The same searched word was attributed to different languages and translations to English. What to make of misleading returns?

Translation errors became a legitimate element of my UDC reading experience. Google frequently couldn't identify one language but several possibilities, and I had to learn by trial and error which were the most likely choices. Without recourse to asking the authors, I would not have been able to check the accuracy of my translations. Google Translate is an unstable tool because its returns reflect the current aggregate of crowdsourced translations at moment of search. For example, the word "továreň," which the native Slovakian Zuzana Husárová identifies in the UDC master word list as a Slovak word for "factory," yields different translation results on different days, both of them erroneous (see Figure 3). I had to "guess and check," but absent conversation with the artists, there would have been no ultimate authority to correct or guide my heuristic method.

Such flaws are pernicious only if we persevere in the tradition of close reading for mastery rather than accurate if nimble approximation. Masterful reading is a luxury borne of a stable medial environment where the object is reproducible. Google Translate is a volatile tool, but that doesn't mean it's useless. Instead that we ought to rethink our expectations of reading, and our investment in textual mastery and control.

If commemoration of medially fragile works joins interpretation as the most important work electronic literature critics do, then the race is on to memorialize not just the sensory-rich and fleeting experiences of installation art, but also the many "surfaces" of Flash-authored, browser-based art that seem durable but are not. A feminist-materialist approach to scholarly documentation could engage the broader M.E.A.L.S. framework: materiality, embodiment, affect, labor, situatedness.[151] Such an approach, developed by the FemTechNet collective and summarized into the memorable M.E.A.L.S. acronym by Elizabeth Losh, reckons with the ways in which readerly drives to mastery are entangled in material and commercial systems. Thoughtful description of reading interfaces is a form of feminist critique, and resistance.

UDC rewards the active reader who augments her reading capacity with software that deforms the Flash output: stopping the cinematic flow by capturing snippets in still images, or silencing the audio loop, or putting 75% of the piece's total text output through Google Translate, or searching for extra bits of context that might make the piece comprehensible. Without these machinic and algorithmic augmentations, *The UpsideDown Chandelier* is surfaces that withhold deeper meaning. Like hyper-reading and distant reading, "augmented reading" is enabled by personal computing and net-

151 See Losh's recorded talk "#GamerGate 101: Public Spheres and Safe Spaces" at Whittier College 2 April 2015, minutes 5-8. Losh's M.E.A.L.S. acronym summarizes work on the FemTechNet collective: http://femtechnet.org.

worked information.[152] Such augmentations impart agency. But it's worth noting that the impulse to "master" every element of a literary text also participates in a larger ideological project that privileges knowledge as disembodied artifact over ephemeral performance.

In my months writing this essay, I observed how intrinsically I seek mastery when I read e-literature. Sampling UDC in the browser activated my bookish impulses toward mastery that in installation I would eschew or forestall. To "read" UDC I had to crack it open: stop it, silence it, or deform it into something other than itself in order to read it. And while I wouldn't call this violence, the process did make me grapple with what's at stake in "mastering" a text. It occurred to me, as I hunted for YouTube videos on how to decompile Actionscript so that I could read UDC's decompiled .swf files, that perhaps my drive to master even the proprietary source code was borne of a bookish mental habit, and a notion of scholarly responsibility borne of print-based scholarly practices.[153] In pushing to know every aspect of UDC, I was in some ways reading against UDC in the manner of a detective grilling the suspect. Mastery is the sterling academic credential. But the drive to "master" the output of volatile new media environments is to import print-based modes of reading better suited to stable medial environments. With its crushing colonialist implications, "mastery" as an outcome of reading ought to give us pause.

With whom or what do we align when we seek mastery? Google exacts a price for using its services, though it's a price we lack sufficient information to tabulate. An individual user is prohibited from paying a subscription fee to Google in exchange for tracking-free access to the Google suite of tools. (Corporations do pay Google a subscription fee for use of its suite of tools.) Google parlays the gleaned information to its clients for the purposes of selling behaviorally-targeted ads pitched to users' particular predilections or vulnerabilities. Every personal search is an expression of desire, no matter how trivial or transient. As Siva Vaidhyanathan, John Cayley, Lori Emerson, and

152 N. Katherine Hayles' work on hyper attention is an analog or precondition to what I call augmented reading. Hayles' remarks on hyper attention have evolved from her 2006 essay "Hyper and Deep Attention: Generational Divides in Cognitive Modes" to her 2010 presentation at the Association of Departments of English (published in 2011 as "How We Read: Close, Hyper, Machine"), to its final form in her third chapter in the book *How We Think: Digital Media and Contemporary Technogenesis.*

153 Decompiled code is stripped of an author's grace notes. The code is functional but does not bear the specific traces of a programmer's (or code author's) language. See *Reading Project: A Collaborative Analysis of William Poundstone's Project for the Tachistoscope*, a book that braids humanities computing and literary criticism. Marino notes: "We should proceed carefully [in looking at code as the "depth" of a medial artifact]. Matthew Kirschenbaum and others have rightly warned against approaching code through such depth-based paradigms as 'looking under the hood.' As Wendy Chun suggests, pursuing the code in such a manner presents the search for an inner essence that is an ideological enterprise, a kind of projection" (16-17).

others have articulated, our digital commons is operated by a for-profit corporation that withholds information about its methods and long term goals. We "augment" our reading capacity of digital literature and other medial objects through these tools, but in doing so our drive to read masterfully ironically subjects us to Google's mastery of our desires. "We recognize digital and other technologies can both subvert and reinscribe oppressive relations of power," notes the FemTechNet Manifesto, "and we work to make these complex relations of power transparent." Such an act of reading acknowledges the limits and costs of interface "mastery."

WORKS CITED

Aarseth, Espen. *Cybertexts: A Theory of Ergodic Literature*. Baltimore: Johns Hopkins University Press, 1997.

Alaimo, Stacy and Susan Hekman, editors. *Material Feminisms*. Bloomington and Indianapolis: Indiana University Press, 2008.

American Association of University Professors. *Annual Report 2012-13*. Accessed 20 July 2015. http://www.aaup.org/report/heres-news-annual-report-economic-status-profession-2012-13

Bell, Alice, Astrid Ensslin and Lyle Skains. *Reading Digital Fiction Project*. Accessed 1 June 2016. https://readingdigitalfiction.com

Berens, Kathi Inman. "Live/Archive: Occupy MLA." *Hyperrhiz*, vol. 11. Accessed 15 June 2016. http://hyperrhiz.io/hyperrhiz11/essays/live-archive-occupy-mla.html

Best, Stephen and Sharon Marcus. "Surface Reading: an Introduction." *Representations* 108, no. 1: 1-21. (2009) http://dx.doi.org/10.1525/rep.2009.108.1.1

Bouchardon, Serge. "Towards a tension-based definition of Digital Literature," forthcoming in *Journal of Creative Writing Studies*, vol. 2, issue 1. http://scholarworks.rit.edu/jcws/

Cayley, John and Daniel C. Howe. *The Readers Project*. Accessed online 25 June 2016. http://thereadersproject.org/

Clement, Tanya. "An Information Science Question in DH Feminism." *Digital Humanities Quarterly*, vol. 9., no. 2 (2015). Accessed 15 June 2016. http://www.digitalhumanities.org/dhq/vol/9/2/000186/000186.html

Cramer, Florian and Matthew Fuller. "Interface" in *Software Studies: a Lexicon*, edited by Fuller. Cambridge, MA: The M.I.T. Press, 2014.

Emerson, Lori. *Reading Writing Interfaces*. Minneapolis: University of Minnesota Press, 2014.

FemTechNet Collective. *Manifesto*. Accessed 26 June 2016. http://femtechnet.org/publications/manifesto/

Fletcher, Jerome. "Introduction." *Performance Research* Vol.18, No.5 (October 2013). [Special issue: On Writing and Digital Media]. DOI: 10.1080/13528165.2013.867168

Fogg, B.J. " "Behavioral Model for Persuasive Design." Accessed online 14 June 2016. http://bjfogg.com/fbm_files/page4_1.pdf

Galloway, Alexander R. *The Interface Effect*. New York: John Wiley and Sons. 2013.

Google, led by Javidan et al. *Patent for Storytelling Device*. http://1.usa.gov/1XxZgBv Accessed online 30 June 2016.

Google Developers. "Upload a SWF." Accessed online 26 June 2016. https://developers.google.com/swiffy/

Grigar, Dene. "Curating Electronic Literature as Critical and Scholarly Practice." *Digital Humanities Quarterly*, vol. 8, no. 4 (2014). Accessed 26 June 2016. http://www.digitalhumanities.org/dhq/vol/8/4/000194/000194.html

Haraway, Donna. "Situated Knowledges: The Science Question in Feminism and the Privilege of Partial Perspective." Feminist Studies, vol. 14, no. 3 (1988): 575–599.

Hayles, N. Katherine. *How We Think: Digital Media and Contemporary Technogenesis*. Chicago: University of Chicago Press, 2012.

———. "Print is Flat, Code is Deep." *Poetics Today*, vol. 25, no. 1 (2004) 67-90. Accessed online 15 June 2016. http://www.cws.illinois.edu/IPRHDigitalLiteracies/Hayles.pdf.

Hutcheon, Linda. *A Theory of Adaptation*, second edition. London and New York: Routledge, 2012.

Kirschenbaum, Matthew. Tweet at ELO 2016 conference: "#ELO16 inchoate thought: lab-based and curatorial practices have emerged in the field as a major counterweight to ergodic formalisms." https://twitter.com/mkirschenbaum/status/742095946729689091

Losh, Elizabeth. "#GamerGate 101: Public Spheres and Safe Spaces." Invited talk at Whittier College 2 April 2015. Accessed online 20 May 2016. https://www.youtube.com/watch?v=hHdGEXPFw_g

McGann, Jerome and Lisa Samuels. "Deformance and Interpretation." Accessed online 1 June 2016. http://www2.iath.virginia.edu/jjm2f/old/deform.html

McPherson, Tara. "DH by Design: Alternative Origin Stories for the Digital Humanities." Talk delivered 5 May 2016 at Washington State University Pullman.

Mencía Maria. Documentation of *The UpsideDown Chandelier* installation. Accessed frequently online http://mariamencia.com/pages/upsidedown.html.

Mencía, María and Zuzana Husárová. *Repurposing in Electronic Literature*. Kociše, Slovakia: ENTER+ Press, 2013. See also the archival website: http://mariamencia.com/pages/repurposing.html

Mencía, María, Zuzana Husárová, Jeneen Naji and Christine Wilks. *The UpsideDown Chandelier*. Created November 2013. Accessed frequently online http://www.mariamencia.com/images/upsidedown_flash/Tabacka-6.html

Pressman, Jessica. "The Aesthetic of Bookishness in Twenty-First Century Literature." *Michigan Quarterly Review*, vol. 48, no. 4 [Bookishness: The New Fate of Reading in the Digital Age, Fall 2009]. Accessed online 14 April 2016. http://hdl.handle.net/2027/spo.act2080.0048.402

Pressman, Jessica, Mark C. Marino and Jeremy Douglass. *Reading Project: A Collaborative Analysis of William Poundstone's Project for the Tachistoscope*. Iowa City: University of Iowa Press, 2015.

Salter, Anastasia and John Murray. *Flash: Building the Interactive Web*. Cambridge, MA: The M.I.T. Press, 2014.

Sample, Mark. "Notes Toward a Deformed Humanities." Accessed online 1 June 2016. http://www.samplereality.com/2012/05/02/notes-towards-a-deformed-humanities/

Sullivan, Mark. "Google Takes Books Through the Looking Glass With Augmented Reality." F*ast Company*, 4 March 2016. Accessed online 30 June 2016. http://www.fastcompany.com/3057464/google-takes-storybooks-through-the-looking-glass-with-augmented-reality

Vaidhyanathan, Siva. *The Googlization of Everything (And Why We Should Worry)*. Berkeley and Los Angeles: University of California Press, 2011.

Vora, Kalindi. *Life Support: Biocaptial and the New History of Outsourced Labor*. Minneapolis: University of Minnesota Press, 2015.

Wilks, Christine. "A crissxross trail < r3/\/\1X\/\/0RX" *(A crissxcross trail [through] remix works)*. Accessed online 4 July 2016 http://crissxross.net/remixworx/indexcxtrail.html

Poetic Tweets from the Avant-Garde to Digital Literature

BY ANGELICA J. HUIZAR

INTRODUCTION

Today *digital media* brings an array of literature that raises questions of analysis and reception that concentrate on the process, the materiality and the interactivity of the text. From the avant-garde to the digital era, poets experiment with poetry that is linguistically translatable into any language where semantics is underplayed and replaced by the phonetic, the visual and the user's interactivity (whether it be through poetic performance or user interactivity). The following samples of poetic experimentation will highlight how poets have a keen sense of this process of communication. These poems show us how language may be used to open us up to novel insights and perspectives, and connect us to philosophical ideas between art and reason. As literary critic, I recognize how artistic language takes on special meaning (semantics), while cognitive scientists might focus on the pragmatics of language. Poetry hails an active exploration and interpretation of language in order to appreciate it, making the reader's engagement particularly relevant. This analysis will explore the trajectory from the Latin American avant-garde with the Chilean poet Vicente Huidobro particularly his *Altazor* (published in 1931, with some fragments written as early as 1919), Argentinean poet Ana María Uribe with her *Anipoemas* (1997), to the native Venezuelan, Spanish local, and London-based María Mencía in her *Birds Singing Other Birds' Songs* (2001). These poets show us that language is not intrinsically poetic, but rather show us how we can cultivate a poetic imagination. We will appreciate how alliterative and nonsense language can emphasize musicality of language while at the same time trying to recapture a more primitive form of communication; perceive how letters in themselves are poetic in the right context; and, revel at how bird songs are poetic when we attune ourselves to the features of the sounds and rhythm of the poem while visualizing its syntax and structure in its visual shape and layout. All three poets guide us through a conceptualization of the poetic that invite us to approach language artistically, and to discover and interpret the world.

TWEETS FROM AVANT-GARDE TO DIGITAL LITERATURE

My analysis is thus focused on the purpose that the poetries serve, and specifically, how these poets bring a keen sense of this process of communication and creativity. In the subject of bird songs and communication, these three poets best resonate for me an ensuing transformation of our curiosity with sound, language and communication in general.[154] From the avant-garde playfulness with alliteration, onomatopoeias, and neologisms, to the emerging digital artistry of sound, moving typography with Flash and intricately immersed in political reproach, to a more contemporary design of the artistic, linguistic and inquisitive performance of the reproduction of bird songs. What is particularly striking is María Mencía does not borrow from nor was inspired by Uribe nor Huidobro's poetries, she specifically notes in an interview that her curiosity with bird songs had not come across either of the poets mentioned.

Vicente Huidobro (1892-1948), a renowned poet, political figure, and non-conformist artist from Chile, founder and best exponent of the literary movement Creacionismo, revolutionizes traditional poetries by animating Stephane Mallarmé's calligrammes, experimenting with sound poetry and fashioning new Spanish words. In the same experimental vein, the Argentine visual poet and web artist, Ana María Uribe (1955-2004) leaves a legacy of animated visual poems, we will focus on two poems: "Spring" and "Spring II" in *Anipoemas* (1997). She draws inspiration from the letter designs and seems almost obsessive about recreating the essence of the figurative mold of the typography, that is, like an artist she finds the spirit representative of the shape of the letter. Her use of humor and symbolic disarray challenges assumptions with substitutions and associations. The phonemes are also important in portraying the intended performance. Her concrete inspired poems playfully interact with the area in-between the visual and the artistic, a revitalized re-imagined existence conjured up by the poet-artist. Most recently, María Mencía, a digital media poet and multi-media artist. Mencía's experimental, textual, generative and sound poetries are in collections such as the Electronic Literature Organization, and her poetry appears in various e-literature and e-poetry databases at research centers, and has been exhibited at art galleries, international conferences and festivals such as: International Symposium of Electronic Arts (ISEA) Japan; Festival Internacional de Lenguas Electrónicas, Brazil; Biennale of Electronic Arts, Perth, Australia; onedotzero Institute of Contemporary Arts, UK; Caixaforum, Spain and the TATE Modern, UK.

154 There are several other literary contributions to the theme of bird songs, such as the Greek playwright Aristophanes (c. 446-386 BC), with his comedy *The Birds* (414 BC, City Dionysia), and most recently the digital texts of the Argentinean Gustavo Romano, a contemporary artist working with installations, net art, video and photography, and Belén Gache with her *Wordtoys*, a hypermedia work in Flash, *El idioma de los pájaros* (2006). In this work, Romano contributes with programming and Gache with idea and direction, their poems draw from verses by Gustavo Adolfo Becquer, Rubén Darío, Edgard Allan Poe, Guillaume Apollinaire, and Charles Baudelaire. While the theme is strikingly similar in terms of its effect on communication, *El idioma de los pájaros* does not echo the same nuances of the linguistic process with sounds and nonsense language as the poems by the artists chosen for this analysis.

To begin my analysis, I'd like to focus on the most contemporary poet, who's poetries on birds really sparked my interest in a comparative analysis with Cantos V-VII from Huidobro's *Altazor*, and the early digital poetries of Uribe. Mencía's *Birds* resonates a literary tradition of sound poetry, moving calligrammes, and non-sense poetry set in a very contemporary digital format that invites user participation. My interest in *Birds* is its ability to create new meaning in mediated image-sound texts bringing into focus cultural, artistic and literary traditions including the imaginative knowledge and performance of semantics. As literary critic I recognize how artistic semantics takes on special meaning and find that Mencía's poem is an interface of signs from different semiotic systems. I find it particularly interesting for what this mediated poetry tells us about the already established literary field: the emerging electronic literary re-conceptualizes the visual and aural experiments found in the literary and the artistic fields.

Mencía remarks on the text's versatility in being able to reshape "into different forms of media and possibilities of presentation and thus exploration" She has designed *Birds* in three different media: video at Medway Galleries at the University of Kent (2001); prints in the 2002 exhibition at La Huella Múltiple at the Fototeca in Havana, Cuba; and, interactive web design published in the ELO *Electronic Literature Collection Volume 1.*

Scholars of electronic and traditional have made significant contributions with their own studies from their situated points of reference, this analysis will focus on a close reading of Mencía, Uribe and Huidobro's poetry as it relates specifically to this topic and few, if any, references to previous readings of the poets' work will be made to focus attention on the close reading.

BIRD SONGS IN TWO MARÍAS

Ana María Uribe is a key pioneer of e-poetries with her semiotic renditions of animated letters performing syntactic relevance. Much like Ana María Uribe, María Mencía makes use of the phonetic and semantic dimensions of language such as letter repetitions to denote syllables, much akin to sound poems. Both poets, at separate times, stress that their poetry is linguistically translatable into any language where semantics is underplayed and replaced by the phonetic, the visual and the user's interactivity. While they don't necessarily use the International Phonetic Alphabet (IPA) the sounds used in their poetry are composed of distinctive qualities of oral speech such as phonemes, intonation, and rhythm. Their selection of bird songs further accentuates their fascination of sound poetry that downplays the role of meaning and structure and foregrounds the performance of the sound, and in a multi-media context the interactivity between the user and the poem.

Ana María Uribe began designing her *Anipoems* in 1997 to have a narrative with a starting point, a climax and a denouement. The main components are still typography motion and sound with rhythm being especially important with her use of repetition and short sequence elements. It very much seems that Uribe saw the world around her as a projection of letters that served as inspiration to her poetry. In ¨Spring¨ and "Spring 2" she depicts the sounds and elements of Spring using as inspiration the letters "p" and "q." The movement upward in each poem displays the silhouette of perching birds on a tree. The recordings on both poems are looped.[155]

"Spring" starts with an escalating "p-q" sequence on white background, followed by the chirping of two distinctive bird songs. "Spring" is reminiscent of the birds' songs in the morning, these are more musical and complex than calls. The white foreground of the screen is only suggestive of morning after we read "Spring 2." According to bird expert Les Beletsky, for most birds, the majority of the signing is in early morning and songs are associated with mate attraction (23). Moving on to "Spring 2" we find that this is the converse of "Spring" displaying a black background and beginning the sequence with "q-p," followed by three distinctive bird callings. The bird songs in "Spring 2" pressed in the black background are suggestive of a night calling. Beletsky points out that the short recordings suggest the birds are using calls that are usually not as musical as songs with only a few short notes. While calls may be used to communicate a variety of things to each other and between members of a flock, these are most often used to give location, to communicate aggression, warning, identification, flocking, and hunger or to announce a food source (54). All calls are used for immediate attention. So, the denouement becomes apparent when we realize that spring, or a renaissance of sorts (political or otherwise), for the poet has its two facets: the dawn of new song or principles and the calls or caveats of looming danger. Uribe's two springs interweave a message with the use of bird sounds. Interestingly enough, ornithologists note that it is birds' hearing of those sounds that is much more complex than what is perceived by the human ear. Symbolically, Uribe is using a communication system that is apparently much simpler—only immediate actions communicated—but with deeper nuances. In a moment in history when Argentineans were not free to express themselves, nor to communicate openly this nuanced system provides a symbolic alternative. Uribe shows us that birds' songs are much more complex and that this emerging digital poetry is more than just images and noise. Her poetry, tragically cut short, has influenced and

155 The poems appear in her website http://vispo.com/uribe/spring.html.

inspired new generations of digital poets, particularly women. Mencía's works show us how far we have come and how much more there is to discover and create.

FROM SOUNDS TO CALLIGRAMMES

While María Mencía's poetics may not resonate a political agenda, we can find similarities in analyzing her bird calligrammes and see how an aesthetic analysis takes into account various levels: the plastic, the geometric and coloristic, a perceptual level, and an emotional-rational level. In *The Semiotics of Visual Languages* Catalina Bogdan posits structures of analysis specific to paintings but the overall scope of interpretation may also apply to visual poetics. First there is a visual scanning that focuses on the elements of the image, it is immediately followed by a perceptual reading that takes into account the overall organization and colors of the visual patterns or forms. Then the image is perceived with plastic or pictorial reasoning followed by the viewer's emotional reactions. The process is re-evaluated and repeated several times, including right after the viewer identifies its title (Bogdan 2002, 4).

To better understand how we naturally "read" images, let's refer to how the semiotics of visual languages takes place. According to Bogdan, viewers process moving images in three levels: visual stimuli, recognition of patterns, and an understanding of the image that bids a prepared response. At the visual stimuli level, data is collected from the image-object, the eye focusing in different parts of it. First a general filtering of the information is scanned, followed by an acknowledgment of the conspicuousness of the points, but more or less at random. At the second level patterns are recognized with criteria of equilibrium and continuity. Then the whole visual field is organized in a structure in which usually a few of these patterns play a determining role. At this level, centration effects are bound to manifest themselves. Viewer feedback affects the filtering of data at the first level, which will disregard what does not fit into a recognizable pattern. The viewer will also give greater weight to recognizable patterns. At the final level the response or understanding may comprise of comparisons, possible restructurings of the whole image perceived (thereby influencing the scanning and filtering at the initial level) with rescaling, reorganizing and other "corrective" actions (Bogdan 2002, 26). The process can certainly be random reflecting the recognition of patterns and the attribution of meaning. The feedback induces more scanning which in turn speeds the analysis.

A LOOK BACK TO THE AVANT-GARDE

The above explanation of visual scanning and understanding of how our eyes perceive images and our minds attribute meaning or visual semiotics is very much akin to how Vicente Huidobro plays with the possibility of such orality in his philosophy of poetics, Creacionismo. In Altazor, poetry is that pure semiotic arrangement of sounds and utterances in its progression toward becoming a song of unrecognizable words as seen in the last Canto. Uribe used a language of sound and symbolism. Huidobro and Mencía search for a new language without grammar, a language with new sounds where consonants and vowels are independent and produce their own resonance, where sound is an imitation of life, and where language is not necessarily a product of civilization. Mencía's *Birds* unsuspectingly puts into practice the precepts of Creacionismo, particularly creating the poem for its own sake without the need to praise, please or even be understood, simply to "flower" as a flower does. Poetry, claims Huidobro, should have its own reality and be separate and distinct from other phenomena.

Huidobro's philosophies of poetry, language, and signification also make reference to the sound performative effects of language in poetry, a characteristic that is prevalent in the poetics of Guillaume Apollinaire in Surrealism, to the symbolist theories of Stéphane Mallarmé which propose the integral relationship between signified and signifier that produces the sign or significance of the word/image. Dadaist theories (1916) of poetic performance may play a role in this poem's search for freedom of expression where the verse intends to replace logic and reason with deliberate madness, particularly with its linguistic effects of primitive language. Much like Dadaist poetry, *Altazor* (the protagonist) seeks to free the word from its semantic function while it embraces a more rhythmical and musical primordial language—a language that is like a bird's song, recognized (by humans) by its sound. *Altazor* is a linguistic "happening" as it attempts to return to the primitive, to incantation and ritual, and to the coming together of music and poetry. Essentially, the poet's skillful and innovative use of linguistic elements presents a performance of how to read the poem, giving the reader many possible ways to recite the poem. One can even say that *Altazor* is an experiment with poetic sound in the style of the Russian Futurists' exploration of trans-rational language.

Similarly, *Birds Singing Other Birds' Songs* (2001) is a multi-textual e-poem that draws from various sources but it is also ultimately a virtual experience of the movement and sound of the letters, the interaction with its audience, be it at the exhibition gallery or on the web. What comes through is Mencía's interest in the transformation of semantics, the forms of human expression, and how communication connects us all, not just humans but other creatures as well. Her thirteen birds scrolling across the screen remind me of Huidobro's final Cantos that progressively deconstruct syntax and words and reduce poetic expression to phonetic bliss. Each bird in Mencía's poem is a new alliterative rendition compounded to the previous ones creating a resonant visual effect of how our ears and eyes perceive sound. Huidobro breaks down Spanish syntax to its phonemes to assimilate bird songs, Mencía recreates bird songs with English phonemes. Either way, the poets rhetorically ponder: Can you hear the poetry in the sounds you hear? The world speaks to us always, are we listening to its poetic song? Are we capable of recreating such poetries?

The interactive web version of *Birds Singing Other Birds' Songs* has thirteen birds that fly across the sky background; each one has its own characteristic song. The birds scroll through the screen, implode into or explode out of their shape as they appear, most are in black font but the fourth bird, whose song is a bit more complicated, is shaped by colorful letters. The sixth bird's song consists of a simpler tweeting and its movement accompanies the sound with a flickering and on-off movements. The vibrating song of the eighth bird is highlighted by the very visible "zee zee zee-zurr" emblem in the shadow of an advancing bird. By the ninth button, the recording is more representative of bird calls and the recording is multiplied to emphasize a passing flock. The movement of the tenth bird toward the viewer accentuates the repetitive and pulsating song of the black bird encrusted with white font. The eleventh bird rapidly chases its own chirping letters as it passes the screen. The twelfth song, is a static white shadow of a bird with movable chirping letters. The small black bird in the thirteenth button moves at a moderate pace as it calls, its phonetic emblem blinking rapidly. The chirpings or tweets are not actual birds, but rather a recording human transcription of what we hear the chirping to be. An attempt at reproducing unstructured communication that is visualized by the splintering letters that come to form the image of the bird, a double-take on the transcription of these sounds given we hear and see how these take effect. Other birds, like the third, flash their figure with the actual sound emitted, "chick-chick" and finally silence reminding us of how language is visual as well and the sound just another element. The transformation of each of birds with its accompanying sound is reflective of the performance of the poem that Huidobro so hankered for: a poetry that defies instituted symbolism and thereby creates its own signification.

María Mencía's *Birds* is an answer to the birth of new poetry dreamed of in Canto I of *Altazor*. Huidobro called for the death of conventional poetic form, which has become stagnant and constricted by linguistic structures. More importantly, it addresses questions of linguistic signification that we later see Julia Kristeva discuss in her essay "Poetry That Is Not a Form of Murder" (1984). She specifically asks:

> Does the course of the "human mind" consist uniquely in learning how to ab-

> sorb the "integrity of the signifier" that is constituted once and for all, by finding corresponding signifieds? (73)

The poem in many ways illustrates Kristeva's theory of language: language in the social order undergoes an instituting symbolism. Kristeva sees how language is a social phenomenon that is codified by the symbolism that the social order imposes on it. This codification is in fact a "sacrifice" that the presymbolic language—or primordial language—must undergo. When this "violence" of the presymbolic language is attributed to some thing or cause, it then becomes part of the symbolic order. Huidobro anticipates Kristeva's interrogations and sets himself up as a philosopher of poetic voice who in the end triumphs over social linguistic structures.

Huidobro's mystical bird tries to escape the encoding of language by privileging sounds and eventually emerging as a song of sounds, of bird tweets. In much the same fashion, María Mencía is influenced by Julia Kristeva's *Revolution in Poetic Language* (1984), specifically by her investigation of the how semiotic and symbolic "maintain their symbiotic identities"; converging but also remaining separate, keeping their own elements, as Mencía cites in her PhD dissertation. The transcript and translation of bird songs from the aural to the written to the visual and then adding the cybernetic movement does interpret the process of communication in its varied forms.

One of Mencía's enquiries in the design of *Birds* was specifically: "How can we create a system of communication using new media, where image-text, semantic-text and phonetic–text converge as new media language?" (Mencía 2003). She makes use of the phonetic and semantic dimensions of language such as letter repetitions to denote syllables, much akin to sound poems. Because of the lack of signification, her poetry is linguistically translatable into any language where semantics is underplayed and replaced by the phonetic, the visual and the user's interactivity. This internationalization may be achieved by its deliberate use of standardized representation of sounds. Her poetry is composed of distinctive qualities of oral speech such as phonemes, intonation, and rhythm. The selection of bird songs further accentuates her fascination of sound poetry that downplays the role of meaning and structure and foregrounds the performance of the sound, and in a multi-media context the interactivity between the user and the poem.

From the above, we can thus say that "Spring" and "Spring II," *Altazor* and *Birds Singing Other Birds' Songs* have pushed the limits of its contemporary literary/artistic traditions, but most importantly the poems reflect on our current discourse practices, sometimes aberrant interaction, and our contemporary wish to be universally understood and desire to create a more unique signification. Such demands on communication are idealistic, but experiments that artists and poets produce do reveal these intricacies. These poets present the poem as a process, language as a metaphor and ultimately they lead us to question how we communicate or what we value in our communication. Huidobro does so by extrapolating a philosophical and poetic explanation of language, Uribe's intricate symbolism veiled in metaphors and sound, while Mencía sets out to create an interactive installation with textual and sound pieces based on the birds' songs inspired from the work of R. Murray Shafer's *The Thinking Ear* (1986). The poetic framework for *Birds* then is the experimentation with multiple and multimodal translations: the translation of birds' songs into linguistic form by the human voice; the interpretation of the birds' songs by the singers; and, the recordings that accompany the first transcription of bird song to recognizable phonemes. The aural and visual components play with the transcripts and the aural human rendition of their song. These recordings are accompanied by calligrammes of birds that bear the transcription of the sounds emitted. Her focus on language thus shifts from the semantic to the visual and the use of code as invisible language. So, for Mencía the literary component stems primarily from her almost philosophical inquiry and artistic rendition of the structure of bird language. Mencía reconstructs language, plays with signification, creates a poesis of sound and visual components, and much like Huidobro's poem, the process is a slow and arduous deconstruction of the poetic genre to its most elemental phase: sound.

THE SEVEN CANTOS OF ALTAZOR

In each of the seven Cantos we can see a progression toward creating a language out of pure sound, devoid of meaning. Although each of the Cantos produces a varying perspective of the poem's theme, there is also a definite and deliberate devolution of the vocalizations. There is a breakdown in syntax and semantics, the words becoming much more independent of their linguistic codifications. There is also a distinct progression toward a free association of language, where the sound of the words is much more evocative than the social and semantic signification. Meaning is derived by the sounds' connotations, by the fluidity of the vocalizations.

Similarly, in *Birds*, the full spectrum of birds and their songs forms a cacophonic assemblage of bird calls and songs, but it also most interestingly gathers a variety of moving calligrammes that personify the poet's fascination with the beauty of sound as poetic, with the artistry of the visual and kinetic in poetry, and with the philosophical idea that language is evolving and new media creates an environment where all can converge. The following analysis of *Altazor* sheds light on how poets have experimented with semantics and sound to show how the intricacies of poetry are all around us. Such inquiries teach us that language is more than direct communication, it is a magical connection between living beings. Ana María Uribe may have drawn from Huidobro's poetic manifesto, María Mencía most certainly brings it to life in her user-interactive poetry.

THE DECONSTRUCTION OF LANGUAGE IN ALTAZOR

The linguistic experiments we start to see in the third and fourth Cantos are the beginning of a disintegration of the semantics and a more deliberate attention to and articulation of the sound (hence, the poetic references to the bird-language of *Altazor*). In Canto IV, linguistic games start to take shape through images composed of a varied combination of two words. While these verses maintain a sonorous, musical quality, they do play on the relationship of words, their semantic as well as their symbolic meaning. As Vicente Huidobro posits in his Creacionismo, poetic language should be rhythmic, uninhibited, alive, drunk; it should be a celebration of sounds, rhythms, and tones. In Canto V, he then presents a dazzling array of new verbal schemes. The poet's "de-writing" has a system: the familiar is de-familiarized, the word order is changed, words are transformed (nouns into verbs, and verbs into nouns). This Canto initiates a conversation in the form of a linguistic game between the swallows and the windmill. The verses specifically referencing the windmill play with the visual and kinetic effect that the mill would produce: it participates in carrying and bringing things. By Canto VI (39-47), the lexicon is still recognizable, but meaning becomes more obscure. Overall, the Canto's verses are made up of nonsense, language is constricted so that the verbs seem to disappear almost completely; the words are in phonic and rhythmic harmony. The seventh Canto finishes with a language that is now an invented one, recognized only by its Spanish phonemes. The poet is experimenting with what Kristeva later posits: the literary practice as an "exploration and discovery of the possibilities of language as an activity which frees man from given linguistic networks" (75). The poem transforms language into an anti-language that performs meaning solely through sound; the significance of the nonsense words is found in how they emulate the singing of a bird. *Altazor*'s language has been freed, and poetry itself is now richer with the freedom to use a more musical tongue.

Altazor's sound performativity is characterized by how the invented words minimize meaning and emphasize sound. Nonsense language, onomatopoeia, glossolalia, neologisms, and rhythmic patterns are all used to revive language with a new set of conventions, all based on sound. This linguistic transformation may in fact be proposing a new logic of meaning: one where meaning results from phonetic association. This new association, in turn, creates new signifiers completely independent of an established social order, as Kristeva puts it, and free of any symbolic codification. As is seen in this last stanza, the bird-like singing of *Altazor* is the poem's last message: poetic language is musical and song-like, and *must be performed to be fully appreciated.*

> Lalalee
> Eeoh eeah
> ee ee ee oh
> Ahee ah ee ahee ah ee ee ee ee oh eeah
> (Canto VII, 63–66)

In essence, Huidobro's *Altazor* is much akin to the Dadaist and Futurist "Happenings," which brought poetry out of the silent written page to oral performances that provoked the imagination by breaking the syntax of the language. A musical composition or a transliteration of the poem might serve to best illustrate the poem's sound performativity.

FINAL CONNECTIONS

At the turn of the twentieth century, Vicente Huidobro deconstructs language to create a new poetics. Not surprisingly *Altazor* has also taken on new forms in screenplays (Mexico, Alan Gómez, 1994, 25 min.), theater productions (Santiago, Chile, Teatroonirus, Horacio Videla, 70 min.), and other mediums. Huidobro's Creacionismo proposed an imaginative poetics that would expose the process of creation and make the art interactive. Digital literature offers exactly that and new media has changed literacy or how we read and how we communicate. Tim O'Connor in *Poetic Acts & New Media* claims that poetic signification does not need to be confined to a codified, verbal-text 'representation' since we no longer live in solely a linguistic/textual universe. Poetic events can be both written as well as read as "minor" productive acts that simulate vectors of multi-sensory transmissions. "An inter-media art can generate a multi-media, poetic literacy that operates within the surfaces/appearances of all cultural (or mass media) information," O'Connor emphasizes (xxiii). Poetry is the genre to best explore that by means of its compact and precise form, new media poetry is effective in conjuring these various elements. In the 1980's Julia Kristeva investigated these same processes. Ana María Uribe began experimenting with that in the late 1990s by making her poems act out their roles: the p/q interplay of pecking birds suggestive of much deeper signification, and most recently María Mencía's *Birds* experiments with and challenges the way new media can help us understand our communicative process.

WORKS CITED

Beletsky, Les. *Bird Songs from Around the World: Featuring Songs of 200 Birds from the Cornell Lab of Ornithology*. New York, NY: Chronicle Books, 2007.

Bogdan, Catalina. *The Semiotics of Visual Languages*. Boulder, CO: East European Monographs, 2002.

Costa, René de. *Vicente Huidobro: The Careers of a Poet*. Oxford and New York: Clarendon P, 1984.

Huidobro, Vicente. *Altazor/Temblor de cielo*. 9th ed. Madrid: Ediciones Catédra, 1998.

Kristeva, Julia. *Revolution in Poetic Language*. New York: Columbia UP, 1984.

Mencía, María. (Sept. 2006) *Birds Singing Other Birds' Songs. Electronic Literature Collection*, Eds. K. Hayles, N. Montfort, S. Rettberg, S. Strickland. UCLA Department of English, Los Angeles. Accessed 23 July 2015. http://collection.eliterature.org/1/works/Mencía__birds_singing_other_birds_songs.html

Mencía, María, Authors' personal website: http://www.MaríaMencía.com/pages/birds.html Accessed 15 July 2016

Mencía, María. *in content |code| process, Authoring Electronic Literature*. Ed. Judy Malloy. http://www.narrabase.net/María_birds.html

Mencía María. *From Visual Poetry to Digital Art : Image-Sound-Text, Convergent Media, and the Development of New Media Languages*. 2003 PhD dissertation.

O'Connor, Tim. *Poetic Acts & New Media*. Lanham, MD: UP of America, 2007.

Shafer, Murray R. *The Thinking Ear: Complete Writing on Music Education*. Toronto: Arcana Editions, 1986.

Uribe, Ana María. "Spring" and "Spring II" (1999). *Anipoems*. 23 July 2015. <http://www.vispo.com/uribe/anipoems.html>.

R(e)orienting Poetics and Lived Spaces "Between"

BY LAURA SHACKELFORD

> If orientations, as sedimented histories, are an effect of what we tend toward, then they point toward the future, to what is not yet present. And yet, orientations are shaped by what is behind us, creating a loop between what is toward and behind. In other words, we are directed by our background. —Sara Ahmed, "Orientations Matter"

This essay approaches an intriguing strain of recent digital literary writing in its largely unrecognized capacity as an emergent, practice-based mode of research into shifting spatiotemporal experiences and knowledges of lived space. Creatively engaging mobile, hand-held, reader-activated, augmented-reality, and locative digital technologies (cellular phones, tablets, GPS technology, Kinect motion-sensing, QR-codes and augmented reality software), these digital writing practices comparatively reconsider a wide range of both analog and digital practices of space-making, and the spatialized environments and interactions they lead us to habitually accept or to confront anew. Influential digital literary works such as Amaranth Borsuk and Brad Bouse's *Between Page and Screen* and María Mencía's *Transient Self-Portrait* tactically read and write with, between, behind, beside, and across emerging digital spacetimes. They reveal that computational processes and architectures, rather than simply replacing or augmenting physical environments, embodied experiences, and other kinds of lived space, are, in fact, complexly interwoven and recombined with existing physical, material, cultural, and symbolic topographies, physical repertoires, and technological scaffolding in ways just beginning to be recognized.

Contemporary senses of space and time are shaped at multiple levels, as critical geographers such as Doreen Massey (2005), Jon May and Nigel Thrift (2001), and Rob Kitchin and Martin Dodge (2011) stress in their various analyses of digital spacetimes. Even as everyday life becomes increasingly reliant on computation-based infrastructure, leading Kitchin and Dodge to describe emergent spatial experience and architectures as "code/space," spatiotemporal experience and knowledge continues to be shaped by the material world[156]; by social disciplines of time, work, family; by our relationships to a range of technological instruments and devices; and by culturally resonant representational practices including writing, literature, visual arts, and poetics. These practices

156 I use the term "code/space" here in terms similar to those laid out by Kitchin and Dodge (2011).

both materially circumscribe and symbolically in-form spatiotemporal experience in distinctive ways. What I describe as "lived space"—extending prior phenomenological inquiries into the experiential and physiological specificity of spatiotemporal experience and action to computation-based spatial practices—emerges through the ongoing intertwining of embodied existence with its, at once, physically, affectively, symbolically, culturally, and technologically distinct relations to the world.

Writing, unfolding from the hand, is oriented by, and, in turn, orients one's physical embodiment and experience of the body and other socially legible lived spaces in multiple ways. As hand-held digital devices, sensors, GPS (global positioning system) technologies, and touch-based interfaces catalyze a circuitous "return to the hand" (Hawk, Rieder, and Oviedo 2008, xiv), key strains of digital literary writing explore these technological practices' impact on lived space, bodily self orientations, and physical and cultural location. Perceptively, their digital writing practices reacquaint readers with writing as a performative practice key to bringing forth distinct social spaces, intersubjectivities, and lifeworlds through its co-productive, material and symbolic enframing of the world. Because spatial practices play a habitual, often unperceived role as background, shaping and symbolically informing social action and experience, it makes sense that these sedimented layers to spatial experience and lived space often remain unremarked even as they fold into and recombine in unexpected ways with more recent spatial practices and architectures.

As I will illustrate in the short readings of recent electronic poetics below, these digital literary engagements with computation-based spatiotemporal experience intently reapproach mobile, sensible and locative digital media, reminding readers of literary writing's prior status as a mode of self-inquiry, navigation—as an affectively-charged social, cultural, and geographical "orientation device," to use philosopher Sara Ahmed's apt concept. The status of writing as a mode of exploration, of orientating oneself to the world, is most obvious in the case of spiritual writings and various forms of autobiography and self writing, perhaps. A consideration of regional and national literary traditions, travel narratives, atlases, and almanacs, though, underscores writing's multidimensional—i.e., physical, geographic, topographic, and symbolic—contributions as a means of culturally-inflected spatiotemporal orientation.[157]

E-poetic practices by Borsuk and Bouse, Mencía, and others, I will suggest, comparatively reimagine predominant modes of digital writing, digital spacetimes, mobility, and intersubjective 'feeling together' in light of these 'sedimented histories' of

157 Intriguingly, Medieval tablet cultures imagined spiritual writing as a productive, i.e., performative individual and communal practice focused on the 'cultivation' of self and of its relations to a larger religious community.

print-based writing and visual arts practices and their habitual spatiotemporal orientations, sensorial regimes, and bodily life. Reading their e-poetic practices in light of a longer trajectory of feminist, queer, and experimental writing, I hope to catalog shared elements and aims in these writers' experimental querying of spatial practices and their nuanced, critical reorientation of digital writing spaces, interface relations, and code/space. As Ahmed stresses in her analysis of the unnoticed role writing and writing tables play in philosophy, as material, phenomenological, and disciplinary orientation devices, women of color, feminists, and queer subjects who are rendered "out of place" by predominant knowledges, writing practices, and their preferred or presumed bodily orientations to the world, "'do things' by claiming spaces that have not historically belonged to them, including the spaces worked out for writing. [They] have to secure a place that is not already given" (20). These acts involve, at once, a physical, phenomenological, and epistemological "re-orientation," or, a tactical making of spaces for women's practices and knowledges within the very social and technological networks and human geographies that forestall, disregard, and delegitimize them. Recent digital writers such as the ones I'll discuss below, tactically re-engage the potential of what often remains part of an unperceived spatiotemporal, cultural, medial and linguistic background to "other" ends. Extending Ahmed's insights to reconsider this strain of digital literary writing practices and emergent e-poetics, I intend to acknowledge key similarities between theirs and prior tactical, feminist and queer engagements with writing spaces. Rather than folding these writers back into this literary historical background, though, I will clarify how such digital literary writing practices—through their, at once, literal and symbolic reorientations of digital technologies, language, modes and media of writing and reading—generate important knowledges about the distinctly twenty-first century spacetimes and intersubjective dynamics currently defining code/space, opening up alternative, unexplored dimensions to these. These digital literary practices encourage readers to reperceive the fundamental relays through which practices of writing and other space-making and spatiotemporal processes, as technics linking subjects and technologies in distinct ways, actively and complexly inflect culturally, and socially distinct perceptions, meanings, and experiences of lived space.[158]

---

158 *Technics*, in my understanding are the mutually transformative interrelations between subjects, technologies, social practices, and lifeworlds. This concept places emphasis on the ongoing, productive, social, cultural, material, and technical relations that generate what later come to be seen as self-apparent subjects, technical objects, social spaces, and spatial relations. This is in keeping with recent thinking about subject-technology relations and digital spacetimes in philosophy, feminist science studies, systems theory, and critical geographies. My conceptualization of technics here also overlap significantly with discussions of "*somatechnics*," coined in 2003 by Susan Stryker, Nikki Sullivan, and others at a conference on "body modification" at Macquarie University. As Sullivan stresses, "techné is not something we add or apply to the already constituted body (as object), nor is it a tool that the embodied self employs to its own ends. Rather, *technés* are the dynamic means in and through which

E-POETIC ORIENTATION DEVICES

Writing, and the literary's historical role as a means of orienting writers and readers to distinct physical, cultural, and affective geographies, is nothing new. Literary writing and reading practices from diverse cultural and historical moments register shifting understandings of self-identity and modes of address. As importantly, such writing practices both explore and help to consolidate intersubjective experience and its shifting embodiments and lifeworlds. Literary writing unfolds as a performative, reciprocal practice through which lived space is regularly informed and co-realized, not simply a secondary representational practice wholly distinct from the lived spaces, experiences, or events it engages and imagines.[159] Writing not only helps to consolidate and stabilize the relative "here and now" of embodied existence, the reference point from which all other human experience unfolds, literary writing has also served as an influential means of hinging embodied subjective experience and self understanding to physical and cultural geographies, and to their socially and culturally distinct modes of spatiotemporal circulation, political economy, agency, and knowledge.[160] Writing is an influential somatechnological support, to draw on Nikki Sullivan's understanding of the heterogenous cultural, technological, material practices that in-form bodily life.

Literary writing and reading orients its readers through its in-forming and shaping of the cultural meaning of lived spaces of self and their multi-leveled physical, cultural, social, and affective geographies. Notably, this occurs at the level of representation, in the "text," and in its implicit paratextual enframing on the page or screen. It also occurs at the level of the literary system's material practices of reading and

corporealities are crafted" (187). Central to discussions of somatechnics is an attention to "operations of power, the soma-techno-logic, that constitute(s) (un)becoming-with in situated ways" (Sullivan) particularly as they are experienced and revealed through transgender and nonbinary orientations. "Transgender, like forms of bodily being commonly pre-sumed not to be technologically produced, is a *heterogeneous* [my ital] somatechnological construct that comes to matter in contextually specific ways and in relation to other discursive formations" (Sullivan 189). *Somatechnics*' attention to the heterogeneous ways in which bodily experiences of lived space come to matter is particularly valuable.

159 While computing and computer science has moved significantly 'beyond the screen' since Mark Weiser's call in 1991 for a computer of the 21st century, moving from desktop and screen to be ubiquitously integrated into the fabric of physical and urban environments, as Jörgen Schäfer and Peter Gendolla note in the introduction to their collection, *Beyond the Screen: Transformations of Literary Structures, Interfaces and Genres* (2010), "digital literature," has always been "beyond the screen" or page, even as web cams, RFID and other sensing technologies, and other hand-held and locative technologies are unquestionably generating "new combinations of physical, virtual, and symbolic spaces" (14). In light of these recent shifts, I encourage careful consideration of how literature and literary systems prior to the digital turn have already, always been 'beyond the screen' or 'page' in multiple ways worth recognizing.

160 Literary writing is, in other words, one "technology of self," in Michel Foucault's terms. And it is through the coordination of "new techniques of self-regulation" at the micro level with 'flexible' "forms of political rule and economic exploitation" at the macro level that literary writing feeds into modern biopower and its normatizing ends. See Lemke (2001), 203.

writing, in their unfolding as events that actively establish and reinforce the spatio-temporal parameters and social priorities of its "imagined communities" (Anderson 1991) through these very practices and their differential, delimited circulations. It is important to address these multiple, coimplicated levels to literary texts and practices of reading and writing to understand the multipotent ways in which they complexly co-inform lived space and spatiotemporal understanding today.[161]

The dynamic interrelations between language, representational practices, and intersubjective lived space are at the core of Gertrude Stein's *Tender Buttons: Objects Food Rooms* (1914), for instance. As an influential precursor to more recent experimental feminist and queer writing, *Tender Buttons* complicates previous literary writing's assumed correlation to interior, subjective space at multiple levels. Its domestic subject matter directly addresses the defining, gendered relations of inside/outside, private/public, interior/exterior to literary writing. In this way, *Tender Buttons* engages with language and literary poetics' performative power as orientation devices. It does so at the material level of the text's spatial organization, separated into visually objectified sections and chunks of text. It also does so at the level of its hybrid generic status as a prose poem (with the relative primacy of narrative space and time, lyrical and narrative registers redistributed accordingly). Additionally, it does so at the level of its written and aural, embodied language practices and distinct usage of linguistic and interpersonal subject/object relations, in its complicated rethinking of domestic spaces and feminine concerns, as well as at the level of its writing and reading from the perspective of a lesbian and expatriate living beside proscribed heterosexist orientations and outside national, domestic space, yet writing about national identities.

Recent twenty-first century digital literary writing by Borsuk and Bouse and Mencía is similarly self-reflexive and multi-leveled in its engagement with literary writing as a co-productive practice that orients readers and writers to lived space according to physical, material, linguistic, subjective, cultural, and affective registers. Amaranth Borsuk and Brad Bouse's 2012 augmented-reality poem, *Between Page and Screen* quite literally occupies, figures, and examines the unperceived spaces between print and digital writing practices, opened up by digital book technologies, machine-readable QR (quick-response) codes, digital interfaces, and visual poetry. *Between Page and Screen* is a print codex book that features black and white, machine-readable QR codes on each of its sixteen pages. Reading this print book involves accessing the book's web site online, holding each page in front of the computer web-cam, and then reading

161 Questions of lived space have been central to discussions of tactical media practices and of locative media works. This article hopes to extend and multiply these considerations, somewhat, by illustrating multiple ways in which e-poetics go "beyond the screen" and reconceive the spatial and temporal parameters and influence of writing in, across, and between digital spacetimes.

the animated, virtual text on each page as it is projected and dynamically unfolds in the space 'between' one's physical body, the hand-held book, its animated projection, and a real-time visual image of oneself reading that appears on the computer screen throughout this e-poetic process.

Devising digital language practices that render the unnoticed perceptual, tactile, technological, linguistic, symbolic, and affective relays between writers, books, screens, and embodied readers more tangible, *Between Page and Screen* physically situates its readers in this unnoticed, multipotent space of interplay between digital computers, interfaces, book technologies, language practices, and the media-specific material practices of reading and writing that are entangled amongst these, at once, physical, virtual, and symbolic "interface relations" (Drucker 2011). Pages and screens, as "interface relations," are understood as productive, differential practices that bring about material transformations in readers, writers, texts, code, and computers, as distinctly co-orchestrated agencies. *Between Page and Screen* actively engages its readers in this *multiagential space of performance*, reminding them that reading and writing are material, media-specific, time and context-dependent practices in space and time to which readers co-contribute in various circumscribed, though "multistable" (i.e., somewhat plastic, playful) ways (Ihde 2010, 13-14)..

Reading *Between Page and Screen* requires significant effort on the part of its readers and some dexterity as one discovers that holding the book upside-down projects the language-based visual animations right-side up. One also quickly realizes that even with perfect alignment and poise, the textual animations (whether the text is dynamic or appears as a static image) require a remarkable, fleeting co-orchestration of hand, book, body, screen, web-camera, web site, machine-reading, animated projection, and linguistic and visual understanding that one cannot easily stabilize for more than a moment or two. In this way, *Between Page and Screen* momentarily opens its multimodal, at once, visual, linguistic and tactile purview onto what it suggests is an ongoing, unfolding process of writing, reading, technics, and language practices. Reading *Between Page and Screen* shifts emphasis away from digital and print book technologies as apparently self-contained, material objects, and towards the languages and practices of reading and writing, and the distinct bodily orientations and intersubjective relations they open up in this complexly unfolding space 'between.'

The ongoing intertwining and interplay between the print book, with its latest page-based spatiotemporal practices and cultural meaning, and the digital screen with its computation-based, processual spacetimes are explicitly personified and examined through the poem's boisterous series of sparring love letters between "P" and "S." The actual format of their alternating letters initially seems to reinforce their personification of predominant characteristics of "page" and "screen." The letters take the page-based format of a print letter or, alternately, the dynamic screen-based, recursive visual animations we associate with more kinetic digital writing, yet these juxtapositions slowly reveal unnoticed commonalities and entanglements in every sense of the word. Most notably, in pursuing many of the Indo-European roots of the words page and screen through its wordplay, the poem underscores how *languages* dynamically and transformatively enter into material practices of reading and writing. Emergent and residual practices of reading and writing, and the performative, intersubjective spatial and spatialized relations these practices enable and constrain, are embedded and disembedded by the language we use to articulate and carry out these practices, by the "metaphors we live by," to borrow George Lakoff and Mark Johnson's conceptualizaton of how language materially orients and cognitively enframes and expresses our thinking and acting in the world. The Indo-European root of the word, *page*: *pag*, for instance, means to *fasten* or *join*, leading to words like *pax*, *pacify*, *appease*, *palus* (to stake to the ground), *pale*, *impale*, and the Latin *pagina*, which is a trellis or frame onto which vines were fastened that has clear similarities to the structure of the print page and its columns of text, like vines on a trellis. Of particular interest here is how the embedded language informing the word page continues to inform our conceptualization of reading and writing the pages of a book. These concepts implicitly inform these material practices and underwrite, if you will, the associated intersubjective orientations supposed to emerge from these media-specific, reading and writing practices. Playing with the Indo-European roots of *screen*, for instance, the e-poem projects an image of a shield in which there are two definitions of its root, "skirm": "to protect, to fight," and "to fight with a sword, or to shield." Skirm is the root of words such as scrimmage, skirmish, and Scaramouch, which also figure prominently in the e-poem. This visual depiction of a shield foregrounds the screen's longstanding status as a literal interface, while it simultaneously underscores the intersubjective orientations the screen with its, at once, physical and phenomenological orientations, rerealizes. The next letter written by Page directly challenges this understanding of the screen's functioning as a particularly divisive, oppositional kind of interface relation, insisting that "A screen is a shield and also a veil. It's sheer and can be shorn." In a later, friendly missive, S seems to concur, writing to P, "We share text's fleshy network- your trellis and my tendency to excoriate." Referring to the structuring of the print page as a "trellis" for its text (and, thus, directly invoking "pagina," a garden trellis or frame for vines, the Latin offshoot of page's root, *pagus*), the e-poem foregrounds the material organization of text in columns on the page, like vines on a trellis. In doing so, it reveals the centrality of embedded language to how we conceptualize print and digital practices of reading and writing and book technologies and the ongoing linguistic, material, and cultural relays between them. P replies, "That trellis is a metaphor – it props me up." This caddy response points to the material organization of the print page as a literal 'prop,' yet it also underscores the *metaphorical* status of this trellis or pagina as a symbolic *bridging across or bringing into relation or joining*, as linguistic metaphors are. The transposition of this trellis or pagina from gardening and the careful cultivation of vines to print textual practices and book technologies presages this latest bridging across or bringing into relation as language practices bring print books and digital screens into new relations. These "lines and vines that link us together," or language practices, as P later seems to recognize, *transform all participants* in the process. As language, poetics, book technologies, and media-specific practices selectively carry their embedded histories with them, they also, therefore, simultaneously (if paradoxically) open onto new possibilities of perception, spatiotemporal dynamics, poetics, and interactions.

Comparatively moving between the predominant languages, material practices, and spacetimes associated with print pages and digital screens, this e-poetic work restages what is often understood in oppositional, mutually exclusive terms as a contest between print books and digital screens (misperceived as distinct, self-contained technological objects), as "a *co-script* [my ital] posthaste postface" [because]: there is no postscript." This phrase is taken from one of S's more conciliatory letters to P, which includes a series of animated digital letters, P and S, tumbling down into a single pile together at the bottom of the screen. *Between Page and Screen* restages their encounters as a "co-script" between print-based language practices and digital writing at the level of its hybrid print and digital execution, at the level of its language and multimodal, visual, textual, and kinetic black and white poetics, as well as at the level of its reading and writing. It is also a co-authored "script" in that the agency of a solitary, disembodied writer or reader alone with a writing implement or a book is clearly re-distributed as a result of these emerging technological relays for writing and reading as well as by the e-poem's explicit co-authorship. In this way, *Between Page and Screen* tangibly revists and restages some of the unnoticed ways in which language, reading, and writing practices differentially enframe as well as co-realize a series of distinct assumptions about subjectivities, their authorship and other kinds of agency, and the lived space and intersubjective relations these culturally, historically, and medially distinct self (and other) regimens help realize and naturalize. Jessica Pressman directly addresses the questions raised by this "Posthuman Reader in Postprint Literature" (2010) as realized through e-poetic practices of writing such as *Between Page and Screen* in her recent reading of the e-poem.

Between Page and Screen and other e-poetic engagements with lived space actively reengage writing as a "multi-layered, distributed activity" (2010), to borrow N. Katherine Hayles' apt terms. They locate writing amidst human, technological, medial, and other nonhuman co-agencies. Importantly, and in keeping with prior feminist and queer literary re-orientations of lived space, their e-poetics explore and evidence the complex affective dimensions to this recalibration of both desire and agency through these computational, technological, medial, and linguistic reroutings. *Between Page and Screen*'s love letters seem to directly ask readers, writers, and computers what kinds of interrelations, as well as what kinds of writing and reading spaces these underappreciated, language-based spaces between page and screen might open onto? Similarly to other tactical feminist and queer engagements with writing spaces by Stein, Virginia Woolf (2014), Audre Lorde(2007), Luce Irigaray (1993), Hélène Cixous (1991), bell hooks (1999), Adrienne Rich (2002), Cherríe Moraga and Gloria Anzaldua (1983), Haryette Mullen (1986), and many, many others this augmented reality e-poem reconsiders how the intersubjective relations consolidated at and through such material practices of writing and reading serve to orient one's desires and self in particular, often explicitly oppositional, as well as proprietary, masculinist, and heterosexist ways, and to foreclose other possibilities. One of *Between Page and Screen*'s digital poetic lines includes the phrase, "A Rose is Eros by another name," directly invoking Stein's "Rose is a Rose is a Rose is a Rose" in which Stein, similarly, plays poetically and visually with the generative recursivity of language practices and their recursive, desiring orientations of desire.

Figure 1: Reading in the ſpace 'between.' Screenshot of *Between Page and Screen.*

Notably, the question of how computers and computational processes impact experiences of embodiment, lived space, and intersubjective relays of desire, affect, language, and agency (not necessarily or exclusively human) has been raised throughout the history of computing and has since been consolidated in unique fields such as Affective Computing, Ubiquitous Computing, Human Computer Interaction, and Computational Linguistics, among others. In 1951 Christopher Strachey and Alan Turing used the first stored program computer, Mark I, to run a combinatory love-letter writing program written by Strachey.[162] One of their computer-generated, co-authored letters, signed by M.U.C. (or Manchester University Computer) reads:

> *Darling Sweetheart,*
> *You are my avid fellow feeling. My affection curiously clings to your passionate wish. My liking yearns for your heart. You are my wistful sympathy; my tender liking.*
> *Yours beautifully, M. U. C.* (Strachey 1954, 26)

Its playful tone, though not its recognizably hackneyed language, is reminiscent of the desiring letters between P and S. The program was simply substituting adjectives, adverbs, verbs, and nouns (selected randomly from a list compiled from *Roget's Thesaurus*) into its pre-formed structure, like an automated *Mad Libs* game. In a journal article published at the time, Strachey acknowledges the simplicity of the program and the computer's rote following of the program's instructions, undercutting any illusion that the computer is "thinking," yet he and Turing were intrigued by the combinatory potential and output of the program, some unexpected results, and clearly appreciated the letters' strange humor. *Between Page and Screen*, i'd argue, like Strachey and Turing's automated love letters sixty-five years prior, creatively engages today's emerging relays between computer programming, writing and lived space to pursue these questions about how computation might co-inform lived space with a difference, eliciting and realizing various kinds of desire for connection and impacting the kinds of intersubjective relations and agency these writing and reading practices open onto.

Their creative interventions into the potential reroutings of human language, desire, and agency through computational processes, technologies, and digital writing go well beyond projecting human attributes across an untroubled human/computational divide. Strachey's love letter generating program, in simulating prior practices

162 Christopher Strachey published an article on this combinatory love letter writing program, "The 'Thinking' Machine" (1954). Andrew Hodges discusses the love letter writing program in his biography of Turing (1992. p. 478). Also, For recent critical readings of the love-letter generator see Wardrip-Fruin (2011).

of writing love letters (equally reliant on highly conventionalized language, modes of address, and exuberant, wistful affect) comparatively aligns and undercuts both the prior human conventions of love letter writing and the computer's equally constrained, yet no less pleasurable, formal, rule-bound, yet variable production of desire. Biographers and literary theorists note that Strachey's motivation to devise this love letter-writing program, in which both addressee and author remain genderless and nameless (aside from the unexplained acronym M.U.C), might have been informed by his and by Turing's experiences living as homosexuals under strict public and legal sanction. Turing publicly acknowledged his homosexuality and, as a result, was later subjected, by the court, to hormone treatment as a "remedy." The pleasure that Strachey and Turing took in this program according to Turing's biographer, Andrew Hodges, suggests that perhaps this was a subtle way of seeking out alternative ways to express this socially unsanctioned, forbidden desire between men via this early computer program and its automated writing process. Whatever playful and creative aspirations prompted these love letters, or *Between Page and Screen*'s e-poetic missives on the affectively-charged medial and linguistic entanglements catalyzing and transforming writing and reading practices, both works are particularly concerned with the potential reroutings of agency and desire as computational processes and digital writing practices alter prior writing practices and their implicit enframings of the human self as unique, standalone, gendered, proprietary, physically self-contained, and as occupying an absolute space and/or time separate from these multiagential technological, literary, and reading practices.

LIVED SPACES "BETWEEN"

Importantly, these digital writing practices explore these lived spaces "between" in their capacity to open up culturally, historically, technically, and affectively in-formed reroutings of agency and desire, not in order to return to some more absolutely absolute human body or bodily experience that they imagine unchanged by these technics. Hand-held, more tangibly performative, bodily responsive, mobile and locative digital technologies have been heralded and pursued by cyberfeminists and designers, alike, for their potential to reprivilege and at times, it is assumed, to recapture the material, tactile, haptic dimensions of our selves, cultural practices, social action, and lifeworlds in all their dynamic agency and complexity. These are the material, spatial, embodied, affective dimensions to self experience that a Cartesian, liberal humanist understanding of subjectivity has feminized, subordinated, and opposed to a superiorly abstract, temporal, disembodied, rational cogito gendered masculine and racialized as white Euro-American. *Between Page and Screen* and other recent digital literary writing reveals how computation-based digital writing spaces do not, in fact, reprivilege or return us to the material specificities of space, time, embodiment, and touch-based interaction. Instead, as dynamic, materially-realized and time-based practices, digital writing spaces and neoliberal code/space, more broadly, effectively contravene this Cartesian, oppositional understanding of space and time and its affiliated gendered, heterosexist differentiations of matter and meaning, feminine and masculine, embodiment and cognition, black and white. The e-poem's comparative stance towards print analog and computation-based writing as technics of the human that co-produce culturally and historically distinct modes of gendered and sexualized, intersubjective relation and dynamic spacetimes, I'll suggest, engages and operationalizes the comparative to open onto a queer space between, beside, alongside predominant computational practices and codespaces, as did Turing and Strachey's comparative, computational writing experiment. The between or "beside," as Eve Kosofsky Sedgwick famously states in *Touching Feeling*, comprises a wide range of desiring, identifying, representing, repelling, paralleling, differentiating, rivaling, leaning, twisting, mimicking, withdrawing, attracting, aggressing, warping, and other relations" (2003, 14). Rather than a third, autonomous space, *Between Page and Screen* unfolds a comparative and co-scripted spacetime 'between' that emerges through this interplay of readers' embodied reading, print book conventions, computer and web-based machine reading, augmented reality text and animated poetry, and generative language change. *Between Page and Screen* encourages readers' self-aware engagement with the combinations of material, virtual, symbolic, linguistic, and computational that now regularly co-inform our experience and knowledges of lived space. It generates appreciation of readers' desire and agency as it feeds into and is transformed in unexpected, still undecided ways by these relays. It elicits alternate modes and means of inhabiting and co-orchestrating lived spaces 'between' digital and analog spacetimes and imagining the intersubjective relations they currently and might otherwise afford.

The e-poem's attention to digital technologies' and interface relations' influences on lived space, to how they differentially encourage subjects to feel good and 'feel together, enhancing (inter)subjective experiences and identifications of many sorts in rewarding, pleasurable ways is, equally, a primary concern of contemporary digital culture, the affective economies currently driving social media and computing today, neoliberal political economies, and their dynamic, processual "architectures of flow" (Knorr-Cetina). A recent series of Apple television and print ads, "Designed by Apple in California," emphasize their defining design principles, opening with the line, "*The First Thing We Ask is… How do we Want people to feel?... Delight. Surprise. Love. Connection… Then we begin to craft around our intention*" (see Figure 2).

Between Page and Screen's (re)turn to the embodied, desiring reader and its awareness of how digital writing practices performatively inform lived space has to be read in the context of this broadscale reprivileging of affective experience and the dynamic time and context-dependent interrelations multimodal digital writing, social media, and dynamic codespace involve us in. The web-based version of this Apple ad campaign includes images of ebullient Apple users in a variety of urban settings that change their racial, cultural, and geographic composition, depending on readers' geographic location, as I discovered accessing this site from Puerto Rico rather than NY. What differentiates *Between Page and Screen* is, therefore, not its concern with desire, agency, and authorship at the interface, per se, but its multiagential understanding of these emergent relays and its efforts to creatively imagine possibilities that might orient readers and writers in unfamiliar ways. It strives to make room (excuse the overdue pun) for more complex experimentation, cross-medial play, and language practices that counter predominant conventions of self-oriented, consumption-based, superficially multicultural "feeling together," and identity-centered control via brand identification, economic mobility, or heterosexist union in the name of (re)production.

Figure 2 "Designed by Apple in California" ad series."

Between Page and Screen literally engages readers in self-reflection on how one co-reads and co-performs lived space and intersubjective relations in complex relation to technologies of language, to poetics, to books, to screens, and to global late capitalist political economies today. In this way, it breaks readers away from the predominant subject-object relations encouraged by hegemonic practices of print and digital reading and writing, through its performative reading as a "co-script." And this is a "co-script" that equally reapproaches the gendered, oppositional intersubjective interface relations these reading and writing practices materially and linguistically engender, rereading predominant semantics of fighting, shielding or joining and appeasing so as to recognize mutual points of entanglement and overlap that complicate and compromise these too easy, binary gender, heterosexist oppositions.

The, at once, comparative and co-scripted lived spacetime *between*, which Borsuk and Bouse explicitly embrace in their title, evidences and tactically engages with these unperceived, nonCartesian, non-oppositional, noninstrumental dimensions to practices of reading and writing that digital writing practices catalyze, though with, as yet, unclear effects. In this way, *Between Page and Screen* registers emergent spatiotemporal orientations introduced by digital spacetimes and cultures that, even as they may significantly contravene former gendered and sexed oppositions and Cartesian understandings of space and time and the or material and cultural domains they segregate, do not necessarily serve feminist ends or signify more enabling spatial architectures or intersubjective relations.

Between Page and Screen, among other e-poetic engagements with digital scenes of writing and their ongoing, material time and context-dependent, performative procesess are part and parcel of a much larger late capitalist reanimation of space that preoccupies itself with time and context-dependent and responsive, material and cultural specificities and frequently disregards Cartesian and Euclidean coordinates in favor of individualized, frame-specific flows. As critical geographer K. Knorr Cetina stresses, in these computation-based "architectures of flow," "static representation becomes subordinated to flow" as a result of the computationally-based, rapid, continuous, recursive calculations.

> In a flow-world…the content itself is processual—a "melt" of material that is continuously in flux, and that exists only as it is being projected forward and calls forth participants' reactions to the flux. Only "frames," it would seem, for example, the frames that computer screens represent in a financial market, are pre-supposed in this flow-world. The content, the entire constellation of things that pass as the referential context wherein some action takes place, is not separate from the totality of ongoing activities. (2003, 4)

The prominence of time, context, and reader-dependent flows in computation-based digital spacetimes calls into question and actively contravenes former boundaries between subjects and objects, readers and texts, and between temporal processes and their spatial background, which were often formerly concieved as absolute, unchanging, and self-contained spaces. *Between Page and Screen*, and other recent e-poetics, participate in digital spacetimes' broader reanimation of space and its reprivileging of dynamic, responsive, spatiotemporal flows, yet they also, I'd argue, tactically engage these spatiotemporal processes and screen-based parameters to quite distinct and distinctly self-reflexive and multistable ends. The "processual melt" of hegemonic "architectures of flow," for instance, typically elicits readers'/viewers' participation in generating and processing specific kinds of information and experiences in real time, while using those queries to generate more information about those readers/viewers and their behavior in order to tailor their processing of information and to further involve readers/viewers in these valuable networks of information retrieval, processing, feedback, and the consumption-driven sharing of experience. The intersubjective relays and circulations afforded by digital language practices, touch-based and place-based, mobile interfaces, real-time, responsive bodily interaction in predominant late capitalist codespace and social media are, thus, circumscribed to very familiar individualistic and consumerist meanings and ends, though not always used in these ways. *Between Page and Screen*, while similarly processual, materially self-aware, and invested in generating and enabling co-orchestrated, physically and affectively responsive context and time-dependent practices, situates and explores its visceral, yet intangible, fleeting spacetime "between" and beside these most typical objects and modes of consumerist, socially-mandated capture. It tactically opens readers to unnoticed intersubjective and perceptual possibilities as these interface relations become differently and differentially sensitive to material bodies, times, and places. Its e-poetic virtualization of the space "between" actively destabilizes the identity of the reader, the text, material and linguistic modes of address, and even one's proprioceptive perception as one holds the book in front of the web camera and rereads one's precarious, momentarily stabilized image and moving text on the screen.

EMERGING SPACETIMES AND SUBJECTS OF DIGITAL WRITING: A PORTRAIT OF THE ARTIST AS A WOMAN WRITING CODE/SPACE

María Mencía's *Transient Self-Portrait* unfolds an equally circumspect, insightful critical engagement with digital writing as a multiagential, performative practice through which historically, culturally, linguistically, and technologically distinct subjectivities, languages, and orientations emerge and are rerealized. *Transient Self-Portrait* reconsiders and, itself, reorients the famed ephemerality and dynamism of code/spaces and digital writing by reapproaching them in relation to prior linguistic, visual, and sensory-rich practices of self writing and portraiture similarly concerned to offset or momentarily capture the ephemerality of material life and the passage of time through their writing. This e-poetic work is concerned, as is *Between Page and Screen*, with the question of how digital writing inflects, transforms, and can creatively retrace, perhaps even reorient the most predominant intersubjective or perhaps, in this context, (inter)selfie relays consolidated through reading, writing, and digital spaces. Its title screen features a portrait of the artist that, under closer examination, is revealed to be comprised of an impressionistic array of small nonlinear, spatially distributed alphabetic letters, as opposed to the typically imperceptible, uniform square pixels that more typically make up digital images (or readable lines of digital typography, for that matter). While evoking the multimodality of digital writing spaces and their multiply encoded, visual, linguistic, aural, tactile, physically responsive capacities, the title screen introduces *Transient Self-Portrait*'s overall concern with writing and self writing as a palimpsest on and through which self experience is recursively figured and refigured and intersubjective relations and modes of address are visually, linguistically, aurally, physically, and affectively reoriented, as well.

Reinforcing this sense of its digital writing space as a performative space of self figuring, self inquiry, and self formation, the title screen tells the reader:

> YOU ARE PART OF THIS POEM
> AS YOU READ THE POEM
> THIS POEM READS YOU
> IT SPEAKS TO YOU
> IT NEEDS TO BE CARESSED
> IT NEEDS LIGHT
> YOU NEED TO SPEAK TO IT
> YOU ARE ITS INK
> ITS COLOUR
> ITS SURFACE
> PLAY WITH IT

This opening text invokes the reciprocal role writing spaces play, serving as a primary 'technology of the self' (Foucault) that both orients writers and readers to a self "image" and, in the process, co-realizes distinct modes of relating to others. "You," as the poem's addressee and reader, are a part of the poem in that portrayals of self and self portraiture, such as this e-poem's, enter into their readers' own sense of acceptable modes of digital self-presentation and self-experience. Just think of how distinct and viral recent representational practices surrounding the "selfie" have become, an integral part of self and identity formation today. In this e-poetic self-portrait, readers are "its ink," "its colour," "its surface" in that this e-poem will similarly render certain aspects of self experience legible and meaningful at the expense of other dimensions. Its use of all capital letters, which are used exclusively for emphasis—if not outright shouting—in digital contexts further reinforces the sense that digital self writing interpellates readers and writers in new ways worth inquiring into. On the other hand, while this poem "reads you" and "speaks to you" and, thus, "orients "you" through its linguistically, culturally, historically, and medially particular second-person addresses in three main sections, it incites its readers to "play with it," to recognize that "you are its ink," "its color," "its surface," and, thus, also not without significant agency in co-realizing what is a multiply, as well as comparatively, transient "self" portrait to which readers of the e-poem can themselves contribute: physically, aurally, visually, and affectively in notable ways.

It is a multiply comparative and transient self-portrait and poem that unfolds through its own and readers' e-poetic rereadings. There are three main sections to the e-poem following this title page. The first section centers on the poem, "En tanto que de rosa azucena" by Garcilaso de La Vega, a Spanish poet writing in the 16th century, the second section of the poem centers on an influential rereading of this first poem by the 17th century Spanish poet, Luís de Góngora in his inventive homage to his predecessor, "Mientras por competir con tu cabello." The third section of the poem recursively reapproaches and reembeds these prior literary portraits/self writing practices in the context of digital writing technologies and their practices of self representation, featuring a four-dimensional digital writing space that projects an image of the reader in front of their web camera and computer screen, which is manipulable in real-time, while a feminine, computer-generated voice recites what appear to be lines of the actual digital code generating the multiple poetic layers of this e-poem in real-time.

Transient Self-Portrait's comparative inquiries into writing as a literary orientation device and self portraiture/self writing as an influential palimpsest for self experience are centered on a series of "love" poems, as are *Between Page and Screen*'s e-poems. These 16th and 17th century poems, in spite of significant differences, are both sonnets written by a masculine writer to his feminine reader positioned as his object of desire. Sonnets are, of course, an encoded writing form, following a preset rhyme scheme and meter. *Transient Self-Portrait*, thus, comparatively flags the sonnet's mathematical and automated formal dimensions as a pre-digital convention of writing and reading.[163] In addition to the sonnets' encoding according to predetermined, culturally resonant rhyme scheme and meter, these poems' intertextuality provides another level of transformative encoding and recoding. Góngora famously takes up La Vega's modes of address and overarching concern with the transience of feminine beauty, masculine desire, and material life, more generally, while creatively readdressing these concerns to his present time and context of writing. Notably, both sonnets realize a distinctly gendered, oppositional, heterosexist scene of writing in which masculine writers (and masculine voices in the e-poem's aural rereading) render the image of their reader and addressee, in language, through a gendered second-person address to her as a time-bound object of (fading) beauty.

Transient Self-Portrait tactically foregrounds the very question of agency at such scenes of writing by documenting this historic absence or relative silence of women and of their agency from the scenes of their own self-depiction and, relatedly, in exploring their own desires. Here the broader question of what happens to agency and desire at multiagential scenes of digital writing, mentioned above, resonates in complex ways with prior delimitations of self writing, portraiture, and authorship. This e-poem adds another layer of intertextuality to these prior two poems through its own encoding and recoding of their sonnets as differently, yet equally transient *self portraits*. Situating contemporary self writing and portraiture enabled by digital code/space within this wider historical, cultural, and linguistic context, *Transient Self-Portrait* suggests how writing, as an interface relation, is always compromised and enabled in different ways by socially and culturally hegemonic technologies of self, and allowable, media-specific modes of linguistic, visual, aural, tactile, and affective address and modes of interrelation.

Through its comparative juxtaposition of these three sections of the poem and their distinct rereadings of these love poems, *Transient Self-Portrait* unfolds a portrait of the artist as a woman writing code/space that creatively rereads, reembeds, and reorients the prior, masculinist and male-authored literary portraits and their privileged modes of affectively-charged address and language from within a similarly, though differently, masculinist code/space. Situating its own digital "transient self portrait" amidst these prior sonnets written by male poets to their feminine objects of desire, the e-poem slyly intimates that these prior poems were likely more reflective of their male authors' self images and desires than they were at registering or depicting those of

163 Oulipo writers also engaged the sonnet as a resource in the mid-twentieth century in light of these underlying similarities and useful contrasts with combinatory computation-based writing.

the women they were addressing. The sonnets were, in other words, self portraits that reflect an image of their masculine authors back to them.

Transient Self-Portrait implicitly confronts readers with the question, "Is digital code/space, in this respect, much different in its privileged encoding of masculinist desires, agency, and self image?" Notably, the third, most contemporary, digitally-inclined section of the poem is, itself, far from unconstrained or without formal rules or conventions. Although its voice is noticeably feminine, it is computer-generated, with an unnerving, uniformity of tone and clearly automated recitation of the lines of digital code the program is in the process of executing.

In this way, it conveys a continued dis-ease with present day, multimodal, digital practices of self-portraiture and writing, even or especially as they may seem to literally give "voice" to women and renewed prominence to historically "feminine" senses of aurality, touch, and spatiality in potentially promising ways. Its comparative rereading of contemporary digital writing and code/space alerts readers and writers to the constraints and affordances of digital writing, as these continue to inform and enframe intersubjective experience, in spite of significant shifts.

Figure 3: "Embodied Codespace in Real Time." Screenshot from third stage of *Transient Self-Portrait*.

At the same time that it registers the politics and technics of self presentation, past and present, I'd suggest that *Transient Self-Portrait* identifies and leans its readers towards the, as yet unrealized, potential of digital writing in its comparative rendering of self-portraiture and self writing beside prior modes of self writing. All three levels of the e-poem are equally, if differently "transient," calling into question self writing and portraiture as mnemonic devices and practices aimed at preserving and stabilizing self experience against this very flow of time. The comparative, embedded, mutually informing and transformative levels to this writing palimpsest open onto a multileveled scene of self writing, which recasts writing as a performative, multiagential practice that reads and writes at once. Its contemporary scene of self writing and performative portraiture allows readers to enter into its reading and to self-reflexively consider how digital self writing practices and web cameras, sensing technologies such as Kinect, and voice-recognition software enter into and inform lived space. It involves its readers in a visceral, physical rereading of these prior sonnets, which generates a crucial, comparative perspective, perhaps even locating readers, in this way, strangely "between these multileveled, multisensory poetic rereadings of self writing practices.

In asking readers to "play" with this fully transient, multileveled, intertextual poem and its rereadings, for instance, *Transient Self-Portrait* takes special advantage of the affordances of digital writing spaces to render the relays between language, media, spaces of representation, writing technologies, lived space, material embodiment, self image and their consequences more tangible, as *Between Page and Screen*, in its own ways, attempts to do. Its initial invitation to "play" with it is furthered in distinct ways in each of the subsequent sections of the poem, which each involve readers in distinct kinds of sensory interactions. In the first section, one's facial and bodily movements in front of the web camera are rendered on screen as a literal palimpsest against which the written text of Garcilaso de La Vega's poem, "En tanto que de rosa azucena," is slowly revealed. One's audible voice is the catalyst for the second section of the poem. As one reads aloud Luís de Góngora's "Mientras por competir con tu cabello" from the screen, more text appears and its colors alternate in response to one's tone, energy, and movement until the letters tumble into a heap and disappear from the screen altogether. The third section visually depicts the reader on the screen, as did the first, though this self image, generated in real time via the web camera, is now juxtaposed against a four-dimensional codespace in which one hears a computer-generated feminine voice read the text-based code underlying and co-realizing this process of self writing through the digital methods of linguistic, visual, and spatiotemporal encoding with which we are just beginning to become familiar. In this way, *Transient Self-Portrait* not only comments on the former, gendered poetic depictions of women as flawed, decaying, quite limited objects of masculine desire, it also underscores how self writing, itself, however paradoxically, functions as a transient, i.e., historically, culturally, cross-modal, and cross-medial spatiotemporal event that enters into our experiences of self and lived space in multiple, complex ways. Notably, these three layers to the poem are further de and re encoded in the alternate versions of the e-poem: their original Spanish language, and their French translation, in addition to the English version on which this essay focuses.

While none of these linguistically, culturally, historically, and technically- distinct language-based writing practices can overcome their material, cultural and historical conditions of existence or their spatiotemporal coordinates and orientations, per se, their comparative juxtaposition affords some greater awareness of their specific affordances and limits and their status as differential, though also similar encounters with and enframings of the transience of life, self experience, spatiotemporal flux, and language. Transience is, after all, a fundamental, though often unperceived 'background' to self experience. *Transient Self-Portrait*'s multilayered e-poem adeptly underscores the sensorial regimens, emphases, and spacetimes each period, poem, medium, technology, and language of self writing privileges and forgets as these inform experiences of gendered self, self experience, intersubjective interactions, and writing. They share in their encounter with "transience," which is itself a condition of being spatially and temporally "in between," critically reframing the digital's exclusive claim to spatiotemporal dynamism, flux, and flow. The distinct layers of this e-poem cast into relief the individual poems' media-specific, language-specific, culturally and historically distinct orientations to transience. In the case of La Vega and Góngora's sonnets, literary critics note the prominence of anaphoric relations between temporal expressions through their usage of words such as "mientras" and "en tanto que." These temporal expressions communicate a sense of temporal drift or transience, yet even more importantly, they establish an anaphoric relation between one temporal expression and its antecedent, leading times to be calculated, comparatively, by using the prior antecedent as a frame of reference. The sonnets' poetic senses and engagements with being 'in between' are accomplished through these anaphoric relations, which situate readers complexly "between" unfolding processes of self expression, material decline, and technical distortion. *Transient Self-Portrait*'s own e-poetics play upon the prior anaphoric temporal expressions, juxtaposing all these three, media-specific spatiotemporal self-portraits so that they serve as frames of reference, modify each other, and continue to unfold in complex spatiotemporal relations to this latest poem's contemporary digital context and vyings with transience. The third section of the e-poem, both similarly and quite differently, invokes contemporary spatiotemporal experiences of transience and being "in between." Listening to the computer program's processing of lines of code, reading those on screen, and manipulating the screen visually, readers experience a transience tied to being between the embodied space of reading, one's visual interface and interactions on screen, the computer program's reading of code, and the larger computational architectures, economies, artists, and material processes co-writing this codespace.

It is a complicated, or perhaps, coimplicated return to the aural, embodied, apparently feminine voice of computer-generated, digital writing spaces and their dynamic, multileveled practices of encoding spacetimes that *Transient Self-Portrait* involves readers in. Its tactical, e-poetic rereadings and reorientations of code/space, like *Between Page and Screen*'s, creatively register the challenges digital writing and computation and these "architectures of flow" pose to Cartesian understandings of absolute space and affiliated understandings of the self as an absolute, self-contained, abstract, singular, singularly gendered identity. These challenges have only increased since Strachey and Turing's time. Rather than continuing to oscillate between the prior gendered, spatiotemporal oppositions and a Cartesian understanding of matter and absolute space outside time, their e-poetic engagements with digital spacetimes generate new practice-based knowledges of digital language, computational processes, interfaces, and intersubjective relations that find comparative, exploratory, experimental ways to self-reflexively r(e)orient these transformative relays between writing, reading, books, physical and symbolic space, processes of computation, intersubjective experience, and the language practices and poetics that join them. In doing so, they bring forth untapped potential in the spaces and relays between digital spacetime, other dimensions of lived space, and performative practices of literary self writing. Their comparative writing practices work with, against, behind, beside, and between twenty-first century codespace, rigorously sidestepping the oppositional, critical methods of much twentieth century literature and criticism. In this way, they provide important, practice-based, immanent models for critical praxis that, because they register emergent spatiotemporal dynamics and interrelations characteristic of code/space, might open onto alternate ways to live through the lived spaces 'between.'

WORKS CITED

Ahmed, Sara. "Orientations Matter." In *New Materialisms: Ontology, Agency, and Politics*. eds. Diana Coole and Samantha Frost. Durham, NC and London, 2010. 234-257.

Anderson, Benedict. *Imagined Communities*. London: Verso Press, 1991.

Borsuk, Amaranth. Personal website. http://www.amaranthborsuk.com/

Borsuk, Amaranth and Brad Bouse. *Between Page and Screen*. NY: Siglio Press, 2012.

Cixous, Hélène. *Coming to Writing and Other Essays*, trans. Sarah Cornell, Deborah Jenson, Ann Liddle, and Susan Sellers. Cambridge: Harvard University Press, 1991.

Drucker, Johanna. "Humanities Approaches to Interface Theory." *Culture Machine* 12 (2011). www.culturemachine.net.

Góngora, Luís. Soneto CLXVI: "Mientras por competir con tu cabello." *Tapas Project.* http://tapasproject.org/gongora/sonetoclxviedicindigital/16624

Hawk, Byron, David M. Rieder, and Ollie Oviedo, ed. *Small Tech: The Culture of Digital Tools*. Minneapolis: University of Minnesota Press, 2008.

Hayles, N. Katherine. "RFID: Human Agency and Meaning in Information-Intensive Environments." *Beyond the Screen: Transformations of Literary Structures, Interfaces and Genres*, ed. Jörgen Schäfer and Peter Gendolla. Verlag, Bielefeld: Transcript, 2010. 95-122.

Hodges, Andrew. *Alan Turing: The Enigma*. London: Vintage Books, 1992.

hooks, bell. *Ain't I a woman: Black Women and Feminism*. NY: South End Press, 1999.

Ihde, Don. *Ironic Technics*. U.S.: Automatic Press, 2010.

Irigaray, Luce. *This Sex Which Is Not One*. Trans. Catherine Porter with Carolyn Burke. Ithaca, NY: Cornell University Press, 1993.

Kitchin, Rob and Martin Dodge. *Code/Space: Software and Everyday Life*. Cambridge, MA: MIT Press, 2011.

Knorr Cetina, K. "How Are Global Markets Global? The Architecture of a Flow World." Paper presented to the Economies at Large Conference, New York, November 2003.

de La Vega, Garcilaso. Soneto XXIII: "En tanto que de rosa azucena." *Centro Virtual Cervantes: 500 años de Garcilaso*. http://cvc.cervantes.es/actcult/garcilaso/versos/soneto09.htm

Lakoff, George and Mark Johnson. *Metaphors We Live By*. Chicago, IL, 2003.

Lemke, Thomas. "'The Birth of Biopolitics': Michel Foucault's Lecture at the Collège de France on Neo-liberal Governmentality." *Economy and Society* 30 (2): 190-207. May 2001, 203.

Lorde, Audre. *Sister Outsider: Essays and Speeches*. NY: Ten Speed Press, 1984, 2007.

Massey, Doreen. *For space*. London, Thousand Oaks, CA, New Delhi: Sage Publications, 2005.

May, Jon and Nigel Thrift, ed. Timespace: Geographies of Temporality. London and NY: Routledge Press, 2001.

Mencía, María. Personal website. http://www.mariamencia.com/

---. Transient Self-portrait (2012). Interactive online version available at http://www.mariamencia.com/pages/transientself_portrait.html.

Moraga, Cherríe and Gloria Anzaldua, This Bridge Called my Back: Writings by Radical Women of Color. 2nd edition (NY: Kitchen Table/Women of Color Press, 1983.

Mullen, Haryette. *Recyclopedia: Trimmings, S*PeRM**K*T, and Muse and Drudge*. St. Paul, MN: Graywolf Press, 2006.

Pressman, Jessica. "The Posthuman Reader in Postprint Literature: Between Page and Screen." *Frame: Journal of Literary Studies*. Utrecht, Netherlands, May 2015. 53-69.

Rich, Adrienne. *The Fact of A Doorframe: Poems 1950-2001*. NY: W.W. Norton Press, 2002.

Schäfer, Jörgen and Peter Gendolla. *Beyond the Screen: Transformations of Literary Structures, Interfaces and Genres*. Verlag, Bielefeld: Transcript, 2010.

Sedgwick, Eve Kosofsky. *Touching Feeling: Affect, Pedagogy, Performativity*. Durham, NC: Duke University Press, 2003.

Shackelford, Laura. "Surviving Codespace: Tracing Lived Space through Digital Literary Writing." *Women's Studies Quarterly: Survival*. 44: 122 (Spring/Summer 2016).

Stein, Gertrude. *Tender Buttons: Objects Food Rooms*. København and Los Angeles: Green Integer Press, 2002.

Strachey, Christopher. "The 'Thinking' Machine." *Encounter Art Journal* (October 1954), 25-31.

Sullivan, Nikki. "Somatechnics." *Postposttransexual: Keywords to a Twenty-First Century Transgender Studies: Transgender Studies Quarterly*. (1.1-2 2014). http://tsq.dukejournals.org/content/1/1-2/187.full

Wardrip-Fruin, Noah. "Digital Media Archaeology: Interpreting Computational Processes" in *Media Archaeology: Approaches, Applications, and Implications*. Erkki Huhtamo and Jussi Parikka, eds. Berkeley: University of California Press, 2011.

Woolf, Virginia. *A Room of One's Own*. 1928. NY: Snowball Publishing, 2014.

A Comparative Study of Shu Lea Cheang's *Brandon*

BY MAYA ZALBIDEA PANIAGUA

This essay offers a close reading of *Brandon* (1998), a hypermedia work by a prominent figure of new media art, Shu Lea Cheang. The metaphors of this hypermedia project explore sexual politics and present the problem of the ideal of the normative sexuality through real cases of transgendered and intersexual people. Cheang's artistic and poetic representations of how the imposition of normative sexuality destroys the subject will be explained using Judith Butler's theories of the body and the self. I will also use Jacques Lacan's theories to interpret in which sense might Cheang be using the concepts of "psychosis," the "Other," "ego," "symbolic," and "imaginary" to develop a systematic analysis of the work. This research shows that Shu Lea Cheang's Brandon is an artistic and literary hypermedia that pays homage to one of the figures who inspired trans and intersexual activism. It is also a text that fosters developments in queer theory. As a hypermedia text it challenges the normative idea of the self and how it is constructed through the apprehension of the self-image and the gendered body. Visual metaphors in Brandon invite spectators of new media art and readers of electronic literature to understand alternative sexualities and subjectivities.

The *Brandon* project by Shu Lea Cheang was originally unveiled on June 30th, 1998, by the Guggenheim Museum. She presented her first artistic project commissioned for the World Wide Web exploring issues of gender fusion and the techno-body in both public space and cyberspace. The project is presently online and can be read and watched freely.[164] *Brandon* will be analyzed to discuss how personal challenges of intersexuals and transsexuals subvert misogynist, homophobic and racist norms of oppression, and how the digital medium permits denunciation of abuses and permits freedom of expression without censorship. *Brandon* consists of digital images and hypertexts which make reference to real and fictional narratives of intersex and transsexual people whom society has discriminated against and constrained. Some of these people such as Brandon Teena were victims of violence and murder. However, Cheang's *Brandon* is not only a Web project about victims but rather a homage for those who, like Brandon Teena, fought against rules and conventions to follow their own needs. "The Website uses his story as a vehicle to explore the broader issues of gender identity and Internet phallocentrism; it interrogates discourses around the intersections of bodies and identities" (Bingaman, Sanders, and Zorach, 237).

164 http://brandon.guggenheim.org. Accessed December 21, 2016.

This web-based project also represents cyberspace as a symbolic place where identities can change without restrictions. According to Verena Kuni:

> the *Brandon* project thematizes the utopias and realities of transgressing gender boundaries, then it appears to be quite characteristic that as transgender subjects, their real and fictitious protagonists are frequently perceived by society as ‹monsters›—while they identify themselves in a positive way as cyborgs. (n.p.)[165]

Apart from using a cyborg identity, a figure popularized through Donna Haraway's philosophy, cyberspace is a convenient place to make reference to Brandon Teena's case because he is an icon for transsexual activism in the World Wide Web. Other real stories of victims of sexual assault on the Internet are remembered in the project. As a review of the project cites: "[t]aking this case into the environment of gender play and multi-identity of cyberspace, *Brandon* extends its case study to include other legal cases where gender ambiguity constitutes points of interrogation" ("Brandon: Bodies of Evidence," n.p.). In this essay I analyze the two interfaces that are currently online in the project: "Bigdoll" and "Roadtrip," as well as the following five hypermedia: "Brandon in transit," "JIM," "GARLAND," "BARBIN," and "VX." Some interfaces which used to be in the project but are currently offline will not be analyzed, these were called: "moo-play" and "panopticon" and these were netlinked to a forum used during the period of time in which the project was under construction.

The title of the project: *Brandon* makes reference to Brandon Teena, a 21-year-old transman from Nebraska, who was raped and murdered in a hate crime in 1993. In Lea Cheang's project the imagotype of the transsexual Brandon Teena embodies those intersexuals and transsexuals who were victims of hatred crimes. When we open the website we find a motion picture of a baby icon whose shape changes into the body of a man and in the end this man turns into a woman.

This image of a baby whose gender changes from male to female is representing the situation of an intersexual or transexual person who may be born with a determined sex but during his/her life begins to feel like a person of the opposite sex. The icons of public toilets symbolize how public institutions have determined the notion of two sexes: male and female. By clicking on the icon of the baby a collage appears.

It consists of a square with pictures and sentences making reference to transgender sexuality and especially to Brandon Teena's transsexuality. The set of images is

165 "Cyborg configurations as formations of (self-)creation in the imagination space of technological (re)production (II): The promises of monsters and posthuman anthropomorphisms, " Verena Kuni, accessed December 20th 2016. http://www.medienkunstnetz.de/themes/cyborg_bodies/mythical_bodies_II/scroll/.

full of symbolism of sexual organs: flowers represent female genitalia, the eggs make allusion to ovaries or testicles and there is a prosthetic penis that may represent one that Teena Brandon used to wear.

According to John M. Sloop, girls used to think that she was a man because she "stuffed socks into his shorts" or would "wear a dildo." There are also images of medical schemas representing how doctors analyze the human body and name its parts. There is even an image of the parts of a penis from a clinical analysis. Clicking on some of the images of the collage there is a hidden collage. Collages in Brandon produce the same effect on the spectator as Dada and Fluxus art: shock, repulsion and incomprehension, and like Dada and Fluxus artists new media artists like Shu Lea Cheang try to stir up scandal. In this collage an arrow whose shape is full of curves represents the tumultuous path of Brandon's life. The whole collage represents a fragmented human body. In "Electronic Literature and the Effects of Cyberspace on the Body," Xiana Sotelo and I explain my theory that in cyberspace bodies are fragmented, distorted and narcissist. Brandon's collage represents how bodies appears in cyberspace.

In one part of *Brandon*, the eyes of the body are reflected on a rear-view window. This is a metaphor of Brandon's conscious of "self," an allusion to Jacques Lacan's theory of the mirror stage. Jacques Lacan explained that the mirror stage "marks a decisive turning-point in the mental development of the child. In the second place, it typifies an essential libidinal relationship with the body image." The rear-view window symbolizes that Brandon's identity is in constant transition, his self is travelling as if it were on a highway. If we look at the hidden collage in the "Bigdoll" interface in detail we will realize that there is a prosthetic arm and a prosthetic leg which symbolize how body organs can be restored artificially.

The prosthetic leg is an allusion to the figure of the cyborg in cyberspace. In the middle of the collage there is a chastity belt, an image of an ambiguous small penis or red vagina and a medical graphic of a pink phallus at the bottom. These hybrid sexes represent the existence of a double sex and red color is a clear symbol of blood. Blood evokes menstruation or a gash in genitalia. This symbol might be an allusion to Brandon Teena's rape. Clicking on several images of the collage reveals the "Roadtrip" interface. This road symbolizes Brandon's trip when he moved from Lincoln to Falls City in order to find a place where nobody knew that she had female genitalia. At the same time the road trip can be seen as a metaphor of the paths followed by users in cyberspace. In this interface, there is an image of a boy who looks like Brandon and the title is: "Brandon in Transit." The use of the word "transit" here refers to his/her condition as a transsexual in transition, a state in which, according to Judith Butler: "Identity is in the process of being achieved" (142).

Clicking on "Brandon in Transit" reaches the hypertext "Fiona McGreggor" in which a narrator tells an imaginary story in which he meets Brandon. He explains that he read about Brandon's murder and when he comments that he was raped he automatically changes the gender of Brandon and starts to use the pronoun "her" instead of "him" in a sexist way, as if only women could be raped. At the end the narrator's discourse turns into Brandon's imaginary discourse: "Brandon returns, we are all haunted. The indistinctness of his voice, embroidering his pauses words chosen by others. Saying: "All I ever wanted was to be a boy. I just wanted to be normal, find a woman and love her, live my life" (Cheang). The name written at the end of the hypertext is Fiona McGregor, the author of this hypertext, one of the artists who collaborated to create *Brandon*. The scroll moves automatically and the reader continues clicking on other images to find another hypermedia. This time it is a collage with a Dada style like the previous one. There is a square with an image of a hand with a cigarette and the picture of a black man smiling. By clicking on the link the destination node is a hypermedia about a woman, Annie Lee Grant, who posed as a man for economic interests. The following image shows another transgendered woman, a she-male wearing a hat. This is a picture of Elvira Mugarietta, a woman who was born female but she passed as a man between 1892 and 1936 becoming first a journalist and later a soldier. Just like Brandon she used false identities and was officially detained several times. According to William N. Eskridge:

> There was nothing new about Mugarietta [...] Fairies had cavorted in New York City before 1890; women passed as men and married other women throughout the modern era. What was new was the publicness and self-consciousness of their deviation from male and female roles, and society's anxious perception that many people shared their inclinations. (17-18)

In "Garland," the reader learns that Elvira's husband hypnotized her so that she could not speak, the spell worked and she had to travel the country using a paper and a pen to communicate. She wrote letters to her husband begging him to release her from the hypnotic spell, then: "he promised to meet her in Oakland, when she should be dressed in female attire, and he would break the spell."

The images of the black person hiding her mouth and the double teeth on the left symbolize Elvira's incapability to speak.

By clicking on the right picture of the black person wearing a hat we will enter into another hypermedia "Under a hypnotic spell." A face of a black person represents Elvira looking at herself in a broken mirror.

This mirror represents Elvira's self-image which is damaged because of the hypnotic spell that her husband cast on her. In the following hypermedia the reader finds some incomprehensible graphics and a hypertext which reads: "Jacques Lacan Schema 1 a psychotic state of mind where Brandon meets Garland." The reader will act as a psychoanalyst of the characters. Like in other hypertext fictions

> the fact that the narrative takes the form of a hypertext influences the perception of the reader, who, like a psychoanalyst, has to find clues to understand the origin of the protagonist's psychological problems which are reflected in loss of the sense of reality and temporality.

Both, Garland and Brandon suffer from a psychotic state because they are punished by society for their transexuality. Psychosis in their case is a consequence of loss of freedom. In *Bodies that Matter* (1993) Judith Butler explains how the normative ideals of gender and sexuality are imposed by society and psychosis takes place as a response to censorship:

> Lacan maintained that sex is a symbolic position that one assumes under the threat of punishment, that is, a position one is constrained to assume, where those constraints are operative relations of cultural life [...] Psychosis appears not only as the prospect of losing the status of a subject, and, hence, of life within language, but as the terrorizing specter of coming under an unbearable censor, a death sentence of sorts. (Webster 2002, n.p.)

We find Lacanian terms in the hypermedia in a chaotic order: mirror, Other, ego, symbolic and imaginary.

This anarchic drawing full of crossing outs and the broken mirror of the previous hypermedia make allusion to Lacanian theory of the mirror stage.

At the beginning of the development of Jacques Lacan's theory of the mirror stage he pointed out that the mirror stage is part of an infant's development from the ages of six to eighteen months. Looking at himself/herself in the mirror the child acquires the dual relationship (*relation duelle*) between the Ego and the body, which is always characterized by illusions of similarity and reciprocity, but also by the relation between the Imaginary and the Real. The visual identity given from the mirror supplies imaginary "wholeness" to the experience of a fragmentary real. In "The Cult of Lacan" (2002), Richard Webster explains that during the 1950s Lacan's concept of the mirror stage evolved: he no longer considered the mirror stage as a moment in the life of the infant, but as representing a permanent structure of subjectivity, or as the paradigm of

"Imaginary order." Garland's self image in the mirror is broken because she does not recognize herself with the image she sees in the mirror. Brandon and Garland have an imaginary conversation:

> Garland: How did you get here? Brandon: I'm having a sexual identity crisis. Garland: A sexual identity crisis? Brandon: I don't know what that is. Garland: How can you have a sexual identity crisis if you don't know what that is?

In this fictional conversation there is a strong criticism of the therapist's diagnosis of Brandon's sexual identity crisis. According to Carolyn Gage:

> Brandon's history would have included twelve pending charges of forgery, a possible charge of sexual assault on a minor, an untreated rape in October 1990, eating disorders, binge drinking, and an ongoing sexual relationship with a fourteen-year-old girl. (n.p.)

The therapist diagnosed a "gender identity disorder" and sent Brandon home with information about "gender reassignment" surgeries. However, the therapist did not take into account that Teena was a survivor of child abuse and what she suffered was rather a Complex Post Traumatic Stress Disorder, "a syndrome commonly associated with survivors of child abuse, and especially survivors of incest." Both Brandon and Garland suffered from homophobic treatments. Brandon Teena presented a record of years of untreated child sexual abuse, a report of a recent rape, an escalation of criminal activity, a history of multiple identities, sexual predation toward under-aged girls, extreme risk-taking behaviors, avoidance of medical care from fear of routine examinations, eating disorders, suicidal ideation, terror of being in a female body, expressed fear of men, preference for protective clothing, and compulsive bathing. Garland was hypnotized and repressed by her own husband for wearing man's clothes when the only reason why she did it was to be allowed to work in a male professions such as soldier.

In the hypermedia the readers can read: "What's the Name of your Father?" which is another allusion to Lacanian psychoanalytical theory. For Lacan, "The Name of the Father" is the fundamental signifier which permits signification to proceed normally. It confers identity on the subject, naming and positioning the subject within the symbolic order, and signifies the Oedipal prohibition, which is the "no" of the incest taboo. If this signifier is foreclosed, in the sense of being excluded from the symbolic order, the result is psychosis. Lacan described how the refusal of "The Name of the Father" operates as a drastic form of self-defense such that psychotic subject is then shut out of the symbolic. The subject refuses the rule of the signifier that names him/

her in the structure of the family. Garland and Brandon both refuse "The Name of the Father," they reinvent their names and identities, escaping from the symbolic order and moving to the imaginary order. Later on, there is another hypermedia in which there is information about Herculine Barbin and quotations from the biography of this transgendered person in the nineteenth century whose biography was published by Michel Foucault in 1980. Alexina B., later officially called Herculine Barbin (1838–1868), was a French intersex person who was treated as a female at birth but was designated a male identity after a physical examination. In *Brandon* there is a hypertext about a sensual chapter of Herculine Barbin in which Alexina embraces a girl whom she used to sleep with when she lived in an ursuline convent. In the images in motion there is an image of a stove symbolizing the gas stove where Herculine Barbin committed suicide. In this hypermedia there is also an image of Brandon with angel wings, Brandon has been historically appreciated by intersexual and transsexual communities, his real case was used as an impulse for transsexual and intersexual social movements in the US.

And finally, following the highway, the reader gets to the last hypermedia. The title has two consonants "VX," representing the acronym of the name Venus Xtravaganza. Gender theorist Judith Butler investigated on the case of Xtravaganza. Venus Xtravaganza was a transgender American man who saved money for sex reassignment surgery while earning a living as a prostitute in New York City. His life was taken by a violent man who mutilated him and killed him when he discovered that "she" was a man. This crime, like Brandon Teena's murder, was a consequence of transphobia. Butler asks, in her analysis of *Paris is Burning*, a documentary by Jennie Livingston about transgender communities in which Xtravaganza was featured, "whether parodying the dominant norms is enough to displace them; indeed, whether the denaturalization of gender cannot be the very vehicle for a reconsolidation of hegemonic norms" (1993, 338).

Having analyzed the symbolic systems in Brandon, as well as documentation on those novels and films about real cases of intersexual and transgendered people it makes reference to, we can conclude that this hypermedia investigates how the imposition of compulsory heterosexuality produces erroneous medical interventions and incites transphobic crimes. According to Judith Butler a way to stop transphobia could be to:

> Undo […] restrictively normative conceptions of sexual and gendered life. Lives and identities of individuals are not static, they are sometimes becoming, in some cases transsexual identity is in transition, it can even be always in transition. And not only the transsexual condition may change, also that one of any

kind of individual. (Butler 2004, page 80)

Shu Lea Cheang's *Brandon* pays homage to one of the figures who inspired trans and intersexual activism. It is a classic work of new media art and exemplary of how new media art has been influenced by the Dada and Fluxus movements. It also vindicates transgender rights by questioning the normative idea of the self and how it is constructed through images of the body. After a semiotic close reading of Brandon by Shu Lea Cheang completed with a comparative study of how psychoanalytical theories by Jacques Lacan and gender theories by Judith Butler are represented in Cheang's work, the result of these studies has been that this interactive hypermedia shows the visual metaphors of intersexual and transgender identities vindicating tolerant attitudes towards LGBIT people.

WORKS CITED

Bingaman, Amy, Lise Sanders and Rebecca Zorach. *Embodied Utopias: Gender, Social Change and the Modern Metropolis.* London: Routledge, 2002.

Butler, Judith. *Bodies that Matter: On the Discursive Limits of "Sex."* London: Routledge, 1993.

Cheang, Shu Lea. *Brandon.* Accessed August 18, 2015. http://brandon.guggenheim.org/.

Eskridge, William N. *Gaylaw: Challenging the Apartheid of the Closet.* Harvard University Press, 2002.

Foucault, Michel. *Herculine Barbin: Being the Recently Discovered Memoirs of a Nineteenth-century French Hermaphrodite.* Trans. McDougall, Richard. New York: Pantheon Books, 1980.

Gage, Carolyn. "Teena Brandon's Inconvenient Truth: Incest and Gender Dissonance." Accessed August 28, 2015. http://carolyngage.weebly.com/teena-brandons-inconvenient-truth.html.

Haraway, Donna J. *Simians, Cyborgs, and Women: The Reinvention of Nature.* New York and London: Routledge, 1990.

Kuni, Verena. "Mythical Bodies II Cyborg configurations as formations of (self-) creation in the imagination space of technological (re)production (II): The promises of monsters and posthuman anthropomorphisms." Accessed December 20th 2016. http://www.medienkunstnetz.de/themes/cyborg_bodies/mythical_bodies_II/scroll/

Lacan, Jacques. *Écrits: A Selection.* Éditions du Seuil. New York and London: Routledge, 1977.

Media Art Projects. "Brandon: Body of Evidence." *London Transgender Film and Video Festival.* Accessed 18 August 2015. http://mediaartprojects.org.uk/brandon.html.

Sloop, John M., "Disciplining the Transgendered: Brandon Teena, Public Representation, and Normativity," *Western Journal of Communication*, 64.2 (2000): 178. Accessed 29 August 2015. https://discoverarchive.vanderbilt.edu/bitstream/handle/1803/3189/SloopDiscipliningTheTransgendered64.2_2000.pdf?sequence=1.

Webster, Richard. "The Cult of Lacan: Freud, Lacan and the Mirror Stage." Accessed August 20, 2015. http://www.richardwebster.net/thecultoflacan.html.

Zalbidea Paniagua, Maya and Sotelo, Xiana. "Electronic Literature and the Effects of Cyberspace on the Body." *CLCWeb: Comparative Literature and Culture* 16.5: (2014): 5. Accessed August 28, 2015. http://docs.lib.purdue.edu/clcweb/vol16/iss5/12/.

Zalbidea Paniagua, Maya. "Psychoanalytic Interpretation of Blueberries by Susan Gibb." *Caracteres. Estudios culturales y críticos de la esfera digital* 3.1 (2014): 201-15. Accessed August 28, 2015. http://revistacaracteres.net/revista/vol3n-1mayo2014/psychoanalytic-blueberries/.

IV. THE MIGRATION OF FORMS

The Legacy of Judy Malloy

BY DENE GRIGAR

> When I began *Uncle Roger* in the mid-eighties, I was working with a database strategy which evolved from the coming together of experiments with non-sequential artists books, of a background which included database programming, and of the growing availability of personal computers. I wanted the reader to step into the narrator's mind, to experience the emerging/submerging of her memories. I thought of the work as a pool of information into which the reader would plunge repeatedly, emerging with a cumulative and individual picture. Rather than provide alternate plot turns and endings, I wanted to build up levels of meaning and to show many aspects of the story and characters. —Judy Malloy, "Interactive Stories, 2015"

NO NEED FOR INTRODUCTIONS

Judy Malloy is a pioneering American artist whose work dates back to the late 1960s. Educated at Middlebury College with training in literature, studio art, and art history, her work spans a broad spectrum of experimental art that includes artists books, installations, performances, non-digital writing, drawings, and electronic literature. Her work has been collected by highly respected libraries and art institutions. Her "database novel" *Uncle Roger* was highlighted in the Wall Street Journal's 1989 Centennial Edition on computing (Miller 1989) and is considered one of the first examples of participatory narratives as well as the first commercial work of electronic literature in the U. S. More recently she was cited as one of the "10 Women Who Changed the Tech Industry Forever" (Cole 2015) published in *The Daily Dot*. Awareness of her contributions to innovation is seen in the 2013 article in Mother Jones entitled "Ladies Last: 8 Inventions by Women That Dudes Got Credit For" (Murphy and Raja 2013). Digplanet lists her in a wide range of categories including an American web producer, digital media educator, American women poet, electronic literature, MUD developer, poet from Massachusetts, and a poet from California.

Even a cursory look at the Judy Malloy Papers listed on the online site for the David M. Rubenstein Rare Book & Manuscript Library at Duke University reveals an art practice spanning well over forty years. Visiting the library, one has access to twenty-seven boxes of Malloy's works, several that include her artists books and experimental work with card catalogs, maps, quilts, information art projects, and other materials that date from the 1970s and writings including poetry, a children's book, and essays, from 1968 onward. Her digital work coincides with the rise of computing, from the introduction of personal computing, to the shift from the net to the web, and in the case of *Uncle Roger* to the development of the computer industry. Along with her art, one also finds a draft of a speech she gave at XEROX PARC in the 1990s, an audio tape of an interview for KPFA in 1982, and a talk she gave at the MLA in 1992, all suggestive of her ongoing influence in and outside of the academic world. Collected also is her correspondence with other noted artists: John Cage, Jill Scott, Carl Loeffler, Sonya Rapoport, and Jim Rosenberg, to name just a few. The 13200 items comprising 15.6 linear feet of space collected at one of the country's best academic libraries[166] as well as recognition Malloy received in the popular press attest to the fact that Malloy has long been recognized as an experimental artist. That her work has been collected by the Museum of Modern Art/Franklin Furnace/Artists Book Collection[167] and at the Stanford University Library[168] speaks to a legacy respected for decades by those in the fields of fine and media art and to a career that has not been solely built on a production of and recognition for electronic literature, but rather on a wide range of art production and scholarship with which electronic literature scholars may be unaware.

Like a lot of electronic literature scholars, I came into contact Malloy's work in 1993 with the publication by Eastgate Systems, Inc. of her hypertext narrative, *its name was Penelope*. Two copies still reside in my personal collection of electronic literature that dates back to its original release.[169] Close to ten years later, I read Stephen Wilson's *Information Arts: Intersections of Art, Science, and Technology* (Wilson 2002), a book that includes numerous references to Malloy's media art practice, and I reviewed for *American Book Review* Malloy's own edited volume *Women, Art, & Technology*, a book that includes artists papers by Donna Cox, Lynn Hersheman, Pauline Oliveros, Char Davies, Allucquère Rosanne Stone, and twenty-one other female media artists. At that time in my career, I had just spent a sabbatical year studying interactive art with the Center for Advanced Inquiry in Interactive Art-Science, Technology, and Art Research (CaiiA-STAR, now called The Planetary Collegium) with Roy Ascott and Michael Punt and had been introduced to the work of many of the women Malloy included in her book. A few years following my book review I began a correspondence with Malloy that included an invitation to her to speak at the public lecture series, "Women on the Edge of the Future: Technology, Culture, and Education," for the Women's Studies Pro-

166 Rubenstein Library, http://library.duke.edu/rubenstein/findingaids/malloyjudy/.

167 See http://www.franklinfurnace.org/research/moma-FF-artist_book_collection.php.

168 See http://searchworks.stanford.edu/view/157646.

169 See The Electronic Literature Lab, http://dtc-wsuv.org/ell-catalog.

gram at Texas Woman's University where I had served on faculty and held affiliate status in that program. I had also included *Women, Art, and Technology* in the readings for a graduate course in Feminist Rhetoric I was scheduled to teach during that same time. From 2006 onward I continued to study Malloy's art and follow her website, Authoring Software (now Content | Code | Process). The opportunity came to write about *Uncle Roger* for Pathfinders, a project that resulted in the production of the multimedia eBook funded by the National Endowment for the Humanities, *Pathfinders: Documenting the Experience of Early Digital Literature* (Grigar and Moulthrop 2015) and in the forthcoming book of criticism also co-authored with Stuart Moulthrop, *Traversals: The Use of Preservation for Early Electronic Writing*. The visit to Malloy's office in the fall 2013 to interview her for Pathfinders provided the opportunity to see, first-hand, some of the early works of art she created and still held in her personal collection. Subsequent email correspondences provided me with further insights into her work. A visit in October 2015 to the Judy Malloy Papers at the Rubenstein Library made it possible for me to study her work more closely and see some of the art that I had previously only read about.

Figure1: Judy Malloy at her Princeton office with her work, Map, in October 2013.

Driving the development of the two books Moulthrop and I were writing that included Malloy was the impetus to make scholars aware of her far-reaching and rich legacy in regards to the production of *Uncle Roger*, the first commercially sold work of electronic literature and perhaps the first example of participatory work of fiction in the U. S. (Inman Berens 2014; Grigar and Moulthrop 2015). This essay, however, takes my research in a different direction: a discussion of Malloy as an experimental artist whose portfolio includes not just important works of electronic literature but also long history of fine art––information that would be helpful to scholars of electronic literature whose community includes, as Scott Rettberg argues, "*artists*, writers, and scholars" (my emphasis, Rettberg 2009). Because Malloy's output covers so many art forms and has spanned over forty years, my essay focuses on her early non-digital experimental art, particularly works with which she explores the "molecular" storytelling technique (Malloy 1991) that greatly influenced the development of *Uncle Roger*, its name was Penelope, and other non-sequential, digital works of electronic literature.[170]

Just as Malloy documented the media art of twenty-six female artists in *Women, Art, and Technology*, she has equally provided scholars with documentation of her own work. Her website, judymalloy.net, lists the many electronic books, visual documents, sculptural books, installations, landscape projects, and performances along with images of her works; Content | Code | Process (narrabase.net) also contains much good information for scholars. Essays she has written and interviews she has given over the years about her art also provide details of her output. Additionally, all three institutions collecting her work provide information about it online and so make it readily accessible to scholars. It is from these resources, along with material developed from the *Pathfinders* interview and private correspondence and information gleaned from the visit to the Rubenstein Library, upon which this essay draws its information.

EARLY NON-DIGITAL EXPERIMENTAL ART

Since 1976 Malloy has been featured in over sixty-five artists books exhibitions, performances, online events, and installations. While her early art had a strong presence on

170 Malloy discusses the influence of her early art upon her later digital work in her interview with Alice McKeever, "Digital Literature Pioneers: Judy Malloy on 'Narrabases,' 80s Silicon Valley and E-Literature Today." She says: "The ideas for the algorithms of *Uncle Roger* and for the use of small but complete units of narrative text that could be combined with other units of text to create a meaningful work of literature occurred in this way: in 1969 I was project head for the creation of an early library database at an aerospace company in Boulder, Colorado. To do this, I studied FORTRAN and Systems Analysis. From this knowledge came the vision to create a non-sequential literature. But at that time computers were often screen-less, room-filling machines. So in 1976 when I began trying to create a databased work of literature, I chose to make one of a kind artists' book. At first I used trays of catalog cards and push button electromechanical books to tell non-sequential stories with words and pictures. Then in 1986, a rare event (in anyone's life) occurred. Everything came together."

the West Coast, particularly in the Bay Area of San Francisco, it gained an international and national reputation through Malloy's participation in prestigious exhibits and installations. She was featured, for example, at Nucleus I, an exhibit at the XVI Biennial de Sao Paulo in Sao Paulo, Brazil (1981); the Book as Art exhibit (1981)—curated by Franklin Furnace—an exhibit that traveled to the Walker Museum (as well as the University of Arizona and the University of New Mexico art museums); Bookworks:1982, curated by Franklin Furnace and held at the National Library of Madrid, in Madrid, Spain; and Planetary Network–Roy Ascott, held at the Biennale of Venice (1986). As Malloy reports in her essay for *Leonardo* in 1991, "*Uncle Roger*, An Online Narrabase," her early work dates back to what she calls "visual books" produced beginning the mid-1970s. In fact, three boxes of slides, photocopies, and supporting material along with original art are available for study at the Judy Malloy Papers and include experiments with maps, quilts, card catalogs, electromechnical books, slide viewers, sculptural artists books, and artists books of photos and drawings.

The Map and *March at Last*, both produced circa 1976 and found among her papers at the Rubenstein Library, constitute some of Malloy's earliest artists books that were "keyed by graphic images and/or text" (Malloy 2015). *The Map* is a drawing produced with pen and ink on a large piece of rice paper that is then folded like a map. As Figure 1 shows, the work relies heavily on images and text and results in a kaleidoscope of color and shapes. The copy held at the Rubenstein Library comes with a folder, or sleeve, as one would find with a well-made street map. Likewise, *March at Last* is comprised of drawings that are then xeroxed and put together in the form of a quilt. While neither of these two works are listed among those on Malloy's personal website, they both fit her category of "visual documents" since they closely resemble the concept of the map included in *The OK Genetic Engineering Briefcase* (1991) she lists in this category. The 1991 work builds on a much earlier project, *OK Research* (1980-1982) that constitutes Malloy's "first technical information project" and explored "the role of technology in our society" (Malloy 1988). As she describes:

> As President of OK Research, I collected over 1,000 pieces of information by contacting scientific equipment vendors, visiting companies in Silicon Valley, going to trade shows and consulting technical libraries [...] . [T]he information included vendor literature, articles from technical journals, charts, graphs, photographs, technical reports, etc. These things were meant to serve as a source of ideas and materials not commonly considered by artists and others outside of the technical community, as well as a collection of source documents that would reflect the habits, resources and products of makers of technology. (Malloy 1988)

The 1991 work entails a wooden briefcase that contains "images, scrolls, documentation, and artists books" (Malloy, N.D., "Judy Malloy: Artists Books"). It was exhibited at (ART) WORD (ART), held at the Trojanowska Gallery in San Francisco from October 28-November 17, 1995. Thus, both *The Map* and *March at Last* may represent early experiments with maps and constructions of quilt-like panels of xeroxed images that came to be part of these two later works.

Malloy's card catalogs (See Figure 2), which followed her work with map and quilt forms, allowed her to continue to experiment with text and images for "simulat[ing] our fragmented, random, repetitious, non-sequential human memory patterns," an interest Malloy continued to explore with *Uncle Roger* in the late 1980s. In her essay, "*Uncle Roger*, an Online Narrabase," Malloy provides details of her card catalog experiments: works that entail "50-200 cards" that contain "text and images on 3 x 5 cards" and are "filed in metal trays." Organized by "dividers that 'key' the cards using small pictures or word phrases," these works provide a narrative intended to be read "non-sequentially." Text and images were combined so that "neither are the words descriptions of the pictures nor are the pictures illustrations of the words" (Malloy 1991).

Figure 2 : Judy Malloy at her Princeton office showing one of her card catalog works.

The Woodpile (1979), one of the first card catalog works Malloy produced, consisted of 165 3 x 5" cards of photos, drawings, or text, "keyed by small photos or drawings and filed in a metal tray" (Malloy 2004). It is listed both at the Rubenstein Library and documented on Malloy's personal website.[171] Other experiments with card catalogs collected at the Rubenstein Library include *Hearst Strip* (1980), exhibited along with *The Woodpile* at Location/Dislocation, held at the Berkeley Art Center from April

171 See the section on Malloy at Pathfinders, http://scalars.usc.edu/works/pathfinders.

25-May 23, 1980; *The TV Blew Up* (1980), described as "a poem made from fifty photos, drawings, and text" that are "filed in a plexiglass box" meant to be "read sequentially or hypertextually;" and *A Party in Woodside* (1987), a non-digital exploration of the kind of experimentation in storytelling Malloy had already begun with Versions 1.0-3.0 of *Uncle Roger*.[172] The Rubenstein Library holds artifacts from the 3x5, Visual Card Catalogs exhibition, held at Artworks, in Venice, CA, from September 18-October 18, 1979 and her single artist exhibition, Judy Malloy: Technical Information at SITE in San Francisco, held March 3-28,1981.[173] This last exhibit was partially funded by a National Endowment for the Arts grant.

The Woodpile and *Hearst Strip* were also featured in Malloy's 1987 article for the *Whole Earth Review*, entitled "Stories, Information as an Artists Material," as well as for the article she produced for *Leonardo* in 1991 (cited in this essay). Her output in this area of fine art is also reflected in the book Malloy published, entitled *500 3x5 Cards and Other Stories*, for the Mail Art Network in 1984. This work is held at the MoMA in its MoMA Manhattan Artists' Books, the Rubenstein Library, and Stanford University Library's Special Collection.[174]

Malloy's electromechanical books, or "electronic books" as Malloy also calls them (Malloy, N.D., "Judy Malloy: Artists Books"), involved narratives accessed via battery-operated address books. *I Don't Care if I Never Get Back* (1985) held at the Rubenstein Library is described as a "[s]equential photo-poem meant to be used in Radio Shack's battery operated address books that electro-mechanically moved a roll of paper on which you could write addresses." Rather than addresses, however, the work features photos "taken of people in the bleachers at Oakland A's games" ("The Judy Malloy Papers" N.D.). *Saturday* (1982) is a work Malloy describes as a "continuing series" of seven works that feature "alternat[ing] photographs of [her] cat killing and eating a bird and of her son eating a cake from a cake mix" (Malloy 1991). Malloy exhibited her electronic books in the 1994 exhibit, Photographic Book Art in the United States, that traveled to The Houston Center for Photography, Houston, Texas; CameraWork, San

172 As Malloy describes SITE: "Site (1976-1983) was an alternative space in San Francisco that allowed artists to conceive and present work in whatever way they chose. Technical Information was partially funded by the National Endowment for the Arts. The following people helped me install Technical Information: Richard Alpert, Penny Dienes, Bill Seely, Shirley Stuart, and the director of Site, Jill Scott" (Malloy 1988).

173 A black and white photograph of *The Woodpile* and *Hearst Strip* is found at http://www.well.com/user/jmalloy/uncleroger/uncle.html.

174 Malloy states in her interview with McKeever this fact, saying "I did not know about Ted Nelson's work until a few years after I had created *Uncle Roger*. I did know about the work of information specialists, such as Henriette Davidson Avram and Ralph H. Parker that enabled the creation of large systems of searchable computerized library catalogs. Occasionally I wonder why the heroes of library automation receive so little Digital Humanities credit" (McKeever).

Francisco, CA; and the Institute for Contemporary Art, New Orleans, LA. They were also featured in 1992 at the exhibit, Cross-Currents held at the Selby Gallery, Ringling School of Art and Design. This show traveled to the University of California Santa Barbara, Hayward State University, and other locations. They were also included in the 1991 Boundless Vision exhibition at the San Antonio Art Institute in San Antonio, TX, among other galleries, libraries, and museums.

What should interest electronic literature scholars about Malloy's card catalogs and electromechanical books is that they represent her early experiments with databases. As she writes in "Notes on *Uncle Roger*":

> Once in a while in a lifetime, everything comes together. In 1986, it was my experience in database programming, the idea I had been working on since 1977 of using molecular narrative units to create nonsequential narrative, the availability of personal computers that would make what I had been trying to do with "card catalog" artists books more feasible, and the arrival of ACEN, a place to create, publish and discuss the work. (Malloy 2015)

For those unfamiliar with *Uncle Roger*, it is a work comprised of three parts—"A Party in Woodside," "The Blue Notebook," and "Terminals—that Malloy published from 1986 to 1988. The first two of these Malloy performed on the Art Com Electronic Network (ACEN) as a serial novel in the form of seventy-five lexias delivered over the net. While developing the serial novel, what Moulthrop and I identify as Version 1.0 of *Uncle Roger*, Malloy had already begun work on Version 2.0, the interactive narrative for the net and Version 3.0, the boxed set of 5 ¼-inch floppy disks of artists' software created with Malloy's database narrative software, Narrabase, produced for use on Apple computers. This version introduced the third part of the story—100 lexias of random generated text. Version 4.0 was similar to Version 3.0 but was produced specifically for IBM computers in GW-BASIC for the purpose of art exhibitions. While Version 5.0 re-created *Uncle Roger* for the web as a hypertext narrative with changes to its content for a broad audience, Version 6.0 is the DosBox emulation that combines the database functionality of Version 4.0 with the content of Version 5.0.

For example, "A Party in Woodside" asks readers to choose one or two characters, places, or things among the twenty listed in a menu (See Figure 3). In response, one or more records associated with the selected item or items is evoked and then can be read. Each record constitutes part of the story—a chunk of information commonly referred to in conjunction with early digital writing as a lexia. Malloy had retained the seventy-five original lexias from Version 1.0 of *Uncle Roger* for subsequent versions of

"A Party in Woodside" and "The Blue Notebook," with some changes to the content beginning Version 5.0 to appeal to the larger web audience. As Malloy points out:

> When I began *Uncle Roger* in the mid-eighties, I was working with a database strategy which evolved from the coming together of experiments with non-sequential artists books, of a background which included database programming, and of the growing availability of personal computers. I wanted the reader to step into the narrator's mind, to experience the emerging/submerging of her memories. I thought of the work as a pool of information into which the reader would plunge repeatedly, emerging with a cumulative and individual picture. Rather than provide alternate plot turns and endings, I wanted to build up levels of meaning and to show many aspects of the story and characters. (Malloy 2004)

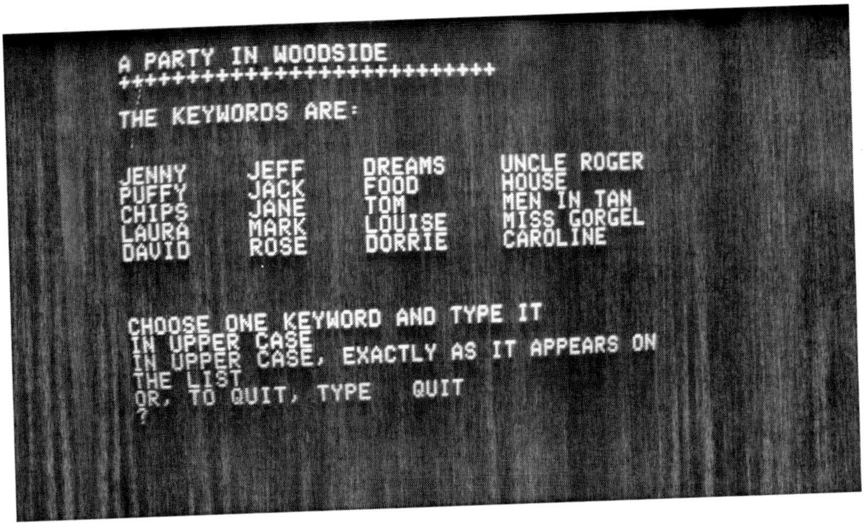

Figure 3: The menu for *Uncle Roger*, Version 4.0

Though she was not familiar with Ted Nelson's work or the hypertext theories that were driving the development of some of the authoring systems in the late 1980s,[175] Malloy arrived at non-sequential storytelling through experiments like her card catalogs that already "combined images and text in non-sequential ways." She sees them

175 Malloy states in her interview with McKeever this fact, saying "I did not know about Ted Nelson's work until a few years after I had created *Uncle Roger*. I did know about the work of information specialists, such as Henriette Davidson Avram and Ralph H. Parker that enabled the creation of large systems of searchable computerized library catalogs. Occasionally I wonder why the heroes of library automation receive so little Digital Humanities credit" (McKeever).

even now as "forerunners of the web-based works that [she] now create[s]" (Malloy, N.D., "Judy Malloy: Artists Books"). As she writes:

> [I]n Berkeley, I developed a series of artists books that combined words and images to create nonsequential narratives. These works that merged visual art and literature were exhibited internationally. They formed the basis for the electronic literature that is now my primary work. (Malloy, N.D., "Biography")

Malloy's long interest in information systems and non-sequential writing began after finishing her undergraduate degree and taking the position of Union Catalog editor for the Library of Congress (Malloy, N.D., "Biography"). There she became aware that libraries were adopting database systems. Years later in 1969 while working for the Ball Brothers in Denver, Colorado, she and a colleague created the company's computer database of engineering literature (Malloy 1991). Thus, it makes sense that many of Malloy's non-digital works of the 1970s and 1980s reflect this knowledge are imbued with an already developed artistic vision.

As evident from her many exhibits, performances, interviews, and writings dating back well over forty years, Malloy has enjoyed a legacy of which fine and media art scholars are and have been well aware. Her recognition in the area of electronic literature came about later after she had already established her name in the art world. We need to remember that Malloy's orbit circled the avant-garde art scene of the West Coast, a scene that included local and global members of The WELL and ACEN communities. Her involvement with the *Leonardo* community (also located for many years in San Francisco) as Associate Editor of its journal, *Leonardo: The International Society for the Arts, Sciences, and Technology*, as well as *Leonardo Electronic News*, and *FineArt Forum*, from 1988-1994, further enhanced her standing as an artist and intellectual. Her reputation gained national and international status because of her highly innovative works that, early on, went beyond traditional fine art. Her path did not cross that of East Coast electronic literature scholars until she published *its name was Penelope* with Eastgate Systems, Inc. in 1993, seventeen years after she completed *The Map* and *March at Last*. Thus, that Malloy was not well known widely to the electronic literature community until 1993 does not mean that she was obscure or that no one collected, read, or exhibited her work. It does however reflect a time when communication was less robust, and public channels like social media were not available for sharing information across communities and groups.

CALL TO ACTION

Much of the feminist scholarship in the 1980s and 1990s has focused on recovering print works by female authors that had become lost or gone unnoticed through time. Shari Benstock's *Women on the Left Bank* (1986) and Bonnie Kime Moore's *The Gender of Modernism* (1990) represent two such examples that focus specifically on female literary artists of the early 20th century. A decade later Malloy helped to highlight work by contemporary female media artists with the production of her book *Women, Art and Technology* (2003). More recent and important endeavors in the area of electronic literature by Jill Walker Rettberg and Kathi Inman Berens have focused on recovering Malloy's legacy. The work that scholars and artists must also share is documenting, that is, providing information about the code, content, functionality, descriptions of material artifacts, and other aspects about works of electronic literature. In this regard, Malloy is a model that so many scholars and artists should follow. She herself has migrated Version 4.0 of *Uncle Roger* to the web (Version 5.0) so that it is available to a large audience, and she has emulated Version 4.0 for use on desktops today. Additionally, she has donated her papers and copies of her art to the Rubenstein Library. MoMA and Stanford University Library have collected her work. Currently, she is re-creating the long lost Version 2.0 from newly found UNIX Shell Scripts so that this version of *Uncle Roger* can be experienced and documented. The time to document works of electronic literature and art is now before much of the artistic output of pre-web digital writing from the late 1980s to the mid-1990s becomes unable to be read and accessed because the platforms on which these works were produced are not longer available. It is particularly crucial to document works by female electronic literary artists, like Malloy, since they reflect women's participation in highly technical intellectual enterprises of the late 20th and early 21st centuries.

THE COLLECTIONS

Mentioned in the essay are three important institutions collecting Malloy's work. These speak to her status as a long established artist.

1. THE MUSEUM OF MODERN ART (MOMA) IS HOLDING TWENTY-FIVE WORKS AND OTHER MATERIALS:

http://tinyurl.com/nc88rcn

l0ve One (1998); link to the works' website

500 3 x 5 Cards (1980); MoMA Manhattan Artists' Books

500 3 x 5 Cards and Other Stories (1984); MoMA Manhattan Artists' Books

And Then (1980); MoMA Manhattan Artists' Books

Artist File: Miscellaneous Uncataloged Material (n.d.); MoMA Queens Artists Files
Bad Information (198?); MoMA Manhattan Artists' Books
The Big Zucchini (1981); MoMA Manhattan Artists' Books
Come Back Kitty, Kitty, Kitty (1979); MoMA Manhattan Artists' Books
Dallas Berkeley: Technical Difficulties (1981); MoMA Manhattan Artists' Books
Eschew Gluttony (1979); MoMA Manhattan Artists' Books
Franklin Furnace Artist File: Miscellaneous Uncataloged Material (n.d.); MoMA Queens Franklin Furnace Artist File
HLIV: Human Lust Inducing Virus (1984?); MoMA Manhattan Artists' Books
Honesty Is the Best Policy (1979); MoMA Manhattan Artists' Books
Housing Problems? Try Shrinking Hormone Gene (1983?); MoMA Manhattan Artists' Books
Is Everybody Done Now? (1980); MoMA Manhattan Artists' Books
its name was Penelope (1990); MoMA Manhattan Special Collections
Keep on Blowing! (1981) two copies; MoMA Manhattan Artists' Books
Lucy Comes Back!: But Mr. Burculosis, I Didn't Mail Your Postcards Yet! (1986); MoMA Manhattan Artists' Books
OK Genetic Engineering: Report (1984); MoMA Manhattan Artists' Books
OKGE Report (1983); MoMA Manhattan Artists' Books
"A Party in Woodside" (1987); MoMA Manhattan Special Collections
Super Lucy (1982); MoMA Manhattan Artists' Books
Values (1987); MoMA Manhattan Artists' Books
Women, Art, and Technology (2003); MoMA Queens Stacks
A Year in Reno: We Want You to Come, a Gratuitous Calendar for 1980 (1980); MoMA Manhattan Artists' Books

2. DAVID M. RUBENSTEIN RARE BOOK AND MANUSCRIPT LIBRARY, DUKE UNIVERSITY

Holds a substantial amount of Malloy's works: as mentioned in the essay, 13200 items taking up 15.6 linear feet of space, too many to list here.
http://library.duke.edu/rubenstein/findingaids/malloyjudy/

3. STANFORD UNIVERSITY LIBRARIES HOLDS FIVE WORKS BY MALLOY

These include:
http://tinyurl.com/q6dw3cl

Forward Anywhere (1995) two copies; Green Library

its name was Penelope (1993); Green Library
Molasses (1989); Special Collections
500 3 x 5 Cards and Other Stories (n.d.); Special Collections
Women, Art, and Technology (2003) two copies; Green Library, Art & Architecture Library

WORKS CITED

Cole, Olivia. "10 Women Who Changed the Tech Industry Forever." *The Daily Dot*. December 15, 2014. http://www.dailydot.com/opinion/women-who-changed-tech-industry-forever/.

Grigar, Dene and Stuart Moulthrop. *Pathfinders: Documenting the Experience of Early Digital Literature*. Los Angeles, CA: Scalar, 2015. http://scalar.usc.edu/works/pathfinders/.

Inman Berens, Kathi. "Judy Malloy's Seat at the (Database) Table: A Feminist Reception History of Early Hypertext Literature." *Literary and Linguistic Computing* 29 (2014): 340-348.

"Judy Malloy." digplanet. http://www.digplanet.com/wiki/Judy_Malloy.

_,_. "Interactive Stories: Writing Public Literature in an Evolving Internet Environment." In *Interactive Dramaturgies: New Approaches in Multimedia Content and Design*, edited by Heide Hagebolling. Kohn, 181-189, NY, NY: Springer, 2004. http://www.judymalloy.net/intaud.html.

_,_. "Judy Malloy: Artists Books." N.D. http://www.judymalloy.net/artistsbooks/artbooks2.html.

_,_. "Biography." N.D. http://www.well.com/user/jmalloy/mybio.html.

_,_. "OK Research, OK Engineering, Bad Information: Information Art Describes Technology." *Leonardo* 21.4 (1988): 371-375. http://www.judymalloy.net/okge.html.

_,_. "The Judy Malloy Papers, 1956-2010." The David M. Rubenstein Rare Book and Manuscript Library. Duke University Libraries. http://library.duke.edu/rubenstein/findingaids/malloyjudy/#c01_3.

_,_. "Notes on Uncle Roger." September 16, 2015. http://www.well.com/user/jmalloy/uncleroger/uncle.html.

_,_. "Uncle Roger: An Online Narrabase." *Leonardo* 24 (1991): 195-202.

_,_, ed. *Women, Art, and Technology*. Cambridge, MA: The MIT Press, 2003.

McKeever, Alice. "Digital Literature Pioneers: Judy Malloy on 'Narrabases', 80s Silicon Valley and E-Literature Today." *The Literary Platform*. April 24, 2014. http://

theliteraryplatform.com/2014/04/digital-literature-pioneers-judy-malloy-on-narrabases-80s-silicon-valley-and-e-literature-today/.

Miller, Michael W. "A Brave New World: Streams of 1s and 0s." *Wall Street Journal* June 23, 1989.

Murphy, Tim and Tasneem Raja. "Ladies Last: 8 Inventions by Women That Dudes Got Credit for." *Mother Jones*. 15 Oct. 2013. http://www.motherjones.com/media/2013/10/ada-lovelace-eight-inventions-women-erasure-credit.

Rettberg, Jill Walker. "Electronic Literature Seen from a Distance: The Beginnings of a Field." *Dichtung Digital* 41 5 (2012). http://www.dichtung-digital.org/2012/41/walker-rettberg/walker-rettberg.htm.

Rettberg, Scott. "Communitizing Electronic Literature." *Digital Humanities Quarterly* 3 (2009). http://www.digitalhumanities.org/dhq/vol/3/2/000046/000046.html.

its Name was Penelope, a Generative Hypertext

BY JUDY MALLOY

Some benevolent muse inspired me to set up a fine large web on my loom. With hand-spun threads, I began to weave, and I said to the princes who wooed me: "Do not be in such a hurry. Wait until I finish this cloth."[176] *its name was Penelope* (Eastgate, 1993, Narrabase Press, 1990, exhibition version 1989[177]) is a collection of randomly-generated memories in which a woman photographer recollects the details of her life. Called one of the early classics of electronic literature by Robert Coover, *its name was Penelope* invites the reader to explore an artist's life through the metaphor of the life of Penelopeia, the central woman in Homer's Odyssey: from "Dawn," the Homeric sun-rise, the years of childhood; to the making of art in "Fine Work and Wide Across"; to the distractions of "That Far Off Island"; to the troubles related in "Rock and Hard Place"; to a concluding "Song" of love and a shared life.

Like photos in a photo album, each lexia in *its name was Penelope* represents an image from the narrator's memory. Housed in a generative hypertext authoring system, the work is the equivalent of a collection of descriptions of photographs that the computer continuously shuffles. The reader sees things as the narrator sees them and observes the events in her life come and go in a constantly changing order, like the raveling and unraveling of Penelopeia's web. As Barbara Page observes in "Women Writers and the Restive Text: Feminism, Experimental Writing and Hypertext":

> A photograph can be read as a composed image of visual objects removed from time and stilled into permanence, or as a momentary arrest of motion in time, pointing back toward a just-gone past and forward to a promised future. Similarly, though the lines of any on-screen writing are set (at least in a read-only text), and may seem as isolated as a single photograph found on the street, in the varied sequences one reads, the words of a text screen float on a motile surface, poised for instantaneous change into another, not fully predictable writing. (196)

176 Homer, *The Odyssey*, Book XIX. This passage and most of the other passages in the iPad edition of *its name was Penelope* were re-translated by Judy Malloy.

177 *Revealing Conversations*, Richmond Art Center, Oct. 3 - Nov. 19. Zlata Baum, curator. The exhibition also included the work of Lynn Hershman, Sonya Rapoport and Stephen Wilson, among others.

The writing and coding of *its name was Penelope* began in 1988, immediately following the completion of the third file of *Uncle Roger*. The initial version, created in BASIC for IBM PC computers, was exhibited as an artists book in 19897 and published as a limited handmade edition (distributed by Art Com Software) beginning in 1990.8 In 1993, the Eastgate Systems version, under the editorship of Mark Bernstein, was released with a Storyspace look and feel. In January, 2016, I reconstructed the 1990 BASIC version, as a code critique for the Critical Code Studies Working Group.[178] The resultant DOSBox edition was made available to scholars in 2016.[179] An IPad version is due to be released by Eastgate.

GENERATIVE HYPERTEXT

Rather than randomly permutating words in phrases and sentences, generative hyper-narrative is created with a database of whole lexias. Generative hypertext (as I have used it) differs from the Gysin-Burroughs "cut-up method"12 in that lexias are not cut from a whole prewritten text but rather are written separately, so that each lexia not only stands by itself but also takes its place in the whole, in such a way that any combination is workable. These lexias, (intuitively but not explicitly linked) are randomly (or more precisely pseudo-randomly) displayed on the computer screen; the reader controls the process only when he or she desires a change in the narrative thread.

Crafted like poetry, the cadence and tone of each lexia in its name was Penelope was carefully constructed, so that in whatever order they were seen, the reading experience would appear natural, and in the same process, I created an authoring system that seamlessly immersed the reader in a work of literature, where you might be reading a poetry chapbook, yet the "pages" are magically brought up at the will of the computer, and the seductive repetition situates the reader in a place of remembered narrative. Poetic narrative is shuffled, continuously changes order, submerges, resurfaces, repeats.

178 Judy Malloy, "Recreating the 1990 GW-BASIC version of its name was Penelope, 2016," Critical Code Studies Working Group, January 2016. Sponsored by the Humanities and Critical Code Studies Lab (USC), and the Transcriptions Center (UCSB).

179 A scholar's edition of the 1990 BASIC Penelope is available for DOSBox at http://www.well.com/user/jmalloy/penelope/penelope.zip with instructions on how to run it at http://www.well.com/user/jmalloy/penelope/how_to_run_penelope.pdf

THE LINEAGE OF GENERATIVE HYPERTEXT: CHAUNCE OF THE DYSE, INDETERMINACY, AND COMPOSITION NO 1

In the rich lineage of aleatory narrative, three works stand out as precursors to computer-mediated generative hypertext. They are the circa 15th century *Chaunce of the Dyse*, John Cage's *Indeterminacy*, and Marc Saporta's *Composition No 1.*

CHAUNCE OF THE DYSE

A cogent example of chance-determined performative storytelling in the late Middle Ages, *Chaunce of the Dyse*,13, 14,15 sometimes attributed to John Lydgate, consists of a manuscript with three introductory stanzas and 56 lexias, each keyed by images of combinations of the throw of three dice. When the ballad was played/performed, a master of ceremonies read the opening words. Each player then rolled the dice, keyed the results to the corresponding text, and read the words aloud. Based on then relatively contemporary works, such as Chaucer's *Troilus and Criseyde* and *The Canterbury Tales*, each brief narrative was both compactly written and intuitively linked to the other nodes, so that as J. Allan Mitchell observes "intertextual allusions produce striking echoes across the texts" (61-68)

INDETERMINACY

A legendary spoken word work with elements of generative hypertext is John Cage's *Indeterminacy*. It began in the late 1950's as a lecture in Brussels with 30 stories. Repeated in other lectures, as the number of stories grew, *Indeterminacy* was most famously performed with David Tudor as "Indeterminacy: New Aspect of Form in Instrumental and Electronic Music." To create this work, Cage read his stories in one room, taking a minute to perform each story, while in another room, out of earshot, Tudor, played selections from Cage's *Concert for Piano and Orchestra*, as well as a pre-recorded tape from Cage's *Fontana Mix*.

Cage's ideas about the composition of *Indeterminacy* are expressed in a 1959 statement that is printed as part of the liner notes to the 1992 Smithsonian Folkways edition of the Cage/Tudor performance:

> The continuity of the 90 stories was not planned. I simply made a list of all the stories I could think of and checked them off as I wrote them. Some that I remembered I was not able to write to my satisfaction, and so they do not appear. Whenever I have given the talk, someone comes up afterwards and insists that the continuity was a planned one, in spite of the ideas that are expressed regarding purposelessness, emptiness, chaos, etc. … My intention in putting 90 stories

together in an unplanned way is to suggest that all things, sounds, stories (and, by extension, beings) are related, and that this complexity is more evident when it is not over-simplified by an idea of relationship in one person's mind.

COMPOSITION NO. 1.19,20

The original French edition of Marc Saporta's *Composition No. 1* was a bookbox containing 150 loose pages. Artists book structures are, to a certain extent, interfaces for the text and images they contain. We open the box of *Composition No. 1* and are confronted with unbound, unnumbered pages. Most pages contain a text that occupies about 3/4 of the page. Without the reassurance of a bound text, we are thrown into the lives of a small group of people at the time of occupied France.

As a unifying device, Saporta immerses the reader in scene-after-scene of distinctly male, same-voiced observations. It is an effective authorial strategy in a work where the author does not know in what order the reader will observe each scene. Contingently, in *its name was Penelope* the centrality of the 1960's male voice in *Composition No. 1*, is subverted by the centrality of a 1980's female voice.

Although, in the past few years, there have been attempts to create computer-generated works from the texts of *Chaunce of the Dyse*, *Indeterminacy*, and *Composition No. 1*, computer mediation was not the intention of any of these remarkable works of (respectively) performative/game text, spoken word text, and artists bookbox-housed text. And as far as I know, other than the third file of my *Uncle Roger*, no computer-mediated works of generative hyperfiction existed before 1988, the year *its name was Penelope* was begun. Thus, *Penelope* stands as the entrance of a computer-mediated feminist voice, differently telling a different story.

Subsequently, I have used generative hyperfiction in four other works, *The Yellow Bowl* (1993), *Forward Anywhere* (with Cathy Marshall, 1996), and the last two parts of *From Ireland with Letters* (2016): "The Not Yet Named Jig" and "when we return again."

BACKGROUND: FROM DATABASE PROGRAMMING TO CARD CATALOGS

Women, in the early years of computer science (WWII, post WWII), were sought out to study computer programming and work on programming projects. Thus, although today it may seem unusual work for an artist/writer, I had worked in the 1960's as editor/searcher for the Library of Congress, as a contract cataloguer for the Goddard Space Flight Center's computerized catalog and as lead programmer for the computerization of Ball Brothers Research Corporation's (BBRC) technical library's computerization. It is therefore, not surprising that these roles seeped into my work as an artist/poet creator of experimental artists books, and later as a pioneer in electronic literature. (Note that my immediate boss at BBRC was pioneer Chicano writer José Antonio Villarreal, who at that time also made a living as a technical writer.)

Along the way, there was a journey from database programmer to creator of series of "card catalog" artists books, beginning in 1976.24 Intended to simulate our fragmented, random, repetitious, non-sequential memory patterns, these works consisted of words and images on 3x5 cards housed in trays and keyed with words or icons. When exhibited, they allowed users to remove cards at random and put them back wherever they so desired. (They were numbered, so eventually the original structure could be restored.) Taking the process a step further, in 1980, I began a series of electromechanical books that housed narrative information in battery-operated address books. When the reader pushed buttons on the unmarked keyboards of these small books, images and text mounted inside revolved and then stopped and displayed one lexia or image on a small screen. These works were precursors to my later electronic literature, in that it was my goal to create non- sequential narrative, and both the card catalogs and the electromechanical books were created with this vision (Malloy 1991).[180] Nevertheless, Noah Wardrip-Fruin's critical repurposing in his paper "Beyond the Complex Surface" is also valid:

> Judy Malloy's card catalog fictions, which have long been discussed as precursors to random-access digital fictions, in today's light may appear with much more emphasis on their specific embodiment. In this way they may seem precursors to work such as genibottles—repurposing familiar objects as the interface to a fictional structure.

BACKGROUND: FROM UNCLE ROGER TO PENELOPE

Once in a while in a lifetime, everything comes together. In 1986, it was my experience in database programming, the idea I had been working on since 1977 of using molecular narrative units to create non-sequential narrative, the availability of personal computers that would make what I had been trying to do with "card catalog" artists books more feasible, and the arrival of ACEN, a place to create, publish and discuss the work.

My early hypertext *Uncle Roger* originally appeared from 1986-1988 on Art Com Electronic Network (ACEN) on the WELL. In June of 1988, when I had finished

180 This paper includes background on the card catalogs and the electromechanical books.

the first two files of *Uncle Roger*, I decided that for the third file, "Terminals," it was important to convey the changed, unsettled nature of the narrator's life. Building on my coding experience and my work with structuring experimental artists books, I surmised that it would be possible to do this not only with words but also by utilizing code and interface to alter the reading experience. Thus in order to create "Terminals," instead of composing hypertextual paths, I used a random number generator (technically a pseudo-random number generator) to produce the narrator's memories at the will of the computer. First using UNIX Shell scripts, so that "Terminals" could be accessed on ACEN DataNet (via The WELL's server) and then using BASIC, so that "Terminals" could also be accessed as artist's software, I created a new authoring system, Narrabase II (Malloy 1991).

When in the same year (1988) I retooled Narrabase II to write the original *its name was Penelope*, I had learned from *Uncle Roger* that indicating different time periods could be difficult for the writer of generative hypertext. For this reason, *Penelope* is structured with six files, and the lexias in each file are related by time period and subject matter; for instance, "dawn" contains childhood memories. The authoring system allows the reader to move between these files and the time periods they represent. To provide concluding structure, the sixth file of *Penelope* is a sequential "Song."

CONCEIVED, WRITTEN, PROGRAMMED, AND NARRATED BY A WOMAN

In Cambridge, UK, the female/male team of Margaret Masterman and Robin McKinnon-Wood created a working authoring system, "Computerized Haiku," which was exhibited at Cybernetic Serendipity in 1968 (Funkhouser 2012:259-260). At Yale, Natalie Dehn explored the use of artificial intelligence in authoring systems. A few realized works were written by woman, including Alison Knowles's wonderful *House of Dust* (1967, implemented by James Tenney). The entrance of women in the introduction of graphic adventure games was marked by *Mystery House* (1980), written and designed by Roberta Williams and programmed by Ken Williams. And Judith Kerman created the generative poetry system *Colloquy* (programmed by Robert Chiles) beginning in 1988.

However, in the stream of works of realized early generative poetry, early hypertext, and Interactive Fiction most were both written and programmed by men. Thus, for me, one of the most important things in creating both *Uncle Roger* and *Penelope* was that they were not only conceived and programed entirely as literary fiction and not as games, but they were also purposefully conceived, written, and programed by a woman. And they featured women narrators telling their stories from a female point of view.

As Jaishree Odin notes about *Penelope*:

> If the epigraphs stand for the sections that the father reads to his children, the textual spaces in between epigraphs tell the story of Anne, a photographer, who has faith and courage in her personal vision and embarks on her journey to become an artist in a patriarchal culture [...] The multiple readings of the text finally exist not so much in what the lexias say but rather in the relations they forge with one another. These relations come into existence and dissolve with each reading and unfold into different versions of the text [...] the female text exfoliates outward, spilling over the boundaries in multiple directions that reveal to the reader the significance of the social, the political, and the historical in any artistic endeavor. (1997)

THE NARRATIVE; THE NARRATOR

In later works I returned to the hypertextual structures I had created in the first two "files" of *Uncle Roger*. But in 1988, when I began *its name was Penelope*, it was my vision to create an entire work that the reader would experience in a completely unpredictable manner. I thought of this in terms of approximating memory, particularly non sequential early memories which surface in one's mind when keyed by contingent events.

To a certain extent I was thinking of James Joyce's *Portrait of an Artist as a Young Man* and *The Dubliners* when I began this work about an artist's memories and the looking at life through past memories and seemingly small incidents that are formative.

In the tradition of visual writing, such as Dorothy Richardson's *Pilgrimage* that could be considered the writing equivalent of impressionist painting, I selected a photographer as the narrator. She is a contemporary, conceptual photographer, who, intertwined with memories of the California art world in the 1980's, retells childhood incidents and remembers past love affairs. Beginning with a quote from *The Odyssey*—

> Of these events,
> Muse, daughter of Zeus,
> tell us the story again,
> beginning where you will.

—the composition process was based on the creation of a series of word pictures that could be combined in many different ways.

Dawn is an ever-changing-in-order collection of memories of clanking wooden toy trains, toy sailboats launched in tidal pools, painted furniture, sand dunes, snow storms, Fenway park bleachers, summer backseat journeys, ice skates slowly laced, and the songs of grandfathers.

The narrator's visual way of expressing the events in her life was sometimes precise and sometimes incorporated elements of magical realism:

> There was a woman in a long, white dress
> standing in the center of my studio,
> right beside the ladder I had used in a performance
> at Target Video about six years ago.
> The wind was blowing her dress around her ankles.
> Long, blond hair was braided around the top of her head.
> I was just getting ready to say something to her
> when she disappeared.
> "Where did she go?" I said out loud.
>
> "She went away," said my cat.
> He was curled up at the foot of my bed.
> When his mouth moved, he looked like the old man
> who lives across the hall.
> (Lexia 23)

Iconic and at times pop-conceptual (as opposed to the pure conceptual work of New York-based artists, such as Hans Haacke and Sol LeWitt) the San Francisco Bay Area art world, in which photographer Anne Mitchell's work is situated, was/is memorable. And it was partially the social and virtual elements (in the sense of real but different) of the world model of the performance and conceptual art world in California, that informed the decision to use that core part of my life as a virtual world model for *its name was Penelope*: for instance, Tom Marioni, whose "The Art of Drinking Beer with Friends is the Highest Form of Art" was central in the social character of the San Francisco Bay Area art world; for instance Paul Cotton, whose finely crafted props and persona in challenging outfits (or lack of any outfit) appeared impromptu on the lawns and in the courtyards of Bay area museums; the adventures of Lynn Hershman's fictional persona Roberta Breitmore; Bonnie Sherk, who had lunch served to her behind the bars of the San Francisco Zoo; Carl Loeffler, who traded "galleries, contacts, bank accounts, houses, clothes, and cars" when he and his staff changed places with the staff of Toronto's A-Space; Michael Pepe's performative rants unfolding like midnight twitter storms; the words slowly emanating from Richard Alpert's rotating wheel at Bonnie Sherk's *The Farm*; the sound of Australian Artist Jill Scott's didgeridoo echoing through 80 Langton St; and my own work as an artist/poet, for instance, engaging the public in dialogue as "President" of OK Genetic Engineering, as I drove the streets of Berkeley in the hand painted OK Genetic Engineering Company Car (Malloy 2014).

It is not as if this world is completely visible to the reader of *its name was Penelope*. Indeed, as Tom Marioni observes in his Crown Point Press memoir.

> I am fascinated by work that can only be seen if you know it is art [...] You can probably see the ideas behind an artwork that seems to be invisible if you look for more than just a few seconds. You can try to figure out the artist's intention, and usually you have a clue from the title. If you stay with it, eventually you get most of the story. You never get it all. The artist doesn't get it all either, and may get something different after he steps back from the work when he is finished [...] (111-112)

"A GATHERING OF SPIRITS"

> Now the spirits gathered....
> Weeping together,
> the souls of warriors killed in the prime of life
> thronged to that place from every side...[181]

But there was a darker side to the California art world of the 1980's. The section titled "A Gathering of Spirits" references Book XI of *The Odyssey*, where Odysseus enters the dwelling of the dead, and it alludes to the tragedy that stalked the San Francisco art world of the mid 1980's: the constant AIDS-dying of friends and fellow artists. You could not go to an opening without hearing of another death (Shnayerson 1987).[182] 43,44

Among the visual artists, poets, and performing artists who died of AIDS were Carlos Almaraz, Joe Brainard, Barton Lidice Beneš, Crawford Barton, Keith Haring, David Cannon Dashiell, Herb Ritts, David Wojnarowicz, Sam D'Allesandro, James

181 Homer, *The Odyssey*, Book XI quoted in Malloy, 1993. lexia "shintro." In the early editions, the section this quote introduces was titled "A Gathering of Shades" (from the Fitzgerald translation). In the iPad edition it is "A Gathering of Spirits," based my translation.

182 See the Visual AIDS Artist Registry, https://www.visualaids.org/artists.

Merrill, William Dickey, Max Epstein, Andrew Meltzer, Arnie Zane, Alvin Ailey, Robert Joffrey, Tomm Ruud, Allan B. Estes, and Rudolf Nureyev.[183]

Notable in *its name was Penelope* are the deaths of friend artists David Mott and Terry Ellis, who created the art space WINDOW and performance artist writer Irwin (Richard) Irwin. It was Irwin who sat down beside me at La Mamelle, as described in a lexia that was true but not completely understandable in today's world. Irwin's obituary is included in *its name was Penelope*:

> A memorial gathering for Richard Irwin, a poet and performance artist who died of AIDS-related pneumonia will be held tomorrow night in San Francisco. Mr Irwin, while a student at the San Francisco Art Institute, organized a series of weekly performances at the Hotel Utah in the 1970's and early 1980's.[184]

Judith Hoffberg's notice of the death of Ulises Carrion also appears in *Penelope*:

> In addition, we wish to dedicate this issue and the rest of all publications of UMBRELLA to the memory of our dear friend, Ulises Carrion, who died in October of AIDS. He was an important friend, one who loved books and was the proprietor of the famous Other Books & So shop which distributed artists' books to all of Europe. He was also a video artist, had a great archive of mail art, performed, and was one of the foremost theoreticians on bookworks. I shall miss him a great deal. We all will.[185]

THE NARRATIVE STRUCTURE

At the time of the telling *Uncle Roger* in a virtual town square on the Internet, I revisited Homer's effective storytelling devices, rereading several translations—primarily Rouse and Fitzgerald—and observed how narratives from different places and times were seamlessly and non-sequentially introduced. This rereading, as well as the childhood memory of my father reading *The Odyssey* out loud to my brother and I, informed the idea of using *The Odyssey* as a way to structure *its name was Penelope*. *The Odyssey*'s sophisticated ordering of poetic narrative would, I envisioned, work well for the narrative I wished to create. Thus in *its name was Penelope*, the reader moves between six "files"

183 See The Estate Project for Artists with AIDS, http://www.artistswithaids.org.

184 Richard Irwin's obituary, published in the San Francisco Chronicle (March 14, 1989), is lexia 13 in *its name was Penelope*.

185 Judith Hoffberg's obituary for Ulises Carrion, in *Umbrella* 12:2 (December, 1989) is lexia 48 in *its name was Penelope*.

that are loosely based on sections of *The Odyssey*. *The Odyssey* was also significant in that the resourceful Penelopeia, a woman whose weaving is central to her life and the story, is a primary character in Homer's narrative. Since I did not desire to rewrite a classic story, the main character was named Anne, not Penelope. However, in order to key the work in such a way that the analogy to *The Odyssey* would be evident to the reader, the toy boat that Anne played with as a child was used as a primarily image. And this boat bore the name the name "Penelope."

> The little boat veered from the shore
> and began to sail out into the middle of the pond.
> I took off my sneakers, rolled up my pants,
> and waded in after it with my camera in my hands.
> I moved gingerly because although the bottom
> was soft and slimy in some places,
> in other places it was covered with sharp little stones.
> The boat was moving faster than I was,
> and it stayed several feet ahead of me. (Lexia 320)

WEAVING AND REWEAVING ITS NAME WAS PENELOPE

Although the migration of *its name was Penelope* to different platforms was a response to changing technologies (as opposed to the subterfuge and delaying action of the original Penelopeia's craft), the reweaving of its name was Penelope on different "looms" has—echoing the countless translations of *The Odyssey*—become in itself a component of the work.

As writers, artists, and scholars approach the issue of reissuing works of electronic literature, it should be noted that creators of work in the realm of hybrids of literature and coding are partially on the territory of software-centered disciplines, where such updating is a part of the culture. Nevertheless, on this hybrid territory, techno-creatives have the choice to leave the "translation" of our works to scholars or to embark on a lifelong practice of learning and updating. If, as I have done, we choose the latter path, nevertheless, aesthetically we can choose to define and preserve our works with the context of aspects of our original vision. It should be noted that throughout all the iterations listed below, the basic algorithms have remained remarkably similar. In an era, where creators in the digital arts, face platform and software changes, exploring approaches to translation issues is important.

The versions of *its name was Penelope* are as follows.

1. The writing and the programming in BASIC of *its name was Penelope* was begun in 1988. It premiered in the exhibition Revealing Conversations, curated by Zlata Baum at the Richmond Art Center (RAC) in October 1989. Because, at that time, reading/viewing on a computer was not usual, Zlata asked the artists in the exhibition to create installations that would draw the viewer into their works. Thus—in addition to creating a disk with the lexias and the program that accessed them—on heavy watercolor paper panels, I drew the text from 66 core lexias. *Penelope* was installed at the RAC on a table with an IBM 286 computer, where the work was running in luminous yellow text on a black background. In front of the table was a hand-painted chair. Beside the computer, were disk packaging and instructions on reading the work. Echoing the computer-mediated lexias, the graphic panels were displayed like a manuscript, pinned to the wall.
2. Beginning in 1990, for the self-published by Narrabase Press version of *its name was Penelope* (distributed by Art Com),[186] I polished the program and text. Then I drew an image for the cover, copied it, and hand-glued it to a disk sleeve, which was created with folded heavy watercolor paper. I had received an order for multiple copies from Belgium and was laboriously creating the disks and packaging, when Mark Bernstein, who was rapidly becoming the primary publisher of literary hypertext, offered *its name was Penelope* Eastgate publication. Mark had published Michael Joyce's *afternoon* and would soon publish, Stuart Moulthrop's *Victory Garden*, Sarah Smith's *King of Space*, and Carolyn Guyer's *Quibbling*, as well *its name was Penelope* and many other works.[187]
3. The first Eastgate version of *its name was Penelope* (1993) was a floppy disk with a rubbery but substantial blue cover that later metamorphosed into evocative blue-green and white packaging, which housed a CD. To create Eastgate's definitive versions, Mark Bernstein retooled my original BASIC program in a Storyspace look and feel design, that both situated my work in the school of the other early Eastgate classics of literary electronic fiction, and emphasized the magical poetry chapbook nature of the work.[188] Eastgate's its name was Penelope was published with an introduction by Carolyn Guyer in which she wrote:

> ...In this work of computer fiction, Judy Malloy has created something very akin to the mélange of snapshots most of us have shut away somewhere in a cabinet

186 Emulated in the scholar's edition, Malloy, 2016.

187 More information about Eastgate is available at http://www.eastgate.com.

188 Note that although *its name was Penelope* follows my algorithms, Eastgate subsequently created their own "sculptural hypertext" authoring system. See Bernstein 2001.

on the back shelf. Here, in this work, the reader finds these same sort of casual, almost meaningless—and thereby potentially most meaningful—images of people meandering in a park, of tightly knotted skate laces, plates of food, or toy sailboats at the beach. Indeed, the visual imagery is strikingly vivid, as clear and lucid as one might expect from a visual artist, which Malloy is. At times the descriptions are almost cinematic, at other times, especially in the *Dawn* section, they are so concrete I expect to see a color illustration immediately next to the text in the manner of children's books... (Guyer 1993, 7).

4. Implemented by Mark Bernstein, Eastgate's elegant iPad version of *its name was Penelope* is in press. With touch, this version involves the reader more intimately in the changing of the screens. The authoring system and algorithms are basically the same as the original, but I slightly edited the text to deal with some awkward places in the original, and iPad authoring guidelines necessitated some interface changes. Additionally, for the iPad version, in order to avoid copyright problems that might arise from using quotes from translations of *The Odyssey* to each section. I made my own translations (made with the English text of four translations and a dictionary). Because I wrote these translations with their place in my narrative in mind, they were satisfactory within the context of *its name was Penelope*.

> And so they went to the bed they had shared so many years ago.
>
> ...They took their fill of sweet love, and afterwards they lay together, telling each other the stories of their years apart. (Lexia 500)

WORKS CITED

Bernstein, Mark. "Card Shark and Thespis: Exotic Tools for Hypertext Narrative." In *Hypertext 2001: Proceedings of the 12th ACM Conference on Hypertext and Hypermedia*, (2001), 41-50.

Cage, John. "Indeterminacy: New Aspect of Form in Instrumental and Electronic Music, 1959." Included in Richard Kostelanetz' liner notes to the recording: *John Cage and David Tudor. Indeterminacy*. Smithsonian Folkways, 1992.

Chaunce of the Dyse, MS Fairfax 16 and MS Bodley 638.

"Colloquy." *The Electronic Labyrinth*. Available at http://elab.eserver.org/hfl0272.html

Coover, Robert. "Literary Hypertext: The Passing of the Golden Age." Keynote Address, Digital Arts and Culture, Atlanta, Georgia. October 29, 1999. Web. http://www. nickm.com/vox/golden_age.html

Dehn, Natalie. "Story Generation after TALE-SPIN." *IJCAI'81 Proceedings of the 7th International Joint Conference on Artificial intelligence* 1 (1981), 16-18.

Foley, Suzanne. *Space/Time/Sound—Conceptual Art in the San Francisco Bay Area: The 1970s*. SF, CA: San Francisco Museum of Modern Art, 1981.

Funkhouser. Christopher T. "First Generation Poetry Generators, Establishing Foundations in Form." In *Mainframe Experimentalism: Early Computing and the Foundations of the Digital Arts*, eds. Hannah B. Higgins and Douglas Kahn. Berkeley, CA: University of California Press, 2012. 243-265.

Guyer, Carolyn, "Introduction," liner material for Malloy, 1993.

Gysin, Brion. "Cut-ups: A Project for Disastrous Success." In *Back in No Time: The Brion Gysin Reader*. Ed. Jason Weiss. Middletown, CT: Wesleyan University Press. 2001, 125-132.

Hammond, E.P. "The Chance of the Dice." *Englische Studien*: 59 (1925), 1-16.

Higgins, Hannah B. "An introduction to Alison Knowles's The House of Dust." In *Mainframe Experimentalism: Early Computing and the Foundations of the Digital Arts*, eds. Hannah B. Higgins and Douglas Kahn. Berkeley, CA: University of California Press, 2012. 195-199.

Homer. *The Odyssey*. Trans. W.H.D. Rouse. NY: American Library, 1937.

_, *The Odyssey*. Trans. Robert Fitzgerald. NY: New Anchor Books, 1963.

Loeffler , Carl E. and Darlene Tong, eds. *Performance Anthology: Sourcebook for a Decade of California Performance*. SF, CA: Last Gasp, 1990.

Malloy, Judy. *its name was Penelope*. Berkeley, CA: Narrabase Press, 1990.

_,_. *its name was Penelope*. Cambridge, MA: Eastgate, 1993.

_,_. *The Yellow Bowl*. Narrabase Press, 1993.

_,_. "Recreating the 1990 GW-BASIC version of *its name was Penelope*, 2016." Critical Code Studies Working Group, January 2016. Sponsored by the Humanities and Critical Code Studies Lab (USC), and the Transcriptions Center (UCSB).

_,_. From Ireland with Letters, 2016. Web. Available at http://www.well.com/user/jmalloy/ from_Ireland/opening_page.html

_,_. "Notes on *Uncle Roger*" (November 1, 2014) http://www.well.com/user/jmalloy/uncleroger/uncle.html

_,_. "Uncle Roger, an Online Narrabase." in *Connectivity: Art and Interactive Telecommunications*. eds. Roy Ascott and Carl Eugene Loeffler, Leonardo 24:2, 1991. 195-202.

_,_. "Art Com Electronic Network On The WELL: A Conversation with Fred Truck and Anna Couey." In Judy Malloy, ed., *Social Media Archeology and Poetics*. Cambridge, MA: MIT Press, 2016. 191-218.

_,_. "OK Research/OK Genetic Engineering/Bad Information, Information Art Defines Technology." In *META-LIFE*, eds. Annick Bureaud, Roger Malina and Louise Whiteley. Cambridge, MA, MIT Press, 2014.

_,_. and Cathy Marshall. *Forward Anywhere*. Cambridge, MA: Eastgate, 1996.

Marioni, Tom. *Beer, Art and Philosophy: A Memoir*. SF, CA: Crown Point Press, 2003.

Mitchell, J. Allan. "Playing Pandarus in Chaunce of the Dyse." In *Ethics and Eventfulness in Middle English Literature*. Ed. J. Allan Mitchell. Palgrave Macmillan, 2009, 61-68.

Nyhan, Julianne. "The Influence of Algorithmic Thinking: An Oral History conversation between Judy Malloy and Julianne Nyhan", in *Computation and the Humanities: Towards an Oral History of Digital Humanities*. eds. Julianne Nyhan and Andrew Flinn (Berlin: Springer, 2016).

Odin, Jaishree K. "The Edge of Difference: Negotiations Between the Hypertextual and the Postcolonial." *Modern Fiction Studies* 43.3. (1997), 598-630.

Page, Barbara. "Women Writers and the Restive Text: Feminism, Experimental Writing and Hypertext." *Postmodern Culture* 6:2. January, 1996. Web. http://pm6.c.iath. virginia.edu/text-only/issue.196/page.196

Saporta, Marc. *Composition No. 1*. Paris: Éditions du Seuil, 1961.

_,_. *Composition No. 1*. London: Visual Editions, 2011.

Sergi, Matthew. "Interactive Readership in the Chance of the Dice," presented at *Reading the Middle Ages*, U.C. Berkeley, March 26, 2011.

Wardrip-Fruin, Noah. "Beyond The Complex Surface." In *Beyond the Screen: Transformations of Literary Structures, Interfaces and Genres*. Eds: Jörgen Schäfer and Peter Gendolla. Bielefeld, Germany: Transcript 2010. 227-248.

Williams, Roberta and Ken, *Mystery House*. On-Line Systems, 1980.

Marble Springs: A Journey of an Electronic Work from the Pre-Dawn of the Internet to Today's Golden Age

BY DEENA LARSEN

ORIGINS

In 1989, I found my Holy Grail. Its name was HyperCard, and like the toy boat, Penelope, it was the vessel of my dreams. Now I could connect all of those odd characters that bunked in my little community, formed from years of hiding out in the bowels of the University of Colorado's Western History Archives. People could look on a screen and move a mouse to magically transport themselves along the connective tissue, to ferret out the secrets between Red Birch, a half-blood Indian and the Ladies Aid Society or to track down the illicit connections between Bridget O'Shanty, the town whore, and Pastor Horner.

I was hooked, spending hours upon eons of time programming HyperCard to do what I wanted in my little mining ghost town of Marble Springs, Colorado. I giddily created jails, mines, stores, roads, maps, and other tools for my characters to intertwingle themselves around. I found invisible buttons and secret passageways and eventually created a work so complex that I got lost in its convolutions.

Of course, Hypercard had its limitations, and I had to bend and twist to render my vision into something usable. More than that, as I had submitted this as part of my thesis work (mostly so that I could play on the fanciest computers of the day in the Math Lab, as the English Department was still using typewriters), I also had to bow to the wishes of my early readers: my thesis advisors who wielded the ultimate power over me—a diploma. None of these worthies had ever worked on a computer or used a mouse, so I ended up putting in back, next, and previous buttons, even though there was no going back and the work had no intrinsic order or organization.

Eastgate Systems published *Marble Springs* (1993), but we had a rough time figuring out how to implement a central tenet of the work: that as a town could never be complete, readers should be able to interact with the work and create their own denizens, connections, and commentary. This is before the internet took off. *Marble Springs* was sold on the 3 by 5 floppy disks, and readers had to pass through a Byzantine maze and leap over tall copyright hurdles to submit their words. HyperCard slowly dwindled into a lamented and abandoned ghost town on the dusty side of the internet.

We did attempt to publish *Marble Springs 2.0* as a read-only HyperCard on a CD, but for various reasons, were unsuccessful.

In the meantime, the internet grew up, taking its first cooing baby steps with cute click here's littering every page, going to elementary school with actual content links, and then shaking off the carefully acquired underlining for freer styles. In 2011, Leighton Christiansen wrote his thesis on digital archiving techniques using *Marble Springs 2.0* as his digital archiving guinea pig. Using his exhaustive lists of links and texts and images, I was able to port *Marble Springs* to a wiki as *Marble Springs 3.0*. Now readers do not have to be superhuman to contribute, and new content can show up in an instant instead of years later. More about the colophonic history lurks at http://marblesprings.wikidot.com/about.

BENDING TO THE FORM

The underlying conceit of *Marble Springs* has always remained the same: a Spoon River like anthology that showcased each story in free verse form, but then added an entire underquilting of connections so that each story thread could be woven into a whole. Like bonsai cats though, the living shapes of the tales had to fit within the tight corset strings of the programming. Transferring *Marble Springs* from HyperCard to wiki was not a simple cut and paste job. Every tiny piece that Leighton gleaned from the tortuous back alleyways of *Marble Springs 2.0* had to be reconsidered and re-glued into a completely new mosaic as a wiki. Even the programming had to be parsed—how could that HyperCard quirk I'd chortled over be rendered in this new format? Should it be? Was the haunting train whistle or fading checkerboard transition triggered on certain links worth the headache of massive reprogramming? (No.) Was an image map function worth the hours of painstaking work it would take? (Well, maybe later.)

Then the wiki presented new ideas and spaces. Ooooh, look at the pretty shiny tags. How could these be manipulated to provide a metareading from the tags themselves? (By emphasizing words like "happiness" and "despair," "respectability" and "secrets," "long" and "love"). What happens if you use tags like "active" and "untold" in the programming to ensure that all the denizens mentioned have their own page? (You get a weird effect in the tags column where active and untold outstrip every other tag in importance, offsetting your carefully written tags. You then decide that this is a happy artifact and that you could let future graduate students create wonderful theories about why this happened.)

Thus, *Marble Springs 3.0* may share words and some links with its ancient ancestress, *Marble Springs 1.0*, but like all generational shifts, similarities are often deceiving and usually coincidental. I'll go through a few of the mosaic pieces that make up this transition to give glimpses into a process I never fully documented.

AESTHETICS

I had always insisted on an old-timey, ghost town look. This, I thought, would insulate me from accusations of not being modern enough, of not keeping up with the latest internet look and feel. But more than that, I wanted readers to feel as if they were sifting through the abandoned shells of lives, to find out what they could about who had gone before. I shifted the black and white of HyperCard to a muted color scheme in the wiki and hoped to maintain that illusion.

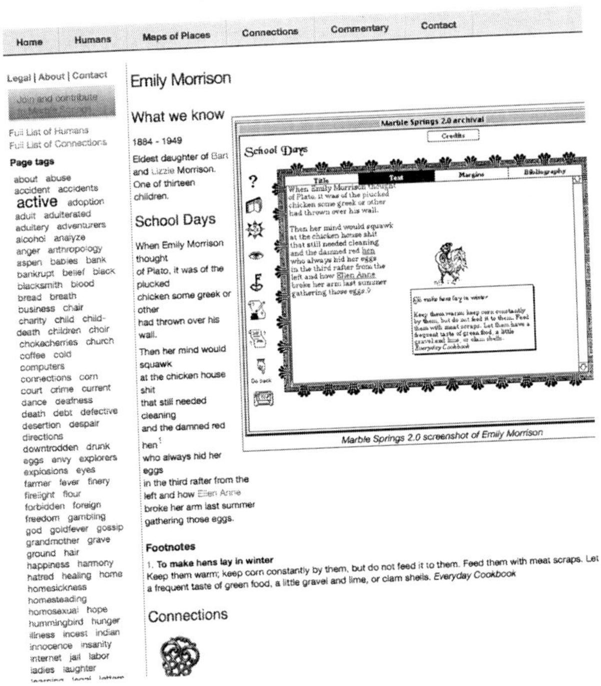

Figure 1: Screenshot from *Marble Springs 3.0* showing the screenshot from *Marble Springs 2.0*.

PAGE LAYOUT

HyperCard provided a blank screen, where any element could be anywhere on the screen. I had four "minicards" or areas of text laid out on each card for a title (which hid a little biography of the character, text (the default screen which told the story), margins to comment in, and a bibliography for source material. This did not work out well in a wiki, where the templates were linear instead of stacked. So I chose a scrolling template and used "What We Know" for the biography, then the story, and then connections and a portal. Some links and graphics would open up a "footnote" on the same card—impossible in a wiki, so I had to add a "footnotes" section to each page as well. The graphic "oddments" on each card in *Marble Springs 2.0* functioned as a connection portal, showing the secret connections between that character and other characters or institutions in the town. As I was loathe to leave the elegance of the HyperCard layout completely behind, I used a screenshot from *Marble Springs 2.0* on each page that came from that work (Figure 1).

LINKS

In the wild west days of *Marble Springs 1.0*, no conventions had settled down for creating links, let alone marking them. Hypercard had a "group text" feature that you could program, and on a special card in the stack, I listed every single link as part of a separately programmed link. The exact text had to be underlined as part of the "group text" function, and the same text to go to two different places, so you will see "hawk" and "hawk." Leighton faithfully documented each link, and as I worked from the ASCII text version Leighton provided, I weighed the merits of each one. Did it advance the character development, the story arc? Was it a good link, in view of the overall whole? I kept many links intact, but changed directions on some links, deleted still more, and added more, now that linking was so easy--all I had to do was type in the link on the ASCII text as I edited: [[[humans:susannah-smith|story]]].

CONNECTIONS

In *Marble Springs 1.0* and *2.0*, each character is associated with a "character connections" card, which are primarily based on family ties (Figure 2). These connections are graphically spaced with a series of patterned lines tying characters to each other and to major institutions (Figure 2). Readers could move buttons or draw new lines, but this was difficult to do and did require some knowledge of HyperCard. Readers could create new buttons for new characters and determine where to place these new buttons. This was a bit more simple than manipulating buttons or graphics.

Each line type portrayed a type of connection, but I deliberately did not include a "legend" to explain which line meant what type of connection. Rather, I tried to create an ambience of connections, a visual atmosphere where these connections could be "grokked" on a visual level and understood intuitively rather than to be categorized and laid out. Remember, this was before the web, and in those days, we saw absolutely nothing wrong with mystery meat—in fact, we thought we were entering an Age of Aquarius where vision would overtake language and we could be able to communicate complex ideas in a series of simple patterns. This did not pan out well—when Leighton asked me to delineate what each line meant, I found I'd forgotten well over half of the connotations.

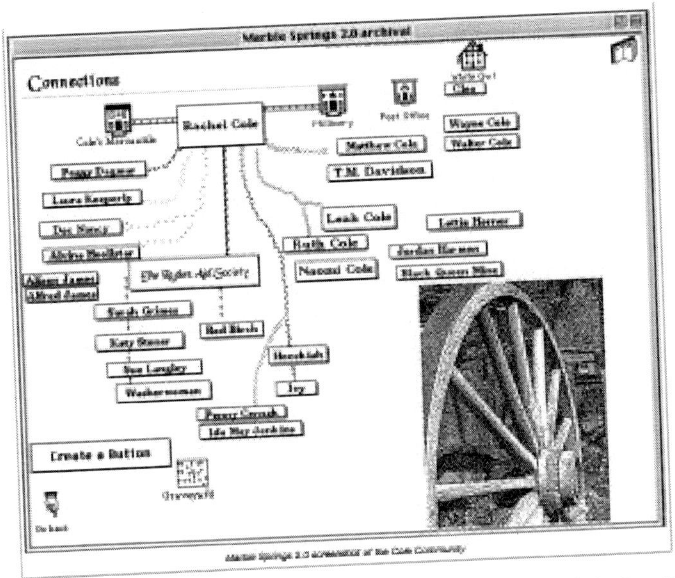

Figure 2. Screenshot of the Cole Connections card in *Marble Springs 2.0*

Rather, I looked to the way social media identifies connective subsets today, with taxonomies include specifying friends or work or relationship status. These still do not go far enough in my opinion. Colleagues and college friends are all very well, but what about the secretive, furtive connections that Marble Springs runs on? For *Marble Springs 3.0*, I recreated every link on every character connections card to conform to a new set of categories. To play off of most social network and Web 2.0 sites, I created an icon for each type of category. I wanted to keep the quilting theme, so I used quilt patterns that the women of *Marble Springs* would have immediately recognized. These quilt patterns are not explained in the work, thus harking back to the unexplained meanings of the line patterns in *Marble Springs 1.0* and *2.0*.

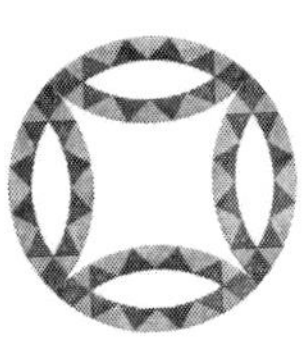

The Marriage icon is a double wedding ring quilt. While these connections are not emphasized at all in *Marble Springs 1.0* and *2.0*, I brought them out in the text of *Marble Springs 3.0* to clarify who was married to whom.

The family icon is a variation of a log cabin quilt pattern. Note that not all families in *Marble Springs* share a loving nature. I did not emphasize the love with its own category, as there are too many different types of love in *Marble Springs*, and I felt that these should be handled via other categories.

The hatred icon is a crossed quilt pattern. In the Cole Community in *Marble Springs 2.0*, this hatred was shown through the crossed lines emanating from the Ladies' Aid society. I deliberately did not repeat these subtle accusations in the text connections of *Marble Springs 3.0*.

The friends icon is based on a pattern that was popular as a friendship quilt given to someone about to embark westward. In the Cole community, I did not emphasize friend relationships in *Marble Springs 1.0* or *2.0*, but I added them in *Marble Springs 3.0*.

The business icon is based on a tumbling blocks pattern. Note that in Marble Springs, business can mean anything from a paid work relationship to business partners to trade to institutional relationships. In *Marble Springs 3.0*, I clarified who was related to whom via business by showing the institution first and listing the characters most associated with that business relationship beneath that.

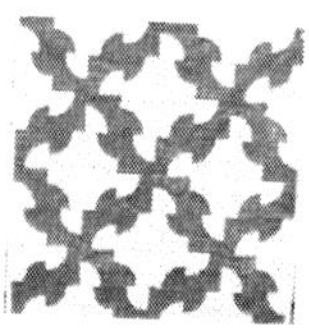

The complicated icon is reserved for any relationship that is not straightforward. The suffragette movement adopted a blue on white drunkard's path pattern for raffling quilts. There is a legend that this pattern meant "take a zigzag route" in the underground railway. As many of the relationships in this category are complicated by either alcohol or temperance or politics, this pattern's history becomes even more significant.

The icon for secrets tearing at the soul is a variation on a flying geese pattern. In *Marble Springs 1.0* and *2.0*, there was only one type of secret relationship. However, I realized that there could be secrets that destroyed as well as created, and that it was better to elucidate the type of secret being kept.

The icons for secrets growing in the soul is a variation on the basket of plenty pattern. In *Marble Springs 3.0*, these secrets could be held by one person and not another (and, indeed, one character in the secret relationship may not even know a secret relationship even exists.)

The icon for outside the wall is the one icon I deliberately blurred to show the edges. In *Marble Springs 2.0*, these relationships were usually indicated spatially by an icon far away from the main action and not connected with any line. But I had to create an icon in *Marble Springs 3.0* as I was constrained to a linear, scrolling format.

I created a one-to-one link for connections in all versions, mostly because anything else would have meant more massive programming. I still have visions of incorporating n-ary links in *Marble Springs 4.0*.

UNTRACKED COMMUNITIES

As part of the wiki programming in Marble Springs 3.0, every character was required to be in a community—which had not been required in HyperCard. Several characters, by their very nature, can not belong within a community: Jedediah Grasslands serves as the undertaker who comes only to bury and envy the denizens of *Marble Springs*, the Washerwoman comes to beg and to be reviled, and no one knows anything really about the Mulatto with Green Eyes. I felt that creating a community for these outliers would be too forced and would not fit with their outcast nature. Thus I created an untracked community page, further delineating the shadows of longing and absence by describing the connections in tantalizing tones.

MAPS

Marble Springs 1.0 and *2.0* treat the three maps (of the valley, town, and graveyard) as spatial connections—because you can put a button anywhere on the card. However, this would not work within these templates for connections in *Marble Springs 3.0* as wikis require linearity on the page. Thus, I eschewed any templates for the maps, opting instead for a generic "content." Again, *Marble Springs 1.0* and *2.0* relied solely on visual cues. The reader could glean content and meaning from which plot in the graveyard was bigger or smaller, which was where, and who was buried "outside the walls" or in the segregated and walled off Potter's field. However, given the current textual expectations of the web, I needed to make these more explicit. Thus, I added a short sentence about the icon I chose and the people living there. For example, rather than just showing the little house on Carlton Avenue for the Coles, the text expands on their positions:

> home with clean lines and a lilac bush icon
>
> The Coles lived just far enough away from the White Owl to be respectable, but close enough for business purposes. (Figure 3)

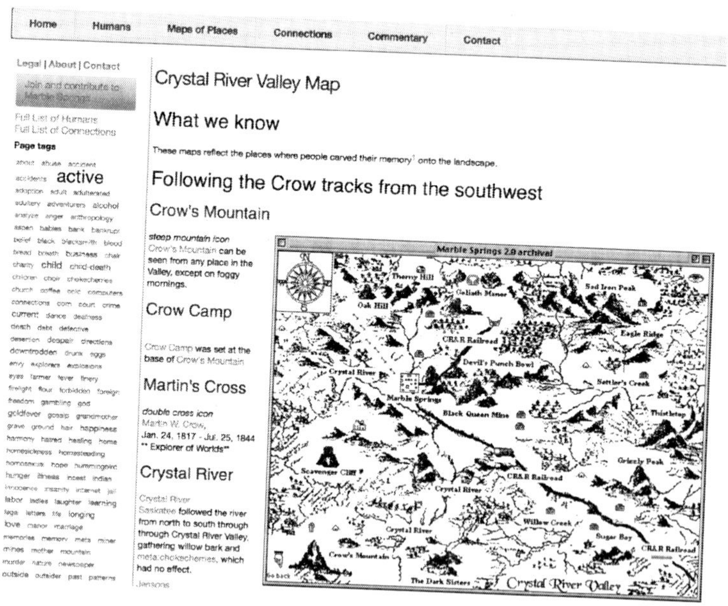

Figure 3. Screenshot comparing the map directions from *Marble Springs 3.0* (text on the side) with the embedded screenshot from *Marble Springs 2.0*

NEW FEATURES

Reforming *Marble Springs* allowed for some new features as well as new content to explore some ideas left unfollowed in the previous iterations.

NAVIGATION

When I wrote *Marble Springs 1.0*, we thought that just being able to poke around and click on links would hold a reader's attention. That was a very quaint and silly notion—completely destroyed by the 5-second world of YouTube and Reddit and other quick fixes. I just had to create more hooks. Along with page tags, a full list of humans and a full list of connections on the left hand side, I created several other directories for a more complete navigational experience:

The Forbidden Index. These are topics that would not have been discussed in a Victorian household. Rather, everyone would simply understand these things by osmosis somehow. I thus teased out what the reader would find for adultery, death, children, crime, etc.

The Census. This provides an alphabetized list of characters so that it is easier to find someone mentioned someplace else—especially if you did not follow the link at the time. The old Directory is listed by last name, but the last name is buried a bit and harder to find. On the new net, every second counts.

Communities. In *Marble Springs 1.0* and *2.0*, the only way to determine which characters belonged to which community was to look on the connection card . Now you can click on a community and get a list.

Connections. In *Marble Springs 1.0* and *2.0*, the only way to access a connection card was to stumble upon it from a person's story. Now we have a list of all the connections in one place.

Top menu. *Marble Springs 1.0* and *2.0* rely on icons (explained only on the help page) to steer readers through the help pages, a map, a directory of stories, or connections. This is a limited palette. So I expanded this to a top menu in *Marble Springs 3.0*, allowing readers to find humans through the forbidden list, a list of humans with stories, or a full list of humans. Allowing all of the maps makes it easier to navigate, but it does lose that focused navigation of going from the wide valley into the town and then into the narrower constraints of the graveyard. So, some meaning is lost. I put all of the help into the commentary, or a "meta" category. This meta category includes Chokecherry wine, which is the only real artifact of the town. Originally, I was going to put chokecherry wine into a "things" category, and if I get more things, that may yet happen.

ANALYSIS

I added a new analysis feature to showcase connections and to provide ideas for students to write papers on. *Marble Springs* can be read on several levels: as a simple piece to enjoy, as a class project, or as an in-depth analysis for a thesis. I wanted to provide an easier entry for students and teachers to show how electronic literature works and how it can be read. E-lit has now been around for a mere two decades—a blip in literary study and criticism, and a lifetime in internet terms. Yet we still grapple with how to tease out the meanings behind connections and navigation and imagery. So, I hope to help out with giving hints on ways to analyze in Nodalities ("We see several characters in *Marble Springs* only in terms of others—we get their story only in how they view the world. Take one of these and determine what she is really like based on her observations.")

CONNECTIONS

In *Marble Springs*, the actual character story is just the tip of the iceberg. To understand these characters, you need to read about how they react in various situations. Thus, to flesh out characters, I also added quite a few institutional connections. Some of these, such as the Marble Springs Bank, Crystal River, Settler's Creek, church choir, had already been mentioned in *Marble Springs 2.0*. However, I wanted to bring these connections out into the open and to allow readers to experience characters through more and more facets. Some of these, such as the Marble Springs Café and Charity Relief, I added as new institutions mentioned in new poems or in new histories of the institutional connections.

I also wanted to tie more into history, and not rely on a reader's knowledge of the west, so I added more connections and drew out the history to hint at the segregation, prejudice, poverty and suffering. As each connection card in the wiki is text based, words can take the place of too-subtle spatial cues:

> Hope Town was a separate little part of Marble Springs, between the Crystal River and the rise of Boot Hill. The land here flooded often and had no mineral values that anyone could see, and thus Matthew Cole leased the land for a pittance. Yet it was Pastor Horner's fondest desire that the inhabitants of Hope Town look upon the closeness of the Church to them as a way to be closer to God.

CHARACTERS

I wanted to flesh out *Marble Springs* with several types of new characters. I expanded the Paines, Vernons, and Pitkins to show various aspects of prejudice and domination in America.

I also wanted to focus on generations and families. *Marble Springs 1.0* and *2.0* are pretty good at lateral relationships—who influences whom for business, friends, gossip, etc. But how family traditions with their hopes and fears, dreams and nightmares handed down through generations was more elusive. So I concentrated on several families (the Millers, Vernons, and Pitkins) to show more of a generational handing down of secrets and obsessions. Now, for instance, we know why Asa Miller is so obsessed with hair—for his grandmother, Gertrude learned from her grandmother, "in long, even strokes of her hair brush as it travelled from her scalp to her waist."

I also wanted to show the other side of issues, and thus Jud Heollstar (Ears) becomes a counterpart for his wife (Eyes), showing how Alvina's bitterness evolved from the fever that took their family on the crossing into the West.

GOING FORTH BY INTERNET

The internet shifts daily as Moore's law propels us to new and dizzying heights in programming. I'll keep *Marble Springs* in its little backwater wiki for now, inviting anyone to come and play and write among the forgotten aspens and abandoned gold mines. And if I port again, then it will be into an entirely different shape—perhaps this is the only true constant in *Marble Springs*:

> Like old women huddled behind vegetable carts, we hawk the wares of our minds, calling out over the noise of data, of interlinks, of electronic networks—hoping someone will hear us, will drop a half- penny into our laps, knowing we will yet live. —Sophie Smith Weaver, Susannah Smith's great-granddaughter, 1993.

WORKS CITED

Larsen, Deena. *Marble Springs 1.0*. Massachusetts: Eastgate Systems, 1993.

Larsen, Deena. *Marble Springs 3.0*. http://marblesprings.wikidot.com

Malloy, Judy. *its name was Penelope*. Massachusetts: Eastgate Systems, 1993.

Masters, Edgar Lee. *Spoon River Anthology*. Macmillan & Co, 1916. http://spoonriver-anthology.net/spoon/river/

The Making and Unmaking of *Califia*

BY M.D. COVERLEY // MARJORIE COVERLEY LUESEBRINK

CALIFIA: "Once upon a time there was an Island named California where dreams came true." *So begins the opening address to the reader in the electronic narrative, Califia, a story of five generations of Californians on a quest for a lost stash of gold. The gold was buried, it seems, in the Southern California mountains some few years after the great gold rush of 1849. And then, through a series of California dust-ups, it got lost. From the discovery of the earliest clues—the Baja Map and the blue-blanket embroidery of Willing Stars—the characters puzzle though earthquake, fire, a mysterious train wreck, Hollywood nights, strange land-buying expeditions in the desert, flight plans, and Chumash legends to link together the elusive path to the dream of riches, and the longing that makes seekers of us all.* —*Califia* (2000), Eastgate Systems), by M. D. Coverley (pen name for Marjorie Coverley Luesebrink). The descriptions in italics are from the M.D. Coverley website.

Figure 1: Opening screen for readers of *Califia* invites them to come ashore.

INTRODUCTION

By now, all of us (or at least everyone reading this) have probably marveled at the speed of change in the world of digital communications technology. Who would have thought that Flash, a central element in the development of interactive web sites, would be gone in a flash (pun intended)? Nonetheless, we move from desktop to laptop to tablet to hand-held or wearable devices, from browser to browser, and from software to cloudware in rapid succession. For users and readers, this has made our digital experience a swift ride. But for writers and artists, a rollercoaster in the dark.

When digital electronic writers began creating for the computer, the rate of tech change came as a sneaky surprise. Certainly, there were examples of newer inscription technologies not preserving as well as previous ones (words written on stone last longer than papyrus, vellum lasts longer than paper). We also had ample evidence of early 20th century film either becoming unplayable or orphaned without machines to play it on. Still, there just wasn't any precedent for the lightning-fast loss of digital material.

Califia was begun in hypertext form in 1995. It was published by Eastgate Systems in 2000. By 2010, it would no longer play on most computers. Holy crumbling stone, a shelf life of ten years!

And, although *Califia* is longer and technically more complicated than most other e-lit fiction, the trajectory of its creation and loss, the pattern of its life-span, bears many similarities with other e-lit writing.

It took a long time to make and a relatively short time to unmake.

Califia is a multimedia, interactive, hypertext fiction for CD-ROM. Califia allows the reader to wander and play in the landscape of historic/magic California. It is a computer-only creation of interactive stories, photos, graphics, maps, music, and movement.

Figure 2: Augusta, Kaye, and Calvin set off for the gold mine.

EARLY STIRRINGS

As a print writer, I had always been interested in multi-voice, multiple point-of-view narratives, what is now termed the "networked novel." I particularly liked the structure of John Dos Passos' *USA Trilogy*, a "four-way conveyor system" as he called it. I tried this approach in print, but the possibilities were limited. In my first novel *Love and The Dragonfly*, written in the 1970's, I experimented with multiple modalities by using the "elements" feature on my IBM Selectric typewriter; this allowed me to assign different typefaces to each kind of segment/fragment. However, using conventional print, I could do no more than change fonts on a static page. The opportunity for layering, multiple linkages, imagery, sound, and symbolic architecture—the technology to actually do that—would not come into my hands for another fifteen years.

As with many ambitious, epic-like narrative works (both in print and in digital form) the idea for *Califia* germinated long before the writing began. For many years, while I was "working" on the concepts for *Califia*, the technology did not exist for its creation.

Like the characters in *Califia*, I had a legacy of gold from my ancestors, but most of it was in the form of photographs, documents, brochures, old newspapers, diaries, and family myths. I started assembling these. And I began to teach myself the skills I would need to write the novel that I imagined. In addition to word processing, I learned to manipulate images and photos, create animations, do some programming, and edit sound. It was to be a montaged, multi-modal, interlinked story of three California families as their lives intersected over five generations of Los Angeles history.

Califia: *The moment I began to create the first screen on the computer, I could see it happening: the weary and beleaguered Samuel Walker—leaving the Tejon Ranch with his wife, Willing Stars, and the renegade mission Indians—desperate to find a place to hide the heavy gold he had mined in the Sierras.*

And the generations that followed, dreamers all, risking their lives for the belief that the gold was still there, buried and waiting for the one who could decode the clues, read the hypertext of star lore and plot maps and legends of gold and movies and airplanes and the history of water and land combines: find pattern in a seeming chaos of desire. Erskine Summerland was in my imaginary California, flying a plane from San Simeon to Tehachapi and straight into a mountain. Quintana, of Chinatown, lost to fire and water. I saw Augusta, just the other day, digging in her own back yard the morning after her father was buried, certain he had left a stash of gold coins under the eucalyptus grove above Hollywood Boulevard. . . .

And you, too, were there. All of us at the interface between acceptance and passion. The western edge is a place where, as Joan Didion once wrote: "the mind is troubled by some buried but ineradicable suspicion that things had better work here, because here, beneath that immense bleached sky, is where we run out of continent."

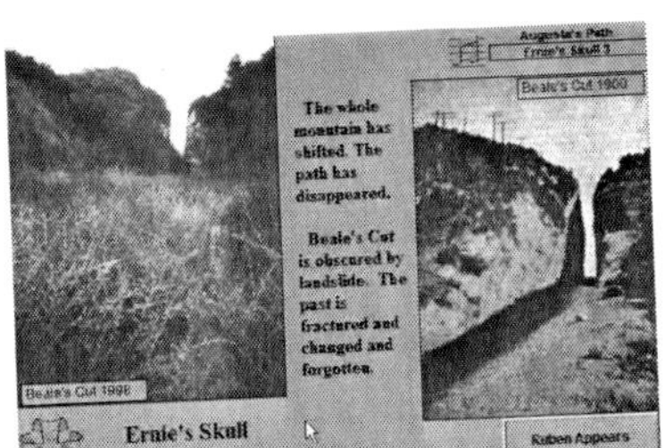

Figure 3: The past is fractured and changed and forgotten.

NEH SEMINAR - LITERATURE IN TRANSITION, UCLA

In 1995 I was awarded an NEH fellowship to attend Katherine Hayles' seminar, "Literature in Transition: The Impact of Information Technologies" at UCLA. The seminar provided an overview of recent scholarship on electronic textuality and offered participants the opportunity to develop their own electronic texts. It was a watershed time for me. This experience served as a catalyst for bringing *Califia* from concept to finished coding. Kate was a knowledgeable and inspired leader; she arranged for our group to become familiar with the new fiction and poetry, the authors and artists working in this medium (in fact, many of the students in her seminars subsequently became pioneers of e-lit), and the tools for creating digital projects. I first tried Storyspace, but I wanted to use color images and sound, which Storyspace did not support, so I moved to Toolbook. Happily, by the end of the seminar, I had a start on *Califia* in electronic form.

Califia *was written in Toolbook software. Platform requirements: Windows 95, 98, 2000, or later (Mac/Windows emulator), Pentium-speed processor, and sound card. It has Three Narrating Characters, Four Directions of the Compass, Star Charts, Map Case, Archives Files, 500 Megabytes, 800 Screens, 2400 Images, 30 Songs, and 500 Words. Graphics were prepared using Photoshop and Micrografix Picture Publisher. Music was edited with Cakewalk.*

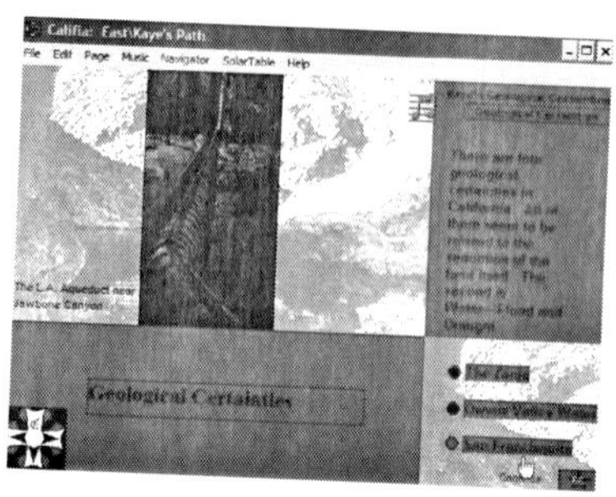

Figure 4: The four certainties of Southern California: water, wind, earthquake, fire

THE SOFTWARE SCRAMBLE

Once I was set with an authoring system that met my needs, the writing of *Califia* was rooted and running. I had the rough outline of a story, the raw images, and a structure that would allow me to integrate the characters, history, myths, and popular culture into what I hoped would be truer than reality. Oh, but I needed sound. I set out to get some tunes.

Califia *features the work of excellent California musicians. The flamenco music is written and performed by Michael Olsen. The classical lute and mandolin music is performed by John Schneiderman. Clips from The Grateful Dead were made available by the Grateful Dead organization with the valuable assistance of Alan Trist.*

Califia was a joy to write. It took some experimenting to build the structure in a way that the navigation would be seamless: one keystroke could take the reader to any section of the story. Having the freedom to indicate relationships between characters, places, symbols, and events (present and past) gave the story a vitality and dimensionality that I could not have conveyed in traditional print. Each working day was an opportunity to invent something new.

Califia *traces five generations of Californians from 1849 to the present; its layered histories contain legends of early sea and land explorers, Chumash Indian tribes, lost gold mines, and the Dream of Islands that makes all Californians seekers.*

By far the most time-consuming and headache-producing part of constructing *Califia* was getting the software and the early computer hardware to do what I had in mind. Fortunately, technology improved as the writing went on and seemed to deliver additional functionality. When I started, I could only use 256 colors; by the time I finished, every shade in the rainbow was possible, millions of colors. Someone less delighted with the medium might have anticipated trouble on the horizon: but not me, not then.

GOLDEN DAYS

The year 2000 was a great year in the *Califia* journey. The tech problems were solved, the piece was pretty much finished, and Eastgate Systems had agreed to publish it. Reviewers were kind, friends were congratulatory, and readers were enthusiastic.

Califia: *consists of four journeys that the reader can choose among:*

> *The Comets in the Yard - The Journey* **South** *is just a few blocks down Fairfax Avenue in Hollywood to Paradise Home, where Violet Summerland forgets among the palms.*
>
> *Wind, Sand, and Stars -* **East** *takes the characters into the desert-land of Windmills and Goldmines to meet the Man from Windpower. The Dipper Mines begin to appear in the sky and on the ground.*
>
> *Night of the Bear - In the* **North** *is San Simeon, but along the way our characters get visits from the spirits, an unexpected plane ride, and another look at the Summerland-Beveridge history.*

The Journey Out - The golden **West** *brings a choice of endings and a suggestion of beginnings. Augusta, Kaye, and Calvin find the Blue Blanket, and, with it, the message from Willing Stars.*

THE WRITING ON THE WALL AND THEN, SUDDENLY, THE WALL ITSELF

"Perhaps the dream they sold us is not quite the dream we got."

The way in which these fragile works begin to fray, the edges to crumble, and the center fail is now somewhat well known. The disturbing signs are much the same, although they may not happen in the same order. The company that makes the software to process photos, animation, or sound goes out of business. The authoring software platform is sold to another company, which declines to support it. The method of storage and transfer evolves (from floppy disk to zip disk to CD-ROM to thumb drive to cloud), and corresponding changes in machine hardware won't accommodate a work. The machine rendering advances so far that the work is all but unrecognizable. Successive browsers do not support the coding. All of these happened to *Califia*.

And then, one fine morning, it was not possible for me to play *Califia* on my own desktop. The center had collapsed.

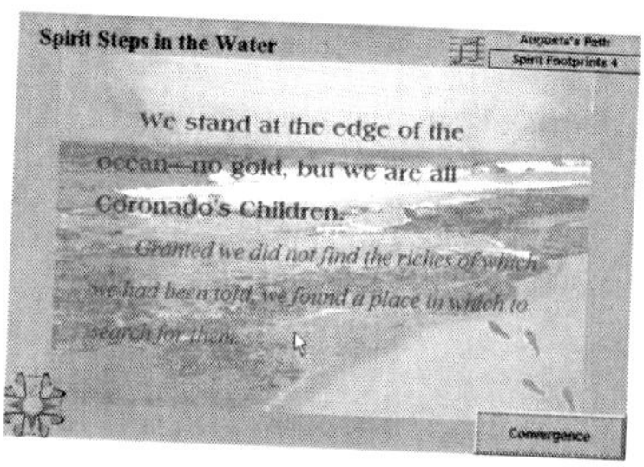

Figure 5: Violet's spirit steps in the water.

Califia*: is narrated by three contemporary California types:*

Augusta, the day-trader, lives in Whitley Heights in Hollywood, California. She is looking for the stash of coins she believes her father buried on the hill behind the house.

Calvin, the would-be movie director, lives next door. He is between film projects and hopes to find out more about the mysterious death of Jack Summerland.

Kaye, the mystic visionary, floats in one day in her midnight-blue cape, decorated with moons and stars, and tells the legends and family myths that set our characters on a journey of discovery.

CALIFORNIA OPTIMISM

Today, *Califia* sits in a technological limbo. But, as a child of the West, I am hopeful about the prospects. New techniques of archiving and preservation are being developed. "Virtual Machine" software is emerging that can replicate the operating system of an obsolete computer, provided that a working model still exists. These developments may bring a future when a copy of *Califia* can be called up and experienced just as it was in the beginning.

And the promise of a literature that combines text, image, sound, and architecture still beckons.

Califia: *Even now, Augusta, Kaye, and Calvin are out in the Mojave Desert, looking for the lost paradise.*

The Death and Re-Distribution of *V*

BY STEPHANIE STRICKLAND

I. BRIEF HISTORY

V is a multi-part poem that explores a weave of ways to cast and map text.[189] *V: WaveSon.nets / Losing L'una* (2002), a double book published by Penguin, won the Poetry Society of America's Alice Fay Di Castagnola Award. Its two components, bound upside-down to each other, lead to a URL printed on the V of pages at their joining midpoint. Arriving from either direction, a reader can upend the book to continue print reading—or go online to read *V: Vniverse*, a Director project created with Cynthia Lawson and published in *The Iowa Review Web* concurrently with the book's appearance. A fourth, earlier, part of *V* exists, *Errand Upon Which We Came*, a Flash interpretation of one poem in *Losing L'una*. It was created with M.D. Coverley and published in *Cauldron and Net* in 2001.

V explores configuration vs. sequence, time-based vs. fixed access, and alphabetic vs. diagrammatic display in its evocation of modes of knowing from the Ice to the Information Age. The play-read process is an iterative one, both within the Shockwave file and across the print/digital divide. *V: Vniverse* was selected to appear in the *Electronic Literature Collection Volume 2*, 2011, edited by Laura Borràs, Talan Memmott, Rita Raley, and Brian Kim Stefans.

The demise of Director/Shockwave after its lack of support by Apple and purchase by Adobe, the out-of-print status of the Penguin book, and the summary withdrawal of the server to which the *Cauldron and Net* issue linked raise the question of the death of *V*, differing deaths of its differing parts. *The Iowa Review Web* (TIR Web) has also largely disappeared, but some portions, including *V*, are still accessible on the Wayback Machine. *Errand* and Shockwave *Vniverse* are available via the author's website (2015).

In 2014 a new edition of *V* in print, *V : WaveTercets / Losing L'una*, was published by SpringGun Press. Together with a coordinating app for iPad, a new *Vniverse* created with Ian Hatcher, this brings *V*'s parts to six. *Son.nets* in the Penguin edition

189 http://vniverse.com; http://collection.eliterature.org/2/; http://www.springgunpress.com/vstephanie-strickland; http://califia.us/Errand/title1a.htm; https://search.itunes.apple.com/WebObjects/MZContentLink.woa/wa/link?path=apps%2fvniverse; http://www.amazon.com/V-WaveSonnets-Losing-Stephanie-Strickland/dp/0142002453.

became *Tercets* in the SpringGun edition. The "new" text of the *Tercets* is in fact the original form in which *V* was written, one long standing wave of numbered units that did not align page or unit boundaries with punctuated closure—a long scrolling that, at the time, I felt was *not* appropriate for a codex. Current familiarity both with scrolling and with small numbered units used online to track location have since changed expectations in the codex environment.

While six parts, approachable in any order, give rise to a large number of combinatory modes, the actual state of affairs with the *V* project has stayed constant—it only ever existed partially on any one platform; it has always posed the problem/choice for the reader of not only which platform to read it on, initially, but also how to read it on that platform. It always exists most intensely in the space between platforms, or media, as one becomes aware of completely different aspects as salient.

Long investigation of "the book," from tablet to scroll to manuscript, from artist's to print-on-demand, has elucidated many of its features. Far less explored are the potentials for poetry introduced by digital technology, such as the potential for concurrent sequences with divergent timings, a capability that goes far beyond the scope of ordinary rhythmic synchronizations. In a digital literature, written less with "places" and more with "transitions," space opens up to a world of currents and transcodings. One does not see spaces full, so much as feel them fill. They are performed, partly in connection with others, in processes of transfer that propagate.

Digital reading practice is also necessarily inflected both by mathematical constraint and lines of code. In the print text of *V* many different kinds of number occur (some of which are described in the TIR Web interview).[190] Very often these disrupt or puncture the text. They always punctuate it in some way, but not in the conventional way numbers are used to separate stanzas. One must decide whether to read across the number, to actually read it, or to treat it as a pause of varying length.

V marks as well a suspended interim-interval where astronomy and astrology split apart, the proto-science of Tarot hanging on. One exemplary figure is that of Katarina Kepler, imprisoned witch, mother of Johannes Kepler who gave us the laws of the planetary orbits. His work on the "lunar observer" had been rejected by authorities who connected it to old wives' tales of the witch's flight to the moon. *V* as a poem is positioned between these two, or three, modes of thought, in itself a claim that the in-between is where we live, that a kind of continual translation or negotiation or cross-border activity is what gives lives their pith, that there is ever a need to move on and ask about the more that is submerged in any one presentation.

190 https://web.archive.org/web/20060218053351/http://www.uiowa.edu/~iareview/tirweb/feature/strickland/index.html#.

II. LOSS OF HOVER: RECREATING SHOCKWAVE VNIVERSE AS AN APP FOR IPAD[191]

The *V* project is dedicated in the Penguin and SpringGun editions to Simone Weil—

For *Simone Weil*, her Life & Thought;
her need to touch;
her gut, her mouth

—and thereby dedicated to embodied knowing. Weil faulted the Greeks only in this, that they counted the work of hands as less important than the work of mind. Her essay "Factory Work," completed after she had spent a backbreaking year as a factory worker, expands specifically on how arbitrary scheduling of the body undercuts the mind's ability to evolve embodied knowing. The *V* project's various modes of idiosyncratic manual interaction, analog and digital, together explore and are a tribute to gestural routes for thought.

Essays by Maria Angel and Anna Gibbs (2013; 2014) have directed our attention to e-writing's embodiment. They quote Bronowski, "the hand is the cutting edge of the mind," and lay out Marcel Jousse's view of gesture as the body's "direct resonance" with the energies of the environment. A 2014 *New York Times* article, "What's Lost as Handwriting Fades" (Konnikova 2014), claims that young children's brains activate more, they learn to read more quickly, and they remain better able to generate ideas and retain information when they learn their letters by drawing freehand, as compared with typing or tracing. In both lab and real-world settings, students who take notes by hand learn better than when they keyboard.

Angel and Gibbs view words as material architectures. Diagrams, notation, and images should be considered material architectures as well. The hand is the point of contact with these architectures. The hand both manipulates and gestures, and these two actions should be recognized as separate; however, they are often metaphorically mapped onto one another by the e-writer, and this mapping is often at the heart of both the significance and the affect of a piece.

Davin Heckman, in his paper "Technics and Violence in Electronic Literature" (2011), explores e-lit as a form of violence against technical systems by way of explicating Serge Bouchardon's hand-to-hand battles in his works, *The 12 Labors of the Internet User*, *Touch*, and *Loss of Grasp*. Heckman stresses that, for Bouchardon, grasp signifies control. The loss of it arouses an anxious desire in the protagonist of *Loss of Grasp*, as well as in the reader who is shown a man whose grasp of his place in city, cosmos,

191 A portion of this section of the paper is based on a talk given with Ian Hatcher at ELO 2014 in Milwaukee and subsequently published in the special issue of *Cultural Studies Review* on Literary Practices and Performances in Transmedia Environments.

marriage, and parenthood is troubled, as are his perceptions of homophones and of sequence. The hand actions in all three of Bouchardon's Flash pieces, including the hit, move, caress, stretch, and scrub-like motions of *Touch*, are mouse-strokes or movements of the cursor. Two other kinds of digital touch exist, the resistive pressure touch required at an ATM machine and the capacitance contact of tablets and cell phones.

One work for the multi-touch screen that maps the manipulation use of the hand to a gestural meaning is the novella *Pry* by Samantha Gorman and Danny Cannizzaro. Here a two-finger pinch-apart gesture is used to pry open an onscreen eye. As manipulation, this action yields what used to be called stretch-text, a new insertion of text in an existing writing; as plot or framing device, it accesses subconscious awareness of the protagonist. It may also, imagistically, refer to *Un Chien Andalou* by Buñuel. The cursor gestures of Bouchardon's touch pieces, the eye-stretching gesture of *Pry*, and the gestures of first-person shooter literary games are all metaphorically meaningful and so too are those of the *Vniverse.*

V is a poem of *migration*, not only in form but also in referenced content: Ice Age/Information Age, equally nomadic, explored one against the other. Ice Age nomads in their life of travel paid obvious attention to glaciers and plant life and the migratory patterns of fish and mammals. Equally they attended that distant, unreachable but readable realm, the night sky, full of what we call stars, planets, comets, but really a night filled with traveling patterns, whether brilliant pixels or nodes, or neurons perhaps.

For nomadic people, strategies of signification are inherently time-based. Their paths are loops created in interaction with the weather. Ice-Age nomads invented a Zodiac of constellations, the clock, calendar, and map by which they tracked animals and seasons together. Information Age migrants crawl, physically and virtually, a globe-spanning network run on satellites and towers. *Vniverse* is a Star-Body grid accessed on an Information Power grid. To it we bring what the Ice Age reader brought to the circling sky—either impulses, go here, go there, or survival-oriented questions: for people of the Ice Age, how to intersect with migrating animals, or how to keep from bearing children when temperatures reach minus sixty degrees. For them, the sky was an Oracle, a constructed relation to a natural world probed with calculations. For us, the digital world is precisely that.

The original Shockwave *Vniverse* aimed to create an interface of gestures with an analogy to the hunting of animals or stars: choose to hunt them, discern them in their disappearing, linger, learn their signs, retrace their paths, and then engage with some persistence or force; cause disappearance, go back and inquire, re-associate, make your own meanings to justify the interference or death you have caused.

V visually can suggest hands of a clock, a volumetric wedge of sky, a witch's conical hat; it suggests an opening, an interim, an interval, a space-between extreme positions. *V* exists in the space between its variations in print and online, and in this it resembles ancient oral poems that have no canonical original with respect to which other versions are derivative. They consist, instead, in the set of performances and notations that exist and can be expanded or compressed at any time should some be amplified or lost.

The *Vniverse* does not have colored pictures or soundtracks that many associate with hypermedia projects. Cynthia Lawson and I took a decision not to include these, although originally we considered a large set of images, because our primary interest was in exploring an extensive text project online. The diagrams work together with colored text and the visual images of the letters themselves, as these move, disappear, and are replaced or overlaid. The *Vniverse* interface uses text as it is broken and assembled and "constellation" shapes to create a world of new meanings. The ten constellations are not those of either astronomy or astrology but shapes associated with the material of the poems. They are named in the SpringGun text.

Though either the book or the digital *Vniverse/s* can be read alone, the richest meanings will occur to people who are reading between them. Within the Shockwave *Vniverse* itself many opportunities for "reading between" arise: the spelling out of triplets enables the reader to engage, in an almost auditory manner, successive letters of the poem; the WaveSon.nets associated with each constellation may be read from it—and colored keywords at each star create a "compressed" mini poem; assembled poems may be toggled back and forth between WaveSon.net and five-triplet forms that share a set of words, but not the same organization or title; both WaveSon.nets or triplet sets in decay can be read as dense visual palimpsests; the WaveSon.nets assemble differently depending on which star is clicked to initiate them; WaveSon.nets or triplet sets, while they are spelling out or decaying, can be overlaid with new text as the reader moves the cursor across the sky.

The entire *Vniverse* is designed to reward an exploration and persistence such as Ice Age nomads must have shown. It is also, however, an always renewable, forgiving space where all options are open at any time. Though responsive and renewable, it is not in every respect re-playable. Fill and decay, transitions, intermediaries, fades and residues are a great part of the matter of this sky. As the reader moves on by pressing "next," the highlighted tercet will be one chosen at random by the computer, making the temporal fragility of reading palpable. One can exactly recapitulate a reading experience only when the *Vniverse*'s sibylline space is probed directly by number, by entering any star's number in the small circular dial in the upper right of the screen.

The Shockwave *Vniverse* was created all in one frame of Director's timeline. This choice took advantage of the speed of imaging Lingo to control both animation and interaction, permitting swift gestural command of language as it appeared to emerge without lag from "the sky." Time never advances—so far as the Director timeline is concerned—but it is highly active. All of the time resources go toward responsiveness and the production of language rather than visual display, space fashioned to amplify the sense of resonance that internal timings create.

The Shockwave interface presents a text-less dot-sprinkled screen (after the loading of a twirling screen of such dots which seemed from the start to be spontaneously read as stars). It requires the reader to interact *without* directions (though some are accessible via the small X at lower screen left). One must choose to "read the stars," just as Ice Age nomads facing a sky they could not mark—but could interact with—made it into something they could read. As eyes sweep the night sky, a corollary swinging, sweeping gesture of the hand/cursor reveals diagrammed constellations, numbers, and words that appear and *immediately disappear*.

Hovering, or lingering *without* clicking, an analog to Ice Age focus on a particular part of the sky, produces the spelling out text of a keyword-tagged-and-numbered Tercet. The moment the hand leaves that spot, interactive response is lost. There is a sense of releasing text by lingering on it. As a corollary to what must have been repeated and devoted Ice Age focus, actually clicking a star stabilizes its constellation—the shape remains onscreen even as the hand moves away. One may trace the constellation *without clicking* to create compressed poems consisting of keywords—one can also *hover without clicking* over any star in the sky to read its released text against the shape of the currently stabilized constellation.

To produce knowledge of multi-year differences in the sky required enormous, persistent communal attention. In the *Vniverse*, a second click on the same spot releases the text of a 15-line WaveSon.net assembled, not sequentially, but beginning with that star's Tercet and in relation to it. Metaphorically one follows, or tracks, this assembling. The need for multi-directional awareness—natural in Ice Age hunters—is recruited as well in the Information Age. Clicking a third time, and thereafter, toggles between Tercet and Son.net form. Clicking for the third time in the same place is the most obsessive/aggressive gesture required. Persistence, persistent re-seeing, requires one to imagine that each node has an unexamined depth.

Clicking a "next" triggers a second Son.net bleeding through the first. A text-decay process takes place that leaves many states of the poem co-present onscreen: time of break-up, time of emergence, and time of cross-layer existence between dissolving and emerging co-exist with the time of reading forward. At any point in this sequence of responses by the sky, the hand can hover, overlaying any diagram or assemblage or bleed-through of text with a new number, a newly colored keyword, or Tercet from any place in the sky. Finally, clicking on the darkness—made possible by the pixel precision of the hovering cursor—makes everything disappear. The play-read process is massively iterative. Iterative processes of return overwhelm individual differences in sampling, just as years of sky observation yielded recognizable astronomical cycles, or significant conjunctions. Extinction, as much as production, is to be read.

These cognitive gestures are distinct and complementary to those required by print forms of *V*. As Edward Picot wrote:

> reading…in this hopping-and-dipping manner rather than in sequence seems to bring out more quickly the themes which run through the whole group—references to astronomy, to cosmological time, to mathematical sequences, to Tarot cards, to Simone Weil, and the letter *V*, symbolizing fertility and virginity both at the same time [...] the spreading-out of stars in "a wedge of the sky" and the spreading-out of electrons in a cathode-ray tube. (2003)

Indeed, to arrive at so *summary* an understanding from the print book could take hours.

Phones and tablets do not support Flash/Director. For the Vniverse to live, or be resuscitated, newly distributed, it needed new co-creators and new coding, becoming part of the larger family of works all of which bear on its vitality.

The iPad *Vniverse* was first attempted in Titanium, which translates JavaScript code into native languages for both Apple and Android devices. Ian Hatcher was eventually forced to reject this insufficiently stable environment, even though he had hoped to avoid learning Objective-C, the proprietary language of Apple platforms. As he noted, Objective-C code is verbose, hard to learn, and Apple is an arbitrarily-dictating, black-box-engineering profit monster.

The Objective-C *Vniverse* is built with new gestures and with gesture "translations." In the necessary trade-off between what is reasonably done in time available, "hover" is lost: no lingering, sweeping, prosthetic cursor—no cursor at all to operate as a pacing device; no clicking, single or repeated. Instead, under capacitive touch, the sky is brought down under our hands. On that sky, readers discover—recover—the distinct pleasure of shaping constellations, freely connecting stars as they wish in Draw Mode. These novel shapes do not immediately fade but persist until actively cleared. Exploring space this way is something like building a simulation, whereas cursor sweeps of the original *Vniverse* more closely resemble a searching inspection of what cannot be directly touched.

Options for interaction on the iPad *Vniverse* are signaled by five Mode buttons along the length of the screen: Draw, Constellations, WaveTercets, Oracle, and Clear. A complete linear play-through of the 232 Tercets is available in WaveTercets Mode, something the Shockwave *Vniverse* did not provide. Steve Tomasula says:

> I was reading it, then carried the iPad into a dark room, so dark I couldn't see the iPad, only *Vniverse*, and the constellations stood out in a way that was so evocative [...] I lay on a bed with the iPad above me, like lying in a field, looking up at a starry night as the poetry played across the constellations. [...] Such a great reading experience. (Private email communication, 2014)

Here touching the iPad is self-inhibited; Steve is not looking down on it, but up! Certainly this reading (a kind of *reading-to-you*) is both more oral and more active than print. The ongoing play-through of the Tercets can be shifted or re-begun at any point by touching any star at which one wishes to initiate the sequence.

A pausing or paused attention is hard to achieve on the multi-touch screen. To touch it is to commit to an act. The pause is most closely approached in Constellations Mode. In this Mode, the text of any Tercet stays still as you read it, and one can explore the keyword outline of the Constellation to learn that this order is not identical to the sequential order of Tercets.

The iPad *Vniverse*, unlike its predecessor, features an Oracle which the reader may consult, choosing from seven supplied questions. The Oracle's responses are unpredictable and enigmatic—it is a black box, a closed system within the closed system of the compiled app which in turn resides within the black box of the iPad, a proprietary consumer device. The Oracle, like the iPad, can be asked for information or operated as a tool, but its borders of acceptable usage are strictly controlled and its secrets as a system remain hidden. The inclusion of the Oracle, however, is an example of using gesture and interaction metaphorically to engage, contest, or comment on literature's—and society's—organization.

To move from one platform to another, from a Flash to an iPad environment, is to affect the meaning of directionality, trajectory, and haptic space. The translation can entail the loss of a manipulation—the mouse-down movement no longer exists, the moment of touch is a mouse-release moment—which then entails a loss of gesture: the non-clicking pause/linger/hover. As well there is a loss of location—a point is no longer a fixed place—and a loss of overview, or revelation, as sweeping gestures become swipes and no longer reveal, but re-scale, though Ian Hatcher and I ultimately inhibited zooming in order to insure legibility of the text. Though almost every effect possible in the Shockwave environment is reproducible in Objective-C, implementation decisions are made using different categories: instead of manipulating mouse-gesture, one plays with time delays and scale.

Emotional coloring shifts when an expansive swinging hand-arm movement is substituted by fingers' contractive pinch-zoom. This more physiologically constrained motion—instead of gaining in precision as expected in the physical world—is in fact less precise, less pixel-specific.

How do these shifts relate to the handwriting studies with children? A theorized part of the value of freehand writing is the variability of the child's output: it is non-standardization which activates the child brain. Politically an environment exists in which millions of readers are trained in an eccentric set of gestures. As screen real estate decreases, more pressure is brought to bear on allowed movements and toward standardized visualizations. One senses that the ultimate goal is attempted direct reading of neurons via some kind of sensor jewelry worn by the user, as if the ideal were to bypass the conscious plane altogether.

To what extent do the movements permitted us for manipulation, which always map onto metaphoric gestures, feed back onto our forms of knowing, both cultural and neuronal? Never have so many people been routed through such a minimal number of highly routinized gestures—not the gestures of hunting or planting that were developed over generations, but rather those devised quickly in some few laboratories of design—and never have these gestures been so widely needed, to obtain a job, to obtain knowledge, to obtain access—even to one's own information. The very youngest are being taught aggressive intervention and one right answer; they are given no occasion to pause, linger, consider, or return for the particular response that is, at that moment, idiosyncratically right.

Quoting Davin Heckman, from a 2014 email exchange with which I deeply agree:

> I struggle constantly with being able to explore the space and scale of the screen [...] because my finger is a very literal material part of me [...] while the cursor functions as a true prosthetic, capable of extending my reach into the space, but not being actually me in that space [....] With touch screen, I have no control over the representation of myself...I do not manipulate the space. Instead, I participate directly in it, and am thus manipulated by the space itself."

Can one critique media from within by doing something like modding? Or by significantly varying pacing or gesture—perhaps especially introducing variability into gestures by creating a family or swarm of works? Or is the proprietary black box the deck of the Titanic—on/in which we play at our peril? Or, indeed, do "on" and "in" lose any of the oppositional quality they have in a gravitational world? Are we already at sea, having lost overboard our children's freehand gestures and perhaps thereby part of their ability to engage, and contest, , the enormous concentration of global power that knows them, and manipulates them, through computation?

WORKS CITED

Angel, Maria and Anna Gibbs, "At the Time of Writing: Digital Media, Gesture, and Handwriting." *electronic book review*, August 30, 2013. http://www.electronicbookreview.com/thread/electropoetics/gesture.

_,_. "The Ethos of 'Walking': digital writing and the temporal animation of space." *Formules* 18 (2014): 155-167.

Heckman, Davin. "Technics and Violence in Electronic Literature." *Culture Machine* 12 (2011). http://www.culturemachine.net/index.php/cm/article/view/435/464

Konnikova, Maria. "What's Lost as Handwriting Fades." *New York Times*, June 2, 2014.

Picot, Edward. "Hyperliterature: The Apotheosis of Self-Publishing?" *Slope* 17 (2003). http://www.slope.org/archive/issue17/hyper_intro5.html.

Reeves, Eileen Adair. "Old Wives' Tales and the New World System: Gilbert, Galileo, and Kepler." *Configurations* 7.3 (1999): 301-354.

Contributor Biographies

Maria Angel and **Anna Gibbs** both teach at Western Sydney University. This research was supported by the Australian Government through the Australian Research Council's Discovery Projects funding scheme (project DP 110105548). They have published widely on e-literature and their most recent work is forthcoming in a book *Exscryptions: Memory, Movement and the unfolding of Space in Digital Writing*, to be published by Open Humanities Press.

Kate Armstrong is a writer, artist and curator based in Vancouver, Canada. She is the author of *Crisis & Repetition: Essays on Art and Culture* (Michigan State University Press, 2002) in addition to numerous essays. She has written for *P.S.1/MoMa*, *Blackflash*, *Fillip*, *SubTerrain*, and the *Kootenay School of Writing*, and is the editor of *Electric Speed* (Surrey Art Gallery, 2013) and *Art and Disruption* (New Forms Press, 2015). Her interdisciplinary practice merges networked media, written forms and urban experiences and engages with open forms of production that bring poetics and computation together in physical or network space. Her works are held in public and private collections including Rhizome, the Rose Goldsen Archive in the Division of Rare and Manuscript Collections at Cornell University, the Clara Thomas Archives and Special Collections at York University, the Library of the Printed Web, and the Whitney Museum of American Art. As a curator she has 15 years international experience producing exhibitions, events and publications in contemporary art and technology. Armstrong is the Director of Living Labs at Emily Carr University of Art + Design.

Kathi Inman Berens, Assistant Professor of Digital Humanities and Book Publishing in Portland State University's English department, researches and make electronic literature. She was the 2014-15 Fulbright Scholar of Digital Culture at the University in Bergen, Norway. Her scholarship has been published in *Digital Scholarship in the Humanities* (Oxford) and her poem "Tournedo Gorge" is anthologized in the *Electronic Literature Collection Volume 3*.

Mez Breeze's award-winning creations have helped shape digital fiction for over two decades. *#PRISOM*, her Augmented Reality game created with Andy Campbell, is "... the digital equivalent of Orwell's 1984" (according to James O'Sullivan). Mez is a Coproducer, Creative Director and Writer of the upcoming *Inanimate Alice: Perpetual Nomads* Virtual Reality/Novel Series, co-creator of *All the Delicate Duplicates*, Advisor to The Mixed Augmented Reality Art Research Organisation, and is developing a comprehensive career archive with Duke University.

Amaranth Borsuk is a poet, scholar, and book artist interested in textual materiality across media. Her most recent book is *Pomegranate Eater* (Kore, 2016). Previous books include *As We Know* (Subito, 2014), with Andy Fitch; *Handiwork* (Slope, 2012); and *Between Page and Screen* (Siglio, 2012; SpringGun, 2016), with Brad Bouse. Her intermedia project *Abra* (1913 Press, 2016), created with Kate Durbin and Ian Hatcher, received an NEA-funded Expanded Artists' Books grant and was recently issued as a limited-edition hand-made book and free iOS app. Her digital collaborations include *The Deletionist*, with Nick Montfort and Jesper Juul, which creates erasures from websites; and *Whispering Galleries*, with Brad Bouse, a LEAP interactive textwork for the New Haven Free Public Libraries. Borsuk's essays appear in *Media-N*, *Writing Technologies*, *The Journal for Cultural and Religious Theory*, *The Journal of Electronic Publishing*, *EBR*, and *Jacket2*. After receiving her Ph.D. in Literature and Creative Writing at the University of Southern California, Borsuk served as Mellon Postdoctoral Fellow in the Humanities at the Massachusetts Institute of Technology. She is currently Assistant Professor Interdisciplinary Arts and Sciences at the University of Washington, Bothell, where she also teaches in the MFA in Creative Writing and Poetics.

J. R. Carpenter is a Canadian-born UK-based artist, writer, performer, and researcher working in the intersecting fields of digital literature, performance writing, and media archaeology. Her work been exhibited, published, performed, and presented in journals, galleries, museums, and festivals around the world. She is a winner of the CBC Quebec Writing Competition, the QWF Carte Blanche Quebec Award, the Expozine Alternative Press Award for Best English Book, and the Dot Award for Digital Literature. Her website is http://luckysoap.com.

Giovanna Di Rosario received her PhD in Digital Culture at the University of Jyväskylä, Finland. Di Rosario is currently a researcher at the Université Catholique de Louvain, Belgium (Marie Curie Actions), where she conducts research on digital literature and digital rhetoric. Previously she has worked in Denmark, Finland, Italy, Spain, and Switzerland. She is also the associate director of Hermeneia Research Group (University of Barcelona) and the managing editor of the "International Journal of Transmedia Literacy."

Odile Farge has a Ph.D. in information and communication sciences. Her research activities focus primarily on such areas as software tools, digital culture, digital literature, digital humanism. Working at the junction of computer science, the arts, humanities and social sciences, she uses a socio-semiotic approach to digital writing and concentrates her research on the digital humanities, analyzing creation tools from a critical perspective. Her thesis entitled A "rhetoric for creative authoring" dealt with becoming aware of the strategies inherent in creative authoring tools, proposing a typology for authors' positions. Farge has been associate researcher of UNESCO ITEN Chair (Innovation, Transmission, Digital Publication) since 2015, in charge of the Digital Humanism Program which brings together an international network of experts and researchers from various disciplines, with the aim of questioning the methods and policies of regulations, the representations and challenges of digital tools for individuals and tomorrow's society.

Natalia Fedorova is a new media poet, a digital literature scholar and a 101.Mediapoetry Festival curator. In collaboration with a sonic artist Taras Mashtalir she founded a media poetry project Machine Libertine. *Noor*, a brain opera with her libretto, was presented at ISEA, 2016. Her audio and video poems appeared in *TextSound*, *Rattapallax*, *LIT* magazine, and *Ill-Tempered Rubyist*, *räume für notizen | rooms for notes* as well as number of international festivals and biennales (ISEA 2016, ELO 2015, 6th Moscow Biennale of Contemporary Art, Manifesta 10, Krasnoyarsk Book Culture Fair, REVERSE, Moscow Book Festival, E-Poetry, LUMEN EX, Interrupt II, VideoBardo, Liberated Words, Tarp and others). Natalia holds a PhD in literary theory from Herzen State University (St-Petersburg). Natalia won a Fulbright scholarship to do her first year postdoctorate term at the Trope Tank at MIT, where she worked on translating e-lit; and SPIRE to develop Russian Electronic Literature Collection in a specialized knowledge base at the University of Bergen for her second year term. She is currently teaching creative writing with new media and text-based art in Smolny College (St-Petersburg State University – Bard College) and curating a Mediapoetry lab at the New Stage of Alexandrinsky Theatre. Natalia is a member of editorial board of Translit an almanach for contemporary poetry.

María Goicoechea teaches English and US-American literature at the University Complutense of Madrid. Goicoechea's recent publications include the edited volume *Alicia a través de la pantalla. Lecturas literarias en el siglo XXI* (2013), and the articles "The Mechanic Ear: North American Sound Poetry in the Digital Age," *Complutense Journal of English Studies* (with Víctor Salceda, 2015) and "Literary Reading Rituals and Practices on New Interfaces," *Literary and Linguistic Computing* (with Amelia Sanz, 2012).

Dene Grigar is Professor and Director of The Creative Media & Digital Culture Program at Washington State University Vancouver whose research focuses on the creation, curation, preservation, and criticism of Electronic Literature, specifically building multimedial environments and experiences for live performance, installations, and curated spaces; desktop computers; and mobile media devices. She has authored 14 media works such as "Curlew" (2014), "A Villager's Tale" (2011), the "24-Hour Micro E-Lit Project" (2009), "When Ghosts Will Die" (2008), and "Fallow Field: A Story in Two Parts" (2005), as well as 52 scholarly articles. She also curates exhibits of electronic literature and media art, mounting shows at the Library of Congress and for the Symposium on Electronic Art (ISEA) and the Modern Language Association (MLA), among other venues. With Stuart Moulthrop (U of Wisconsin Milwaukee) she is the recipient of a 2013 NEH Start Up grant to support the digital preservation of early electronic literature, a project that culminated in an open-source, multimedia book entitled *Pathfinders* and book of criticism, entitled *Traversals*, for The MIT Press. She is President of the Electronic Literature Organization and Associate Editor of *Leonardo Reviews*.

Angelica Huizar is Chairperson and Associate Professor of Spanish and International Studies at Old Dominion University. Her research and teaching interests focus on avant-garde poetry, Latin American digital poetics, and graduate seminars on Cultural Studies. She has authored several refereed publications and presented more than forty professional conference papers in the United States, Canada and Mexico. Her book entitled, *Beyond the Page: Latin American Poetry from the Calligramme to the Virtual* (Academica Press, 2008), focuses on the aesthetic and theoretical relationships between art, music, sound, visual typography and the word in avant-garde poetry including digital poetics of Mexico, Uruguay, Chile, Peru and Brazil. Her most recent research interests center on digital poetics and aesthetics through a cultural studies lens.

Zuzana Husárová is a Slovak author and scholar of literary theory and (post)digital media, teaching at the Comenius University (SR) and at the Universität für angewandte Kunst (AT), an ex- Fulbright scholar at the MIT. She creates electronic, sound and experimental poetry across media, transmedia projects (liminal and lucent) and co-edited monographs on electronic literature research and practice: *V sieti strednej Európy* (with Bogumila Suwara) and *ENTER+ Repurposing in Electronic Literature* (with María Mencía). Her website is http://zuz.husarova.net.

Claudia Kozak (Ph.D, University of Buenos Aires) is Professor and Researcher at the Departments of Literature and Communication Studies, University of Buenos Aires. She also teaches at the Masters in Latin American Literary Studies, National University of Tres de Febrero, Argentina. Chair of Ph. D. Program in Social Sciences, National University of Entre Rios (Paraná City, Argentina). She sits at the Academic Council of the Erasmus Mundus Masters "Crossways in Cultural Narratives" and at the Academic

Council of Ph. D. Program in Comparative Theory of Arts, National University of Tres de Febrero. Researcher of Argentinean National Council for Scientific and Technological Research (CONICET) on the Arts/Technology/Society axe. Currently, she coordinates LitElat (Red de Literatura Electrónica Latinoamericana). Her most recent books include: *Poéticas/Políticas tecnológicas en Argentina, 1910-2010* (Ediciones La hendija, 2014); and *Tecnopoéticas argentinas. Archivo blando de arte y tecnología* (Caja Negra, 2012 and 2015). Her website can be found at http://ludion.org/.

Deena Larsen has been addicted to hypertext since before the internet. As a child, she spent hours at the Colorado History Museum's library, searching out the women's stories and connections. Homesick during a stint in Japan, she wrote *Quilts*. Laura's story led to Sadie's and Rachel's, and then the prostitutes at the White Owl and the Washerwoman. These character connections wove themselves mercilessly into complex tangles, which Deena has been unravelling ever since.

Dolores Romero López is Associate Professor in the Department of Spanish Literature (Complutense University of Madrid, Spain). She has edited *Literatures in the Digital Age: Theory and Praxis* (2007) and *Literaturas del texto al hipermedia* (2008). She has also published many articles on Spanish digital literature. She was Founder and Chair of the Research Committee on "Comparative Literature in the Digital Age" (CLDA) of the International Comparative Literature Association (ICLA) from 2005 to 2010 and Vice-President of the International Committee on EOLSS (Encyclopedia of Life Support System-UNESCO) Theme 6.87 Comparative Literature in Digital Age (http://www.eolss.net/). She collaborates with the LEETHI Research Group (Literaturas Españolas y Europeas del Texto al Hipermedia / Spanish and European Literatures from Text to Hypermedia). Ciberia, Digital Library for Spanish Electronic Literature is one of its collections. She is the director of LOEP Research Group (La Otra Edad de Plata). They are developing Mnemosyne, Digital Library for Rare and Forgotteen Text (1868-1936). Her website is https://www.ucm.es/leethi/dolores-romero.

Marjorie Coverley Luesebrink writes hypermedia fiction as M.D. Coverley. Her full-length interactive, electronic novel, *Califia*, is available on CD-ROM from Eastgate Systems. *Egypt: The Book of Going Forth by Day* was published in 2006. Coverley's Web short stories and essays have appeared in many zines including *The Iowa Review Web Review*, *BeeHive*, and *frAme*. She is a member of the Board of Directors of the Electronic Literature Organization and was given the Marjorie C. Luesebrink Career Achievement Award in 2016. Her website is http://califia.us.

Judy Malloy is a poet/researcher who works at the conjunction of hypernarrative, generative literature, social media narrative, magic realism, artists books, and information art. A pioneer in electronic literature, in 1986 she wrote and programmed the early hyperfiction, *Uncle Roger.* In the ensuing years she created a series of hypernarratives published by Eastgate, including *its name was Penelope*, called one of the early classics of electronic literature by Robert Coover. She has taught at Princeton as a distinguished fellow, as a Digital Studies Fellow at the Rutgers Camden Digital Studies Center, and as visiting faculty in the digital arts at San Francisco Art Institute. Her research and practice includes artist/consultant at Xerox PARC; Content Coordinator for *Arts Wire*, a program of the New York Foundation for the Arts; and Editor of the MIT Press compendium, *Social Media Archeology and Poetics*. Her work has been exhibited and published internationally including, among many others, the Library of Congress; Sao Paulo Biennial; Walker Art Center; Hammer Museum; Bibliothèque Nationale de France, Eastgate Systems; E. P. Dutton, MIT Press; and *The Iowa Review Web*. Her papers are archived at the David M. Rubenstein Rare Book & Manuscript Library at Duke University.

María Mencía is a multimedia artist and practice-based researcher. She lectures at Kingston University, London, UK. Her research explores hybrid textualities at the intersection of language, art and digital technologies, which has been published internationally, including the *Electronic Literature Collection, Volume 1* and the *ELMCIP Anthology of European Electronic Literature*. María has curated and edited e-lit shows and journals, as well as exhibiting worldwide. Her website is at http://mariamencia.com.

Dr. Jeneen Naji is Digital Media Faculty in the Department of Media Studies in Maynooth University, Ireland where she lectures on the B.A. Media Studies and the B.A. Media Technology run with the Department of Computer Science. Dr. Naji's research is in the area of digital culture specifically exploring the impact of the digital apparatus on poetic expression. She is also a founding member of the Maynooth University Digital Arts & Humanities Research Cluster. Dr. Naji is also a member of the international editorial review board of the *International Journal of Game-Based Learning* (IJGBL) and a Fulbright TechImpact Scholar.

Maya Zalbidea Paniagua works as Associate Professor at Complutense University of Madrid. She holds a Ph.D in Literary Studies (UCM). She has worked as visiting scholar in the ELMCIP E-literature Knowledge Base (2013-2014) at the University of Bergen. She has published: "New Works on Electronic Literature and Cyberculture"

(*CLCWeb*, 2014), "Cyberfeminist Theories and the Benefits of Teaching Cyberfeminist Literature" (*InTech*, 2012) among others. She was consulting as editor for the *ELO Collection: Volume 3* (2016).

Laura Shackelford is Associate Professor of English and Chair of the Women's and Gender Studies Program at the Rochester Institute of Technology. The author of *Tactics of the Human: Experimental Technics in American Fiction* (2014), her research explores comparative literary and media studies, digital literary practices, and their relation to bioinformatic knowledge production and circulation, particularly from the perspectives offered by feminist science studies.

Laura Sánchez is a PhD candidate in Literary Studies at Complutense University of Madrid (UCM). She is member of LEETHI (European and Spanish Literatures from Texts to Hypermedia), an interdisciplinary research group located at UCM, and she is also co-founder of Ciberia Project (http://www.ciberiaproject.com/), a platform dedicated to community building around digital literature and the study of new forms of literary digital publishing. Her research interests concern mainly the relationship between digital literature and digital arts.

Hazel Smith is a Research Professor in the Writing and Society Research Centre at Western Sydney University, and is the author of several academic books including *The Contemporary Literature-Music Relationship* (Routledge 2016). Hazel is a poet, performer and multimedia artist, and a member of austraLYSIS, the sound and intermedia arts group. She has published four volumes of poetry, including *Word Migrants* (Giramondo Publishing, Sydney 2016), three CDs of performance work, and numerous collaborative multimedia works. Her website is http://australysis.com.

Stephanie Strickland has published eight books of poetry and ten electronic poems. *Zone : Zero*, book + CD, features the digital work *slippingglimpse* which maps text to Atlantic waves. *V : WaveTercets / Losing L'una* has a complement, the *Vniverse* app for iPad, written with Ian Hatcher. Recent work includes *Hours of the Night*, an MP4 PowerPoint poem with M.D. Coverley. Strickland is a Director of the Electronic Literature Organization. Her website is http://stephaniestrickland.com.

Sue Thomas is a writer and a Visiting Fellow in The Media School at Bournemouth University. Her books include *Technobiophilia: nature and cyberspace* (2013), a study of the impact of the natural world on digital culture; *Hello World: travels in virtuality* (2004), a travelogue/memoir of life online, and *Correspondence* (1992), short-listed for the Arthur C. Clarke Award for Best Science Fiction Novel. In 1995 she founded the trAce Online Writing Centre, an early global online community which ran for ten years. From 2005-2013 she was Professor of New Media in the Institute of Creative Technologies at De Montfort University where she researched biophilia, social media, transliteracy, transdisciplinarity and future foresight. She now lives in Bournemouth, Dorset, UK, where she writes about nature and technology at http://technobiophilia.com. She is a member of the EU COST CyberParks Network, forecasting the technological future of urban parks. Her website is http://suethomas.net.

Christine Wilks is a digital writer, artist and developer of playable stories. Her digital fiction, *Underbelly*, won the New Media Writing Prize 2010 and the MaMSIE Digital Media Competition 2011. Her work is published in online journals, exhibitions and anthologies, including the *Electronic Literature Collection, Volume 2* and the *ELMCIP Anthology of European Electronic Literature*, and at her website. She is currently engaged in a practice-based PhD at Bath Spa University, UK.